THE PAPERS OF
BENJAMIN FRANKLIN

SPONSORED BY

The American Philosophical Society

and Yale University

Silver *Libertas Americana*

THE PAPERS OF

Benjamin Franklin

VOLUME 39 *January 21 through May 15, 1783*

ELLEN R. COHN, *Editor*

JONATHAN R. DULL, *Senior Associate Editor*

KAREN DUVAL, *Associate Editor*

KATE M. OHNO, MICHAEL SLETCHER,
AND PHILIPP ZIESCHE, *Assistant Editors*

ALICIA K. ANDERSON, *Editorial Associate*

ELIZABETH MORRIS, *Editorial Assistant*

CLAUDE A. LOPEZ, *Consulting Editor*

New Haven and London   YALE UNIVERSITY PRESS, 2008

As indicated in the first volume, this edition was made possible through the vision and generosity of Yale University and the American Philosophical Society and by a substantial donation from Henry R. Luce in the name of Life Magazine. *Additional funds were provided by a grant from the Ford Foundation to the National Archives Trust Fund Board. Subsequent support has come from the Andrew W. Mellon Foundation. Major underwriting of the present volume has been provided by the Barkley Fund, the Florence Gould Foundation, the Norman and Lyn Lear Foundation, the National Trust for the Humanities, the Packard Humanities Institute through Founding Fathers Papers, Inc., and The Pew Charitable Trusts. We gratefully acknowledge the bequest of Raymond N. Kjellberg, which will continue to sustain our enterprise. We offer particular appreciation to Richard Gilder, Charles and Ann Johnson, Mason Willrich, the Yale Class of 1954, and the Benjamin Franklin Tercentenary for generous donations that will insure the future of the edition. We are grateful for the generous support of Curran W. Harvey, Jr., Candace and Stuart Karu, Richard N. Rosenfeld, Phyllis Z. and Fenmore R. Seton, Malcolm N. Smith, and Ralph Gregory Elliot. Gifts from many other individuals as well as donations from the American Philosophical Society, Yale University, the New York Times Foundation, the Friends of the Franklin Papers, and the* Saturday Evening Post *Society help to sustain the enterprise.* The Papers of Benjamin Franklin *is a beneficiary of the generous and long-standing support of the National Historical Publications and Records Commission under the chairmanship of the Archivist of the United States. The National Endowment for the Humanities, an independent federal agency, has provided significant support for this volume. For the assistance of all these organizations and individuals, as well as for the indispensable aid of archivists, librarians, scholars, and collectors of Franklin manuscripts, the editors are most grateful.*

Publication of this volume was assisted by a grant from The Pew Charitable Trusts.

Library of Congress catalog card number: 59–12697
International standard book number: 978-0-300-13448-3

⊗ The paper in this book meets the requirements of ANSI/NISO Z39.48-1992 (Permanence of Paper).

Printed in the U.S.A.

To

RICHARD GILDER

with gratitude

Contents

Foreign-language surnames and titles of nobility often run to great length. Our practice with an untitled person is to provide all the Christian names at the first appearance, and then drop them; a chevalier or noble is given the title used at the time, and the full name is provided in the index.

*Denotes a document referred to in annotation.

CONTENTS

CONTENTS

List of Illustrations

The first known example of a dinner invitation printed by Franklin on his press at Passy. Reproduced by courtesy of the University of Pennsylvania Library.

The Franklin/Folger chart of the Gulf Stream engraved by George-Louis Le Rouge with Franklin's marginalia, written by his secretary L'Air de Lamotte and Franklin himself (the additional note in the right margin). Franklin's text clarified and amplified Folger's original sailing instructions, which Le Rouge had translated and engraved in the upper right corner. The "Remarks" explained how to navigate into New England ports while avoiding the strong Gulf Stream current and the treacherous shoals off the Georges Banks. The added "Note" explained how navigators could tell whether they were in the Gulf Stream. Reproduced by courtesy of the Centre Historique des Archives Nationales.

Medal by Jean-François Bernier for the Lodge of the Nine Sisters. The medal was presented to Franklin and distributed to guests at the lodge's fête académique on May 12. Reproduced by courtesy of the American Philosophical Society.

Contributors to Volume 39

The ownership of each manuscript, or the location of the particular copy used by the editors of each rare contemporary pamphlet or similar printed work, is indicated where the document appears in the text. The sponsors and editors are deeply grateful to the following institutions and individuals for permission to print or otherwise use in the present volume manuscripts and other materials which they own.

INSTITUTIONS

The American Museum of
   Historical Documents
American Philosophical Society
Archives du Ministère des affaires
   étrangères, Paris
Archives Nationales, Paris
Bibliothèque de Carcassonne
William L. Clements Library,
   University of Michigan
Columbia University Library
Dartmouth College Library
Harvard University Library
Historical Society of Delaware
Historical Society of Pennsylvania

Library of Congress
Massachusetts Historical Society
National Archives
National Heritage Museum
New Hampshire Historical Society
New-York Historical Society
Princeton University Library
Public Record Office, London
South Carolina Historical Society
Svenska Riksarkivet, Stockholm
University of Pennsylvania Library
University of Pittsburgh Library
Yale University Library

INDIVIDUALS

Barclay Giddings Johnson, Jr., Watertown, Connecticut
Robert J. Walker III, Jupiter, Florida

Statement of Methodology

Arrangement of Materials

The documents are printed in chronological sequence according to their dates when these are given, or according to the date of publication in cases of contemporary printed materials. Records such as diaries, journals, and account books that cover substantial periods of time appear according to the dates of their earliest entries. When no date appears on the document itself, one is editorially supplied and an explanation provided. When no day within a month is given, the document is placed at the end of all specifically dated documents of that month; those dated only by year are placed at the end of that year. If no date is given, we use internal and external evidence to assign one whenever possible, providing our explanation in annotation. Documents which cannot be assigned a date more definite than the entire length of Franklin's stay in France (1777–85) will be published at the end of this period. Those for which we are unable to provide even a tentative date will be published at the conclusion of the series.

When two or more documents have the same date, they are arranged in the following order:

1. Those by a group of which Franklin was a member (*e.g.*, the American Commissioners in Paris)
2. Those by Franklin individually
3. Those to a group of which Franklin was a member
4. Those to Franklin individually
5. "Third-party" and unaddressed miscellaneous writings by others than Franklin.

In the first two categories letters are arranged alphabetically by the name of the addressee; in the last three, by the name of the signatory. An exception to this practice occurs when a letter to Franklin and his answer were written on the same day: in such cases the first letter precedes the reply. The same rules apply to documents lacking precise dates printed together at the end of any month or year.

Form of Presentation

The document and its accompanying editorial apparatus are presented in the following order:

1. *Title.* Essays and formal papers are headed by their titles, except in the case of pamphlets with very long titles, when a short form is substituted. Where previous editors supplied a title to a piece that had none, and this title has become familiar, we use it; otherwise we devise a suitable one.

Letters written by Franklin individually are entitled "To" the person or body addressed, as: To John Adams; To John Adams and Arthur Lee; To the Royal Society.

Letters to Franklin individually are entitled "From" the person or body who wrote them, as: From John Adams; From John Adams and Arthur Lee; From the Committee of Secret Correspondence.

Letters of which Franklin was a joint author or joint recipient are titled with the names of all concerned, as: Franklin and Silas Deane to Arthur Lee; Arthur Lee to Franklin and Silas Deane. "Third-party" letters or those by or to a body of which Franklin was a member are titled with the names of both writers and addressees, as: Arthur Lee to John Adams; The American Commissioners to John Paul Jones.

Documents not fitting into any of these categories are given brief descriptive headings, as: Extract from Franklin's Journal.

If the name in the title has been supplied from external evidence it appears in brackets, with a question mark when we are uncertain. If a letter is unsigned, or signed with initials or an alias, but is from a correspondent whose handwriting we know, the name appears without brackets.

2. *Source Identification.* This gives the nature of the printed or manuscript version of the document, and, in the case of a manuscript or a rare printed work, the ownership and location of the original.

Printed sources of three different classes are distinguished. First, a contemporary pamphlet, which is given its full title, place and date of publication, and the location of the copy the editors have used. Second, an essay or letter appearing originally in a *contemporary* publication, which is introduced by the words

"Printed in," followed by the title, date, and inclusive page numbers, if necessary, of the publication. Third, a document, the manuscript or contemporary printed version of which is now lost, but which was printed at a later date, is identified by the words "Reprinted from," followed by the name of the work from which the editors have reproduced it. The following examples illustrate the distinction:

Printed in *The Pennsylvania Gazette,* October 2, 1729.

Reprinted from William Temple Franklin, ed., *Memoirs of the Life and Writings of Benjamin Franklin* . . . (3 vols., 4to, London, 1817–18), II, 244.

The Source Identification of a manuscript consists of a term or symbol (all of which are listed in the Short Title List) indicating the character of the manuscript version, followed by the name of the holder of the manuscript, as: ALS: American Philosophical Society. Because press copies replicate the manuscripts from which they were made, we indicate the character of the original manuscript, as: press copy of L. Since manuscripts belonging to individuals have a tendency to migrate, we indicate the year in which each private owner gave permission to publish, as: Morris Duane, Philadelphia, 1957. When two or more manuscript versions survive, the one listed first in the Source Identification is the one from which we print.

3. An editorial *Headnote* precedes some documents in this edition; it appears between the Source Identification and the actual text. Such a headnote is designed to supply the background of the composition of the document, its relation to events or other writings, and any other information which may be useful to the reader and is not obtainable from the document itself.

4. The *Text* of the document follows the Source Identification, or Headnote, if any. When multiple copies of a document are extant, the editors observe the following order of priority in determining which of the available versions to use in printing a text: ALS or ADS, LS or DS, AL or AD, L or D, and copy. An AL (draft) normally takes precedence over a contemporary copy based on the recipient's copy. If we deviate from the order set forth here, we explain our decision in the annotation. In those instances where multiple texts are available, the texts are collated, and sig-

nificant variations reported in the annotation. In selecting the publication text from among several copies of official French correspondence (*e.g.*, from Vergennes or Sartine) we use the version which is written in the best French, on the presumption that the French ministers used standard eighteenth-century spelling, grammar, and punctuation.

The form of presentation of the texts of letters is as follows:

The place and date of composition are set at the top, regardless of their location in the original manuscript.

The signature, set in capitals and small capitals, is placed at the right of the last line of the text if there is room; if not, then on the line below.

Addresses, endorsements, and notations are so labelled and printed at the end of the letter. An endorsement is, to the best of our belief, by the recipient, and a notation by someone else. When the writer of the notation has misread the date or the signature of the correspondent, we let the error stand without comment. Line breaks in addresses are marked by slashes. Different notations are separated by slashes; when they are by different individuals, we so indicate.

5. *Footnotes* to the Heading, Source Identification, Headnote, and Text appear on the pages to which they pertain. References to documents not printed or to be printed in later volumes are by date and repository, as: Jan. 17, 1785, APS.

Method of Textual Reproduction

1. *Spelling* of all words, including proper names, is retained. If it is abnormal enough to obscure the meaning we follow the word immediately with the current spelling in brackets.

2. *Capitalization and Punctuation* are retained. There is such variety in the size of initial letters, often in the same manuscript, that it is sometimes unclear whether the writer intended an upper or lower case letter. In such cases we make a decision on the basis of the correspondent's customary usage. We supply a capital letter when an immediately preceding period, colon, question mark, exclamation point, or dash indicates that a new sentence is intended. If a capital letter clearly indicates the beginning of a new thought, but no mark of punctuation precedes it, we insert a period. If neither punctuation nor capital let-

ter indicates a sentence break, we do not supply them unless their absence renders comprehension of the document nearly impossible. In that case we provide them and so indicate in a footnote.

Dashes were used for a variety of purposes in eighteenth-century personal and public letters. A dash within a sentence, used to indicate a break in thought, is represented as an em dash. A dash that follows a period or serves as a closing mark of punctuation for a sentence is represented as an em dash followed by a space. Occasionally correspondents used long dashes that continue to the end of a line and indicate a significant break in thought. We do not reproduce the dash, but treat it as indicating the start of a new paragraph.

When there is an initial quotation mark or parenthesis, but no closing one, we silently complete the pair.

3. *Contractions and abbreviations* are retained. Abbreviations such as "wd", "honble", "servt", "exclly", are used so frequently in Franklin's correspondence that they are readily comprehensible to the users of these volumes. Abbreviations, particularly of French words, that may be unclear are followed by an expanded version in brackets, as: nre [navire]. Superscript letters are brought down to the line. Where a period or colon is a part of the abbreviation, or indicates that letters were written above the line, we print it at the end of the word, as: 4th. for 4.th. In those few cases where superscript letters brought down to the line result in a confusing abbreviation ("Made" for "Mad^e"), we follow the abbreviation by an expanded version in brackets, as: Made [Madame].

The ampersand by itself and the "&c." are retained. Letters represented by the "y" are printed, as: "the" and "that". The tailed "p" is spelled out, as: "per", "pre", or "pro". Symbols of weights, measures, and money are converted to modern forms, as: *l.t.* instead of ⅄ for *livres tournois*.

4. *Omissions, mutilations, and illegible words* are treated as follows:

If we are certain of the reading of letters missing in a word because of a torn or taped manuscript or tightly bound copybook, we supply the letters silently.

If we cannot be sure of the word, or of how the author spelled it, but we can make a reasonable guess, we supply the missing letters in brackets.

When the writer has omitted a word absolutely required for clarity, we insert it in italics within brackets.

5. *Interlineations* by the author are silently incorporated into the text. If they are significant enough to require comment a footnote is provided.

Textual Conventions

/	denotes line break in addresses; separates multiple endorsements and notations.
⟨roman⟩	denotes a résumé of a letter or document.
[*italic*]	editorial insertion explaining something about the manuscript, as: [*one line illegible*]; or supplying a word to make the meaning clear, as: [*to*].
[roman]	editorial insertion clarifying the immediately preceding word or abbreviation; supplies letters missing because of a mutilated manuscript.
(?)	indicates a questionable reading.

Abbreviations and Short Titles

AAE	Archives du Ministère des affaires étrangères.
AD	Autograph document.
Adams Correspondence	Lyman H. Butterfield, Richard A. Ryerson, *et al.*, eds., *Adams Family Correspondence* (8 vols. to date, Cambridge, Mass., 1963–).
Adams Papers	Robert J. Taylor, Gregg L. Lint, *et al.*, eds., *Papers of John Adams* (14 vols. to date, Cambridge, Mass., 1977–).
ADB	*Allgemeine Deutsche Biographie* (56 vols., Berlin, 1967–71).
Adm.	Admiral.
ADS	Autograph document signed.
AL	Autograph letter.
Allen, *Mass. Privateers*	Gardner Weld Allen, ed., *Massachusetts Privateers of the Revolution* ([Cambridge, Mass.], 1927) (Massachusetts Historical Society *Collections*, LXXVII).
Almanach des marchands	*Almanach général des marchands, négocians, armateurs, et fabricans de France et de l'Europe et autres parties du monde . . .* (Paris, 1779).
Almanach royal	*Almanach royal* (91 vols., Paris, 1700–92). Cited by year.
Almanach de Versailles	*Almanach de Versailles* (Versailles, various years). Cited by year.
Alphabetical List of Escaped Prisoners	Alphabetical List of the Americans who having escap'd from the Prisons of England, were furnish'd with Money by the Commissrs. of the U.S. at the Court of France, to return to America.

A manuscript in the APS, dated 1784, and covering the period January, 1777, to November, 1784.

ALS — Autograph letter signed.

Amiable, *Une Loge Maçonnique* — Louis Amiable, *Une Loge maçonnique d'avant 1789* . . . (1897; reprint, followed by an introduction, commentary, and notes, separately paginated, by Charles Porset, Paris, 1989).

ANB — John A. Garraty and Mark C. Carnes, eds., *American National Biography* (24 vols., New York and Oxford, 1999).

APS — American Philosophical Society.

Archaeol. — Archaeological.

Assn. — Association.

Auphan, "Communications" — P. Auphan, "Les communications entre la France et ses colonies d'Amérique pendant la guerre de l'indépendance Américaine," *Revue Maritime,* new series, no. LXIII and LXIV (1925), 331–48, 497–517.

Autobiog. — Leonard W. Labaree, Ralph L. Ketcham, Helen C. Boatfield, and Helene H. Fineman, eds., *The Autobiography of Benjamin Franklin* (New Haven, 1964).

Bachaumont, *Mémoires secrets* — [Louis Petit de Bachaumont *et al.*], *Mémoires secrets pour servir à l'histoire de la république des lettres en France, depuis MDCCLXII jusqu'à nos jours; ou, Journal d'un observateur* . . . (36 vols. in 12, London, 1784–89). Bachaumont died in 1771. The first six vols. (1762–71) are his; Mathieu-François Pidansat de Mairobert edited them and wrote the next nine (1771–

79); the remainder (1779–87) are by
Barthélemy-François Mouffle
d'Angerville.

Balch, *French in America*   Thomas Balch, *The French in America
during the War of Independence of the
United States, 1777–1783* (trans. by
Thomas Willing Balch *et al.*; 2 vols.,
Philadelphia, 1891–95).

BF   Benjamin Franklin.

BF's accounts as   Those described above, XXIII, 20.
commissioner

BF's journal of the peace   Described in XXXVII, 291–346. This
negotiations   refers to the copy in Josiah Flagg's
hand with corrections by BF, at the Library of Congress.

BFB   Benjamin Franklin Bache.

BFB's journal   Described above, XXXVII, 682n.

Bigelow, *Works*   John Bigelow, ed., *The Works of Benjamin Franklin* (12 vols., New York
and London, 1887–88).

Biographie universelle   *Biographie universelle, ancienne et mo-
derne, ou histoire, par ordre alphabé-
tique, de la vie publique et privée de tous
les hommes qui se sont fait remarquer . . .*
(85 vols., Paris, 1811–62).

Bodinier   From information kindly furnished us by
Cdt. Gilbert Bodinier, Section études,
Service historique de l'Armée de
Terre, Vincennes.

Bodinier, *Dictionnaire*   Gilbert Bodinier, *Dictionnaire des officiers
de l'armée royale qui ont combattu aux
Etats-Unis pendant la guerre d'Indépendance* (Château de Vincennes,
1982).

Bowler, *Logistics*   R. Arthur Bowler, *Logistics and the Fail-*

ure of the British Army in America,
1775–1783 (Princeton, 1975).

Bradford, *Jones Papers*   James C. Bradford, ed., *The Microfilm*
Edition of the Papers of John Paul
Jones, 1747–1792 (10 reels of mi-
crofilm, Alexandria, Va., 1986).

Burke's Peerage   Sir Bernard Burke, *Burke's Genealogical*
and Heraldic History of the Peerage
Baronetage and Knightage with War
Gazette and Corrigenda (98th ed., London, 1940). References in exceptional
cases to other editions are so indicated.

Burnett, *Letters*   Edmund C. Burnett, ed., *Letters of*
Members of the Continental Congress
(8 vols., Washington, 1921–36).

Butterfield, *John Adams*   Lyman H. Butterfield *et al.*, eds., *Diary*
Diary   *and Autobiography of John Adams*
(4 vols., Cambridge, Mass., 1961).

Cash Book   BF's accounts described above, xxvi, 3.

Chron.   *Chronicle.*

Claghorn, *Naval Officers*   Charles E. Claghorn, *Naval Officers of*
the American Revolution: a Concise
Biographical Dictionary (Metuchen,
N.J., and London, 1988).

Clark, *Ben Franklin's*   William Bell Clark, *Ben Franklin's*
Privateers   *Privateers: a Naval Epic of the Ameri-*
can Revolution (Baton Rouge, 1956).

Clark, *Wickes*   William Bell Clark, *Lambert Wickes, Sea*
Raider and Diplomat: the Story of a
Naval Captain of the Revolution (New
Haven and London, 1932).

Clowes, *Royal Navy*   William Laird Clowes, *The Royal Navy:*
a History from the Earliest Times to the
Present (7 vols., Boston and London,
1897–1903).

Cobbett, *Parliamentary History*	William Cobbett and Thomas C. Hansard, eds., *The Parliamentary History of England from the Earliest Period to 1803* (36 vols., London, 1806–20).
Col.	Column.
Coll.	*Collections.*
comp.	compiler.
Croÿ, *Journal*	Emmanuel, prince de Moeurs et de Solre et duc de Croÿ, *Journal inédit du duc de Croÿ, 1718–1784* (4 vols., Paris, 1906–7).
d.	*denier.*
D	Document unsigned.
DAB	*Dictionary of American Biography.*
DBF	*Dictionnaire de biographie française* (20 vols. to date, Paris, 1933–).
Dictionary of Scientific Biography	Charles C. Gillispie, ed., *Dictionary of Scientific Biography* (18 vols., New York, 1970–90).
Deane Papers	*The Deane Papers, 1774–90* (5 vols.; New-York Historical Society *Collections,* XIX–XXIII, New York, 1887–91).
DF	Deborah Franklin.
Dictionnaire de la noblesse	François-Alexandre Aubert de La Chesnaye-Dubois and M. Badier, *Dictionnaire de la noblesse contenant les généalogies, l'histoire & la chronologie des familles nobles de la France . . .* (3rd ed.; 19 vols., Paris, 1863–76).
Dictionnaire historique	*Dictionnaire historique, critique et bibliographique, contenant les vies des hommes illustres, célèbres ou fameux de tous les pays et de tous les siècles . . .* (30 vols., Paris, 1821–23).

Dictionnaire historique de la Suisse	*Dictionnaire historique & biographique de la Suisse* (7 vols. and supplement, Neuchâtel, 1921–34).
DNB	*Dictionary of National Biography.*
Doniol, *Histoire*	Henri Doniol, *Histoire de la participation de la France à l'établissement des Etats-Unis d'Amérique. Correspondance diplomatique et documents* (5 vols., Paris, 1886–99).
DS	Document signed.
Duane, *Works*	William Duane, ed., *The Works of Dr. Benjamin Franklin* . . . (6 vols., Philadelphia, 1808–18). Title varies in the several volumes.
Dubourg, *Œuvres*	Jacques Barbeu-Dubourg, ed., *Œuvres de M. Franklin* . . . (2 vols., Paris, 1773).
Dull, *French Navy*	Jonathan R. Dull, *The French Navy and American Independence: a Study of Arms and Diplomacy, 1774–1787* (Princeton, 1975).
Ed.	Edition or editor.
Edler, *Dutch Republic*	Friedrich Edler, *The Dutch Republic and the American Revolution* (*Johns Hopkins University Studies in Historical and Political Science,* ser. XXIX, no. 2; Baltimore, 1911).
Elias and Finch, *Letters of Digges*	Robert H. Elias and Eugene D. Finch, eds., *Letters of Thomas Attwood Digges (1742–1821)* (Columbia, S.C., 1982).
Etat militaire	*Etat militaire de France, pour l'année* . . . (36 vols., Paris, 1758–93). Cited by year.
Exper. and Obser.	*Experiments and Observations on Electricity, made at Philadelphia in America,*

by Mr. Benjamin Franklin . . . (London, 1751). Revised and enlarged editions were published in 1754, 1760, 1769, and 1774 with slightly varying titles. In each case the edition cited will be indicated, *e.g., Exper. and Obser.* (1751).

f.   florins.

Fauchille, *Diplomatie française*   Paul Fauchille, *La Diplomatie française et la ligue des neutres de 1780 (1776–1783)* (Paris, 1893).

Ferguson, *Power of the Purse*   E. James Ferguson, *The Power of the Purse: a History of American Public Finance* . . . (Chapel Hill, N.C., 1961).

Fitzmaurice, *Life of Shelburne*   Edmond George Petty-Fitzmaurice, *Life of William, Earl of Shelburne, Afterwards First Marquess of Lansdowne, with Extracts from His Papers and Correspondence* (3 vols., London, 1875–76).

Fitzpatrick, *Writings of Washington*   John C. Fitzpatrick, ed., *The Writings of George Washington* . . . (39 vols., Washington, D.C., 1931–44).

Ford, *Letters of William Lee*   Worthington Chauncey Ford, ed., *Letters of William Lee, 1766–1783* (3 vols., Brooklyn, N.Y., 1891).

Fortescue, *Correspondence of George Third*   Sir John William Fortescue, ed., *The Correspondence of King George the Third from 1760 to December 1783* . . . (6 vols., London, 1927–28).

France ecclésiastique   *La France ecclésiastique pour l'année* . . . (15 vols., Paris, 1774–90). Cited by year.

Freeman, *Washington*   Douglas S. Freeman (completed by John A. Carroll and Mary W. Ashworth),

George Washington: a Biography (7 vols., New York, 1948–57).

Ga*z*.   *Ga*ʒ*ette.*

Ga*z*. de Leyde   *Nouvelles extraordinaires de divers endroits,* commonly known as *Gaʒette de Leyde.* Each issue is in two parts; we indicate the second as "sup."

Gen.   General.

Geneal.   *Genealogical.*

Gent. Mag.   *The Gentleman's Magaʒine, and Historical Chronicle.*

Giunta, *Emerging Nation*   Mary A. Giunta, *et al.,* eds., *The Emerging Nation: a Documentary History of the Foreign Relations of the United States under the Articles of the Confederation, 1780–1789* (3 vols., Washington, D.C., 1996).

Harlow, *Second British Empire*   Vincent T. Harlow, *The Founding of the Second British Empire, 1763–1793* (2 vols., London and New York, 1952–64).

Hays, *Calendar*   I. Minis Hays, *Calendar of the Papers of Benjamin Franklin in the Library of the American Philosophical Society* (5 vols., Philadelphia, 1908).

Heitman, *Register of Officers*   Francis B. Heitman, *Historical Register of Officers in the War of the Revolution . . .* (Washington, D.C., 1893).

Hillairet, *Rues de Paris*   Jacques Hillairet, pseud. of Auguste A. Coussillan, *Dictionnaire historique des rues de Paris* (2nd ed.; 2 vols., [Paris, 1964]).

Hist.   Historic or Historical.

Hoffman and Albert, eds., *Peace and the Peacemakers*   Ronald Hoffman and Peter J. Albert, eds., *Peace and the Peacemakers: the Treaty of 1783* (Charlottesville, Va., 1986).

Idzerda, *Lafayette Papers*   Stanley J. Idzerda *et al.*, eds., *Lafayette in the Age of the American Revolution: Selected Letters and Papers, 1776–1790* (5 vols. to date, Ithaca, N.Y., and London, 1977–).

JA   John Adams.

JCC   Worthington Chauncey Ford *et al.*, eds., *Journals of the Continental Congress, 1744–1789* (34 vols., Washington, D.C., 1904–37).

Jefferson Papers   Julian P. Boyd, Charles T. Cullen, John Catanzariti, Barbara B. Oberg, *et al.*, eds., *The Papers of Thomas Jefferson* (34 vols. to date, Princeton, 1950–).

Jour.   *Journal.*

JW   Jonathan Williams, Jr.

Kaminkow, *Mariners*   Marion and Jack Kaminkow, *Mariners of the American Revolution* (Baltimore, 1967).

Klingelhofer, "Matthew Ridley's Diary"   Herbert F. Klingelhofer, ed., "Matthew Ridley's Diary during the Peace Negotiations of 1782," *William and Mary Quarterly*, 3rd series, XX (1963), 95–133.

L   Letter unsigned.

Landais, *Memorial*   Pierre Landais, *Memorial, to Justify Peter Landai's Conduct during the Late War* (Boston, 1784).

Larousse   Pierre Larousse, *Grand dictionnaire universel du XIXe siècle* . . . (17 vols., Paris, [n.d.]).

Lasseray, *Les Français*   André Lasseray, *Les Français sous les treize étoiles, 1775–1783* (2 vols., Paris, 1935).

Laurens Papers   Philip M. Hamer, George C. Rogers, Jr., David R. Chestnutt, *et al.*, eds., *The*

Papers of Henry Laurens (16 vols., Columbia, S.C., 1968–2002).

Le Bihan, *Francs-maçons parisiens* — Alain Le Bihan, *Francs-maçons parisiens du Grand Orient de France* . . . (Commission d'histoire économique et sociale de la révolution française, *Mémoires et documents,* XIX, Paris, 1966).

Lee Family Papers — Paul P. Hoffman, ed., *The Lee Family Papers, 1742–1795* (University of Virginia *Microfilm Publication* No. 1; 8 reels, Charlottesville, Va., 1966).

Lewis, *Walpole Correspondence* — Wilmarth S. Lewis *et al.*, eds., *The Yale Edition of Horace Walpole's Correspondence* (48 vols., New Haven, 1939–83).

Lopez, *Lafayette* — Claude A. Lopez, "Benjamin Franklin, Lafayette, and the *Lafayette*," *Proceedings* of the American Philosophical Society, CVIII (1964), 181–223.

Lopez, *Mon Cher Papa* — Claude-Anne Lopez, *Mon Cher Papa: Franklin and the Ladies of Paris* (rev. ed., New Haven and London, 1990).

Lopez and Herbert, *The Private Franklin* — Claude-Anne Lopez and Eugenia W. Herbert, *The Private Franklin: the Man and His Family* (New York, 1975).

LS — Letter or letters signed.

l.t. — *livres tournois.*

Lüthy, *Banque protestante* — Herbert Lüthy, *La Banque protestante en France de la Révocation de l'Edit de Nantes à la Révolution* (2 vols., Paris, 1959–61).

Mackesy, *War for America* — Piers Mackesy, *The War for America, 1775–1783* (Cambridge, Mass., 1965).

Madariaga, *Harris's Mission* — Isabel de Madariaga, *Britain, Russia, and the Armed Neutrality of 1780: Sir James Harris's Mission to St. Peters-

	burg during the American Revolution (New Haven, 1962).
Mag.	*Magazine.*
Mass. Arch.	Massachusetts Archives, State House, Boston.
Mazas, *Ordre de Saint-Louis*	Alexandre Mazas and Théodore Anne, *Histoire de l'ordre royal et militaire de Saint-Louis depuis son institution en 1693 jusqu'en 1830* (2nd ed.; 3 vols., Paris, 1860–61).
Medlin, *Morellet*	Dorothy Medlin, Jean-Claude David, Paul LeClerc, eds., *Lettres d'André Morellet* (3 vols., Oxford, 1991–96).
Métra, *Correspondance secrète*	[François Métra *et al.*], *Correspondance secrète, politique & littéraire, ou Mémoires pour servir à l'histoire des cours, des sociétés & de la littérature en France, depuis la mort de Louis XV* (18 vols., London, 1787–90).
Meyer, *Armement nantais*	Jean Meyer, *L'Armement nantais dans la deuxième moitié du XVIIIe siècle* (Paris, 1969).
Meyer, *Noblesse bretonne*	Jean Meyer, *La Noblesse bretonne au XVIIIe siècle* (2 vols., Paris, 1966).
"Mission of Col. Laurens"	"The Mission of Col. John Laurens to Europe in 1781," *The South Carolina Historical and Genealogical Magazine*, I (1900), 13–41, 136–51, 213–22, 311–22; II (1901), 27–43, 108–25.
Morison, *Jones*	Samuel E. Morison, *John Paul Jones: a Sailor's Biography* (Boston and Toronto, 1959).
Morris, *Jay: Peace*	Richard B. Morris *et al.*, eds., *John Jay, the Winning of the Peace: Unpublished Papers, 1780–1784* (New York, Cambridge, London, 1980).

Morris, *Jay: Revolutionary* Richard B. Morris *et al.*, eds., *John Jay, the Making of a Revolutionary: Unpublished Papers, 1743–1780* (New York, Evanston, San Francisco, 1975).

Morris Papers E. James Ferguson, John Catanzariti, Mary A. Gallagher, Elizabeth M. Nuxoll, *et al.*, eds., *The Papers of Robert Morris, 1781–1784* (9 vols., Pittsburgh, Pa., 1973–99).

Morton, *Beaumarchais Correspondance* Brian N. Morton and Donald C. Spinelli, eds., *Beaumarchais Correspondance* (4 vols. to date, Paris, 1969–).

MS, MSS Manuscript, manuscripts.

Namier and Brooke, *House of Commons* Sir Lewis Namier and John Brooke, *The History of Parliament. The House of Commons, 1754–1790* (3 vols., London and New York, 1964).

NNBW *Nieuw Nederlandsch Biografisch Woordenboek* (10 vols. and index, Amsterdam, 1974).

Nouvelle biographie *Nouvelle biographie générale depuis les temps les plus reculés jusqu'à nos jours* . . . (46 vols., Paris, 1855–66).

ODNB H. C. G. Matthew and Brian Harrison, *Oxford Dictionary of National Biography* . . . *to the year 2000* (60 vols., Oxford, 2004).

p. pence.

Pa. Pennsylvania.

Pa. Arch. Samuel Hazard *et al.*, eds., *Pennsylvania Archives* (9 series, Philadelphia and Harrisburg, 1852–1935).

Palmer, *Loyalists* Gregory Palmer, ed., *Biographical Sketches of Loyalists of the American Revolution* (Westport, Conn., 1984).

xlix

Parry, *Consolidated Treaty Series*
Clive Parry, comp., *The Consolidated Treaty* Series (243 vols., Dobbs Ferry, N. Y., 1969–86).

Phil. Trans.
The Royal Society, *Philosophical Transactions.*

PMHB
Pennsylvania Magazine of History and Biography.

Price, *France and the Chesapeake*
Jacob M. Price, *France and the Chesapeake: a History of the French Tobacco Monopoly, 1674–1791, and of Its Relationship to the British and American Tobacco Trade* (2 vols., Ann Arbor, Mich., 1973).

Proc.
Proceedings.

Pub.
Publications.

Quérard, *France littéraire*
Joseph Marie Quérard, *La France littéraire ou Dictionnaire bibliographique des savants, historiens, et gens de lettres de la France, ainsi que des littérateurs étrangers qui ont écrit en français, plus particulièrement pendant les XVIIIe et XIXe siècles . . .* (10 vols., Paris, 1827–64).

Rakove, *Beginnings of National Politics*
Jack N. Rakove, *The Beginnings of National Politics: an Interpretive History of the Continental Congress* (New York, 1979).

RB
Richard Bache.

Repertorium der diplomatischen Vertreter
Ludwig Bittner *et al.*, eds., *Repertorium der diplomatischen Vertreter aller Länder seit dem Westfälischen Frieden (1648)* (3 vols., Oldenburg, etc., 1936–65).

Rev.
Review.

Rice and Brown, eds., *Rochambeau's Army*
Howard C. Rice, Jr., and Anne S.K. Brown, eds., *The American Campaigns of Rochambeau's Army, 1780, 1781,*

1782, 1783 (2 vols., Princeton and Providence, 1972).

s. *sou.*

s. shilling.

Sabine, *Loyalists* Lorenzo Sabine, *Biographical Sketches of Loyalists of the American Revolution* . . . (2 vols., Boston, 1864).

SB Sarah Bache.

Schelle, *Œuvres de Turgot* Gustave Schelle, ed., *Œuvres de Turgot et documents le concernant* (5 vols., Paris, 1913–23).

Schulte Nordholt, *Dutch Republic* J. W. Schulte Nordholt, *The Dutch Republic and American Independence* (trans. Herbert M. Rowen; Chapel Hill, N.C., 1982).

Sellers, *Franklin in Portraiture* Charles C. Sellers, *Benjamin Franklin in Portraiture* (New Haven and London, 1962).

Sibley's Harvard Graduates John L. Sibley, *Biographical Sketches of Graduates of Harvard University* (17 vols. to date, Cambridge, Mass., 1873–). Continued from Volume IV by Clifford K. Shipton.

Six, *Dictionnaire biographique* Georges Six, *Dictionnaire biographique des généraux et amiraux français de la Révolution et de l'Empire (1792–1814)* (2 vols., Paris, 1934).

Smith, *Letters* Paul H. Smith *et al.*, eds., *Letters of Delegates to Congress* (26 vols., Washington, D.C., 1976–2000).

Smyth, *Writings* Albert H. Smyth, ed., *The Writings of Benjamin Franklin* . . . (10 vols., New York, 1905–7).

Soc. Society.

Sparks, *Works* Jared Sparks, ed., *The Works of Benjamin Franklin* . . . (10 vols., Boston, 1836–40).

Stevens, *Facsimiles*	Benjamin F. Stevens, ed., *Facsimiles of Manuscripts in European Archives Relating to America, 1773–1783* (25 vols., London, 1889–98).
Taylor, *J. Q. Adams Diary*	Robert J. Taylor *et al.*, eds., *Diary of John Quincy Adams* (2 vols. to date, Cambridge, Mass., and London, 1981–).
Tourneux, *Correspondance littéraire*	Tourneux, Maurice, *Correspondance littéraire, philosophique et critique par Grimm, Diderot, Raynal, Meister, etc. revue sur les textes originaux comprenant outre ce qui a été publié à diverses époques les fragments supprimés en 1813 par la censure les parties inédites conservées à la Bibliothèque Ducale de Gotha et l'Arsenal à Paris* (16 vols., Paris, 1877–82).
Trans.	Translator or translated.
Trans.	*Transactions.*
Van Doren, *Franklin*	Carl Van Doren, *Benjamin Franklin* (New York, 1938).
Van Doren, *Franklin-Mecom*	Carl Van Doren, ed., *The Letters of Benjamin Franklin & Jane Mecom* (American Philosophical Society *Memoirs*, XXVII, Princeton, 1950).
Villiers, *Commerce colonial*	Patrick Villiers, *Le Commerce colonial atlantique et la guerre d'indépendance des Etats-Unis d'Amérique, 1778–1783* (New York, 1977).
W&MQ	*William and Mary Quarterly,* first or third series as indicated.
Ward, *War of the Revolution*	Christopher Ward, *The War of the Revolution* (John R. Alden, ed.; 2 vols., New York, 1952).
Waste Book	BF's accounts described above, XXIII, 19.
WF	William Franklin.

Wharton, *Diplomatic Correspondence*	Francis Wharton, ed., *The Revolutionary Diplomatic Correspondence of the United States* (6 vols., Washington, D.C., 1889).
Willcox, *Portrait of a General*	William B. Willcox, *Portrait of a General: Sir Henry Clinton in the War of Independence* (New York, 1964).
Wolf and Hayes, *Library of Benjamin Franklin*	Edwin Wolf 2nd and Kevin J. Hayes, eds., *The Library of Benjamin Franklin* (Philadelphia, 2006).
WTF	William Temple Franklin.
WTF, *Memoirs*	William Temple Franklin, ed., *Memoirs of the Life and Writings of Benjamin Franklin, L.L.D., F.R.S., &c . . .* (3 vols., 4to, London, 1817–18).
WTF's accounts	Those described above, XXIII, 19.
Yela Utrilla, *España*	Juan F. Yela Utrilla, *España ante la Independencia de los Estados Unidos* (2nd ed.; 2 vols., Lérida, 1925).

Note by the Editors and the Administrative Board

As we noted in volume 23 (pp. xlvi–xlviii), the period of Franklin's mission to France brings with it roughly two and a half times as many documents as those for the other seventy years of his life. In the present volume once again we summarize a portion of his incoming correspondence in collective descriptions; they appear in the index under the following headings: emigrants, would-be; offerers of goods and schemes; favor seekers; consulship seekers; verse, composers of.

As we noted in volume 30 (p. lx), Franklin's French secretary Jean L'Air de Lamotte was responsible for keeping the official letterbook. Many of his copies contain errors of spelling, punctuation, and syntax that could not have been present in Franklin's originals. Regrettably, these copies are in many cases the only extant versions. We publish them as they stand, pointing out and correcting errors only when they threaten to obscure Franklin's meaning.

A revised statement of textual methodology appeared in volume 28 and is repeated here. The original statement of method is found in the Introduction to the first volume, pp. xxiv–xlvii. The various developments in policy are explained in xv, xxiv; xxi, xxxiv; xxiii, xlvi–xlviii.

We are pleased to announce the digital edition of *The Papers of Benjamin Franklin,* conceived and sponsored by the Packard Humanities Institute, at www.franklinpapers.org. It contains texts of our entire archive up to Franklin's death, including those papers we either summarize in our volumes or mention in annotation, as well as biographical sketches of Franklin's correspondents and an introduction by Edmund S. Morgan. Readers should be aware that papers to be included in future volumes, marked "unpublished," are only preliminary transcriptions and will be verified before publication. Dates and attributions may also change as our research proceeds.

While this volume was in preparation, Associate Editor Karen Duval and Administrative Assistant Elizabeth Morris left the project. We thank them and wish them well.

Introduction

This volume chronicles the transition from war to a provisional peace and with it the gradual recognition of the United States of America as an independent nation in the eyes of the world. It begins the day after the preliminary peace treaty between the United States and Great Britain took effect, treaties were signed at Versailles between Great Britain and its European enemies, and general terms for the cessation of hostilities were agreed upon by all the belligerents.[1] It ends as formal negotiations for the definitive British-American peace treaty are finally poised to begin, after having been stalled by political events in England. In the intervening months, despite the frustrating delay in negotiations for the definitive treaty, the American peace commissioners as a group and Franklin as minister plenipotentiary had a great deal to do. Transatlantic trade had to be reestablished and trade regulations clarified. The United States was being courted for treaties of amity and commerce by governments wary of signing formal agreements before the definitive British-American treaty was signed; Franklin negotiated the first of them, a treaty with Sweden that was signed in secret. As the Loyalists in Britain bitterly demanded reparations and helped bring about the fall of the Shelburne government, individuals from all over Europe clamored to emigrate and begged Franklin for help. Franklin helped plan a transatlantic packet boat service, advising the French on how to navigate into New England ports, and continued his personal campaign to publicize American ideals.

One of the first tasks for the American peace commissioners was to exchange ships' passports with Great Britain that would protect merchant vessels until the armistice took effect in different parts of the world. (The preliminary peace treaties called for an incremental cessation of hostilities based on distance from Europe.) The issue reawakened Franklin's rage at the British for

1. See the Preliminary Articles of Nov. 30, 1782, and the Acceptance of the British Declaration of the Cessation of Hostilities of Jan. 20, 1783: XXXVIII, 382–9, 605–8.

imposing the Prohibitory Act. Assuming that he, as minister plenipotentiary, was authorized to compose the American passports for British ships, Franklin produced a form that allowed British vessels to carry cargo anywhere in the world other than the United States. Jay and Adams overruled him, and Franklin was forced to approve more general language that was issued in the name of all three commissioners.[2] These passports were exchanged for British counterparts prepared by Alleyne Fitzherbert, the temporary British minister at the French court. Once George III formally declared a cessation of hostilities on February 14, the American commissioners followed suit and issued a declaration of their own on February 20. The terms of the armistice that had been agreed upon at Versailles on January 20 now took effect.

The Americans were still in desperate need of money. Less than a week after the preliminary peace was declared, Franklin cautiously petitioned French Foreign Minister Vergennes for an additional 6,000,000 *l.t.* to supplement the 6,000,000 *l.t.* loan the French had granted the previous month. This request was quickly refused.[3] On May 10 the Americans' banker Ferdinand Grand informed the commissioners that he lacked the funds to meet their anticipated expenses.

The French treasury was also in trouble. With war's end the government suspended payment on all bills of exchange drawn from the United States, the West Indies, and India. One victim of this new policy was Franklin's nephew Jonathan Williams, Jr., who was unable to collect the 184,000 *l.t.* due him from bills he held. Franklin obligingly sought an exemption on Williams' behalf, but the request was denied.[4]

Franklin's skills as a diplomat continued to be vital. As soon as the British-American preliminary peace treaty took effect on January 20, he revived the secret negotiations for a commercial treaty that he had started in December with the Swedish ambassador, the comte de Creutz. Congress had instructed him to obtain a treaty as soon as possible, even if it meant compromising

2. The two passports are published below, Feb. 1 and 3.
3. BF to Vergennes, Jan. 25; Vergennes to BF, Feb. 1.
4. JW to BF, March 5; Joly de Fleury to BF, March 15.

on certain articles. Sweden, too, wanted to conclude a treaty as soon as possible, but its position was complicated by the ongoing Parliamentary debates over the terms of the preliminary peace agreement. Gustavus III was determined to be the first monarch to sign a treaty with the United States after peace was declared, but he feared reprisals from Great Britain should that treaty be signed before American independence was absolutely assured. On February 5, after news arrived in Paris that the British crown had ratified the Anglo-French preliminary articles, Creutz and Franklin signed their treaty. Hours later, Creutz received strict instructions from Gustavus not to sign anything until the preliminary articles were officially published in London. Franklin agreed to destroy the dated treaty and sign a new, undated version while awaiting the London publication. That publication was not forthcoming. A month later, under pressure from both Franklin and Vergennes, Creutz decided that he could wait no longer. He and Franklin met on March 5, agreed on five additional articles that granted the remainder of what Congress had requested, and signed the treaty in secret. To appease the king, Franklin was willing to date it April 3, a date Creutz had selected for practical reasons of his own.[5] Despite this discrepancy in dates, both negotiators immediately sent the treaty to their respective governments for ratification.

As minister plenipotentiary to the French court, Franklin continued to work with Vergennes, signing a new contract for the repayment of American loans and submitting a memoir on removing obstacles to American trade.[6] He was also inundated with requests from people all over Europe for help in establishing trade with America, assistance in emigrating, or support of their bids for consulships.

The major unfinished business of the American peace commissioners was the negotiation of a definitive peace treaty with Great Britain. They hoped to incorporate a commercial treaty into that document. Unfortunately, discussions were delayed be-

5. See the the headnote and text of the Swedish-American treaty published under [March 5].

6. The contract was signed on Feb. 25; BF's letter to Vergennes was written on March 16.

cause of the political circumstances in Great Britain. Prime Minister Shelburne was forced to resign in February, and it was not until April that a new government took office. It was only at that point that the British appointed a negotiator to treat with the Americans. Their choice was Franklin's old friend David Hartley, who arrived in Paris at the end of April. Hartley's credentials were unacceptable to the Americans, however, so initial discussions were perforce informal while the negotiators waited to see whether Hartley would be issued the full powers that they demanded. George III issued Hartley those powers on May 14, which allowed formal negotiations to begin. Those negotiations, which culminated in the Treaty of Paris of September 3, will be covered in Volume 40.

During the months of this volume Franklin continued his work on two major projects that helped launch the United States as an independent nation in the eyes of Europe and publicized American ideals. One was the so-called *Libertas Americana* medal, which commemorated American independence, the victories at Saratoga and Yorktown, and France's aid in the war. He distributed gold medals to the king and queen of France, silver medals to the diplomatic corps, and copper medals to special friends of America. They became such coveted objects that Franklin ordered a second striking, distributing more medals in France and sending one to every member of Congress. The image of Liberty that he certainly helped design—a strong young woman in profile whose loose hair streamed behind her—would prove to be enduring in both France and America.[7]

Franklin's second project was the French edition of the founding documents of the United States: the thirteen state constitutions, the declaration of independence, the articles of confederation, and the treaties with France, Holland, and (because publication was delayed) Sweden. He continued to work on this edition with the duc de La Rochefoucauld, who had translated many of the documents, and the printer Philippe-Denis Pierres. Largely printed during the period of this volume, *Constitutions des treize Etats-Unis de l'Amérique* was not issued until July.

When the American commissioners' dispatches informing

---

7. See BF and Morellet's "Explanation of a Medal," [c. May 5].

Congress of the provisional preliminary articles that they had signed with the British on November 30 finally reached Philadelphia in the middle of March, they were met with deep uncertainty as to whether Congress could ratify that preliminary treaty without breaking the terms of the Franco-American alliance, which forbade either party to make a separate peace. Two weeks later, when news of the armistice signed on January 20 arrived, Secretary of Foreign Affairs Robert R. Livingston scolded Franklin and the entire peace commission for failing to consult France before signing the preliminary agreement.[8] By the time Livingston wrote that letter, Franklin had long since mollified the French, and a general euphoria prevailed in Europe. Franklin was inundated with congratulations and adulatory verses and was honored at elaborate ceremonies held by the Lodge of the Nine Sisters and the Musée de Paris.[9]

Privately, Franklin was both elated and bitter, energized and wistful. He continued to reflect on the treachery of those former Americans who called themselves Loyalists, and on the evils of war. As he wrote to Mary Hewson on January 27, "All Wars are Follies, very expensive & very mischievous ones. When will Mankind be convinc'd of this, and agree to settle their Differences by Arbitration? Were they to do it even by the Cast of a Dye, it would be better than by Fighting & destroying each other." He was conscious of his own mortality, as well, particularly as he had lost several of his close friends over the previous year. He felt one of those losses particularly keenly: that of Mary Hewson's mother, Margaret Stevenson, his former London landlady. He continued his letter to Hewson by begging her to visit him in the spring, "when Travelling will be delightful," and concluded by writing to her what he regretted not having been able to tell more of his old friends: "*the fewer we become, the more let us love one another.*"

8. Livingston to the American Peace Commissioners, March 25; Livingston to BF, March 26.

9. The invitation from the masonic lodge was issued by the marquis de la Salle (Jan. 30, below). For the latter celebration see Court de Gébelin to the Secretary of the American Philosophical Society, March 15.

Chronology

January 21 through May 15, 1783

January 23: Franklin is sent designs for *Libertas Americana* medal.

February 3: American peace commissioners approve language of passports for British ships; Britain and France exchange treaty ratifications.

February 14: George III issues declaration of cessation of hostilities.

February 18: Alleyne Fitzherbert sends passports for American ships.

February 20: American peace commissions issue declaration of cessation of arms.

February 23: French government suspends payment of bills of exchange from United States.

February 24: The Earl of Shelburne resigns as prime minister.

February 25: Franklin, Vergennes sign new contract for American repayment of French loans.

March 3: Board of Admiralty orders exchange of all American prisoners in Britain; Pitt introduces "American Intercourse Bill" in House of Commons.

March 5: Franklin, Creutz sign Swedish-American commercial treaty.

March 12: News of preliminary American-British peace agreement reaches Philadelphia.

March 15: Washington addresses dissatisfied officers at Newburgh, New York.

March 23: News of end of hostilities reaches Philadelphia.

c. March 26: Striking of *Libertas Americana* medals.

April 2: Duke of Portland becomes prime minister of Great Britain.

April 8: Franklin presents *Libertas Americana* medal to Louis XVI.

April 11: Congress proclaims cessation of arms.

April 15: Congress ratifies preliminary peace articles.

April 17: George III approves repeal of Prohibitory Act.

April 24: David Hartley arrives in Paris for commercial discussions, negotiation of final peace treaty.

May 6: Conference between Washington and Carleton; Livingston presents to Congress a draft American-British commercial treaty.

May 12: George III assents to bill granting him power to issue orders in council on trade matters.

May 14: Order in council allows non-manufactured American goods to enter British ports. George III issues Hartley full powers to sign treaty.

THE PAPERS OF
BENJAMIN FRANKLIN

VOLUME 39

January 21 through May 15, 1783

Editorial Note on Franklin's Accounts

The following previously identified accounts cover the period of this volume: VI and VII (xxiii, 21); XVII (xxvi, 3); XIX and XXII (xxviii, 3–4); XXV, XXVII, and XXVIII (xxxii, 3–4); XXX (xxxvi, 3); and XXXI (xxxviii, 3). We offer here a summary of items that have not found a place elsewhere in our annotation but that provide insights into Franklin's private and public life.

Account XVII (Franklin's Private Accounts with Ferdinand Grand, xxvi, 3) reveals, as usual, a variety of personal and household transactions. On January 31 Franklin ordered Grand to remit 4,800 *l.t.* to Benjamin Vaughan. No request for this sum survives, though one of several requests from Benjamin's brother does.[1] M. "Sikes," undoubtedly the optician and scientific instrument dealer H. Sykes, presented a bill for 300 *l.t.* 4 *s.* on February 1, which Grand paid three days later. Mlle Chaumont and Brunel the carpenter both provided unspecified services. A request for payment from Gabriel-Louis Marignac, Benjamin Franklin Bache's tutor, was accepted on March 20. Jean L'Air de Lamotte, Franklin's secretary, received 380 *l.t.* on February 27 and 193 *l.t.* on April 1. Franklin's servant Arbelot received 150 *l.t.* on March 3. Jacques Finck, the new *maître d'hôtel*,[2] was paid 600 *l.t.* on February 18 for expenses not summarized in his monthly bill.

Franklin was credited on January 21 with interest of 4,800 *l.t.* arising from his shares in the *caisse d'escompte.*

Account XXV (Account of Postage and Errands, xxxii, 3) was at this time being kept by L'Air de Lamotte. Franklin received letters and packets almost daily, for which he paid postage. The most costly packet by far was the one delivered on February 19, which required a payment of 83 *l.t.* On two occasions in April, Franklin hired carriages to distribute *Libertas Americana* medals. William Temple Franklin franked a packet containing another medal that was sent by post. On April 28 and 29, contrary to usual practice, loans were recorded in this account to three Americans who had escaped from British prisons.[3]

---

1. Samuel Vaughan, Jr., to BF, April 3, below.
2. Finck assumed the position at the beginning of 1783: xxxviii, 3, 530–1.
3. On April 28 Thomas Cave signed a promissory note for 24 *l.t.*, one section of which is interfiled in this account; see also the Editorial Note on Promissory Notes. On April 29 loans of 18 *l.t.* were recorded for two illiterate seamen who could not fill out forms. L'Air de Lamotte understood the name of one of them to be J. Mercer; he noted the other as "Prisonier Ameri-

We presume that L'Air de Lamotte was the one who authorized those expenditures, and that it was he who took the trip by carriage noted on May 8 both to obtain from Ferdinand Grand the funds for those prisoners, and to settle an account "for the public" with the bookseller Pissot. Finck and Bonnefoÿ the gardener[4] each submitted bills for errands, which were paid. Those bills are interfiled in the account, as are the itemized bills of Berthelot the postman.

Account XXVII (Accounts of the Public Agents in Europe, XXXII, 4) records quarterly salary payments of 360 *l.t.* to L'Air de Lamotte in January and April. William Temple Franklin's quarterly payment of 1,800 *l.t.* was issued on April 8. On April 30 Franklin received 43,750 *l.t.*, salary for the previous three quarters at 14,583 *l.t.* 6 *d.* 8 *s.* per quarter. Franklin ordered Grand to pay John Jay 20,000 *l.t.* on March 11.[5] On April 17 the Nantes firm of Schweighauser & Dobrée was reimbursed 2,796 *l.t.* for "sundry disbursements" made by Pitot Duhellés, their agent in Morlaix, on behalf of the 138 Americans who had arrived from Plymouth aboard the cartel *Molly.*

Account XXXI (Jacques Finck's Accounts of Household Expenditures, XXXVIII, 3) provides the most detailed glimpse into Franklin's larder that we have had since the Household Accounts of 1779 (Account XXI, XXVIII, 3). Among the meats, fish, songbirds, fowl, vegetables, fruits, spices, nuts, pasta, dairy goods (including heavy cream for making ice cream), condiments, wine, spirits, coffee, and chocolate, Finck also records household staples such as ice, wood, candles, writing paper, and kitchenware. He pays wages and a wine allowance to the cook, M. La Marque, and buys milk, cream, and fine herbs from Mlle Chaumont; otherwise, his suppliers and the household staff are listed only by function. Pots were mended, wood was stacked, water was carried, dishes were washed. In February Finck purchased a pair of three-branch silver candelabras and a pair of smaller ones, a bucket for washing feet, and enough cloth and ribbons to make 50 aprons and 80 dishcloths. In April, on an unspecified date, he paid the expenses of

---

cain." These men must have arrived at Passy when BF and WTF were meeting with the other American commissioners in Paris; see Adams and Jay to BF, April 28.

4. XXXVII, 4.

5. This payment was "on account of monies due to him from Congress," according to the May 11 letter WTF sent Jay, enclosing the order on Grand. WTF told Jay in that letter that BF thought this method of payment "the best manner of settling for the present." Columbia University Library.

bringing from the customs house two large books that had arrived from England.[6]

Editorial Note on Promissory Notes

Seventeen escaped prisoners made their way to Passy and received financial assistance from Franklin during the period covered by this volume.[7]

Benjamin Ramsdell of Massachusetts,[8] captured aboard the ship *Three Sisters*, received 96 *l.t.* on February 10. Thomas Moore was given 48 *l.t.* on February 23. Four men applied for assistance on March 9, each of whom received 24 *l.t.* They were Richard Cockshott of Pennsylvania and James Leigh, Mourning Richardson, and R. Roxbury, all of Virginia.[9] On March 16 four more men were given 24 *l.t.* each: William Bird of Maryland, John Dorsey of Harford County, Maryland, Thomas Jones of New York, and John Stidart of Edenton, North Carolina. Richard Haynes of South Carolina signed a note for 36 *l.t.* on March 23. On April 27 John Baker, Peter Green, William Hoadley, Timothy Parmele, and John Peet each signed notes for 24 *l.t.* Thomas Cave received the same amount on April 28.[1]

---

6. Among BF's papers at the APS is an otherwise mysterious note from A. Raibaud in Paris, dated March 4: he had received "your Box," but not knowing the contents, was afraid it would be "taken." If BF (or possibly WTF) would send word, he would give it to his man at Calais "to pass it by assurance," if it was not too large.

7. All the promissory notes described below are at the APS.

8. Ramsdell was aided in Calais on Jan. 4 by Jacques Leveux: Leveux to BF, March 30, 1784 (APS). His name was not recorded on the Alphabetical List of Escaped Prisoners.

9. Francis Coffyn aided all four men before their arrival in Passy: Account XXVII (XXXII, 4). Richardson, captured aboard the *Pocahontas*, was committed to Forton Prison on Nov. 18, 1780, and pardoned for the Royal Navy on March 27, 1781: Kaminkow, *Mariners*, p. 161.

1. Cave was committed to Forton on Jan. 23, 1778, and pardoned for exchange on May 31, 1779: Kaminkow, *Mariners*, p. 35. None of the men who signed promissory notes in April was included on the Alphabetical List of Escaped Prisoners.

From Charles-Gabriel de Messey[2]

ALS: American Philosophical Society

Monsieur   [after January 20, 1783][3]

Jay apris avec la mesme Satisfaction lheureuse nouvelle de la paye finie que selle de la liberté que nos hommes ont procuré au quatorze provinse de la Merique, Evenement qui Eternise a james la mémoire dun des plus grant homme de notre siecle en votre Respectable persone. Permette moi monsieur davoir lhoneur de vous an faire mon compliment, je doit set omage a toutte les marque de bonté et damitié dont il vous a plut mhonorer pandan mon séjour ché monsieur et madame le roy mes anfants qui mont procure lavantage de ferre votre conessance insy que selle de monsieur votre fils bien digne dimiter les tallants et les vertu Eroique dun ausy grant homme que vous monsieur.

Permetté quil trouve isy mes tres humbles complimant il ne me restroit a désirer que destre themoins de tout Les omages que votre nasion randront a vos vertus Eroique qui leurs procure tout les avantages dont ils vont jouire je desir que se que le roy mon maitre et la nasion a fet an faveur dun peuple ausy belliqueu unise pour tous les siecles avenir les deux nasions et quil vous plaise de ne james doutter du respectueux attachement avec le quel jay lhoneur Monsieur Votre tres humble et tres obeissant serviteur   MESSEY

---

2. Charles-Gabriel de Messey, baron de Braux-Le-Chatel, a former cavalry officer, was the father of Le Roy's wife Pétronille de Messey: David Smith *et al.*, eds., *Correspondance général d'Helvétius* (5 vols., Toronto, Buffalo, and Oxford, 1981–2004), IV, 130n. We previously misidentified Pétronille's father as the comte de Milly.

3. This letter was enclosed with Le Roy's letter of Feb. 10, below. The congratulations it offers are for the British-American peace agreement of Jan. 20 (XXXVIII, 605–8).

To Robert R. Livingston

Two ALS[4] and transcript: National Archives; press copy of ALS: Myron Kaller and Associates, Asbury Park, New Jersey (1991)

Sir,   Passy, Jany. 21. 1783.
I have just received your Letters of Novr. 9. & Decr. 3.[5] This is to inform you, & to request you would inform the Congress, that the Preliminaries of Peace between France, Spain, and England were yesterday signed, and a Cessation of Arms agreed to by the Ministers of those Powers, and by us in Behalf of the United States: Of which Act, so far as relates to us, I inclose a Copy.[6] I have not yet obtained a Copy of the Preliminaries agreed to by the three Crowns, but hear in general that they are very advantageous to France and Spain. I shall be able in a Day or two to write more fully and perfectly. Holland was not ready to sign Preliminaries, but their principal Points are settled.[7] Mr

---

4. With minor differences in phraseology.

5. XXXVIII, 292–5, 405–6. The *Heer Adams,* which carried them, arrived in Lorient on Jan. 18: Barclay to JA, Jan. 19, 1783 (Mass. Hist. Soc.).

6. On Jan. 20 Fitzherbert presented BF and JA with a Declaration of the Cessation of Hostilities between Great Britain and the United States, a general statement vowing to observe the same terms and timetable as were included in the preliminary articles he signed that day with France and Spain. The American commissioners drafted and signed a document that both accepted the British declaration and made a reciprocal one: XXXVIII, 605–8. Because the terms were not specified in those documents, the commissioners had WTF transcribe the relevant articles of the Anglo-French preliminaries, Articles 1 and 22. BF enclosed a copy of those articles in this letter to Livingston. (It was a press copy in L'Air de Lamotte's hand, now at the National Archives. A copy in WTF's hand is at the Mass. Hist. Soc.) Article 1 stated that as soon as the preliminaries were ratified, orders would be sent to all armies, squadrons, and subjects of the two powers to stop hostilities; each power would likewise issue sea passes for the ships carrying the news to their possessions. Article 22 spelled out the timetable by which the armistice would take effect in different parts of the world, starting from the date of the ratification: 12 days for ships in the Channel and in the North Sea; one month for the area from the Channel and North Sea to the Canary Islands, in either the Atlantic Ocean or the Mediterranean; two months from the Canaries to the equator; five months for anywhere beyond the equator: Parry, *Consolidated Treaty Series,* XLVIII, 238–9.

7. They were settled by Alleyne Fitzherbert and the comte de Vergennes: XXXVIII, 595n.

Laurens is absent at Bath, and Mr Jay in Normandy, for their Healths,[8] but will both be here to assist in forming the Definitive Treaty. I congratulate you & our Country, on the happy Prospects afforded us by the Finishing so speedily this glorious Revolution; and am with great Esteem, Sir, Your most obedient & most humble Servant   B FRANKLIN

Honble. R. R. Livingston Esqr

From Marie-Anne Le Page Fiquet, Dame Duboccage[9]

AL: American Philosophical Society

[after January 21, 1783][1]

Mde. Duboccage rend mille tres humbles graces a Mr. franklin; la Vision de Colomb donne une champ bien vaste a l'imagination du poëte et l'ange avoit Sans doute prévu qu'il naîtroit un

---

8. Laurens, who described himself as extremely ill, arrived in London on Jan. 15 and set out for Bath the next day, after receiving permission from the king to stay in England to recuperate: XXXVIII, 515n; *Laurens Papers*, XVI, 129–30. Jay returned on Jan. 23: XXXVIII, 596n.

9. This is the only extant letter from Mme Duboccage (du Bocage, du Boccage), a poet and translator to whom BF had recently sent a prospectus for Joel Barlow's nine-book epic poem, *The Vision of Columbus*. Mme Duboccage is remembered for her own epic poem, *La Colombiade, ou la foi portée au Nouveau Monde*, first published in 1756 to great acclaim: XXIII, 60n; *DBF;* Anne-Marie du Boccage, *La Colombiade . . .* , ed. Catherine Jardin (Paris, 1991), pp. 23–8.

Among BF's papers at the APS is a copy of a letter Mme Duboccage received from Voltaire dated Nov. 2, 1777, written in response to her having praised his tragedy, *Alzire ou les Américains*. Voltaire returned the compliment, writing, "Vous, Madame, et les insurgens, me rendez l'Amérique précieuse." The copy is in her hand; it is the text published in Theodore Besterman, ed., *The Complete Works of Voltaire: Correspondence and Related Documents* (51 vols., Toronto, Buffalo, and Geneva, 1968–77), XLV, 81.

1. The day by which BF had received Joel Barlow's handwritten prospectuses for his *Vision of Columbus*, circulated to elicit subscribers. They were enclosed in Livingston's letter of Nov. 21, which BF received along with Livingston's of Dec. 3: XXXVIII, 331n, 405n. BF acknowledged receipt of the latter on Jan. 21, the preceding document.

législateur tel que le tres docte franklin pour donner la liberté, de bonnes loix et Beaucoup de gloire a son païs.

Mde. Duboccage ne renvoie point l'imprimé en cas qu'elle trouve quelqu'un qui voulut souscrire.[2]

From Jean-Jacques Caffiéri ALS: American Philosophical Society

Monsieur De Paris ce 22 janvier 1783

L'europe entiere a Les yeux sur L'epoque à jamais memorable de La liberté de l'amerique, votre patrie Scait apprecier L'etendue de vos Lumieres, et combien vous ave contribué a La Rendre L'egale Des Roys—peutetre S'empressera t'elle de Transmettre a La Posterité Cette Epoque qui L'immortalise, par un Monument qui en atteste La Gloire, ou Rendre a vos Compatriotes Sacrifies pour La Cause Commune Le Tribut De Reconnoissance et de Regrets qu'elle leur Doits,[3] Dans L'une ou L'autre de ces circonstances je vous Suplie de vouloir bien contribuer a faire emploïer mes Talens, et D'etre persuadé que je mettrai tous mes Soins et mon Zele a me Rendre Digne de votre choix.

J'ay Lhonneur D'etre avec Respect Monsieur Votre tres humble et tres obeïssant Serviteur[4] CAFFIERI

Notation: Caffiery 22 Janr. 1783.

2. We have not found any printed prospectus. The only two Frenchmen listed among the subscribers of the first edition were Louis XVI, to whom the poem was dedicated, and the marquis de Lafayette: *The Vision of Columbus; a Poem in Nine Books* (Hartford, 1787), pp. iii–v and the unpaginated list of subscribers at the end of the book.

3. Caffiéri had been offering since the previous April to sculpt commemorative monuments for the Americans: XXXVII, 84, 741.

4. Caffiéri wrote to WTF the same day suggesting that Americans residing in Paris commission him to sculpt a statue of BF in marble or bronze to send to Philadelphia. APS.

From —— Gebhard and Other Favor Seekers[5]

ALS: American Philosophical Society

As usual, Franklin receives a steady stream of requests for favors of all kinds. The first of these, printed below, asks him to forward a letter.

Four other letters request a similar favor. On March 29 Wilhelm Augustine von Steuben, writing in German from Cüstrin, begs Franklin once again to forward a letter to his son the general, and in return will pray for His Excellency and the sons of the United States. He wishes Franklin to say whether he and the general have received his earlier missives, for he has had no word from his son.[6]

Two days later, H. Adolphe Hoffmeister sends a letter from Heidelberg to be forwarded to his brother-in-law Doll and thanks Franklin for his continuing assistance.[7]

The abbé de Floirac, vicar-general of the archbishopric of Paris, tells Franklin on April 9 that, in the "Nouvel empire que vous Venez de créer," there is a young Frenchman, the chevalier d'Anterroches, who is married and has children.[8] The chevalier has complained to his mother, the comtesse d'Anterroches,[9] that her letters are not delivered

---

5. Unless otherwise indicated, all the documents discussed here are in French and at the APS.

6. A contemporary English translation of this letter also is at the APS. This is von Steuben's last communication; he died less than a month later: Friedrich Kapp, *The Life of Frederick William von Steuben* . . . (New York, 1859), p. 43.

7. BF had received letters for George Jacob Leonard Doll twice before: XXXVI, 309; XXXVIII, 473.

8. Joseph-Louis d'Anterroches (Anterroche) (1753–1814), chevalier and later comte, as a younger son was intended for the church. He was sent to study under his uncle Alexandre-César d'Anterroches, Bishop of Condom (*DBF*), but ran away to England where he joined the British army, and was sent to America in 1777. Taken prisoner by the Americans, he wrote to Lafayette, a relation through his mother, and soon was paroled. He married Mary Vanderpoel in 1780, settled in Elizabethtown, N.J., in 1784, and distinguished himself during the Whiskey Rebellion. He died in France on a visit to his parents: Mrs. Emeline G. Pierson, "Some Records of the French in Elizabethtown," N.J. Hist. Soc. *Proc.*, 2nd ser., XIII (1894–95), 161–70.

9. Jeanne-Françoise Teyssier (Tessier) de Chaunac was the wife of Jean-Pierre d'Anterroches: *ibid.*, p. 165; *DBF,* under Marie-Thérèse d'Anterroche, the chevalier's sister.

promptly. The comtesse hopes that Franklin will agree to forward her letters in the future.

The peace has renewed the worries of one family: Françoise de Brahm writes from Coblentz on April 27 to ask for news of her brother,[1] who has not answered any of her letters for the past year. His last letter, a year ago, was sent from Philadelphia. Franklin forwarded the family's letters earlier in the war; would he again forward one to her brother and find out if he is still alive?

In February, Franklin received three requests for ships' passports. The first one, in English, comes from London on February 7: Thomas Backhouse,[2] thinking that an English ship might not be safe entering an American port "at this Crisis," wishes a pass for the *Active* (J. Powell, master),[3] loaded at Liverpool with salt and other merchandise bound for Philadelphia.

The Ostend firm of De Vinck & Co. asks Franklin's protection on February 13 for a business they intend to establish in either Boston or Philadelphia. They already have an agent in the latter place, Rodolph Tillier.[4] While in The Hague, Tillier became acquainted with John Adams, who gave him letters of recommendation. They hope that Franklin will be likewise obliging, by advising them and sending passports for the two ships they intend to send to one or the other city under the Imperial flag. Their "Sieur De Vinck," who will deliver this to

1. Ferdinand-Joseph-Sébastien de Brahm, whose father had enlisted BF's help six years earlier: XXIII, 593.

2. Probably Thomas Backhouse (1750–1824), who later became chairman of Lloyd's (c. 1796–1806): Joseph Foster, comp., *The Descendants of John Backhouse, Yeoman, Of Moss Side, Near Yealand Redman, Lancashire* (London, 1894), p. 16; Warren R. Dawson, *The Treasures of Lloyd's* (London, 1930), p. 82. Thomas Backhouse & Co., merchants, first appear in *Kent's Directory . . .* for 1785, p. 11.

3. *Lloyd's Register of Shipping* for 1783 (reprint, London, 1963–64), under *Active*.

4. Rodolphe Tillier, a native of Berne, became the third husband of Sarah Biddle Penrose Shaw (c. 1745–1794) of Philadelphia. During the early years of their marriage he was engaged in business with her brothers Owen and Clement Biddle (XV, 262n; XX, 185n), and just before the turn of the century he managed the Castorland colony in northern New York State: *Jefferson Papers*, XIII, 146n; XV, 160; Thomas R. Hay, "Letters of Mrs. Ann Biddle Wilkinson from Kentucky, 1788–1789," *PMHB*, LVI (1932), 44n; Harold C. Syrett *et al.*, eds., *The Papers of Alexander Hamilton* (27 vols., New York, 1961–87), XXVI, 41n.

Franklin, is commissary in Flanders for the navy of the States of Holland; he lives in Dunkirk and is a French subject.[5]

Louis Vivier writes on February 22 from La Rochelle,[6] optimistic that the arrival of peace will occasion commercial relations between the United States and the ports of France. To that end he is prepared to send a ship to the Chesapeake and desires a passport if one is necessary to unload the cargo.[7]

Other merchants require assistance to further their enterprises or help with ventures gone awry. The vicomte de Faudoas[8] writes on February 4 to ask a favor for Captain Harel of the *Marie-Thérèse*, a merchant ship about to leave Le Havre with a cargo for Philadelphia. Harel would like to be able to say that he has had the honor of Franklin's acquaintance, and wishes a few letters of recommendation. He is truly a man of merit and worthy of these kindnesses. Moreover, he will be one of the first Frenchmen to arrive in America since the peace.

On February 13 the chevalier de Mailly, marquis de Neelle,[9] seeks information for a venture not yet undertaken: he has heard that the United States is prepared to grant vast tracts of uncultivated land on very advantageous terms and that there is an agent at Paris in charge of handling these concessions. He would be most grateful if Franklin could inform him of the arrangements the United States has made.

Jean-Pierre Carayon and the widows Blaud and Ducastel, inhabi-

---

5. François Devinck is identified as a merchant at Dunkirk and consul general of the States of Flanders in Lüthy, *Banque protestante*, II, 528, and mentioned in Christian Pfister-Langanay, *Ports, navires et négociants à Dunkerque (1662–1792)* (Dunkirk, 1985), p. 472n.

6. Prominent merchant and shipowner, Louis Vivier belonged to an affluent, Protestant, merchant-outfitter family long established in La Rochelle: John G. Clark, *La Rochelle and the Atlantic Economy during the Eighteenth Century* (Baltimore, 1981), pp. 45, 47–8, 53–4, 92, 123–4, 212–13.

7. Vivier's optimism at the end of the war was misplaced; he and other Rochelais merchants who invested in American markets and the slave trade failed in 1787: *ibid.*, pp. 108–9.

8. XXV, 248n.

9. Louis-Marie-Joseph-Augustin, chevalier de Mailly, marquis de Neelle (Nesle) (1744–1810), entered the army in 1764 and rose to the rank of *maréchal de camp*. In April, 1789, he was elected to the Estates General as a deputy of the nobility, but resigned in protest in October and emigrated. He returned after the coup d'état of 18 Brumaire: *Dictionnaire de la noblesse*, XII, 870; Adolphe Robert, Edgar Bourloton, and Gaston Cougny, *Dictionnaire des parlementaires français* (5 vols., Paris, 1889–91), IV, 230.

tants of Nîmes, write on February 16.[1] At the end of 1781 the husbands of the two widows, associates of Carayon, embarked with a cargo for America. The following August they arrived at New Bern, North Carolina, by way of Martinique, and had set about selling or exchanging their merchandise when they both fell ill and died. Vanschellebeck and Mailhot,[2] French merchants with whom they had deposited their effects, have notified the survivors and offered to represent them before the state. Their confidence in the French firm has been bolstered by the recommendation of Monsieur Chaponel,[3] a resident of the state who is to become French consul. Will Franklin please ensure that the powers to represent their interests, which they have sent to the firm, are respected by the state authorities?

Two merchants from Germany, N. Westerwick of Lübeck and Friedrich Steyn of Berlin, write in English from Paris on February 17 requesting the letters for Philadelphia and Boston that Franklin has promised them. They travel separately to pursue individual business opportunities and request separate letters.

J.-Fr. Ruellan de Gallinée, a merchant of Saint-Malo, writes on February 20 for friends who wish information about letters of exchange received for a cargo sold in Charleston, South Carolina, in 1778. If Franklin has the time, could he tell them what the Carolina pound is worth in *livres tournois* and what return they might expect? In a postscript Ruellan adds that, although he does not have the honor of knowing Franklin, his visits to Paris have taken him often to houses that Franklin has honored with his presence.

1. Our text of this letter, which BF presumably forwarded to America (though no cover letter exists), comes from a French transcript with an English translation at the National Archives. Blaud & Comp. was a firm of cloth and woolen merchants of Nîmes: *Almanach des marchands*, p. 352. The widows signed "Chabert, veuve Blaud" and "Chadenede, veuve Ducastel."

2. Van Schellebeck and Mailhol, French merchants at New Bern, were factors of the marquis de Brétigney (Brétigny), agent for North Carolina at Martinique until the summer of 1782: William L. Saunders *et al.*, eds., *The Colonial and State Records of North Carolina* (30 vols., Raleigh, 1886–1914), XVI, 327, 394–6, 494. For Brétigney's arrival in America see XXIV, 96–8; XXXVI, 310.

3. The copyist mistakenly wrote "Chapomt." The correct spelling comes from the trio's next letter, dated July 9, 1784, which summarizes the story thus far and adds new details (APS). A M. Chaponel at New Bern received approval in 1789 to emancipate a three-year-old mulatto slave: Saunders *et al.*, *Colonial Records*, XXV, 37.

J.-P. Viollier,[4] a Geneva merchant, writes on March 17 concerning the estate of Denis Pallard, a former captain in the Geneva army who absconded to America with a part of his small fortune, leaving behind certain "désagrémens" and a wife and four young children.[5] Viollier, who has learned that Pallard probably died in Charleston before the city was taken by the English, has been appointed guardian to the children, and wishes now to retrieve the remains of Pallard's fortune. Could Franklin recommend him to someone to whom he could address his power of attorney? He encloses a two-page memoir about Pallard's activities since his departure in early 1778.

The Baron de La Marck et Stein, *seigneur de la libre imperiale seigneurie de Stein,* writes from Stein in Germany on March 23. He had traveled to America from Surinam in the hope of settling there and establishing a commercial firm, but has had to return to Europe, where he and his wife own land. Dutch bankers, ignorant of North America, have refused him the credit he needs for his venture. His youngest son has remained in Boston with Martin Brimmer[6] to learn the language and the commerce of the country. He has other contacts among the local merchants there and in Providence. On his return to America he will take with him a number of people who will contribute to improving agricultural practices. Will Franklin please extend credit to him and recommend him to some French merchants?

That same day but closer to home, the marquis de La Salle, Franklin's successor as *vénérable* of the Neuf Sœurs,[7] requests a letter of recommendation for the son of M. Poulletier, a wealthy and respected merchant of Paris, who is being sent to Philadelphia with a large cargo of goods. La Salle has been pressed on all sides to intervene for the merchant; indeed, Mme la marquise Dervillers, "femme aussi aimable que jolie," will be grateful to Franklin for helping this gallant man whom she has known for a long time. He adds that the lodge has decided on May 5 as the date of the celebration of the peace, an event Franklin has promised to attend.

4. Possibly Jean-Pierre Viollier (1755–1818), who became a member of the provisional government under the Restoration in December, 1813, and a *conseiller d'état* the following year: *Dictionnaire historique de la Suisse.*

5. Evidently, BF had agreed to write a letter of recommendation for Pallard in 1778: XXVI, 274.

6. A Boston merchant (d. 1804): James H. Stark, *The Loyalists of Massachusetts and the Other Side of the American Revolution* (Boston, 1910), p. 196; Mass. Hist. Soc., *Commerce of Rhode Island, 1726–1800* (2 vols., Boston, 1914–15), II, 41–2.

7. XXXIV, 470n.

M. Mazue, a merchant from Marseille, writes on March 24 to beg Franklin's help. He sank his entire fortune into merchandise sold in America; unfortunately, the captain accepted paper money for the goods, not realizing that the currency had depreciated. Could he exchange this money for land in America? If Franklin does not think this likely, could he at least help Mazue obtain a passage to America, where he could petition Congress in person? A month later, on April 23, the chevalier de Cachard, a captain in the grenadiers of Saluce and a vassal of the king of Sardinia, writes a letter urging Franklin to reply to Mazue, who faces certain ruin unless he can find some livelihood more reliable than that of commerce.

On March 26 the firm of Devoulx frères of Marseille[8] writes for information on exchange rates and on how to cash in loan office certificates received for cargo shipped on the *Hazard,* Captain Nicolas, and sold at Baltimore in 1778.

Daniel Astruc writes to Franklin from Bordeaux on May 6, asking for help in recovering the 576 *l.t.* 9 *s.* 2 *d.* he is owed by "sieur Grive de la Nouvelle Angleterre" for textiles purchased on January 17, 19, 30, and March 13. A copy of Grive's account is enclosed.[9] Astruc extended unlimited credit to him over his four-month stay in Bordeaux because he believed him to be a New Englander acting under Franklin's authority. Grive left for Paris on the public coach, commonly called the "Turgotine," two days ago. Astruc is acquainted with Vergennes, and hopes that Franklin will forgive this request out of consideration for that minister.[1]

---

8. The family was among the city's principal grain merchants and shippers: Louis Bergasse et al., eds., *Histoire du commerce de Marseille* (7 vols., Paris, 1949–66), IV, 381, 521.

9. The account lists him as "Grive Anglois." This was undoubtedly George Greive (Grieve), an Englishman who swore allegiance to the United States in 1781, told BF he planned to settle in Virginia, and procured from him a letter of recommendation. Greive stayed in America for only a year, where, according to Howard Rice, he transacted business for English acquaintances and seems to have been speculating in either war supplies or land. He sailed from New England in November, 1782, arriving in Bordeaux in January, 1783: XXXIV, 581–2; XXXV, 25–6, 28, 319; Marquis de Chastellux, *Travels in North America in the Years 1780, 1781 and 1782,* ed. and trans. Howard C. Rice, Jr. (2 vols., Chapel Hill, N.C., 1963), I, 30–2.

1. Astruc repeated this request on June 10, adding how unfortunate it was for a father of six children to see himself taken advantage of in such a way. Vergennes always replied by return mail; Astruc hoped that BF would do the same. APS.

Several people seek positions for themselves or others. Alexandre-Andronique Gika, who has come to Paris to search for employment, writes the first of three letters on March 6. He was born in Turkey to a family of some standing, has received the most careful education, and has traveled throughout Asia, Europe, and most of Africa. His applications at Versailles have met with promises and even a kind of pension, but now he offers his services to the United States. He speaks many languages, knows almost every district on earth, has contacts everywhere, and is persuaded that he can manage almost any business. If Franklin permits, he will present his letters of recommendation in person. Having received no response, Gika repeats his request on March 21, adding more about his career. He served with the Russians during the Russo-Turkish War, but when he did not receive payment, he went to London and sought the help of John Elphinston, formerly a rear-admiral in the Russian navy.[2] Finding that Elphinston could do nothing for him, Gika came to Paris. The marquis de Castries has made promises to him these past six months, but Gika is tired of waiting and wishes to sacrifice the rest of his days to the republic of the United States. A third letter from Gika, this one undated, asks on behalf of a friend if the Americans would appoint a Jew as consul at Marseille. A person of quality desires to solicit the position for a merchant there named Sylva.

M. de Boisroger, honorary inspector of manufactures at Chartres, writes from that city on March 14. Although he is not well enough known to Franklin to ask anything for himself,[3] he solicits a position for a fellow native of Chartres who will present this letter. Chauveau, now 25 or 26 years old, had so impressed the late bishop Fleury[4] that he found a place for the young man at the seminary of Saint-Sulpice and paid his way. Before completing his degree, he was diverted from his studies by the comte d'Albon, who wished the young man to accompany him on his travels. Chauveau later left d'Albon to become preceptor to the children of M. de La Linière, a colonel in the cavalry, *régiment du roi*,[5] but again was disappointed in his hopes for advance-

2. Elphinston left the Russian service in 1771 and was reinstated in the British Navy: *ODNB*.

3. Boisroger had been acquainted with BF since at least 1778: XXVII, 55–6.

4. Pierre-Augustin-Bernardin de Rosset de Rocozel de Fleury (1717–1780), consecrated bishop in 1746, was known for his charity toward the poor. He was almoner first to Queen Marie Leczinska and later to Marie-Antoinette: *DBF*.

5. D'Albon had written an account of these travels, and in December, 1782, sent BF a copy of the expanded edition: XXXVIII, 497–8. For Antoine-

ment and returned to Paris where he has been teaching geography and mathematics. Boisroger hopes also to be useful to Franklin in his exchanges with the French court.

The mayor of Abbeville, M. de Pioger, writes a general letter of recommendation on April 17 for young M. Le Febvre de Villers, the son of a distinguished local magistrate and the scion of a military family. The young man is endowed with talents, vigor, enterprise, and rural knowledge.

Several correspondents send Franklin samples of their work for his approbation or evaluation. On March 13 M. Bonzon, the rector of a school in Trévoux, where he teaches grammar, submits to Franklin his idea for this year's dialogue, an annual end-of-year exercise. The topic is the "Anglo-Franci-Américaine" war. Characters will be England, the mother country who imposed taxes upon taxes; the malcontented Americans, inspired by the genius of France; the king of France, who assured them of protection; Spain, who joined France; and so on. To succeed, Bonzon needs the names of the leaders of the revolution, the most illustrious members of Congress, and certain key generals. If Franklin does not have the goodness to supply him with "Matériaux Solides," he will have to make things up out of thin air and his own imagination.

On April 7 the comtesse de Malarme sends Franklin a copy of a book she has written, her third, inspired by a journey she made to America five years before. She would be flattered if Franklin would read it; she glories in her occupation, an unusual one in France for a woman so young. When she began to write, she was animated solely by glory. Now that she has lost her fortune, she asks Franklin for a donation of whatever amount he thinks appropriate.[6]

François de Guichard de La Linière (1724–1808) see the *DBF,* under Guichard, and *Etat militaire* for 1782, p. 351.

6. Charlotte de Bournon, comtesse de Malarme (1753–*c.* 1830), was at the beginning of a prolific literary career. Her previous book, *Le Fripon parvenu* . . . (1782), was deemed libelous and landed the young woman and her co-author in the Bastille. Her new work was a novel, *Anna Rose-Tree, histoire anglaise,* announced the following day for sale at 3 *l.t.: Jour. de Paris,* issue of April 8. Malarme, who was the sister of the mineralogist Jacques-Louis de Bournon and the wife of Jean-Etienne de Malarme, went on to publish more than 30 novels, many with English characters or settings, and was made a member of the Accademia degli Arcadi of Rome. *DBF,* under her brother's name; *Nouvelle biographie;* Quérard, *France littéraire;* Anna Maria Giorgetti Vichi, ed., *Gli Arcadi dal 1690 al 1800, onomasticon* (Rome, 1977), p. 106, under Eudora Afrodisea, her Arcadian name.

The parish priest of Arpajon, curé Guinchard,[7] seeks Franklin's advice on April 25 concerning the medical case of one of his parishioners, a six-year-old girl who has been paralyzed in both legs since the age of two. He hopes that Franklin is still able to engage in making precious discoveries in physics and medicine, in which he himself is an amateur.[8] Wanting to help this girl, he bought an electrical machine from Mr. Rouland, demonstrator of physics at the University of Paris,[9] and for the past two months he and a local surgeon have been administering electric therapy. The treatments, lasting 45 minutes and administered twice daily, were given first by bath, then by sparks and commotions.[1] Guinchard begs Franklin to read the enclosed account of the treatment, add his remarks in the margin, and return it by post.[2]

As always, some writers simply want money. Andrew Kirwan writes in English from Passy on April 5 and encloses an account of his "case."[3] Hearing that Franklin "is possessd. of a most Tender good heart, Especially towards the distressd.," Kirwan is emboldened to ask him and his friends to put together "a little Mony" for him.

Acknowledging that this is his second letter, Sebastian Hartwig,[4] musician at the ducal court at Gotha, writes in German on May 9 to wish Franklin a safe journey when he returns to America. He requests 100 louis d'or, or at least 50, to be forwarded by Privy Councillor von Grimm to chief court mistress von Buchwald. Hartwig's brother will repay the loan when Franklin arrives in America. Should Franklin decline to send the money, would he please transmit the enclosed letter to his brother? It might be Hartwig's last, for they are both very old and have one foot in the grave.

Finally, in a category of his own, Jean-Chrétien Schuster writes from Vienna on February 8 reminding Franklin that in March, 1778, he had written to say that he had named his newborn son after the three American commissioners Franklin, Deane, and Lee. He now

7. François-Marie Guinchard is mentioned in A.-E. Genty, *Histoire de La Norville et de sa seigneurie* (Paris, Brussels, and Geneva, 1885), p. 259.
8. BF discussed his experiments with electric-shock treatment in a Dec. 21, 1757, letter to John Pringle (VII, 298–300), which was included in Dubourg, *Œuvres*, I, 191–3.
9. XXXVIII, 177n.
1. For the three electrotherapeutic techniques see Geoffrey Sutton, "Electric Medicine and Mesmerism," *Isis*, LXXII (1981), 384–6.
2. The two-and-a-half page journal, with unannotated margins, remains with Guinchard's letter.
3. Not found.
4. Hartwig wrote in 1778 asking for the same favor: XXVI, 365–6.

gives details on the baptism of little Benjamin Silas Arthur, whom they call "le petit Americain." Schuster, who signs himself a banker, congratulates Franklin on the peace, renews his expressions of admiration, and asks whether, as a particular favor, the minister could give him the names of merchants in Boston, Philadelphia, New York, and Charlestown.

Monseigneur!   a strasbourg Le 22: Jany 1783.

Je prie en grace Son Exellence, de me pardonner la grande Liberté, que je prends par celleci de Vous recomander à Vos graces Ci jointe cette Lettre à mon frère, de qui notre famile n'a pas reçue aucunne avis depuis la rupture existe dans cet Etat.

Votre humanité fondé partout me fait esperer que Son Exellence, ne réfusera pas la Grace à celui, qui se mette à vos pieds. Monseigneur. Votre très devoué Valet   GEBHARD

Notation: Gebhard, Strasbourg 22 Janr. 1783.

From Joseph Trout and Richard Davis

ALS: American Philosophical Society

Honoured Sir!   Niort Castle Jany 22. 1783

We hope you will pardon the Liberty we take in sending you these few lines, was it not on Account of your general good Character, and the Distress we labour under we assure you we should not be so bold; but thinking our Situation very hard and more than ever our true Countrymen met with since the Commencement of the present Hostilities, encourages us to be so bold as to address ourselves to you in hopes of once more regaining the liberty to see our Mother Country. The first hereunder signed was born at Boston, brought up in the same place, and gave his Mind to the Sea to which he has serv'd ever since in the Service of his Country, the latter was born in Newberry in Massachusetts Bay, brought up in the same manner as above, in the Sea Service.[5] These two having been taken in a Brig from Point

5. Davis may have served aboard the sloop *Republic* in 1776 under Capt. John Foster Williams: Mass. Secretary of State, *Massachusetts Soldiers and Sailors of the Revolutionary War* (17 vols., Boston, 1896–1908), IV, 535.

Peters bound to Newberry, by an English Privateer and carried into New York, where they laid upwards of 8 Months on board of a Prison Ship[6] enduring the greatest hardships. We were then taken out, though much against our Inclination to man a fleet bound to England, where when we arrivd, rather than go on board an English Man of War, or go in a Prison, we found ourselves obligated, to go on board a Vessell bound to the West Indias, in hopes of there gaining our Releasement, but however we did not reach so far, before we were taken by a french Man of War, which carried us into Rochelle, from whence we were marchd to this place, notwithstanding all our Applications of being Americans. We therefore Hond Sir now beg leave to desire a little of your kind Consideration on our present Circumstances, hoping you will be so good as to gain our Releasement, to go in the Service of the Country which gave us birth therefore in Expectation of your kind Answer by return of post, directed as at foot, informing us whether we may expect our Desires or not We also beg you will be so good in Case of the Affirmative, to send a Line with your Orders to the Commandant at this place (as at foot) with our Passport.

Therefore hoping to hear from you with the News according to our Wishes, We have the Honour to remain with the greatest Esteem Honoured Sir Your mo: Hble & Obt: Servts:

JOSEPH TROUT
RICHARD DAVIS

NB to us under Cover to the Commandant to Him, A Monsieur Monsieur de la Pomelie Lieutenant du Roi Commandant du Chateau de Niort en Poitou

Addressed: A Monseigneur / Monseigr: Franklin / Ambassadeur des Etats / Americains / à / Paris

Notation: Richd. Davis, Janvier 22. 1783.

---

6. Perhaps the *Jersey,* the most notorious prison hulk during the war: XXXVII, 228n.

Cliché of Unfinished Reverse of *Libertas Americana*

From Alexandre-Théodore Brongniart[7]

ALS: American Philosophical Society

paris le 23. janvi 1783

J'ai L'honneur d'Envoyer a Monsieur franclin deux Nouvelles Epreveuves de la medaille, en observant que La tete[8] n'est pas encore au point de perfection ou elle doit etre, que Les Serpens que tient L'enfant Seront plus grands et plus Caracterisés; en outre Le graveur a mis *intans,* au lieu d'*infans* et qu'il Corrigera Ce deffaut d'Ortographe—[9]

J'ai L'honneur de Rapeller au Souvenir de Monsieur franclin qu'il m'avoit promis Ce qu'il doit faire Ecrire des deux Cotés en Bas de la Medaille et que Ce Seul objet en retient La perfection.[1]

---

7. The architect who had solicited sketches for the *Libertas Americana* medal and was now serving as an intermediary between BF and the engraver, Augustin Dupré; see XXXVIII, 128–9, 577–8. On April 23 Brongniart was paid 1,136 *l.t.* "in full on Account of the Medal": Account XXVII (XXXII, 4).

8. "Tête" has a double meaning in this case: its numismatic sense is "obverse," but Brongniart could also be referring to the head of Liberty, which would amount to the same thing.

9. The proof of the obverse has never been located. The unfinished reverse came to light in May, 2006, as part of the John J. Ford, Jr., Collection sold at Stack's. It is shown on the facing page, where the misspelling of "infans" is obvious, and the snakes are somewhat shorter than in the final version illustrated in the frontispiece. The snake in the infant's right hand was given a longer tail; the one in his left hand was given a longer tongue with an exaggerated tip.

The motto BF selected for the reverse was from Horace's *Odes,* book 3, ode 4, line 20: "Non sine diis animosus infans" (not without divine help is the infant courageous). For the obverse, he chose "Libertas Americana." They had been suggested by the classicist William Jones, whom BF thanked on March 17, below.

1. The blank sections at the base of each side were reserved for dates. For the reverse, there was a question of how best to fit the two dates of the surrenders of Burgoyne and Cornwallis in such a small, curved space. BF sketched a design on the verso of the present letter. Taking advantage of the fact that both battles occurred in October, he wrote "Oct." in the narrow space on the left (centered, top to bottom), drew a brace, and to the right of it wrote the day and year of each battle, one above the other. Either BF or Dupré later altered this design by moving "Oct." to the center; see the illustration of the finished medal.

J'ai Celui de L'assurer du tres humble Respect de Son tres de-
vouè Serviteur   BRONGNIART

Endorsements: Jeudy en huit chez Mad D'uteto / Jan. 31. 83[2]

Notation: Brognant, Paris 23 Janvr. 1783

From the Marquis de Saint-Auban, with Franklin's Note for a Reply
ALS: American Philosophical Society

Monsieur   paris le 23 janvier 1782 [*i.e.*, 1783][3]
Vous etes au comble de la gloire, veullie le ciel que vous
jouissies long tems de votre triomphe, les dieux vous ont bien
privilegié en vous acordant autant de superiorité de genie,
puisque vous vous etes aquis la plus haute celebrité dans les sciences sublimes, et que vous les avès apliquées a la conservation
de lhumanité; vos vues se sont ensuite tournées vers votre nation
dont vous devenès le libérateur. Jouissés long tems de la venéra-
tion qui vous ets [est] due, votre nom sera a jamais celebre dans
les fastes de lhistoire de tous les pays; jay ete et seray toujours
votre admirateur, je partage bien sincerement vos sucés, et vous
suplie de ne jamais douter de la verite et de la sincerité de tous
les sentiments que vous mavès inspires et avec les quels jay
lhoneur detre Monsieur votre tres humble et très obeissant serviteur   ST. AUBAN

Endorsed: That I am sensible touché de la part qu'il a le bonte de
prendre de notre heureux Sort. C'est l'ouvrage de Dieu & le Roy
de France. J'aurois bientot l'honneur de faire mes Compliments
respectueuses a lui & Made de St Auban en personne.[4]

2. This appears to have been jotted after the comtesse d'Houdetot issued
an invitation for a musical performance on Thursday, Feb. 13; see her note to
BF of Feb. 4.
3. Saint-Auban is offering congratulations for the conclusion of the general preliminary peace agreement of Jan. 20, 1783.
4. For the marquise see XXXVI, 257n. The last extant correspondence from
Saint-Auban is an exchange of notes in April. On April 13 he asked WTF to
thank BF for the medal (doubtless one of the *Libertas Americana* medals), and

Notation: St. Auban. 23 Janvr. 1783.

From Sarah Bache: Two Letters, with a Note from
Richard Bache   (I) and (II) ALS: American Philosophical Society

I.

Dear & Honoured Sir   Philadelphia Jan 24th. 1783
    Coll Cambray,[5] who we shall miss very much, is the bearer of
this, he will tell you how all the Family do, I paraded all the Children to day on purpose for him to tell you how they look'd, and
if he does not say they are fine and handsome, I know not were
he will find his beauties—the news papers that came since Major Franks' paket[6] was made up I now give to Coll Cambray—
Miss Beckwith, who is every thing that is Clever is with us, give
me leave to thank you for introducing her to us,[7] I look upon myself particularly fortunate to have it in my power to make Philad
in some measure agreable to her, every effort in Mr B. power and
mine shall be exerted to serve her— Mr Bache is not at home, my
love to Temple and Beny I am as ever your Dutiful Daughter
                                                            S Bache

Addressed: The Honble. / Dr. Benjamin Franklin / Minister
Plenepy. from the United / States of No. America / at / Passy.

---

expressed his hope that the Franklins would dine with him and his wife after
Easter. On April 18 he and his wife wrote BF to set the date for April 23. On
April 20 they sent a note postponing that dinner until April 25. APS. Saint-
Auban died on Sept. 5, 1783 (*DBF*, under Baratier).

    5. For the chevalier de Cambray-Digny see XXXVIII, 535.
    6. She had entrusted her Jan. 7 letter (XXXVIII, 558–60) to David Franks.
For his mission see the annotation of that letter.
    7. Sally Beckwith, who had been warmly recommended to BF by William
Strahan (XXXVII, 425), wished to establish herself in America as a teacher or
milliner. She was in Paris in the summer of 1782, when she met BF, and sailed
to Philadelphia in company with William Bell in early October. BF's letter
recommending her to the Baches is missing: XXXVIII, 7, 109–10n.

II.

Dear and Honoured Sir   Philadelphia Jan. 24. 1783

 As soon as we receiv'd Your letter by Miss Beckwith, both Mr Bache and myself waited on her, and requested her to stay with us, till she could be agreeably setled. She more than answers the recommendation given her, and if my fortune was as large as my heart should never leave us, but warm Friends she shall never want while in Philad. I answer for Mr Bache and myself— I wrote you already by this opportunity, but wished to tell you Miss B was with us, she will write to you herself[8] we all continue well— I am as ever Your Dutiful Daughter   S BACHE

[*In Richard Bache's hand:*] Inclosed is the 4th. Bill of a Sett— three of which are already sent, & I hope some of them got to hand by this time—[9]   R BACHE

Addressed: Dr. Franklin

From James Hutton   ALS: American Philosophical Society

Dear Old Friend   Pimlico 24 Jan. 83

 You may remember my Tears of Jan. 20. 1778. They are wiped off. They were made an Article of Scoffing in a Lr. to Lord Chatham published by Almon.[1] My Congratulations on Peace attend you. I thank you again & again for your very kind & ready granting my Request of a Passport for our Labradore Ship.[2] & for sending my Lr. to America wrote in your Room at

---

 8. Her letter is below, Jan. 25.

 9. The bill was a copy of a Robert Morris draft on Ferdinand Grand for 3,200 *l.t.*, a transfer of money from Christian Schneider to Catharine Höklin. For the first three copies sent see XXXVII, 576–7, 665, 715, and for one that BF had received see XXXVIII, 237.

 1. Hutton had wept "floods of Tears" (his own description) when his attempt to negotiate a peace at Passy failed: XXV, 401–2; XXXVII, 666. This was reported in the British daily press (for which see Lewis, *Walpole Correspondence*, XXVIII, 360) and in a letter to Chatham dated Feb. 12, 1778, published anonymously in Almon's *Remembrancer*, VII (1778–79), 80–1.

 2. Being sent to the Moravian mission there. BF regularly granted such

Passy Jan. 1778. which by your Means was of Service in America for the Repose of my Brethren.[3] How many Personal and interesting kindnesses have you not shewn me? I beg you not to fail to let me know, if you come to England on a short visit to your friends, that I may thank you in person once more before we are removed to another Country. Mrs Hewson was well & her three Children last Monday, but you have had very painful Illnesses, and an Irish Gentleman whom I saw yesterday tells me you was a little lame last Friday.[4] God bless you my old dear kind Friend. Continue to Love me & my Brethren. Ever obliged to you as I am JAMES HUTTON

excuse haste & agitation.

Addressed: To / Doctor Franklyn / Passy

From the Comte de La Touche[5]

ALS: American Philosophical Society

Monsieur a paris le 24 Janvier 1783

Lespoir que jai eu jusqua ce moment que ma Sante me permetterait davoir lhonneur de vous presenter mon hommage res-

---

passports; see, for example, XXVI, 667–8. The most recent was sent the previous March: XXXVI, 691.

3. Probably his letter to Bishop Nathaniel Seidel. Hutton was concerned about reports of attacks on Moravians at Bethlehem, Pa.: XXV, 403–4, 412.

4. On Feb. 14 Receiver General of Finances Jean Chanorier (*DBF*), acting at the request of former minister of state Bertin, forwarded to WTF a letter addressed to BF that had been sent to Bertin's care (APS). This was probably the present letter, as Hutton often used Bertin as a conduit for his correspondence with BF. Also enclosed may have been the undated "Extrait d'une Lettre Ecrite de Londres à M Bertin Ministre d'Etat par M Huton," now among BF's papers at the Library of Congress. Having heard that BF suffered from the stone, Hutton described a remedy that he thought would be effective.

5. This celebrated naval officer (XXVII, 78n), sailing on the *Aigle*, had been captured by a British squadron in September, 1782, while entering the Delaware. He was sent to England as a prisoner, arriving on Dec. 8, and was released around the time the peace was signed: XXVIII, 117–18n; G. Rutherford, "The Case of M. de La Touche," *Mariner's Mirror*, XXXIV (1948), 34–41. He must have just arrived in Paris.

pectueux et vous faire agreer mon compliment Sur la paix et la recconnaissance de lindépendance des etats unis ma empéché de vous remettre La lettre cy jointe qui ma été remise a londres par chr Sargeant[6] votre ami. Me trouvant for incomodé et craignant de ne pouvoir d'ici a quelques jours me rendre a passi pour avoir lhonneur de vous y voir jai pris le parti davoir Celui de vous ladresser en vous priant de recevoir toutes mes excuses ainsi que les assurances des sentiments respectueux avec les quels je suis Monsieur votre tres humble et tres obeissant Serviteur

LE CTE DE LA TOUCHE

hotel de louis le grand Rue de la Bastienne

Notation: Touche le Cte de 24 Janr. 1783.

From Antoine-Laurent and Marie-Anne-Pierrette Paulze Lavoisier[7]

AL: American Philosophical Society

Ce vendredy [January 24, 1783][8]

Mr. et Mde. Lavoisier sont passés mercredy au soir ches M. francklin pour le feliciter Sur la grande revolution que son genie

6. Probably he enclosed John Sargent's letter of Jan. 3: XXXVIII, 547–8.

7. Mme Lavoisier (1758–1836), daughter of farmer-general Jacques Paulze, married Lavoisier in 1771, when he was her father's assistant at the *ferme*. She completed her education in Latin and foreign languages under her husband's direction and collaborated with him in his laboratory, translating for him chemistry texts in English and Italian, taking notes on his experiments, and drawing skillful illustrations. Her translation of Richard Kirwan's *An Essay on Phlogiston, and the Constitution of Acids* (London, 1787) was published at Paris in 1788 with Lavoisier's notes refuting Kirwan's theories. She studied drawing and painting with Jacques-Louis David, and in 1788 painted a portrait of BF after Duplessis which she sent to him in America; she also engraved the plates for Lavoisier's *Traité élémentaire de chimie* (Paris, 1789). *DBF;* René Fric *et al.*, eds., *Œuvres de Lavoisier: Correspondance* (6 vols. to date, Paris, 1955–), V, 274–6; Sellers, *Franklin in Portraiture*, pp. 273–4.

8. The Friday following the signing of the preliminary general peace treaties. The Lavoisiers mention "next Monday" as being the 27th; Jan. 27, 1783, did fall on a Monday.

avoit preparée et qui vient d'etre affermie par la signature de la Paix.

Ils Se proposoient de l'engager a venir diner avec eux lundi prochain 27 a l'arsenal.[9] Ils auront un peu de musique apres diner et ils seroient bien flattés quelle put amuser M. francklin quelques instans.

Cette invitation est Commune pour lui et M. son petit fils.

Notation: Lavoisier

From ———— Perrault[1] and Other Applicants for Emigration   ALS: American Philosophical Society

The number of people applying to Franklin for help in emigrating to America increases markedly during the months following the signing of the preliminary peace treaty. Those letters for which no responses have been located are summarized here, with Perrault's letter published as a sample.[2]

Johann Philipp Breidenstein writes in Latin from Giessen on February 1. Now that the United States has established its freedom, he foresees the flowering of administrative, commercial, and cultural institutions and the need for experts in these areas. He is a professor of agriculture and accounting at the University of Gießen, has studied theology, and has held a number of high administrative posts. He is fully able to teach the doctrines of the Reformed Church as well as

9. The Lavoisiers had been hosting Monday dinners at the Arsenal for their friends and visiting scientists since 1776: *DBF*.

1. Perrault, writing from the duchy of Deux-Ponts in Mannheim, signs himself as editor of "la Gazette," which we take to mean the *Gaz. des Deux-Ponts*, a journal of political opinion. It was launched in 1770, along with a literary journal, by the duc de Deux-Ponts, Christian IV, who had ties with the *philosophes*. From 1778 to 1782 it appeared as the *Gaz. ou journal universel de politique*, but resumed its original title in 1783: Jochen Schlobach, "Conditions politiques et matérielles de l'imprimerie et des gazettes à Deux-Ponts," in *Les Gazettes Européennes de langue française (XVIIe–XVIIIe siècles)*, ed. Henri Duranton *et al.* (Saint-Etienne, 1992), pp. 269–80.

2. All these documents are at the APS. Unless otherwise specified, they are in French.

music and the German language.[3] Breidenstein cannot say what draws him, his wife, and their 18-year-old son to trust themselves to the ocean, but honors and an annual salary would be sufficient inducements to emigrate. Franklin should reply, upon receipt of this letter, in either German or Latin.

On February 3 M. Feron from Vernon asks whether Franklin could procure him a free passage to America, or, if not, at least advise on the cheapest method of travel, and let him know whether he might expect to earn a living with only bookkeeping skills. His savings amount to 1,200 *l.t.;* will this, invested in land, be enough to sustain him?

De Lenoble, a retired captain living in Hanau, explains on February 4 that he wishes to return to America, where he once spent some time. He now regrets the fact that ten years ago, while in Saint-Domingue, he resigned his position in the French service to enter the Prussian army under his uncle, head of a regiment and governor of the county of Glatz. He has no doubt that Franklin's protection will gain him entry to the American service at his present rank.

J. François Amaudruz confides in Franklin on February 13 that for the past 18 months he has wanted to go to America. A native of Bern, he has lived in Paris for 20 years and worked at perfecting his skills as a clockmaker. Eight-and-a-half years ago he fell in love and married; after seven glorious years his wife and child died, and he despairs of ever finding happiness in France. He longs now to live under the laws and customs of America. He asks Franklin's protection for himself and the young man who will deliver this letter, also a native of Bern.

Also on February 13 Captain Siegmüller, in the service of the Holy Roman Emperor, writes in Latin from Linz to say that he would like a

---

3. Breidenstein (1729–1785) published several piano sonatas and musical treatises, in addition to works on agriculture: Walther Killy, ed., *Deutsche Biographische Enzyklopädie* (12 vols., Munich, 1995–2000). He was no longer teaching, however. Having been appointed Professor of Agriculture and Accounting when the Economic Faculty was founded at the University of Giessen in 1777, he was dismissed on Feb. 16, 1782, for "having fallen into debt and mental confusion": Diethelm Klippel, "Johann August Schlettwein and the Economic Faculty at the University of Giessen," *History of Political Thought*, XV (1994), 204, 215. Breidenstein must have enclosed with this letter a copy of the published address he delivered on the occasion of that appointment, *Oratio inauguralis de formanda ante omnia aerarii cvivsvis administrandi vel publici vel privati designatione statvs . . .* (Giessen, 1777); his letter is tucked inside a copy of that address, which itself is bound with other pamphlets BF owned.

better and more humane life in the United States; with Franklin's support he is certain to achieve it. He has spent 16 of his 28 years in the Austrian military, and he can write in his native German and Latin, as well as speak French and some Polish. He was educated at the University of Vienna, passed his exams *cum laude*, and is now a judge. He would be grateful for some honorable office in America appropriate to his talents.

M. Schopman, a Frenchman, writes from Antwerp on February 17 inquiring whether Franklin will offer him free passage to Philadelphia, Boston, or Charleston, to "exercise his talents." He is an architect and building contractor who also knows about rivers and canals. He worked in Paris for 15 years before trying his fortune first in Brussels and now Antwerp. He adds in a postscript that another Parisian living nearby would like the same privileges so that he might teach French, accounting, or something else altogether; the friend speaks English fairly well.

On February 24 Madame Dufour, the wife of a master tailor on the rue Saint-Honoré, throws herself on Franklin's mercy. They have suffered considerable losses, they have sacrificed to meet their contractual obligations, and now they and their infant child live in misery. If Franklin could help them get to America, her husband could continue his profession, and she could work in the fashion industry or as a tutor to some young person.

After expressing the usual compliments on the peace, De Wolff, a major of grenadiers who has served with the duke of Württemberg for 22 years,[4] expresses his desire to be among the new nation's citizens. Writing from Stuttgart on March 4, he explains his situation: for the past year he has been assistant director of the duke's military academy, but he has reached an impasse with his proud and rigid superior, Colonel de Seeger,[5] over the need for improvements at the school. He has resolved to quit his post, and though the King of Prussia offered him a position, he would rather go to America, where he

---

4. Friedrich Wilhelm von Wolff (1744–1816), later colonel: Axel Kuhn *et al.*, *Revolutionsbegeisterung an der Hohen Carlsschule: ein Bericht* (Stuttgart, 1989), pp. 83–4; *ADB*.

5. Christoph Dionysius Freiherr von Seeger: *ADB*. The Stuttgart military academy, founded in 1770, was known for its strict discipline. It attained university status in 1782, and until its closing in 1794 trained many distinguished army officers, physicians, and scientists, including the poet Friedrich Schiller: *ADB*, under Seeger and Karl Eugen Herzog von Württemberg; Hans-Joachim Harder, *Militärgeschichtliches Handbuch Baden-Württemberg* (Stuttgart, 1987), p. 348.

would gladly renounce his noble titles in order to be a useful citizen. He knows America will need farmers; he hopes that his example will serve to inspire many citizens of Württemberg, skilled in the arts of farming and forestry, to participate with him in the grand project of settling the American empire. He is the enemy of luxury and ostentation. Scion of a military family (his father was a lieutenant general who served under the maréchal duc de Broglie), he has a wife and two children, a modest fortune (6,000 francs), and the hope of an inheritance. All he asks is reimbursement for an exploratory trip to America, a modest allowance while there, and the assurance of a pension for his family should he die during the voyage.

From Bruges comes a letter from M. de Lafosse, written on March 7, declaring that he awaits the first opportunity to emigrate with his family to Pennsylvania, where under the happy influence of liberty he may raise his children to be hardworking, sober, and virtuous. He had planned also to develop a code of laws in which virtue and kindness would be inculcated not by negative example but by philosophic and religious maxim, but he hears that Franklin himself is to undertake such a project, and he offers to share in the work: to Franklin would go the framework of the code, while Lafosse would take on the trifling details of distinctions and exceptions necessary to legal precision.

M. Ferrier writes from Lille on March 9. Is it true that the republic Franklin helped found is offering advantages to Genevans skilled in clockmaking? He would like to be among the first to offer his talents in a land where liberty flourishes, and expects that other Genevans will also wish to join him and throw off the yoke that oppresses them. He may be reached through Mr. Bacle, clockmaker on the rue Déquermoise in Lille.

From Ganges in Languedoc, the merchants Vincent & fils write on March 9 about their intention to remove to America to set up a manufactory.[6] Joining them in this design are several others of their Protestant faith, all with the hope that Franklin will extend to them his protection and that Congress might help them to defray their expenses.

"Pinelli née Costanzia" writes on March 12 from Hondschoote to assure Franklin of his expertise in all aspects of engineering: theoretical and practical, civil, military, hydraulic and mechanical. He was employed until recently by the Dutch East India Company, and now offers his services to the Confederation of the Thirteen United Prov-

---

6. A Monsieur Vinsent is listed as one of the principal tanners of Ganges in the *Almanach des marchands*, p. 217.

inces. He proposes an elaborate scheme involving all phases of linen production, from cultivation of the plant to construction of small spinning machines. He himself will lead a team of Flemish carpenters and weavers. He can provide plans for the factories and housing, as well as assist in the construction. In addition he could teach young people drawing, mathematics, artillery, and the arts of fortification and of selecting sites for military camps.[7]

On March 13 Anthony Mikoviny,[8] a native of Hungary who obtained the rank of major in the army of His Imperial Majesty during the Seven Years' War, writes in English from London to describe his "lang intending Dessein & Inclination" to be servicable to "their great and High Mighteness of America." He is not unacquainted with several languages nor inexperienced in agriculture, mining, smelting, and the mechanical arts; the discoveries he has made in mechanics since being in England can be attested by certificates from reputable people. Mr. Lawrence,[9] who has given him encouragement, will convey this letter.

Carrouge, the parish priest at Monceaux,[1] expresses on March 15 his regret that, as a religious man, he was not able to join the Americans in their fight for liberty. Now, however, he wishes to contribute to the republic's prosperity by recommending a talented young bachelor, fluent in French and Latin, with a knowledge of Spanish and German, and a little English. He paints well, has a superior epistolary style, and would be a suitable secretary to a man of influence. He might also keep the books for a merchant house or serve as interpreter in a port city. He is prepared to leave for America if Franklin will honor him with his support and obtain passage for him to Boston. If America is in need of smiths, Carrouge knows of many excellent workmen from the local ironworks who would gladly make the trip.[2]

7. Having had no reply, Pinelli writes again on Aug. 5 to say that for the past three months he has been working for the Merseman brothers at Dunkirk to establish a factory there with the understanding that he may depart at any time to work elsewhere. He renews the offer of his engineering and architectural skills, adding that he is a subject of the king of Sardinia.

8. The Mikovinys (Mikowinh) were an old aristocratic family of Hungary: Constant von Wurzbach, ed., *Biographisches Lexikon des Kaiserthums Oesterreich* (60 vols., Vienna, 1856–91), XVIII, 287–9; Ján Purgina, *Samuel Mikovíni, 1700–1750* (Bratislava, 1958).

9. Possibly Henry Laurens, who was in London at this time. He did not go to Paris until July, however: *Laurens Papers,* XVI, xlv.

1. Montceau-les-Mines in southern Burgundy.

2. The coal mines of Montceau were near the industrial complex centered

A shipsmith from Morlaix hopes that his small talents might be useful in one of America's port cities. "Mi:l" [Michel?] Guillaume, who writes on March 19, has just finished making pumps, pulleys, bells, and other necessities for the royal navy. If his services would be useful in America, he hopes that Franklin will grant a passport and passage; he even dares hope for a letter from Franklin that will help him establish a foundry, where he promises to train apprentices who might then set up their own foundries. Franklin may signal his intentions in a letter to him care of Mr. Pitot Duhellés, Congress' agent at Morlaix.

Jo. McIntosh, writing in English from London on March 18, is experienced in the design and printing of calicoes, and wishes, with Franklin's protection, to relocate to America, where he hopes "to Provide more Amply" for his family. Franklin is surely aware of the dangers to manufacturers seeking to emigrate from Britain, and will understand the need for delicacy in this matter.[3] Should Franklin respond favorably, McIntosh will come immediately to Paris armed with recommendations.

Born noble, and having served his king with honor for 23 years, M. de Croust was forced to retire in 1781. He writes Franklin on March 23 that, having been harassed by two wives, he has decided to finish his days under the skies Franklin has rendered peaceful, hoping to taste liberty under America's wise laws. If the government were to grant passage for him and four or five vintners with their families (his own family includes five children and three valets), he could bring 30,000 *livres* and enough rootstock from the vineyard in Champagne where he resides for a trial planting in Virginia. He thinks he might be able to buy property from one of the royalists.[4]

---

at Le Creusot, where in 1782 a foundry and blast furnace using coal rather than wood were begun: XXXIV, 175–6n; J. R. Harris, *Industrial Espionage and Technology Transfer: Britain and France in the Eighteenth Century* (Aldershot, Brookfield, Vt., and Singapore, 1998), pp. 253, 256; Christian Devillers and Bernard Huet, *Le Creusot: Naissance et développement d'une ville industrielle, 1782–1914* (Seyssel, 1981), pp. 20, 22.

3. British legislation against the emigration of skilled workers and manufacturers as well as the export of machinery was passed in 1719, and further laws aimed at artisans and tools employed in the textile industries were passed in 1750, 1774, and 1781. In 1782 an act extended these prohibitions to the machines for calico-printing: Harris, *Industrial Espionage and Technology Transfer*, pp. 7–12, 361–2, 455–60.

4. He neglected to specify his location. On May 2 he wrote again, this time with more details: he signed himself "Cordier de Croust," retired infantry officer, living in Laon. He would gladly pay the cost of the journey if BF

Also writing on March 23, Joachim Heinrich Ludewig, from Büt-
zow in Mecklenburg-Schwerin, recounts in excellent English the time
in 1773 when he called on Franklin with a recommendation from the
late Mr. Achenwall of Göttingen.[5] He was then a poor German scholar
wanting to go to Philadelphia to sell books; Franklin was both kind
and generous. Now he congratulates Franklin on the peace, and, because he is still unmarried, proposes again to go to America, but only
if he has Franklin's recommendation or assured employment at the
University of Philadelphia as a professor or lector of German and
Dutch, or an instructor of history or political science. For the past
eighteen months he has been a *lector publicus* at the university in Büt-
zow,[6] where he has taught those subjects.

A prominent physician from Bruyères in Lorraine writes on March
24 that he yearns to practice his art in the homeland of "le Grand
Franklin." M. Poma's fortune is small, but he is a member of several
academies in Europe as well as the societies of medicine of Paris[7] and
Nancy.

On March 25 a German builder of keyboard instruments who signs
himself "J. Geib" writes in imperfect English from London.[8] Ten
years earlier he left the Palatinate with the intention of going to America, but went first to London where he had heard the arts were highly
developed. Forced to remain there when war broke out, he wishes to

---

could assure him of land for his children to cultivate. He has 60,000 *livres* at
his disposal, and will need 1,000 acres along a navigable river; he understands
that Georgia and South Carolina need settlers. He would even take up military service again.

5. For Gottfried Achenwall, who died in 1772, see XIII, 346–77.

6. The university was founded by Duke Frederick of Mecklenburg in
1760: *Catholic Encyclopedia* (16 vols., New York, 1912–14), XIII, 205.

7. Poma was elected a corresponding member in 1780: *Histoire de la Société royale de médecine . . .* for 1779, pp. 29–30.

8. Johann or John Geib (1744–1818) was born into a family of prominent
organ and piano builders. The composite instrument he says he invented was
called an "organized piano"; composites of organs and clavichords or harpsichords had existed since the late fifteenth century. His letter to BF is strik-
ingly modest; his factory completed eight to ten pianos a week, and in 1786,
still in London, he patented a double action for the square piano. Geib, his
wife, and their seven children finally emigrated to New York in 1797, where
he became a leading builder of organs and other keyboard instruments. His
sons joined his firm and continued the business after his death: Stanley Sadie,
ed., *The New Grove Dictionary of Music and Musicians* (2nd ed., 29 vols.,
London, 2001), under Claviorgan; Geib.

resume his plan now that "all thoss calamiteis" are over. He is afraid to undertake the journey without a recommendation, having heard that strangers are lost without one. For his part, he was brought up to be a maker of organs, harpsichords, and grand and small pianos; since being in England he has also made pedal harps. Eighteen months earlier he invented "a Flute with Sixty pipes, with a Stopd. in treble with therty pipes, unter a little Pianoforte." He has turned down several offers to go to St. Petersburg, and hopes that Franklin will give this request a favorable reception.

The vicomte de Lomagne-Tarride writes on March 31 from the château de Berenx in Béarn. Assuring Franklin that he is not going to trouble him to obtain payment of his loan office certificates,[9] the vicomte proposes to lead a group of his own vassals, the most industrious and skillful people in all of France, to America, where they will cultivate the land. He would like permission to name the little Béarnaise colony in Franklin's honor; he also seeks the title to a suitable tract (the due of every military man who has served in America) and an answer before the Easter holiday so that he might depart for America with Franklin's orders.

M. Desbrossée writes from Le Mans on April 4 that he has been waiting for the peace in order to fulfil his dream of going to America. Would Franklin support him as he seeks a position as an engineer or architect in one of the American provinces? He is a student in the *Bureau des ingénieurs* and of M. Blondel, *architecte du roi*.[1]

M. Dubeaucage, writing from Marseille on April 4, gets right to the point. On March 17, just as he was about to get on the coach to take him from Geneva to Lyon, he dashed into a bookstore for something to read. Chance guided his hand to the abbé Robin's *Nouveau Voyage dans l'Amérique Septentrionale, en l'année 1781.*[2] The depiction of such a beautiful country of virtuous inhabitants has captivated him; above all he was struck by the letter from Yorktown dated November 15, 1781, stating that the Americans would one day be the most enlightened people of the world. He asks Franklin to advise him as a father

9. See XXXVII, 64.
1. The renowned architect Jacques-François Blondel (*DBF*) had established an art school in which he taught architecture and which came to serve as a preparatory school for the Ecole des Ponts et Chaussées, one of the two principal engineering schools in Europe at the time: Gaston Serbos, "L'Ecole royale des ponts et chaussées," in *Enseignement et diffusion des sciences en France au XVIIIe siècle*, ed. René Taton *et al.* (Paris, 1964), pp. 349–56; Michel Delon, ed., *Dictionnaire européen des lumières* (Paris, 1997), pp. 402–3.
2. XXXIV, 164–5.

34

would. He offers all his personal details: his birthdate (in 1755), the fact that he was orphaned as an infant, how he ended up as a merchant in Rouen. He wants to go to America and establish a firm. Should he go to Boston or elsewhere? His health is good, he is gentle and sensitive, he loves virtue, he minds his elders, and he is sure to find friends among the good people of America. If he is fortunate enough to obtain Franklin's trust, he will repay it by becoming a good citizen. He will be back in Rouen by July, but Franklin can write to him in Toulouse, *poste restante*, where he will be by the 25th.

M. Bourdillon has been waiting impatiently for American independence to be established. Now that it is assured, he writes to Franklin from Montferrand on April 8. He and his family are ready to leave for Virginia, the region he feels will be most suitable, for both its climate and its constitution. He needs a sponsor, however, and asks Franklin to supply the names of a few people around Williamsburg whose counsel will guide him as he sets up his business. He hopes to acquire a spread of 6,000 acres and needs to know how much this will cost; he will bring his family as soon as he is in a state to offer them shelter. He intends to leave for Bordeaux in June, and from there take the first American ship leaving for Williamsburg. He plans to spend the crossing learning English and familiarizing himself with the inhabitants of his new country. Should Franklin honor him with a reply, Bourdillon and his family will be infinitely grateful.

L. J. de Grobert,[3] describing himself as a Tuscan man of letters, writes from Marseille on April 14. He has been planning for some time to write the history of the American Revolution. He has communicated this idea to several Americans, among them Samuel Curson of Baltimore,[4] but now turns to Franklin. Having been plagued by persecution and misfortune, he asks whether Franklin can provide him asylum in America. He is trained in military tactics and mechanics, and has served the House of Austria for some time. He stands ready to provide further information on his birth and talents.

On May 13 C. F. Schmidt writes in German from Frederiksberg,

3. Possibly Jacques-François-Louis Grobert (*DBF*), born of French parents in Algiers in 1757. In 1773 he joined the Tuscan artillery where he rose to the rank of sub-lieutenant; he subsequently entered the Spanish service and, in the 1790s, the French artillery. He published books on artillery, mechanics, and the pyramids of Giza. The title page of his work *Des Fêtes publiques chez les modernes* (Paris, [1802]) lists him as a member of the "Institut de Bologne, l'Académie de Florence et de plusieurs Sociétés savantes et littéraires."

4. Who wrote BF from Marseille on Jan. 16: XXXVIII, 591.

near Copenhagen, where he is inspector general of the royal Danish garden. He submits a list of questions about settling in America. Does Congress admit foreign citizens and extend to them the rights of citizenship? Are they offered the same constitutional protections that native-born citizens enjoy? Is land distributed freely to immigrants, or must it be purchased? Can land be held without taxes for 50 years? Schmidt is eager to take up his homestead and wishes Franklin to lay his questions before Congress and inform him by post of their answers.

On May 15 Gelatte, a 29-year-old obstetrical surgeon, writes from Bouguenais, near Nantes. In 1777 he was captured aboard a vessel from Nantes and taken to Halifax. On his return to France he completed his degree requirements and began his medical practice. He now hopes that his meager talents might be useful in America, in a hospital or in some city.

Also on May 15 J. A. C. Siek, formerly postmaster at Göttingen, writes in German from Berlin. He wishes employment as postmaster in America and alludes to the secret information he has concerning the United States.[5]

Finally, we present several hopefuls who press their cases through intermediaries. Louis-Germain Dupin d'Assarts from Nivernois was determined to go to America, and sought the protection of both Franklin and Mrs. Izard, whom he knew was about to return to the United States.[6] He made this request through the duc de Nivernois,[7]

---

5. He writes three more times, signing his name Sieck in the last two letters. On May 17 he refers to the present letter and requests money for traveling expenses. On Aug. 19 he repeats his request for a position in America and says he has valuable secret information about the Revolution. He refers to an earlier letter to Mr. Adams and mentions Secretary Bonhomme in the Dutch secret service. On Aug. 23 he explains that his previous letter was sent to Dumas at The Hague and that he is enclosing a duplicate of it.

6. Dupin d'Assarts had written to BF twice in 1780 about his wish to serve in the American army and to find a refuge for his family; he would write again in 1784: XXXIII, 46–7.

7. Louis-Jules-Barbon Mancini-Manzarini, duc de Nivernois (Nivernais or Nevers), a celebrated diplomat, was also governor of the last great fief independent of the French crown and was known for his solicitous protection of his duchy's inhabitants: XIV, 248n; *Dictionnaire de la noblesse*, under Mancini; Paule Beaud-Ladoire, *Mancini Mazarin, dernier duc de Nevers, 1716–1798: une injustice de l'histoire* (Paris, 2001), pp. 162–6, 171; André-Marie-Jean-Jacques Dupin, *Eloge de M. le duc de Nivernois, pair de France* . . . (Paris, 1840), pp. 19–20.

who was pleased to recommend his honest "vassal" to Franklin's notice in a letter of March 16. The duke, not knowing Franklin personally, asked Claude-Henri Watelet, who did, to deliver his letter. Watelet enclosed it in an undated letter of his own, which intimated that the duke deserved an audience. Watelet and his wife took the opportunity to send all good wishes to the honorable and immortal doctor. On Watelet's letter Franklin jotted the following note for a reply: "Make an Answer to this that I shall be glad to see the Gentleman, and will with Pleasure do what is desired by M le Duc de Nivernois."

J. de Sparre, this time signing himself "Docteur," addresses his final letter to Franklin on March 1.[8] Writing from the *imprimerie de la Société littéraire* at Kehl, he says that Fournier, the typefounder, and the sieur Mahon told him that Franklin had once wanted to send them to America to set up a printing house. Now is the time: Fournier and some talented printers of Kehl have asked de Sparre to communicate their interest in the project. He and Fournier will meet with Franklin in Paris and can assemble papermakers, bookbinders, and others skilled in the trade. If he has not received a response in 12 days, he will conclude that Franklin has changed his mind.

On March 28 Col. de Prehn[9] addresses a request for assistance to the comte des Roches.[1] Prehn, no longer commandant in the service of Holland at the Cape of Good Hope, is now at Bremen. He has decided not to re-enlist with the Dutch East India Company, which refused to provide a pension for his wife in the event of his death. He wishes instead to settle with his family in Charleston, South Carolina.

---

8. For de Sparre and a list of his extant correspondence see XXIII, 301. His previous letter, of April 17, 1781, came from Strasbourg, where he said he was a professor of tactics.

9. Hendrik Prehn or von Prehn (1733–1785), born at the Cape of Good Hope, was educated in Holland and had a long and varied military career. While serving as commandant of the troops at the Cape, he and several other officials were accused of financial and political irregularities; Prehn was allowed an honorable discharge and repatriated in 1780. He took an active interest in science and first brought to Europe the mineral prehnite, named for him: W. J. de Kock, ed., *Dictionary of South African Biography* (5 vols., [Pretoria], 1968–87), II, 558–9.

1. Comte François-Julien du Dresnay des Roches (1719–1784), *chef d'escadre* since 1776, had been governor general of the Iles de France et de Bourbon and was one of the founders of the Académie de marine, an affiliate of the Académie des sciences (XXXV, 42n). He contributed several articles to the *Dictionnaire de marine: DBF; Almanach royal* for 1783, p. 169. We have no record of how the present letter was delivered to BF.

He asks the comte to apprise Franklin of his intentions and to elicit Franklin's opinion of the plan.

Deux ponts le 24 Janvier 1783. A l'Imprimerie Ducale
Monsieur

Vos momens doivent être Si remplis que si vous en avez quelques-uns à m'accorder, je ne dois pas les perdre à Vous redire ce que Vous devez être plus las d'entendre que de mériter: Je vais donc en peu de mots vous faire la demande la plus Simple du monde.

Vous allez, disent toutes nos gazettes que je copie dans la mienne, retourner dans un pays où l'humanité & la liberté appelleront bientôt la foule des hommes las du joug de L'Europe que vous avez secoué: hélas! j'en suis un. Seroit-il possible qu'au moyen des milliers d'individus que la Soif de l'or ou l'amour d'un repos non oisif vont vous conduire, vos pertes fussent Si bien réparées que vous ne sussiez plus que faire d'un homme à qui de trop foibles talens n'auroient pas été inutiles dans cet hémisphère. S'il eût pu y joindre ce qui les supplée tous Aujourdhui, le manège & l'intrigue: qui un peu mûri par Sept Lustres & demi d'infortunes, désespère avec la misérable besogne dont il S'est chargé depuis quelque tems, d'être jamais utile ni à lui-même ni aux personnes pour l'amour de qui seules il a encore le courage de vouloir faire quelque Chose. Est-il décidé que dans le Globe entier on aura beau découvrir de nouveaux Terrains ou dépeupler ailleurs des régions immenses il ne se trouvera pourtant jamais un coin de terre que les Autres hommes veuillent lui céder à moins qu'il ne l'achète par le mensonge ou l'infamie, un coin où il puisse prendre racine & Végéter, & dire enfin en mourant à la mère commune, "O toi qui m'as nourri, reçois ma dépouille!" Si, dis-je, il est ainsi écrit à mon article, il faut bien s'y soumettre. Mais Si vous voulez & pouvez rouvrir à l'espoir de l'existence un cœur flétri, il faut vous faire voir d abord toute l'étendue de ma demande, que vous aurez cependant déja pressentie, si je ne me trompe: C'est que je n'ai point de fonds à porter sur cette Terre, & qu'il ne S'agiroit de rien moins que de me mettre dans une position à pouvoir aquérir ou rembourser ces fonds avant que l'âge, toujours hâtif, vienne me dérober non seulement au plaisir de la jouissance, mais à celui même de l'exécution.

Je n'entre pas dans d'autres détails, parcequ'ils ne seroient utiles qu'autant que, d'après ceci, vous pourriez réellement concevoir des Vues dont vous auriez la bonté de m'instruire par un mot de réponse, & que par-là vous donneriez au foible espoir, source de ma démarche un peu singulière, la consistance qu'il tireroit bien de Votre Seul Caractère si je ne sentois trop qu'il vous est impossible de Vous y livrer dans tous les cas innombrables qui doivent se présenter.

J'ai l'honneur d'Etre avec les sentimens de tant de personnes plus éclairées que moi, & en un mot de toute l'Europe, Monsieur Votre très humble & très obéissant Serviteur

PERRAULT
Rédacteur de la Gazette

Si vous m'honorez d'une réponse quelconque, Vous m'obligeriez de Vouloir bien l'adresser Sous le Couvert de *Mr. Bettinger directeur de la Poste Impériale.*

Notation: Perrau 24 Janvr. 1783.

Three Draft Replies to Applicants for Emigration

(I) AL (incomplete draft): Library of Congress; (II) and (III) AL (incomplete draft): American Philosophical Society

Following the signing of the preliminary peace treaty, Franklin was inundated with requests for assistance from people all over Europe who wanted to emigrate to America. More than 30 are summarized in the headnote to Perrault's letter of January 24, above; they represent only those applications for which no responses have been located. The documents published below are undated responses written by Franklin to recipients who have not been identified. The first of them has much in common with BF's March 17 letter to the Earl of Buchan, but the differences convince us that this draft was intended for another applicant. Letters II and III are more generic and could have been intended for any number of hopefuls who wrote during 1783. They may, in fact, have been intended as models for responses that Franklin wanted sent out in French. Ultimately, he composed a general pamphlet on emigration, *Information to Those Who Would Remove to America,* which was printed shortly before March 9, 1784.[2]

[between January 24, 1783, and March 9, 1784]

I.

Your Queries concerning the Value of Land in different Circumstances & Situations, Modes of Settlement, &c &c are quite out of my Power to answer; having while I lived in America been always an Inhabitant of Capital Cities, and not in the way of learning any thing correctly of Country Affairs. There is a Book lately published in London, written by Mr Hector St. John, its Title, Letters from an American Farmer,[3] which contains a good deal of Information on those Subjects; and as I know the Author to be an observing intelligent Man, I suppose the Information to be good as far as it goes, and I recommend the Book to your perusal.

There is no doubt but great Tracts may be purchased on the Frontiers of Virginia, & the Carolinas, at moderate Rates. In Virginia, it used to be at 5£ Sterling the 100 Acres. I know not the present Price, but do not see why it should be higher.

Emigrants arriving pay no Fine or Premium for being admitted to all the Privileges of Citizens. Those are acquired by two Years Residence.

No Rewards are given to encourage new Settlers to come among us, whatever degree of Property they may bring with them, nor any Exemptions from common Duties. Our Country offers to Strangers nothing but a good Climate, fertile Soil,

2. On that date BF sent a copy to Charles Thomson, explaining, "I am pestered continually with Numbers of Letters from People in different Parts of Europe, who would go to settle in America; but who manifest very extravagant Expectations, such as I can by no means encourage; and who appear otherwise to be very improper Persons. To save myself Trouble I have just printed some Copies of the enclosed little Piece, which I purpose to send hereafter in Answer to such Letters." National Archives.

3. St. John de Crèvecœur, *Letters from an American Farmer* (London, 1782), which BF received in July, 1782: XXXVII, 628–9.

wholesome Air, Free Governments, wise Laws, Liberty, a good People to live among, and a hearty Welcome. Those Europeans who have these or greater Advantages at home, would do well to stay where they are.

II.

The civil Employments are few, not very profitable, and all fill'd by Persons elected by the People from a Knowledge and Approbation of their Characters & Conduct. A Stranger cannot expect that any of these will be displac'd for his Accommodation.

A Settlement there he may undoubtedly make; Coming with that Intention he will be kindly receiv'd; and will soon be consider'd as a Citizen. By a prudent Conduct he may in a few Years acquire the Esteem and Confidence of the People, and obtain in Consequence some publick Employ either civil or military.

III.

That Employments are not given in America but to Persons known. That if he can transport himself thither and maintain himself a Year or two till the Inhabitants are acquainted with his Character and Merits, he may possibly obtain one of the Employments he mentions; but nothing of the kind can be promised to him by me.

From Jacob Smith[4]

ALS: American Philosophical Society

Mister franklin   Mil preason Jenary the 24 1783.

Sur I take This Opurtunety to inform You Of the Onhapy Setuation of Our People Now in this Prison. I Must inform You that thay Are Entering Out of Prison Averry Day for the Wont of Close and Vitels for thare Are Sum of them that Have Ben Hear this Aight Monts And Have Not Had the Lest Asistance from Any Body. And thare is the french and Duch and Spanish

4. A Jacob Smith was captured aboard the *Franklin* and committed to Mill Prison on Dec. 6, 1781: Kaminkow, *Mariners*, p. 175.

that Reseave both Close And Mony. Sur I Must inform You that thare Are Now in Prison One Hundred and Sixty Men And Out of that Number thare Are One Half of the [them] Without Shous or Stockins And thar Are forteen of them that Had Entered Out Within this fotnet [fortnight] and thare Will Be More of them Go Out Sun if No Help—⁵ I think that it is A Shame for Our Congres that for the Sake O A letel Expence that thay Will Let Our People Sufer in this Maner. I Must inform You that there Are Not One of the Amaracan Ofarsurs that get thare Porole So I Have No more At Present But I Remane Your Humbel Sarvant

Jacob Smith

of Providence

Addressed: To / Mi / Jeames(?) franklin / in Paris / in france

To the Comte de Vergennes

AL (draft) and copy: Library of Congress

Sir,   Passy, Jan. 25. 1783

I received the Letter your Excellency did me the honour of writing to me the 31st. of the last Month, relative to the fresh pecuniary Aid which the King was dispos'd to grant to the Congress.— I received also a second Letter on the same Subject, dated the 16th Instant.⁶ I am extremely sensible of his Majesty's Goodness in according a new Loan to the United States of Six

---

5. By the early summer of 1782, all American prisoners held at Forton and Mill—except for those in hospitals—had been exchanged and sent to America in cartel ships. New prisoners continued to arrive, however, and by mid-October there were more than 200. The inhumane conditions induced some to defect (as Smith here discusses). Those who remained were engaging in such "riotous behavior" that in October the Commissioners for Sick and Wounded Seamen requested assistance from the Admiralty. A planned cartel was repeatedly postponed: XXXVII, 31–3, 625; XXXVIII, 225n, 305, 441, 568, 583; Sheldon S. Cohen, *Yankee Sailors in British Gaols: Prisoners of War at Forton and Mill, 1777–1783* (Newark, Del., and London, 1995), pp. 204–5.

6. Vergennes told BF on Dec. 20 that France would loan the United States 6,000,000 *l.t.* (XXXVIII, 487, 487–8n). The letters BF mentions here have not been located. (The Jan. 16 letter from Vergennes published in vol. 38 does not concern the loan.)

Millions, and I accept the same in their Behalf with the most perfect Gratitude. Considering the enormous Expence this extensive War must occasion to his Majesty, I did hope to avoid the Necessity of repeating their original Request of a larger Sum;[7] and with that View have had many Consultations & considered various Schemes with our Banker Mr Grand for procuring Money elsewhere. This with other Circumstances occasioned my so long Delay in Answering, which I beg you would excuse.— None of those Schemes proving practicable, I am constrain'd by my Orders humbly to request that the Matter may be reconsidered; and that at least Six Millions more may be added. As Peace will diminish both the King's Expence and ours, I hope this Request may be granted and that it may be sufficient for our Occasions. I am however ready to enter into and sign the Contract your Excellency mentions for whatever Sum his Majesty's Wisdom & Goodness shall think fit to direct. I inclose the Resolutions of Congress, impowering me to borrow the Twenty Millions; in which their Sense of his Majesty's Friendship is strongly express'd. I am, with great Respect, Sir, Your Excellency's most obedient & most humble Servant

M. le Comte de Vergennes—

From Sally Beckwith   ALS: American Philosophical Society

Sir   Philadelphia January 25th [1783]
    Encouraged by the assurances of my Dear Friend Mrs. Bache that you will not think my writing a peice of presumption I take this method at once of assuring you of my gratitude for past favors & to beg that when you shall hear that your Friends here have so very far outdone your utmost intention of serving me it may not so much be atributed to any art I have had of availing myself of your Excellencys reccomendation as to the desire Mr.

7. Congressional resolutions of Sept. 14 directed BF to borrow four million dollars, roughly equivalent to 20,000,000 *l.t.* (the figure BF cites below), and to communicate the request to Louis XVI. BF notified Vergennes on Nov. 8: XXXVIII, 103n, 289–90.

& Mrs. Bache seem to have to find occasions of *loading* with favors any who have been So fortunate as to meet with the smallest countenance. I am very happy in finding that my scheme cannot fail of success. I dont know whether I ought to say it with joy or regret that the cultivation of European manners will hardly be an innovation. Tis be hoped that Nature being so bountifull it will be a long while before they are reduced to the mean arts of avarice to suport their luxurys, for such I doubt not will the be(?) [be the?] applicable term to a lively people who love french finery & English Neatness.

I am ordered to describe your dear Grandchildren & first for Master Bache who is a tall big Boy with a fine open countenance who when he smiles & he is very gay displays two Broad white teeth set apart that promises long life & good Health, he has moreover a great deal of sensibility, which is a weakness not easily cured. Miss Betsy who is my bedfellow is of a small delicate figure has dark hair is attentive inquisitive & retentive & very affectionate & thinks still better than she reads, Louis is a perfect peice of good nature & has two Beautifull Eyes with which he gives occasionally gives some little Squints which are esteemed a great Merit. Miss Debby is pretty & has More little tricks than most Misses of her age.[8] I beg my compliments to Mr Franklin & remain with the most perfect respect & gratitude your Excellancys most Obdt & very Hle Servant　　　　S BECKWITH

Notation: Beckwitt

---

8. Deborah was almost 16 months old. William, Elizabeth, and Louis were, respectively, nine, five, and three: 1, lxiii–lxiv.

From Jean-Baptiste Le Roy AL: American Philosophical Society

[January 25, 1783?]¹

Tout le monde veut ici Mon Illustre Docteur que votre Excellence ait fait un discours au Roi et tout le monde me le demande et que je le traduise. Un mot un Seul mot mon Illustre confrere pour Savoir ce qui en est ou Si ce Sera pour Mardy Ou envoyez moi confiez le moi pour que je le traduise. Je ferai tous mes efforts pour y faire passer cet esprit de sagesse et de profondeur qui regne dans tout ce que vous dites et que vous écrivez. Adieu Mon illustre Docteur je ne veux pas par mes paroles abuser de votre tems. Recevez de nouveau Mon Compliment sur la fin glorieuse de la plus belle revolution qui se soit opèree depuis le renouvellement des lettres. Dinez vous chez vous demain Dimanche Selon l'usage

Addressed: a Monsieur / Monsieur Franklin Ministre / des treize Provinces Unies de / L'Amèrique

From L. Martineau aîné and Other Offerers of Goods and Schemes ALS: American Philosophical Society

Once the general peace was declared, merchant firms and individuals all over Europe wanted to form connections with the United States. For many of them, writing to Franklin was the first step. The letters we summarize in this headnote did not, to the best of our knowledge, receive responses. The earliest letter, published below, seeks a generous advance from Congress to establish a sugar refinery and flour mill in Philadelphia.²

1. Though we cannot trace the rumor Le Roy mentions of a speech BF had written for the king, his reference to "demain dimanche" places this letter on a Saturday, and Jan. 25 was the first one after the signing of the general peace agreement on Jan. 20. Le Roy's congratulations on the end of the war places this letter either here or after the signing on Sept. 3 of the final peace treaty.

2. The writer was probably Louis Martineau, a wealthy Bordelais businessman: Michel Figeac, *Destins de la noblesse bordelaise (1770–1830)* (2 vols., Bordeaux, 1996), II, 606. All the letters summarized in this editorial note are in French and are at the APS unless otherwise noted.

A sieur Boyer, writing from Bordeaux on February 1,[3] has heard that Congress is looking to encourage foreigners to establish manufactories in America—encourage and also sustain. Acknowledging that Franklin's title of Liberator of his Country is well deserved, Boyer hopes he will endorse his plan to establish a glassworks in or near Virginia, a project that occurred to him during the two years he spent in the United States. Boyer studied glassmaking for 15 years in France and Switzerland. He knows that in America there is an abundance of the necessary raw material, and of the wood required for smelting and constructing the necessary buildings. If Congress agrees, he will recruit partners (one of whom already owns land between Virginia and Maryland, with access to the sea) and import workers from France and Switzerland. He would make window glass of all types, bottles, *dame-jeannes* (large bottles), and drinking glasses of all qualities, all for less than imported glassware. If Franklin thinks his project worthwhile, he asks the honor of a response.

Du Radier, writing on March 4 from Nantes, has heard a similar rumor: that Franklin is looking for workmen and a manager for a calico manufactory in America. He proposes himself, as he has been waiting for four years for just such an opportunity. He has three associates whose superior talents would be impossible to reunite in another group. He hopes for a prompt answer from Franklin under cover to his friend M. Blin l'aîné, a medical doctor at Nantes.[4] As soon as Franklin responds, he will send the qualifications of his syndicate. If Franklin will underwrite a trip to Paris, he can explain his ideas in person.

Having received no reply, Du Radier writes again on an unspecified day later in March. He begs Franklin to charge Jonathan Williams, Jr., with the task of meeting him and investigating his claims; he can be contacted through the Nantes firm of Walcker, Scholl & Cie. He has only recently started with that firm, after eight years elsewhere. He cannot anticipate any barriers to working in America that cannot be surmounted by industry. If he is permitted, he will use slave labor; if there are no capable workmen in America, his associates will send

3. The Boyers, a prominent Bordelais family of merchants and *armateurs*, were Protestants who had come from Périgord a century earlier: Paul Butel, *Les Négociants bordelais: l'Europe et les îles au XVIIIe siècle* (Paris, 1974), pp. 205, 307–8, 379; Paul Butel, *Les Dynasties bordelaises* (Paris, 1991), pp. 49, 103, 122.

4. Possibly François-Pierre Blin (1756–1834), who established himself as a physician in Nantes in 1783 and later became a Revolutionary politician: *DBF*.

some from France. If Franklin is not interested in his venture, he plans to go to America and explain his plan directly to Congress and wealthy investors. He is a man of a good, but too numerous, family, and would like either a certificate attesting to his character or letters of recommendation to Congress.

Several of Franklin's correspondents seek to market their products in the United States. John Woddrop writes two letters from Glasgow on February 17. In the first, he seeks Franklin's opinion on the marketability of certain Scottish textiles such as silk gauze, muslins, and lawn (suitable for the coming summer season). Also, what encouragement could Franklin give to young tradesmen, farmers, and gardeners who wish to emigrate with their families? He requests a passport, if one is needed for the journey.[5] The second letter contains a list of members of the Mississippi Land Company, including the Lee brothers and George Washington, which Woddrop received some years earlier from William Lee. Woddrop plans to contact the members as potential trading partners.[6]

Isaac Lynen le jeune writes from Stolberg in Prussia on February 19.[7] Now that peace is near and the independence of the United States is recognized throughout Europe, he explains, merchants and manufacturers are vying for new outlets. Lynen's brass mill produces all kinds of goods, among them nesting kettles, casseroles, basins, plates, wire of various gauges, needles, and brass rods for the slave trade. His firm has supplied metal for foundries of all kinds and articles suitable to the tastes and needs of any region.

From Saint-Pol in Artois, Heroguelle Hermans writes a letter on March 9. Hermans has been manufacturing calamanco for the last

5. Woddrop (Wardrop) was a Glasgow tobacco merchant who had lived in Virginia for some years before returning to Scotland. Having received no reply he sent a copy of this letter to Henry Laurens in June. Laurens excused BF's silence: he was not only fully employed with "the proper Business of his Mission," but he was also "incompetent to the subject you referred to him." W. W. Abbot et al., eds., *The Papers of George Washington*, Confederation Series (6 vols., Charlottesville and London, 1992–97), II, 76n; *Laurens Papers*, XVI, 220n.

6. For the Mississippi Land Company see XXXI, 531; W. W. Abbot et al., eds., *The Papers of George Washington*, Colonial Series (10 vols., Charlottesville and London, 1983–95), VII, 219–25, 415–17; VIII, 62–5, 149–53.

7. Lynen was the scion of a brass and copper dynasty based in Stolberg; he helped found a glassworks there in 1790: August Brecher, *Geschichte der Stadt Stolberg in Daten* (Aachen, 1990), p. 34; August Brecher, *Stolberger Alltag in zwei Jahrhunderten* (2 vols., Stolberg, 1993–95), II, 99.

three years, some of which has surely made it to America, though probably third or fourth hand and therefore at a higher price than had it been purchased directly. He therefore offers to Franklin everything his firm manufactures at wholesale prices: all kinds of calamanco (wide, narrow, ribbed, and plain) as well as Turkish satin, Minorcan serge, and prunella. If the Americans would like to send samples of desired fabrics, he can make them and dye them to specification. This is the moment to place an order; English cloth will be 12 to 15 percent more expensive because so many of their workers were impressed as seamen during the war and practically nothing was manufactured. He encloses samples in the colors of his region, lists prices, and requests Franklin to put him in touch with a reliable American merchant with whom he may correspond or meet at some local seaport.

A merchant firm also dealing in fabric—mainly linen—seeks to establish trade with the United States in a letter dated April 10 from Leipzig. Writing in English and signing themselves Godfrey Grosser's Widow & Co., they assure Franklin that nothing makes a Saxon merchant happier than the idea of negotiating with "a people who freed himself in such a distinguishing manner as the american did." The Saxon court, they understand, has made some trade proposals through its ambassador at Versailles.[8] Having heard that some of their compatriots have already shipped considerable quantities of linen to America, the firm cannot sit by idly. As they are financially solvent and knowledgeable, they vow to "do more then others." Can Franklin furnish the names of the best mercantile houses in Philadelphia and other ports, along with advice about what is most needed?

Johann Wilhelm and Johann Gottfried Spangenberg, also from Saxony, write in German on March 14 from Sühla (Suhl) with a business proposition. Arms from their factory in Henneberg were sent to America by an indirect route during the war. Now that peace has been concluded, they expect that the United States will set up arsenals in the various provinces and may require new arms, which they propose to supply. The iron from their region is of an excellent quality, and their manufactory is one of the best in the world. They ask Franklin to supply the name and address of the party they should deal with; they propose as an intermediary John Frederick Droop of Hamburg, who would forward to them any model that the Americans might want duplicated. The Saxon ambassador in France, Schönfeld, who will de-

8. For the commercial proposals forwarded to BF by the Saxon minister Schönfeld see his letter below of March 9.

liver this letter,[9] is available to discuss the export of other products from Saxony. They promise to "incessantly offer up to heaven our prayers and goodwishes for the continuance of [Franklin's] precious health."[1]

From the other end of Germany comes a letter from another arms manufacturer. The firm of Jean & Gaspar Halbach & fils writes from Remscheid near Cologne on April 11. One of their associates plans to leave for Philadelphia in three weeks, by way of Amsterdam, and they request a letter of recommendation addressed to Congress. That unnamed associate will be in Amsterdam for a week, at the address of their banker Jean Texier.[2] Their arms are of the best quality and are offered at competitive prices; they have been in operation for 70 years and have the largest and best facilities. They have furnished arms to nearly every European war department. If their partner finds Philadelphia suitable, he may choose to open a branch there, and in time, maybe even a factory if the rivers can provide water power. They enclose a one-page list of articles they manufacture: guns, rifles, pistols, musketoons, pikes, swords, and sabers for the infantry, cavalry, and navy, as well as all sorts of hardware, steel bars, and barrels.

Besides those merchants who are offering specific goods, a number of merchants seek Franklin's general help and advice concerning the establishment of commercial ties in America.

Writing from Lyon in fractured English on January 27, the firm of Charles Gilibert & Cie. begs for advice. Through Wallace, Johnson & Muir they have received an order worth about 40,000 *l.t.* from an Annapolis merchant named John Hoskins Stone.[3] Is he trustworthy? The reputation of their firm has spread to America by way of Nantes and Lorient, and this is not the first invoice they have received from America. They have declined to fill such orders until the peace was de-

9. We summarized Schönfeld's cover letter, dated only April 5, at its earliest possible date; see XXVI, 171, where we mistakenly said that the enclosure was missing. Schönfeld characterized the Spangenberg factory as "la plus estimée de toute l'Allemagne."

1. This quotation is taken from an English translation of the present letter that was prepared for BF. It is in an unknown hand.

2. XXXII, 593n.

3. For Wallace, Johnson & Muir see XXXVI, 598–9n. Stone (1750–1804) was the nephew of Daniel of St. Thomas Jenifer (XXXV, 179n). He later became governor of Maryland: Edward C. Papenfuse et al., eds., *A Biographical Dictionary of the Maryland Legislature, 1635–1789* (2 vols., Baltimore and London, 1979–85), II, 784–5.

clared. They await Franklin's counsel, and hope to trade with their new friends to mutual advantage.

Jean Guild Wets writes in English from Bruges on January 30 on behalf of a syndicate comprising 40 of the "most substantial marchants" of Flanders and Brabant. He has Mr. Naghel[4] to thank for the favor of their acquaintance with Franklin. His firm intends to send ships to North America if this can be done with safety and "a moral succes." Having no knowledge of the country or its manufactories, he requests the names of some reliable mercantile houses.

The next day, January 31, Veuve d'Aubremé & fils writes from Brussels. Winning the peace and American independence will cover Franklin with immortal glory. The firm wishes now to establish a direct correspondence with the United States. Are its ports open to ships flying the Imperial flag? If so, would Franklin indicate a mercantile house in Boston and in Philadelphia where they might consign the ships they intend to send as soon as hostilities cease? They will be shipping goods that they believe to be the most useful and necessary to the inhabitants.

Charles Paleske, writing in English on March 7 from Danzig, reminds Franklin that he had called on him four years earlier to propose "advantageous connections" with his country. He now congratulates Franklin on the peace, predicts that this will cause "quite a new turn to the commercial transactions of all Europe," and hastens to offer his services for business in his city and the neighboring ports in the Baltic. He also wants to know what encouragement is being offered to merchants (with or without capital), tradesmen, and manufacturers to settle in America. Would they receive grants of land or relief from taxes for a certain period? Would Franklin likewise provide him with names of mercantile houses in the capital city and elsewhere, to which cargoes and ships might be addressed?[5]

In a March 16 letter from Paris, J. M. Delamarche extols the suitability of goods from Languedoc for the American market, including wine, eau de vie, and salt. He assures Franklin that American products

4. Probably the Naghel who wrote to BF about outfitting ships in 1779: XXXI, 51.

5. Paleske emigrated to Pennsylvania in 1784, and was appointed Prussian consul to the U.S. in 1791. By 1797 he settled in Montgomery County, Pa.: Thompson Westcott, *Names of Persons Who Took the Oath of Allegiance to the State of Pennsylvania between the Years 1777 and 1789* . . . (Philadelphia, 1865), p. 105; King Frederick William II, Commission for Charles G. Paleske, Aug. 14, 1791 (National Archives); *Jefferson Papers*, XXIV, 99–101; *Pa. Gaz.*, Aug. 16, 1797.

would likewise sell to advantage in Languedoc. Virginia tobacco is in great demand, and Carolina rice has been highly esteemed ever since the firm of Falconnet, Brérnet & Delamarche received the first shipment. This firm, established in both Montpellier and Sète, the only seaport of the province, can provide further documentation and testimonials to Americans who wish to do business. He signs himself *Commissaire de la Marine d'hollande en Languedoc.*[6]

Fiott & Patriarche, a firm from the Island of Jersey, writes in English on April 3. They have heard that Franklin views the Channel Islands as the best entrepôt for trade between Europe and America. Their island is preferable to the others: they are only seven leagues from France, and they charge lower fees for unloading, loading, warehousing, and shipping. They hope to be honored with Franklin's protection and recommendation, and refer him for information respecting their character to General Conway, the island's governor, and any London merchant who has had dealings with their island.[7]

Josef Utzschneider of Munich, signing himself "bailiff to Anger in Bavarie,"[8] writes in English on April 10, apparently on behalf of a Bavarian firm which remains unnamed. They know very little about America, and would like Franklin to advise them regarding what merchandise is needed there and what American products they could sell in Europe. They intend to send an agent to Philadelphia in the coming year.

The comte de Wied (or so he signs himself)[9] writes from Neuwied

6. Delamarche is listed as the Dutch representative in Sète in the *Almanach royal* for 1783, p. 268. On the bottom of this letter is written, in another hand, "Mr Vieussieux negociant à Naples demandent la meme faveur."

7. This letter is at the Hist. Soc. of Pa. The writers may be William Patriarche, who became president of the Jersey Chamber of Commerce when it was revived in 1785, and Nic. Fiott, who served on the Chamber's executive committee: A. C. Saunders, *Jersey in the 18th and 19th Centuries* . . . (Jersey, Channel Islands, 1930), p. 38. Henry Seymour Conway, with whom BF had dealings before the Revolution (XII, 209n; XIV, 242), spent prolonged periods of time on Jersey during the war in his capacity as governor: *DNB.*

8. Utzschneider (1763–1840) was the private secretary and estate manager of Maria Anna, Duchess of Bavaria (1722–1790). He later studied philosophy and law and became a prominent agronomist: *ADB.* This letter may have been conveyed by the duc de Deux Ponts; see the duchesse de Deux Ponts to BF, April 21, and Kéralio to BF, letter (II), April 26. On a blank leaf of Utzschneider's letter the comte de Proli wrote BF a request for a passport; see our annotation of his letter of May 14.

9. Probably Friedrich Alexander Graf zu Wied-Neuwied (1706–1791):

on March 19 that the United States could not have entrusted its affairs to better hands. He assures Franklin that liberty and prosperity are his "devises favorites," which he always keeps in mind for his subjects and the county of which he is regent. He recommends the products of his region, which he hopes will form the basis for commerce between the "protégés" of America and his own subjects, and asks Franklin to grant an interview to his commercial advisor, Sr. Rœngen.[1]

Various individuals other than manufacturers and merchants send Franklin ideas for schemes that will benefit either the new nation, themselves, or, more often, both. Knowing that America will need to understand and evaluate the various currencies of her new trading partners, Adam Christian Kümmel tells Franklin that he has spent about 30 years working out currency conversion charts of all the gold coins of Europe. Writing in German from Brieg in Silesia on January 28, he encloses nine of these to serve as examples.[2] There are 53 more, he writes, of which he has only handwritten copies. Believing that these will be infinitely useful to the United States, he asks whether Franklin would help get them printed and convey them to America.[3]

Jean-Louis Stourm, signing himself chevalier de Saint-Louis, writes from Belfort on February 4. He had written Franklin the previous year, and because the reply was so gracious, he is now emboldened to offer congratulations on America's having won independence.[4] He encloses a three-page essay entitled "Le Royaume Imaginaire: Election du Roi," which he wrote during a long period of unemployment.[5] When one has nothing to do, one concerns oneself with every-

---

Wilhelm Tullins, *Die wechselvolle Geschichte des Hauses Wied* (Neuwied, 2002), pp. 65–75.

1. This may be David Roentgen (1743–1807), who in 1780 became a master cabinetmaker of Paris and furnished Louis XVI with pieces from his workshop. The cabinetmaker Abraham Roentgen, his father, founded one of the most successful enterprises of this type in the eighteenth century. Father and son were natives of Neuwied: Joseph M. Greber, *David Roentgen, Der königliche Kabinettmacher aus Neuwied* ... (Neuwied, 1948); *New Encyclopædia Britannica*.

2. Not found.

3. Kümmel's German is not always clear. We base our summary in part on a French résumé prepared for BF by an unknown translator, now among BF's undated papers at the APS.

4. Stourm had written on Dec. 19, 1781: XXXVI, 314. We have not located BF's answer to that letter, and have found no indication that BF replied to this one, Stourm's final communication.

5. Having found that a hereditary monarchy poses problems, but being

thing. Stourm also has ideas on fortifications and the best organization of the military. He knows that Franklin will tell him *laus propria sorda* (self-praise is to be despised), but he has no one to champion him. He is obliged to boast. He hopes Franklin will not take offense at what he has written.

On February 16 Johann Michael Ortlieb, a farmer and wine-grower with long experience in Riquewihr, Alsace, presents three projects on ways of cultivating the vine in sterile regions and on employing common lands and pastures for subsistence farming. Included in his 13-page letter, a mixture of French and German, are excerpts from correspondence he has exchanged with Joly de Fleury in an attempt to interest the king in his projects.[6]

Johann Rodolph Valltravers, writing in his characteristically effusive English, offers congratulations from Vienna on February 19. Does not the United States wish to (1) protect its freedom with a "respectable military Establishment," (2) make up for the loss of all those killed or fled during the war, (3) introduce an annual supply of husbandmen and tradesmen at the least expense, and (4) form alliances with the most prosperous European republics? All this he promises to effect, once Congress grants him citizenship and a tract of land. In addition to this proposal, he submits a second scheme on behalf of an old friend from Lincolnshire who lived in North America for many years, who received considerable land grants in northern New York from Governor Tryon, and who is now back in England.[7] This friend, who recently spent five years in Bengal, owns four ships there; he desires a commission from Congress to send those ships on expeditions "to make profitable discoveries and settlements." He would like to be

---

unwilling to embrace a democracy (which tends towards anarchy), Stourm proposed a representative system of voting for king. Every province would elect one candidate, preferably between 25 and 30 years old and certainly no older than 40, who would have undergone a rigorous examination as to education, morals, talent, and family. Votes would be cast by placing balls of gold, silver, and copper into sealed urns. The candidates would then go to Paris and be examined by a national corps; whoever was not chosen king would constitute the Secret Council.

6. Six years later Ortlieb published his ideas in a work which he dedicated to the king: *Plan and instructions based on experience, in order to improve the products of the land, in particular the vineyards, dictated by patriotic instinct . . .* (Strasbourg, 1789). The work appeared in French and in German the same year.

7. In an earlier letter Valltravers identified him as Jas. Creassey: XXXVIII, 184.

commodore of the squadron, with full powers to sail and trade in any part of the world. He would begin by taking possession of two small uninhabited islands, which are unclaimed by any European power but are ideally situated for trade with India. He asks for no money, only one or two fully outfitted vessels from Congress, manned and freighted in Europe with naval stores. Valltravers would prefer to discuss both of these plans in person; he awaits Franklin's summons, which Ingenhousz will forward.[8]

August Friedemann Rühle von Lilienstern introduces himself as a jurist and an economist in a letter of March 14, written in German.[9] He writes from Dillenburg where he is lieutenant general of police and a magistrate for the region. He has published a collection of all the constitutions of Nassau, going back several centuries. Work on the collection has given him insight into the underlying causes of misery and famine among the peasantry, and has made him determined to gather the unfortunates from all over Germany and transplant them to another part of the globe. He considered St. Petersburg, but he and his associates would now prefer the United States. Graf von Wied-runkel[1] has already proposed to him a colony of several hundred families, and offered his land as a depot. The new colonists—who have nothing—will need to be given money for the journey, tools and animals, access to shops for various services, and above all a large area of land that is wooded and preferably near a navigable river. They also must have tax relief for a period of ten to twelve years and freedom from military service. All now depends on Franklin's response, which should be prompt if he wants to eliminate competition from a Canadian colony being promoted by British Americans. The first country to meet his offer will be chosen. The writer is a member of the Reformed Church, 39 years old, with a wife and children and a large

8. A duplicate of this ALS is also at the APS; we do not know when Valltravers sent it.

9. Rühle von Lilienstern (1742–1828) was a magistrate in Isenburg, Dierdorf, and Dillenburg, and a newspaper editor. He published several books on legal and religious subjects: *ADB;* Walther Killy *et al.,* eds., *Deutsche Biographische Enzyklopädie* (14 vols., Munich, 1995–2000), under Rühle. A French translation of this letter was prepared for BF by the baronne de Bourdic, who enclosed it in her letter of [April 20?], below.

1. Christian Ludwig Graf von Wied-Runkel: Ernst Heinrich Kneschke, ed., *Neues allgemeines Deutsches Adels-Lexicon* (9 vols., Leipzig, 1859–70). The county of Wied in the Duchy of Nassau was divided into two districts: Dierdorf was the administrative center of Wied-Runkel, and Neuwied was that of Wied-Neuwied: Larousse.

number of relatives, many of whom work in various courts of Germany. He also has a brother in the Royal–Deux-Ponts Regiment serving in America.[2] He is not wealthy, but he is healthy and has a desire to be useful and maintain his reputation for uprightness.

Having received no response, Rühle von Lilienstern writes again on April 3, in German. He fears that the colonists will apply to an English agent or to Graf Romanzow, the Russian ambassador in Frankfurt.[3] He asks to be appointed American agent to various German districts, and encloses a four-page 16-point plan of colonization.

Herbert Jones, writing in English on April 9 from his estate of Llynon on the Isle of Anglesey in North Wales,[4] proposes a very different colonization scheme. Overpopulation and crushing taxes have made the inhabitants of his principality eager to emigrate to North America. May they have Franklin's protection? Jones and "other men of Property and Opulence" will take a colony of at least 1,000 people; they will be craftsmen of different sorts but mostly weavers, as they intend to establish a woolen cloth manufactory. Jones asks permission to wait on Franklin and deliver his credentials in person.

On March 17 a M. de Coch, writing from Brussels and signing himself as a pensioner of the States of Brabant, asks rhetorically whether all the arts should not be used to celebrate the most remarkable event ever to occur on earth; doubtless the subject of the ingenious medal that Franklin has had struck[5] would be no less imposing on canvas than it is in bronze. Surely Franklin knows that the Flemish school has produced excellent painters; de Coch recommends one who follows in the steps of Rubens, by the name of Herreyns.[6] This artist is well known

2. Charles-Guillaume Rühl de Lilienstern (b. 1740) went to America with Rochambeau's corps: Bodinier, *Dictionnaire.*

3. Count Nikolaj Petrovié Rumjancev served as Russian minister to the Upper Rhenish Imperial District from June 19, 1782, to Oct. 1, 1795: *Repertorium der diplomatischen Vertreter,* III, 353.

4. Jones inherited Llynon from an uncle, also Herbert Jones, in 1767, and in 1775–76 built a large flour mill on the estate in Llanddeusant which still stands. He was high sheriff in 1791: Aled Eames, *Ships and Seamen of Anglesey, 1558–1918* (Llangefni, Wales, 1973), pp. 155–7; Helen Ramage, *Portraits of an Island: Eighteenth Century Anglesey* (Llangefni, Wales, 1987), p. 296.

5. The *Libertas Americana* medal.

6. Guillaume-Jacques Herreyns (1743–1827) studied at the Academy of Antwerp and later became its director. Considered the last of the school of Rubens, he painted portraits as well as historical and religious subjects. In 1771 he settled in Mechelen where he founded a drawing school which in five

to John Adams, who was enchanted by his work when he went to see him in Mechelen.[7] The king of Sweden has given him several commissions and has named him his history painter. Roslin, Pierre, David, and van Spaendonck[8] have all visited Herreyns' studio and can testify about him.

Writing on March 22 from Bergamo, Italy, in a combination of German and Latin, Nicolaus ab Albrecht identifies himself as a professor of languages. After congratulating Franklin on the peace, he offers to introduce him to some unnamed Italian bankers who might be willing to supply the American government with a loan of several million florins. They are based in a seaport that may form an advantageous relationship with the United States. Albrecht can furnish Franklin with the particulars, and would expedite the negotiation. The rate of interest would be five percent, and the repayment of principal could stretch over 30 years or more. They could also arrange to supply the United States with a couple of million in copper coins as well as three-and-a-half million in smaller denominations, enough so that every American province would have half a million coins. He may in time have other advantageous proposals to offer.[9]

J. M. Wintmülle writes from Hamburg on April 18 with a number of proposals to recommend. The first is for General Washington. The news from London is that Congress has resolved to establish a standing army, and has offered a premium for the best formula for powder for cannons, guns, and pistols. A friend of Wintmülle's has made many as-yet secret discoveries regarding the perfection of musket design, including one that allows the gun to fire three times as fast. Wintmülle may be able to persuade his friend to give a more detailed explanation; if interested, Franklin should indicate the best way to send this proposition to Washington. His friend might be willing to go to America, with or without a group of trained gunsmiths. If Franklin

---

years became a royal academy. He was the *premier peintre* of the States of Brabant and painter to the king of Sweden, and in 1783 refused the position of director of the Brussels Academy: Jane Turner, ed., *The Dictionary of Art* (34 vols., New York, 1996).

7. JA probably passed through Mechelen on Aug. 3, 1780, when traveling from Brussels to Antwerp: Butterfield, *John Adams Diary*, III, 31–2, 305. He took great interest in the paintings in Antwerp: *ibid.*, 444.

8. The painters Alexander Roslin, Jean-Baptiste-Marie Pierre, Jacques-Louis David, and Gerard van Spaendonck were all living in Paris: Turner, ed., *Dictionary of Art*.

9. An English translation of this letter in an unknown hand is also at the APS.

should agree to this first proposal, they will send details of a new kind of explosive device and a special sort of bullet. The inventor is well known to General von Steuben, who can furnish references. In a postscript, Wintmülle asks if painters are in demand in America, because he knows one who wants to emigrate. This artist knows a secret technique for gilding, invented in Copenhagen, which uses false gold or base metal; it is almost better than gold leaf. The Danish king has awarded to the inventor a pension of 300 *écus* to teach the art to two subjects before he dies. Wintmülle will send Franklin the whole explanation (on six sheets of paper), which he will translate from Danish into German. In the royal castle of Copenhagen the gold leaf has been replaced in large rooms by the technique he describes because it is more durable than gold. Wintmülle has used it himself, and anyone who knows a little about gilding can master the method. He also asks if Franklin has any interest in the works of northern philosophers; if he should want the works of the late Baron von Holberg[1] or others for his library in Philadelphia, he has only to ask. Franklin's response should be directed to him at the "Bureau des Postes de Sa Majesté Danoise à Hambourg."

Several undated notes in Wintmülle's hand, the first of which accompanied a four-page printed announcement in German, were possibly enclosed in this letter.[2] The printed brochure announced for sale in Hamburg an "ingenious planetary system" and a "great and magnificent art turner's lathe." A note on a small square of paper explains that the sellers, heirs of Simon Peter Meyer, are asking 600 *écus* for the planetary system, which is "unique de son genre." If they do not find a buyer by the end of May, they will sell it at auction on June 2. On the verso Wintmülle says that some 33 years earlier he invented a miniature printing press on which he printed in French *Lettre à Monsr. Le Baron de Holberg*, a response to one of Holberg's letters. A second note offers to procure any book Franklin might want, no matter how rare or in what language. The possibilities in his city exceed those of Paris; Hamburg merchants have correspondents in Philadelphia, Boston, and Quebec. Voght and Sieveking[3] control about half the shipments from Hamburg to North America. The latter is a reputable

1. Ludvig Holberg (1684–1754), made a baron in 1747, was the major literary figure of the Scandinavian Enlightenment, best remembered for his comedies and moralist essays: *New Encyclopædia Britannica*.

2. These handwritten notes and the printed announcement are filed together at the APS.

3. Caspar Voght (1752–1839) and Georg Heinrich Sieveking (1751–1799) were partners: *ADB*.

and reliable man, as well as a personal friend. If Franklin wants more information about the moralist Holberg, Wintmülle could send his memoirs, written in Latin but now translated into German and Danish.[4] The third undated piece, this one in German and filling four sides of a folded sheet of writing paper, appears to be a summary of the contents of Holberg's *Vergleichung der Historien und Thaten verschiedener.* Wintmülle adds, in French, that this book is Holberg's masterpiece, and he lists Holberg's other publications.

Monsieur   Bordx ce 25 Janver. 1783./.

J'aÿ eû lhonneur de vous ecrire & de vous faire part de mon projet pour Letablissement dune Raffinerie â Sucre, â philadelphie, ainsy Que dune manufacture a minot,[5] Joze Croire que J'ai des Connaissances sur ces objets ayant pluzieurs annees de travail dans ces deux Branches de Commerce, Jai dans cette ville & aux environs deux manufactures que Jai Etablies, dans Le meme Genre Lune & Lautre sont En activitté, & Je les Cederais a mon frere qui en dirige une, esperant Trouver des plus grands avantages dans ce pais, dittes moy Je vous prie votre Sentiment & si le Congrés ferait Les fraix de letablissement. Il faudrait une avance de 300 m L. & en Meme temps La liberté entiere de porter dans Les Collonnies francaises Tous les Minots que Je ferais fabriquer pour du produit Raport et des sucres bruts pour Les Raffiner. Si cette entreprize pouvait se faire ainsy Je ménerais avec Moy dans ce pais les ouvriers necessaires Et Je prendrais des mezures pour avoir Tout ce quil y aurait de mieux.

Honnorés moy de votre reponce & croyés moy avec un proffond respec Monsieur votre Tres humble et ot[6]

L Martineau ainé

negt. Raffineur a bordeaux

---

4. *Ad virum perillustrem epistola* (Frankfort and Leipzig, 1736).

5. "Minot," or "farine de minot," referred to a kind of refined white flour made from hard wheat, which kept well in humid climates and on long sea voyages. Bordeaux specialized in producing this flour and shipping it to the French West Indies; its chief competition was inexpensive flour smuggled to the French Islands from North America: François Crouzet, "La Croissance economique," in *Bordeaux au XVIIIe siècle,* ed. François-Georges Pariset (Bordeaux, 1968), pp. 208–9. Martineau's earlier letter is missing.

6. On March 1 Martineau wrote again, thanking BF for his letter of Jan. 17. He is determined to pursue the project he outlined earlier, but now asks noth-

Addressed: A Monsieur / Monsieur de francklin / Embassadeur des Etats unis / a Paris

Notation: Martineau 25 Janvr. 1783.

From Jonathan Williams, Jr.: Two Letters

(I) ALS: American Philosophical Society; (II) ALS: American Philosophical Society; copy: Yale University Library

I.

Dear & hond Sir   Nantes Jan. 25. 1783

The present Serves to hand you some Letters brought by my Father who is in my house in perfect Health.[7] When I have arranged my Business so as to be able to leave it I shall wait on you with him & bring home Mrs W[8] in return.

I thank you for your Note to Lord Shelburne[9] which I hope he will feel.

I am with the greatest Respect Your dutifull & affectionate

JONA WILLIAMS J

I have just recvd your Packet sent Mr Livingston with the news of Peace. Vessells will not go to sea without Passeports untill the time is elapsed.[1]

---

ing from Congress but their permission. No one would know better than BF whether such an enterprise would prosper.

7. Jonathan Williams, Sr., newly arrived in France, carried letters from Jane Mecom: XXXVIII, 200, 506; see also his letter to BF, Jan. 26.

8. Mariamne Williams had been staying with her relatives in St. Germain: XXXVIII, 233, 261.

9. Regarding JW's claim on the *Trio,* which had been carried into Kinsale by mutineers; see XXXVIII, 570–1, 587–9.

1. JW had written anxious letters to WTF on Jan. 21 and 23, begging for confirmation of the rumors he had heard that a peace was signed. He needed BF to send commissions for two brigs that were ready to sail, the *Olive* and *Hetty,* which he co-owned with Samuel White; in the event of peace, he would need passports instead. APS. Now that JW had seen BF's Jan. 21 letter to Livingston and its enclosures, he knew that American ships would need the protection of English passports for the time periods specified in the preliminary articles (for which see the annotation of that letter, above).

II.

Dr & hond Sir.   Nantes Jan. 25. 1783
    The Bearer is my Friend Saml White Esqr who is on the Busi-
ness of obtaing Passports from England for the american Ships
outward Bound.[2] He will Show you my Letter to Lord Shelburne
& Mr Vaughan; If you think the application useless, or unlikely
to Succeed please to tell Major White so that he may not proceed
on a false Errand.[3] I beg leave to introduce my Friend, to your
kind Notice & am Dr & hond Sir most dutifully & affecy Yours
                                                JONA WILLIAMS J

I shall take it as a favour if you will give Mr White an Introduction to some of your Friends in London.

His Excelly Doctor Franklin.

Addressed: His Excellency.— / Doctor Franklin.

Notation: Jona. Williams June 25. 1783

From John Bondfield   ALS: American Philosophical Society

Sir   Bordeaux 26 Jany 1783
    An Express arrivd yesterday proclaimd Peace permit me to
renew my Compliments of Congratulation.[4]

---

    2. See the preceding note. Samuel White (XXXVIII, 258, 259n) had not yet
been to Passy. JW recommended him warmly to WTF in a letter of this same
day, Jan. 25: APS.
    3. White was hoping to recover the *Trio*. JW's Jan. 25 letter to Benjamin
Vaughan introduced White and asked Vaughan to recommend him to Shelburne; a copy is in the Yale University Library. JW's letter to Shelburne has
left no trace.
    4. On Jan. 20, the day the preliminaries were signed, the French court sent
circulars to the ports, announcing the news and issuing a temporary embargo
on shipping: *Gaz. de Leyde*, Feb. 4, 1783. That circular, probably the proclamation Bondfield mentions here and in the third paragraph, must have either
described or quoted Article 22 of the Franco-British treaty, which specified
that once the preliminary treaty was ratified, the armistice would take effect
at sea on different dates depending on the distance from France and England.
See the annotation of BF to Livingston, Jan. 21.

Mr Barclay wrote me some posts past from Lorient to have the returns of the prisoners at this City which I have transmitted and expect his further instructions by return of Post.[5]

I took the liberty to request a protection for two small Brigs I have which will very speedily be ready for Sea and as their Proceeding without Protections if met by English Men of War or Cruizers in Latitudes or Longitudes precribed by the proclamation before the Stipulated term allowd is expired will subject them to Capture and condemnd as legal Prizes we have Recourse to your protection which will preserve our Vessels from being Molested on their Voyage.

I receivd a few Days past a Letter from Mr Bache acknowledging the receipt of part of the Wine you orderd for his Account[6] ten Cases shipt per the Maclanachan had the misfortune to be carried to Halifax.[7]

With due Respect I have the Honor to be Sir Your most Obedient servant   JOHN BONDFIELD

The Brig Sophia Cap Allin for Philadelphia
The Brig Mimi Cap Walls for Charles Town

Addressed: a Son Excéllance / Benjm. Fránklin / Ministre Pre. des Etats Unis / de Lamerique / à Paris

---

5. Hodgson wrote BF on Dec. 12 that Townshend had decided to send a cartel ship to Lorient for the exchange of prisoners. BF was asked to have all the British prisoners sent to Lorient: XXXVIII, 441. On Dec. 25 WTF wrote to Thomas Barclay (then at Lorient) with these instructions. Barclay immediately sent word to Bordeaux, La Rochelle, Nantes, and Rochefort: Barclay to WTF, Jan. 6, 1783 (APS).

6. For which see XXXVIII, 363.

7. For the capture of the *McClenachan* see XXXVIII, 569–70.

From Alleyne Fitzherbert[8]

AL: Library of Congress

Hotel du Parc Royal rue des Marais le 26 Janvier 1783

M. Fitz-Herbert est venu pour avoir l'honneur de faire part qu'il a eu Mardi 21 de ce mois ses premiéres audiences du Roi, de la Reine, et de la famille Royale en qualité de Ministre Plenipotentiaire de Sa Majesté Britannique.

From William Hodgson

ALS: American Philosophical Society

Dear sir   London 26 Jany 1783

I have Rec'd your favor of the 14th per Mr Oswald & am much obliged to you for your friendly Intentions,[9] I have the Satisfaction to inform you that after all the Alarms & Apprehensions the upshot was tolerable, much better than I expected.

I without delay waited upon the Secretary of State with the discharges of the Officers you sent me & he readily consented to do every thing you requested & desired I woud return you his best thanks[1] & this day I have been again at the Office desiring the Cartel Vessell might go to L'Orient instead of Morlaix which was promised me[2] I hope they will be soon sent away, if you

---

8. Fitzherbert had been appointed minister plenipotentiary the preceding summer (XXXVII, 685n), but was received by the royal family only when peace was restored. We assume that this announcement, written in French, was one of several that Fitzherbert prepared in advance to leave at the residences of the ministers who were not at home when he called.

On Jan. 25 Fitzherbert reported to Grantham that the American commissioners had accepted his credentials to treat with France as "a full-power to treat with them likewise," in Oswald's absence: Giunta, *Emerging Nation*, I, 759.

9. Included in the "note" dated Jan. 14: XXXVIII, 583–4.

1. On Jan. 8 Hodgson had relayed Secretary of State Townshend's request for the exchange of three British officers: XXXVIII, 568–9. BF's answer is missing; it might have been in the now-missing section of his letter of Jan. 14 (XXXVIII, 583).

2. Preparations for an exchange of prisoners at Lorient were well under way when Hodgson wrote on Jan. 8 that the site had been changed to Morlaix; see our annotation of Bondfield to BF, Jan. 26, and XXXVIII, 568. BF must have insisted on Lorient in a now-missing response.

judge a Passport still necessary I will endeavour to procure one
& send before the Cartel Vessell goes— I do now most sincerely
congratulate you on the happy Issue to the horrors of War,
which in my Opinion has terminated in such a Manner as to be
a general Blessing to the human Race & to yourself nothing
coud be more glorious & honorable—there Remains yet a good
deal to settle & arrange— I recollect when at Passy you was
pleased to say that you woud turn your thoughts to the Consideration of which wou'd be the wisest & best Conduct for this
Country to pursue with respect to America, after Independence
shou'd be acknowledged & you gave me reason to hope you
wou'd favor me with them, I take the Liberty of reminding you
because I think you will do thereby an Essential Service to this
Country & it will be highly honorable to me to be the Commu-
nicator of your Ideas on such a Subject to the Minister— War
being now no more, Commercial Ideas, begin to occupy my
Mind, I wish to have Connections with America & I think there
is a fair prospect that those who get first to Market will do best
—3 I have a Ship of my own Called the Mary, Jno Muir master
which I design to send to the Chesapeak with a Cargo of goods
as soon as I possibly Can, Hostilities, I expect, will cease in the
Channell before the Vessell can possibly be ready, but I am apprehensive she may get into War Latitude before the Cessation
of Hostilities for this reason I request the favor of you to give
me a pass for her both in her Voyage & on her arrival in America shou'd it so happen that she gets there before the final Settlement & as I wish her to be protected att all Events if Mr W. T.
Franklin will oblige me so far as to procure a pass for her both
from the French & Spanish Ministers I shall be much obliged to
him & the sooner it is done the more likely to prove beneficial—
I am well informed that there is not any thing novel in this request— After the Preliminaries of the last General Peace were
signed the different Powers granted Passports for such Vessells
as were to sail after the signing & were intended for long Voyages, where they might run the risque of being captured as the

---

3. European imports flooded American ports in the spring and summer of
1783: Richard Buel, Jr., *In Irons: Britain's Naval Supremacy and the American Revolutionary Economy* (New Haven and London, 1998), p. 247.

Time limited for the Cessation of Hostilities woud not be expired.[4]

I submit it to your Consideration whether it may not have some weight in Case of any Demur, to certify the pass to be given to the Ship as belonging to me, (which she actually does)—as I am apt to flatter myself my Conduct wou'd entitle me to some favor in America. I hope soon to furnish you with my Ballance Acct for the prisoners, I recd upwards of a Month ago a small Bill from Mr Wren belonging to a Prisoner twas a Continental Loan Note I enclosed it you in a Letter per a friend of Mr Vaughans be pleased to signify if you recd it.[5]

The favor of an Answer to this Letter the first opportunity will much oblige. Your's most Sincerely   WILLIAM HODGSON

P.S. pray am I to prosecute Digges,[6] I totally forgot to mention it to you—

Addressed: To / His Excellency / Benj. Franklin Esqr

---

4. As in the current preliminary agreement, the preliminary treaty of Nov. 3, 1762, between France and Great Britain provided for time limits, based on distance, for the armistice to take effect. Article 22 of the 1783 preliminary articles (for which see the annotation of BF to Livingston, Jan. 21) was in fact adapted from Article 25 of the 1762 preliminaries: Parry, *Consolidated Treaty Series*, XLII, 225–6. The geographic zones were identical, but the amount of time allowed for sailing to them was shortened.

5. Hodgson's letter of Dec. 12: XXXVIII, 442. Hodgson wrote to Samuel Vaughan, Sr., on the same evening as he penned the present letter to BF, complaining that the letters he had entrusted to Vaughan six weeks earlier for forwarding to Passy did not appear to have been delivered, and asking for the name of the prisoner whose bill of exchange was in question. That letter was conveyed to Paris, where Samuel Vaughan, Jr., wrote and signed a statement that "The above letters came by Mr. Watson," and thence to Passy, where WTF noted on the verso that the bill, no. 499 dated April 16, was accepted on Dec. 17, 1782, and was to the order of E. Baker for 36 dollars: APS. Elkanah Watson, Jr., arrived in Paris on Dec. 15, after an extended stay in England: XXXVIII, 501n. He is most likely the "friend of Mr Vaughans" mentioned here by Hodgson.

6. For embezzling funds intended for prisoner relief: XXXVII, 25–6n, 627.

From John Jay

ALS (draft) and AL (draft):[7] Columbia University Library; copies: Library of Congress (two), Massachusetts Historical Society, New-York Historical Society

Sir   Paris 26. Jany. 1783

It having been suspected that I concurred in the appointment of your Grandson to the Place of Secretary to the american Commission for peace, at your Instance,[8] I think it right thus unsollicited to put it in your power to correct that Mistake.

Your general Character, the opinion I had long entertained of your Services to our Country; and the friendly Attention and aid with which you had constantly favored me, after my Arrival in Spain, impressed me with a Desire of manifesting both my Esteem & Attachment by stronger Evidence than Professions. That Desire extended my Regard for you to your Grandson, He was then indeed a Stranger to me, but the Terms in which you expressed to Congress your opinion of his being qualified for another place of equal Importance[9] were so full & satisfactory as to leave me no Room to doubt of his being qualified for the one abovementioned. I was therefore happy to assure you in one of the first Letters I afterwards wrote you from Spain, that in Case a Secretary to our Commission for peace should become necessary, and the Appointment be left to us, I should take that opportunity of evincing my Regard for you by nominating him or words to that Effect.[1] What I then wrote was the spontaneous Suggestion of my own Mind, unsollicited, and I believe unexpected by you.

When I came here on the Business of that Comn I brought with me the same Intentions & should always have considered

---

7. The ALS (draft) is a revision of the AL (draft). Changes made during the drafting process are detailed in Morris, *Jay: Peace*, pp. 488–9.

8. These three words must have been underlined on the ALS sent to BF, since all the copies made from that ALS reflect it. The suspicions Jay alludes to were those of JA: XXXVIII, 164–7, 257; Arthur Lee to James Warren, Dec. 12, 1782, in *Warren-Adams Letters . . .*, II (Mass. Hist. Soc. *Coll.*, LXXIII [1925]), 186.

9. XXXIV, 447–8.

1. XXXVI, 497.

myself engaged by Honor as well as Inclination to fulfil them; unless I had found myself mistaken in the opinion I had imbibed of that young Gentleman's Character and Qualifications but that not being the Case, I found myself at Liberty to indulge my wishes & to be as good as my word—for I expressly declare that your Grandson is in my opinion qualified for the place in Question, & that if he had not been no Consideration whatever[2] would have prevailed upon me to propose or join in his appointment. This explicit and unreserved State of Facts is due to you, to him, and to Justice; and you have my Consent to make any use of it that you may think proper.

I have the Honor to be Sir with great Respect & Regard Your obliged & obedt. Servt   JOHN JAY

His Excellency Doctr Franklin

To Dr. Franklin 26 Jan. 1783

From Jonathan Williams, Sr.

ALS: American Philosophical Society

Hond sr   Nantes Janry 26. 1782 [*i.e.*, 1783]

I take the Liberty to Inform you that after a passage of twenty days I have ariv'd hear in Nantes hope the pleasure of Seing you Soon, I Left all our friends Well in America.[3]

I most hartly Congratelate you On the good News of Peace thanks to God.

Belive me ever your most Dutyfull Nephew & Hble Servant
JONA WILLIAMS

Notation: Jona. Williams Jany. 26. 1782.

2. Jay dropped this word in the version sent to BF, judging by the copies.
3. He had been planning this trip since early fall, and carried letters from Jane Mecom: XXXVIII, 335; see also JW to BF, Jan. 25, letter (I).

To Mary Hewson

ALS: Yale University Library; press copy of ALS: American Philosophical Society; AL (draft) and copy: Library of Congress

Passy, Jany. 27. 1783.

The Departure of my dearest Friend, which I learn from your last Letter,[4] greatly affects me. To meet with her once more in this Life, was one of the principal Motives of my proposing to visit England again before my Return to America. The last Year carried off my Friends Dr Pringle, & Dr Fothergill, & Lord Kaims, and Lord Le Despencer;[5] this has begun to take away the rest, and strikes the hardest. Thus the Ties I had to that Country, & indeed to the World in general, are loosned one by one, and I shall soon have no Attachment left to make me unwilling to follow.[6]

I intended writing when I sent the 11 Books, but I lost the Time in looking for the 12th.— I wrote with that; and hope it came to hand.[7] I therein ask'd your Counsel about my coming to England. On Reflection I think I can, from my Knowledge of your Prudence, foresee what it will be; viz. not to come too soon, lest it should seem braving & insulting some who ought to be respected. I shall therefore omit that Journey till I am near going to America; and then just step over to take Leave of my Friends, and spend a few Days with you. I purpose bringing Ben with me, and perhaps may leave him under your Care.[8]

At length we are in Peace, God be praised; & long, very long may it continue. All Wars are Follies, very expensive & very

---

4. Her Jan. 13 letter reported that her mother, Margaret Stevenson, had died on Jan. 1: XXXVIII, 578–9.

5. Actually, these friends died during the previous two years: John Fothergill on Dec. 26, 1780 (XXXIV, 260), Sir Francis Dashwood, Lord Le Despencer, on Dec. 11, 1781 (Namier and Brooke, *House of Commons*, II, 301), Sir John Pringle on Jan. 18, 1782 (XXXVI, 407n), and Henry Home, Lord Kames, on Dec. 27, 1782: *ODNB*.

6. On the draft BF here wrote and deleted: "The [*struck out:* Time] Period of my Days cannot now be far distant, having now entred my 78th. Year."

7. The books were monthly installments of Arnaud Berquin's *L'ami des enfants* for 1782. BF sent the twelfth on Jan. 8: XXXVIII, 566.

8. BF had been considering enrolling BFB in the Cheam school with Hewson's sons: XXXVIII, 567.

mischievous ones. When will Mankind be convinc'd of this, and agree to settle their Differences by Arbitration? Were they to do it even by the Cast of a Dye, it would be better than by Fighting & destroying each other.

Spring is coming on, when Travelling will be delightful. Can you not, when your Children[9] are all at School, make a little Party, and take a Trip hither? I have now a large House delightfully situated, in which I could accommodate you & two or three Friends; and I am but half an Hours Drive from Paris.

In looking forward,—Twenty-five Years seems a long Period; but in looking back, how short!— Could you imagine that 'tis now full a Quarter of a Century since we were first acquainted!— It was in 1757. During the greatest Part of the Time I lived in the same House with my dear deceased Friend your Mother; of course you and I saw and convers'd with each other much and often.[1] It is to all our Honours, that in all that time we never had among us the smallest Misunderstanding. Our Friendship has been all clear Sunshine, without any the least Cloud in its Hemisphere. Let me conclude by saying to you what I have had too frequent Occasions to say to my other remaining old Friends, *the fewer we become, the more let us love one another.*

Adieu, and believe me ever, Yours most affectionately,

B FRANKLIN

Mrs Hewson

Endorsed: Franklin Jan 27 83 / Passy Jan 27 — 83 40

To John Sargent   Press copy of ALS: American Philosophical Society

My dear Friend   Passy, Jany. 27. 1783

I received and read the Letter you were so kind as to write to me the 3d Instant,[2] with a great deal of Pleasure, as it inform'd

9. William, Thomas, and Elizabeth: XXXIV, 524n.
1. BF lived at Craven Street from 1757 to 1762 and again from 1764 to 1775. He met Mary when she was eighteen and spending most of her time as the companion to an elderly aunt about 10 miles distant: VIII, 122n; *Autobiog.,* pp. 306, 308–9, 313; Lopez and Herbert, *The Private Franklin,* p. 83.
2. XXXVIII, 547–8.

68

me of the Welfare of a Family whom I have so long esteem'd and lov'd and to whom I am under so many Obligations, which I shall ever remember. Our Correspondence has been interrupted by that abominable War: I neither expected Letters from you, nor would I hazard putting you in Danger by writing any to you. We can now communicate freely; and next to the Happiness of seeing and embracing you all again at Halstead,[3] will be that of Hearing frequently of your Health and Prosperity.

Mrs Sargent and the good Lady her Mother, are very kind in wishing me more happy Years. I ought to be satisfy'd with those Providence has already been pleas'd to afford me, being now in my seventy-eighth; a long Life to pass without any uncommon Misfortune, the greatest Part of it in Health and Vigour of Mind & Body, near Fifty Years of it in continu'd Possession of the Confidence of my Country in public Employments, and enjoying the Esteem & affectionate friendly Regard of many wise and good Men and Women, in every Country where I have resided. For these Mercies and Blessings I desire to be thankful to God, whose Protection I have hitherto had, & I hope for its Continuance to the End, which now cannot be far distant.

The Account you give me of your Family is pleasing, except that your eldest Son continues so long unmarried. I hope he does not intend to live and die in Celibacy. The Wheel of Life that has roll'd down to him from Adam without Interruption, should not stop with him. I would not have one dead unbearing Branch in the Genealogical Tree of the Sargents. The married State is, after all our Jokes, the happiest, being conformable to our Natures. Man & Woman have each of them Qualities & Tempers in which the other is deficient, and which in Union contribute to the common Felicity. Single and separate they are not the compleat human Being; they are like the odd Halves of Scissors;[4] they cannot answer the End of their Formation.

I am concern'd at the Losses you have suffer'd by the War. You are still young and active enough to retrieve them, and Peace I hope will afford the Opportunity.

---

3. BF was a guest at the Sargents' country house in Kent during 1774: XXI, 547, 570.
4. BF frequently used this analogy: XXXVI, 204n.

You mention nothing of my good Friend Mrs. Deane, or her amiable Sisters[5] whom I sometimes saw with you, nor of Mr Chambers.[6] I hope they are all well & happy. Present my Respects to Mrs. Sargent whom I love very much, and believe me ever My dear Friend, Yours most affectionately   B FRANKLIN

John Sargent Esqr.

From Nathaniel Fanning[7]   ALS: American Philosophical Society

Dunke: Goal 27th: Jany: 1783

May it please your Excellency

That having wrote your Excellency several Petitions in justification of my Conduct, during my last Cruise on Board of the Eclipse, which has made such a Noise in this Part of the World relative to my Crew having Plundered a certain danish Vessel which has been transacted without my Knowledge, or consent, as appears by my Interogation as well as those of my People.— I have thought fit by and with the Advice of some of the first Men in this place not to cease of Petitioning your Excellency, 'till I shall have some redress or at least an Answer as I am well assured

5. Elizabeth Chambers Deane (XVIII, 37), now deceased, was the sister of Sargent's wife, Rosamond (XXXVI, 551n), and of Theodosia and Jane Chambers (who died in 1778 and 1771, respectively): David Hancock, *Citizens of the World: London merchants and the integration of the British Atlantic community, 1735–1785* (Cambridge, New York, and Melbourne, 1995), p. 405; Stephen Glover, *The History and Gazetteer of the County of Derby . . .* (2 vols., Derby, Eng., 1831–33), II, 494. Mrs. Deane's death is noted in a letter from Theophilus Lindsey to William Turner, July 22, 1779 (Dr. Williams's Library, London): information kindly provided by G. M. Ditchfield, University of Kent, England.

6. Possibly Christopher Chambers, Sargent's partner in the merchant firm of Sargent, Chambers & Co., and his wife's cousin: XXIX, 175n; Hancock, *Citizens of the World*, pp. 11, 74–5, 405; G. M. Ditchfield, "The Revd. William Chambers, D.D. (*c.* 1724–1777)," *Enlightenment and Dissent*, IV (1985), 6.

7. A Connecticut native who was given command of a French privateer and was arrested for boarding a neutral vessel and robbing its French passengers. For the background of this incident see Fanning's previous appeal of Nov. 23 (his only other extant letter) and the annotation there: XXXVIII, 340–3.

that it lays in your Excellency's Power to procure me my Enlargement.—[8] I presume the reason of your Excellency's not having deign'd to answer my former Petitions has been on acct: of your Excellency's having as I am told been often deceiv'd by Englishmen's imposing on your Excellency for Americans & consequently my being thought by your Excellency to be one of the former; If so, I can prove by many Americans now resident in France, of my having been Born of a very reputable Family in New London in America.— I hope & beg most sincerely that this Petition may have the desired effect.

Thus Prayeth Your Excellency's Humble Petitioner & most Obdt. Servant   NATHL: FANNING

His Excellency Benjamin Franklin Esqr: Passy.

Notation: Fanning Nathaniel Dunkerque 27. Janvr. 1783

From the Chevalier de Kéralio, with a Note by the Duchesse de Deux-Ponts   ALS: American Philosophical Society

Forbach, le 27e. janvier, 1783.

Nous avons appris aujourd'hui, mon Respectable ami, que les préliminaires de la paix avoient été signés le 20e entre les puissances belligérantes, et sur le champ la Dame du chateau[9] a ordonné à son secrétaire intime[1] de mettre son tendre hommage aux pieds du libérateur de l'amérique, du Vengeur du droit des Nations, en attendant qu'elle puisse l'embrasser de tout son cœur. Vos jours sont comme ceux du juste, ils sont bien remplis: Convenés, malgré vôtre excessive modestie, que jamais il ne fut une Carriere plus brillante que la Vôtre; le bienfaiteur des hommes approche seul de la divinité; Continués à les éclairer, à les instruire, mais restés parmi nous, s'il vous est possible; c'est le Vœu de Votre digne amie, et d'un des hommes du monde qui

8. Receiving no answer from BF, he enlisted the help of Thomas Greenleaf, who wrote on April 16 (below).

9. The duchesse douairière de Deux-Ponts, or, as she signs herself below, the comtesse de Forbach.

1. Kéralio himself.

dans tous les temps se fera gloire d'avoir mérité vos bontés et de vous donner des preuves de l'inviolable et respectueux dévouement avec lequel je ne cesserai d'être, Mon Respectable ami, Votre très humble et très obeissant Serviteur.

LE CHR. DE KERALIO

[*Note by the duchesse de Deux-Ponts:*] Approuvé, Confirme, rattiffié, par Le Coeur d'une amie qui vous cheris avec tendresse exelant homme parcequil aime le bien et adore La Vertue.

CTESSE DE FORBACH

douairiere du sme [sérénissme] Duc de deuxponts

Notation: Le Chevr. de Keralio Forback le 27 Janvr. 1783.

From Jacob Duché, Jr.[2]   ALS: American Philosophical Society

Sir   Asylum, Lambeth Jan. 28, 1783

I take the earliest Opportunity, since the Signing of the Provisional & Preliminary Articles of a General Peace, of express-

2. The former rector of Christ Church and St. Peter's, Philadelphia (VII, 170–1n), who was elected Chaplain of Congress on July 8, 1776. His early sympathies for the revolutionary cause changed, however. On Oct. 8, 1777, he wrote a long, intemperate letter to George Washington urging Congress to rescind the Declaration of Independence and negotiate a peace. America's prospects were dismal, he argued: the members of Congress (many of whom he named) were incompetent; the army was undisciplined and cowardly; the navy was practically nonexistent; the expectation of French aid, fueled by intelligence from BF, was "a fiction from the first." Washington was stunned by this "ridiculous, illiberal performance" and forwarded the letter to Congress. It was copied by many members and widely circulated, with versions also appearing in the New York and Philadelphia press. Duché was denounced, and sailed for England in December, 1777; when he arrived, he learned that his assets had been confiscated and his wife and children had been evicted from their home. They joined him in 1780. Whitfield J. Bell, Jr., comp., *Patriot-Improvers: Biographical Sketches of Members of the American Philosophical Society* (2 vols. to date, Philadelphia, 1997–), II, 9–19; W. W. Abbot *et al.*, eds., *The Papers of George Washington*, Revolutionary War Series (18 vols. to date, Charlottesville and London, 1985–), XI, 430–7, 528; Smith, *Letters*, VIII, 150–1, 158, 161, 168–9, 182–3, 194, 213; *Rivington's New-York Loyal Gaz.*, Nov. 29, 1777; *Pa. Evening Post*, Dec. 13, 1777.

ing my sincere Congratulations to your Excellency on that happy Event, and at the same Time of communicating to you my most ardent Desire of returning to my Native City; earnestly requesting you to honour me with your Opinion & Instructions with Respect to my Conduct in an Affair so interesting to my own & my dear Family's future Welfare.

I address your Excellency, as the Friend of my Father, and of my Wife's Father;[3] and flatter myself, that my own Name is not so entirely blotted out from your Remembrance, but that these Lines may remind you, that I had once the Happiness of enjoying your good Opinion, as well as that of all my Countrymen.[4]

Your Excellency has known me from my Infancy— You have known my Character to be uniformly & unexceptionably moral; and could not have been a Stranger to the reciprocal Affection, that subsisted for Years betwixt me and my Congregations, and the Unanimity, with which they elected me their Rector, on the Resignation of Dr Peters.[5]

To preserve their Affection & the same Unanimity, was the Object I have ever had in View: And to this alone I can truly refer every Part of what has been called my *Political Conduct*. For as to Politics I profess myself totally ignorant. I never had either Abilities or Influence to display, in that Line, nor had I ever the smallest Inclination to deviate from that happy & retired Path of Life, which I had made Choice of in my earliest Years.[6]

My Letter to Genl. Washington was the only Cause of Offence, which I ever gave to my Countrymen. The Circum-

3. Duché was married to Elizabeth Hopkinson, the sister of Francis Hopkinson and daughter of Thomas Hopkinson (I, 209n; IV, 208). BF had known Thomas Hopkinson and Duché's father, Jacob Duché, Sr. (VII, 170n), since their service together as directors of the Library Company of Philadelphia. The elder Duché and his son had witnessed BF's 1757 power of attorney to his wife Deborah: VII, 169–70.

4. BF expressed that good opinion in a 1765 letter: XII, 125–6. A member of the APS since 1768, Duché was also a trustee along with BF of the Dr. Bray Associates of London.

5. The Rev. Richard Peters (III, 187n) resigned in 1775.

6. For an account of the tensions that Duché experienced as a clergyman of the Church of England accountable to an American vestry see Clarke Garrett, "The Spiritual Odyssey of Jacob Duché," APS *Proc.*, CXIX (1975), 146–9.

stances attending this Letter, both previous & subsequent to the sending it, are not known. I trust, I may one Day have an Opportunity of giving your Excellency a fair & just Account of them.

I never communicated the least Intelligence nor had I ever the least Intercourse with the British Army, whilst I was in America— And since my Arrival in England, I have cautiously avoided all Kind of Political Connexions, or Political Meetings, & confined myself wholly to the Duties of my Profession— Of this my most amiable Friend Lady Juliana Penn, Mr Baker, & Mr R. Penn[7] can give your Excellency the fullest Information.

I am at present very pleasantly situated, as Chaplain & Secretary of the Asylum, a Charitable Female Institution, which you may remember to have seen near Westminster Bridge. My Salary & other Emoluments, with my Pension from Government, which they now talk of exchanging for a Church Living of equal Value, amounts in the whole to more than £300 per Annum.[8]

This, with every Prospect of farther Preferment I would most chearfully resign, could I have any Assurance of being re-instated in the good Opinion of my Countrymen, and particularly of being restored to my Congregations, for whom, as my First Love, I feel a most ardent Affection.

I should be very happy, therefore, if your Excellency would condescend to inform me, as soon as may be convenient to you, whether the Act of Attainder[9] in which my Name among others

7. Juliana Penn, widow of Pa. proprietor Thomas Penn, was currently in Paris, trying to gain BF's assistance in recovering her family's property in America: XXXVIII, 343–4, 464n. Her son-in-law William Baker, a member of Parliament and the executor of part of Thomas Penn's personal estate (Namier and Brooke, *House of Commons*, II, 42–3), and her nephew Richard Penn, Jr., were also with her: Richard Penn, Jr., to BF, Feb. 25, below; Benjamin Vaughan to the Earl of Shelburne, Jan. 28, 1783 (APS); Howard M. Jenkins, "The Family of William Penn," *PMHB*, XXI (1897), 346, 421.

8. Duché was appointed to this position in July, 1782. The pensions of American Loyalists were reevaluated in early 1783, though there is no indication that Duché's was threatened: Garrett, "The Spiritual Odyssey of Jacob Duché," p. 150; George A. Ward, ed., *Journal and Letters of the Late Samuel Curwen* . . . (London, 1842), pp. 367–8.

9. On March 6, 1778, the Pa. Assembly passed an act for "the attainder of divers Traitors," which provided that if certain persons, including Duché,

JANUARY 28, 1783

is mentioned will be repealed in Consequence of the Treaty of Peace; whether there is the least Prospect of my being re-imbursed any Part of the Sum for which my House &c was sold; and whether, if the present Rector[1] & Vestry should agree to reinstate me in the Churches, it could be done under the Sanction of the State of Pennsylvania.

I should be happy to pay my Respects to you in Paris, if I could have your Permission, and you would condescend to give me your candid Advice on these Subjects.

I can very readily obtain Permission of the Guardians of the Asylum to make such an Excursion for a few Weeks; and as I am well known to the Marquis of Carmarthen who will set out in a few Days, as Ambassador from hence to Paris,[2] and his Chaplain & private Secretary is my most intimate Friend & Kinsman, I am sure of a kind Reception from them, in Case your Excellency should think such a Visit proper & necessary.

I have the Honour to be With the Greatest Respect Your Excellency's Most obedient humble Servant   J DUCHÉ

P.S. I take the Liberty of inclosing to your Excellency, Mr White's Form of Acceptance of the Rectorship, which he sent to me, soon after his Election—[3] Mrs Duché begs to be affec-

---

failed to appear for trial by a specified date, the Commonwealth would seize their estates. The Supreme Executive Council was empowered to attaint other individuals, and in eight subsequent proclamations between 1778 and 1781, the Council designated 453 persons as traitors. James T. Mitchell and Henry Flanders, comps., *The Statutes at Large of Pennsylvania from 1682 to 1801* (17 vols., [Harrisburg], 1896–1915), IX, 201–15; Wilbur H. Siebert, *The Loyalists of Pennsylvania* (Columbus, Ohio, 1920), pp. 57–8.

1. William White (XVII, 246n) succeeded Duché as rector. The large house Duché and his family had owned on Third Street was now occupied by Thomas McKean: Bell, *Patriot-Improvers*, II, 11, 17; Smith, *Letters*, XVI, 742n.

2. On Jan. 25 Grantham notified Francis Osborne, Marquess of Carmarthen, later 5th Duke of Leeds (1751–1799), that he would be appointed ambassador to France. Carmarthen received official notification on Feb. 9. He never served, however, because of the change in ministry two weeks later: *ODNB;* Oscar Browning, ed., *The Political Memoranda of Francis Fifth Duke of Leeds . . .* (London, 1884), pp. 77–9.

3. Duché only copied one paragraph of White's acceptance, a declaration that if Duché were permitted by the civil authorities to return, and if the vestry desired to reinstate him, White would resign. This "Extract from the

tionately remembered, and particularly enquires after Mrs Bache
& her Children—

From ———— Pitot Duhellés[4] and Other Consulship
Seekers   ALS: Historical Society of Pennsylvania

Once the preliminary peace treaties were signed, applications for
American consulships came streaming into Passy from all over Europe. Most of the applicants expected their home ports would soon begin a vigorous trade with America and that Congress would appoint
consuls immediately. Franklin, on the other hand, believed that the
United States could not appoint consuls in foreign ports until it had
concluded commercial treaties with the countries in question.[5]

We summarize first the requests for positions in France that are not
mentioned elsewhere in the volume. The undated appeal from Rouen
merchant Philippe Taillet reminds Franklin of the two previous memoirs he had submitted, which the American had received with kindness
(though he had promised nothing). Now that the peace is settled and
Franco-American trade is sure to be established, Taillet renews his request for a consulship and asks Franklin either to make the appointment himself or else to recommend him to Congress.[6]

Minutes of Vestry" was taken from White's letter of April 15, 1779: Benjamin Dorr, *A Historical Account of Christ Church, Philadelphia, from Its
Foundation, A.D. 1695 to A.D. 1841; and of St. Peter's and St. James's, until
the Separation of the Churches* (New York and Philadelphia, 1841), pp. 194–
6.

4. Pitot Duhellés (du Hellés), the American agent at Morlaix: XXIX, 90.

5. He expressed this view in a letter to Jan Ingenhousz, May 16, 1783 (Library of Congress). Unless otherwise noted, all letters cited in this headnote
are in French, are at the APS, and elicited no known response.

6. This letter is at the Hist. Soc. of Pa. One of Taillet's earlier petitions is
above, XXVI, 214. Like that one, this memoir was evidently delivered by
Kéralio, who wrote at the bottom, "Recommandé par le chr. De Keralio."
Taillet's second memoir (now missing) was probably delivered by the abbé
Morellet, to whom he was distantly related through marriage: Taillet was the
cousin of the wife of Morellet's cousin Toussaint-Jacques-Paul Morellet.
Cousin Morellet wrote to the abbé on Jan. 28, 1783, explaining Taillet's re-
lationship to them and begging him to intercede with BF on Taillet's behalf
(APS). We have tentatively dated the present letter, therefore, as [after Jan.
28, 1783].

From Dunkirk comes a February 4 letter in perfect English from Connelly & Sons & Arthur, a merchant firm that has been established in Dunkirk for more than 70 years with a house also in Ostend.[7] They ask Franklin to recommend them to good houses in Boston, Charleston, Philadelphia, and New York and request the American consulship in Dunkirk for either Phillip or Joseph Connelly. They give the names of ten references in France, America, and London, including Jacques Necker, Matthew Ridley, Jonathan Nesbitt, and John Holker.

Le Grand de Castelle also seeks the consulship in Dunkirk. He writes from there on February 24 but asks Franklin to send his reply to the town of Saint-Omer in Artois.[8]

On February 4 Nicolas Reboul, a former ship captain, writes from La Ciotat in Provence to request the post of consul in that city, whose virtues he enumerates.[9] Reboul writes again on May 13, suggesting that Franklin ask Beaumarchais to consult M. Guys, *secrétaire du roi*, about his qualifications.[1]

On February 17 Madame Price, writing from Paris in phonetic French, explains that since she did not have a chance to speak to Franklin in person "yére," she must let her pen make this supplication. She asks that her husband[2] be appointed American agent in Marseille. She writes again on February 22 to remind Franklin that she had spoken and written to him. Now that the "conçule"[3] is there, it might not be a bad idea for Franklin to talk with him about the matter.

Laurent Councler,[4] an associate of the firm Councler, Rigot & Sollicoffre, announces from Marseille on February 19 that he has wanted

7. The firm was one of the most prominent in Dunkirk. It sponsored at least six voyages to North America in the 1780s, and Connelly alone sponsored at least five more: Christian Pfister-Langanay, *Ports, navires et négociants à Dunkerque (1662–1792)* (Dunkirk, 1985), pp. 416, 459.

8. Le Grand de Castelle had written BF once before, from St. Omer: XXXVI, 8–9.

9. Reboul may have been associated with the firm Reboul & Cie. of nearby Marseille: Lüthy, *Banque protéstante*, II, 89n. BF endorsed the letter, "Consuls" (University of Pa. Library).

1. This letter is at the Hist. Soc. of Pa.

2. Possibly the Montreal merchant James Price (XXII, 360–1n), who offered his services to Congress before embarking for France in 1781: Smith, *Letters*, XVII, 343.

3. Thomas Barclay.

4. Councler had been the Dutch consul in Safi, Morocco, in 1762: Lüthy, *Banque protestante*, II, 90n.

the American consulship ardently for two years but was told by M. Grand of Paris that he would have to wait until the peace. Now he will speak forthrightly of his hopes. He assumes that prospective American consuls must be Protestant, English-speaking, and in possession of a good reputation and good credit. He approaches Franklin under the auspices of M. van de Perre. Two months ago he discussed his situation with M. de Jaucourt, but he does not know whether Jaucourt has mentioned him to Franklin. He also wants to discuss his plans with Matthew Ridley, with whom his firm has correspondence.

Councler's two recommenders had already written. The letter from Paul Ewaldus van de Perre,[5] dated February 18 from Marseille, praises "Conclair" as a first-rate Protestant English-speaking merchant known for his zeal, probity, exactitude, and good sense. No one could fill the post with greater honor and success. The marquis de Jaucourt,[6] writing on February 15, addressed his appeal to the comte de Maillebois, asking him to intercede with Franklin: Councler's firm is very well known and has ties with several American firms; Matthew Ridley can supply more information. Maillebois forwards this letter to Franklin with one of his own on February 20, hoping that Franklin will dine with him some evening in the coming week (but not Tuesday).

On February 20 Pomaret[7] writes from Ganges, where he has been pastor of the Reformed Church for 40 years, asking Franklin to forward a letter to Miss Laurens and recommending Marc-Antoine Bazile of Montpellier for the consulship in Sète. Bazile is an able merchant who trades on a large scale.

Another candidate for the consulship in Sète is Grangent,[8] nominated by M. Marignié, his nephew, in an undated letter to Philip Keay which asks Keay to intercede with Franklin.

5. Van de Perre (1745–1786) was a partner in the Zeeland firm Van de Perre & Meÿners (XXXII, 221) and an administrator of the Dutch East India Company: *NNBW*, v, 490–1.

6. Possibly Louis-Pierre-Antoine, usually called the comte de Jaucourt (1726–1813), a *maréchal de camp* and first gentleman-in-waiting to the prince de Condé, but more likely his son Arnail-François, *dit* marquis de Jaucourt (1757–1852), an officer in the French army who became a statesman after the Restoration: *Dictionnaire de la noblesse*, XI, 61; *DBF*.

7. Jean Gal, *dit* Pomaret or Jonvals (1720–1790), who corresponded with Voltaire and Rousseau and wrote on religious subjects: *DBF;* Emile du Cailar and Daniel Benoit, *Gal-Pomaret, Pasteur de Ganges: son temps, son ministère, ses écrits* (Paris, 1899), pp. 5–7.

8. A merchant of that city and the consul for Prussia and Monaco: *Almanach royal* for 1783, pp. 267, 269.

On March 9 Jean-Baptiste Le Roy forwards an undated memoir from Bérian frères of Bayonne, who passionately desire to be the American consuls in that city.[9] Franklin must be overwhelmed by such solicitations, but Le Roy asks him to give this one special consideration, as the firm also is recommended by the comtes d'Ornano and d'Angiviller.[1] He regrets not having the opportunity to hand Franklin the memoir in person but hopes to see him before the week is out. In their memoir soliciting the consulship, Bérian frères mention that they have assisted Mr. Emery, an American merchant who sought to establish himself at Bilbao.[2]

Two people hope to become the American agent in Lyon. Claude Charton, a merchant there, requests the position in an undated memoir, explaining that he is on the verge of retiring and will be able to devote his time solely to the affairs of the United States. He encloses testimonials dated April 3 from the Lyon commercial syndicate and other notables.[3]

Jacques de Flesselles, intendant of Lyon,[4] writes from Paris on May 15 to recommend M. Dainval for the post, adding that the marquis de Vergennes[5] will vouch for Dainval as well. Flesselles even offers to send Franklin a sample commission which Congress could review. Franklin evidently answered the same day, offering to forward Flesselles' draft commission to America. That letter is unlocated, but the intendant thanks Franklin for it and sends him the draft commission on June 3.[6]

The first of the appeals from Italy comes from Civitavecchia on February 3. M. Vidaú, French consul in that city (known as the port of

9. Le Roy's letter and the enclosure are at the Hist. Soc. of Pa.

1. Jean-Baptiste, comte d'Ornano (1742–1794), was the governor of Bayonne: Larousse. Angiviller was the director of the royal buildings and gardens: XXXV, 529n.

2. John Emery: XXV, 499n. Le Roy reminded BF of this application in his letter of March 23, below.

3. Charton's petition and the testimonials are at the Hist. Soc. of Pa. He is listed in the *Almanach des marchands*, p. 303.

4. Flesselles (1721–1789) had been intendant since 1767: *DBF*.

5. Jean Gravier, marquis de Vergennes: XXIV, 551n; XXXVI, 589n.

6. The four-page document, entitled "Projet d'une Commission d'Agent et de Banquier a Lyon des Etats unis de L'Amerique," includes the draft commission for Michel-Catherine Dainval, an enumeration of the different products of Lyon and the surrounding area, and the claim that the applicant was recommended by the comte de Vergennes. BF must not have forwarded the draft commission, as it remains among his papers.

Rome) and the father of many children, is enchanted to congratulate Franklin on the peace, and offers the services of himself and his family. In particular, his son Paul would like to be appointed either American agent or consul.[7] Vidaú assures Franklin that his son will fulfill his duties on behalf of the "nation Anglameriquaine" with the same zeal and exactitude with which he himself has protected the commerce and laws of France. Franklin soon learns that the Vidaús had begun this campaign the previous fall. On September 9, 1782, believing peace to be imminent, Paul Vidaú wrote at his father's urging to Philippe-Athanase Täscher in Paris,[8] whom they thought was a close friend of Franklin's, begging him to intercede with the American minister to obtain this consulship. Täscher forwards this letter to Franklin on March 3, 1783, along with a letter of his own in support of Vidaú's application. He adds that he forgot to mention this when he saw Franklin at Passy two days earlier. On May 12 the elder Vidaú writes again, fearing that his first letter has been lost. His superior, the marquis de Castries, has undoubtedly informed Franklin of his good qualities and conduct as French consul. If his son Paul is fortunate enough to obtain the consulship, he pledges to supervise him.[9]

Several applicants seek the consulship in Naples. Thomas Plumer Byde, though British and a former member of Parliament, evidently thinks himself qualified for the position because he voted to repeal the Stamp Act and showed himself on numerous other occasions to be a friend of America.[1] He writes on February 8 from Naples, where he now resides, sure that Franklin must have forgotten him. He is a friend of Wharton's, who will certainly vouch for him. He encloses a letter to Wharton, which he asks Franklin to forward.

Antoine Liquier applies to the American commissioners from Naples on April 5. He is sure that the king of the Two Sicilies will soon sign a commercial treaty with the United States, which will necessitate

7. Both Vidaús are listed in the *Almanach royal* for 1783, p. 262 (the younger as consul *en survivance*). This letter is at the Hist. Soc. of Pa.

8. Täscher (XXIX, 48) was the honorary *président au parlement* at Metz and a former intendant at Martinique (1771–77): *Jefferson Papers,* VII, 387; Michel Antoine, *Le Gouvernement et l'administration sous Louis XV: Dictionnaire biographique* (Paris, 1978).

9. This letter is at the University of Pa. Library.

1. Byde (*c.* 1720–1789) was an M.P. for Hertfordshire from 1761 to 1768; his contemporaries found his political opinions unpredictable and difficult to classify. After losing two subsequent elections, he became a banker, went bankrupt in May, 1779, and died in poverty in Naples: Namier and Brooke, *House of Commons,* II, 166–7.

the appointment of an American consul in his city. Liquier is familiar with the duties of a consul: he works for his father, the Dutch consul in Naples and the head of a firm of nearly 50 years' standing.[2] He is Protestant, too, which only can work in his favor. He ends with a series of recommendations for products that could be traded between the two countries.

On April 21 Louis-Berton Hortal, writing from Valence in Dauphiné,[3] recommends his cousin Charles Forquet, a French merchant in Naples, for the latter city's consular post. Forquet's partner M. André, the Swedish agent in Naples, thinks that Forquet might be charged with the same responsibilities for the United States. Forquet has asked Hortal to solicit recommendations for him; accordingly he has applied to Vergennes and Necker but has been told they do not meddle in other states' affairs. On reflection, Hortal realizes that he does not need letters of recommendation: all honest souls have easy access to Franklin. Forquet is a man of spirit, merit, and solid fortune.

From Leghorn comes an application from the merchant Joseph du Pranoul (Preissoul?) père, who writes on February 14 under the auspices of Chalut de Vérin. His firm has enjoyed a certain reputation in Leghorn for a century and a half.[4] Feeling certain that the grand duke (Leopold, Grand Duke of Tuscany) is well disposed toward the Americans and will allow their ships entry into the port, he begs Franklin to allow his son and his firm to extend their services to Congress. Chalut de Vérin forwards this letter to Franklin on February 28 with a note recalling that he already spoke to Franklin and Adams about his friends in Leghorn. Adams, in fact, should have received a memorandum on the subject a few days ago.

2. Antoine Liquier (1762–1849) was a member of a prominent commercial family with bases in both Marseille and Naples. His father, Marc-Antoine Liquier, served as Dutch consul general in the latter city from 1769 to 1793: Gilles Bancarel, "Autour du rouergat Liquier, lauréat de l'Académie de Marseille en 1777," *Studi Settecenteschi*, XXI (2001), 141–7, 155–8. This letter is among JA's papers at the Mass. Hist. Soc.

3. Where Hortal (1725–1791) was a judge and assessor of the *commission de conseil:* Justin Brun-Durand, *Dictionnaire biographique et biblio-iconographique de la Drôme* (2 vols., Grenoble, 1900–01). This letter is at the Hist. Soc. of Pa.

4. The French had been granted commercial privileges at Leghorn in 1593. It became a free port in 1676: Jean-Pierre Filippini, "La Nation française de Livourne (fin XVIIe–fin XVIIIe siècle)," in *Dossiers sur le commerce français en Méditerranée orientale au XVIIIe siècle*, ed. Jean-Pierre Filippini et al. (Paris, 1976), pp. 235–6, 239–40, 244–8. This letter is at the Hist. Soc. of Pa.

Christian Andrew Tilebein, writing in English from Barcelona, reminds Franklin on February 26 that he applied for the American consulship in that city in 1778.[5] He renews that solicitation now, adding that he has also written to John Jay. The letter is addressed to "Dr Samuel Franklin."

Several applications arrive from Portugal. Dominick Browne, acting French consul in Oporto during the absence of his uncle "Emel. [Emanuel] De Clamouse,"[6] writes in English on February 8 to request the American consulship there. Born in Portugal to Irish parents, he was educated in England and speaks several languages. In keeping with Sartine's March 30, 1778, instructions, Browne has assisted American subjects as zealously as French ones, providing them with passports to Spain and cash when needed. His letter will be forwarded to Franklin by M. O'Dunn, French ambassador at the court of Lisbon.[7]

John Keating writes in perfect English from Faro on February 25.[8] He works for the French consul in Lisbon and aspires to serve the United States as well. He asks Franklin to recommend him for the deputy consulship in the province of Algarve.

The baron de Jumilhac[9] writes from Lisbon on March 1 to recommend Wilhiam Wiliamson for the vice-consulship in Setuval (Setúbal) and Edward Clarke for the vice-consulship in Belém. He has known both men for nearly three years and can vouch for their good conduct and intelligence. Franklin endorsed the letter, "Recommended by Made Bertin."[1]

Dominique-François Belletti, a partner in the firm Belletti, Zaccar & Cie. and the Tuscan consul in Trieste, launches an aggressive campaign on February 21 for the American consulship in that city and throughout Austria. Offering his services to the United States free of charge, he encloses copies of two letters of recommendation.[2] In the

5. See XXVI, 210. The present letter is at the Hist. Soc. of Pa.

6. The honorary French consul in Oporto, and probably a relative of Bernard Clamoux (d. 1760), who had held that position earlier in the century: *Almanach royal* for 1783, p. 261; *DBF*, under François de Clamouse.

7. Jacques-Bernard O'Dunne: XXXI, 316n; *Repertorium der diplomatischen Vertreter*, III, 130. Browne's letter is at the Hist. Soc. of Pa.

8. Hist. Soc. of Pa.

9. Henry-François-Joseph, baron de Chapelle de Jumilhac (1752–1820), then serving as French envoy to Lisbon: *DBF*.

1. See BF to Mme Bertin, [after March 1]. The present letter is at the Hist. Soc. of Pa.

2. The one that survives is from Karl Graf von Zinzendorf, writing in

next several weeks he writes four more times. On April 7 he tells Franklin that his sovereign is eager to establish an active commerce between Austria and the United States and has dispatched Chancellor de Rossier to Trieste to discuss the project; furthermore, the comte de Brigido[3] has been instructed to present the plan to the city's leading merchants. What are Franklin's sentiments on the proposal? On April 11 Belletti adds that he intends to sail for Philadelphia with a vessel laden with Austrian and Levantine products and manufactures; because there is no commercial treaty yet, he asks Franklin to send a ship's passport and a letter permitting him to purchase merchandise in Philadelphia.[4] Franklin should address his reply to Messrs. Fries et Comp., bankers, in Vienna, whither Belletti will soon be traveling. On April 14 he reminds Franklin that he still needs a letter for Philadelphia. On April 25, confounded by Franklin's silence, he writes to announce his departure for Vienna the next day; he can only hope that he will receive news of his consular appointment while there. He encloses a copy of the Austrian chancellery's reply to the memoir by the comte d'Oeinhaussen[5] on Belletti's election as Tuscan consul.

A 45-year-old native of Bordeaux, Guillaume Sazÿ, writes in stilted English from Fiume on February 11. Able to speak Dutch, German, Italian, Spanish, and Latin as well as French and English, he has worked in Trieste and Fiume for seven years under Jean Jaques Kick[6] and now seeks an American consulship in any port on the Adriatic or Mediterranean or elsewhere.

From St. Petersburg comes a March 31 letter from a man by the

---

Italian from Trieste on Jan. 19, 1780. Zinzendorf was governor of Trieste from 1776 to 1782 and subsequently headed the Austrian court's financial office (XXIX, 54n; *ADB*).

3. Pompeo, conte de Brigido (1729–1811), Zinzendorf's successor as governor of Trieste: Pietro Stancovich, *Biografia degli uomini distinti dell'Istria* (2nd ed., Capodistria, 1888), pp. 448–9.

4. Belletti may have been involved in outfitting the *Capricieuse*, which sailed from Trieste in the summer of 1783, reaching Philadelphia by early December. Soon after the ship's return to Trieste, Belletti formed an Austro-American trading company with three other men, including two who had financed the *Capricieuse*'s first expedition: *Pa. Gaz.*, Dec. 10, 1783; Hanns Schlitter, ed., *Die Berichte des ersten Agenten Österreichs in den Vereinigten Staaten von Amerika Baron de Beelen-Bertholff . . .* (Vienna, 1891), p. 589.

5. Georg Ludwig Graf Oeynhausen (1734–1811), a German military man: *ADB*.

6. Jean-Jacob Kick, the Austro-Hungarian consul in Marseille: *Almanach royal* for 1783, p. 265.

name of Horn, an instructor of the cadet corps who, in his youth, was secretary to M. Soermann, the Dutch resident at Danzig.[7] He has been a courtier in Dresden and Warsaw, has traveled widely, and speaks French, Italian, Latin, German, Polish, and mediocre Russian. Now, at the age of 40, he requests an appointment as consul in St. Petersburg, Hamburg, or Lübeck.

Jean Bernard Linckh, writing from Hirschberg, Silesia, on February 12, reminds Franklin that he called on him in the autumn of 1780 and gave him information about his cloth factory. He now wants a recommendation to American merchants interested in the cloth trade, and offers to serve as consul. He gives several references, of whom the most distinguished is M. de Thulemeyer at the Hague.[8]

Finally, we offer letters sent from the British Isles, all written in English. David Williams,[9] acknowledging that he and Franklin have not corresponded since the beginning of the war, writes on February 14 to recommend a gentleman named Mace[1] for a position as consul, ambassador, or secretary to the ambassador in Constantinople. Mace, who was secretary to the late British ambassador in that city, Mr. Murray,[2] is Cambridge-educated, trained for the clergy (a profession he dislikes), knowledgeable about business, and particularly adept at using cipher, and he speaks French and Italian fluently. A speedy reply is requested.

On February 15 Arthur Bryan and William Bryan, Jr., write from Dublin and acknowledge Franklin's kind notice of their previous applications.[3] They are now preparing several ships to sail to America, one of which, the *Adjuter* bound for Baltimore, will soon be ready. Unsure of whether it will be admitted into an American port, they request a passport; the ship will carry a number of "people of property"

7. Hendrik Soermans was the Dutch commissioner in Danzig from 1754 until his death in 1775: *Repertorium der diplomatischen Vertreter*, III, 261.

8. Friedrich Wilhelm von Thulemeier was the Prussian envoy to the Netherlands from 1763 to 1788 and the son of Prussian minister Wilhelm Heinrich von Thulemeier: *Repertorium der diplomatischen Vertreter*, III, 333; *ADB.*

9. A friend from BF's second mission to London: XXI, 119.

1. Charles Mace, who was the rector of Halsham, Yorkshire, from 1770 until his death in 1825 and served as British consul in Algiers: John and J. A. Venn, comps., *Alumni Cantabrigienses* . . . (2 parts in 10 vols., Cambridge, Eng., 1922–54), part II, IV, 262; *Gent. Mag.*, XCV (1825), part I, 474.

2. John Murray, ambassador to the Ottoman Empire from 1766 to 1775: *Repertorium der diplomatischen Vertreter*, III, 179.

3. See XXVI, 528.

who intend to settle in the United States. They also offer themselves for the American consulship in Dublin. In a postscript they add that William soon will pay his respects to Franklin in person.

Also from Ireland comes a series of long and, to some degree, repetitive letters from an Englishman who is reluctant to divulge his name but wants to be consul in either Dublin or Waterford. He signs his letters "J. F.," as near as we can tell; the later ones instruct Franklin to direct replies to "Mr. Freeman" under cover to "G: M: Coote Esqr. M: P: Dublin."[4] The first letter, written on March 31 from Dublin, explains that he was a successful merchant in London before the war and traded indirectly with America through George Hayley's firm and Lane, Son & Fraser.[5] He claims to have written pro-American letters and essays in the press and has associations with prominent Whigs: Beckford, the Duke of Richmond, and the Marquess of Rockingham.[6] He has been in Ireland for two years and is involved with a mining operation located on the lands of an unnamed Irish peer. On April 3, writing from Wicklow, he adds more personal details: he is the son of an Oxford-educated Warwickshire clergyman and is now widowed; even his friends George Hayley and the banker James Browne[7] are dead. He has debts with American merchants, having supported distressed colleagues whose remittances failed after the outbreak of the war; perhaps a powerful American could help him reclaim the money. Friends in Ireland offered him a share in their mining venture in an area discussed by the Rev. Dr. Henry in the *Philosophical Transactions*.[8] One of the investors from Dublin has erected mills for rolling

---

4. The only Irish M.P. of that name in 1783 was Charles Henry Coote (1754–1823) of Dublin: Edith M. Johnston-Liik, ed., *History of the Irish Parliament, 1692–1800* . . . (6 vols., Belfast, 2002), III, 496–8.

5. Both of these London firms would have been known to BF through their involvement with American trade. Hayley was identified with the Whig party; he had married John Wilkes's sister: XX, 19–20n. For Lane, Son & Fraser see XVI, 162.

6. Merchant William Beckford served in Commons and for two terms as lord mayor of London: XV, 287n; Namier and Brooke, *House of Commons*, II, 75–8. Richmond and Rockingham were leading Whig politicians.

7. Probably the London banker James Brown: XXXVII, 175.

8. William Henry, "A Letter from Rev. William Henry, D.D. to the Right Honourable the Lord Cadogan, F.R.S. concerning the Copper-Springs in the County of Wicklow in Ireland," *Phil. Trans.*, XLVII (1751–52), 500–3; "A second Letter of the Rev. William Henry, D.D. to the right honorable the Lord Cadogan . . . ," *Phil. Trans.*, XLVIII (1753–54), 94–6. The mines of Ballymurtagh and Cronebane were operated in the 1780s by John Howard Kyan and his partners: Des Cowman, "The Mining Community at Avoca, 1780–

copper and lead. "J. F." already has sent samples to Bordeaux and is prepared to send some to Philadelphia and New York. He goes on to describe other Irish products suitable for the American trade: fish, woolen goods, and linen second to none. His final letter, written on May 14 from Dublin,[9] indicates that he sent a now-missing letter from Rathdrum on April 11. Since his return from the mines he has mentioned his applications to Franklin only to Major Brooke,[1] the owner of a large and important cotton factory which already has shipped goods to America; Brooke has promised him assistance. Furthermore, having read in the newspapers about America's financial straits, he proposes a plan for introducing into circulation "a very large Sum in Specie," about which he wishes to talk with Franklin in person in either Paris or London. In a postscript he adds that he visited the Rev. and Mrs. Bladeen of Dorsett Street, the latter of whom claims to know Franklin quite well; they will be glad to recommend him. Another postscript, now separated from its letter but possibly belonging to the missing one of April 11, requests a personal interview and mentions the writer's 20-year-old son, a merchant in England, who could assist his father.

Monsieur   Morlaix le 28e. Jer. 1783.

Le Préliminaires de Paix étant Signés, l'indépendance de l'Amerique est assurée á Jamais. Je ne puis m'empecher de vous en témoigner ma Joye, et de Vous felicitter de l'heureux Succés d'une affaire dont la réussitte doit Vous immortaliser, puisqu'on la doit a vos grandes Lumieres et a votre zéle infatigable.

Sans doutte que vous ne tarderez pas (á l'exemple des autres puissances Commercantes) á établir des Consuls et Vice-consuls dans le principaux ports de Mer. Le Notre merittera quelque attention Rapport a la Manufacture du tabac et a notre fabrique de toille.

Comme en qualitté de Correspondant des Agents Génereaux J'ay Servi les Americains toutte la Guerre, Je Supplie Votre Ex-

---

1880," in *Wicklow: History and Society,* ed. Ken Harrigan and William Nolan (Dublin, 1994), pp. 762–4.

9. Hist. Soc. of Pa.

1. Probably Capt. Robert Brooke, the owner of Temple Mills in Prosperous, west of Dublin: xxxviii, 108n; Robert Glen, "Industrial Wayfarers: Benjamin Franklin and a Case of Machine Smuggling in the 1780s," *Business Hist.,* xxiii (1981), 316–18.

cellance de Vouloir bien Se Souvenir de moy Si elle établit un quelqu'un à Morlaix Sous quélque dénomination que ce Soit. Je puis me flatter d'être en etat de Répondre a vos vuës et J'y apporteray toûjour le plus grand zele.

Je Suis avec un proffond Respect de Votre Excellence Le trés humble et trés Obeissant Serviteur   PITOT DUHELLÉS

S. Exe. Mr. le Docteur franklin

From the Comte de Grasse   LS: American Philosophical Society

Paris Rüe du faubg St. honnoré No. 4 Le 28. Janvier 1783.
Permettez, Monsieur, que J'ay l'honneur De faire a Votre Exececellence mon sincere Compliment Sur la Signature des preliminaires De la Paix & Sur l'Independance Reconnue & Definitive Des Etats unis De l'amerique. J'ose me flatter que Votre Exececellence Sera plus Convaincüe De la sastifaction que J'ay Ressentie De Ce grand Evenemement que Je ne puis La luy Exprimer Par la Part Essentielle que J'ay le Bonheur D'avoir a L'action qui l'avait Decidé Depuis la fin De 1781.
Je Desirois Temoigner le meme Sentiment a Son Excelence M. le president Du Congrés, si vous voulez Bien avoir la Bonté de vous charger De ma lettre.[2] J'ose Esperer que Ce Second hommage De mon Respect Pour votre Republique ne luy Sera pas moins agreable que Celuy que Je luy a Rendu a york-town. Je voudrois qu'Il me fut Permis D'y joindre un De mes memoires Sur Le Combat naval Du 12 avril,[3] Pour luy Prouver, que quoiqu'Il n'ait En Rien Retardé la Paix, & la Reconnoissance De la Souveraineté De la Republique americaine, Elle ne Scauroit Sans Injustice m'attribuer la Cause De Cet Echec, tout Infructueux qu'Il a Eté Pour Ses Enemis & m'assurer par là la plenitude De Son Estime. Il Doit m'Etre Permis D'avoir cette ambition.

2. The enclosures are no longer with this covering letter.
3. De Grasse was defeated at the Battle of the Saintes on April 12, 1782. He wrote and printed privately a 28-page memoir justifying his conduct, *Mémoire du comte de Grasse, sur le combat naval du 12 avril 1782 . . . .:* Rice and Brown, eds., *Rochambeau's Army,* I, 311.

J'ay l'honneur D'Etre avec Respect De votre Excelence Le tres humble & Tres obeissant serviteur LE COMTE DE GRASSE

Notation: Le Comte de Grasse Paris 28 Janvr. 1783.

From Jan Ingenhousz   ALS: American Philosophical Society

Dear Friend   Vienna 28 Jan. 1783.

As I expected every day to hear that peace was actualy made, I postponed to write to you, fearing to interrupt your attention now engaged in more whighty affaires than the Content of my lettres. I hope you have put the wire inclosed in my last to the test in a phial filled with fine dephlogisticated air. If you have, I am Sure you will have been pleased with the experiment.[4] I burn'd some days ago a watch-spring in a large jarr filled with dephlogisticated air. The appearance was magnificent and inspired some terror in som of the bystanders, tho there is not the least danger in it, if you leave open the orifice of the jarr, or, which is still better, if the jarr has the bottom taken away: a lock for an air pump having an open neck instead of a nob is the best, for a common jarr must be unavoidably broken by the melted metal falling down upon the bottom, at which it Stiks, and which therefore must breake, tho there was water kept in it at the hight of two inches. I dare say you will be equaly delighted to see a small piece of Phosphorus burn in a jarr filled with very fine dephlogisticated air in the way described in my book.[5] You will dowbt, whether even the sun it self has more splendour than the Smoak issuing from it. The piece must be only of this sice[6] for [*if*] it is a thick piece, the conflagration is too quick, and the flame too large, and the jarr will be broken. A cylindrical piece of phosphorus as thick as a common quill must be divided in four at

4. See XXXVIII, 379–80.

5. *Vermischte Schriften physisch-medizinischen Inhalts* ... , the German translation of Ingenhousz' text (written originally in French) which the author sent to BF the previous spring. BF replied that he could not read German, and was waiting for the French version: XXXV, 549; XXXVII, 211.

6. Here Ingenhousz drew a small, vertical rectangle.

least. There is in my german book, I sent you, a figure of a small iron or brass leadel fixed to a long wire for this purpose. The orifice of the jarr for this experiment must be open or loosely stopt during the experiment.

I am very sorry that Dr. le *Begue* keeps my M.S. without putting them to the press.[7] I propos'd him to get the assistance of some other gentleman, as for inst Mr. Le Roy,[8] if he should be sick, out of town or taken up by his own occupations. But he promish'd me to doe himself what he could for me, and yet I recieve not a single sheet of the impression, which vexes me a great deal. If you could rouse Mr. le Begue out of his inaction on this head you would oblige me. You will highly oblige me to Grant me leave to dedicate this work to you, that it may be a publick and lasting testimony of a long an uninterrupted friendship between us, and so honorable for me. Thus both my books will be stamped with two very respectfull names, which my [may] conduct mine with more security to posterior ages, and prevent it being lost within the crowd of contemporary and futur philosophers.

Ten or twelf sheets are allready printed of a dutch translation of this very book printed on fine paper and with a very fine tipe. But I Stopt the progress of this edition till the original Frensh one is come out.[9] It is now a year since the German translation is printed. If my old Gracious Imper. Mistress was still alive this business should induce me to ask her leave to goe to Paris on purpose to forward the edition as I did with my book on vegetables;[1] but I am afrayed of meting now with a narrow minded answer, and can not bear those disdainfull frowns, of which the great soul of M. T. was incapable of. If Mr. Wharton had acted as I had a right to exspect,[2] my fortune would have inspired me with

7. Lebègue de Presle had agreed to handle the publication of Ingenhousz' French text: XXXVI, 221.

8. As suggested by BF: XXXV, 548.

9. Both the French edition and the Dutch translation appeared in 1785: XXXV, 548n; J. van Breda, trans., *Verzameling van verhandelingen, over verschillende natuurkundige onderwerpen* (2 vols., The Hague, 1785).

1. XXXI, 121–3, 139–40; XXXII, 406n.

2. Samuel Wharton was supposed to remit Ingenhousz the profits from several commercial ventures: XXXIV, 124n; XXXVII, 212, 468n.

my former republican principels; and made me act with a manly resolution.

The Composition of the Self-lighting candels was sent from the inventor mr. Paybla[3] of Turin half a year ago to the Emperour, and delivred to me. I made them immediately and gave more than ten dozain to the Emperour.

I recieved yesterday a very civil lettre from the great Duc of Russia written by his own hand, thanking me for the Copy of the German translation of the book now to be printed at Paris, and requesting me a copy of the french edition allso. This very distinguish'd honour makes me wish so much the more, that mr Le Begue would forward the book. He will certainly find one or other bookseller how [who] will undertake it under the Condition of giving me 160 copies, which I want for distributing among my numerous friends I have scattered through Europe. They were very ready to undertake it in Holland upon this Condition.

I have heard of a machine for raising water by means of a rope, but have as yet no idea of it. I should be obliged to you if you could, as you are so good as to propose me, send me a description of it.[4]

This moment I am interrupted by a visite of one mr. *Waltravers* F.R.S. a swish [Swiss] gentleman, who has been here several month for a law suit.[5] He has often strongly pressed me to give you his best respects, which I forgot to doe. Now he begs from me to put you in mind of what he wrote to you about his circumstances, which are indeed very distressing. He wants even common necessaries, unable to pay a very homely lodging, and to redeem his cloath watch, ring &c, which are seized for payement, his law suit having turn'd out conntrary to his wishes. He looks out for a shelter on what ever condition it may be. I have a long while employed my good offices to get him in some or other family of rang, where he Could be employed in writing

---

3. Louis Peyla: XXXVIII, 175.

4. BF referred to Vera's "corde sans fin" in a Nov. 23, 1782, letter to François Steinsky, and probably mentioned it to Ingenhousz in the letter (now missing) written on Nov. 12: XXXVIII, 338, 378.

5. Valltravers wrote to BF about this lawsuit on Oct. 2, 1782: XXXVIII, 183–5.

Copying, being a compagnon or a kind of tutor to children &c: but his age seems to obstruct my endeavours, and his wants are to great for my own pecuniary habilities, as to afford him a material relief. He beggs with the strongest expressions that you should look over his lettres and consider whether you could help him in Som or other way in America. Common charity does not admit of refusing this service to a man in such distress. As I never before this time knew him, you will be a better judge than I, whether his dismal condition, in an advanced age, has been the effect of former irregularities and imprudencies, or of unavoidable misfortunes.

I told you in my last, that in your case I should reather exspect a good effect from moderate exercise of body and keeping up the Cutaneous perspiration by softening the skin by a tepid bath used now and than, than by such medecines from whose manifest power some effect could seem to be exspected in remooving or prevening the fits of gravel and gout. For all the powerfull remedies, which have been employed doe hurt the stomach too often; and the want of propre digestion may hurt you more materialy than a fit of those diseases, by which fits a long intervall is commonly obtained. A rigourous diet would probably have the same effect as heroic medicines, it would weaken the constitution at your age. A milk diet and abstaining from animal food, would suit a young man and keep him cool. It would tend only to keep you low, and very probably have very little material effect, if at all, on remooving the disease. I publish'd in Latin Some years ago a dissertation on curing the gout, gravel &c. which I translated from Dr. Hulme, in which is recommended Water or any other liquor impregnated with fixed air either by means of mr. Parker's Machine or by putting togeather two equal quantities of water, in one of which is melted som salt of tartar in the other are put as many drops of spirit of vitriol as by a previous experiment is found necessary to saturate the quantity of salt of tarter adhibited. The two liquors being put togeather quietely, the fixed air extricated by the meeting of the *acid* and *alkaly* remains thus almost all mixed with the liquor, which is than immediately fit for use. It has done indeed much good in some and can doe no harm. Mr. Nairn, to home I adresed it, found no benefit from it. I believe I gave you a copy of it. The titel is *Nova*

91

tuta facilisque methodus curandi calculum, podagram destruendi vermes &c. . . . it is a pamphlet in small octavo.[6] Upon the whole I shoud advise you not to thrust too much to the common officiousness of Physicians in your Condition, and believe, that more mischieve is to be apprehended by doying to much than by doying too little. This is still the advise, which I give you as a friend, who has so much sincere attachement for your person, as to expose him self to being looked by you as not knowing enough of the matter by not recommending you boasted medecines. May you be preserved, by kind Nature, still a great many years for the benefit of your Country, philosophy and mankind!

I have allready a good deal of sollicitations of men of the first rang to be introduced to you by me, when you will fulfill my ardent wishes to see you here.

But what bad *omen* gives us that procrastination of making a peace. With what pride and insolence England, after openly declaring the unjustice of the attack on my Country, can refuse to restore the town of *Trinconomale* on Seilon? This is an open declaration of their intention of turning by the first oportunity the Duch out of the whole Island. I hope they will not submit to Such an indignity.[7] A year more of war can't doe but good tho our republic. It will oblige them to restore their navy so shamefully negleted and to overturn the English party. The English here give now openly fore, that the Declaring America independent is a very sound political stroke to crush Frensh; for, say they, the Americans having obtained what they wanted will renew their commerce with old England, and England no more at any expense in America, will now fall upon france with all that tremendous power they have now on foot. Thus they look now on the Americans as on a nation as ungenerous to their protectors as the English have been to the Americans how allways had assisted them in their quarels. I wonnder all Europe is not revolted at the genious of such a haughty people.

6. This translation of Nathaniel Hulme's work was published in Leyden in 1778. BF's copy has not been located.

7. In the end, Vergennes succeeded in negotiating the return of Trincomalee to the Dutch: Nicholas Tarling, *Anglo-Dutch Rivalry in the Malay World, 1780–1824* (St. Lucia, Australia, 1962), pp. 6–11.

If you have recieved some more German American news papers. I have not yet recieved the American Almanack.[8] Has count Mercy forgot it?

If you can give me any thing news, pray doe not forget your old friend.

I hope you will find time to compleat your remarks on the *furnus acapnus* or fire place without smoak.[9] I prepare a very powerfull Electrical machine with two plats of 2 feet diameter, and will make some decisive Experiments. I have now a good deal of notes on various subjects taken from your correspondence which the public may be instructed, but when I will have put them in order I will send you the m.s.

I am with as much due respect as sincere friendship your affectionate   J. INGEN HOUSZ

Pray either burn this lettre or strik out he [the] lines opposit the Barr.[1]

Endorsed: Dr. Ingenhouse Vienna 28th Jany. 1783

From John Sargent

ALS: American Philosophical Society

Dear Sir   London 28 Jany. 1783—

Mr. Charettier, the Bearer hereof, who had the Honour of paying His respects to You two Years agoe being about to set for Paris again, in a few Hours, to give an account of a Trust He hath executed for that Court, as Commissary for Their Prisoners of War, with great Credit, I beg Leave to recommend Him to Your Favour, & Protection, as a very honest deserving Man—[2]

The Time is short, and will not allow me to say more than to congratulate You once more on the Peace, & the great Things Providence hath made You a principal Instrument of effect-

8. Forwarded by BF six months earlier: xxxv, 547.

9. See xxxviii, 177.

1. Ingenhousz drew a vertical line in the left margin of the third paragraph, next to the sentence beginning "If my old Gracious Imper. Mistress . . ."

2. John Charretié had asked BF to help him obtain the position he evidently now held: xxxiv, 101n, 152.

ing,—which I do most sincerely,—and to convey to You the most affectionate Regards of my Wife,—old Mrs. Chambers, who still hopes to see You again,—My Sons,—& all our Family—

I say nothing of our Politicks, knowing You are like to be acquainted with Them thro' a surer Channell; by which You will learn, We are the same unhappy ill Governed, distracted Nation—

May all Happiness attend You, and a better Disposition take place with Us!

Favour me with a Line, when You have a few Minutes to throw away, & be assured I am with the sincerest Esteem, & affection Dear Sir Your devoted Friend & Servant J SARGENT.

Dr. Franklin Paris—

From Jonathan Williams, Jr.

ALS: American Philosophical Society; copy:[3] Yale University Library

Dear & hond Sir.   Nantes Jan. 28. 1783.

As It is proper for every prudent Man to know on what Ground he proceeds before he engages too far, and as now we have a general Peace there can no longer be a Reason for keeping the Terms of it Secret, I beg you will kindly resolve the following Questions.

1 Does the Prohibition of English Goods in America cease, on Britains ceasing to be an Enemy?

If you cannot inform this positively, does it not appear probable it will be so, as that prohibition was the declared Consequence of the War?

2 May Tobacco already imported into France go to England, as it does to other Powers without any infringment of the Treaty, in short, will Tobacco be received there?

I have 800 hhds Tobacco on Sale, & I have some Vessells which propose to go to Liverpool & take Crockery Ware from thence

---

3. The copy, in JW's letterbook, is misdated Jan. 23.

to America, you therefore see the importance of these Questions & I trust you will answer me decisively excusing the Freedom.

My Father joins in the most respectfull Affection I am as ever most dutifully Your affectionate Kinsman   JONA WILLIAMS J

As there will be vessells now soon going hence to England I can get a passage for the few Prisoners remaining here if by treaty you are obliged to send them home, if not I will let them go as they can.

Notations: Jonath. Williams Nantes Jany. 28 1783 / [*In William Temple Franklin's hand:*] Ansd by WTF.[4]

From Thomas Barclay   ALS: American Philosophical Society

Sir   L'Orient 29 Januy. 1783
I had the Honour of receiving the Letter which your Excellency was so kind as to Write me the 21st. instant[5] and I very heartily and sincerely Congratulate you on your having seen such Important Events take place as the Independence of America, and General Peace of Europe.

There are now in this port several American Vessels ready to push to Sea, and if there is nothing improper in the application, I woud be very glad that Passports from the British Minister

---

4. WTF's letter of Feb. 2 is missing. JW acknowledged it in his response of Feb. 6: he "did not intend to do anything unworthy an American," he wrote, and assured WTF that his cargo would be confined to crockery and tools for the fishery, "both of which articles America want[s], & the latter will be a public Benefit." He had heard from Samuel White that blank passports would arrive from England, and that in order to fill them out, BF would need from him a list of names. He enclosed it, but anticipating that the personnel might change, he requested that he be sent blank passports on the assurance that he would return an exact account of how he had used them. He requested 30 blanks to serve for the Americans in Bordeaux, Nantes, and Lorient. APS. JW wrote to White on Feb. 6, as well, informing him that their Liverpool scheme was disallowed; he had heard from BF that the prohibitory laws remained in effect in England and America until repealed, which might take up to a year, and there could be no trade until a treaty of commerce was signed: JW to Samuel White, Feb. 6, 1783, Yale University Library.
5. Not found.

cou'd be obtaind to permit them to Sail without delay. It is of much consequence to the owners, as the Seamen are shipped upon the terms usually allow'd in time of War, and an other reason I have to wish to see them get away is, that all of them have Public supplies onboard.— If those supplies can be got to Philadelphia before the Shipments from England &c get there, Mr. Morris will be enabled if he chuses to Sell them, to raise a very considerable sum from them.

I am not clear as to the practicability of procuring such Passports, but as I am told they will be granted to the French Ships[6] I hope you will excuse my mentioning it.

I have the Honour to be very respectfully Sir Your Most Obt. Most Huml servt. THOS BARCLAY

The Vessels here are,
The Ship St. James,   Alexr. Cain Master
 "   Heer Adams . . . . . . Collins
 "   America . . . . Robt. Caldwell
 "   Washington   Jams. Josiah[7]
And at Nantes,
The Ship Prince of Liege Isaac All[8]

His Excellency Benjamin Franklin Esqr.

Notation: T. Barclay L'Orient 9 June 1783

6. This information may have come from the circular issued by the French court; see the annotation of Bondfield to BF, Jan. 26. The Franco-British preliminary articles had not yet been published; they appeared in the *Courier de l'Europe* of Jan. 31, and were printed as a pamphlet by the *imprimerie royale* on Feb. 3 (*Gaz. de Leyde*, issue of Feb. 11).

7. Barclay had informed BF on Dec. 16 that the *St. James, America,* and *Washington* were at Lorient, loading public goods that had been stored at Brest: XXXVIII, 463. The *Heer Adams* arrived on Jan. 18; see our annotation of BF to Livingston, Jan. 21. Barclay had loaded about 700 bales on the first three ships: Barclay to WTF, Jan. 24, 1783 (APS). Morris received at least some of the cargo by mid-April: *Morris Papers,* VII, 711.

8. Around this time, Barclay estimated that the *Prince de Liège* would carry about 600 bales of goods. The bales at Rochefort, he had discovered, were in need of substantial repair: Barclay to WTF, Jan. 24, 1783 (APS). The *Prince de Liège* sailed for America in mid-April: *Morris Papers,* VII, 625n.

From Maxwell Garthshore[9]   AL: American Philosophical Society

Hotel de Tours Rue Paon 29 Jan: *1783*

Dr. Garthshore returns His respl. Compts. & Thanks to Dr. Franklin, it is with infinite regret He finds Himself oblidged to leave Paris this day, where He has only staid a very few & without having it once in His power to wait on Dr. Franklin but that single time on His return from Versailles, which He was conscious was an improper Hour, but was owing to His Coachm's. getting drunk & misleading Him for two Hours— Dr. Garthshore would have been happy to have seen & conversed with Dr. Franklin of their old Friends in England, but want of Time deprives Him of almost every Thing He wish'd to see, & to know here.— The widow Pollhill[1] desires to join Him in respl. Comps. & Thanks for His oblidging attention on their passage thro' Paris.—

Addressed: A Son Excellence / Benjamin Franklyn / Ecuyer / Passy.

Notation: Dr. Garthshore Paris 29 Jany 1783

From John Jay   ALS: American Philosophical Society

Dr Sir   Paris 29 Jany 1783

Two Days ago I requested the favor of Mr. W. Franklin to mention to you the Case of Mr. Johnsons Bills,[2] and to inform me whether it would be convenient to You to provide for their paymt. & when, in Case I accepted them. Mr Johnson is anxious to know my Determination, and offers to be the Bearer of this note—

I am Dr. Sir your obliged & obt Servt   J. JAY

His Exy Dr Franklin

9. The London physician who had been attending the late Nathaniel Polhill on his travels through France. Garthshore had applied to BF in October for a passport: XXXVIII, 256–7.

1. Ursula Polhill; see the letter cited above.

2. Possibly those of the merchant Joshua Johnson, a correspondent of Jay: XXXVII, 497; Morris, *Jay: Peace*, pp. 208, 459.

Addressed: His Exy Dr. Franklin

Notation: Mr. Jay Paris Jany. 29. 1783

From Samuel Cooper Johonnot

ALS: University of Pennsylvania Library

Respected Sir   Geneva 29 Jan 1783.
Your kind Favour of the 7th Inst.[3] came to hand safe the 16th.— Please to accept my sincere & hearty thanks for your good Advice, & the many Obligations I am under to so good a Benefactor, & permit me also, to congratulate You upon the Peace lately concluded, which gives me the greatest Joy as a Patriot & by the Hopes I have that it will ease You of a major Part of your laborious Occupations.

I am striving to merit if possible, another Prize which however will afford me less Contentment than the good Will You are pleas'd to profess for your most humble Servant

S. COOPER JOHONNOT

His Excellency Doctor Franklin.

Addressed: A Monsieur / Monsr le Docteur Franklin / Ministre plenipotentiare des Etats / unis de l'Amerique auprès de sa Ma- / jesté tres chretienne, / A Passy / pres Paris.

From François-Félix Nogaret

ALS: American Philosophical Society

Vlles. Le 29 Janvr [1783]
Aimable Docteur! homme utile! Votre santé est-elle retablie? Personne ne le desire plus que vos respectueux amis de versailles homme et femme f. nogaret. Je vous prierai d'agréer, pour vos etrennes, Le portrait de notre archevêque de Paris, qui paraîtra

3. XXXVIII, 557–8.

dans les premiers jours de janvier,[4] et qu'on vous portera. Menagés une Santé precieuse à tout le monde, et continués d'avoir quelqu'amitié pour celui qui est avec tous les Sentimens d'estime et de veneration que vous inspirez Monsieur votre très humble et très obeissant Serviteur   FELIX-NOGARET

Mes respectueuses civilités, je vous prie, à Monsieur votre fils.

Notation: Felix Nogaret.

From Charles Pettit[5]   ALS: American Philosophical Society

Sir,   Philadelphia 29th. Jany. 1783
    Presuming on some Degree of personal Acquaintance and the Respect I have long entertained for your Character, I take the Liberty of recommending to your Notice my Son, Andrew Pettit, who will have the Honor to present this Letter.[6] As a Citizen of the United States I doubt not he would receive your Countenance and Protection, and I flatter myself that neither his own Conduct nor the Circumstances of his Introduction will diminish his Claim to your favorable Notice and friendly Advice.
    I have the Honor to be with perfect Respect, Sir Your most Obedient & most humble Servant   CHAS. PETTIT

His Excellency Dr. Franklin

Notation: Petitt 26 Janvr. 1783

4. Nogaret must have meant to write "février"; the engraving, by Fessard, was announced in the *Jour. de Paris* on Feb. 2. Nogaret had commissioned a portrait of the archbishop the previous spring: XXXVII, 411–12. By November he designed the surrounding allegories, which were described in detail (and deemed too elaborate) in Bachaumont, *Mémoires secrets,* XXI, 198–200.
    5. Pettit (XXII, 552n) had returned to private life after serving as assistant quartermaster general of the American army: *ANB.*
    6. His son Andrew, who had served as an aide to Joseph Reed, was preparing to leave for Amsterdam on the *Congress,* which finally sailed on March 23: Richard K. Showman *et al.,* eds., *The Papers of General Nathanael Greene* (13 vols. to date, Chapel Hill, N.C., 1976–), VI, 227n; XII, 424–5, 569. In later life Andrew became a merchant and insurance executive: *DAB,* under his son Thomas.

From Benjamin Vaughan and Samuel Vaughan, Jr.

AL:[7] American Philosophical Society

Wednesday morning, Jany. 29, 83.

Messrs: Vaughan have the honor to present their respects to Dr: Franklin. A prior engagement obliges them with the most extreme regret to decline the pleasure of waiting upon him on sunday, agreeable to his kind invitation.

Mr: Vaughan has the honor to inclose a list of some books sold by the same bookseller who furnished Mr V with the copy of the Politique Naturelle,[8] the mention of which is omitted in the list. The two first pencil-marks upon the list stand opposite to two other works by the same author.[9] The marks in the second page stand opposite to books which appear to relate to the subject of criminal laws, but which perhaps are not new to Dr. Franklin.— Mr Vaughan begs the favor to have his list returned at the Dr's leisure.

Best regards attend Mr Franklin Junr:

Addressed: a son Excellence / Monsr Franklin, / Ministre Plenipotentiaire des Etats Unis de L['amerique] / a Passy, / pres Paris.

Notation: Messrs. Vaughan Jany 29th. 1783

From Benjamin Franklin Bache

ALS: Historical Society of Pennsylvania

My Dear Grand Papa   Geneva 30 jan 1783.

I Reciv'd your Letter dated the 7 January[1] the 18 of the same month. I wrote your Letter a little in a hurry because the night was coming on and that I wanted to put the letter to the Post

---

7. In the hand of Benjamin Vaughan.

8. Paul-Henri Thiry, baron d'Holbach, *La Politique naturelle, ou Discours sur les vrais principes du gouvernement* . . . , first published in 1773. BF knew the author; he invited him to dine, along with Turgot: XXVII, 546n.

9. The list is missing, but probably included Holbach's most celebrated work, *Le Système de la nature* . . . (2 vols., London and Amsterdam, 1770).

1. XXXVIII, 556–7. BF there instructed BFB to date his letters, and to acknowledge by date those he received.

office that made me forget the date but I will try to forget it no more.

I have not receiv'd the parsel of Books you mentioned me in your letter that you had sent to me. I shall mention when I receive them. I heard yesterday with a great deal of pleasure that the peace was made Because that gives me hopes of seeing you soon if you have not Changed your resolution of coming and Because that takes away a great part of your occupations.[2]

Beleve me for ever your Most Dutiful and affectionate Grand son   B Franklin Bache

My Dear grand Papa Finding a watch a very necessary Instrument I beg you to permit Mr Marignac to procure me a good goden one. I schall have I peculiar care of it

Addressed: A Monsieur / Monsieur Le Docteur Franklin / Ministre plenipotentiare des etats / unis de l'Amerique auprès de sa / Majesté très Chretiene / a Passy / pres Paris

From Angélique-Michèle-Rosalie Jogues de Martinville Lafreté[3]

LS: American Philosophical Society

Paris le 30. Janver. 1783.

Mr. et Madme. La Vicomtesse de la héréria[4] prennent le plus grand intêrét, mon cher Docteur a Mr. De La barre, ancien Receveur des Tailles de Villefranche, qui vous remettra cette lettre.

2. Not long after BF sent BFB to Geneva, he mentioned plans to visit his grandson the next spring: XXIX, 600. Late in 1780 BF again had thoughts of visiting Geneva: XXXIV, 140.

3. This is the last extant letter from BF's good friend. Her health remained poor all that winter; on March 1 her husband suggested to BF that more frequent visits from him would have a salutary effect. She died that spring: *Jour. de Paris,* issue of April 22, 1783.

4. Alvaro de Navía Osorio y Bellet, vizconde consort de la Herrería, and his second wife, Francisca Javiera Güemes de Pacheco Padilla. The vizconde was the Spanish minister plenipotentiary in the Netherlands until 1780, when he was appointed to the court of Naples. He did not arrive at that court until early 1784, spending much of the intervening time in Paris: Didier Ozanam, *Les Diplomates espagnols du XVIIIe siècle: introduction et répertoire*

Il désireroit passer en amérique, honnoré de Votre protection. Vous nous obligeriéz infiniment si vous daignéz l'accorder a un homme honnête et malheureux. Je ne vous dis rien de ma santé qui est toujours languissante. Vous me feréz grand plaisir de venir me voir. Je n'ai pas de plus douce consolation que de voir mes amis et vous Savéz bien, mon cher Docteur, que vous êtes un de ceux à qui je suis le plus tendrement Attachée.

MARTINVILLE DE LA FRETÉ

Notation: La Freté Mde. De 30 Janr. 1783.

From the Marquis de La Salle

ALS: American Philosophical Society

A L'O.∴ de Paris Ce 30e. j.∴ du 11e. mois de
L'an de V.∴ L.∴ 5782.∴ [January 30, 1783][5]

T.∴ C.∴ &.∴ T.∴ R.∴ f.∴[6]

La R.∴ L.∴ des IX Soeurs qui a eû L'avantage de vous avoir pour Son Vénerable, Enchantée d'une paix qui rendant Le repos au monde assurre l'indépendance de votre patrie qui doit bien vous nomer son père, Dèsireroit faire passer jusqu'à vous l'expression de Sa joyë. Elle a nomée une députation pour aller vous feliciter Sur cet heurreux évenement; & j'ai la faveur de vous prier en son nom de vouloir bien me marquer quel jour & a quelle heure Vos frères pourront vous porter ses voeux & Son homage.

J'ai la faveur d'être avec les sentiments fraternels que je vous dois comme maçon, avec l'admiration qu'inspirent La Sublimité de vos talents & la profondeur de vos lumieres & le respect dû au grand homme d'état & au bienfaiteur de l'humanité, T.∴ C.∴ &.∴ T.∴ R.∴ F.∴ Votre trés afectionné Serviteur & frere

LE MIS. DE LA SALLE
Vble. de La L.∴ des IX soeurs.

---

biographique (1700–1808) (Madrid and Bordeaux, 1998), pp. 364–5; *Repertorium der diplomatischen Vertreter*, III, 435, 443.

5. The abbreviations stand for Orient, jour, and Vraie Lumière. The masonic year began on March 1.

6. Très Cher & Très Respectable Frère. In the next line the abbreviations are for Respectable Loge.

rue St. Rock près la rue poissonniers à Paris

Notation: Marquis de La Salle Paris 30 Novr. 1782

From the Chevalier de Meyronnet de Saint-Marc[7]

LS: American Philosophical Society

Monsieur   A Lisbonne ce 30 Janvier 1783

J'ai L'honneur de vous prevenir, que j'ai reçû il y a quelques jours une Lettre du Vice Consul de françe à L'Isle de Fayal;[8] dans la qu'elle cet officier me donne Avis; qu'ayant reçû du Consul Anglois cinq Americains pris par le Corsaire *la Hornett de Bristol* Sur le *Brigantin la Betsey de Boston.* Il Les embarquera sur un des Vaisseaux qu'on expedie de Fayal pour L'Amerique Septentrionale; et qu'il m'addressera à lors la nôte de Ses Avances dont il demande le remboursement. Cet Officier juge, Monsieur, que la Depense de leur nourriture et de leur passage pourra Monter à vingt Monoïës D'or; ce qui revient apeupres à £600 Tournois. Je vous prie, Monsieur, de Vouloir bien donner des ordres ici pour le remboursement de cette Somme, qui Sera tirée sur moi par une Lettre de Change à vue.

Je Suis enchanté, Monsieur, d'avoir cette occasion de me rappeller dans vôtre Souvenir et de vous temoigner combien je Suis faché de n'etre plus à portée de vous exprimer tous les Sentiments d'estime dont je Suis penetré pour vous; comme je le faisois, Lorsque j'avais l'honneur de vous voir à Passy Chez feu Madame la Marquise de Boulanviliez,[9] Chez M. le Comte D'Estaing et aux termes, Chez Mr. le Mis. de Gallifet.

Si je puis vous être de quelque utilité, Monsieur, dans ce Pays ici; je vous prie de me donner la prefference. Je Serois très flatté que vous me mettiez à portée de vous convaincre de mes Sentiments respectueux.

---

7. On an April 19, 1783, certificate on behalf of Jean-Baptiste Pecquet (National Archives), he signed his Christian names as Jean-Pierre-Balthazard.

8. Faial Island in the Azores.

9. She died in 1781: XXXVI, 179n.

Je Suis avec respect Monsieur Vôtre tres humble & tres Obeissant Serviteur   LE CHEVALIER DE MEYRONNET DE ST. MARC
ançien lieutenant des vaisseaux de roy
consul general de france en portugal

Notation: Meyronnet 30 Janvr. 1783

From the Chamber of Commerce of Aunis and Others Concerning the Selection of Free Ports

LS: Historical Society of Pennsylvania

Article 32 of the 1778 Franco-American Treaty of Amity and Commerce promised that the king of France would provide one or more
free ports in Europe for American produce and merchandise.[1] During
the war all French ports were open to American ships, the choice of
free ports being left until the peace.[2] Once France reached peace terms
with Britain, various French cities sought to influence the coming
choice of free ports. The present letter extolling the advantages of La
Rochelle is the first of many appeals sent to Franklin.[3]

The municipal officers of Port Louis (across the bay from Lorient)
begin their campaign with a letter of February 14. They have already
spoken to Barclay and Moylan, and have addressed a petition to the
marquis de Castries. On April 7 they send a three-page memoir on the
commercial advantages of their city. Franklin also received, probably
around this time, a copy of an undated memoir petitioning Louis XVI
to make Port Louis a free port for trade with the United States.[4] It is
signed by the abbé Rugnebourg, *député* of the city.

On February 15 Mayor Etienne Lalanne writes on behalf of the municipal magistrates and city council of Bayonne,[5] urging the advantages of their port and introducing a deputy named Galart, who is

1. XXV, 624–5.
2. XXVIII, 430.
3. Unless otherwise noted, the letters described below are in French and
at the APS.
4. On March 19 Lafayette wrote Vergennes criticizing Port Louis as being
too small, and arguing that Lorient was more convenient and "agreeable" to
the Americans: Idzerda, *Lafayette Papers,* V, 112–13, 376.
5. Lalanne was mayor of Bayonne from 1782 to 1785: Josette Pontet, ed.,
Histoire de Bayonne (Toulouse, 1991), p. 322.

coming to Paris and would be pleased to speak with Franklin. Galart arrived by March 1, and finally obtained an interview with the American minister through the perseverance of their mutual friend Jean-Jacques Lafreté.[6] Galart himself writes Franklin on April 10, recalling Franklin's statement that American commerce will eventually settle upon whichever port proves to be the most convenient. Under present circumstances Bayonne will not be favored on account of the high duties and heavy regulations placed on it by the French government, which prevent the entry of goods destined for the Spanish interior. Making Bayonne a free port, the subject of the memoir he encloses, would open avenues of trade not available elsewhere. If his translator had not delayed, Franklin would have had it two days earlier.[7]

In a memoir of February 25, chevalier Louis-Honoré Froger de La Rigaudière[8] argues that nothing would be more advantageous to the United States than having a free port in the province of Saintonge, be it Marennes, La Tremblade, or the Ile d'Oleron. In a continuation dated March 8, the author urges Congress to name his brother as consul at Marennes; he will serve without pay.[9] Froger undoubtedly added the second section after being assured by his friend Jean-Jacques Bachelier that the latter had obtained for him an audience with Franklin.[1] On March 8 he also wrote a memoir addressed to Congress for Franklin to forward, the first part of which concerned free ports, the second part of which was a copy of what he had written about his brother. He had the memoir signed by Baron Anne-Léon de Montmorency, commandant general of Aunis, Saintonge, and Poitou.[2] After meeting Franklin Froger made a summary of his arguments, adding that Franklin should

6. See Lafreté's letters of March 1 and 10.

7. Both the ten-page memoir and its English translation are among Franklin's papers at the APS. The latter is entitled, "Superiority of the Bayonne's Port above others harbours, for the trade of North America." Lafayette, in the letter to Vergennes cited above, said that he had been visited by deputies from Bayonne, who were grateful for Vergennes' interest.

8. He and his brother Henry-André were half-brothers of the celebrated Lieutenant Général des Armées Navales Michel-Joseph Froger de l'Eguille (1702–1772): *DBF;* Michel Vergé-Franceschi, *Les Officiers généraux de la marine royale (1715–1774): Origines-conditions-services* (7 vols., Paris, 1990), I, 281, 294.

9. Two signed copies of this Feb. 25–March 8 memoir survive, one at the APS and the other at the Hist. Soc. of Pa.

1. The dinner took place on March 12; see Bachelier to BF, March 3.

2. The signed document and an unsigned copy are at the Hist. Soc. of Pa. For Montmorency see *Dictionnaire de la noblesse,* XIV, 387.

recommend his petition to the court; he sent this "Extrait des deux mémoires présentés le 12 mars 1783 à Son Excellence Monsieur de Francklin" to Vergennes.[3] On March 30, in a letter to Franklin, he explains that his recent silence was due to a terrible cold. Has Franklin yet given his March 12 memoir to Barclay to translate into English, and has he spoken with Vergennes? In a letter of April 8, written at Passy, he explains that he wants to see Franklin, who should know that the maréchal de Richelieu is interested in speaking to him as well. He is giving Franklin a map of Saintonge.

On February 26 the marquis de Luce-Seillans, reminding Franklin of their conversations in September, 1777,[4] writes from Grasse extolling the advantages of Antibes and remarking that the consuls of the port had petitioned the French government on its behalf.

Writing from Paris on April 12, Perrot de Chezolles, director general of the Bureau royal de correspondance,[5] reminds Franklin of his promise to support the application of La Ciotat (between Marseille and Toulon) and encloses a copy of a memoir on the subject addressed to the French naval ministry.

Finally, we take note of three undated memoirs. One, insisting that no port would be more convenient for the Americans than Lorient, was signed by the mayor of that city, Esnoul Deschatelets.[6] The Chamber of Commerce of Montpellier proposes nearby Sète as a free port and urges the "Ameriquains Anglais" to take advantage of all the products the Languedoc has to offer.[7] A five-page memoir in the hand of Francis Coffyn outlines the advantages of Dunkirk to the commerce of the kingdom.

The French government did not reach a final decision on free ports for another year. By an *Arrêt du Conseil d'Etat du Roi* of May 14, 1784, it selected Lorient, Bayonne, Dunkirk, Marseille, and St. Jean de Luz.[8]

3. The so-called extract is at the AAE; an incomplete copy is among BF's papers at the Hist. Soc. of Pa.

4. XXIV, 544–5n.

5. *Almanach royal* for 1783, pp. 435–6.

6. He signs as both mayor and merchant; he is listed in *Almanach des marchands*, p. 295. BF endorsed it, "Memoire Recommending L'Orient for one of the Free Ports."

7. Hist. Soc. of Pa.

8. François-André Isambert, ed., *Recueil général des anciennes lois françaises . . .* (29 vols., Paris, 1821–33), XXVII, 405. Numerous memoirs were sent directly to the French government on behalf of various cities wishing to be free ports: Waldo G. Leland, ed., *Guide to Materials for American His-*

Monseigneur   La Rochelle le 31 Janvier 1783.

La paix qui met une fin glorieuse à la tâche importante dont vous étiés chargé, est une époque que nous croyons devoir saisir pour réclamer l'intérêt que nous avions déjà suplié Votre Excellence de nous accorder. Daignés permétre, Monseigneur, que nous remetions sous vos yeux notre Mémoire[9] à l'effet d'obtenir que la Rochelle soit un des ports francs promis par le Roi aux États-unis de l'Amérique.

Si, comme nous l'en suplions de nouveau, VOTRE EXCELLENCE veut bien prendre en considération la situation de cette ville, l'émulation de ses habitans, la comodité & la sureté de ses Rades, la nature des productions de son sol, la proximité des manufactures propres à alimenter un commerce naissant, les liens de parenté dont nous rapellons les traces, nous ne craindrons point, Monseigneur, de fonder les plus grandes espérances dans votre crédit, ainsi que dans les vues d'utilité qui vous animent.

Nous sommes avec respect Monseigneur Vos très humbles & très obéissans serviteurs Les Directeur & Syndics de la Chambre de Commerce du Pays d'Aunis   RANJARD Directeur
                                                      LEGRIX
                                                      GOGUET
                                                      JACQ. GUIBERT
                                                      B GORAUDEAU[1]

Monseigneur de Francklin.

---

tory in the Libraries and Archives of Paris (2 vols., Washington, D.C., 1932–43), II, 603–9.

9. The enclosed memoir is missing. It was sent to a number of French officials, as well, and is printed in Emile Garnault, Le Commerce rochelais au XVIIIe siècle . . . (5 vols., Paris and La Rochelle, 1888–1900), V, 250–3; for an earlier memoir see ibid., V, 244–9.

1. Three of the five signatories were still members of the La Rochelle Chamber of Commerce in 1791: J. D. Goguet was director, Ranjard a syndic, and Jacques Guibert a member. Ibid., V, 402.

From Brongniart

AL: American Philosophical Society

paris Rue St Marc. le 31 janvier 1783

M. Brongniart a L'honneur de presenter Son Respect a Monsieur franklin et Le prie de Lui faire Sçavoir Si on lui a remis Vendredi de L'autre Semaine, deux Nouvelles Epreuves de la Medaille, et entre autres Celle de la tete de la libertè.[2]

Monsieur franklin oublie apparemment d'envoyer a Mr Brongniart Ce qu'il desire faire mettre au Bas de la Medaille de chaque Cotè, et Cela retient Le graveur qui desireroit terminer Cet ouvrage—

Notation: Brognart 31 Janvr. 1783

From ——— de Illens

ALS and copy:[3] American Philosophical Society

Monsieur! Marseille 31 janvier 1783

J'ay bien reçu en son tems la Lettre dont vous m'avez honoré en datte du 6. aoust 1780.[4] Elle me donnoit bon espoir pour la rentrée des fonds considerables qui me sont dus par le Tresor de la Caroline du Sud.

Aujourd'huy qu'une paix avantageuse & honorable pour votre nation, la reconoit independante & libre, j'espere qu'elle se fera un devoir de satisfaire honorablemt. aux engagemens contractés bien solidement et par contract avec les negotians francois qui come moy ont porté des secours, et ont fait credit dans des momens pressés et de detresse.— Mon Contract original est en mains du consul de france qui en quittant Charles

---

2. See Brongniart's letter of Jan. 23.

3. Illens sent this copy on May 16 with a brief note asking for a response (APS). We have found no further correspondence.

4. Recommending that he seek reimbursement from the state of South Carolina for the notes he held. These had been given in exchange for a cargo sent to Charleston: XXXII, 588–9; XXXIII, 152–4.

Town etoit alle à Philadelphie.[5] Je lui ecris pour comencer à le presser sur les demarches necessaires a mon payement. Oserois je Monsieur, vous demander votre protection dans cette legitime prétention & me dire quand & coment vous croyés que l'on remboursera. Si on remettoit des marchandises, j'ai des Vaisseaux qui pourroient aller les chercher, Si au pis aller on payoit en bonnes terres, je pourrois m'en contenter.

Vous m'avez fait la grace monsieur de me promettre des eclaircissemens, et c'est ce qui m'enhardit de vous en demander.

Recevez mon compliment Sincere sur le grand ouvrage, ou vous avez tant operé, & les assurances de la respectueuse Consideration avec laqlle. j'ay l'honeur d'etre const. [constamment] Votre très humbe. & très obeïssant Serviteur   DE ILLENS

Monsieur

Notation: Illens 31 Janvr. 1783.

From Mathurin Roze de Chantoiseau[6]

ALS: Historical Society of Pennsylvania

Monsieur.   Ce 31. Janvier 1783.

Oserois-je vous offrir Le fruit de plusieurs années d'un travail assidu et reflechi, dont le resumé n'exige pas un quart d'heure de Lecture, et dont le resultat seroit d'operer, d'une maniere simple et peu dispendieuse, la Liquidation de la majeure partie des Dettes d'un Etat, Sans en alterer les fonds, et Sans en diminuer les revenus, ny en aggraver les charges.

5. French consul J. Plombard (XXXII, 588n) was released on parole by the British after they captured Charleston: *Laurens Papers,* XV, 296n.

6. In the 1760s the enterprising Roze de Chantoiseau was celebrated for inventing the *restaurant,* directing the bureau général d'indication (a privately managed information center closed by the state in 1766 when it established a monopoly on such businesses), and publishing an annual *Almanach général d'indication d'adresse personnelle et domicile fixe des Six Corps, Arts et*

Emprunter une somme quelconque a interêt, doubler les impots, ou en creer de nouveaux, n'est chose rare ny difficile; mais Éteindre Les interets et le Principal d'une somme quelconque Sans alterer Ses fonds actuels, Sans diminuer ses revenus, sans creer aucun Emprunt et Sans Etablir ny doubler aucun impot paroîtra Sans doute chose neuve, et digne, Si jose dire, d'un accueil favorable et des suffrages de Votre Excellence.

On Cherche depuis longtemps des moiens Simples et peu dispendieux pour Liquider tout ou Partie des Dettes d'un Etat Sans en diminuer les revenus ny en aggraver les charges. Le Ministere qui connoit combien il seroit interessant de trouver un objet aussi essentiel reçoit tous les Projets d'œconomie, de finances, d'aggriculture, et de Commerce qu'on lui propose, les examine, les discute, et paroit jusqu'a ce jour n'en n'avoir trouvé aucun qui dut etre adopté.

En Effet quand on a pesé et combiné tous ces differents sistêmes, et que l'on reflechit Sur les difficultés et l'immensité de tems qu'il faudroit Employer pour les mettre à execution avant de pouvoir en recueillir le fruit, on S'apperçoit qu'ils ne peuvent remedier pour L'instant aux besoins pressants d'un Etat; et dès lors on seroit tenté de regarder le mal comme desesperé et Sans remede si l'on n'offroit de demontrer qu'il en est un aussi prompt qu'efficace pour Subvenir a tous les besoins urgents des Citoyens par une operation Simple, facile, uniforme, et peu dispendieuse dont l'effet seroit de procurer a tous les Creanciers de L'Etat le

---

Métiers, a comprehensive business directory for Paris which continued through the 1780s. His chief interest, however, was in seeing the French state abolish the national debt by means of his system of letters of credit. In 1769 he published his concept in *L'Ami de tout le monde, précis d'un plan de banque générale du crédit public, sociale & commerçante* . . . . Bachaumont, praising Roze de Chantoiseau for his singular ingenuity and resourcefulness (displayed in his myriad inventions), featured the pamphlet in the *Mémoires secrets,* but its unauthorized publication resulted in the author's arrest and imprisonment. Thereafter, except for the present attempt to interest BF in his banking scheme, Roze seems to have kept these ideas to himself until 1789, when he renewed his unsuccessful attempt to get France to adopt his system. Rebecca L. Spang, *The Invention of the Restaurant* (Cambridge, Mass., and London, 2000), pp. 12–14, 17–21, 255n; Bachaumont, *Mémoires secrets,* V, 40–2.

moyen de se Liberer envers leurs creanciers et de mettre ceux cy a couvert des poursuites quils seroient dans le cas d'essuier en leurs transmettant pareillement les memes droits et facultés a legard de leurs creanciers personnels de maniere que les peines de Saisie et d'enprisonnement ne seroient pour ainsi dire plus desormais reservées qu'a l'inconduite ou a la mauvaise foi.

Ce Sisteme quelque Specieux qu'il paroisse par les avantages inestimables qu'il presente n'est pas une speculation Vague et denuée de fondements; Ce nest pas même un sisteme a proprement parler; C'est un moyen unique et certain de Simpliffier toutes les operations de finances et de reduire presque toutes les operations de Commerce a une Seule forme connüe, avoüée et generalement reçue qui en desobstruant les canaux de La circulation ouvre a jamais, a LEtat qui en fera Usage, une Source de richesse et Ecarte au loing tous les Funestes Effets de la fraude, du Vol, de la Surprise et de l'usure.

Tel est, Monsieur, Lobjet important que jai à proposer à Votre Excellence, et que je me fais fête de lui justiffier dès qu'il lui plaira m'accorder un moment d'entretien particulier, et m'indiquer Le jour et Lheure qui lui seront les plus commodes.[7]

Je Suis avec un tres profond respect Monsieur Votre tres humble et tres obeissant Serviteur

Roze de chantoiseau
Directr. du Beau. [Bureau] d'Indications generales des artiste celebres
Rue comtesse d'artois

A Monsieur francklin Ministre Plenipotentiaire des Etats unis de L'Amerique.

---

7. They met on Feb. 7; see Roze de Chantoiseau to bf, Feb. 8.

From Benjamin Vaughan[8]

Reprinted from William Temple Franklin, ed., *Memoirs of the Life and Writings of Benjamin Franklin* . . . (3 vols., 4to, London, 1817–18), I, 59–63.

My Dearest Sir,   Paris, January 31, 1783.

When I had read over your sheets of minutes of the principal incidents of your life, recovered for you by your Quaker acquaintance; I told you I would send you a letter expressing my reasons why I thought it would be useful to complete and publish it as he desired.[9] Various concerns have for some time past prevented this letter being written, and I do not know whether it was worth any expectation: happening to be at leisure however at present, I shall by writing at least interest and instruct myself; but as the terms I am inclined to use may tend to offend a person of your manners, I shall only tell you how I would address any other person, who was as good and as great as yourself, but less diffident. I would say to him, Sir, I *solicit* the history of your life from the following motives.

Your history is so remarkable, that if you do not give it, somebody else will certainly give it; and perhaps so as nearly to do as much harm, as your own management of the thing might do good.

It will moreover present a table of the internal circumstances of your country, which will very much tend to invite to it settlers of virtuous and manly minds. And considering the eagerness with which such information is sought by them, and the extent of your reputation, I do not know of a more efficacious advertisement than your Biography would give.

All that has happened to you is also connected with the detail of the manners and situation of *a rising* people; and in this respect I do not think that the writings of Cæsar and Tacitus can be more interesting to a true judge of human nature and society.

---

8. This is one of the two letters BF included in his autobiography between parts I and II; see XXXVIII, 425–9. The "Quaker acquaintance" mentioned in the first sentence is Abel James.

9. See XXXVIII, 426–7n.

But these, Sir, are small reasons in my opinion, compared with the chance which your life will give for the forming of future great men; and in conjunction with your *Art of Virtue,* (which you design to publish)[1] of improving the features of private character, and consequently of aiding all happiness both public and domestic.

The two works I allude to, Sir, will in particular give a noble rule and example of *self-education.* School and other education constantly proceed upon false principles, and shew a clumsy apparatus pointed at a false mark; but your apparatus is simple, and the mark a true one; and while parents and young persons are left destitute of other just means of estimating and becoming prepared for a reasonable course in life, your discovery that the thing is in many a man's private power, will be invaluable!

Influence upon the private character late in life, is not only an influence late in life, but a weak influence. It is in *youth* that we plant our chief habits and prejudices; it is in youth that we take our party as to profession, pursuits, and matrimony. In youth therefore the turn is given; in youth the education even of the next generation is given; in youth the private and public character is determined; and the term of life extending but from youth to age, life ought to begin well from youth; and more especially *before* we take our party as to our principal objects.

But your Biography will not merely teach self-education, but the education of *a wise man;* and the wisest man will receive lights and improve his progress, by seeing detailed the conduct of another wise man. And why are weaker men to be deprived of such helps, when we see our race has been blundering on in the dark, almost without a guide in this particular, from the farthest trace of time. Shew then, Sir, how much is to be done, *both to sons and fathers;* and invite all wise men to become like yourself; and other men to become wise.

When we see how cruel statesmen and warriors can be to the

---

1. A project BF never finished, but did partially incorporate in the next section of his autobiography: IX, 104n, 375n; *Autobiog.,* pp. 148–60.

humble race, and how absurd distinguished men can be to their acquaintance, it will be instructive to observe the instances multiply of pacific acquiescing manners; and to find how compatible it is to be great and *domestic;* enviable and yet *good-humoured.*

The little private incidents which you will also have to relate, will have considerable use, as we want above all things, *rules of prudence in ordinary affairs;* and it will be curious to see how you have acted in these. It will be so far a sort of key to life, and explain many things that all men ought to have once explained to them, to give them a chance of becoming wise by foresight.

The nearest thing to having experience of one's own, is to have other people's affairs brought before us in a shape that is interesting; this is sure to happen from your pen. Your affairs and management will have an air of simplicity or importance that will not fail to strike; and I am convinced you have conducted them with as much originality as if you had been conducting discussions in politics or philosophy; and what more worthy of experiments and system, (its importance and its errors considered) than human life!

Some men have been virtuous blindly, others have speculated fantastically, and others have been shrewd to bad purposes; but you, Sir, I am sure, will give under your hand, nothing but what is at the same moment, wise, practical, and good.

Your account of yourself (for I suppose the parallel I am drawing for Dr. Franklin, will hold not only in point of character but of private history), will shew that you are ashamed of no origin; a thing the more important, as you prove how little necessary all origin is to happiness, virtue, or greatness.

As no end likewise happens without a means, so we shall find, Sir, that even you yourself framed a plan by which you became considerable; but at the same time we may see that though the event is flattering, the means are as simple as wisdom could make them; that is depending upon nature, virtue, thought, and habit.

Another thing demonstrated will be the propriety of every man's waiting for his time for appearing upon the stage of the world. Our sensations being very much fixed to the moment, we are apt to forget that more moments are to follow the first, and consequently that man should arrange his conduct so as to suit the *whole* of a life. Your attribution appears to have been applied to your *life*, and the passing moments of it have been enlivened with content and enjoyment, instead of being tormented with foolish impatience or regrets. Such a conduct is easy for those who make virtue and themselves their standard, and who try to keep themselves in countenance by examples of other truly great men, of whom patience is so often the characteristic.

Your Quaker correspondent, Sir, (for here again I will suppose the subject of my letter resembling Dr. Franklin,) praised your frugality, diligence, and temperance, which he considered as a pattern for all youth:[2] but it is singular that he should have forgotten your modesty, and your disinterestedness, without which you never could have waited for your advancement, or found your situation in the mean time comfortable; which is a strong lesson to shew the poverty of glory, and the importance of regulating our minds.

If this correspondent had known the nature of your reputation as well as I do, he would have said; your former writings and measures would secure attention to your Biography, and Art of Virtue; and your Biography and Art of Virtue, in return, would secure attention to them. This is an advantage attendant upon a various character, and which brings all that belongs to it into greater play; and it is the more useful, as perhaps more persons are at a loss for the *means* of improving their minds and characters, than they are for the time or the inclination to do it.

But there is one concluding reflection, Sir, that will shew the use of your life as a mere piece of biography. This style of writing seems a little gone out of vogue, and yet it is a very useful one; and your specimen of it may be particularly serviceable, as it will make a subject of comparison with the lives of various public cut-throats and intriguers, and with absurd monastic self-tormentors, or vain literary triflers. If it encourages more writings of the same kind with your own, and induces more men to spend lives fit to be written; it will be worth all Plutarch's Lives put together.

2. XXXVIII, 427–8.

But being tired of figuring to myself a character of which every feature suits only one man in the world, without giving him the praise of it; I shall end my letter, my dear Dr. Franklin, with a personal application to your proper self.

I am earnestly desirous then, my dear Sir, that you should let the world into the traits of your genuine character, as civil broils may otherwise tend to disguise or traduce it. Considering your great age, the caution of your character, and your peculiar style of thinking, it is not likely that any one besides yourself can be sufficiently master of the facts of your life, or the intentions of your mind.

Besides all this, the immense revolution of the present period, will necessarily turn our attention towards the author of it; and when virtuous principles have been pretended in it, it will be highly important to shew that such have really influenced; and, as your own character will be the principal one to receive a scrutiny, it is proper (even for its effects upon your vast and rising country, as well as upon England and upon Europe), that it should stand respectable and eternal. For the furtherance of human happiness, I have always maintained that it is necessary to prove that man is not even at present a vicious and detestable animal; and still more to prove that good management may greatly amend him; and it is for much the same reason, that I am anxious to see the opinion established, that there are fair characters existing among the individuals of the race; for the moment that all men, without exception, shall be conceived abandoned, good people will cease efforts deemed to be hopeless, and perhaps think of taking their share in the scramble of life, or at least of making it comfortable principally for themselves.

Take then, my dear Sir, this work most speedily into hand: shew yourself good as you are good, temperate as you are temperate; and above all things, prove yourself as one who from your infancy have loved justice, liberty, and concord, in a way that has made it natural and consistent for you to have acted, as we have seen you act in the last seventeen years of your life.[3] Let

3. Perhaps this refers to the 17 years that had passed since BF began working in late 1765 for the repeal of the Stamp Act, a key stage in the identification of BF with the causes of "justice, liberty, and concord."

Englishmen be made not only to respect, but even to love you. When they think well of individuals in your native country, they will go nearer to thinking well of your country; and when your countrymen see themselves well thought of by Englishmen, they will go nearer to thinking well of England. Extend your views even further; do not stop at those who speak the English tongue, but after having settled so many points in nature and politics, think of bettering the whole race of men.

As I have not read any part of the life in question, but know only the character that lived it, I write somewhat at hazard. I am sure however, that the life, and the treatise I allude to (on the *Art of Virtue*), will necessarily fulfil the chief of my expectations; and still more so if you take up the measure of suiting these performances to the several views above stated. Should they even prove unsuccessful in all that a sanguine admirer of yours hopes from them, you will at least have framed pieces to interest the human mind; and whoever gives a feeling of pleasure that is innocent to man, has added so much to the fair side of a life otherwise too much darkened by anxiety, and too much injured by pain.

In the hope therefore that you will listen to the prayer addressed to you in this letter, I beg to subscribe myself, my dearest Sir, &c. &c. Signed BENJ. VAUGHAN.

From Jonathan Williams, Jr. LS: American Philosophical Society

Dear & hond. Sir   Nantes Jan. 31. 1783

The Bearer is the Honble. John Wheelock President of Dartmouth College, who has come to Europe with a Deputation from the Trustees, supported by strong Recommendations from the first Characters in America, in order to obtain Donations for an Institution for the propagation of Knowledge & Virtue.[4]

---

4. See XXXVIII, 134–5. John Wheelock and his brother James arrived in Nantes on Jan. 24 after a three-week passage from Boston: Leon B. Richardson, *History of Dartmouth College* (2 vols., Hanover, N.H., 1932), I, 205–6.

The respectable Recommendations Mr. Wheelock has with him make it unnecessary for me to add to them & I assure myself his personal merit joined to the Importance of his mission will entitle him to your Friendship and support.

Mr. Wheelocks Brother accompanys him and I equaly recommend him to your Notice.

I am with the highest Respect Your dutifull & affectionate Kinsman[5]   JONA WILLIAMS J

His Excelly Benjn Franklin Esqr.

Notation: Williams Mr. Jona. Nantes Jany. 31. 1783

From Jonathan Williams, Sr.

ALS: American Philosophical Society

Hond sr   Nantes, Janry. 31, 1783

The bearer is the Honble. President Wheelock (in Company with his Brother) he is on a Benevolint Design & has the Best Recommendations, he wishes to Lay the Plan & his Credentials before you, for your Opinion or Advice.[6]

I take the Liberty to Recommend the above Gentm. to your Civilities as strangers in your City, which will ad to the many Obligations all Ready Conferd On Your Dutyfull Nephew & Most Hbe Servant   JONA. WILLIAMS

Notation: Williams Jona. Nantes Jany. 31. 1783.

---

5. JW wrote a similar letter to JA the same day (Mass. Hist. Soc.).

6. Jonathan Williams, Sr., sailed to France on the same ship as the Wheelocks. The brothers reached Paris on Feb. 5: Leon B. Richardson, *History of Dartmouth College* (2 vols., Hanover, N.H., 1932), I, 205–6.

From Antoinette-Cécile Clavel, *dite* Mademoiselle Saint-Huberti, and Christian Karl Hartmann[7]

AL: American Philosophical Society

[before February 1, 1783]

Votre Excellence est invitée d'honorer de Sa présence le Concert des Amateurs qui Se donnera le 1er. février 1783, dans la Salle du Contrat Social, Rue Coqhéron[8] de la part de Madelle. St. huberti et de Mr. hartman Directeur dudit Concert./.

Son Excellence voudra bien accepter les deux Billets d'Entrée ci-joints./.

7. The celebrated soprano Saint-Huberti (-Huberty) (1756–1812) performed regularly at the Concert Spirituel and in 1783 became a principal singer at the Opéra: Stanley Sadie, ed., *The New Grove Dictionary of Music and Musicians* (2nd ed., 29 vols., London, 2001); Henriette-Louise von Waldner, baronne d'Oberkirch, *Mémoires de la baronne d'Oberkirch sur la cour de Louis XVI et la société française avant 1789*, ed. Suzanne Burkard (Paris, 1970), pp. 328–9, 335–6. Her performances around this time were praised in the *Jour. de Paris*, issues of Feb. 16 and March 15, 1783.

Hartmann (1750–1804), born in Germany, moved to Paris around 1774 and was renowned as a flutist and composer: *New Grove Dictionary;* John S. Sainsbury, ed., *A Dictionary of Musicians from the Earliest Times* (2 vols., London, 1825; reprint, New York, 1966), I, 334.

8. This prestigious concert series was performed by an orchestra of accomplished amateurs who were often joined by virtuoso performers from the Opéra and the king's household. Founded in 1769 by farmer general Charles-Marin de La Haye (XXIII, 492n) and Claude-Jean Rigoley, baron d'Ogny, the series was dissolved around 1781 but was shortly thereafter revived under the auspices of the masonic Loge Olympique. Performances were held at the *Hôtel de Bullion* on the rue du Coq Héron until they moved to larger quarters in 1786, and often involved musicians from other lodges, including the Contrat Social (of which Hartmann was a member): Michel Brenet, *Les Concerts en France sous l'ancien régime* (Paris, 1900; reprint ed., New York, 1970), pp. 357–66; Marcelle Benoît, ed., *Dictionnaire de la musique en France aux XVII et XVIII siècles* (Paris, 1992), pp. 170–1; Le Bihan, *Francs-maçons parisiens*, pp. 17, 245; Roger Cotte, *La Musique maçonnique et ses musiciens* (2nd ed., Paris, 1987), pp. 45–8.

Franklin's Passport for British Ships

ps:[9] Massachusetts Historical Society, American Philosophical Society

Exchanging ships' passports was the first official act between the former belligerent nations, whose vessels needed protection until the news of the armistice was generally known, and whose merchants were anxious to race their cargo to newly opened ports. But were those ports truly open? Franklin maintained that until the Prohibitory Act was repealed by Parliament, America could not admit British manufactures. This, rather than the passports themselves, was the first substantive issue he discussed with Fitzherbert when the two met on January 24. Franklin told Fitzherbert that "an article for that purpose had been inserted in the project of preliminaries transmitted by himself and his colleagues, but that it had been left out in that which was brought back from England by Mr Strachey." Fitzherbert replied that the article in question (Article 4 of the first draft treaty, which gave American merchants the same commercial privileges as their British counterparts, and vice versa)[1] was so broad as to be applicable to all Britain's trade laws, including the Navigation Act, "which, [Franklin] knew, could not be meddled with, Without the most serious and mature deliberation." Fitzherbert recommended that the two countries agree to an article that confined itself "to such acts as had been passed on both sides on account of the war." Franklin then mentioned that additional articles might have to be inserted into what would become the definitive treaty. The British negotiator was both alarmed and adamant that "no fresh matter was to be introduced on either side." Unless, as Franklin urged, both sides should agree to it.[2]

It appears that Fitzherbert called at Passy on the morning of February 1 and informed Franklin (as he would later that day inform Jay) that the British were prepared to issue passports for American merchantmen if the Americans would do likewise. Franklin, who was used to writing such documents, composed one immediately, adopting much of the language verbatim from the British passport that Fitzherbert must have shown him. He insisted, however, on inserting a clause restricting British ships from entering the United States.

9. Both are in L'Air de Lamotte's hand, with WTF filling in the date and writing the phrase above his signature (elements we italicize). It is not known how many were prepared before BF was informed that they were not valid.

1. XXXVIII, 193–4.

2. Fitzherbert to Grantham, Jan. 25, 1783, in Giunta, *Emerging Nation*, I, 759–60.

When Fitzherbert returned to Paris, he informed Jay that Franklin was preparing passports in his own name as minister plenipotentiary. The two men agreed that the authority to issue the forms resided not with a minister to any particular court but rather with the commissioners authorized to negotiate peace. Jay immediately wrote to inform Adams. "Would it not be proper to apprize the Doctor of our Sentiments," he concluded, "before the passports he is now making out shall be delivered?"[3]

The following day, Adams summoned Franklin and Jay to a meeting at his house on February 3, at which passports would be discussed. Franklin obviously brought to that meeting the present document,[4] as Adams wrote a notation on the verso and kept it among his papers. It was probably Adams, also, who was responsible for editing the manuscript; Franklin's and Temple's signatures were crossed out, and certain phrases that were disputed that morning were underlined. Chief among them was the restriction on British trade with America. In this, Franklin was overruled by his colleagues.[5] The American commissioners' passport adopted on February 3 is published below under that date.

The British passport[6] reads as follows:

George the Third, by the Grace of God, King of Great Britain, France and Ireland, Defender of the Faith, Duke of Brunswick and Lunenburg, Arch-Treasurer and Prince Elector of the Holy Roman Empire, &ca. &c. &c.

To all our Admirals, Vice Admirals, Captains, Commanders of our Ships of War, or Privateers, Governors of our Forts and Castles, Customers, Comptrollers, Searchers, and to all and singular Our Officers, both Civil and Military, our Ministers and Subjects, whom it may concern, Greeting:

Our Will and Pleasure is, and We do hereby strictly charge and require

3. Morris, *Jay: Peace*, p. 493.
4. It is illustrated in *Adams Papers*, XIV, facing p. 226. JA's note is below, Feb. 2.
5. "Dr Franklin chicaned to the very last upon the business of the Passports," Fitzherbert reported, "and finally moved for the inserting in them this odious & ungracious Clause 'that they should not be considered as Protections for *any Ship bound to Ports in North America.*' This Motion was founded upon the Prohibitory Acts passed by Great Britain which he affects to consider as still in force, but he was overruled in it by his Colleagues without any Instance from me." Fitzherbert to Grantham, Feb. 9, 1783, in Giunta, *Emerging Nation*, I, 765.
6. Mass. Hist. Soc.

you (as We do likewise pray and desire the Officers and Ministers of all Princes and States in Amity with Us) to permit and suffer the American Ship called the [blank] to sail with her Lading, or in Ballast, from the Port of [blank] or any other Port of America, to [blank] and to return from thence to [blank] or any other Port of America, without any Lett, Hindrance, or Molestation whatsoever; Provided that the said Ship do not carry any Goods or Merchandizes which are prohibited or contraband, or import from America into this Realm, or any other of his Majesty's Dominions, or carry out from hence, any Goods prohibited by Law.

Given at our Court at St. James's the [blank] day of [blank] 1783, in the twenty-third Year of our Reign.

By his Majesty's Command,   GRANTHAM

[February 1, 1783]

To all Captains or Commanders of Ships of War or Privateers, belonging to the United States of America, or Citizens of the same. Greeting.

We the Underwritten, Minister Plenipotentiary from the Congress of the said States to the Court of France, do hereby in their Name, strictly charge and require of you, as we do likewise pray and desire the officers and Ministers of all Princes and Powers in Amity with the said States, to permit & suffer the Merchant Vessel called the [blank] commanded by [blank] belonging to Great Britain to sail from any of the Ports thereof to any Port or Place whatsoever, except those of the said States in North America, together with the marchandize wherewith she may be laden, without any Let, Hindrance or Molestation whatsoever, but on the contrary affording, the said Vessel, all such Aid and Assistance as may be necessary. Given at Paris, this *First* Day of *Feby* 1783.   B FRANKLIN

By Command of the Minister Plenipotentiary

W. T. FRANKLIN
secy

Notation:[7] Form of a Passport

7. In JA's hand.

From Martha Laurens AL: American Philosophical Society

Hotel d'Yorcke. [before February 2, 1783][8]
Miss Laurens presents her respectful Compliments to his Excellency Doctor Franklin, & will be much obliged to him if he has any Letters directed for her, to send them by the Bearer of this Billet—

Addressed: His Excellency Dr Franklin / Passy—

Notation: Miss Laurens.—

From John Adams[9]

AL: Library of Congress; copy: Massachusetts Historical Society

Paris 2 Feb. 1783
Mr Adams having Something of Consequence to communicate to the American Ministers Plenipotentiary, for the Peace, requests the Honour of His Excellency Dr Franklin's Attendance, with the other Ministers, at Mr Adams's Lodgings, at Eleven O Clock Tomorrow Morning. The Points to be considered, are 1. Passports to be given to and received from the British Minister, for British and American Vessells,[1] and 2d. Preparations for the

---

8. The day she left for London, after a brief stopover in Paris. Accompanied only by a maid, Martha Laurens was hastening from Le Vigan in southern France to England, in order to join her ailing father. Their first day's journey had been cut short by the loss of a carriage wheel; Samuel Vaughan, Jr., sent a replacement carriage the following morning: Samuel Vaughan, Jr., to WTF, Feb. 3, 1783 (APS). They arrived in London on Feb. 8: Joanna B. Gillespie, *The Life and Times of Martha Laurens Ramsay, 1759–1811* (Columbia, S.C., 2001), pp. 102–3; *Laurens Papers,* XVI, 145, 150.

While she was in Paris, Martha visited BF accompanied by Benjamin Vaughan. During the conversation BF recommended to Vaughan that Britain send a "plain, downright, honest man" as its new ambassador to the French court and expressed his belief that such characteristics were essential to an ambassador at any court. He suggested the appointment of the Duke of Richmond: Benjamin Vaughan to Shelburne, Jan. 28, 1783 (typescript, APS).

9. JA sent a similar letter to Jay (N.-Y. Hist. Soc.).

1. The language of these passports would be vigorously debated; see the headnote to BF's Passport for British Vessels, Feb. 1.

Signature of the definitive Treaty.[2] Both upon the Propositions of the British Minister Plenipotentiary.

Hotel du Roi. Feb. 2. 1783.

Addressed: A Son Excellence / Monsieur Franklin, / Ministre Plenipotentiaire / des Etats Unis de L'Amerique pour la Paix / en Son Hotel a Passy / Pres Paris

From Michel-Alain Chartier de Lotbinière[3]

ALS: American Philosophical Society

paris, Rue de Bourgogne En face du palais Bourbon
petit hôtel de Lordat,
Monsieur   Ce dimanche matin 2 fevrier 1783.

Vous Etes trop Certain de l'intèrêt que j'ai pris dez le principe a la Cause des Etats-unis de l'amérique, pour pouvoir douter de la joye Extrême que j'ai ressenti En apprenant que vous Etiez Enfin reconnus indépendans par Ceux même qui vouloient vous Jetter dans les fers. Mais En même tems Je ne puis Cacher a Votre Excellence ma peine de ne vous pas voir le Canada unis Comme quatorziéme province, Et il Se pourroit que sous bien peu d'an-

2. JA drafted a definitive treaty on Feb. 1, which contained only minor changes from the preliminary treaty. After the Feb. 3 meeting he noted on the verso that Jay and BF had approved it, but "Some Additions were proposed." *Adams Papers*, XIV, 227–30. One of those additions undoubtedly concerned trade, a topic BF had already broached with Fitzherbert on Jan. 24; see the headnote to BF's Passport for British Vessels, Feb. 1. For the next seven months the American peace commissioners would attempt in vain to overcome British resistance to amending the preliminary agreement of Nov. 30, 1782.

3. A Canadian-born engineer and landowner (V, 504–5n), who had not written BF, as far as we know, in more than four years. His last extant letter (XXVIII, 273–5) sought BF's help in recovering his former seigneuries at the head of Lake Champlain. Twice in 1782 he sent Vergennes memoirs urging that France regain Canada and warning of the dangers of a British-American reconciliation: *Dictionary of Canadian Biography* (15 vols. to date, Toronto, 1966–), IV, 144; Sylvette Nicolini, "Michel Chartier de Lotbinière: l'Action et la pensée d'un Canadien du 18e siècle" (Ph.D. diss., University of Montreal, 1978), pp. 166–8.

nées vos Etats Eussent beaucoup a se repentir de n'avoir pas tenu plus fermement sur Cet article. Comme En Ce moment il n'est plus question que de retarder le mal qui En doit résulter autant qu'il vous Est possible, C'est a bien fixer vos limites Entre vous Et vos voisins que vous pouvez trouver quelque ressource Contre tout Ce que j'envisage pour l'avenir. J'entend dire sourdement que le 41e degré de latitude septentrionale doit faire la ligne de démarcation Entre vous Et Eux. Il ne me paroit pas possible que vous y Consentiez a moins que ce ne soit audelà des limites fixées pour chacune des provinces de new-york et de pensylvaine qui S'Etendoient jusqu'au 45e. degré sur le *lac champlain* Et la *Riviere de Katarakoui* [Cataraqui],[4] Et de la bordoit (Si je ne me trompe) Cette Riviere, tout le lac *ontario,* Et une partie de Celui *d'Erié* auprès du portage de *Niagara;* autrement vous Consentiriez a Céder a Cette Couronne la partie la plus précieuse Et pour ainsi dire la plus peuplée de Vos Etats. D'ailleurs Vôtre Excellence sent trop de quelle Conséquence il Est a vos Etats de ne lui pas livrer la navigation Exclusive de toutes ces parties; Et la ligne desja tirée, En vous y tenant fixément Et formant des Etablissemens solides a ses bords, vous donne incontestablement la navigation Exclusive sur le lac Champlain, Et vous met dans le Cas de les gesner [gêner] au moins autant sur celle des grands lacs (ayant a vous la partie de Riviere intermédiaire) qu'ils le peuvent pour vous.— Un moment de conversation avec vous, Monsieur, ou Monsr. adams accompagné d'une bonne Carte de Ces parties, vous feroit sentir Mon idée beaucoup Mieux que je ne le puis dans une simple lettre. Mais a présent que le Canada est décidé rester à la grande Bretagne, Et que ma famille Et ses Biens y sont, pour ne la point Exposer a perdre immédiatement Et peut Etre a des accidens plus funestes Encore, Je me vois forcé de ne pouvoir Communiquer a découvert avec Vous Messieurs Car que ne peuvent-ils pas Surtout ce qui habite Ce pays, avec le Conseil legislatif qu'ils y ont Etablis?—[5] S'il Etoit donc possi-

4. The portion of the St. Lawrence River between Lake Ontario and Montreal. Lotbinière is describing the border actually adopted.

5. Lotbinière had fought unsuccessfully against the establishment of an appointive governor's council under the Quebec Act: Nicolini, "Lotbinière," pp. 94–112; M. Elizabeth Archer, "French-Canadian Participation in the

ble, ou a vous Monsieur, ou a Monsr. adams de vous porter jusqu'a ma demeure a heure Et jour Connu au moins Vingt quatre heures En avance, Je pourrois vous y Exposer toutes mes Craintes a vôtre sujet, Et le meilleur remede que j'y vois voulant prévenir pour un tems les accidens les plus grands.

J'ai Eu l'honneur a mon retour de l'Amérique, de remettre a Votre excellence les papiers pour mes seigneuries *d'hocquart* (en face de Crown-point &c.) Et *d'allainville* (qui Commence a une lieue de Crown-point et s'étend de Suite Jusqu'a l'Entrée du lac george, Comprenant ticonderoga)[6] qui sont a présent mon unique appui, ne m'etant plus permis sans le risque le plus Certain, après tout Ce que J'ai fais pour vos Etats, de me replacer sous l'autorité Britannique. J'espere que vous aurez, dans le tems, fait valoir mes droits incontestables auprès du Congrès, Et que vous voudrez bien le faire aujourd'hui plus que jamais; puisque ma proscription, Et peut-etre sous peu Celle de Ma famille Entiere, ne vient uniquement que du vif intèrêt, Et des mouvemens multipliés Et Constans Jusques dans ces derniers momens, que je me suis donné pour le Succés de Votre Cause.

J'ai l'honneur d'Etre avec l'attachement le plus réel, Et Beaucoup de Respect Monsieur de Votre Excellence le tres humble Et tres obeissant serviteur   LOTBINIERE

Notation: Lotbiniere 2 Fevr. 1783.

From Matthew Ridley   ALS: American Philosophical Society

Sir,   Paris February 2d: 1783.

I take the Liberty inclosing you a power of Attorney executed by me & to beg you will affix a Certificate there to with your Seal annexed— I should not have given your Excellency this Trou-

---

Government of Canada, 1775–1785," *Canadian Hist. Rev.*, XXXII (1951), 303–14.

6. Lotbinière visited the United States between November, 1776, and May, 1777: Nicolini, "Lotbinière," pp. 148–54. In a Dec. 24, 1778, letter he mentioned having given the papers to BF: XXVIII, 274.

ble had not some difficulties been made by the Notary here as to the Form—

I would not pretend to dictate to you the form of a Certificate but wish if agreeable to you that it might run something in the following State.

"I do hereby Certify that the Signature to the annexed Power of Attorney is the proper hand Writing of Matthew Ridley a Subject of the United States of America & that all due faith & Credit ought to be given thereunto &ca."

Any alterations or additions you may please to make will be perfectly agreeable to me— I have only to beg it may be returned by the Bearer as I am desirous of sending it away to night.[7]

Mrs. Ridley joins me in respects & wishes to be informed that you enjoy good health. I have the Honor to be Your Excellencys Most Obedt & hble Sert   MATT: RIDLEY

Notation: Matt. Ridley Feby. 2 1783.

From Vergennes   L: Library of Congress

Vlles. [Versailles] le 2 fevr. 1783
M le Cte. de Vergennes a l'honneur d'envoyer à Monsieur franklin deux exemplaires des articles preliminaires de paix convenus entre le Roi et le Roi de la Grande Bretagne.[8]

7. BF's response has not been found.
8. Signed on Jan. 20; see XXXVIII, 605n. Those preliminary articles had in fact been ratified by both governments, as Vergennes may have known; he and Fitzherbert exchanged ratified treaties the following day, Feb. 3: *Courrier de l'Europe*, XIII (1783), 91, issue of Feb. 11.

The American Peace Commissioners: Passport for British Ships[9]

Copies:[1] Massachusetts Historical Society (three), Library of Congress

[February 3, 1783]

We John Adams, Benjamin Franklin and John Jay, three of the Ministers Plenipotentiary of the United States of America for making Peace with Great Britain.

To all Captains or Commanders of Ships of War, Privateers or armed Vessels belonging to the said States, or to either of them, or to any of the Citizens of the same, And to all others whom these Presents may concern send Greeting.

Whereas Peace and Amity are agreed upon between the said United States and his Britannic Majesty, & a Suspension of Hostilities to take place at different Periods in different Places hath also been agreed upon by their respective Plenipotentiaries. And Whereas it hath been further agreed by the said Plenipotentiaries, to exchange one hundred[2] Passports for Merchant Ves-

9. For background see the headnote to BF's Passport for British Ships, Feb. 1. The language of this passport, which superseded BF's, was debated at the meeting JA called for eleven o'clock on Feb. 3. At two o'clock that afternoon JA sent a note to Fitzherbert informing him that the American peace commissioners "have determined to exchange an hundred Passports, which are now printing and will be ready for Signature Tomorrow." *Adams Papers*, XIV, 231. Fitzherbert sent them to England on Feb. 9 along with the French and Spanish passports; they arrived on Feb. 13: Morris, *Jay: Peace*, pp. 492, 493n; Fortescue, *Correspondence of George Third*, VI, 238.

These first hundred passports were soon distributed, causing the American commissioners to order a second hundred printed. In the second printing, they deleted the phrase "one hundred," as noted below. Once they discovered that British merchants were being charged for the forms, they had a third set printed with the word "GRATIS" added; see Hodgson to BF, Feb. 25, and BF to Hodgson, March 9, where the third printing is shown as an illustration.

1. The one we publish is a freestanding copy in the hand of JA's secretary, John Thaxter, Jr. The other copies listed are from the commissioners' letterbooks.

2. In a letterbook copy by John Thaxter, Jr., he added a note explaining that, after the first hundred passports were sent, "one hundred more were added of the same Form, except the Omission of the Words 'one hundred'— In the second hundred, it is, 'to exchange Passports,' instead of 'one hundred'". Mass. Hist. Soc.

sels. To the End that such as shall be provided with them shall be exempted from Capture, altho' found in Latitudes at a time prior to the taking place of the said Suspension of Hostilities therein.

Now Therefore Know Ye, that free Passport, Licence and Permission is hereby given to the [*blank*] Commander now lying at the Port of [*blank*] and bound from thence to [*blank*]

And we do earnestly enjoin upon and recommend to You to let and suffer the said Vessel to pass unmolested to her destined Port, and if need be, to afford her all such Succour and Aid as Circumstances and Humanity may require.

Given under our Hands and Seals at Paris on the [*blank*] day of [*blank*] in the Year of our Lord 1783.

Passport to Ships given by the Commisios. for making Peace

Copy

From John Adams

AL: Library of Congress; copy:[3] Massachusetts Historical Society

Monday Evg. Feb. 3. 1783.[4]

Mr Adams has the Honour to inform Dr Franklin that the American Ministers for the Peace, are desired by the British Minister to meet him at the Hotel du Parc Royal, Wednesday, at Eleven, for a Conference concerning the Definitive Treaty.

Addressed: A Son Excellence / Monsieur Franklin / Ministre Plenipotentiaire / des Etats Unis de L'Amerique, pour / la Paix / en son Hotel a Pasy / Pres Paris.

3. In JA's hand, with a note that he sent a similar letter to Jay.
4. In the note JA wrote to Fitzherbert at two o'clock that afternoon (see the annotation of the preceding document), he added that the American peace commissioners were "ready to enter into Conferences concerning the Preparations for the definitive Treaty of Peace," and requested Fitzherbert to appoint the time and place.

From Richard Bache ALS: American Philosophical Society

Dear & Hond: Sir   Philadelphia Febry 3d, 1783
    Permit me to introduce to your Acquaintance & Civilities, Mr. Petitt, Son of my Friend Mr Charles Petitt of this place;[5] I believe him to be a young Gentleman of merit, and as such beg leave to recommend him to your Notice & Esteem— Sally & the Children are well, I am ever Dear Sir Yours affectionately
                                                      RICH BACHE
Dr. Franklin

Addressed: His Excellency / Dr. Franklin / at / Passy / Favored by Mr. Pettit

From Fizeaux, Grand & Cie. LS: American Philosophical Society

Monsieur   Amsterdam le 3 de fevrier 1783.
    Conformément á la lettre que vous nous avéz fait l'honneur de nous écrire le 23 du mois dernier,[6] nous avons acquité la traitte de M. Morris Sur nous de L2458.10. & Suivant vos ordres nous nous en remboursons par la nôtre Sur vous Monsieur de 820 écus, á 20 jours de date, á nôtre ordre.[7]
    Nous en créditons le Compte des Etats unis au che. [change] de 54 5/16[8] en B f. 1113.8.— Veuillés l'accepter.
    Nous avons l'honneur d'être avec un Respectueux dévouement, Monsieur, Vos trés humbles trés obeissans Serviteurs
                                          FIZEAUX GRAND COMP
S. E. Monsieur Franklin, à Passi.

Notation: Fizeaux Grand & Co. Amsterdam 3 Fevrier 1783

5. Andrew Pettit had been introduced by his father on Jan. 29, above.
    6. Not found.
    7. For Morris' explanation of this circuitous arrangement see XXXVII, 164, and for previous examples of his drafts on Fizeaux, Grand & Cie. see *Morris Papers*, VI, 165, 473–4. On March 5 Ferdinand Grand paid the firm 2,460 *l.t.*: Account XXVII (XXXII, 4). An *écu* equalled 3 *l.t.*
    8. The firm is giving the current exchange rate between *grooten* and *écus*, which then is converted to *florins;* see XXXVII, 442–3n.

From ———— Loyseau   ALS: American Philosophical Society

Monsieur   Le 3 fevrier 1783.

La Revolution de L'amerique etant heureusement achevée, il est permis de penser aux objets du commerce qu'il est dorenavant possible de faire avec elle. Je m'interesse Beaucoup a une Manufacture d'acier etablie a 20 lieues de paris, elle opére par cementation pour parvenir a La conversion du fer de Suede en acier. Elle veut S'ouvrir un débouché en amerique, elle peut quant a present en fournir plus de 300 milliers. Les interessés a cette manufacture dans le nombre desquels je Suis, desirent Savoir S'ils trouveroient a vendre cet acier en L'envoyant en amerique et comment on Le leur payeroit; ils prendroient, a defaut d'argent des objets d'echange en amerique, mais qu'ils pussent esperer de vendre ici avec quelqu'avantage. Voulés vous, Monsieur, me fournir quelques Renseignemens Sur ce point de vue. L'on pourroit faire une fourniture chaqu'année de 3, 4 5 ou Six cent Milliers et meme davantage. La Maniere de traiter Sera aussi Loyale qu'on pourra le desirer.

Je Suis avec Respect Monsieur votre tres humble et tres obeissant Serviteur   LOYSEAU

                    avocat au parlement Rue Ste. anne

L'acier est aussi bon que celui d'angletere.[9]

9. Incredulous that he had received no reply, Loyseau wrote again on Feb. 11, specifying that the steelworks in question was the one at Néronville, and expressing his fear that BF resented him for having written on behalf of Benyowzky (XXXVIII, 10). The Néronville factory was one of two established by Pierre-Clément Grignon (*DBF*), who conducted some trials with government support. Despite Loyseau's claims, French steel was still inferior to British. See Denis Woronoff, *L'Industrie sidérurgique en France pendant la Révolution et l'Empire* (Paris, 1984), pp. 351–3; [Pierre-Clément] Grignon, "Mémoire . . . des expériences faites en 1780 par ordre du Gouvernement, dans les Forges du Comte de Buffon en Burgogne, & dans la Manufacture Royale d'Acier fin de Néronville . . . ," *Jour. de Physique*, XX (1782), 184–216; Hubert and Georges Bourgin, *L'Industrie sidérurgique en France au début de la Révolution* (Paris, 1920), p. 431; J. R. Harris, "Attempts to Transfer English Steel Techniques to France in the Eighteenth Century," in *Business and Businessmen: Studies in Business, Economic and Accounting History*, ed. Sheila Marriner (Liverpool, 1978), p. 210. As for Benyowzky, he returned to France on April 14, 1783: Christian Gut *et al.*, eds., *Inventaire des archives coloniales: sous-séries C^{5A} et C^{5B}* (Paris, 1970), p. 103.

131

Notation: Loyseau 3 Fevr. 1783.

From David Hartley   ALS: American Philosophical Society

My Dear friend   London feb 4 1783

As I enclose this in the same cover as one from my Brother, his letter anticipates every thing that I have to say to you at present.[1] I beg leave to join in the recommendation to you of Mr Joshua Grigby who with the Spirit of Youth & activity wishes to see the new world.[2] I hope the future intercommunication between this Country and America will obliterate temporary animosities & restore the antient harmony & connexion. I heartily rejoice to see & hear of the public tokens of an approaching pacification. Whenever I shall see the general proclamation for a suspension of hostilities between all the belligerent parties my heart will be at rest. We are encouraged to expect such a proclamation in this Country very speedily. Every future view of my life upon this subject will be to cultivate conciliatory principles between our two Countries, in the reciprocity of common interests & common affections. Believe me to be a friend to the rights of Mankind and of all those who are friends to them; & therefore ever Most sincerely and most affectionately Yours   G B

To Dr. Franklin &c &c &c

1. The letter from Winchcombe Henry Hartley has not been located. He made copies of his half-brother's letters and papers for BF in the spring of 1782: XXXVI, 624n; XXXVII, 410–11.

2. Joshua Grigby, Jr., the eldest son of the future M.P. Joshua Grigby (*c.* 1731–1798) and his wife, Jane Bird, had served four years in the English militia and now wished to settle in one of the mid-Atlantic states: Namier and Brooke, *House of Commons,* II, 556; Benjamin Vaughan to JA, Feb. 25, 1783 (Mass Hist. Soc.). See also Vaughan to BF, Feb. 25.

From the Comtesse d'Houdetot

L:[3] American Philosophical Society

Mardy 4. fevrier 1783.

Madame La Comtesse D'houdetot Se Conformera aux intentions De Monsieur franklin avec Le Regret De le Voir huit jours plus tard. Elle Espere qu'il n'a point oublié qu'il Luy a promis De Luy faire L'honneur de Venir Entendre De la Musique Chez Elle De jeudy prochain En huit treize de Ce Mois.[4] Elle aura Soin De prevenir Mr. De St. Lambert[5] pour Le Mercredy douze; Elle prie Monsieur franklin De Vouloir Bien agreer Ses plus tendres Complimens.

Notation: La Ctesse. d'Houdetot

From ———— Brossière
ALS: American Philosophical Society

Monsieur   L'orient le 5. fevrier 1783.

Mille pardons si Je prens la liberté de vous détourner un instant de vos immenses occupations; mais la Circonstance dans laquelle Je me trouve, demande un éclaircissement qu'on m'a assuré que vous pouviés me donner. Voici le fait.

Une certaine Demoiselle, nommée Desbois, originaire de cette Province, est venû demeurer dans cette Ville; elle y est entré, y vit Et n'est connuë que Sous le nom de Madame Loch.[6] Ce Monsieur Loch qu'on dit né à Block-island dans l'amerique Septentrionnale, fut pris en 1780. Conduit, comme prisonnier de guerre, dans la Ville de Dinan, Et ayant manqué à sa parole

---

3. In the hand of Girard: XXXVI, 583n.

4. The comtesse held these musical evenings from 8:00 to 10:00 P.M. every other Thursday: XXXVIII, 594.

5. Her *ami intime:* XXXV, 350n.

6. When last BF heard about John Locke and Mlle Desbois, in 1779, they were seeking his help in getting Locke released from prison so that they could marry. BF embraced their cause until he learned that Locke already had a wife: XXXI, 170–1, 180–1, 244–5, 266. Now, it seems, Mlle Desbois ("Mme Loch"), who had been living with him for years, wanted to marry another. We have found no trace of a response from BF, and, as far as we know, the couple does not reappear in his papers.

d'honneur, fut mis au Chateau de Nantes: ayant eu Son échange, il partit pour l'angleterre, la dlle. Desbois, dont il avoit fait la Connoissance pendant qu'il étoit à Dinan, le suivit à Londres Et elle y a demeuré près de deux années. Revenuë en france Sous le nom de Madame Loch, il est à présumer qu'elle S'est mariée en angleterre avec ce monsieur. Il Se presente aujourd'hui un établissement, elle veut l'accepter. Dans les renseignemens que j'ai pû prendre Sur sa qualité de femme, elle m'assure qu'elle ne l'est point Et que, quoiqu'elle porte le nom de M. Loch, elle n'est point mariée avec lui, Et que ledit Sieur Loch est lui même depuis long tems marié Et qu'il a Sa femme Et un enfant à Nantuchest. Je lui en ai demandé la preuve; elle n'a pû me la fournir; mais elle m'a dit que je pouvois m'adresser à vous, Monsieur, Et que vous me donneriés un certificat qui constateroit le vrai mariage du sr. Loch, Et l'existence actuelle de sa femme. Si le récit de cette personne est vrai, Et que vous daigniés, Monsieur, me certifier que ledit Sieur Loch etoit marié avant d'etre fait prisonnier de guerre environ 1780, Et que Sa même femme éxiste encore, tout est fini, les difficultés Sont levées Et rien ne m'empêcheroit de procéder au mariage qu'elle desire contracter dans cette Ville. Je vous Supplie donc Monsieur, de vouloir bien me dire ce que vous en pensés; votre Sentiment fera la regle de ma conduite.

J'ai l'honneur d'etre avec un respect infini Monsieur Votre très humble Et très obeissant serviteur

BROSSIERE
Recteur de l'Eglise Royale de L'orient

Notation: Brossiere 5. Fevr. 1783.

From ―――― Campo-de-Arbe[7]

ALS: American Philosophical Society

Monsieur   paris 5 fevrier 1783

Le temoignage que je me rends au fond de mon Cœur, de n'avoir aucun reproche a me faire pandant le tems que j'ai eü L'honneur de vous appartenir, tant a l'egard de la probité, que de

---

7. BF's maître d'hôtel from the spring of 1781 until June, 1782: XXXIV, 503; XXXV, 4; XXXVII, 3, 502–3, 503–4.

mon zéle a chercher en tout, les occasions de vous plaire, et de vous Servir utilement; me fait esperér, Monsieur, que vous voudrés bien m'honorer de vôtre protection pres des personnes de votre connaissance, et me permétre de vous Saluer;

Je prie M. de lamotte de vouloir bien me faire connaitre vos intentions, et dans tous les cas, quelque chose que vous determiniez pour moi, je me rendrois promptement a vos ordres.

J'ai lhonneur d'etre avec un profond respet Monsieur votre tres humble et tres obeisant Serviteur   CAMPO-DE-ARBE

Endorsed: Campo d'Arbe

From Alleyne Fitzherbert

AL: Library of Congress

Paris Wednesday afternoon. [February 5, 1783?][8]
Mr. Fitz-Herbert presents his Compliments to Dr Franklin and many Thanks for the passports.— He purposes sending away a Messenger to England tomorrow about noon and will be happy to charge him with any letters or packets which Dr Franklin may have to send.

From Matthew Ridley

AL: American Philosophical Society

Rue de Clery Wednesday Morning [February 5, 1783][9]
Mr. Ridley presents his Respects to His Excellency Dr. Franklin & informs him that he is going for Nantes today & will take

8. If Fitzherbert is referring to the first set of American passports for British ships, then this date is likely. See the annotation of that passport, [Feb. 3], and JA to BF of the same date.
9. The day Ridley told Thomas Barclay that he planned to leave for Nantes: Ridley to Barclay, Feb. 4, 1783 (Mass. Hist. Soc.). At the end of the present letter Ridley alludes to BF's dinner invitation for the following Monday. BF did entertain on Monday, Feb. 10. Anne Ridley attended that dinner, though her husband, delayed in Nantes while waiting for Barclay to arrive, was unable to accompany her. Ridley and Barclay returned to Paris together around Feb. 18: Anne Ridley to Matthew Ridley, Feb. 13, 1783; Ridley to French & Nephew, Feb. 19, 1783 (both at the Mass. Hist. Soc.). Our thanks to Priscilla Roberts for providing us with information from all three letters.

charge of anything for Mr Williams or others that his Excellency will have to send. Mr Ridley does not know that a pass is necessary but will be thanful for one in case it should be asked for.

Mr. Ridley will with Mr Hunt[1] have the honor of waiting on His Excellency at dinner on Monday next.

Addressed: His Excellency / B Franklin Esqr. / Passy

From George Walker

ALS: American Philosophical Society

Dear Sir,   Calais 5th February 1783.

I did myself the honour of writing to you in the beginning of December to request your advice and assistance.[2] Mr. Laurens, whom I saw on his return from Paris, told me I was not to wonder at your silence, for that your time was so taken up with matters of State, that your private friends must excuse you, nor impute to a seeming inattention to them, what arose solely from a multiplicity of publick business. I can easily conceive such a situation, and should therefore have been unwilling to have repeated the same trouble so soon, if Mr. Laurens had not recommended it to me to apply to you again.

Since my first application, the suspense, whether peace or war, is decided, and peace is to take place. Allow me to congratulate you on the happy issue of your negotiation: it will be the task of the historian to record your praise; it is the part of the humble friend to admire and be silent.

Mr. Oswald passed thorough this place on his return.[3] Entire strangers as we were to each other, I could not resist an impulse I felt to introduce myself to him. I wished to know what was intended to be done by England for the planters of Barbadoes, whose ruin begun by the late ministry, had been compleated by

1. John Hunt, a cousin of Ridley's wife, Anne, had obtained a passport from BF to return to England at the beginning of 1782. He was back in Paris by mid-December: XXVIII, 248; XXXVI, 378; Matthew Ridley's Journal, entries of Dec. 7 and 13, 1782 (Mass. Hist. Soc.).
2. XXXVIII, 396–7.
3. Oswald left Paris for London on Jan. 15: XXXVIII, 584n.

the hurricane. Mr. Oswald was very civil, blamed where I blamed, and entered into a good deal of conversation with me: but I found no redress of a publick nature was thought of, not even an act of insolvency upon liberal principles. However he had no doubt of success in an application to my creditors for liberty and a moderate allowance. I had already vested all my property in trustees for those purposes. He even offered to undertake the necessary solicitations himself. It was an offer not to be declined, although all former efforts of the sort have been ineffectual: neither have I much hopes from this new attempt. Indeed my favourite wish is to be put into some decent way of earning a livelihood; you know me and can judge wherein I may be useful to myself or others.

I remain, Dear Sir, Your most obedient humble servant

GEORGE WALKER.

From William Carmichael   ALS: Library of Congress

Dear Sir   Madrid 6th Feby. 1783

Altho Mr Jays acquaintance with Mr Gardoqui, who will have the honor to deliver this to your Excy. Might excuse me from taking the present Liberty, yet I cannot refuse this Gentlemans request to be the bearer of a Line from myself to your Excy;[4] His friendly conduct to me intitles him to every mark of Consideration in my power to shew him & I hope to the many proofs of regard which You have had the goodness to manifest in my favor you will add of convincing Mr Gardoqui that you still interest yourself in what Concerns one who has the honor to be With

---

4. James Gardoqui (Diego María de Gardoqui y Arriquibar), formerly the liaison between Jay and Spanish Chief Minister Floridablanca, was accompanying to London the new minister plenipotentiary, Bernardo del Campo, who left Madrid on Feb. 6. Gardoqui became interim Spanish consul general in June and titular consul general in January, 1784: Didier Ozanam, ed., *Les Diplomates espagnoles du XVIIIe siècle: Introduction et répertoire biographique (1700–1808)* (Madrid and Bordeaux, 1998), pp. 205, 270.

the greatest Respect & Affection Your Excys Obliged & Humble Sert[5]   WM. CARMICHAEL

His Excy Benjamin Franklin

From Mademoiselle ———— Defay

ALS: American Philosophical Society

Monsieur   Paris 6 fevrie 1783
    Cest Avec tout le Respect La Reconnoissance que je doit a vos Bontees que je vous prie de Recevoir Mon Compliment Sur Lanonce de la paix que vous procuree aux puissances interessee.
    Je joint icy une nouvelles Supliques de Mr Gastellier[6] Sur la quelle je vous Suplie de Vouloir bien a Cordée La grace quil demande.
    Si je nestoit pas incomodee jauroit eü lhonneur de vous la presenter.
    Jay Lhonneur dEstre Avec Respect Monsieur Votre tres heumble Et tres obeissantte Servantte   DEFAY

Mlle defay Rue beauregard ou Mr Gastellier a Montargis

Notation: De Fay 6. Fevr. 1783.

From Frédéric-Samuel Ostervald

ALS: American Philosophical Society

Monsieur,   Neuchâtel en Suisse le 6. fevrier 1783.
    Puisje me flatter que Votre Excellence Se rappellera encore, l'hommage respectueux, qu'eut l'honneur de lui rendre, il y a pres de deux ans un homme de Lettres, directeur de la Société

---

5. Carmichael also recommended Gardoqui to WTF, in a letter of Feb. 7; WTF noted that he received it on April 7. Carmichael had written to WTF on Feb. 4, as well, thanking him for sending news of the peace settlement. Both letters are at the APS.
    6. René-Georges Gastellier's letter of Jan. 19: XXXVIII, 599–600.

Typographique de neuchâtel en suisse, en sollicitant humblement Sa puissante protection, dans la vue de faire connoitre cet
établissement, chès les Etats unis de l'amerique Septentrionale?[7]
Je pris alors la liberté de Lui présenter le plan génèral qui dirige
notre travail en ce genre. Elle daigna me donner quelques espérances de pouvoir le rendre utile aux peuples dont les plus précieux interrests lui ont été confiés à si juste titre, lors que la paix
leur auroit rendû la tranquilité, fruit nécessaire de leurs soins
généreux. J'ose donc Saisir aujourdhui cette heureuse èpoque,
pour lui rappeler ces faits interressants avec une legére esquisse
de ce même établissement.

Votre Excellence sait que tous les premiers typographes
étoient gens de Lettres, & il eut été sans doute à Souhaiter que
l'exercice de ce bel art ne fut jamais Sorti de leurs mains. Nous
avons entrepris, mes associés & moi, de fonder & de diriger une
imprimerie considérable, pour l'utilité de ceux qui font le commerce de livres en nous attachant à ne produire que des éditions
propres & correctes & en leur cédant à des prix très modiques,
& même ordinairement à un sol argent de france la fueille tous
frais compris, les fruits de nos travaux, ensorte qu'il est de l'in-
terrest de tous les Libraires de tirer de nous, comme de la premiere main. Mais nous ne nous bornons pas à la simple exècu-
tion typographique, nous cherchons de plus à augmenter de
quelque mérite les ouvrages qui occuppent nos presses, lors que
l'occasion s'en présente. Nous savons que Votre Excellence a
bien voulû acquérir un Exemplaire de nos Descriptions des Arts
4o. lequel lui a été fourni par Mr. l'abbé Morrelet qui nous honnore de ses bontés[8] & Elle aura pû juger par cette production, de
la maniere dont nous travaillons. C'est même dans le dessein de
lui en donner une idée plus complette que je prends la liberté
de lui en prèsenter ici le Tableau géneral, qui fera connoitre en

7. Ostervald and his partner Abraham Bosset Deluze called on BF in the
spring of 1780: XXXII, 300, 328–9.

8. BF's subscription to this quarto edition of *Descriptions des arts et métiers*
came through Morellet. It was not only cheaper than the original being published by the Académie des sciences; it included additional material by other
scholars: Medlin, *Morellet*, 1, 296n, 419, 477–9; Arthur H. Cole and George
B. Watts, *The Handicrafts of France as recorded in the* Descriptions des Arts
et Métiers, *1761–1788* (Boston, 1952), pp. 18–19, 36–7.

même temps à quel point se trouve aujourdhui poussèe de notre part cette utile entreprise, si propre à rèpandre les connoissances les plus interressantes, chès les peuples de l'Amérique unie.[9]

Je ne dois point omettre un avantage qui nous est acquis dans le lieu de notre domicile & dont Vôtre Excellence connoit le prix mieux que personne. C'est une honnête & raisonnable libertè de la presse, qui sans jamais dègènérer en licence, nous permet de publier bien des ouvrages qui quoi que n'offensant rien de tout ce qui doit étre respectè ne pourroient pas s'imprimer dans le royaume de France.[1] Nous avons enfin, toutes les facilitès nécessaires pour le transport de nos marchandises & notre correspondance s'etend aujourdhui à tous les principaux pays de l'Europe.

Je prends donc la libertè de Supplier, Votre Excellence de vouloir me faire èprouver aujourdhui ses bontès en daignant prendre ma Typographie Sous ses auspices, en la faisant connoitre aux Libraires des principales villes de l'Amérique unie & les engageant à m'accorder leur confiance.[2] L'usage de la langue Françoise ne pourra que s'ètendre de plus en plus dans ces heureuses contrèes, à qui nous fournirons avec plaisir & à un prix bien infèrieur, tout ce que la Littèrature Nationale produira de mieux, & jaurai l'honneur de présenter à Votre Excellence, si

9. Ostervald enclosed a four-page "Tableau de la nouvelle édition augmentée des Descriptions des arts & métiers . . . ," a table of contents of the 20 projected volumes that listed the additions exclusive to the Sociéte typographique de Neuchâtel edition.

1. In addition to Enlightenment works like the *Descriptions* and d'Holbach's *Système de la nature,* the STN's book list included "livres philosophiques" of a licentious nature, a Protestant Bible, novels, plays, travel books, and works of jurisprudence: Robert Darnton, "Le livre prohibé aux frontières: Neuchâtel," in *Histoire de l'édition française,* ed. Henri-Jean Martin and Roger Chartier (4 vols., [Paris], 1982–86), II, 343–5.

2. In January Ostervald had written to Morellet asking him to discuss with BF his desire to supply American booksellers. Morellet replied on Jan. 25 that few in America would want books in French and that English-language books printed in London would be far less expensive. Moreover, BF was at the moment "bien occupé." Morellet wrote again on March 27, promising to remind BF to answer Ostervald. On May 31 the abbé excused BF's silence by explaining that the American minister was "fort occupé" with negotiating the definitive treaty with England as well as commercial treaties: Medlin, *Morellet,* I, 470–1, 476–9, 488–9.

Elle me le permet, le catalogue de tous les livres que nous sommes à même de céder actuellement.

Tels Sont les dètails dans lesquels l'accueil flatteur dont il a plût à Votre Excellence de me favoriser, sembloit m'inviter d'entrer, mais que la discretion me deffend de prolonger. Je ne pourrai cependant point finir sans lui offrir mon très humble compliment Sur l'heureux Sucès qui vient de couronner ses travaux patriotiques en lui assurant & comme philosophe & comme nègotiateur, un double titre à l'immortalité.

J'ai l'honneur d'être avec un tres profond respect Monsieur De Votre Excellence Le très humble & trèz obéissant serviteur

LE BANNERET[3] D'OSTERVALD

Notation: Le Banneret Portewalez 6 Janvr. 1783.

From Vergennes   LS: American Philosophical Society

Versailles le 6. fevrier 1783.

Daprès la Lettre que vous m'avez fait l'honneur de m'écrire, Monsieur, le 25. Janvier dernier, j'ai pris définitivement les ordres du Roi touchant le nouveau prêt d'argent que le Congrès des Etats-Unis de l'Amérique Septentrionale, Sollicite des bontés de Sa Majesté; Elle a bien voulu le fixer à *Six millions* de livres payables dans le Cours de la présente année; J'ai fait dresser en conséquence le projet d'articles d'un nouveau Contrat à passer pour cet objet, à l'instar de celui que nous Signâmes le 16. Juillet de l'année derniere pour les précédentes avances fournies par Sa Majesté au Congrès;[4] J'ai l'honneur de vous envoyer ci-joint les articles projettés;[5] Par le premier le Roi veut bien prêter au Congrès *Six millions* de livres, payables à raison de Cinq cent mille livres par chacun des douze mois de la présente année, à charge

---

3. A member of the city council. Ostervald had been forced to give up his position in the outcry that followed the publication of d'Holbach's *Système de la nature* in 1771; he was reinstated in 1782: *Dictionnaire historique de la Suisse.*

4. XXXVII, 633–9.

5. The draft articles have not been found. The contract is below, Feb. 25.

de remboursement de cette avance au Trésor Royal à Paris, avec les intérêts à Cinq pour cent par an.

L'article 2e. récapitule les precédens Secours fournis par Sa Majesté au Congrès, et les divise Selon leurs differentes Classes.

Le 3e. fixe les termes de remboursement des *Six millions* au Trésor Royal.

Vous verrez, Monsieur, que le premier terme est combiné sur la derniere époque de remboursement de l'emprunt de hollande, Stipulé par la Convention du 16. Juillet 1782.[6]

Par l'article 4e. le Roi veut bien faire don et remise au Congrès, des intérêts partiels du Capital à payer, et fixe le terme où les intérêts subséquents commenceront à courir.

Les articles 5e. et 6e. ne contiennent que les Stipulations d'usage.

Je vous prie, Monsieur, d'examiner ce projet et de me communiquer les observations que vous pouvez avoir à y faire, afin de mettre ensuite le Contrat Sous la forme qu'il éxige et que vous connoissez déja par celui de l'année derniere.

J'ai l'honneur d'être très parfaitement, Monsieur, votre très humble et très obéissant Serviteur. DE VERGENNES

M. franklin.

From Jean-Guillaume Backhaus,[7] with Franklin's Note for a Reply

ALS: American Philosophical Society

Monseigneur, à Hannovre ce 7. fevr. 1783.

J'ai l'honneur de feliciter VÔTRE EXCELLENCE de la paix glorieuse, qui vient être conclue, & dont l'histoire èternisera VÔTRE nom très réspectable & Vos insignes merites.

A Son rétour me vinrent quelques considerations en égard de

6. The third article of the Feb. 25 contract specifies that repayment would begin in 1797, the year after the scheduled conclusion of the repayment of the Dutch loan guaranteed by France (XXXVII, 638).

7. Who had written on Jan. 20 to request a consulship at Hamburg: XXXVIII, 316–17. As with that letter, this letter was sent by way of Genet: Backhaus to BF, March 8, 1783 (Hist. Soc. of Pa.).

l'Armée des Etats Souvrains de l'Amerique Septentrionale, les quelles mon Zêle m'inspira, & ma confiance réspectueuse aux gracieux faveurs de VÔTRE EXCELLENCE m'engage d'exposer ici très humblement. Elle est formée d'indigênes que le patriotisme a armé & qui Sont rappellés par la paix à leurs occupations ordinaires lesquelles ils ne Sauroient abandonner Sans faire une perte notable à leurs compatriotes.

Mais puisqu'il Sera necessaire d'entretenir un Corps d'armée, il paroit profitable d'y faire entrer des Etrangers, qui remplaceröient autant d'indigênes augmenteröient l'industrie, & dont la posterité—Si l'on ne les empeche pas de Se marier, ce qui les oblige à une plus grande fidelité & au Soin de leur famille profitable au public—fourniroit nombre de natifs.

Les Trouppes allemandes, qui ont Servi contre Les Etats Souvrains durant la guerre passée, Sont accoutumées au Climat & à la nourriture, habillées, armées & exercées. Le Prince Marggrave d'Anspac en a fait Transporter pour payer des Subsides les dêttes de feu son pere,[8] qui en a chargé Son païs par des depenses enormes pour la fauconnerie des housards. Il ne Se consolera de voir cesser Ses Subsides avant de S'étre entierement dechargé de ces dêttes, que par l'idée que la paix y ait mise Ses trouppes hors de fonction.

A leur rétour il ne lui reste qu'à les reformer & a garder leurs armes au l'arsenal, jusqu'a ce qu'après Sa mort S. M. Prussienne[9] trouve bon de les en rétirer.

Le Prince de Waldec, dont la revenue principale font les Eaux de Pyrmont, Se trouve dans le même cas, & je crois d'y pouvoir ajouter celui d'Anhalt Zerbst.[1] Ils ne Seront pas éloignés de vendre leurs régiments, lesquels il leur faudroit réformer à leur rétour, Sans aucun dédomagement, ce qui plongéroit bien de gens, dont leurs païs abondent, dans la misêre.

8. Karl Wilhelm Friedrich, margrave of Anspach, was the father of Christian Friedrich Carl Alexander, margrave of Anspach-Bayreuth (XXXVI, 493n): Walther Killy, ed., *Deutsche Biographische Enzyklopädie* (12 vols., Munich, 1995–2000).

9. Frederick II, King of Prussia.

1. Frederick Augustus, Prince of Anhalt-Zerbst, and Frederick, Prince of Waldeck: Edward J. Lowell, *The Hessians and the Other German Auxiliaries of Great Britain in the Revolutionary War* (New York, 1884), pp. 3, 15, 300.

Ayant de mes amis aux conseils des Princes d'Anspac & de Waldec, j'offre mes très humbles Services pour entamer cette negociation, qui n'est pas Sans exemple, vû que la cour d'Hannovre a acheté l'an 1760 un Regiment d'Infanterie du Duc de Saxe Gotha,[2] qui garde Son nom. L'avantage qui en Suivra, est, que l'on Sauroit établir une levée perpetuelle de récrues pour ces regiments allemands dans les Cercles de la Franconie, de la Suabe & du Rhin, & veritablement à les augmentér Successivement de plusieurs bataillons.

Il n'y a païs au monde qui Soit Si facile à cette permission & je me charge avec mille plaisirs du plan & de l'arrangement de Son execution, ayant la parfaite connoissance de ces cercles.[3] Mon depart d'ici Se tardant jusqu'aux Paques, j'abandonne très humblement à VôTRE EXCELLENCE de SE Servir de l'addresse, que j'ai donné l'autrefois à Hambourg,[4] ou de me faire écrire directement ici, si ELLE me fait la grace d'une reponse.

C'est avec le plus profond respect que j'ai l'honneur d'être MONSEIGNEUR DE VôTRE EXCELLENCE le très humble & très Soumis Serviteur   JEAN GUILLAUME BACKHAUS
Docteur en Droits

Endorsed: That It is probable that the United States will not keep up a Standing Army, having every where a well disciplin'd Militia. That many of the Germans have already deserted the English Colours & settled in the Country,[5] and it is probable most of them will do the same rather than return to Europe. That I am not authoriz'd to set on foot any such Negociations. Am how-

2. Friedrich III, Duke of Saxe-Gotha-Altenburg (1699–1772). He signed a subsidy treaty on Nov. 17, 1756: Killy and Vierhaus, eds., *Dictionary of German Biography*, II, 479; Carl W. Eldon, *England's Subsidy Policy Towards the Continent During the Seven Years' War* (Philadelphia, 1938), pp. 83, 105.

3. As a former representative of the duchy of Holstein: XXXVIII, 316.

4. Care of Lagau, the French vice-consul in Hamburg: Backhaus to BF, Jan. 20, 1783 (APS). In the *Almanach royal* for 1783 Lagau is listed as vice-consul in nearby Rostock (p. 263).

5. Of about 30,000 German mercenaries who fought in America, approximately 5,000 deserted and more than 17,000 returned to Europe: Lowell, *The Hessians and the Other German Auxiliaries*, p. 300.

In 1776 BF had devised a strategy to entice German troops in the vicinity of Philadelphia to desert: XXII, 578–9.

ever oblig'd to him for his good Will to our Service, & request he would accept my Thanks.[6]

From Christoph Diedrich Arnold Delius[7]

ALS: American Philosophical Society

Sir!   Bremen the 7 feber 1783

I am established in this City near 20 Years and carry on Business for my own proper Account particularly in the Linnen Trade & other Manufactories & Merchandizes for Exportation, especially the produces of the Dominions of HIS MAJESTY THE KING OF PRUSSIA and with some tolerable good Success. These different Kind of Goods were formerly sold to the English Men and by them exported for America: however this Trade is greatly

6. Backhaus' final letter to BF, dated March 8 and cited above, was written before he received this reply. He repeats his proposals, and adds that Heyne, secretary of the Göttingen Royal Society of Sciences, will attest to his good reputation. Since BF is a member of that organization, surely Heyne's endorsement will provide an adequate introduction. Christian Gottlob Heyne (1729–1812) was Professor of Poetry and Rhetoric and library director at the University of Göttingen as well as the editor of *Göttinger gelehrten Anzeigen:* Killy, ed., *Deutsche Biographische Enzyklopädie.* BF had been a member of the Society since 1766: XIII, 315.

7. This Bremen merchant (1742–1819) had for two years been trying to find investors for his plan to outfit a ship and establish trade with the United States. In 1782 two well-established merchants agreed to be his partners: Herman Heyman, Sr., and Heinrich Talla, with Talla serving as the firm's director. Heyman was at this time very ill; his two sons were in business with him, and when BF did not respond to the present letter, Talla petitioned BF on behalf of Herman Heyman's Sons. Those two letters are below, Feb. 17 and March 24.

Delius' scheme ultimately failed. His ship, delayed by storms and poor navigation, arrived in Philadelphia with much of the cargo ruined. Delius stayed in America until 1785, trying to establish other business ventures. Upon his return to Bremen he was sued by Heymans and Talla in a much-publicized case, and in 1788 he declared bankruptcy. He finally emigrated to America and in 1794 became a naturalized citizen. *Neue Deutsche Biographie* (23 vols. to date, Berlin, 1953–), III, 583–4; Sam A. Mustafa, *Merchants and Migrations: Germans and Americans in Connection, 1776–1835* (Aldershot and Burlington, Vt., 2001), pp. 29–37, 92–5.

diminished & almost totally lost by the long duration of the present War, which was undertaken & carried on by the said 13 United Provinces in order to obtain freedom and independency, in which at last they have gloriously succeeded and Preliminaries of Peace have actually been signed, in which YOUR EXELLENCY's unremitted zeal & Patriotism had a great Share.

For many Years past I have wished to get in direct Connexions with the 13 united States of America in order to establish a mutual Trade equally beneficial to both parties: about 2 Years ago I had the pleasure to get acquainted at Amsterdam with Mr Nathan Blodget[8] of Boston, by whom I was recommended to Mr Smith of that place who both encouraged my Plan of sending a Cargo of Goods to Boston, as YOUR EXELLENCY will find by the inclosed Original Letter of Mr Smith.[9]

Before the Preliminaries of Peace were signed I had already resolved in Conjunction of my Friends Mr. Heyman & Mr. Talla, both Merchants of this place, to set out a Ship of about 400 Tons upon the Plan of the aforesaid Mr. Blodget, which actually has been executed & she is loaded with Linnen, Manufactured & other goods: but as that time the Præliminaries of Peace were not yet signed, we resolved not only that our Friend & Copartner Mr. Heymann should apply to His Prussian Majesty for leave & to permit the Ship sailing under Prussian Coulours, which was not only granted, but at the same time we received the necessary Passport, of which I have the Honour to present to Your Exellency inclosed a Copy;[1] but also to direct the said Ship first to the Isle of St. Thomas and there it was to be regulated & settled whether she should go to Boston or Philadelphia, because in consequence of the said Passport & other Circumstances we did not dare venture to go directly to the Continent.

But now as the Præliminaries of Peace between England and the 13 free & United States of America are signed, we could indeed directly sail for the Continent, but the Ship beeing already

8. Blodget (xxix, 31), purser of the *Alliance*, was in Holland with John Paul Jones's squadron between October, 1779, and February, 1780: xxx, 444; xxxii, 12n.

9. The enclosure is missing.

1. The passport has not been located.

loaden and a few Goods must be left at St. Thomas, we can not make any Alteration in the Plan.

In order not only to sell the present Cargo of Goods & take in Exchange the Products of the 13 united States, but also to examine whether it would not be possible to establish for the future a Treaty of Commerces or make such regulations that either we in particular or our City in general should & might enjoy all such *Beneficia & Emolumenta* as have been and are to be granted to other Powers, I am resolved to make the voyage to America as Supercargo with the aforesaid Ship, which is called the 3 Friends & comanded by Captain Havinghorst.[2]

However as we are for Want of Acquaintances and Connextions in that part of the World afraid, that great Difficulties may arise or some obstructions may be put in our way, I find it not only necessary to acquaint YOUR EXELLENCY of our intended Plan, but humbly beseech You at the same Time To grant me a Letter of Recomendation to the President of the Congress or Regency of the 13 united free & independent States, That they would graciously be pleased to take me, my Ship & Cargo under their particular protection & that if any Beneficia or Emolumenta, which are granted to other Powers should or might be thought Necessary, that they may be granted to me as also to give all possible assistance to establish a Trade equally Beneficial to both Parties.

I beg at last most humbly YOUR EXELLENCY that You'll favour me with a Resolution and answer accompanied with such Letter of Recomendation I have prayed for, & to deliver the Same as soon as possible to the Bearers Messrs. Laval & Wilfelsheim[3] who will take care to forward it to me as fast as possible, for we intend to set sail in abt 16 Days at farthest.

Having the Honour to subscribe myself YOUR EXELLENCY'S most humble & most obedient Servt.   ARNOLD DELIUS
                                                   Mercht

2. Delius signed a contract with Talla on Feb. 25 for the use of *Die Drey Freunde* (The Three Friends). That contract named a different captain, but Havinghorst did end up commanding the vessel. The ship arrived in Philadelphia in early June: Mustafa, *Merchants and Migrations*, p. 30; *Pa. Gaz.*, June 11, 1783.

3. Parisian bankers; see their letter of March 6.

P.S We believe to make it possible if we are honoured with a Letter of Recomendation from Your Exellency, to direct the Cours of our Ship & loading aforesaid to Philadelphia & beg Your Exellency's advice upon this Subject whether it can be done with Safety.

To His Exellency Benjamin Francklin Esq. Ambassador of the 13 United States of America. at the Court of France.

Notation: Delius 7 Fevr. 1783.

From Vergennes   LS: American Philosophical Society; AL (draft): Archives du Ministère des affaires étrangères

A Versailles le 7. fever. 1783.
Jai l'honneur, Monsieur, de vous envoyer copie d'une lettre que je viens de recevoir de M. le Mis. de Castries.[4]

Vous y verrez la maniére indécente dont le Capitaine smith s'est conduit envers quatre officiers distingués des troupes du Roi qui s'etoient embarqués sur son bâtiment pour repasser en france, et les exactions par lesquelles il a terminé ses procédés injurieux et violents à leur égard.

Je Suis bien persuadé que vous serez aussi indigné que nous le sommes nous-mêmes de cette conduite du Capne. smith, et

4. Castries' Jan. 30 letter reported the mistreatment at sea of four French captains discharged from Rochambeau's army who had arrived at Bordeaux aboard the American privateer "*General Garveret*" (*General Galvez*, 18, of Salem, Thomas Smith, master: Claghorn, *Naval Officers*, p. 288, and Charles H. Lincoln, comp., *Naval Records of the American Revolution, 1775–1788* [Washington, D.C., 1906], p. 309). The captains were Julien Drudes de La Caterie, Alexis Dujast de Vareille or Vareilles, Jean-François Le Bret, and Jacques Scott de Coulanges, for whom see Bodinier, *Dictionnaire*, pp. 149, 163, 296–7, 429. They complained that even though they had paid 100 guineas for their passage, they were forced to survive on salt pork and biscuit because the provisions they had brought aboard were eaten by the ship's officers and crew. When they reached France, Smith claimed he was owed ten guineas more for the passage of a servant and refused to permit them to land their trunks until the Bordeaux *commissaire* intervened. Castries asked Vergennes to inform BF so that Smith could be punished and justice done the wronged officers.

que vous employerez volontiers l'autorité dont vous êtes revêtu pour rendre justice à nos Officiers, et pour punir ceux du Corsaire américain *Le Général Gaveret,* qui se sont réunis avec leur Capne. pour les maltraiter.

J'ai l'honneur d'être trés-sincérement, Monsieur, votre très humble et très-obéissant serviteur./. DE VERGENNES

M. francklin

From John Wright[5]

ALS: American Philosophical Society

Dear Friend   London 7th. of 2nd month 1783

I take the liberty to inclose a letter from my ffrd Charles Eddy[6] late of Philadelphia but now of Dublin respecting which I doubt not thy doing what shall be proper & expedient and if his request appears so to thee thou wilt be so kind to Comply therewith.

I congratulate thee on the peace which I hope will be permanent & mutually beneficial to both Countries and that we shall have the pleasure of seeing thee here wherein I promise myself great satisfaction.

I understand my ffrd David Barclay wrote thee on the Subject of Tim Matlocks affair & recd. an agreable answer.[7] I could not entertain a doubt of the justice of Your government in the business.

5. An old friend of BF's from his London years: X, 350–1; XI, 179–80.

6. Eddy (*c.* 1754–1804) was a Quaker merchant and ironmonger who was accused of being a Loyalist and whose estate in Philadelphia was confiscated in 1777. He eventually went to Great Britain; in the late 1780s he was based in London, where he imported American plants: Elaine F. Crane *et al.*, eds., *The Diary of Elizabeth Drinker* (3 vols., Boston, 1991), III, 2141; Sabine, *Loyalists,* I, 402; John W. Harshberger, "Additional Letters of Humphry Marshall, Botanist and Nurseryman," *PMHB,* LIII (1929), 270–82. His letter is missing.

7. Neither Barclay's letter nor BF's response has been located. Radical politician Timothy Matlack (XXXII, 282n), secretary of the Pa. Supreme Executive Council, had been accused of mismanaging government funds in the midst of an electioneering campaign in the autumn of 1782. The newly elected Republican legislature unanimously declared the secretary unworthy of public trust in March, 1783.

I shall esteem a letter from thee a favour & hearing of thy welfare always affords me pleasure being with great Esteem Thy very Respectful Frd JOHN WRIGHT

A ship from Massachusets bay or Rather from Nantucket is arrived in the Thames & reported at the Customhouse—[8] The first ffrdly 13 stripes may she be the forerunner of thousands

Addressed: Doctr Benjamin Franklin / Minister Plenepotentiary / From the Congress / of the United States of America / Paris

From Lotbinière

ALS: American Philosophical Society

paris, petit hôtel de Lordat Rue de Bourgogne
Monsieur   Ce samedi matin 8 fevrier 1783.

J'ai Eu l'honneur de vous faire Compliment dernierement Sur la signature des préliminaires de la paix, sans savoir Encore Ce qui Concernoit particulierement vos Etats.[9] Je vis le tout hier dans le Courrier de l'Europe,[1] Et suis tres satisfait des limites que vous avez fixé Entre vous et Vos voisins Bretons; ils sont par Ce moyen beaucoup moins En Etat de Vous nuire, que vous a Eux.

J'ai pris au même tems la liberté de rappeller a Votre Excellence le souvenir de mes deux seigneuries a la tête du lac Champlain (allainville, Et hocquart); de la promesse que vous me fites a mon retour du Continent de l'amérique, En 1777, que vous recommanderiez le plus particulierement Cette affaire au Congrès, En lui faisant passer Copie des papiers que j'eus l'honneur de Vous remettre alors; Et J'Espère, ayant pris date de si longue main, que la Chose doit desja avoir Été déterminée intèrieurement, beaucoup avant les derniers arrangements, de maniere a me louer de la justice Complette que me doivent vos Etats a Cette occasion Et Conformément a mes titres Et aux traités qui m'assuroient la pleine propriété de Ces biens, pour En jouir a

---

8. The *Bedford*, Capt. Morris, arrived on Feb. 5: *Morning Herald and Daily Advertiser*, Feb. 7, 1783.

9. Above, Feb. 2.

1. A French translation of the American-British treaty was printed in the Jan. 31 issue: *Courier de l'Europe*, XIII (1783), 69–70.

perpétuité de la maniere dont j'en avois joui Et du jouir avant. J'ose vous réitérer ma priere a ce sujet, regardant Ces seigneuries Comme mon appui unique Et le lieu de mon azile a venir. J'en ai prévenu dez longtems, Et tout recemment encore M. le Comte de Vergennes, qui, je l'espere, aura pû vous En toucher desja quelques mots.—²

J'ai l'honneur d'Etre avec beaucoup de Respect Monsieur de Vôtre Excellence le très humble Et tres obeissant serviteur

LOTBINIERE

Notation: Lotbiniere 8 Fevr. 1783.

From Roze de Chantoiseau

ALS: Historical Society of Pennsylvania

Monsieur   Ce 8 fer. 1783.
Jai Lhonneur de vous adresser cyjoint Le Plan de Banque Generale de Credit Public, qui a fait hier Le Sujet de notre entretien.³

2. In January Lotbinière had asked Vergennes to speak on his behalf to the Americans so that his right to full possession of Allainville and Hocquart would be acknowledged, and had asked him to forward a memoir to BF on the subject. (The memoir is at the AAE.) Sylvette Nicolini, "Michel Chartier de Lotbinière: L'Action et la pensée d'un Canadien du 18e siècle" (Ph.D. diss., University of Montreal, 1978), p. 185.

3. The four-page enclosure, dated Feb. 8, was signed by Roze and written in the form of a first-person address to BF. Entitled "Developpement du Plan proposé pour operer La Liquidation des Dettes d'un Etat . . . ," his proposal for a "national bank of public credit" involved a system whereby the state would issue a limited number of letters of credit to purveyors, who would in turn exchange them for goods and services. With each transaction, the letters (which were not backed by specie) would decrease in value by one percent until they were negligible. Their worth was based solely on their scarcity and the trust of the people; see Rebecca L. Spang, *The Invention of the Restaurant* (Cambridge, Mass., and London, 2000), pp. 17–19. Roze's plan was written on a sheet of the marbled, wove paper that BF had commissioned from England for the printing of loan certificates for the French treasury; see XXX, xxxii, 345–6, 609–12, and the illustration facing p. 346; XXXI, 284–5, 341, 363. On the marbled strip he wrote "Banque Nationale des treize Provinces unies d'amerique / Lettre de credit public de 300 *l.t.* &c."

Je n'entrerai point Monsieur, dans de nouveaux details sur les produits immenses qui peuvent et doivent necessairement resulter de ce nouvel Etablissemt. Vous en connoissés comme moi toutes les ressources et ne sentés pas moins la necessité d'en tenir caché le grand ressort et faire quil ne soit connû que de Ceux qui seront en quelque sorte initiés dans Le Sacré mistere.

Je sens bien que de proposer de Liquider toutes Les dettes d'un Etat Sans en alterer les revenus, et d'en augmenter les revenus Sans en aggraver les charges paroitra une assertion hazardée et invraisemblable a quiconque ne Sera pas dans la Confidence; Mais qu'importe pourvû que l'on ne promette que ce qu l'on poura tenir, et que l'on tienne ce que l'on aura promis aussi inviolablement, et aussi constamment que les sentimens de respect et d'attachement avec les quels je Suis et Vous promets d'etre toute ma vie Monsieur Votre tres humble et tres obeissant serviteur   ROZE DE CHANTOISEAU

From René-Georges Gastellier[4]

ALS: American Philosophical Society

Mgis [Montargis] 9 fevrier 1783
Monsieur et trés illustre docteur

Mr le marquis dusaillant Gendre de Mr le Mquis de mirabeau[5] doit vous remettre le petit ouvrage que vous me permettés de vous dédier, mais auparavant que de lui faire voir le Grand jour, j'ai crú devoir le soumettre à votre examen afin de rectifier de Corriger ce qui pourroit vous déplaire, et même d'y enlever jusqu'a votre nom si l'ouvrage ne vous semble pas digne de toute votre indulgence. J'attends sur cela une reponse décisive et je me resigne par avance à tout ce qui vous plaira d'ordonner, voici le seul exemplaire qui paroît, l'imprimeur ne tirera pas la derniere feuille que je ne sache votre décision, j'ose me flatter qu'elle me

---

4. Author of the forthcoming *Des spécifiques en médecine*, dedicated to BF: XXXVIII, 599–600. This letter and the page proofs it mentions were forwarded to BF by the marquis de Mirabeau on Feb. 13; see the marquis' letter of that date.
5. For Mirabeau's son-in-law see Du Saillant to BF, March 14.

sera favorable surtout vous etant demandée par une personne aussi respectable que l'est le Gendre de l'ami des hommes.[6]

Je suis avec respect Monsieur et trés illustre docteur votre trés humble trés obeissant serviteur GASTELLIER

Endorsed: Gastellier 9 Fev 83

Reuben Harvey[7] to the American Peace Commissioners

LS: National Archives[8]

Cork 10th Febr. 1783

Respected Friends John Adams, Benjamin Franklin John Jay & Henry Laurens, Esquires.

Although my Name may be unknown to you, it is not so to many of your Countrymen whom the chance of War threw into Captivity at Kinsale & here during the late War, so unnaturally waged, & persisted in by a weak, wicked Ministry— In the early part of it some few warm Friends to America assisted me in collecting a handsome Sum to buy Cloaths & other Necessaries for 33 American Prisoners who had been taken near Montreal in 1775 & sent to England from Quebec— These poor Men were brought here on board the Solebay (one of Sir Peter Parker's Fleet) in Decr. 1775 & had comfortable Supplies of every thing suitable provided for their Winter Passage—[9] From July till Octr. 1781 there were several Hundred Americans captured in those Seas & confined in Kinsale Prison: their Treatment was not

6. "L'ami des hommes" refers to Mirabeau, author of *L'Ami des hommes, ou Traité de la population:* XV, 182n.

7. Harvey (1734–1808) was a Quaker merchant who had been involved in trading ventures with North America: Sheldon S. Cohen, "Reuben Harvey: Irish Friend to American Freedom," *Quaker History,* LXXXVIII (1999), 22–39; Reuben Harvey to George Washington, Feb. 12, 1783 (National Archives).

8. This copy was enclosed in Harvey's letter to Washington, cited above.

9. The most famous of these prisoners was Col. Ethan Allen, whose treatment at the hands of the British had enraged BF: XXII, 393; J. Kevin Graffagnino, ed., *Ethan and Ira Allen: Collected Works* (3 vols., Benson, Vt., 1992), II, 18–21; John J. Duffy *et al.,* eds., *Ethan Allen and His Kin: Correspondence, 1772–1819* (2 vols., Hanover, N.H., and London, 1998), I, 54–5.

good, & I applied to Government for their relief, but under the Administration of Lord North little or no attention was paid to any Distress of this kind, however, I availed myself of the change that happened in April 1782 & on the Duke of Portland's Arrival at Dublin as Lord Lieutenant I wrote him concerning the hard Treatment (in many respects) endured by the poor Americans at Kinsale;[1] & a Correspondence on that Subject continued some Months between his Secretary Col. Fitzpatrick & me, as you will perceive by two of his letters to me now enclosed—[2] A great many of the Prisoners escaped from Kinsale to this place & were maintaind by me & a few other Friends to America for Months, until I could get them Passages to different parts of France & the Continent.

I have been severely reflected upon during the American War for my open & avowed Attachment to your just cause: I have been threatened with the vengeance of Ministry & was once obliged to appear before the Mayor of this City to answer a charge brought against me by Robert Gordon Esqr. Commissary: no less a charge than that of assisting the American Rebels, which however had no effect, for I told both Gordon & the Mayor; that I abhorred the American War; that I must ever wish Success to a People who bravely opposed "the tyrannick Attempts of a vile Ministry, & that if the Americans were reduced to their last Province, I would still adhere to their Cause, believing *it* to be a just one & *them* an oppressed People."

Though my Fortune is but moderate & I have 10 Children, my Feelings for the poor ill-clothed Prisoners from New England, Pennsylvania & other parts of America (whose Fate cast them amongst us) were so prevalent that I have expended large Sums of my own Property, besides the Subscriptions & Collections that I made, in maintaining, cloathing, & paying Passage

1. For the community's response to the prisoners' distress see XXXVI, 606–7.
2. The Hon. Richard Fitzpatrick (1748–1813) was the Earl of Shelburne's brother-in-law. He had served in the British army in North America in 1777–78, and as a member of Parliament he opposed the American War: Namier and Brooke, *House of Commons*, II, 433–5. In Harvey's letter to Washington of Feb. 12 (cited above) he enclosed at least three of Fitzpatrick's letters written in May, 1782, and his own replies; these copies are at the National Archives.

Money for those Prisoners, the Truth of which you'll have confirmed by living Witnesses, when you shall happily return to your Native Country— I was a principal Person in effecting a Remonstrance & Petition against the American War so early as 1776 which was signed by about 600 respectable Inhabitants of Cork & delivered to the King by Lord Middleton[3] the 10th of May following. At that time an Address for carrying on the War & ending the Rebellion (so called) in America was set on foot here by Commissary Gordon, Paul Benson a Contractor & others who were immediate Gainers by this War, but it was only signed by Men of that Stamp, Revenue & other Crown Officers, together with the Mayor & Corporation, in the whole 150.[4]

I don't expect by thus acquainting you with the little Services which I have done for the Cause & People of America to receive any Emolument, but I hope for your Friendship in recommending me to the Congress, should they think proper to appoint any Person here or in other Ports of Ireland as a Consul, for managing Matters of Commerce: Sufficient Security should be given, & my Character will bear the test of Enquiry.

Your Consequence, Gentlemen, in different parts of America must give great weight to your Recommendation of me as a Merchant and I flatter myself that you will be so kind as to mention my Name to your Friends at Boston, Philadelphia, New York Charlestown, Maryland, Virginia &c &c that I may be favoured with some Business from a Country, for whose Wel-

---

3. George Brodrick, 4th Viscount Midleton (1754–1836), an Irish peer who opposed the North ministry, wrote in August, 1775, "we are all Americans here." The 1776 petition was the result of the embargo on provisions; with Cork's American trade prohibited and its West Indies commerce in ruins, the signers called on the king to dismiss his ministers and stop the war: R. B. McDowell, *Ireland in the Age of Imperialism and Revolution, 1760–1801* (Oxford, 1979), pp. 241–2; *Burke's Peerage*, p. 1733.

4. The March, 1776, address by the mayor, sheriffs, merchants, traders, and inhabitants of Cork expressed the signers' abhorrence of the "American Rebellion" and their support of the king. It was sent to the city's parliamentary representatives for forwarding to the Lord Lieutenant of Ireland: Richard Caulfield, ed., *The Council Book of the Corporation of the City of Cork, from 1609 to 1643, and from 1690 to 1800* (Guildford, Eng., 1876), p. 906.

fare & Independence no Person has been a more strenuous & steady Advocate than—Your very sincere Friend

REUBEN HARVEY

P.S. Should any of you visit London, Col. Barré⁵ will readily tell you his opinion & Knowledge of my Principles & Conduct during the American War—

(Copy)

From Ingraham & Bromfield⁶

ALS: American Philosophical Society

Sir,   Bordeaux February 10th: 1783.

The Letter which we have the Honor to enclose reach'd us Yesterday under a Cover dated so long ago as last October.

We proffit of this Opportunity to mention that we have here a Ship which will be ready to sail for New England in a few Days & beg Leave to ask whether a particular Passport will be necessary for Security against Capture, or whether any Act of the Commissioners will give sufficient Protection without one. If the first be the Case we must be oblig'd to trouble you for the Papers requisite & shall esteem ourselves greatly indebted for them by the earliest Opportunity.⁷

We have the Honor to be With great Respect Sir, Your most obedient Humble Servants   INGRAHAM & BROMFIELD

His Excellency Benjamin Franklin Esqr.

Addressed: A Son Excellence / Benjamin Franklin / Minister des Etats unis / d'Amerique / á / Passy.

Notation: Ingraham & Bromfield Bordeaux February 10th. 1783

---

5. Col. Isaac Barré: XVI, 69–70n.
6. Two Bostonians whose firm was based in Amsterdam: XXXVI, 119–20.
7. JA sent Ingraham six passports on Feb. 19, one of which was for Neufville (Mass. Hist. Soc.).

From Le Roy

ALS: American Philosophical Society

De Paris ce lundy 10 Fevrier 1783

J'ai lhonneur de vous renvoyer mon Illustre Docteur La lettre de mon beau Père[8] et le projet de rèponse que j'y ai fait tant bien que mal car Je suis bien loin d'y avoir fait parler comme je le désirois, et comme Il le feroit lui même, Le Libérateur de L'Amérique; mais enfin je vous l'envoye telle qu'elle est. Si je n'avois été un profane J'aurois éte vous demender à dîner avec Le détachement de La Loge des neuf Soeurs que vous traitez aujourdhui à ce que m'a dit M. De La Lande[9] qui a bien voulu Se charger de cette lettre. Adieu Mon Illustre Docteur vous savez combien Je vous suis passionnément attaché pour la vie

LE ROY

[On a separate sheet:][1]

J'ai reçu Monsieur La lettre que vous m'avez fait L'honneur de m'écrire au Sujet de la paix et Je suis fort Sensible à tout ce que vous me marquez de flatteur à cette Occasion. Je ne puis esperer d'y répondre comme je le désire. Je vous prie ainsi de vouloir bien Suppléer à mes expressions car votre langue est Si difficile qu'un etranger et surtout quand il a mon age doit renoncer au plaisir et à la Satisfaction de S'y exprimer d'une manière qui réponde à ce qu'il sent le mieux. Cependant je puis vous dire que je me flatte de l'entendre assez bien pour avoir parfaitement distingué votre compliment de la foule de ceux que m'ont attirré ce grand évenement. Il y a une tournure de franchise et de vérité qui n'appartient qu'aux anciens militaires François et que j'ai déja eu lieu d'observer plusieurs fois. Je joins avec grand plaisir Monsieur Mes Voeux aux Votres pour la prosperité et L'Union èternelle des deux nations. Pour la mienne elle n'oubliera jamais que sans les secours d'un Roi puissant et génereux et les efforts de ses braves troupes elle n'auroit pu être delivrée aussi rapidement du Joug tyrannique de la grande bretagne. C'est une verité

8. The letter from Charles-Gabriel de Messey is above, [after Jan. 20].

9. Lalande had preceded BF as *vénérable* of that lodge: XXIX, 528–9.

1. Le Roy's draft of a letter BF might send his father-in-law. We have no record of its being sent. Messey did acknowledge a now-missing letter from BF in an undated reply we publish below under [April].

qu'elle se plaira à répandre jusques dans les forets les plus reculées de LAmérique et d'age en age jusques à la derniere Posterite.

J'ai Lhonneur détre, &c

Mon petit fils Monsieur qui a èté fort sensible à votre Souvenir me charge de vous en marquer Sa reconnoissance et de vous assurer de son respect.

From Franz Ulrich Theodor Aepinus[2]

ALS: Historical Society of Pennsylvania

Monsieur,   à St. Petersbourg. ce 1 [*i.e.*, 12][3] Fevrier. 1783.

Vous pardonnerez sans doute, à l'empressement, que je montre, à l'occasion de la grande nouvelle, qui nous est arrivée, ces jours-ci, de me rappeller à Votre souvenir, qui me sera aussi precieux, que me l'a été dans le tems, l'approbation, que Vous avez crû pouvoir accorder autrefois, à mes travaux pour l'avancement des sciences.[4]

J'ai l'honneur de Vous feliciter, Monsieur, non pas tant sur ce, que la posterité ne cessera de citer Votre nom avec respect, et avec admiration. Les ames, comme la Votre, n'ayant pas besoin d'être remuées, par ce qu'on appelle la gloire, n'en font pas tant de cas. Pour produire un effèt surprenant, un corps grand en soi-même, n'a pas, comme une bâle de fusil, besoin d'être poussé par l'elasticité de vapeurs comprimées, capables de lui communiquer un degré de vitesse, qui puisse en quelque sorte compenser la modicité, ou plutôt le néant de son énergie, et de son poids origi-

2. A distinguished scientist: VIII, 393n.

3. News of the Jan. 20 peace hardly could have reached St. Petersburg by Feb. 1; Aepinus obviously is using the old style or Julian calendar, differing by 11 days from the Gregorian calendar used in western Europe and America.

4. On June 6, 1766, BF congratulated Aepinus for his work on electricity and magnetism and sent him a scientific article of his own (Hist. Soc. of Pa.). That letter, which will be published in the addenda to our series, has been published in Nina N. Bashkina *et al.*, eds., *The United States and Russia: the Beginning of Relations, 1765–1815* ([Washington, D.C., 1980]), p. 12; an English translation of the present letter is on pp. 173–4.

naire. Si je crois avoir lieu de Vous feliciter, c'est que Vous jouis-
sez maintenant, Monsieur, du plaisir pur, de Vous pouvoir dire à
Vous même, que Vous avez commencé la carriere, que la Providence Vous fait parcourir, par porter une lumiere éclatante et
inattendue, dans la branche des sciences humaines, qui s'occupe
du developpement des ressorts et des loix, par lesquels l'Etre
supreme anime et gouverne son éternel et immense ouvrage; et
que Vous l'avez terminée, cette heureuse carriere, par procurer,
et par assûrer à Votre patrie la liberté, événement, dont les effets
bienfaisans, s'etendront, par la suite des siècles, sur tout le genre
humain.

Avec les voeux, les plus sinceres, pour Votre prosperité con-
stante, et avec le respect le plus vray, et le plus inalterable, j'ai
l'honneur d'être Monsieur Votre très-humble et très-obeissant
Serviteur,

AEPINUS,
Cons: d'Etat actuel au College des Affaires étrangeres.

Addressed: A Monsieur / Monsieur Francklin, / Ministre Plenipotentiaire de 14 Provin / ces unies de l'Amerique Septentrionale / à la Cour de Sa Majté tres Chretienne, / à / Paris.

From Ferdinand Grand

L:[5] University of Pennsylvania Library

Monsieur   Paris le 12. fevrier 1783.
J'ai examiné, suivant vos ordres, la lettre de Mr. Le comte de
vergennes du 6. de ce mois, ainsi que le Projet du nouveau contrat qu'elle renfermait.

J'observe qu'effectivement Mr. Le Comte de vergennes ne fait
point mention du nouveau secours que vous lui avés demandé,
et parait s'en tenir aux Six Millions ci-devant accordés pour le
Service de cette année, les quels font l'objet du premier article de
ce projet, qui porte:

1°. Que ces six Millions seront remboursés au Tresor Royal *au
domicile du Sr. Grand.* Ce Domicile n'a point été Stipulé dans le

5. Written and signed on Grand's behalf by his eldest son, Jean-François-
Paul (XXIX, 424n).

premier traité, il semblerait qu'il devrait y etre exprimé, ou annullé dans celui-ci pour etre uniformes.[6]

2°. Que les termes du payement de ces Six millions par £500,000. chaque mois, *ne pourront etre anticipés.* Cette condition devient extremement gênante, comme la Suite de cette lettre le fera voir. Le Second article recapitule les payemens des 18. millions précédents. Cette récapitulation me parait d'autant plus inutile, que cette Somme fait l'objet du premier traité, et que consequemment elle Se trouve déplacée dans celui-ci.

J'en dirai de même du 3me. article qui est aussi une recapitulation des Dons précédemment faits par le Roy, montant à 9. Millions, des quels il semble inutile de parler dans ce nouveau Traité, d'autant plus qu'il y a erreur dans l'énoncé des 3. millions accordés antérieurement au traité du mois de fevrier 1778. Je connais bien 3. Millions payés en 1777. mais je ne connais point de traité de 1778. ni les 3. Millions dont il entend parler.[7]

6. The final contract (below, Feb. 25) retained this provision. The "premier traité" is the July 16, 1782, contract signed by BF and Vergennes (XXXVII, 633–9). Throughout this letter, Grand uses the £ symbol to mean *livres tournois.*

7. Grand's accounts showed that the American commissioners had received 3,000,000 *l.t.* in 1777, prior to the February, 1778, Treaty of Alliance. Two million was in outright gifts paid quarterly under the guise of private contributions; the other million was through a tobacco contract with the farmers general: XXXVII, 570; XXXVIII, 142–3, 223. Subsequent payments were loans (except for a 6,000,000 *l.t.* gift in 1781: XXXIV, 444); they are listed in the July 16, 1782, contract.

On July 11, 1786, BF wrote Grand to inquire about the additional 1,000,000 *l.t.* because Congress had been unable to find receipts for it. BF assumed that this was the 1,000,000 *l.t.* advanced by the farmers general and deposited with Grand and wondered why, if it was a gift from the king, deduction had not been made of the tobacco sent to the farmers general in partial repayment: Smyth, *Writings,* IX, 527–8. When Grand inquired at the foreign ministry, *premier commis* Jean-Baptiste Luton Durival (XXXIII, 221n) informed him that this 1,000,000 *l.t.* had not been loaned by the farmers general, but had been delivered by the royal treasury on June 10, 1776: Wharton, *Diplomatic Correspondence,* I, 377–8. Although the French government refused to acknowledge the recipient, BF deduced this was money provided to Beaumarchais' trading company Roderigue Hortalez & Co. (XXII, 454): BF to Charles Thomson, Jan. 25, 1787 (Wharton, *Diplomatic Correspondence,* I, 378–9).

In attempting to impress the peace commissioners with the king's gen-

Quoique j'aie reçu par anticipation le premier Quartier d'avril de £1500,000. la rapidité successive des traites de Mr. Morris[8] ne m'en mit pas moins en engagemens actuels pour lui de £1042,030.
et je suis à la veille d'en contracter de
nouveaux pour   <u>1099699.</u>
pour Ses traites avisées qui paraissent
successivement, ce qui forme un
découvert de   £2,141,729.
d'autant plus instant à pourvoir que toutes ses dernieres traites sont à 30. jours de vue. Comme Mr. le Comte de vergennes annonce que les payemens de £500,000. par mois ne pourront etre anticipés, je ne vois de possibilité d'atteindre la premiere échéance des £500,000. qui va au 1. may, et moins encore de pouvoir faire face aux sommes ci dessus sans le secours le plus immédiat.

Je ne pense pas cependant que dans aucun cas, et sur tout aujourd'hui que nous pouvons dire etre arrivés au port, le Gouvernement consentit à laisser retourner à protest les traites de Mr. Morris, vu les conséquences facheuses qui en resulteroient, et ce Serait cependant l'équivalent si je les acceptais, comme il me l'a été proposé, pour les payer *aux termes des quartiers* aulieu de celui qu'elles portent.

Vous connaissés, Monsieur, mon zèle, et vous ne doutés surement pas que je fisse usage de mon crédit si cette somme ne surpassait pas ses limittes, et si sa conservation n'était pas plus utile à la chose; mais je puis cependant en faire usage pour une partie si vous m'y autorisés.

---

erosity, Vergennes had told a half-truth; the money had been loaned to Beaumarchais rather than given to him, but as he had been unable to repay the loan, the supplies he provided to the United States ended up being a gift from the king. Vergennes' exaggeration would have serious consequences for Beaumarchais and his heirs. Because of the question of this missing million *livres*, it would take half a century to resolve the Beaumarchais family's financial claims on the United States: Brian N. Morton and Donald C. Spinelli, *Beaumarchais and the American Revolution* (Lanham, Md., Boulder, Colo., and New York, 2003), pp. 46–7, 292–9, 317–26.

8. Faced with numerous expenses, including the need to pay the American army to keep it from dissolving, Morris had overdrawn his accounts: *Morris Papers*, VII, 265–7n.

Mr. Adams que j'ai été voir ce matin ignore si l'Emprunt de Hollande va, et si ceux qui en sont chargé ont des fonds libres. Je pense qu'il conviendrait de leur écrire, soit pour les engager, vu la circonstance a se pretter a des avances étant munis d'un Emprunt, soit pour m'ouvrir un crédit chès eux. Mais comme ce moyen ne poura pas suffire aux besoins, il faut en employer d'autres. Je croirais qu'en représentant la Situation des choses à Mr. Le comte de vergennes, qui Sent mieux que personne la necessité de Soutenir le crédit naissant de l'amérique, il Se determinerait a engager Mr. de fleury a me remettre des rescriptions avec les quelles je pourais m'aider pour faire face à mesure de mes besoins, et comme en attendant les traites de M. Morris paraissent tous les jours, je vous Supplie, si je ne dois pas les accepter de vouloir bien me le marquer, ou m'autoriser à les accepter payables aux échéances des Quartiers si vous l'approuvés, ce que j'attends pour m'y conformer à l'égard de £400,000. que l'on vient de m'apporter à l'acceptation, car il est instant de prendre un parti définitif à tous ces égards.

Je vous prie d'agréer les assurances des sentimens respectueux avec les quels j'ai l'honneur d'etre Monsieur votre tres humble et trés obeissant serviteur.   GRAND

Na. [Nota] les traites de Mr. Morris, s'elevent à £2,469,240. dans l'intervalle seulement du 23. Novembre au 28 Décembre.

Endorsed: Mr Grand Mr Couteulx &c relative to the Money Affairs—1782 & 83

From Le Roy   ALS: American Philosophical Society

ce Mercredy 12 Février [1783][9]
Je Suis chargé Mon Illustre Docteur de la part de M. Le Cte de Maillebois de vous demander si vous pouvez lui faire L'honneur de venir dîner chez luï ruë de Grenelle, Vendredy prochain 14 de ce mois. Vous y trouverez M O Connell que Je Sais qui vous a

9. The only Wednesday, Feb. 12, when BF resided in Passy.

demandé un rendez vous.[1] Je Souhaite bien Mon Illustre Docteur que vous acceptiez La proposition de M. De Maillebois parce-qu'elle me procurera L'honneur et le plaisir de vous voir et de diner avec vous. Je n'ai pas besoin de vous dire qu'il espere bien que Monsieur Votre petit Fils Sera de la partie. Recevez Mon Il-lustre Docteur mille et mille Complimens   LE ROY

réponse S'il Vous plait parceque je l'ai promise pour ce Soir.

Addressed: a Monsieur / Monsieur Franklin / en son hôtel / à Passy

From Daniel Charles O'Connell[2]

AL: American Philosophical Society

Paris wednesday morning [February 12, 1783][3]

Mr. O'Connell has the honour to present his respects to his Ex-cellency Dr. Franklin, requests he may be so good to grant him a quarter of an hour's Audience on friday Morning about some business, If that Day shu'd not be convenient to his Excellency Mr. O'Connell shall wait on him any other moment he shall be pleased to appoint.

Notation: O'Connell.

1. Daniel O'Connell's letter requesting a meeting is immediately below. Maillebois had long been a friend to O'Connell and had facilitated his rise in the French army: Mary Anne Bianconi O'Connell, *The Last Colonel of the Irish Brigade, Count O'Connell and Old Irish Life at Home and Abroad, 1745–1833* (2 vols., London, 1892), I, 188–9, 197, 201, 203, 207, 253; II, 23.

2. O'Connell (1745–1833), officer in the Royal Suédois and chevalier de Saint-Louis, had distinguished himself at the siege of Gibraltar and been promoted to Colonel Commandant of his regiment. Supposedly he saved the life of the comte d'Artois, who was instrumental in conferring on him the colonelcy of the Salm-Salm regiment and the title of count: Mary Anne Bianconi O'Connell, *The Last Colonel of the Irish Brigade, Count O'Connell and Old Irish Life at Home and Abroad, 1745–1833* (2 vols., London, 1892), I, 278, 281–95, 300–2; II, 3–7, 304; Mazas, *Ordre de Saint-Louis,* II, 273–4; *État militaire* for 1784, p. 235; *ODNB.*

3. Dated on the basis of the preceding letter.

From Ferdinand Grand

LS: Historical Society of Pennsylvania

Monsieur   Paris le 13. fevrier 1783.

J'ai l'honneur de vous renvoyer la lettre de Mr. Le Comte de Vergennes et le projet d'Acte qu'elle renfermait, que l'on a omis d'insérer dans celle que j'ai eu celui de vous écrire hier. Je n'ai rien a ajouter a ce que j'ai eu l'honneur de vous marquer au Sujet de ces piéces. Mais je dois vous observer encore que le Traité du 16. Juillet 1782. n'ayant pas fait mention des Sommes accordées ci devant en don gratuit au Congrès, il doit paraitre extraordinaire, ou du moins l'on aura peine à comprendre pourquoi le nouveau traité en fait mention.

J'ai eu l'honneur de vous remettre l'année derniere le tableau des fonds accordés par le Roy au Congrès, et des Payemens faits en consèquence.[4] Je fis dans le tems ce tableau pour vous aider à vous reconnaitre, et reconnaitre les Promesses que vous aviès fournis depuis 1778. qui est l'époque où ont commencé les 18. millions que porte le traité. La totalité des Sommes que porte ce tableau ne S'éleve qu'à 34. millions et le projet du nouveau traité les fait monter à 37. millions, parcequ'il y comprend Sans doute les 3. millions de 1777. car je n'ai pas connaissance qu'il en ait été payé d'autres.[5]

Je Souhaite que ces éclaircissement vous Satisfassent, Monsieur; S'il en est d'autres en mon pouvoir, je suis à vos ordres. Je me conformerai à ceux que je vous ai demandé, et que j'attends, relativement aux traites de Mr. Morris que l'on me presse de rendre acceptées ou non.

Je vous renouvelle les assurances des Sentiments respectueux avec les quels j'ai l'honneur d'etre Monsieur votre très humble et trés obéissant Serviteur   GRAND

---

4. Not found.
5. See Grand's letter of Feb. 12.

From Le Roy

AL: American Philosophical Society

Jeudy matin [February 13, 1783][6]

J'espere Mon très cher Docteur, que vous n'avez point oublié La proposition de M. De Maillebois, pour demain dîner. Il m'a bien recommandé de vous en faire Souvenir, ainsi que Monsieur Votre petit fils Sur Lequel il compte pareillement et de graces ne manquez pas de L'Amener car M. De Maillebois m'en voudroit beaucoup. Je vous Souhaite bien le bon Jour à tous Les deux. Voila Docteur un beau tems à Echecs.

Addressed: a Monsieur / Monsieur Franklin / Ministre Plenipotentiaire / des Etats Unis

From John MacMahon

AL: American Philosophical Society

feby. the 13th. 1783

Doctor Mac Mahon presents his sincere respects to Dr. Franklin, and thanks for his obliging invitation. He is very sorry not to have had it in his power to wait upon him these three or four weeks past, but will break off a previous engagement to have that honour next sunday.

Addressed: A son Excellence / Monsieur le Docteur Franklin / Ministre Plénipotentiaire / des Etats unis de l'Amerique / à Passy

Notation: Mac mahon

From the Marquis de Mirabeau[7]

ALS: American Philosophical Society

Monsieur   de paris le 13e. fevrier 1783

Mr. gattelier, très digne et utile mèdecin dans le canton ou se trouve la campagne que j'habite une partie de l'année,[8] m'adresse

---

6. Based on Le Roy's invitation of the previous day.

7. For the marquis, whom BF had known since 1767, see XXIV, 335–6. He was forwarding Gastellier's letter of Feb. 9, above.

8. Montargis in the Gâtinais, where Gastellier practiced medicine and had

le livre et la lettre que vous trouverez cy jointe pour vous etre offerts. Il me charge de scavoir 1°. si vous voulés bien donner par ècrit le consentement a la dédicace, dont vous l'avés flaté par tierce personne;[9] 2°. si vous daignerés prendre prèalablement lecture de l'ouvrage, pour y ordonner les corrections ou suppressions que vous desireriés, 3°. il me charge de solliciter une aussy prompte expedition que vos affaires le permettront attendu que son dèvouement a cet ègard a déja fort retardé son libraire qui s'empatiente, et nuy a ses arrangements.

Ce que je puis ajouter a cecy Monsieur cest que Mr gattelier est notoirement un homme de mèrite et qui vaut d'etre encouragé. Je ne scaurois assurément prononcer en thèorie, mais quand à la pratique, il à la confiance de tout le païs. Né de parents très pauvres, n'ayant pu avoir qu'une èducation de village il s'est fait tout seul—ayant la confiance de touts le païs et chateaux il ny à prèsque pas de jour ou dans toute saison il ne fasse douze et quinze lieues et ne lasse plusieurs chevaux; et cest au milieu d'une vie si agitèe qu'il trouve encor la nuit le temps dècrire et de travailler mème dans ses courses et dans sa voiture; et le feu dont il est animé ne tourne qu'a bien, ne procure que du bien, car il est fort heureux dans ses traitements et grand observateur de tout dans ses courses.

Ce sont choses Monsieur dont je puis et dois rendre témoignages et qui apuyent la prière que je vous fais de vouloir bien lèxpédier promptement et amiablement. Je saisis avec plaisir cette occasion de vous renouveller les assurances des sentimens Rèspectueux avèc lèsquels j'ay l'honneur d'etre Monsieur votre très humble et très obeissant serviteur   LE MIS DE MIRABEAU

Notation: Marquis de Mirabeau Paris 13 Fevrier 1783

---

recently been elected mayor, was south of Mirabeau's estate at Bignon: *DBF*, under Gastellier; Barbara Luttrell, *Mirabeau* (New York, London, and Toronto, 1990), p. 10.

9. Mlle Defay: XXXVI, 547–8; XXXVII, 30; XXXVIII, 599–600.

From Samuel Vaughan, Jr.   AL: American Philosophical Society

Thursday 13 Feby. [1783] Hotel de Vauban,
Rue de Richlieu.

Mr Vaughan presents his most respectful compliments to Dr
Franklin, & will do himself the honor of accepting his kind invitation to dinner on Sunday next: Mr Vaughan would have done
himself the pleasure of sending an earlier answer, but having
changed his abode, Dr Franklin's obliging note came late to
hand. If any letters should be laying at Dr Frankins for Miss Laurens, & he had an opportunity of sending them to Town tomorrow, Mr V would be particularly thankful, as Mr Storer sets off
for London in the evening.[1]

Addressed: A son Excellence, / Monsieur Franklin, / Ministre
Plenipotentiare des Etats Unis &c &c, / a Passy.

Notation: Vaughan

From Alleyne Fitzherbert   AL: Harvard University Library

Hotel du Parc Royal Friday Feby. 14th [1783]

Mr Fitz-Herbert presents his Compliments to Dr Franklin & has
the honour of transmitting to him herewith a letter which he received Yesterday evening by a Courier from England.

Notation: Fitz-Herbert.

1. The following day, Feb. 14, JA wrote letters of introduction for Charles
Storer, his secretary (XXXVIII, 285n), to Benjamin Vaughan and Richard Oswald in London, and to Edmund Jenings (saying that Storer would look for
him in Brussels). Eleven days later Benjamin Vaughan replied that Storer had
arrived. *Adams Papers,* XIV, 260–2, 295.

From ———— Perret ALS: American Philosophical Society

Excellence. Nantes ce 14. fevrier 1783.

J'ay l'honneur de Vous envoyer cy joint, les grosses des procedures qui ont etés faites par M M. les officiers de l'amirauté de nantes relativement aux Prises, le tartare, la Kitty; la Sally, l'anteloop, & la Betzy;[2] je Supplie Votre Excellence de Vouloir bien m'en accuser la réception, & elle obligera sensiblement celui qui a l'honneur d'estre avec un profond respect.

Votre éxcellence, Le trés humble & trés obeissent Sérviteur.

PERRET

Notation: Perret 14 Fevr. 1783.

From Samuel Vaughan, Jr. AL: American Philosophical Society

Friday morning. Hotel de Vauban Rue de Richelieu
[February 14, 1783][3]

Mr Vaughan has the honor to present his respectful comps. to Dr Franklin. Inclosed is a letter from Mr Hodgson, which Mr V received this morning,[4] & forwards early, as he imagines Dr Franklin may wish to answer it by Mr Storer, who sets off tonight at 10 oClock for London.[5]

Respecting News, Mr Vaughan has the pleasure to inform Dr Franklin, that Lord Surry is *talked* of as Ambassador to Amer-

2. All prizes handled by jw's firm. The *Tartar* was taken by the *Marquis de Lafayette:* XXXVIII, 334n. The *Kitty, Sally, Betsey,* and *Antelope* were taken by the *Buccaneer* (XXXVIII, 93n), and consigned to Williams, Moore & Co. in December, 1782: jw to John and Andrew Cabot, Feb. 22, 1783 (Yale University Library); dossiers des prises, Archives départementales de Morbihan.

3. Dated on the basis of Vaughan's letter of Feb. 13.

4. Probably Hodgson's Jan. 26 letter to BF, above; Hodgson wrote Vaughan the same day.

5. Storer took with him the Ridleys' servant Mary Mingey, whom Anne Ridley was not sorry to see leave: Anne Ridley to Matthew Ridley, Feb. 14, 1783, Mass. Hist. Soc. In a note to BF dated only "Thursday morning," undoubtedly written on Feb. 13, Anne Ridley requested a passport for Mingey, who would leave for London the following evening. APS.

ica;[6] That the ratifications were not arrived in Town the 8th Inst:,[7] & that the subject was not to be discussed by parliament before they were arrived; And, that by letters from Mr Laurens to Mr Manning, Mr L proposed being in Paris by the 11th: Inst., however the latest letters do not speak of his arrival even in London.[8]

Addressed: A son Excellence / Monsieur Franklin, / Ministre plenipotentiare des Etats Unis &c &c, / a Passy.

Notation: Vauhan

From the Baron de Bissy[9] ALS: American Philosophical Society

Votre Excelance.   Bruges en flandre Le 15 fevrier 1783.

Je Benit mille et milles fois Le ciel qui nous donne Cette paix, et je Le Benit dauptems plus de bon Coeur, quelle corone manifiquement vos glorieuses et justes enterprises.

Veulle ausi le just Ciel vous faire vivre Longeus années, pour Le Bonheur et Les delisses de vos chers, braves et interpides patriotes a qui je soite touttes sorte de biens et La gloire de rendre tous les peuples ameriquens, braves, Libres, et unis a eux. . . .j'ay L'honneur detre par des santimens innepriambles . . . De votre Excelance Le tres hemble et tres obisent serviteur.

LE GÉNÉRAL STEPHANO BARON DE BISSY:.

P.S. janbras de tout mon coeur et ame Monsieur. franclin fils. . . .

6. In December Shelburne offered the post to Charles Howard, Earl of Surrey and later Duke of Norfolk (*ODNB,* under Howard), but Surrey declined: Namier and Brooke, *House of Commons,* II, 644–5.

7. The ratifications of the British-French treaty; see Vergennes to BF, Feb. 2.

8. Laurens wrote William Manning from Bath on Feb. 5 about his plans to go to London (S.C. Hist. Soc.). He was in London from Feb. 8 to 11 before returning to Bath: *Laurens Papers,* XVI, 144–5.

9. We have no evidence that he was a general, as he signs himself. Bissy was prone to make inflated claims about himself, as he did in his previous letter to BF (XXIV, 532–4).

A son Excelance. Monsieur Le Docteur franclin ambasadeur plen-ypotansier des Etats unis de L'amerique &. &.

Notation: Bissi Le Baron de, 15 Fevr. 1783.

From Ferdinand Grand   L: Historical Society of Pennsylvania

Saturday night— [February 15, 1783][1]

Mr Grand presents his respectfull Compliments to Doctor Franklin, and takes the liberty of inclosing his Letters for Mr Morris,[2] with the Sketch of the one, about which Mr Grand had the honour to converse with Doctor Franklin; & which proves so much more necessary that Mr Adams has declined in his usual manner* to Sign the Letter for Holland, which had met the approbation of Doctor Franklin, and of course is kept back—

[*Written by Franklin in the margin:*] *i.e. rude Manner

1. On Feb. 12, above, Grand wrote BF about his inability to meet Morris' bills and recommended that a letter be sent to the Dutch bankers who were raising the loan that JA had negotiated (XXXVIII, 574n). On Feb. 15, Grand wrote to Morris explaining the state of the financial crisis and mentioning that he and BF were trying to find solutions: *Morris Papers,* VII, 435. One of Grand's proposals was that the Dutch banking consortium remit to him monies already raised. BF approved this plan, authorizing Grand to write to the consortium. That same day, Feb. 15, Grand sent the letter to JA for his approval so that it could be dispatched the next morning: *Adams Papers,* XIV, 269. The present letter, written by Henry Grand on his father's behalf, indicates that JA refused to sign. On Feb. 23, however, JA wrote the consortium that if Morris had no objection, he would not object to their remitting to Grand whatever balance they held after deducting his own anticipated expenses and the interest on the loan: *Adams Papers,* XIV, 291. By May 22, in response to the deepening crisis presented by Grand in his letter of May 10 (below), JA drafted a letter for the American commissioners to send to Holland proposing that the consortium send 5 million *l.t.:* Butterfield, *John Adams Diary,* III, 125.

2. Grand sent only two letters to Morris between February and May, 1783, as far as the record shows: the one of Feb. 15, cited above, and one of Tuesday, April 15, which is missing, but which enclosed a state of Morris' account and expressed Grand's growing "anxiety": *Morris Papers,* VIII, 315.

From George William René Macarty[3]

ALS: American Philosophical Society

Monsieur   A Vannes ce 15 fer 1783

Je voudrois étre plus agé pour Sentir le bonheur de L'Inde-pendance de mon pays, en partie duë a vos soins, et vous ex-primer en mon particulier ma reconnoissance comme tout Bon Américain doit Le faire, j'es pere par La suite pouvoir m'acquit-ter de ce devoir. Comme j'ai oublié l'adresse de Mon Papa, J'ose vous prier de vouloir bien lui remettre ma lettre, Je vous en au-rai bien de l'obligation. Je prie Dieu de vous Conserver ensanté et suis avec respect Monsieur Votre très humble & très obeissant serviteur.   GEORGE. WILLIAM. RENE. MACARTY

Addressed: A Son Excellence / Son Excellence le Docteur frank-lin / Ministre plenipotentiaire des Etats unis / de l'Amérique a son hotel / A Passy

Notation: Macarty 15 Fevr. 1783

Jonathan Williams, Jr., to William Temple Franklin

ALS: American Philosophical Society

My dear Billy.   Nantes Feb. 15 1783.

The americans here do not understand the 23d Article of the Treaty, & I request you will as soon as may be do me the Favour to explain, whether, By the Canary Islands is meant only the *Latitude* of those Islands, & thus on a line of Latitude, Ships may in one month be in Safety in any Longitude if not to the Southard of the Canaries; or whether it is meant that the Canary Islands are to be considered as a Point which must not be passed either *westward* or *Southward.*[4] You will see that the explanation of this

---

3. Son of William Macarty; see XXXVII, 106.

4. JW is here inquiring about Article 22 (not 23) of the preliminary articles of peace between Great Britain and France, to which America agreed when the general armistice was signed on Jan. 20; see the annotation of BF to Liv-ingston, Jan. 21; Bondfield to BF, Jan. 26. The relevant section of Article 22 said that prizes would be restored for a period of one month if taken between

may save a months Time, or on the other Hand prevent Ships running into Danger. I request an immediate answer & am most affectionately my dear Billy ever Yours   J WILLIAMS J

Addressed: A Monsieur / Monsieur Billy Franklin / chez Son excellence le Docteur Franklin / à Passy / Pres Paris

Note by Franklin: It is the Latitude of the Canary Islands

Notation: Williams, 15. Feby. 1783.

To [American Merchants in France]⁵

Press copy of ADS: Library of Congress

[after February 15, 1783]

By the 22d Article of the Preliminaries of Peace between the Kings of France & Great Britain, signed the 20th of January 1783. it is agreed that all Vessels should be restored that might be taken In the Channel & North Seas 12 Days after the Ratification of the Articles.

Thence as far as the Canaries, whether in the Ocean or Mediterranean, after one Month.

Thence to the Equinoctial after two Months.

Thence in all other Parts of the World after five Months.—

And the Words *as far as the Canaries,* are understood to mean the Latitude of the Canaries, which appears also by adding the Mediterranean to the Ocean.   B FRANKLIN

---

the Channel and North Sea "as far as the Canary Islands, inclusively, either in the Ocean or in the Mediterranean." BF addressed this ambiguity in the following document.

5. This has the appearance of being a circular, and was undoubtedly written in response to JW's letter to WTF, the preceding document. Livingston also requested clarification on the same point: Livingston to JA, April 14, 1783, in Wharton, *Diplomatic Correspondence,* VI, 374.

From J. Torris & Wante[6]

LS:[7] American Philosophical Society

Monsieur [before February 16, 1783][8]

La Conclusion heureuse de la Paix nous determinant à faire l'expedition d'un Navire pour Philadelphie afin d'y déboucher les objets considérables que nous avons fait acheter à Morlaix, à Brest, & dans les autres ports de la Bretagne, provenant des diverses prises faites par Les Differents corsaires de notre Sr Torris, & votre Excellence nous ayant precedemment adressé une Circulaire pour recommander La Maison de Mrs. Bache & Shée,[9] nous souhaiterions leur Consigner ce navire & Sa Cargaison, qui sera assez riche, en consequence, nous Supplions Votre Excellence de nous adresser le plûtôt possible quelques mots de recommandation pour Cette maison qu'elle protege, D'autant que nous nous proposons d'entretenir des Liaisons de consideration avec elle: comme il importe à nos Intérêts de hater cette expedition, nous serions inclinés à La faire Sous pavillon americain. Si aux expeditions americaines, que nous demandons à votre Excellence, elle pouvoit y joindre un passeport du Plenipotentiaire de SA MAJESTÉ Britannique à Paris: cela nous eviteroit bien des risques, de gros frais que le Pavillon Imperial entraineroit: mais si VOTRE EXCELLENCE trouvoit des difficultés à expedier Sous pavillon Americain, nous pourrions encore plus aisement Le faire sous pavillon francais, pourvu qu'elle put egallement procurer un Passeport Britannique contre toutes hostilités.

Notre sr Torris se rappelle toujours avec gratitude ce qu'il doit à vos bontés pour Lui. Il ose se flatter que ces mêmes bontés sont un titre auprès de votre excellence pour en reclamer la Continuation.

Nous Sommes avec respect De Votre Excellence les très humbles & très obeissants serviteurs J. TORRIS & WANTE

Notation: Torris & Wante

6. The Dunkirk mercantile firm: XXXVI, 548.
7. Signed by Wante.
8. Dated on the basis of the firm's letter of Feb. 16, below.
9. Torris' name is on an undated list entitled "Houses Bache & Shees Circular Letters have been sent to" (APS). RB acknowledged the receipt of such a list in early 1780: XXIX, 273n; XXXII, 176.

To Thomas Barclay

ALS: Barclay Giddings Johnson, Jr., Watertown, Connecticut (2001)

Sir   Passy, Feb. 16. 1783
   The within is a Copy of a Resolution of Congress, which I
forward to you, lest you should not have receiv'd it by any direct
Conveyance.[1]
   Your Appointment to this Service gives me great Pleasure, as
I am sure your Execution of it will be of great Use to the United
States. I hope therefore that as soon as you have expedited the
Congress Goods, you will come up to Paris, and enter upon the
Business. In the mean time I will endeavour to prepare every
thing, so far as may depend on me, for rendering the Work easy
to you.
   We daily expect from London 100 Passports that have been
promis'd us, for American Ships. As soon as they arrive We shall
forward a Number to you, to be dispos'd of as you shall judge
proper;[2]
   With great Esteem I have the honour to be, Sir, Your most
obedient & most humble Servant   B FRANKLIN

T. Barclay Esqr

From J. Torris & Wante, with Franklin's Note
for a Reply   ALS: American Philosophical Society

Monsieur   Dunkerque Le 16. fevrier 1783.
   Nous avons appris par Mrs. Maussallè & Bertrand L'acceuil
Obligeant dont Vous les avez honnoré,[3] et la promesse que vous

---

1. BF enclosed a copy of the Nov. 18, 1782, congressional resolution (*JCC*,
XXIII, 728–30) appointing a commissioner "to liquidate and finally to settle
the accounts of all the servants of the United States, who have been entrusted
with the expenditure of public money in Europe, and all other accounts of
the United States in Europe," with a note about Barclay's election. This was
presumably a copy of what Livingston sent him on Nov. 21: XXXVIII, 332.
   2. WTF inserted an asterisk here and added a note in the margin: "Pray inform the Merchts of L'Orient of this."
   3. Maussallé had been Torris' lawyer: XXX, 404n; XXXII, 385; Bertrand, ac-

Leur avoit faite de nous addresser un passeport du Nombre des cent que vous attendez de la Cour de Londres,[4] avec une Lettre de Recommandation pour la maison de Messrs. Bache & Shée à Philadelphie, la multitude d'Armement qui Se fait Tant dans nos ports qu'en Angleterre nous détermine à presser L'Expédition de Notre Brigantin: que nous nommons le franklin. Il a Recu Son Chargement et nous n'attendrons pour le faire partir que L'arrivée de Vôtre passe-port. Nous osons vous prier de nous L'addresser Sans perte de Tems, parce-que nous avons envue une seconde expédition aussi Intéréssante mais qui dépend de la Célérité de la première, et nous prendrons encore la confiance de Reclamer un Nouveau passe-port pour le Second armement que nous projettons. Nous vous prions de Laisser en Blanc dans Votre passeport le nom du Capitaine parce que S'il faut absolument que nous armions Sous Pavillon du congrez nous Serons obligé de faire un nouveau choix.

Nous sommes avec un profond Respect.

De Vôtre Excellence Les Très humbles & Très obeïssants Serviteurs   J: TORRIS. & WANTE

Mr. franklin.

Endorsed: Make a Letter of Recomn. to Messrs. Bache & Shea, and send a Passport. It should be at the Office by 12 oClock tomorrow.[5]

---

cording to the firm's letter to WTF of Feb. 28 (described below), was their representative in Paris. The pair undoubtedly delivered the firm's letter published above, [before Feb. 16].

4. They arrived on Feb. 18; see Fitzherbert's letter of that date.

5. The mail coach for Dunkirk departed daily at noon: *Almanach Royal* for 1783, p. 640. In a letter from Torris & Wante to WTF of Feb. 28, they acknowledged his sending the letter and passport on Feb. 22. The second ship that needed a passport, the brigantine *Haʒard*, would sail under French colors from Dunkirk to Philadelphia. Because the government prohibited French-owned ships from flying anything but the French flag, the *Franklin* had been refused permission to sail under American colors. They therefore requested a replacement passport, as WTF's had identified the ship as American.

On March 13 the firm thanked WTF for sending on March 6 the new passport from BF, which was valid only for a ship flying American colors. In the meantime, the authorities had granted permission for the *Franklin* to sail un-

Notation: J. Torris & Wante Dunkerque 16 Fevrier 1783

To Charles-Guillaume-Frédéric Dumas

Transcript: National Archives

Dear Sir   Passy Feb. 17. 1783.
It is a long time since I have had the Pleasure of hearing from you.[6] I hope however that you and yours continue Well. The Bearers, Mr. President Wheelock and his Brother go to Holland on a Publick spirited Design, which you will find recommended by many eminent Persons in America.[7]

---

der the American flag. They no longer needed the second passport; they did, however, want a list of drugs that could be sold at advantage in America, which should be given to the bearer, Bertrand. Further, they had bought another ship which they hoped to sell to Congress, and wanted advice.

The last extant letter from Wante is written from Paris to WTF and undated. He is about to depart for America; he encloses a petition to BF and requests letters of recommendation for himself and a certain Morgand, who was also bound for Philadelphia to establish a mercantile house. All the letters summarized in this note are at the APS.

6. Dumas' last extant letter was written the previous September: XXXVIII, 67.

7. John Wheelock, president of Dartmouth College, and his brother James had come to Europe to raise desperately needed funds; for their arrival see the Jan. 31 letters from JW and his father, above. The brothers carried letters of recommendation as well as a document on parchment signed by 39 prominent Americans describing the college's history and present circumstances: XXXVIII, 134–5. These they presented to BF the day after they arrived in Paris, according to the narrative Wheelock wrote upon his return. BF received the brothers with "much personal politeness, kindness, and civilities," and lauded their endeavor as "noble and liberal." He invited them to dine the following day, when he introduced them to Morellet and promised to have their "credentials" translated into French. (A French translation of the parchment document, made by L'Air de Lamotte and corrected by Morellet, is at the APS.) BF declined to present their case at Versailles, however, as he was on the verge of presenting a new application for funds from Congress, and he feared that the French might think that "our applications and solicitations might never end, and there would be a real danger of some disgust & national disservice." John Wheelock agreed not even to deliver La Luzerne's letter of introduction to Vergennes and to desist from other fund raising in France. BF suggested that he try England and Holland, and offered, with

I beg leave to request for these Gentlemen your civilities and best Counsels, as they will be entire Strangers in your Country. With great Esteem, I am ever, Dear Sir your faithful humble Servant.   B. FRANKLIN.

M. Dumas.

From Herman Heyman's Sons,[8] with Franklin's Note for a Reply   LS:[9] American Philosophical Society

Sir!   Bremen the 17. feb. 1783.

It is with the greatest Satisfaction, that we Observed by the Publick papers the Declaration of Independence from Great

---

Morellet, to introduce him to potential donors in Britain including Shelburne; Wheelock politely turned down this offer, as he expected little sympathy for a school in the former colonies. He and his brother departed for the Netherlands on Feb. 21, armed with the present letter and several recommendations from JA. In addition, BF, JA, and Jay each donated 20 *louis d'or:* Dick Hoefnagel, "Benjamin Franklin and the Wheelocks," Dartmouth College Library *Bulletin,* new ser., XXXI (1990), 20–1; *Adams Papers,* XIV, 271, 293.

Wheelock prepared two documents around the time BF penned the present letter, which remained in BF's possession: on Feb. 15 he made an extract of a 1768 declaration by the English board of trustees of Moor's Charity School (XXXVIII, 295n) regarding a fund-raising trip to Britain in 1766–67, and on Feb. 17 he certified an eight-page history and description of the institution entitled "Historical Anecdotes . . . ." Both are at the APS.

The following year, in response to a solicitation from another college, BF recalled the Wheelocks' visit. Friends had advised him, he wrote, that Dartmouth's attempt to seek assistance abroad "hurt the Credit of Responsibility we wish to maintain in Europe, by representing the United States as too poor to provide for the Education of their own Children." One circumstance in particular made BF "somewhat ashamed for our Country": that all but one of the 39 signatories of Wheelock's document had refused to make personal donations. BF to John Witherspoon, April 5, 1784, quoted in Hoefnagel, "Benjamin Franklin and the Wheelocks," pp. 22–3.

8. Heyman, Sr.,'s sons were Gerhard (1748–1831) and Herman, Jr. (1754–1810): Karl H. Schwebel, *Bremer Kaufleute in den Freihäfen der Karibik: von den Anfängen des Bremer Überseehandels bis 1815* (Bremen, 1995), pp. 172–3n. For background on this letter see Delius to BF, Feb. 7.

9. In the hand of Heinrich Talla: Sam A. Mustafa, *Merchants and Migra-*

Brittain to the United States, a Situation which we Have heartily wished to the latter for many Years past, and by which means our Country, will be now abel to enter in the most frindly & advantageous Alliance with the same; to convince the United States from our wishes to accept the first Opportunity to enter in Connection with them, we purchased a Vessel and made an Expedition of the products of our Country by the same, in the latter end of last year, and such is now quite compleat, so that it will sail in about 3 Weeks, Our partners in this Expedition are Mr. Henry Talla & M Arnold Delius, the latter has taken the Liberty to write to you the 7 Inst. to which beg leave to refer ourselves, he is going along with the Cargo in the Rank as Supper Cargo, but afterwards, at first makes some stay in Nord America, to establish, if possible an uninterrupted traide between the United States and our place, which will be carried on under the Firm of Heymans Talla & Delius; Mr. Delius has mentioned to you allready that our first intention has been to send the Vessel to St. Thomas to sell the part of her Cargo, which was consisting of provisions, and to take an Opportunity to go with the Remainding to Philadelphia or Boston, but now the Declaration of Independency and the preliminares of peace being signed from great Brittain, made a material Alteration in the Destination of the Vessel, and we are determined to send it now direct to Nord America. We conceive that our Reception, in a Country which never had any direct Dealing with our part of the World might at first be somewhat Cool, and trade not be carried on in such a Spirit & Confidence as Merchand, which have been already in Connection before. We should therefore be infinitly Obliged to your Excelency to favour us with some Letters of Introduction & recommendation as well to the first houses in the most principal traiding places of the United States, as likewise to the Congress or Regency of the same, it would be against Delicacy, to say you much of the Security of our House, but we may say without vanity, that it is of the first Rank of our place, so the two other interested houses, above mentioned, enjoy likewise the first Credit. May we Still take the Liberty to beg of you the

---

tions: Germans and Americans in Connection, 1776–1835 (Aldershot and Burlington, Vt., 2001), pp. 30–1.

favour to address yourself by Mess: Giardot Haller & C: Mess. Cottin fils & Jauge at Paris, or Mess. fizeaux Grand & Comp. & Mess. Hope & Comp. & Mess. Luden & Comp in Amsterdam,[1] and you'll get convinced, that you introduce people to your good Country, which honesty & good Character, as well as their Security intitles them, to recive the best reception in the United States, We formerly recived at our house alone every year 5 or 6 Cargoes of Rice & 3 of Tobacco as the produce of Nord America by way of England, and our port at least Imported of the first 20 and of the Latter about 15 Cargoes in all.

You'll excuse our Liberty to trouble you with the present but the Assurance of your Patrotism and uninterrupted Zeal for your Country makes us flatter ourselves, that you'ill take such in the light, that our Sincere Wishes and our only Views are, to make both our Country become in mutual Advantageous and the most amicabel Connections. We are convinced that it lays in your power to promote such, and to procure us and our City all such benefices or Emoluments, which are granted to other powers; may we therefore request from you these assistences and that you'ill favour us with such Letters as necessary to fullfill our most earnest Wishes, in particular that to the Congress, that we may recive their protection, and enjoy all the Benefice, which they grant to other Nations.

We have the honour to remain with the most Sincerest Regard Sir! Yr. most Obedient, & devoted humble Servants

HERMAN HEYMANS SONS

Endorsed:[2] The Inhabitants of N. A. are accustomed to treat Strangers with Hospitality and Kindness, and a Recommendation to the Government to protect them is neither necessary nor usual. Enclose a Letter to Friends who will give Mr Delius any

1. The first three firms appear frequently in recent volumes. BF was first introduced to Hope & Co. more than 20 years earlier: IX, 367n. Luden & Co. was a leading mercantile house: Johan E. Elias, *De Vroedschap van Amsterdam, 1578–1795* . . . (2 vols., Haarlem, 1903–05), II, 1037.

2. The letter based on these notes, now missing, was sent on March 10; see Herman Heyman's Sons to BF, March 24. The firm also asked JA for letters of recommendation. JA's letter to Robert Morris, dated March 11, is in *Morris Papers*, VII, 555.

Advice that as a Stranger he may stand in need of [*written in margin:* Mr Bache / Mr Williams]

Notation: Herman Heymans Sons Bremen 17th. Febry. 1783

From Loyseau   ALS: American Philosophical Society

Monsieur   Le 17 fevrier 1783.

Mon intention en vous demandant des Renseignemens pour envoyer avec quelque Sureté des aciés dans Le continent de L'amerique,[3] a d'abord eté d'ouvrir un débouché de plus a La Manufacture a la quelle je m'interesse, mais encore je me Suis proposé d'offrir aux etats unis un Moyen d'avoir a Mellieur Marché qu'en angleteré des aciers dont ils doivent faire une Consommation assés abondante. Personne ne voit de plus grandes Suites que moi a L'importante revolution de L'amerique, de plus avantageuse a L'humanité, et personne aussi n'a plus fortement desiré qu'elle Se terminat a votre Satisfaction. D'apres cela je Serois affligé que vous recussiés des impressions qui me fussent contraires; comme M. William alexandre que j'ay obligé tres essentielement, a tenu des propos capables de me nuire, en Supposant Calomnieusement que j'avois Sacrifié Ses interets a L'affection de M. Necker pour M. Walpol, tandis que je me Suis mis Si fort audessus de cette affection que j'ay eloigné de moi des objets d'interet personnel tres essentiels pour Repondre a la confiance de MM alexander[4] avec La pureté d'intention qui est

3. See his letter of Feb. 3, above.
4. In 1779 Loyseau drafted petitions to Sartine, Vergennes, and Maurepas on behalf of William and Alexander J. Alexander, whose estates on Grenada had been sequestered to satisfy a mortgage held by Walpole & Ellison. After the French capture of the island, BF had promoted the brothers' interests with the French government. Loyseau's relationship with the Alexander brothers subsequently soured, and by 1781 Alexander J. Alexander was claiming that improper influence had been used against him in France. Finance Minister Necker's circle is known to have included banker Thomas Walpole (XVI, 163–4n): XXX, 579; XXXI, 242n; XXXV, 314; Robert D. Harris, *Necker, Reform Statesman of the Ancien Régime* (Berkeley, Los Angeles, and London, 1979), p. 211.

toujours ma Regle de conduite; j'ay craint que M. William[5] ne vous eut tenu Sur mon compte quelques-uns de ces propos empoisonnés qu'il S'est permis avec d'autres personnes qui ne lui en ont pas gardé Le Secret. Je n'accuse que lui de cette ingratitude Monstrueuse, car je pense tout autrement Sur Son frere jean.[6] Non Seulement je lui crois un bon coeur mais aussi une tête Beaucoup Mieux faite.

Sur M. de Benyowsky, j'ay craint que vous n'ayes pas bien compris ma demarche en Sa faveur. Je voulois, Sans doute, le Servir et c'est encore mon intention, mais jamais il n'entrera dans mon esprit de le faire aux depens de La justice et je L'ay Reconnue dans L'explication que vous avés bien voulu avoir avec moy, des lors je Suis Resté tranquile Sans pour cela me Moins interesser a M. de Benyowsky, parceque je lui trouve plus de grandes qualités que de défauts, et que je pense qu'il peut Rendre au Royaume des Services importans.

Je Suis avec Respect Monsieur Votre tres humble et tres obeissant Serviteur. LOYSEAU

Lorsque vous voudrés, Monsieur, des aciers dont je vous ay parlé, vous pouvés vous adresser a moy, je vous indiquerai, avec plaisir, les Moyens de traiter Raisonnablement. Peutetre les americains fatigués par une Longue guerre et Les Suites d'une grande Revolution, doivent-ils eviter, S'il est possible, Les Benefices de La Seconde ou meme de la troisieme Main.

Notation: Loyseau 17 Fevr. 1783.

From Roze de Chantoiseau ALS: American Philosophical Society

Monsieur   Ce 17 fevr. 1783.

Oserois-je vous offrir et vous prier de vouloir bien aggreer L'ouvrage que vous m'avés parû desirer. C'est une foible es-

5. Undoubtedly JW. The dowry of Mariamne Williams, his wife, was at issue in the legal battle of William and Alexander J. Alexander (her father and uncle) against Walpole & Ellison: XXXI, 242n.

6. John (Jack) Williams had visited France in 1777: XXIII, 533; XXXIV, 548n.

quisse d'un Projet mieux conçu que des circonstances particulieres ne m'ont pas permis d'executer, pour me livrer tout entier au Plan bien plus important que jai eu lhonneur de vous
adresser il y a environ huit jours et que d'autres occuppations ne
vous ont peut-etre pas permis d'examiner.[7]

Je desire ardemment, Monsieur, que L'Etablissement proposé
qui l'emporte Sans contredit sur tous les moiens dont on a fait
usage jusque a present, pour operer La Liquidation des dettes
d'un Etat puisse etre praticable en faveur d'une Nation qui me
devient aussi chere que ma Patrie, et a La Félicité de laquelle je
Voudrois consacrer tous les instants de mon existence, sils ne
vous etoient particulierement devoüés.

Je suis avec un tres Profond respect de Votre Excellence Le
Plus humble et le plus affectionné serviteur.

ROZE DE CHANTOISEAU

Notation: Roze de Chantoiseux 17 Fevr. 1783.

Alleyne Fitzherbert to the American Peace Commissioners

ALS and two copies: Massachusetts Historical Society; copy: Library
of Congress

Gentlemen,   Paris February 18th 1783.

I have the honour to transmit to you herewith a packet containing one hundred passports for American Vessels[8] which I
have this moment received by a Courier from England.

I take this opportunity of acquainting you that a proclamation
was issued out in the King's Name on the 14th Instant, making

7. The enclosure has not been located; for their previous meeting see
Roze's letter of Feb. 8. Wolf and Hayes claim that the enclosure was Roze
de Chantoiseau's *La Richesse du peuple républicain* . . . , which they assert was
published in 1783: Wolf and Hayes, *Library of Benjamin Franklin,* p. 692.
Their source, however, the published catalog of the Bibliothèque nationale,
lists no publication date for the pamphlet, whose full title suggests a date of
at least 1789. Current online catalogs list versions of the pamphlet from 1789
through 1795.

8. In the margin Fitzherbert wrote "100".

known the cessation of hostilities which has been agreed upon between the several belligerent powers, and declaring farther that the several epochas at which the said armistice is to commence between His Majesty and the United States of North America are to be computed from the third day of this Instant February, being the day on which the Ratifications of the Preliminaries were exchanged between His Majesty and The Most Christian King. I must add that His Majesty was induced to take this step under the firm & just expectation that you, Gentlemen will correspond to it in your parts, by adopting the same measure reciprocally in the name of the States Your Masters.[9]

I have the honour to be with great Regard and Esteem, Gentlemen, Your most obedient and most humble Servant

ALLEYNE FITZ-HERBERT

J. Adams, B. Franklin, & J. Jay Esqrs &c &c &c

To J. Adams, B. Franklin and J. Jay Esqrs Plenipotentiaries of the United States of North America

Notation: Mr. Fitzherbert 18t. Feby. 1783.

From Christopher Baldwin[1] ALS: American Philosophical Society

Clapham Common 18 Febry 1783

Look my dear Sir at the place from whence this letter is dated—have you forgot it? I am sure you have not.—have you forgot the many pleasant hours you have passed here? No, you have not. Have you forgot your throwing oil on the Pond near me, and instantly smoothing the troubled Water—impossible![2] But a far, infinitely far greater object rises before me! Tis you my dear Sir who have troubled the mighty Ocean!—tis you who have raised

---

9. The proclamation is published in *Adams Papers*, XIV, 264–6; copies are in the commissioners' letterbooks at the Mass. Hist. Soc. and the Library of Congress. The American declaration of Feb. 20, below, is a close adaptation of its language.

1. A London merchant and BF's old friend: XX, 466n.

2. For the experiment and Baldwin's involvement see XX, 466; XXIX, 51.

billow upon billow & called into action, Kings, Princes & Heros!—& who after engaging the attention of every individual in Europe and America, have again poured the oil of Peace on the troubled Wave, and Stiled the mighty Storm!

God of his infinite mercy grant it may tend to the happyness of all our fellow creatures in every part of the World!—for narrow indeed are the ideas of those, whose views are confined to particular districts—little, very little, are they intitled to the name of Philosopher.

I write this in the room in which we have often sat & enjoyed ourselves & our friends, and in the moment in which I am writing, in pops Mrs. Baldwin[3] and says—my dear to whom are you writing?— I smile and say—to your friend Dr. Franklyn—O! pray make my best compliments to him, tell him I long to see him again & hope it will be soon—tell him that in spite of politics, I have shewn his Picture which he sent me to all our friends,[4] at all times & boasted of his acquaintance—thus much for a favorite of yours—and no sooner is she gone, than in comes my Son[5] from Town, and he also asks to whom I am writing, I tell him to you—when he says I am very glad of it, for I have a good deal to say to you as I have brought in my pocket a letter I have just received from Mr. Van Moorsel, in which he mentions to me a matter that I should be exceedingly happy to oblige him in. Here I must tell you that my Son for some time past, has had considerable commercial connections with Mr. Van Moorsel, & has procured to the House of Theodore Van Moorsel & Co at Ostend, West India consignments to the amount of 7 or 8000 hhds. Mr. Van Moorsel is the Cheif in the house, & his partner is a most worthy Gentleman of large fortune. Mr. Van Moorsel & my Son have a great regard for each other— I have seen Mr. Van Moorsel and he is one of the most amiable men I ever met with. His House at Antwerp and Ostend, is in high repute, and they have a very great capital, and what my Son is very anxious to have me mention to you, is, that Mr. Van Moorsel, is desirous of

3. Née Jane Watkins: XXVIII, 243n.
4. Probably one of the porcelain medallions made at Sèvres: XXVIII, 244; XXIX, 51.
5. XXVIII, 243–4.

being appointed Consul at Ostend & Antwerp for the American States. If this matter lies with you, you'l highly oblige us all, by naming Mr. Van Moorsel to that Office.—if not with you, but must come from Congress, do my dear Sir favor him with your recommendation, for be assured it will be impossible to find a Gentn. more highly qualified in every respect than he is. If we are to have the pleasure of seeing you here again, and it was with a view to ask you that question that I took up my pen—do come by way of Antwerp, & there, go directly to Mrs. Van Moorsel, you'l find her the most lovely of women and trust me, she will take all the care of you that Mrs. Baldwin would gladly do. Tho I am sure it is needless, yet allow me to assure you our Kindest wishes attend you and that I am Dear Sir Your very sincere friend & humble Servant   CHRR. BALDWIN

Addressed: a Son Excellance / Monsr. / Monsr: B. Franklyn / Plassey / Paris

From Joseph-Etienne Bertier[6]

ALS: American Philosophical Society

Monsegneur   à Paris à st. Honoré le 18 fevrier 1783

Je prends trop d'interet a vôtre victoire complète sur les en-nemis des insurgens, victoire de laquelle vous êtes de ma con-noissance le principal auteur, pour ne pas vous en marquer ma joye. J'ay vu le commencement, la continuation, et la fin de cette guerre par votre sagesse; et l'on peut dire que vous êtes l'auteur d'un peuple nouveau. Je remercie le Segneur de s'être servi de votre canal pour cette grande oeuvre.

Je n'ose pas envoyer à un grand homme occupé à de si grandes choses un ouvrage que je viens de donner, c'est l'histoire des pre-miers tems du monde et des commencemens des hommes prou-

6. An old acquaintance of BF's, Bertier retired from teaching around 1756 and took up the study of physics: VIII, 358; James Evans, "Fraud and Illusion in the Anti-Newtonian Rear Guard: the Coultaud-Mercier Affair and Ber-tier's Experiments, 1767–1777," *Isis*, LXXXVII (1996), 81–5.

vée par l'accord de la Physique avec la Génèse.[7] Si cependant vous avez quelques momens à perdre et que vous me la demandássiés dans une réponse, je seray bien honoré de vous l'envoyer.[8] J'attens votre réponse avec impatience, et suis avec un très profond respect Monsegneur de votre excellence le très humble et très obeissant serviteur   BERTIER

prêtre de l'orat. [oratoire]

From the Earl of Buchan[9]   ALS: American Philosophical Society

Sir,   Edinburgh, 18th. February 1783.

You was entitled to a Civick crown on my account a great many years ago when at the University of St. Andrews you gave a turn to the carreer of a disorder which then threatned my Life.[1]

You have since that time done so much and Heaven has at last been pleased to bless & to Crown your endeavours with so much success that Civic Crowns of a more importent nature are due to you, and certainly await you if there is any such thing as Publick Gratitude on the face of the Earth.

Many of my acquaintance in this part of — seem disposed to seek for an asylum on the other side of the Attlantick and knowing my steady attachment and affectionate regard to a People who received my Great Grand Father when an exile or rather a

---

7. Bertier had long opposed Newton's law of attraction, advocated by what he called latter-day "jeunes épicuriens," as contrary to the notion of God as the first mover. He wrote the *Histoire des premiers temps du monde, prouvée par l'accord de la Physique avec la Génèse, par les philosophes; contre des petits écrits des jeunes épicuriens que les ignorans leur attribuent* (Paris, 1778) to show "the agreement between Cartesian physics and the biblical account of creation": Evans, "Fraud and Illusion," pp. 85, 106.

8. Bertier did send BF a book under cover of an undated letter; we published that letter around the time *Histoire des premiers temps . . .* was published (XXVII, 481), but now realize that it must postdate this letter of Bertier's. After BF returned to America, he presented the volume to the APS: APS *Trans.*, II (1786), [407]. Bertier died on Nov. 15; his obituary appeared in the *Jour. de Paris* on July 31, 1784.

9. This is his first letter since 1774; see XXI, 203.

1. For Buchan's fever see our annotation of BF's reply, March 17.

fugitive from his Country during the Administration of Lauderdale in Scotland[2] have applied to me for informations on the subject of Settlement in the Dominions of the United States.

Before the troubles commenced I had meditated a Settlement in the Estates of the Lord Fairfax in Virginia, but Lord Fairfax being since dead and my connections alterd in that family I have not thought of renewing my Inquiries in that quarter.[3]

What I wish to promote is the happy settlement of my Countrymen in N. America in the Territory of the United States, such Countrymen being Friends to the Principles which gave independence to that Country, Persons also of good characters & virtuous conduct who find themselves crampt & unhappy in a Country now very unfit for the residence of such individuals who have not very considerable fortune to attach them to home.

I forsee a spirit of Emigration, and I wish as much as possible to give it a direction which might tend to the happiness of those in whom from a similarity of Sentiment I must necessarily find myself very much interested.

I have the Honour & pleasure to be Sir with great respect & attachment your most Obedient & Obliged H: Servt.

BUCHAN

Notation: Buchan 18 Feby. 1783

2. Buchan's great-grandfather was Henry Erskine, Lord Cardross (1650–1693), an ardent Presbyterian who opposed the administration of John Maitland, second Earl and first Duke of Lauderdale. He was imprisoned in Edinburgh for almost four years, beginning in August, 1675, and shortly after his release was accused by the Scottish Privy Council of misrepresentation. Cardross emigrated to South Carolina and established a plantation; when the Spaniards drove him out, he went to Holland, where he accompanied William of Orange to England during the Glorious Revolution: George E. Cokayne *et al.*, eds., *The Complete Peerage of England, Scotland, Ireland, Great Britain, and the United Kingdom, Extant, Extinct, or Dormant* (rev. ed., 13 vols., London, 1910–59), III, 19–20; *DNB*, under Henry Erskine and Maitland.

3. Thomas Fairfax, sixth Baron Fairfax of Cameron and related to Buchan's grandmother, died on Dec. 9, 1781, and Robert Fairfax became the seventh baron, inheriting the "Northern Neck" proprietorship: Stuart E. Brown, Jr., *Virginia Baron: the Story of Thomas, 6th Lord Fairfax* (Berryville, Va., 1965), pp. 187, 197–9; *Burke's Peerage*, pp. 421–2, 977–8.

From Reichsfreiherr von Weinbrenner[4]

ALS: American Philosophical Society

Excellence!   Vienne le 19. Fevrier 1783.[5]

La Liberté du commerce des états unis de l'Amerique étant fondée, les sujets de notre cour ont aussi l'envie, de tenter un commerce droit avec ces Provinces heureusses et abondantes en plusieurs Articles pour notre bésoin, et il ne leurs ÿ manque que la connoissance des maisons de toute la solidité, auxquelles ils se pourroient confier.

A ce sujet je prends la liberté, de prier votre Excellence, de me communiquer quelques Adresses des maisons solides à Boston, Philadelphie, et nouvel york. J'en serai infiniment obligé, et je

---

4. Joseph Paul Reichsfreiherr von Weinbrenner (1728–1807), an extremely wealthy and well-connected Austrian merchant who acted as an informal commercial advisor to Empress Maria Theresa and after 1771 as commercial counselor to Joseph II: Constant von Wurzbach, ed., *Biographisches Lexikon des Kaiserthums Oesterreich* (60 vols., Vienna, 1856–91). It was Prince Kaunitz, imperial chancellor and minister of foreign affairs, who instructed him to write the present letter. Having received no response, he asked Ingenhousz to forward a copy to BF; it was enclosed in Ingenhousz's letter of April 8 (below).

5. On Feb. 18 Joseph II had written to Mercy-Argenteau, his minister to the French court, that commerce with the Americans would be extremely important for the future. Because the Low Countries would most profit from this trade, he had charged the prince of Starhemberg (its interim governor general: *ADB*) to look into the matter. Joseph also indicated that he would welcome an American overture to establish diplomatic relations. He thought that the best occasion to discuss matters would be when BF visited Ingenhousz in Vienna: Alfred d'Arneth and Jules Flammermont, eds., *Correspondance secrète du comte de Mercy-Argenteau avec l'empereur Joseph II et le prince de Kaunitz* (2 vols., Paris, 1889–91), I, 165.

Joseph II must have written to Starhemberg immediately upon hearing news of the preliminary peace. On Jan. 22 Starhemberg wrote to Mercy-Argenteau that he should informally let BF know that the time was propitious to discuss a trade agreement. He suggested that BF send a representative to speak to him in Brussels, but cautioned Mercy-Argenteau to maintain secrecy unless the impression could be created that BF had made the first overture on establishing commercial relations. He also directed that his letter be burned. Mercy-Argenteau had not so much as hinted anything about this to BF by March 1, to Starhemberg's disappointment: Hanns Schlitter, ed., *Die Berichte des ersten Agenten Österreichs in den Vereinigten Staaten von Amerika Baron de Beelen-Bertholff . . .* (Vienna, 1891), pp. 233–4.

me protesterai toute ma vie d'être avec la plus parfaite Réconnoissance Excellence! votre très-humble et très-obeïsst. Serviteur   JH v WEINBRENNER

Mon Adresse:
A Monsieur Joseph de Veinbrenner, conseiller du commerce de sa Majesté Imperiale Royale / â Vienne / en Autriche.

Notation: Veinbrenner 19 Juillet 1783.

The American Peace Commissioners to Alleyne Fitzherbert

AL (draft):[6] Massachusetts Historical Society

Sir   [February 20, 1783]

We have recd. the Letter wh you did us the Honor to write on the 18th. Inst, together with the Passports mentioned in it.

His britannic Majesty's Proclamation of the 14th. Instant has our entire approbation, and we have the Honor of transmitting to you, herewith enclosed, a Declaration perfectly correspondent with it.[7]

It appears to us important to both Countries that a System be speedily adopted to regulate the Commerce between them; and it gives us pleasure to inform you that we are authorized to form one, on Principles so liberal, as that british Merchants shall enjoy in America & her Ports & Waters, the same Immunities and Priviledges with her own; provided that a similar Indulgence be allowed to those of our Country, in common with british Merchts. in general—[8]

6. In Jay's hand.
7. The following document.
8. JA suggested such a clause in his 1776 model Franco-American commercial treaty. In 1780 he anticipated the British would suggest such a clause in the peace treaty: *Adams Papers*, IV, 260, 266, 290–1; IX, 84–5. BF made a similar suggestion to Oswald on July 10, 1782, as the third of his advisable articles (XXXVII, 600), and the American commissioners included it in Article 4 of their first draft treaty (XXXVIII, 193–4). See also BF's sketch of articles to be included in the definitive treaty: XXXVIII, 434. This proposal resembles Article 24 of the third Family Compact (*pacte de famille*) signed by

We presume that such a System will on consideration appear most convenient to both; if so, we shall be ready to include it in the definitive Treaty—

We flatter ourselves that this overture will be considered as a Mark of our Attention to the Principles adopted in the Preamble of our Preliminaries, and of our Desire to render the commercial Intercourse between us free from Embarrassing & partial Restrictions—

We have the Honor to be with great Regard & Esteem Sir Your most obt & very hble Servt

Sketch of a Letter.
to Mr Fitzherbert.[9]

The American Peace Commissioners: Declaration of the Cessation of Arms[1]

ADS and AD (draft):[2] Massachusetts Historical Society; copies: Massachusetts Historical Society, Library of Congress; transcript: National Archives

[February 20, 1783]

By the Ministers Plenipotentiary of the United States of America for making Peace with Great Britain:

France and Spain on Aug. 15, 1761, and later joined by the Bourbon rulers of the Duchy of Parma and the Kingdom of the Two Sicilies: Parry, *Consolidated Treaty Series*, XLII, 97–8. It too envisaged a commercial relationship deeper than that between two unrelated states.

9. These two notations appear on the verso. The first was written by John Thaxter, Jr. JA added the second.

1. This declaration was subsequently printed, most likely by Philippe-Denis Pierres; the dual-sided folio sheet is described in Luther S. Livingston, *Franklin and his Press at Passy . . .* (New York, 1914), pp. 194–5. The printed version differs from the ADS and all the American commissioners' copies in one regard which has not hitherto been noticed: any time the French king ("his most Christian majesty") is mentioned, he is listed before any other monarch or government.

2. Both of which are in JA's hand. (Jay made corrections to the draft, which are detailed in Morris, *Jay: Peace*, pp. 495–6.) Fitzherbert sent a signed copy to Grantham on Feb. 22: Giunta, *Emerging Nation*, II, 70.

A Declaration

of the Cessation of Arms, as well by Sea, as Land, agreed upon
between His Majesty the King of Great Britain and the United
States of America.

Whereas Preliminary Articles, were Signed, at Paris, on the
thirtieth Day of November last, between the Plenipotentiaries of
his Said Majesty the King of Great Britain, and of the Said
States, to be inserted in, and to constitute the Treaty of Peace, to
be concluded, between his Said Majesty and the Said United
States, when Terms of Peace Should be agreed upon between his
Said Majesty, and his most Christian Majesty: And Whereas Preliminaries for restoring Peace, between his Said Majesty the King
of Great Britain, and his most Christian Majesty, were Signed at
Versailles, on the twentieth Day of January last, by the respective Ministers of their said Majesties: And Whereas Preliminaries for restoring Peace, between his said Majesty the King of
Great Britain and his Majesty the King of Spain, were also
Signed at Versailles on the Twentieth Day of January last, by
their respective Ministers: and Whereas, for putting an End to
the Calamity of War, as Soon and as far as possible, it hath been
agreed, between the King of Great Britain, his most Christian
Majesty, the King of Spain, the States General of the United
Provinces, and the United States of America as follows, that is
to Say.

That such Vessells and Effects, as should be taken in the Channel, and in the North Seas, after the Space of Twelve Days, to be
computed, from the Ratification of the said Preliminary Articles, Should be restored on all Sides; That the Term should be
one Month from the Channel and the North Seas as far as the Canary Islands, inclusively, whether in the Ocean or the Mediterranean; Two Months from the Said Canary Islands, as far as the
Equinoctial Line or Equator, and lastly five Months, in all other
Parts of the World, without any Exception, or any other more
particular Description of Time or Place.

And Whereas the Ratifications of the said Preliminary Articles, between his said Majesty, the King of Great Britain, and his
most Christian Majesty, in due Form were exchanged by their
Ministers, on the third day of this instant February, from which

Day the Several Terms abovementioned, of Twelve Days, of one Month of two Months and of five Months, are to be computed, relative to all British and American Vessells and Effects.

Now therefore, We, the Ministers Plenipotentiary, from the United States of America, for making Peace with Great Britain do notify to the People and Citizens of the Said United States of America, that Hostilities on their Part, against his Britannic Majesty, both by Sea and Land, are to cease, at the Expiration of the Terms herein before Specified therefor, and which Terms are to be computed, from the third day of February instant. And We do, in the name and by the Authority of the Said United States, accordingly warn and enjoin all their Officers and Citizens, to forbear all Acts of Hostility, whatever, either by Land or by Sea, against his Said Majesty, the King of Great Britain, or his Subjects, under the Penalty of incurring the highest Displeasure of the Said United States.

Given at Paris the Twentieth Day of February, in the year of our Lord, one Thousand Seven hundred and Eighty Three.

JOHN ADAMS [seal]

B FRANKLIN [seal]

JOHN JAY [seal]

From Amelia Barry

ALS: American Philosophical Society

My Dear Sir,   Pisa 21st. Feb. 1783

The important contest between America and Great Britain being finally decided, I cannot deny myself the pleasure of making you my sincere felicitation upon it. Condemned as I am to humble fortunes, I am aware that there is an impropriety in my concerning myself with the affairs of states and empires; but while I invade not the Politician's province, and only in the shades of retirement, breathe wishes for the happiness of persons most dear to me, and success to a glorious cause, and exult when they are effected, I hope that the events on which they depended being of a Public nature, gives not culpability to sentiments, which, had they had a reference to Private events, might have been deemed virtuous.— You my dear Sir, are most immediately concerned in the decision of the late contest, & must feel a very superior pleasure in finding that it has terminated in the Independance of America.— Your decline of life cannot now fail to be calm and serene: may you long be a witness of the happy fruits of your labours and may the new Empire be, thro' a series of ages, the envied seats of virtue, science, and grandeur. At times I look back to the scenes of my childhood, & feel a desire arise in my breast to revisit them once more;—but the severity of my fortune keeps me here an exile, nor even admits of my return to England.

I return you Sir, my best thanks for your having condescended to honor my recommendation of Doctor Burrows with notice.[3] Miss Burrows wrote me that they had dined with you; how I envy them the happiness of having conversed with you! Miss Burrows said you disapproved of my remaining in Italy, and mentioned your having hinted to her father an intention to give your Banker instructions to remit me a sum of money, to enable me to conduct my little helpless family to England. This is near 4 months ago; and as I know you never say what you do not mean, I am apprehensive that you have put your kind intention into execution, & that the letter has miscarried, in which case, you must deem my silence an act of flagrant ingratitude— Yet do not my dear Sir, imagine that my motive in this address, is to put a tax upon your friendship. I value it too much to risque the loss of it by appearing mean enough to sollicit pecuniary favors:—to poverty my mind is tolerably subdued; all my cares now centre in my children, and were I but enabled to give them tolerable educations, (as I have nothing else to bestow) and to find that their progress in virtue [*torn:* had] responded to the culture of their minds, all my wishes would be accomplisht.

I hear that it is expected you will soon return to England— May Heaven direct your steps, and grant you health & happiness. When you write to my dear Mrs. Bache, do me the favor to present my affecate. comps. to her, and ever believe me with the sincerest veneration and respect, Most Dear Sir Your faithful, obliged & Obedt. Servant   A. BARRY.

3. XXXVIII, 120.

Be pleased to direct to me sulla Piazza San Nicola, Pisa.

His Excelly. B. Franklin Esqr.

Addressed: His Excelly. B. Franklin Esqr. / Ambassador, & Plenepotentiary / from the United-States, / Paris.

Endorsed: A Barry 21 Feb. 83 / Feb. 21. 83

From John Fottrell,[4] with Franklin's Note for a Reply

LS: American Philosophical Society

Sir   Ostend the 21 february 1783

I had the honour of writing you About Sixteen Months ago per Mr DeClerck; the Subject whereof was for advice of a Draft on your Excellency for a Trifling Sum advancd to one Mr Robeson:[5] I only mention this Circumstance to facilitate your recalling me to mind, and you was So Kind sir at that time to give him a List of Such articles as were then most In Demand in the united States of America. Having Last year sent Several Cutters Loaded to those parts, and having at present one ready to Sail in Ten Days, I Should be under the greatest obligation, were your Excellency pleased to honour me with a few Lines of advice, whether I may or not, venture yet to Send any goods of English manufactory, for tho' Peace be Concluded, I am apprehensive Notwithstanding that the act of Congress prohibiting the Entry of Such goods may not be yet repeald at the time of her arrival, & Such goods be Still Liable to Confiscation. As she is a remarkable fast Sailer I Expect She'll Gett there in a Short time: having been Intended to perform the voyage During the war, when men & Every thing in General were very Dear, her fitting out has been very Expensive.

If it was possible, & your Excellency pleased to honour me with a pass of Safety in respect to the act. Should it not be re-

4. An Irishman, formerly based in Dunkirk: Christian Pfister-Langanay, *Ports, navires et négociants à Dunkerque (1662–1792)* (Dunkirk, 1985), pp. 334, 447.

5. XXXV, 664–5.

peal'd at the vessell's arrival, for the Speculation of these articles would help for the great Charges I have Been at, and I shall Ever acknowledge with real Sentiments of Gratitude the favor Conferred on me.

Should your Excellency be inclin'd to Send any thing by this opportunity to America, I Shall in the Strongest manner recommend Same to the particular Care & attention of the person who goes in the Cutter, and to whom I Entrust the whole manadgment of Vessell & Cargoe.

She is Called De Stadt Weenen, John Standbank Junr Commander under Imperial Colours,—& in about two hundred & twenty Tuns Burthen destin'd for Philadelphia.

The Chief Magistrates of this Town in Consequence of orders from Government have Desird me (Knowing the Connection I have with America) that I would acquaint all my friends there, that Every Encouragement & facility that Can be desird will be granted to the American trade here, ardently wishing to See it flourish; it's with pleasure I Do my Self the honour of Informing your Excellency thereof, and of Subscribing my self with the Greatest Respect— Your Excellency's most obedient and most humble Servant   JOHN FOTTRELL

Endorsed: I cannot advise Mr Fottrel to send any British Goods to America till he hears that the Trade is open. No Passpt. of mine will be sufficient to secure them from Seizure. Thanks for his Offer of Service.— Glad to hear of the good Disposition of the Magistrates.

Notation: Tottrell Mr. John, Ostend 21 Feby. 1783.

From Triol, Roux & Cie.   ALS: American Philosophical Society

Monsieur,   à Marseille le 21e. février 1783.

Le 12e. Avril 1781, vous eútes la bonté de nous écrire pour nous assurer que vous enverriez au Congrès copie de notre lettre du 4e. du même mois,[6] & que vous le prieriez d'en prendre le

6. See XXXIV, 535–6.

contenu en considération. Depuis lors, nous attendions à ce sujet quelques nouvelles de Mr. Oster, Vice Consul de France à Philadelphie, qui avoit été chargé de nos effets par le Capitaine de notre navire, mais jusqu'ici nous n'en avons reçû aucune.[7] La circonstance actuelle d'une heureuse paix, qui fixe par vos soins le sort de l'Amérique Angloise, nous fait prendre la liberté de vous mettre de nouveau sous les yeux l'objet de notre demande.

Au mois de septembre 1778, le Capitaine Guillaume Reboul, commandant notre navire la Louise Marie, arriva dans la rivière de Bedfort, après avoir passé pendant la nuit au milieu d'une escadre Angloise, & il y vendit une partie de sa cargaison à Mr. Rossel,[8] pour les besoins de l'armée de Providence; le papier du Congrès étoit alors au pair de l'argent. Quelque tems après, il se rendit à Boston où il finit sa vente, mais quand il voulût prendre des lettres sur la France contre le papier du Congrès, pour le retour de ses fonds, personne ne voulût lui en fournir qu'à deux ou trois pour un: il n'osa se soumettre à une si forte perte, & il cherchoit à employer ses fonds de quelque autre manière, lorsque le Congrès suspendit deux émissions de son papier, dont notre Capitaine se trouvoit pour cinquante six mille six cens soixante quatre Dollars; il fût obligé de les remettre au Congrès, qui ne lui rendit de nouveau papier en échange que huit mois après, époque à laquelle il étoit tellement en discrédit, qu'il ne vit d'autre parti à prendre que celui de le déposer au Congrès pour trois ans, à l'intérêt de six pour cent par an. Les Capitaines qui firent leur vente lors de la remise du papier, tirerent de leurs cargaisons des sommes immenses; mais comme nous ne sommes pas dans la classe de ceux qui ont fait d'aussi grands bénéfices, nous espérons que le Congrès voudra bien avoir égard à l'époque à laquelle notre Capitaine a vendu, & à la détention d'une partie de ses fonds, qui l'a tenu en suspends pendant huit mois; de sorte que nous ne serons pas dans le cas de supporter des réductions

7. François Barbé de Marbois reported on the firm's continued struggle to realize its profits in a Dec. 20, 1784, letter to Castries: Abraham P. Nasatir and Gary E. Monell, *French Consuls in the United States: a Calendar of Their Correspondence in the Archives Nationales* (Washington, D.C., 1967), pp. 177–8. For Martin Oster see xxvii, 334n.

8. Probably Joseph or William Russell: xxxiv, 329n.

s'il s'en faisoit. Nous osons espérer, Monsieur, de votre justice, que vous voudrez bien nous faire la grace de présenter nos raisons au Congrès sous leur vrai point de vuë, pour que nous ne soyons pas confondus avec ceux qui ont vendu leurs cargaisons à vingt ou trente pour un, & que nous soyons payés de notre capital & des intérêts, comme nous avons lieu de l'attendre de son équité. Cela ne nous dédommagera pas des pertes que nous & nos intéressés avons souffertes par la prise de nombre d'autres batimens que nous avions armés pour la même destination.

Nous avons l'honneur d'être avec respect, Monsieur Vos très humbles & très obéïssants Serviteurs   TRIOL ROUX & CE.

Notation: Triol Roux & Co Marseille 21. Fevr. 1783.

From Patience Wright

ALS: American Philosophical Society

My dear honourable Friend—   London Feb 22th 1783

I This moment made up my Packet for america Sent by a old faithful Servant of Doct Franklin Sons: from New Jersey of govonr Franklins— This man is Sent off to america from his master who is now Lodging in Suffolk Street no 16 where he Sd. govonor has undertaken to pettition in aid on behalf of all the tories together with the famous of that Partie—⁹ His late disopintm. in aplying to Parliment together with his Convection of Bad Politicks: his health is bad looks old and Excites in me the old feelings of Friendship the death of his Wife¹ has added to his other Losses &c.

---

9. At the beginning of February, Loyalists living in Britain formed a board of representatives to petition Parliament for compensation. WF was chosen as the representative for New Jersey and was one of four members, all former governors, who presented Shelburne with a draft petition dated Feb. 8. Despite Shelburne's refusal of support, the Loyalists proceeded to submit their petition to Parliament. They also published a pamphlet, described in the headnote to Franklin's Answers to "Claims of the American Loyalists," [during or after February]. This campaign was one of the factors that contributed to the fall of the Shelburne government at the end of the month: Mary Beth Norton, *The British-Americans: the Loyalist Exiles in England, 1774–1789* (Boston and Toronto, 1972), pp. 185–9.

1. WF's wife Elizabeth died in 1777: XXII, 621n.

His Servent now Sets out to leve the Place and his master the news of my own Son Jos Wright being Cast away nere Boston from Nantz in the Ship Argo . . Stranded &c.[2]

Those unhapy tidings makes me feal the Parent, and Joyne in Comforting them—may god whom I trust Make your heart to do and Contunue to do good and Keep you a Blessing to mankind is the Pray[*torn:* er of] your faithful old friend and very humble much obl'gd   PATIENCE WRIGHT

I hope to See you in Phila this Sumr as Human Nature Seems Changd I no longer Prophesie But only say time will bring all my Romantick Ideas Round and Convince my Friend I am no MAD but Speak the old Quaker truths—

—My daughter and husband[3] is Well my health good my Spirits Rise and feal Rightous Indignation at the parliment of England. They adopt the faults of george and Charlott.[4] And as they pertake of ther Sins they will also have their Plagues I hope you will visit London the great Joy will by Expresd *mentiond* heretofore and a publick Entry into London; not only 2 hundred but 2 thousand to attend you. Major Labilliere is Ready with his Christian Armie[5] 7 thousand whom have not bow'd down to george or *Beal* my Kind love to your grand Son I hope his Experienc and Wisdom will make him a great Minister We all Wait for the Season to Set out for america all the wise and prudent are going Depend on the great fall of Publick Credit oh the Bank must go before Pharoh will go to hanovor[6] my daughter Joyne me in love and Esteem I hope you have health Pleas to mention me to those who Enquire after P Wright

2. For Joseph Wright's shipwreck see XXXVIII, 507n.

3. She may have been living at this time in St. James's Square with her daughter Phoebe and son-in-law John Hoppner: Charles C. Sellers, *Patience Wright: American Artist and Spy in George III's London* (Middletown, Conn., 1976), pp. 173, 175.

4. The king and queen. For Parliament see Hodgson's letter of Feb. 25.

5. For Peter Labilliere, a retired major, and his "Christian Army" see XXIII, 449; XXXVI, 222–5.

6. She hoped George III would abdicate and retire to his Electorate of Hanover, which he had been ruling in absentia; see Sellers, *Patience Wright*, pp. 159, 172.

Addressed: His / Excellency / Doctr. Franklin / Passey / Paris

Notation: Wright Feby. 22 1783—

From Jonathan Williams, Jr.

ALS: American Philosophical Society; copy: Yale University Library

Dear & hond Sir.   Nantes Feb. 23, 1783.

I inclose you a Letter I have received from Mr Dalton of New-bury, you will see by it that he is in hopes another Application will procure a greater allowance from Government for the Brig Fairplay.[7] I have promised (not with a view of having ⅙ of the Property) to write you once more though it does not appear [*to*] me likely to meet any Success. If you imagine otherwise I shall be obliged by your Answer, and to forward the Papers and such a Letter to the Minister as you may think the affair merits.[8]

I am obliged to you by your kind Notice of Mrs Williams who I hear is with you, my Father will thank you for himself, I should be happy if my Business would permit me to make one of the Party but I must mind the main chance.[9] Now we are at Peace the

7. The *Fair Play* was mistakenly sunk by the French in 1779, and BF's intervention had failed to obtain the full value of the ship; see XXXVIII, 11. The letter JW enclosed was Dalton's to him of Dec. 24, 1782, begging that BF try once more to procure the full value of 26,666 Spanish milled dollars. One-sixth of any sum in excess of the 15,000 *l.t.* already awarded was promised to the man who secured the increase.

A week after Dalton sent that letter, JW wrote to him with the news that on Nov. 14 Castries informed him that the award would not be increased. The money was ready to be delivered, but they needed Capt. Giddings' signature on a receipt that JW enclosed (JW to Dalton, Dec. 30, 1782, Yale University Library).

8. JW did not wait for BF's response. On the same day that he wrote the present letter he sent a discouraging reply to Dalton. Castries, he said, claimed that the captain was responsible for the fate of his ship, and the settlement was more of a favor than the discharge of an obligation: JW to Dalton, Feb. 23, 1783 (Yale University Library).

9. JW had intended to go with his father to Paris and escort Mariamne Williams home to Nantes. On Feb. 6 he notified WTF that because of business-related matters, he was postponing his trip and his father would travel alone: JW to BF, Jan. 25, above; JW to WTF, Feb. 6, 1783 (APS).

americans are flocking to England. Poor Richard's Advice makes me incline to remain where I am at least 'till I see some certainty of being better elsewhere which does not appear likely to happen soon.

I am as ever most dutifully & affectionately Yours

JONA WILLIAMS J

Please to return me the Letter.

His Excelly Doctor Franklin

Notation: Williams Jona. Nantes Fevr. 23 1783.

From the Abbé André Morellet

ALS: American Philosophical Society

Cher et respectable ami   lundi. [February 24, 1783][1]

Vous m'avez promis que vous me donneriés un jour pour venir diner chés moi avec mr. le chevalier de chatelux. Vous devez cette complaisance (car c'en est une) à son amitié à la mienne et aux desirs de toute ma petite famille.[2] Il faut absolument que vous me donnies ou *samedi* ou *lundi* de la semaine prochaine et que vous me fassies savoir votre reponse demain matin en venant à paris, ou plutot encore si vous le pouves. Consultés votre cher fils qui sait mieux que vous si vous etes libre ou non car vous voyes bien qu'après vous etre affranchi vous et toute votre patrie de la tyrannie brittanique il vous reste encore celles que l'indiscretion francoise vous impose. Je vous enverrai demain chés mr.

1. Dated by two clues. This is the first Monday after Feb. 18, when Rochambeau, along with Chastellux and the rest of his general staff, arrived at Versailles. They sailed on the frigate *Emeraude,* which anchored at the mouth of the Loire on Feb. 10: *Gaz. de Leyde* of Feb. 28; Rice and Brown, eds., *Rochambeau's Army,* 1, 84n. The allusion to WTF's social life also signals that this letter had to have been written during the season of balls that ended with the beginning of Lent on March 5.

2. Which included his brother Jean-François Morellet and sister Françoise Lerein de Montigny, as well as his niece Marie-Adélaïde, her husband, Jean-François Marmontel, and their children, Albert-Charles-François and Charles-Paul: Medlin, *Morellet,* 1, 467n.

de maillebois la copie de la traduction du discours de mylord dont vous feres l'usage que vous jugeres convenable.[3] Si vous n'aves pas pû me repondre plutot sur le choix du jour vous voudres bien faire la reponse au porteur qui vous remettra le papier. Je n'ai pas besoin de dire que si les plaisirs de mr. franklin le fils l'emportoient ce jour là à quelque bal et l'empechoient de venir avec vous il nous feroit un mortel chagrin. Je vous prie de recevoir les assurances de mon tendre et respectueux attachement pour la vie.   L'ABBÉ MORELLET

tout consideré je vous envoie un exprés afin d'avoir la réponse tout de suite choisisses du *samedi* ou du *lundi*

Addressed: à Monsieur / Monsieur Franklin / ministre plenipotentiaire des etats / unis / à Passy.

Notation: L'abbè Morellet

Contract between Louis XVI and the United States, Signed by Vergennes and Franklin

DS: Archives Nationales,[4] National Archives; two copies and transcript: National Archives; press copy of copy: American Philosophical Society

[February 25, 1783]

Contrat entre le Roi et les Treize Etats Unis de l'Amérique Septentrionale, passé entre M. le Cte. de Vergennes et M. Franklin, le 25. Fevrier 1783./.

3. Shelburne's speech of Feb. 17 in the House of Lords defending the peace terms (Cobbett, *Parliamentary History*, XXIII, 407–20). Morellet translated a summary of it published in the *Morning Post:* Medlin, *Morellet,* 1, 475n, 480, 484. We have found no record of Morellet's translation being published; another translation appeared in the *Gaz. de Leyde* of March 11 and the supplement of March 14. BF's copy is at the APS.

4. Docketing on the cover sheet indicates that BF was given a duplicate copy on the day of the signing, along with a copy of Vergennes' full powers. An English translation of the contract along with its ratification by Congress on Oct. 31 are in *JCC,* XXV, 773–8.

Contrat entre le Roi et les Treize Etats-Unis de l'Amérique Septentrionale.

La paix rétablie entre les Puissances belligérantes, les avantages d'un Commerce libre dans toutes les parties du Globe et l'Indépendance des Treize Etats-Unis de l'Amérique Septentrionale, reconnüe et fondée sur une base solide et honorable, promettoient de voir les dits Etats en situation de pourvoir dès apprésent à leurs besoins par les ressources qui leurs sont propres, sans être forcés d'implorer la continuation des secours que le Roi leur a si libéralement accordés pendant la durée de la guerre; Mais le Ministre plénipotentiaire desdits Etats-Unis près Sa Majesté, lui ayant exposé l'épuisement où les a réduit une guerre longue et désastreuse, Sa Majesté a daigné prendre en considération la demande faite par le Ministre susdit au nom du Congrès desdits Etats, d'une nouvelle avance d'argent pour subvenir à une multitude d'objets de dépenses urgentes et indispensables dans le Cours de la présente année; Sa Majesté s'est déterminée en conséquence, malgré les besoins non moins pressants de son propre service, à accorder au Congrès une nouvelle assistance pécuniaire qu'Elle a fixée à la somme de Six millions de livres tournois, à titre de prêt et sous la garantie solidaire des Treize Etats-Unis, Ce que le Ministre du Congrès a déclaré accepter avec la plus vive reconnoissance au nom desdits Etats.

Et comme il est nécessaire au bon ordre des finances de Sa Majesté et même utile aux opérations de la finance des Etats-Unis, d'assigner les époques de payement des Six millions de livres dont il s'agit et de régler les conditions et les termes du remboursement qui doit en être fait au Trésor-Royal de Sa Majesté à Paris, à l'exemple de ce qui a été stipulé pour les précédentes avances, par un premier Contrat du 16 Juillet 1782.[5]

Nous Charles Gravier Comte de Vergennes &ca. Conseiller du Roi en tous ses Conseils, Commandeur de ses ordres, Chef du Conseil Royal des finances, Conseiller d'Etat et d'Epée, Ministre et Secrétaire d'Etat et de ses Commandemens et fi-

5. XXXVII, 633–9.

nances,[6] muni des pleins pouvoirs de SA MAJESTÉ à nous donnés à l'effet des présentes.

ET NOUS BENJAMIN FRANKLIN Ministre plénipotentiaire des Etats-Unis de l'Amérique Septentrionale, pareillement muni des pouvoirs du Congrès desdits Etats au même effet des présentes, après en avoir conféré et nous être düement communiqué nos pouvoirs respectifs, avons arrêté les articles qui suivent,

Article Per. [Premier]

Le payement des Six millions de livres argent de france énoncés ci-dessus, sera fait des fonds du Trésor-Royal, à raison de Cinq cens mille livres par chacun des douze mois de la présente année, sur les reconnoissances du Ministre desdits Etats-Unis, portant promesse au nom du Congrès et Solidairement pour les Treize Etats-Unis, de faire rembourser et restituer en argent comptant au Trésor-Royal de SA MAJESTÉ, au domicile du S. Grand Banquier à Paris, ladite Somme de Six millions de livres, avec les intérêts à Cinq pour cent l'an, aux époques stipulées par les articles Trois et Quatre ci-après; Les avances que SA MAJESTÉ a bien voulu permettre qui soient faites à compte des Six millions dont il s'agit, seront imputées sur les payemens des premiers mois de cette année.

Article 2.

Pour l'intelligence de la fixation des termes de remboursement des Six millions au Trésor-Royal, et pour prévenir toute ambiguité à ce sujet, il a été trouvé convenable de récapituler ici le montant des précédens secours accordés par le Roi aux Etats-Unis, et de les distinguer suivant leurs différentes Classes; La pre-

6. Two days before signing this contract Vergennes was promoted to *chef du conseil royal des finances*, which effectively made him chief minister as well as foreign minister. The king's decision resulted from the political challenge mounted by Joly de Fleury against Castries, who was also a rival of Vergennes. (See the annotation of JW to BF, March 5; Joly de Fleury to BF, March 15.) BF must have learned of Vergennes' appointment when he signed this contract at Versailles. He made a note on a fresh sheet of paper of the minister's new address: "A Monsieur / Monsieur le Comte de Vergennes / Chef du Conseil Royal des Finances / Ministre & Secretaire d'Etat / à la Cour" (APS).

miere est composée des fonds successivement prêtés par SA MA-JESTÉ, montans ensemble à la Somme de Dix huit millions de livres, remboursables en especes au Trésor-Royal en douze parties égales de Quinze cens mille livres chacune, outre les intérêts, et en douze années à commencer seulement de la troisieme après l'époque de la paix; Les intérêts commençant à courir de l'époque de la paix pour être acquittés chaque année, doivent diminuer à mesure et en proportion du remboursement des Capitaux, dont le dernier terme écherra dans l'année 1798.

La seconde Classe comprend l'emprunt de Cinq millions de florins de Hollande, montant par évaluation moderée à Dix millions de livres tournois,[7] ledit emprunt fait en Hollande en 1781. pour le Service des Etats-Unis de l'Amérique Septentrionale, sous l'engagement du Roi d'en restituer le Capital avec les intérêts à 4. per%. l'an, au Comptoir général des Etats généraux des Provinces-Unies des Pays-Bas, en dix parties ègales à compter de la sixieme année de la datte dudit emprunt; Et sous pareil engagement de la part du Ministre du Congrès et solidairement pour les Treize Etats-Unis, de faire le remboursement des Dix millions du dit emprunt, en argent comptant au Trésor-Royal, avec les intérêts a 4. per%. par an, en dix parties égales d'un million chacune et en dix termes d'année en année, dont le premier écherra au mois de Novembre 1787. et le dernier dans le même mois de l'année 1796., Le tout conformément aux conditions exprimées au Contrat du 16. Juillet 1782.

Dans la troisieme classe sont compris les secours et Subsides fournis au Congrés des Etats-Unis, à titre d'assistance gratuite de la pure générosité du Roi, dont Trois millions accordés antérieurement au Traité du mois de fevrier 1778.[8] et Six millions en 1781., desquels secours et Subsides montans ensemble à Neuf millions de livres tournois, SA MAJESTÉ confirme ici, en tant que de besoin, le don gratuit au Congrès desdits Treize Etats-Unis.[9]

7. 10,000,000 *l.t.* was worth approximately 4,400,000 *f.*: XXXVI, 190n.

8. The amount provided became a source of controversy; see our annotation of Grand's Feb. 12 letter.

9. By contrast, in the Seven Years' War France paid Empress Maria Theresa nearly 35,000,000 *l.t.* in outright subsidies (the total is for the years 1757–66): P. G. M. Dickson, *Finance and Government under Maria Theresia, 1740–1780* (2 vols., Oxford, 1987), II, 180–2.

Article 3.

Le nouveau prêt de Six millions de livres tournois qui fait la matiere du présent Contrat, sera restitué et remboursé en argent comptant au Trésor-Royal de SA MAJESTÉ, en six parties égales d'un Million chacune avec les intérêts à Cinq pour cent par an, et en six termes dont le premier écherra en l'année 1797. et ainsi d'année en année jusqu'en 1802. que le dernier remboursement sera effectué.

Article 4.

Les Intérêts à Cinq pour cent l'an, du Capital de Six millions énoncé en l'article ci-dessus, commenceront à courir du Per. Janvier de l'année 1784. et seront payés comptant au Trésor-Royal de SA MAJESTÉ à Paris, au même jour de chacune année dont la premiere écherra le premier Janvier 1785. et ainsi d'année en année jusqu'au remboursement définitif du Capital, SA MAJESTÉ voulant bien, par un nouvel acte de générosité, faire don et remise aux Treize Etats-Unis, des intérêts partiels de la présente année, ce que le Ministre soussigné du Congrès a déclaré accepter avec reconnoissance, au nom des dits Etats-Unis.

Article 5.

Les Intérêts du Capital de Six millions diminueront dans la proportion des remboursemens aux époques fixées en l'article ci-dessus; Le Congrès et les Etats-Unis se réservent néanmoins la faculté d'accélerer leur libération par des remboursemens anticipés, si l'état de leur finance pouvoit le leur permettre.

Article 6.

Les parties contractantes se garantissent réciproquement l'observation fidèle des articles ci-dessus, dont les ratifications seront échangées dans l'espace de Neuf mois, ou plutôt s'il est possible, à compter de la datte du présent Contrat.

EN FOI de quoi Nous Ministres plénipotentiaires de SA MAJESTÉ et du Congrès des Treize Etats-Unis de l'Amérique Septentrionale, en vertu de Nos pleins-pouvoirs respectifs, avons signé le présent Contrat et y avons fait apposer le Cachet de Nos armes.

FAIT à Versailles le Vingt cinquieme jour du mois de Fevrier Mil sept cent quatre vingt trois./.

GRAVIER DE VERGENNES   B FRANKLIN
[seal]   [seal]

From Benjamin Franklin Bache

ALS: American Philosophical Society[1]

My dear Grand Pappa   Geneva 25, Feb 1783

Full of Impatience to recieve a letter from you in order to know the state of your health & whether you consent to my having a wathch as I Desir'd by my Last,[2] I write yo the present Letter, to ask again that Favour and repeat to you that I have not reciev'd the Parcel of Books mention'd in your Letter of the 7 Jan. 1783.[3] I have receiv'd Lately a letter from Mrs Montgomery to wish I have not yet ans werd having had a sore hand. I have heard also By madame Cramer that you think of going to London as I should have a very great Desire of nowing those Contries, & being estremely fund of Voyagin and above all other Reason being full of Impatience to see you. I ask of You as a particular favour to permit Me to go with You. You will lay under a great obligation Your Most Dutiful & Affectionate Grandson

B. FRANIN. BACHE

Addressed: A Monsieur / Monsieur Franklin Ministre / Plenipotentiaire des Etats unis / D'Amerique auprès de [sa] Majesté / très chretienne. / á Passy Près Paris.

1. Castle-Bache Collection, available on microfilm.
2. Jan. 30, above.
3. XXXVIII, 556–7.

From the Comte de Beaujeu ALS: American Philosophical Society

à champlitte, en franche comtè,
Illustre Ministre.   ce 25. fevrier, 1783.
Daignés agrèer la foible production d'une mûse Séptuage-
naire! J'avoüe mon insufisance pour L'èxpréssion du Sentiment
Relatif à une matière aussi Riche qu'intèrèssante; mais, mon admiration pour le heros de l'amerique, et ma vènèration pour
votre Excèllence, ÿ suplèront à ce que J'éspère.[4]

J'ai encore Monsieur, une grace éssentielle a vous dèmander;
c'èst de faire passer la Rèspéctable médaille *cÿ jointte,* à notre immortel général Monsieur de Waginsthon. Ses glorieux èxploits,
ont tant de raport, avec ceux du cèlébre henry quatre (le plus
Brâve et le meilleur de nos Roÿs) que, j'aime a me pèrsuader que
ce paralèle lui Sera aussi agrèable que L'Effigie de ce grand
prince . . .[5]

Et Vous, Monsieur? qui, à juste titre, mèritès celuy du mo-
derne Sullÿ, je vous ferois, de grand cœur L'hommage de Son
portrait, si J'avois pû me le procurer, pour faire le pendant de
celuy du grand henry?[6] je supplie, instament Votre Excèllence,
de me tenir, un peû compté, de ma bonne volontè: peut ètre que,
mes Ulterieures Rechérches seront plus fructueuses. Mes Vœux
seroient à leur comble, si Vos Excèllences daignaient Se resou-
venir de moi, lors de la distribution de vos Rèspèctables Bustes,
et médailles, qui doivent Eterniser, Monsieur, vos profonds
travaux politiques, et les victoires accumulées du vrai *Mars* des
Etats unis . . .

4. Beaujeu enclosed a seven-stanza "chanson militaire" set to the tune of
"du haut en Bas," which employs seven lines to the stanza; it is in praise of
brave "Waginsthon" and wise BF, the new Sully. In a note on the bottom
of the sheet he calls it "très mediocre," begging BF's indulgence because he
is as old as Herodotus. The effort is not so much mediocre as charmingly col-
loquial; few poets unknown to BF praised him using the informal "tu," and
rhymed "Amérique" and "politique" with "aux anglois tu fais la nique": you
thumbed your nose at the English.
5. Beaujeu wrote again on April 1, begging for a reply; in that letter he explained that the medal depicted a bust of Henri IV and was made of "argent
dorée." APS.
6. Maximilien de Béthune, duc de Sully (1560–1641), served Henry IV in
various essential capacities, and helped negotiate the Peace of Savoy.

Je n'ai point l'honneur d'ètre connu de vous Monsieur; Mais, Monsieur le comte de Vérgennes qui m'honnore de Sa protéction et de Ses Bontés, poura certifier à Votre Excéllence, que j'ai quelques droits aux votres, par mes voeux Redoublès pour le bien de la cause commune c'est dans ces invariables sentimens que je Suis avec bien du Réspèct, Monsieur, de Votre Excéllence, Le très humble et très obeissant serviteur,

Le cte. de Beaujeu
ancien chambellan et capitaine aux gardes
du feû Empereur charles Sept &c.[7]

From William Hodgson

ALS: American Philosophical Society

This letter reports what proved to be a fatal setback to American hopes that Britain would adopt liberal trade policies toward the United States or would include such provisions in a revised final peace treaty. In the early morning hours of February 22, after an all-night debate, the House of Commons voted to approve the provisional peace treaties but censured Shelburne for the concessions they contained. Having lost a vote on the peace terms four days earlier, Shelburne saw his position as hopeless. He submitted his resignation as First Lord of the Treasury on February 24, though it would be another month before the king accepted it.[8]

Shelburne's defeat was the result of a coalition between North and Fox, former political opponents but both rivals of Shelburne. The king refused to accept Fox as a member of any new cabinet. When the North-Fox alliance remained firm, he sought to form a government without them, but William Pitt the Younger and others refused to make the attempt. It was not until the beginning of April that a new government was formed under the Duke of Portland, with North and Fox as its secretaries of state.[9]

7. Charles Albert, Elector of Bavaria, was elected Holy Roman Emperor in early 1742, with French support, three years before his death: *ADB*, under Karl VII.

8. Cobbett, *Parliamentary History,* XXIII, 435–571; Fortescue, *Correspondence of George Third,* VI, 244–5, 247–8; John Norris, *Shelburne and Reform* (London and New York, 1963), pp. 264–70.

9. Fortescue, *Correspondence of George Third,* VI, 265–8, 329–30, *passim;* Alan Valentine, *Lord North* (2 vols., Norman, Okla., 1967), II, 345–64; John

Dear Sir   London 25 feby 1783

I rece'd your favor of the 2d per Major White[1] & Credit your Acc't per Bill on Mr Vaughan Two hundred & Sixty pounds, per Contra I debit you for Ten Guineas paid Mrs Hewson & £7..17.6 for the Bills of 180 Livres Tournois. I have got a pass for my Ship the Mary but they made me pay £23 for it at our Secretary of State Office; a most shamefull Imposition in my Mind.[2]

You express a doubt in your Letter, respecting its being adviseable to send a Vessell out untill some Treaty of Commerce shou'd be settled, it gives me much Concern how to govern myself—for in point of Fact such arrangments had been made with respect to the purchase of goods, jointly betwixt Mr. S. Vaughan & myself that, if we do not send the Ship we shall be saddled with a large parcell of goods, with which we shall not Know what to do & if we delay the sending them the first Blush of the Business, our whole Plan will be frustrated; We flatterred ourselves we might, under the Sanction of the Treaty att all Events be secure from any thing like Confiscation or Seizure, & we further had reason to hope if any Indulgencies were shewn we were as much entituled to them as any other Persons, as our Cargo will go consigned to Mr Vaughan's Son[3] either to Baltimore or Philadelphia as may be judged best, the Vessell calling for Instructions at Lewes in the Delaware.

There is no doubt but our Parliament will do away every Hostile Act—& permit American Vessells to come in (without any Treaty) they have allready admitted two Vessells to an Entry from Nantucket; When Particular Stipulations are settled by Treaty, they do away the general Rule, but it is by no Means necessary there shou'd be a Treaty for the Subjects of different

---

Ehrman, *The Younger Pitt* (3 vols., New York and Stanford, Calif., 1969–96), I, 101–4.

1. Not found. The portions concerning trade, which Hodgson mentions in the next paragraph, must have echoed BF's message to JW of Feb. 2, which JW conveyed to Samuel White; see our annotation of JW to BF, Jan. 28.

2. BF agreed; see his reply of March 9. Hodgson later charged the state with extortion, and on Feb. 20, 1784, the court ruled in his favor: *Universal Magazine* for February, 1784, pp. 108–9.

3. Samuel's son John went to Philadelphia in 1782: XXXVI, 450n.

States to Trade with each other— If I understand att all what is a first Principle in the Law of Nations this is one— That the Subjects, of every State in Amity with any State may navigate to & from such State without hindrance or Molestation Conforming themselves to the general Laws of the State with which they intend to Trade. This is however only my Idea of things I may be wrong & shall be much obliged to you for your Advice & direction, we cannot undo what we have done but if you apprehend any Danger, we can send the Vessell to New York; Perhaps Sr you may without Impropriety write a Letter to some of the Leaders in Congress, Stating our Case & recommending us to their Friendship & Assistance, If you can do this Mr Vaughan & myself will both esteem ourselves much obliged to you & pray be so Kind as favor me with an Answer the very first Opportunity after you receive this for we were in hopes our Ship woud be ready to Sail in a fortnight.

We have had a strange Revolution in the Political World within the last week, Mr Fox & the Discontented part of the late Ld R'ms[4] Friends having made a Coalition with Ld North, the combined Army has in two Engagements totally routed the Shelburnites, & this day I understand the New Arrangement in Administration is to be made, I do not, in my own Judgment think this will be the worse for America—the *Inns* are as much for Peace as the *Outs*, & perhaps it may, upon the whole, have a Tendency to make a more permanent Establishment, Lord S— had very few personal Friends, & his whole Manner was such, that every Man who had access to him, soon Saw, he had nothing like Friendship in his Composition. I am with the greatest Respect Dr sr your Obliged Hble Servant   WILLIAM HODGSON

From Richard Penn, Jr.   ALS: American Philosophical Society

My Dear Sir.   Cavendish Square Feb. 25th. 1783

I hope you continue to enjoy perfect good health, it woud give me great pleasure to hear from you & have that confirm'd to me,

---

4. Rockingham. In 1782 Fox had been a member of the Rockingham government.

I myself was not quite Well for a few days before I left Paris which prevented me from calling upon you to take leave of you, but your Grandson was with me & I desir'd him to apologize for me, which I dare say he did in a proper manner.[5]

There was a matter that I cou'd have wish'd to have open'd my mind to you upon but I had not an Opportunity. It is not imprabble but that the Congress of the United States may think it expedient to fix upon some Order or Mark of distinction for those who they may think have deserv'd well of them. Now if such an Honour coud be extended to One an Alien & who has not the happiness of having been born amongst them I shou'd be Proud to wear it, & Altho' I have not been actually employ'd in their Service either Civil or Military, yet I have always thought with the greatest satisfaction of the Confidence they plac'd in me in making me the Bearer of that admirable Petition which was intended to have prevented the distresses & Calamities that since that time have befall'n both Countries.[6] If the Order of distinction cou'd in any shape be merited, by the Dictates of the heart & the feelings of an Individual ever anxious for their wellfare & Success I think I might with propriety put in some claims to it, but give me leave to rest the matter entirely with you, if you think my Request improper you will of course think no more of it, if otherwise I beg your protection & Friendship in speaking the good word for me, I flatter myself that when you come to England my House in Cavendish Square will not be the last that you will come to, for altho' you undoubtedly have a great many Friends amongst the Literati & Great Men of this Country, perhaps there is not one of them who is a greater Admirer of your Abilities & who wish's more for your happiness & Prosperity than does My Dear Sir Your sincere Friend   RICHD. PENN

5. Penn had delivered to WTF a letter from Maj. Richard England, taken prisoner at Yorktown and now in London, asking him to intercede with BF to obtain a release from his parole. England had first asked WF to intercede for him but was refused; he enclosed a copy of WF's reply, which explained that WF had not corresponded with either WTF or BF since they arrived in France: Richard England to WTF, Dec. 29, 1782 (APS).

6. Penn carried the Olive Branch Petition to England: XII, 94n; XXII, 280–1.

Mrs. Masters, my Wife & her Sister join me in desiring to be kindly remember'd by you[7]

From Benjamin Vaughan   ALS: American Philosophical Society

My dearest sir,   London, Feby 25, 1783.

The return of Mr White[8] enables me to send you some of the articles you asked of me to procure. You will find the list inclosed, and in my next I will try to send you a bill of my disbursements, both now & formerly.—[9] Mr Franklin's glasses will be forwarded by Mr Storer,[1] or earlier, if an opportunity offers. They would have gone now by Mr White, had I received a longer notice of his intentions of returning to Paris.

7. Penn's wife, Mary Masters Penn, was the daughter of BF's late friend William Masters (VI, 312n) and Mary Lawrence Masters (XVI, 275n), and the sister of Sarah Masters: Charles P. Keith, *The Provincial Councillors of Pennsylvania . . .* (Philadelphia, 1883), pp. 428, 453–4.

8. Samuel White, whose departure was delayed because of illness, never returned to France, as far as we can determine. See Vaughan to WTF, March 5, below.

9. The list is missing. On Jan. 31, shortly before Vaughan left for London, BF remitted to him 4,800 *l.t.* (Account XVII, XXXII, 4); it is likely that part of this sum, at least, was for the articles BF and WTF wished to obtain from England. For reasons that will emerge in these pages as the months unfold, Vaughan did not send them until early June, by which time the number of items had increased. He sent WTF an account of what was in the four boxes he shipped, some of which was destined for other friends in Paris. That account largely corresponds to the inventory, undated and in French, that seems to have accompanied the boxes themselves, though that inventory lists five boxes: Vaughan to WTF, June 6, 1783; List of Boxes Containing Articles for BF *et al.;* both at the APS.

1. This scientific glassware for WTF was from William Parker & Sons (XXXVII, 698n). Contrary to what Vaughan writes here, it was included in the June shipment of boxes described in the previous note. Storer returned to Paris on March 11: JA to Laurens, March 12 (*Laurens Papers*, XVI, 160). He did deliver to the Franklins, on the part of Samuel White, "some late papers, some Curious Cuts of the Times, the Debates of House of Parliament, for your Amusements." When White heard from WTF that the "Cuts" had pleased them, he replied, "the English foks are a Curious set of beings, their print shops are full of their Abuses of their Great": Samuel White to WTF, March 5 and April 15, 1783, APS.

You now see verified all that I said about binding down England to so hard a peace.[2] It has put many good people into ill humor, and it has given a thousand pretexts to the bad people among us. But the overthrow of parties, is nothing to the overthrow of systems relative to English commerce, which was intended to be placed on a footing that would have been an example to all mankind, and probably have restored England to her pinnacle again. America I am sure we should have had as much of, as could be expected, upon the proposed systems of liberality. But However the ministry shall finally arrange itself, I cannot but hope on all hands, that we shall be more or less cured of our fighting & monopolizing notions, and look to an American's *friendship.*— The boldness of my friend's[3] conduct therefore has done infinite service to men's minds, as his conversation has done to the royal mind.— You will take pleasure in hearing that he talked of making England a free port, for which he said we were fitted by nature, capital, love of enterprize, marine, connections, & position between the old & new world & the north & south of Europe; and that those who were best circumstanced for trade, could not but be gainers by having trade open. Indeed I may now say to you with courage, that I have scarcely seen or heard any thing of what has passed already, or was meant to take place hereafter, that I do not approve and applaud, as conducted upon grand principles. In short, I think that at last England will mend, not her parties indeed, but the proceedings of those who remain in office, whoever they may be.

The public are not yet instructed in the system of their peace; but pains are taking for this purpose by a respectable friend of yours.[4] And more too will be said in the house. But the ministry were confounded, all but one or two men, at the junction of parties against them; for had the crisis of the peace been missed for an attack, opposition as politicians knew that no other would offer, and the ministry would become fixed & even popular.— I

2. During his extended visits while BF was conducting peace negotiations: XXXVII, 672–3, 719–25; XXXVIII, 368–70, 596–8.
3. Shelburne.
4. Possibly David Hartley.

do not however find that the man of the people[5] has gained much in the public estimation, for his union with Lord North, or his conduct about the peace.

To you I need not point out any of the absurdities of the public proceedings; but you will now see who has been your friend, and upon what principles; for he *might* have made closer terms with you, had he thought either the measure or *manner* wise.— I am much satisfied at having heard him say, that he repented of nothing of all that he had done, that he would do it all over again, and that he sees that he alone had the resolution to go through it— God be praised that it is done, & that no one asks to have it undone.

They are hurt here to think of your apprehensions about coming to London,[6] which reflect on those of your friends who have been in power, and suppose them wanting in manliness & every thing else.— I am preparing your apartments, and would not make over my guests to the first man in the world. And I say that you are coming likewise, and that you are coming to honor one who of all others upon earth will most taste it.— Nothing can be more snug than the place where we live. Your son & you will both have your apartments, and a range of three sitting rooms besides to yourselves, besides the one we have for the family. Music will be going forwards in the house, and the child we have got is too well educated & tempered to spoil it by its cries.[7] As to our company, it will be your own; and my wife bids me add, that she is prepared to love you as much as I do.

Before I close, I have the favor to ask you of a *single* short letter in behalf of Mr Joshua Grigby Junr:, Mr Bird's cousin; who though of a good family, county connections, with £500 per annum of his own, & eldest son to parents who have £2000 per

5. Charles James Fox; see the headnote to Hodgson's Feb. 25 letter.

6. On Jan. 20, after the signing of the preliminary peace, Vaughan heard BF respond to a lady who inquired whether he would now go to London. The answer, as Vaughan recalled it, was "Probably not; I may not be agreeable, & I do not know how I should be received": Vaughan to Shelburne, Jan. 25, 1783 (APS).

7. The Vaughans' first child, Harriet, was born on Nov. 11, 1782: John H. Sheppard, *Reminiscences of the Vaughan Family . . .* (Boston, 1865), p. 26.

annm, is going out to settle in America.[8] His spirit I dare say will strike you, and I think he demands it of us to render his first entrance into the country easy. He seems to have good sense, and has certainly a good character and is a gentleman & one who has seen much of considerable company; but in the midst of it all, he can be struck with a country life & simple manners.— A second, but single letter, I have to request in favor of Mr John Darby, a relation of my own, & of the Admiral of that name.[9] He still remains in a very capital business, but I have little doubt that he will prolong the visit he is going to make to America into a final settlement, as his manners very much lead him to a natural country life. He is an Irishman, and has very wide connections in the North of Ireland. He is honorable, and much beloved by his family & friends, of whom he has an infinite number in all quarters. You have seen him at our house upon a Sunday evening, when my father went to Jamaica, with Mrs Knowles, Dr: Caulder, & others, and were very merry with him.—[1] These two letters, I beg to have as soon as possible, or at least Mr Grigby's.

8. Grigby (for whom see Hartley to BF, Feb. 4) was a cousin of the London bankers Henry Merttins Bird (1755–1818), the husband of Vaughan's sister-in-law Elizabeth Ryan Manning, and his brother Robert Bird (b. 1760). Both had visited Vaughan in Paris the previous December, Henry at the beginning of the month (when Vaughan requested from WTF a passport for him to return to London) and Robert at the end of the month, when he met BF in Vaughan's presence on Dec. 25. Robert returned to London a few days later, carrying correspondence of Vaughan's and, very likely, the gift of children's books BF sent Mary Hewson (XXXVIII, 566, 578; BF to Hewson, Jan. 27, above): W. W. Abbot et al., eds., The Papers of George Washington, Presidential Series (13 vols. to date, Charlottesville and London, 1987–), V, 41n; Vaughan to WTF, Dec. 8, 1782; Vaughan to Shelburne, Dec. 17[–18], 26, and 27, 1782 (all at the APS); Laurens Papers, XVI, 108, 299–300.

9. John Darby was married to Vaughan's sister Ann: Sheppard, Vaughan Family, p. 26. He had been a pupil of Thomas Paine's in London around 1770, and once he arrived in America, Paine recommended him to George Washington: Philip S. Foner, ed., The Complete Writings of Thomas Paine (2 vols., New York, 1945), II, 1222. Vice Adm. George Darby (XXIX, 296n) resigned from his command in March, 1782, but continued to serve as an M.P. for Plymouth (1780–84): ODNB.

1. Samuel Vaughan went to Jamaica in early 1775: XXI, 442n. "Mrs. Knowles" undoubtedly is the poet Mary (Molly) Morris Knowles (1733–1807), wife of the London physician Thomas Knowles, known for her bril-

I am doubtful whether Johnson[2] will have prepared the things I gave orders for, & procured your philosophical books; but I shall be very angry, if he does not, which I hope will excuse me to you.

Your friends are all well. Will you believe the power of party, when I tell you that Jack Lee[3] execrates the peace, and talks of our *fine fleet* &c &c? You do not wonder at his former opposition, after hearing this, or think the worse of my friend for not having had *his* friendship.

With my perpetual & affectionate regards to your son, I am my dearest sir, Yours ever most devotedly, gratefully, & affectionately,   BENJN: VAUGHAN

I shall write your son the first opportunity I learn of.

Some of Johnson's things are arrived. The debates are sewn together out of news-papers by some gazzeteer, in the pamphlet you have sent you.

Some people say in London, that you are now abusing England as much as during the war.[4] I tell them that if you do abuse, it is I believe more as a philosopher & speculator, than as a politician: At least that this was your turn when I saw you.

---

liant conversation as well as her needlepoint portraits. She was a correspondent of the Rev. Dr. John Calder, whose first letter to BF is below, March 13. *ODNB*, under Mary Knowles; John Nichols, *Illustrations of the Literary History of the Eighteenth Century* . . . (8 vols., London, 1817–58), IV, 830–1.

2. Probably Joseph Johnson, who had published Vaughan's edition of BF's writings (XXXI, 210–11).

3. Doubtless BF's former attorney John Lee (XV, 255n; XXI, 38n), who brutally criticized the peace treaty during the debate in the House of Commons: Namier and Brooke, *House of Commons*, III, 26–7.

4. One such critic was Alleyne Fitzherbert; see our annotation of his Feb. 5 letter.

From Clemens August Haxthausen[5]

ALS: American Philosophical Society

Eccellence   Hildesheim le 26 feby 1783

Permettez votre Eccellence qu'un inconnu etrencher [étranger] vous Présenter ses hommages en occasion du glorieux paix que votre Eccellencé avez fait pour gloirs immortell du serenissime Republique des Etats unies en Amerique, et de votre Eccellencé; et quoi jai eu toujour ete un admirateur du heroisme qu'enflame le coeur de votre Eccellence et des touts ses braves Compatriotes, je ne me pouver plus dispensé en attendant le tres honorable paix de faire une inscription latin qu'on pouver mettre a la statu du Roÿ de france, que le très Illustre Congres avez resolu d'erricher [d'ériger] a Philadelff, que j'ai l'honneur de summetre du jugement de votre Eccéllence[6] et de me nommer avec le plus profonde respect du monde Eccellence votre tres humble et tres obeisent serviteur

AUGUST BARON D'HAXTHAUSEN
Trefoncier d'Hildesheim proche d'Hannover

From Ingenhousz

ALS: American Philosophical Society

Dear friend.   Vienna febr. 26. 1783.

You will have recieved my last,[7] by which I asked you leave to dedicate my work, now, as I hope, under the press, to you— I

5. A colonel in the Danish army (1738–1793): Carl Frederik Bricka, ed., *Dansk biografisk leksikon* (16 vols., Copenhagen, 1979–84).

6. On Feb. 25 the *Courier de l'Europe* reported news from Paris (dated Feb. 14) that the Americans, wishing to honor the French monarch, were proposing to erect a bronze statue in the main square of Philadelphia, "en face du Palais du Congrès," with the following French epigraph: "A Louis XVI, Libérateur des Américains." We cannot trace the origin of this rumor. It was in circulation for at least another month, when an unattributed Latin inscription for the statue was published; see Caffiéri's letter of March 25, below. Haxthausen's enclosure has not been found.

Another writer, the abbé "N. st. D.," also proposed an inscription for this monument. His verse (in French, undated, and among BF's papers at the APS) was intended for the pedestal of an obelisk he understood was to be erected at the "place de Boston" where Congress met.

7. Above, Jan. 28.

am rejoiced to be informed by the *chancerie* of the Court, that, according to an advise of Count de Mercy to Prince Kaunitz, you are certainly to come here.[8] Since that time I am courted by many more Gentlemen and Ladies to present them to you. I hope, in that case, to share the most part of time in private Conversation with you. I think the best and most confortable way to go from France to Italie is throh Austria, because from Vienna to the Venitian territory you have not a single difficult or dangerous road; all of them run along the feet of the mountains and are very well kept up. But for all be very carefull to take as aisy a carriage as possible, and suspended upon good springes, which have been used a long while; so that there be no danger of their failing on the road. Such springs, as have the leather stops, by which the carriage is suspended, tyed over them, are the best. They seldom break for a very natural reason. The Frensch use such springs more than the English. You will not be fatigued by such a carriage. The inside of the carriage aught to be large in Italie. Other wise the heat is very distressing; the frensh carriages are in general too narrow and the English too low. You are to reflect at that article. I wish I Could accompany you in your journey thro Italie. Having been twice there and knowing the language and Customs of the people I would be usefull to you. If every thing was now conducted in the liberal way it was before, I would not scrupul to provide a carriage for me for the purpose and keep my self ready at a day's warning.

The inclosed I could not refuse to forward. I gave the writer

8. BF had been telling Ingenhousz for some time that he hoped to visit Italy with WTF, and would stop in Vienna on his way back to Paris; see XXXV, 551. Word evidently circulated that they planned to make the journey as soon as peace was secured. On Jan. 21, the day after the preliminaries were signed, JW wrote to WTF asking if they were going (APS). On Jan. 27 Favi wrote to his government in Tuscany that BF would go to Italy, and thence to Spain, before returning to America. On March 24 Venetian ambassador Dolfin reported to his government that BF intended to visit Italy before leaving Europe, "in order to offer philosophic food to his sublime genius": Antonio Pace, *Benjamin Franklin and Italy* (Philadelphia, 1958), p. 10. At least two Venetians contacted BF as a result; see Pavola to BF, May 10. BF himself explained to Robert Livingston some months later that he wanted to introduce WTF to Italy "as a Reward for his faithful service, and his tender filial attachment to me": BF to Livingston, July 22[–26], 1783, National Archives.

as much temporary assistance as I could: but I doubt whether his exigencies are not above any thing I can afford him my self, or by the liberality of my acquaintances.[9]

Recieve my harty Congratulation on the fulfilling of your prophecie, that *England will never return into the possession of America*. The important share you have had in this revolution, which makes one of the most memorable epocha's in the history of the world, must create a lively joy in your friends, and a sense of shame and envy in those, who laboured in vain to crush you, and to overturn your cause. I should like to observe now, in your presence, the Contenance of Lord North, Sandwich, george Germain, Stormond,[1] and for all of mr. Wedderburn, now, in honour of his short triumph over you, Lord lougsborough;[2] (if I doe not mistake) but I should not wish to see Among them the king, because I would as much pity him as I would laugh at the rest. Now you are a free and independent people you aught to be mindfull of the old proverb. *Felix, quem faciunt aliena pericula cautum!*[3] and prevent disunion among your Self. You have had open ennemies, now you will have inobservable onces. The flattering hope; with which your old master will still feed him Self, that America, finding that the liberty of the people is precarious without a Souverain being the gardian of it, will return again to the old allegiance, will be kept op a long while. Several people here begin to think of setling in a Country, which seems So much the more temting, as this begins to offer a melancholy prospect. For my part I would be the most tempted of all to goe over, if the mercantile undertakings, in which I engaged with mr. Wharton,

9. If the enclosure was a letter from Valltravers, as we suspect it was, that letter is missing. See Ingenhousz' letter of Jan. 28.

1. These men had been members of Lord North's cabinet. John Montagu, Earl of Sandwich (X, 412n), was First Lord of the Admiralty; Lord George Germain (XXI, 185n), Secretary of State for the American Colonies; and David Murray, Viscount Stormont, Secretary of State for the Northern Department (XXXI, 154).

2. Alexander Wedderburn, who had humiliated BF in the Cockpit, was created Baron Loughborough in 1780: *ODNB*.

3. Happy is he whom others' experiences make cautious. BF quoted this proverb twice in *Poor Richard's Almanack*, and repeated it in "Father Abraham's Speech": I, 359; II, 373; VII, 346.

had answered as I had the greated reason to expect. There was time enoug to employe the capital three or four times in the Same undertaking, as was proposed, if he had send remittances as soon as possible, according to his pledge of honour. Have you got no intelligence of my lettre being arrived at Philadelphia, or of his (Mr. Wharton's) circonstances? I can not familiarise my self with the idea of a man, who has allways wore an unsullied caracter, being Such mean sharper, as every circonstance should made suspect him to be to any one but me. He is now a membre of Congres,[4] and must therefore bear still a honorable caracter. I am neither satisfied with the lettres of Dr. Bankroft nor with those of mr. Coffyn,[5] as the former gives me for reason of not communicating to me the contents of Mr. Wharton's lettre, that he thaught mr. Coffyn had done it; whereas mr. Coffyn writes me the reason of his not doing it, was because he did not doubt but Dr. Bankroft had done it; and yet, when they both were informed by my self, that neither of them had informed me of it and that I desired very much to be informed of it, they continued the one as well as the other to conciel it from me. What Dr. Bankroft writes me of having informed me of it in a lettre, which may be lost by not having been payed at the post office, can not be probable, as I ordred my bankers to inform exactly at the post office about it and mr. Le Begue did it allso, and as there is a standing ordre to inform the person to whom the lettre is directed, that a lettre to his adres is stopt till payed for. Besides Dr. Bankroft contradictes him self by writing in the same lettre, that he Should have inform'd me of it, if mr. Coffyn had not wrote him that he had allready done it. I have got constantely such a printed lettre of advise from the post office. There is in the Contents of Dr Bankroft's letter and that of mr. Coffyn an other contradiction. Dr. Bankroft informs me that mr. Coffyn wrote to him, that he mr. Coffyn thaught to have a right to pay him self first out of the remittance send to him by mr. Wharton for our joint concern, and mr. Coffyn informs me, that he kept for him

4. Wharton was elected to Congress by the Delaware Assembly on Feb. 2, 1782: Smith, *Letters*, XVIII, 340n.
5. For Bancroft's recent message see XXXVIII, 366n; for one of Coffyn's letters see XXXVI, 221.

self the most part of the remittance by the direction of Mr. Wharton. Whatever this may be I can not understand why mr. Wharton should Send the money belonging to me thro the hands of an other, and give me not the least information even of having done it. I have nothing to doe with mr. Coffyn, but only with mr. Wharton. And as the case was Such, it would have been an indispensable duty in mr. Coffyn to send me an exact copy of the lettre of mr. Wharton, which he did when the lettre was accompanied with no remittance, and thus when its contents were by no means interesting to me. I am Sure you can not approve the conduct of any one of those three gentlemen towards me.

I entrusted to the care of mr. Wharton, when he set out, a lettre to mr. Williams at Boston, who, according to advice of his Son, of Nantes, had placed in the loan office at Boston on my name the produce of a mercantil advanture which mr. Williams of Nantes had very cairefully Conducted for me, and of which the produce amounted to about two thousand pound sterling in real value at that time. I begged mr. Williams of Boston to send me a certificate of the loan office, and to inform me as soon as possible of the transaction as well as of the increase of the sum by the interst it had gained in the public loan. I requested this information to be Sent either directely to me, to you, or to mr. Sam: Wharton, who would forward it to me. By the strange behaviour of mr. Wharton I doe not know even, whether he did send that lettre to mr. Williams, nor whether mr. Williams has send an answer to me to the care of mr. Wharton. I am thus kept allso in the dark about this transaction, of which however I hope to be soon inform'd in a satisfactory why by mr. Williams of Nantes, how [who] has inform'd me at the time, that, according to his father's letters, the above mentioned sum has been placed in the public loan office—[6] A part of an advanture which mr. Williams Conducted for me was taken by the ennemy, but was duly insured at charlestown soon after, that place becoming in the hands of England, Mr. Williams has not been able to recovre the

6. It was actually JW's brother John (XXIII, 533n) who had made the investment on Ingenhousz' behalf, and JW reported this to Ingenhousz on Jan. 18, 1780: JW to Ingenhousz, Jan. 18, 1780; JW to John Williams, March 6, 1780 (Yale University Library).

money, till it should again return in to possession of America, which is now the case.

By this all, you see, what efforts I made in my humble Situation to secure to my self an independency in a Country, which I saw some probability of becoming an inhabitant, if the old world should once displease me. I doe not want to begg your advise and assistance in these affaires being sur your friendship towards me will induce you to doe for me what may be in your power: and I have faith enoug in the justice of your new republics, to be persuaded that I shall loose neither the capital nor the intrest of the money, which I have intrusted them with before any depreciation of the currency happened—I begg of you to Consider a little on all this at a leasure hour. Your answer will keep up my Spirits.

Mr. Le Begue has not yet send me any sheets of my book, of which delay I can not even so much as guess the reason.

I exspect from the equity of the belligerant powers, that they will not suffer the English to crush our Republique. It seems to me an impolitical step to refuse restoring to my Country what was taken from it by the greatest injustice. It can only tend to alienate the mind of the Dutch from their ancient allies more and more.

Doe not forget your old friend; and, when a little at leasure, remember de new fireplace and keep up my hope to see you here in a favourable season: for you shoud never travel but in the summer, and allways in good easy carriages. Have you burn'd the wire I have sent you in my last?[7]

I am Dear friend you affectionate   J. Ingen Housz

My Respect full Compl. to your grand son

to his Excellency Benj. Franklin, Passy

Endorsed: Feb. 26. 83

7. See Ingenhousz' letter of Jan. 28, above.

From Sarah Bache

Translation:[8] reprinted from Alexandre-Marie Quesnay de Beaurepaire, *Mémoire, statuts et prospectus, concernant l'Académie des sciences et beaux-Arts des Etats-Unis de l'Amérique, établie à Richemond* . . . (2nd ed., Paris, 1788), pp. 22–3.

Philadelphie, le 27 Février 1783.

Mon cher et honorable père,

Avec cette Lettre, vous recevrez un projet pour une Académie Française qui doit s'ériger ici; c'est un plan fort étendu, & qui fera honneur au Monsieur qui l'a tracé, aussi bien qu'à l'Amérique: s'il peut être exécuté, il ne dérangera nullement le plan des Collèges, & sera seulement pour compléter l'éducation des jeunes gens, quand ils en seront sortis. Ceux qui sont déjà sous M. *Quesnay* ont fait de grands progrès.[9]

Il vous regarde comme le père des Sciences dans ce pays-ci,

8. Presumably made by Quesnay de Beaurepaire, who must have asked SB to write this letter on his behalf. He published it in his 1788 prospectus, writing that "Madame Béache" had given him one of the English originals. He issued three editions of that prospectus in 1788; all include this letter and none mentions any endorsement by BF. We have found no trace of the ALS nor of the "projet" it enclosed, and cannot verify that BF received either. We cite here the second edition of the *Mémoire et prospectus*, a copy of which George Buchanan sent BF on March 5, 1789; the cover letter and presentation copy are both at the APS. For bibliographical information see Denis I. Duveen and Herbert S. Klickstein, "Alexandre-Marie Quesnay de Beaurepaire's *Mémoire et prospectus, concernant l'Académie des Sciences et Beaux Arts des Etats-Unis de l'Amérique, établie à Richemond*, 1788," *Va. Mag. of Hist. and Biog.*, LXIII (1955), 280–5.

9. Alexandre-Marie Quesnay de Beaurepaire, grandson of the celebrated political economist François Quesnay (XV, 118n), had established a French school in Philadelphia in 1780 after serving in the Virginia militia. He expanded the school in the fall of 1782, calling it the "French Academy," and offered French, English, and Italian as well as dancing, drawing, and fencing. He spent several years trying to raise money for a larger academy, finally opening a school in Richmond, Va., which he hoped would have branches in Baltimore, Philadelphia, and New York. In 1786 he sailed for France, where his *Mémoire et Prospectus* won the approbation of the Academy of Sciences. He failed to secure sufficient funds, however, and his plans evaporated with the advent of the French Revolution: *DAB;* Bodinier, *Dictionnaire*, under Quesnay; John G. Roberts, "The American career of Quesnay de Beaurepaire," *French Review*, XX (1946–47), 463–70; *Pa. Jour. and Weekly Advertiser*, Oct. 9, 1782; New York *Independent Jour.*, Nov. 6, 1784.

& pour les avis & les leçons que vous n'avez jamais manqué de donner à ceux dont les talens sont louables.

L'argent est l'article qui manque; mais le frère de M. *Quesnay*[1] en vous remettant cette lettre, vous informera de quelle manière vous pourrez lui rendre les services les plus utiles.

Je conçois fort combien vous devez être occupé dans cette crise importante; mais, en mère qui desire donner à mes enfans une éducation utile & polie, sur-tout fière de les avoir formés dans mon pays & sous mes yeux, je vous prie de donner à M. *Quesnay* toute l'aide & l'assistance qui seront en votre pouvoir.

Je vous ai déjà écrit par une autre occasion, & ne vous ajouterai que l'amour & le respect de toute la famille: sur ce, je suis votre affectionnée fille.   J. BÉACHE.

From ———— Saint-Martin   ALS: American Philosophical Society

                     a tonnein sur garonne poste Restante le 27e.
Monsieur   fevrie 1783 a vertueil En albret.

Les affaire venant de changer de face a levenement De la paix, je L'honneur de vous demander de quelle façon Les officier attaché a larmée des treize proveinse unie de lamerique seront traité, j'i est esté Employé En soixante seise Comme Lieutenant Collonel[2] Est n'est discontinué mon servisse que depuis pres de deux mois que je suis arrivé En france pour Retablir ma santé, quoique je Ne sois pas mieux ayant Besoin d'aller aux eau de Barege pour des Blesseure que j'ai Reçu a une affaire que nous

---

1. Quesnay had two brothers: Jean-Marc (Marie) Quesnay de Beauvoir (b. 1750) and Robert-François-Joseph Quesnay de Saint-Germain (1751–1805); see F. Lorin, "François Quesnay," Société archéologique de Rambouillet, *Mémoires*, XIV (1900), 157, 194–203.

2. On July 23, 1776, Congress appointed Saint-Martin an engineer with the rank of lieutenant colonel under Washington's command. A week later they voted to advance him two months' pay. Washington sent him to serve under the command of Maj. Gen. William Heath: *JCC*, V, 602, 624; Lasseray, *Les Français*, I, 74; II, 410; W. W. Abbot *et al.*, eds., *The Papers of George Washington*, Revolutionary War Series (18 vols. to date, Charlottesville and London, 1985–), VI, 132.

eume a white plain,[3] je Repartirois tout de suite si vous me le Conseillé, En attandant Cette Grace de vous, je L'honneur dettre avec Respects Monsieur Votre tres humble est tres obeissant serviteur ST MARTIN

Notation: St. Martin 27 Fevr. 1783.

From Vergennes

L (draft):[4] Archives du Ministère des affaires étrangères

à Versles. le 27. fev. 1783.

J'ai deja eû l'honneur, M. Il y a quelque temps de vous demander des eclaircissements Sur les moyens les plus propres à établir Solidement des relations de commerce entre la france et les Etats unis.[5] Voicy le moment de S'en occuper[6] et je vous prie de vouloir bien me faire part de votre opinion Sur cet objet qui doit etre d'un interêt commun aux deux nations.

M. franklin

From Johann Valentin Embser

ALS: American Philosophical Society

Monsieur,   aux Deux-Ponts ce 28 febrier 1783.

La paix glorieuse, que l'Amérique vient de conclurre, doit remplir de joye tout honnête homme, par la preuve éclatante,

---

3. The Battle of White Plains, which took place on Oct. 28, 1776: Mark Mayo Boatner III, *Encyclopedia of the American Revolution* (New York, 1966), pp. 1200–2.

4. In the hand of Gérard de Rayneval, who returned on Feb. 15 from his final mission to England (for which see XXXVIII, 415n): *Gaz. de Leyde*, Feb. 28, 1783.

5. XXXVIII, 35.

6. On Feb. 27 Vergennes wrote La Luzerne, "Je sens comme vous, M, la nécessité de conclure promptement la convention relative aux Consuls, et je compte men occuper incessamment." AAE. The letter is translated in Giunta, *Emerging Nation,* I, 772–3.

que par le courage & la fermeté, appuyés de la sagesse & de la prudence, la vertu triomphe des ennemis les plus puissans. Je joins mes voeux les plus ardens à ceux de l'Amérique pour les jours précieux de l'Illustre Franklin, dont le nom brillera dans les siècles les plus reculés, pour avoir crée une grande nation, & pour avoir rendu ses droits naturels à l'autre hémisphère— Mais je m'égare. Ce n'est pas à moi, à begayer mes foibles hommages à ce Grand Homme; & je me tais—

La qualité, en la quelle il me convient de parler à Votre Excellence, est celle d'éditeur des anciens auteurs classiques. Et j'ose Lui demander, si ces éditions, destinées à l'usage de la jeunesse, puissent en quelque manière mériter Son approbation? & en ce cas, auquel de Ses Agens en France je pourrois m'addresser, pour en faciliter la vente en Amérique? Les troubles de la guerre étant passés, il ne dépend que du jugement, que Votre Excellence portera de nos auteurs, pour les faire accueillir dans l'autre monde.[7]

Mille voeux sincères pour la santé & la prospérité d'un Homme, qui a tant contribué au lustre de ce siècle, & au bien de l'humanité!

J'ai l'honneur d'être avec les plus profonds respects, de Votre Excellence le très humble et très obéissant Serviteur[8]

EMBSER
Professeur au College Ducal

Addressed: A Son Excellence, / Monsieur de Franklin / Ministre Plénipotentiaire des Etâts / Unis de l'Amérique près Sa Majesté / très Chrêtienne / à / Passy

Notation: Embser 28 Fevr. 1783

7. BF had ordered the *Editiones Bipontinae* the year before, promising to recommend the volumes in America if he found them to be "well and correctly printed." See XXXVIII, 68, and the references there.

8. While this is the last extant letter from Embser, BF's accounts show that he continued to receive books from the Societas bipontina into 1787: XXXVII, 347–8n.

From Thomas Pownall ALS: American Philosophical Society

My Old Friend   Richmond Surrey Feb 28:83
   I write this to congratulate You on the Establishment of your
Country As A Ful & Sovereign Power taking it's equall Station
amongst the Powers of this World.
   I congratulate You in particular as chosen by Providence to
be a principal Instrument of this Great Revolution: a Revolution
that has stronger marks of Divine interposition superceeding the
ordinary course of human affaires, than any other Event which
this world hath experienced. Even where God is supposed to
work miracles, He uses human means; & it hath pleased him to
make You the Means of this Blessing to America; And, under her
establishment in political freedom, of a Blessing to all Men who
are worthy of it & willing to partake of it: of One also who looks
up to it, & does not think himself the less worthy of it for having been a stranger and Exile in his native land, which he can
scarce call his Country— Duas esse censeo patrias (saieth Cicero) Unam Naturæ, Álteram Civitatis: et eam Patriam ducimus
ubi nati, et Illam quâ excepti sumus: Sed necesse est caritate eam
præstare in quâ Reipublicæ Nomen & universæ Civitatis est.[9]
   You expressed a fear that You should not see peace in your
daies— You may now say—"Lett now thy Servant, O Lord, depart in Peace for he hath seen thy Salvation".[1] Solon a real Patriot & Great Philosopher like yourself used to say That it is not
the Man who *Lives* but who *dyes* in happiness [*torn:* who is(?)]
to be acconate *a happy Man.*[2] If ever any Man did [*torn:* you(?)]

9. He quotes from Cicero, *De legibus,* book 2, part 5, beginning in mid-
sentence and omitting a middle portion: Cato and all natives of Italian towns
"have two fatherlands, one by nature and the other by citizenship . . . so we
consider both the place where we were born our fatherland, and also the city
into which we have been adopted. But that fatherland must stand first in our
affection in which the name of republic signifies the common citizenship of all
of us": trans. Clinton W. Keyes (London and New York, 1928), pp. 374–7.
   1. A paraphrase of the words spoken by Simeon when he saw the child Je-
sus in the temple: Luke 2:29–30. BF had quoted the passage in a recent letter
to Livingston: XXXVIII, 416–17.
   2. The response made by Athenian lawgiver Solon when Croesus asked
him to identify the happiest man: Herodotus, *History,* book 1, chapters 30–33.

shall dye happy. If You my Old Friend, "O Lett my last end by like his."[3] You see that the contemplation of this wonderfull Event has thrown my mind into a religious frame & that my words take their form from it: Yet I express but in part what I feel.

I am embarked for another voyage to the Azores I shall write a second Memorial & address it to the Sovereigns of America.[4] I use none of the Gothick Titles of modern Europe, or the Servile ones of Asia. As though I was addressing Myself to the Repub: of Rome. Senatui Populoq Romano[5] I address myself to the UNITED STATES & CITIZENS of America I wish by this to express the most marked & profound Reverence to A SOVEREIGNTY OF FREE-CITIZENS. If the title of Address which I use is wrong or if there is *any Other of Form* yet adopted, sett me right— I should be sorry to be wrong in this *Peace Offering* in these first Fruits.

I have taken the Liberty to enclosed to You two Letters for my Friends Mr Bowdoin & Dr Cooper with a power of Attorney to them to make for me a Deed of Gift to Harvard College of 500 Acres of Land which I have (& were not confiscated) in Pownalborough in the State Massachusetts-bay.[6] I have not directed that which is for Mr Bowdoin as I should be sorry to be wrong

3. From Numbers 23:10. "Who can count the dust of Jacob, and the number of the fourth part of Israel? Let me die the death of the righteous, and let my last end be like his!"

4. *A Memorial Addressed to the Sovereigns of America* (London, 1783) advised America on its political system; for the other see xxxvii, 583n.

5. *I.e.*, to the Senate and People of Rome.

6. Pownalborough (now Dresden, Maine) was near the mouth of the Kennebec River: Lester J. Cappon, ed., *Atlas of Early American History: the Revolutionary Era, 1760–1790* (Princeton, N.J., 1976), pp. 2, 151. The lands had in fact been seized and in 1780 sold for non-payment of taxes. Harvard eventually recovered the property but netted too little to fund a position in political law, as Pownall had wished. Pownall's letter to James Bowdoin, dated Feb. 28, 1783, and Bowdoin's response of Nov. 20 are in *The Bowdoin and Temple Papers*, II (Mass. Hist. Soc. *Coll.*, 7th ser., vi [1907]), 3–6, 21–3. For details about the bequest and taxes see *ibid.*, pp. 23–7, 30–2, 38–40. We have not located Pownall's letter to the Rev. Samuel Cooper, but BF promised to forward it as well: Pownall to BF, Oct. 6, 1783 (APS).

in the mode of Address. Will you be so good as to direct it or to tell the Bearer of this how to do it who will direct it.

I continue under the idea of my schem of making the tour of America, I cannot but think that [*torn:* if(?)] there ever was an Object worth the travelling to see & worthy the contemplation of a Philosopher it is that in which he may see the Beginnings of a great Empire at its foundation.

Our Politicians quarrelling, in their Scramble, with the Peace and House of Commons declaring themselves unsatisfyed with the Line which divides the two Empires, seem like a Caution sett by Providence openly before the Eyes of the States of America to mark to them the danger of Dissension & the Necessity of Union. Where there is a Danger that the internal principle of Attraction is not sufficient to hold the Parts united in their Center. It is happy for that System that the external Compellant Principle shou'd act to the same end.

I hope the Crisis of pain under which you was suffering is gone off & that you are in good health to enjoy the happiness which you must feel. May God bless you is the Wish & prayer of Your Old Friend   T POWNALL

P:S: I am this day made happy by having received & hung up an excellent Portrait of You My old friend—Copied from that which West did for You—[7]

To His Excelly B Franklin Esqr Minister Plenipo: of the United States of America &c. &c &c &c—

Notation: Pownall Feby. 22 1783.

7. See Sellers, *Franklin in Portraiture,* pp. 402–3.

From Daniel Roberdeau[8]

Two ALS:[9] American Philosophical Society

Dear Sir   Philade. Feby. 28th. 1783

I cannot hardly refrain my concratulation although the great Event of peace has not been announced here. From experience of your good offices betwixt my relations & myself,[1] permit me to ask the favor of an immediate conveyence of the inclosed. I am Sir Yr. most obt. huml. Sert   DANIEL ROBERDEAU

Addressed: His Excellency / Doctor Benjamin Franklin / at the Court of France / Passe / Per Ship Nancy

Notation: Roberdeau 28 Feby. 1783.

Answers to "The Claim of the American Loyalists"

AL (draft): University of Pennsylvania Library

In the latter part of February, 1783, William Franklin and the other Loyalist representatives who had submitted a petition to Parliament at the beginning of the month[2] published a pamphlet entitled *The Case and Claim of the American Loyalists Impartially Stated and Considered.* The first section, "The Case of the American Loyalists," reviewed the royal proclamations issued during the war and described the Loyalists' dutiful responses. The second section, "The Claim of the American Loyalists," argued that Great Britain was legally and morally obligated to compensate them for their losses, and that British citizens had to share their burden.[3]

The present manuscript, undated and incomplete, appears to be the start of a response to the "Claim." The two answers Franklin drafted

---

8. A former politician and militia general (XVII, 81n; XXII, 378n), who had returned to his earlier career as a merchant: *ANB.*

9. The other of which is marked "Duplicate."

1. See XXXIII, 47.

2. See Patience Wright to BF, Feb. 22.

3. *The Case and Claim of the American Loyalists Impartially Stated and Considered* (London, 1783). See also Mary Beth Norton, *The British-Americans: the Loyalist Exiles in England, 1774–1789* (Boston and Toronto, 1972), p. 188.

follow directly from the two sentences that form that section's second paragraph, which launches a 22-page argument. Franklin was on the verge of composing a third answer when he seems to have abandoned the exercise. No other versions of this project survive, nor have any references to it been located among his own papers, the papers of his contemporaries, or in the press. He did compose another kind of counter-argument to the Loyalists' claims in the form of an apologue, published immediately below. In that piece, the objections he expresses here are delivered as a speech so persuasive that the claims were summarily rejected.

[during or after February, 1783]

Question 1.[4]

Answer.

Undoubtedly. And when the Chief of any Civil Society, instead of affording that Protection would injure a Part of that Society, and Engages by artful Promises another Part of the Society to assist in destroying that Part, both the Chief and the Partisans so engaged depart from their Duty.

Question 2.[5]

Answer.

Certainly. And therefore if the Chief of a Civil Society shall resolve the Ruin of a Part of that Society, it is the Duty of every Individual to bear his Proportion of the "Expences, Burthens and Sacrifices" necessary for the common Protection. And whoever to avoid bearing that Proportion, and in Expectation of Advantages promised to him, deserts his Fellow-Citizens & joins the Chief in the Attempts against them, departs from his Duty. The Society owes him nothing but Punishment. He has in high

---

4. The sentence we believe BF to be answering reads: "The great aim and end of civil society is protection of the persons and properties of individuals, by an *equal contribution* to *whatever* is necessary to attain and secure it." *The Case and Claim of the American Loyalists* . . . (London, 1783), p. 17.

5. The sentence that follows the one quoted above reads: "For, since *all* the individuals who compose the union are to partake of its protection, and of every other benefit resulting from it, nothing can be more just, than that the *expences, burthens, and sacrifices,* necessary to preserve it, should be equally distributed and proportionably sustained by *all.*" *Ibid.*

Gaming wickedly & foolishly stak'd his own Estate against the Estate of his Neighbour, which he hop'd to win; but has been unsuccessful; and the Society are under no Obligation to repair his Losses.—

Question 3.

Answer.—

"Apologue"

Reprinted from William Temple Franklin, ed., *Memoirs of the Life and Writings of Benjamin Franklin* . . . (3 vols., 4to, London, 1817–18), III, 309–10.

When William Temple Franklin published this piece (for which no manuscript survives), he placed it among the undated bagatelles, noting only that it was "written at the period of, and in allusion to, the claims of the *American Royalists* on the *British Government*." Broadly speaking, that period lasted many years. Because the central drama of the fable takes place in the aftermath of a peace treaty, when a "council of the beasts" was considering whether or not to grant the demands of the loyal "mongrels," we believe that it was probably written between February, 1783, when the board of American Loyalists petitioned Parliament and published a pamphlet to gain public support, and the following July, when Parliament responded by passing a compensation act appointing a commission to investigate the cases of all Loyalists who submitted claims.[6] Moreover, the focal point of this apologue—the speech delivered by the horse—echoes Franklin's argument in his answers to the Loyalists' pamphlet, the preceding document.

In 1787, when a Scottish friend challenged Franklin's views on the Loyalist question, the doctor underscored his explanation by sending a copy of this apologue. By that time, his views had softened to some degree.[7] He expressed sympathy for the "distressed Exiles," allowing

---

6. The work of the commission took more than six years. See Mary Beth Norton, *The British-Americans: the Loyalist Exiles in England, 1774–1789* (Boston and Toronto, 1972), pp. 188–92.

7. During the 1782 peace negotiations, JA remarked that neither he nor Jay

that he was glad that they were receiving some compensation. "It was clearly incumbent on the King to indemnify those he had seduc'd by his Proclamations," Franklin wrote. "But it seems not so clearly consistent with the Wisdom of Parliament to resolve doing it for him. If some mad King hereafter should think fit, in a Freak, to make War upon his Subjects in Scotland, or upon those of England, by the Help of Scotland and Ireland, (as the Stewarts did) may he not encourage Followers by the Precedent of these Parliamentary Gratuities, and thus set his Subjects to cutting one another's Throats, first with the Hope of Sharing in Confiscations, and then with that of Compensation in case of Disappointment? The Council of Brutes in the old Fable were aware of this. Lest that Fable may perhaps not have fallen in your Way, I enclose a Copy of it."[8]

[during or after February, 1783]

APOLOGUE.

Lyon, king of a certain forest, had among his subjects a body of faithful dogs, in principle and affection strongly attached to his person and government, but through whose assistance he had extended his dominions, and had become the terror of his enemies.

Lyon, however, influenced by evil counsellors, took an aversion to the dogs, condemned them unheard, and ordered his tygers, leopards, and panthers to attack and destroy them.

The dogs petitioned humbly, but their petitions were rejected haughtily; and they were forced to defend themselves, which they did with bravery.

A few among them, of a mongrel race, derived from a mixture with wolves and foxes, corrupted by royal promises of great rewards, deserted the honest dogs and joined their enemies.

The dogs were finally victorious: a treaty of peace was made, in which Lyon acknowledged them to be free, and disclaimed all future authority over them.

---

were nearly as "staunch against the Tories" as BF: XXXVIII, 346–7. In this apologue BF expresses a striking intolerance, characterizing all Loyalists as genetically inferior and arguing against their receiving any recompense.

8. To Alexander Small, Sept. 28, 1787, Smyth, *Writings*, IX, 616. BF later asked Small whether his former letter "inclosing the apologue" had come to hand: WTF, *Memoirs*, II, 116–17.

The mongrels not being permitted to return among them, claimed of the royalists the reward that had been promised.

A council of the beasts was held to consider their demand.

The wolves and the foxes agreed unanimously that the demand was just, that royal promises ought to be kept, and that every loyal subject should contribute freely to enable his majesty to fulfil them.

The horse alone, with a boldness and freedom that became the nobleness of his nature, delivered a contrary opinion.

"The king," said he, "has been misled, by bad ministers, to war unjustly upon his faithful subjects. Royal promises, when made to encourage us to act for the public good, should indeed be honorably acquitted; but, if to encourage us to betray and destroy each other, they are wicked and void from the beginning. The advisers of such promises, and those who murdered in consequence of them, instead of being recompensed should be severely punished. Consider how greatly our common strength is already diminished by our loss of the dogs. If you enable the king to reward those fratricides, you will establish a precedent that may justify a future tyrant in making like promises, and every example of such an unnatural brute rewarded, will give them additional weight. Horses and bulls, as well as dogs, may thus be divided against their own kind, and civil wars produced at pleasure, till we are so weakened that neither liberty nor safety are any longer to be found in the forest, and nothing remains but abject submission to the will of a despot, who may devour us as he pleases."

The council had sense enough to resolve,—That the demand be rejected.

From the Marquis d'Amezaga

LS: American Philosophical Society

Paris ce 1er Mars 1783

Ma Santé Monsieur ne ma Pas Permis d'aller vous faire tous mes Compliments Sur la Conclusion de Votre très Grande ouvrage. Vous Connoissé Monsieur, Les Sentiments que Je vous aÿ vouë, dépuis que Jai l'honneur de vous Connoître, Les Circonstances ne Sonts Pas faite Pour les diminuer.

Jai pour amis Intime un homme qui dans un ouvrage, qui và paroître, qui se trouve chez Prault imprimeur, Intitulé Laigle et L'hiboux. Je m'empresse Monsieur de vous faire Part, d'un Article, qui vous Conserne, et J'espere, que vous le trouveré digne de Vous.[9] Je veut être le Premier, qui vous l'aprennent.

Dès que je me Porteré mieux jiré vous demander à dinner et Vous rénouveller la tendre Veneration et le réspect avec lequ'elle Jai l'honneur d'etre, Monsieur, votre très humble et très obeissent Serviteur,   URTADO MIS DAMEZAGA

From Jean-Jacques Lafreté   ALS: American Philosophical Society

Paris le 1er. mars 1783

Mon ami M. Gallard de Bayonne, est chargé, mon Cher Papa de vous voir, et a beaucoup de choses à vous dire;[1] Je vous prie, ou Monsieur votre fils, de me faire savoir le jour et l'heure où il pourra avoir l'honneur de vous voir à Passy. Vous me feréz plaisir de le recevoir avec bonté, et l'écouter avec attention. Il est fort instruit, et entrera avec vous dans des Détails fort interressans pour nos bons amis les Américains. Ce Mr. Gallard est le frere de celui pour qui je vous ai demandé le consulat de bayonne.[2] Je vous le recommande de nouveau.

Ma petite femme est asséz bien pour son Etat Mais elle seroit encore mieux, Si elle avoit le plaisir de vous voir plus Souvent.

---

9. Joseph-Antoine-Joachim Cerutti's *L'Aigle et le hibou,* announced for sale in the *Jour. de Paris* on March 9, was a 15-page fable in verse followed by 38 pages of notes, which celebrates the ideal of enlightened rule. Washington is the American Atlas; BF, "en cheveux blancs," is Jupiter (p. 8). The accompanying note explains that future ages will regard BF as a god, responsible for the most far-reaching changes of the century: the discovery of electricity will alter all of physics, and the founding of the United States will alter all of politics (pp. 39–40).

1. For Galart's campaign with BF and others to have Bayonne named a free port see the headnote to the Jan. 31 letter from the Chamber of Commerce of Aunis.

2. XXXV, 505.

Vous Savéz Combien elle vous aime. Elle vous fait mille compliments, et je vous renouvelle mon cher Papa les assurances de mon tendre et Respectueux attachement.   LAFRETÉ

To Caroline (Charlotte)-Bertrande Chapelle de Jumilhac-Cubjac Bertin[3]

AL (draft): Library of Congress

[after March 1, 1783][4]

Mr Franklin presents his respectful Compliments to Madame Bertine,[5] and acquaints her that he long since gave the Recommendatory Letter and Passport desired, to the Portuguese Ambassador, who had before demanded the same thing:[6] and that[7] the Letter receiv'd thro' her hands from M. le Baron de Jumilhac shall be duly attended to. He begs leave to assure M. Bertin of his sincere Attachement, and his Readiness to do upon her single Recommendation any thing that may be in his Power for her Friends

To be translated.—

3. An old friend, though an infrequent correspondent: XXVI, 422–3, 506n. Her maternal uncle (mentioned in the references just cited) was a Bertin; her husband, Auguste-Louis Bertin, was from a different family of the same name. Their full names, and further details on the family, are in David Smith *et al.*, eds., *Correspondance générale d'Helvétius* (5 vols., Toronto, Buffalo, and Oxford, 1981–2000), IV, 39–40n.

4. The date of a letter BF mentions below, from her brother the baron de Chapelle de Jumilhac; it is described in our headnote on consulship seekers, Jan. 28.

5. Putting "Bertine" in the feminine must be a joking reference to his confusion about French genders. In the last sentence BF refers to her as "M[onsieur] Bertin."

6. Doubtless the passport Ambassador Sousa Coutinho requested on Dec. 20, 1782: XXXVIII, 483–4.

7. BF here drafted and crossed out: "he will communicate with Congress". The letter in question remains among his papers.

To Philip Mazzei[8]   AL: American Philosophical Society

Passy, Sunday [March 2, 1783][9]
Mr Franklin presents his Compliments to M. Mazzei and acquaints him that some unforeseen Business will prevent his being at Versailles on Tuesday;[1] He thinks too that there will be no
Court, it being Mardi-gras.

From Nicolas-Toussaint Le Moyne, *dit* Des Essarts[2]
ALS: American Philosophical Society

Monsieur   paris ce 2. mars 1783./.
Je vous supplie D'aggréer Le Volume que j'ai L'honneur De
vous Envoyer. Il Renferme une Cause qui Doit vous interresser,
celle Du paratonnerre De st. omer.[3] Tous ceux qui sont capables
De sentir Le prix Des Bienfaits Du Genie, Vous Doivent De la
reconnoissance. J'ai saisi avec plaisir L'occasion De vous offrir
L'hommage De La mienne. Ce sera une jouissance Delicieuse

8. Who arrived in Paris around the beginning of February and spent most
of the year in France. He returned to Virginia at the beginning of December: Margherita Marchione *et al.*, eds., *Philip Mazzei: Selected Writings and
Correspondence* (3 vols., Prato, Italy, 1983), I, 394, 410–11.
9. The Sunday before Ash Wednesday (which marks the end of Mardi
Gras) in 1783: *Almanach royal* for 1783, p. 5.
1. For the weekly royal audience for ambassadors.
2. *Avocat au parlement* and author of plays, pamphlets, and works on law,
history, and pedagogy (1744–1810): *DBF*, under Des Essarts.
3. The enclosure has not been found. It was most likely an issue of Des
Essarts' *Causes célèbres, curieuses et intéressantes, de toutes les cours souveraines
du royaume, avec le jugements qui les ont décidées* (Paris, 1773–89), a periodi-
cal reviewing current court cases. It was notable for eschewing sensational-
ist treatment in favor of analyzing the cases' social and psychological aspects
and underlying legal principles: Jean Sgard, ed., *Dictionnaire des journalistes,
1600–1789* (2 vols., Oxford, 1999), II, 622–4; Jean Sgard, ed., *Dictionnaire
des journaux, 1600–1789* (2 vols., Paris, 1991), I, 221.
Des Essarts supplied an extract of his account of the "Affaire du Para-ton-
nerre de St.-Omer" to the *Mercure de France (Jour. politique de Bruxelles)*
where it appeared on April 12, 1783, pp. 94–6. For the controversy surrounding Vyssery de Bois-Valée's installation of a lightning rod in Saint-
Omer see also XXXVIII, 435–8.

pour moi si vous L'aggreés; & si vous Eprouvés quelqu'interêt en parcourant mon ouvrage, ce sera La Recompense La plus flatteuse que je puisse obtenir De mon travail.

Je suis avec Respect Monsieur Votre trés humble & trés obeissant serviteur   Des Essarts

avocat, membre de plusieurs academies
rue dauphine hotel de mouy

From Pierre-André Gargaz   ALS: American Philosophical Society

Monseigneur   A Theze ce 2 mars 1783.

L'aprobation que vous donates, l'anée derniere, a mon projet de Paix perpetuéle,[4] me persuade réelement que vous avez travaillé beaucoup, et trez utilement, pour faire faire la Paix dont on a signé les preliminaires a Londres et a Versailles (selon que j'ai apris par le numero 9 de la Gazete d'avignon) et que vous voudrez bien encore prendre la peine de travailler pour faire adopter ladite Paix perpetuéle.

Plusieurs Pretres françois de l'Eglize Romaine (parmi lesquels se trouve un Eveque d'ici de ces cantons) auxquel j'ai presenté mondit Projet de Paix, trouvent fort mal que j'aie done le titre de Lieutenants de l'Etre supreme aux souverains, parce, disent ils, que ce titre n'est dû qu'au Pape; et que j'aie proposé d'unir tous les souverains sans exception d'aucun, pas meme des Turcs.[5]

Je prends la liberté, Monseigneur, de vous faire cete observation, afin que vous preniez les mesures necessaires, pour que quelqu'un de ces Messieurs, les Pretres Romain, ne vous empechent de reussir a l'etablissement de ladite Paix.

4. See xxxvii, 611–14.

5. Gargaz conceived of a "universal union" that would eventually include nations from all over the world including Europe, Asia, Africa, and America. He made a distinction between hereditary and elected sovereigns, giving preference in certain cases to the former because—as he says here—they were "lieutenants de l'Etre Suprême": *Conciliateur de toutes les nations d'Europe, ou Projet de paix perpétuelle entre tous les souverains de l'Europe & leurs voisins,* pp. [ii], 15.

Je crains, MONSEIGNEUR, de vous importuner, mais l'ardent desir que j'ai d'etre rehabilité (en consideration de l'honeur et des douceurs de la víe que cela me procureroit infaliblement) est cause que je vous demande, très respectueusement, la grace, MONSEIGNEUR, de m'obtenir du Roi, des Lettres de rehabilitation pour etre remis dans le meme Etat que j'etois avant l'arret de 1761 mentioné dans le certificat de Probité ci humblement joint.

L'Eté dernier Mr. le Comte de Vergenes secretaire d'Etat, estima que mondit Projet de Paix pouvoit etre imprimé, je lui en presentai ensuite un exemplaire. Si vous jugiez a propos, MONSEIGNEUR, de lui en rafraichir la memoire, et lui parler desdites Letres de Rehabilitation, pour l'auteur dudit Projet, peut etre qu'il vous eviteroit la peine de les demander (en les demandant lui meme) au Roi ou au Garde des sceaux.

Enfin, MONSEIGNEUR, pardonez moi s'il vous plait la peine que je vous done, quand ce ne seroit que cele de lire cete longue Letre. Si vous ne jugez pas a propos, par quele raison que ce puisse etre, de m'obtenir lesdites Letres de Rehabilitation, je vous prie de me renvoier le certificat ci inclus. Mon adresse est, a Monsieur Gargaz, a Theze par sisteron en Provence./.⁶

MONSEIGNEUR Permetez, je vous en suplíe, que j'insiste a vous demander cete grace avec toute l'instance que votre bonté peut me permetre./.   GARGAZ.

---

6. Gargaz had returned to his native Thèze in October, 1782, and was earning a meager living as a schoolteacher. His two attempts to procure letters of rehabilitation had been unsuccessful: Ferréol de Ferry, *Pierre-André Gargas (1728–1801), Galérien de Toulon* (Paris, 2000), pp. 86–90. The certificate he enclosed is no longer among BF's papers. It must have been returned along with the letter of recommendation BF sent to Gargaz: BF to [Whom It May Concern], May 22, 1783, APS.

From Nicolas Richard[7] and Other Composers of Verse

ALS: American Philosophical Society

Just as the Treaty of Alliance had inspired an outpouring of tributes in verse to Franklin and his fellow commissioners,[8] so too the signing of the preliminary peace was the occasion for a profusion of couplets and stanzas honoring Franklin and the many other French and American heroes of the war. Franklin was sent poems in both manuscript and printed form. In the letter published below, Richard encloses the printed version of his ode as well as six handwritten stanzas that the royal censor had suppressed.

On January 22 the abbé Pierre Duviquet observes that to celebrate the peace between America and England, "c'est Célebrer Votre Ouvrage." In the enclosed verse he hopes to put Franklin's name alongside those of Louis XVI and Vergennes.[9]

On February 12 the comte de Bussy-Dagoneau writes Franklin from the château de Pierre-en-Cize, a prison near Lyon. He recalls the verse he sent Franklin four years earlier foretelling America's success.[1] Now he sends an ode on the peace in which Franklin's name is placed with those whom all nations respect. Because Franklin does not know him, he attaches a précis of his situation: he is 47 years old, the last male of his line, forgotten by his mother, and embarrassed and betrayed by his wife. He has lost everything but is dear to those who do

---

7. Richard had sent BF a poem the previous spring, and was elated at BF's apparent encouragement: XXXVII, 247–8, 262–3. We have since learned his first name (inscribed in a copy of his 1782 verse at the Bibliothèque nationale) and the title of that poem, which was printed as a pamphlet: *Vers sur la Naissance de Monseigneur le Dauphin, addressés à la Reine* (Paris, [1782]). BF's copy is at the APS.

Unless otherwise noted, the letters and poems discussed in this headnote are in French and are at the APS.

8. XXVI, 21–5.

9. Duviquet, who became a writer of some prominence (*DBF*), was at this time a student of rhetoric at the *collège* Louis-le-Grand. His enclosure has not been found. In 1784 he published an eight-page *Vers sur la paix;* BF's copy of that pamphlet is at the Hist. Soc. of Pa. A section of the verse that elaborated on America's gratitude to Louis XVI was excerpted in the *Jour. de Paris,* issue of March 10, 1784.

1. For the comte's earlier letter, written from the refuge of the *enclos du temple,* see XXVII, 195.

not persecute him; he is accused but guilty of nothing, and trusts in the justice of the king and his ministers.[2]

Pierre-Maurice Saunier, writing from Paris on March 17, likens the names of Franklin, Washington, Adams, and Laurens to Brutus, Cato, Cicero, and "all the great Republicans of antiquity." He encloses an ode inspired by the return of peace.[3]

On April 6 the abbé Coquillot, prior of l'Epinay, sends Franklin his newly published *Couplets sur la paix* along with his veneration.[4]

Philippe de Saint-Mars, *écuyer*, also sends an ode on the peace in a letter of April 15 from Mantes. He apologizes for the liberty he takes in writing, but since his ode mentions Franklin, custom requires that he send him a copy before it is made public. He adds in a postscript that, because he understands that Franklin does not care about honorary titles, he has left off those that by rights are due him. The enclosed manuscript poem praises the American code of laws as the best way to guarantee to the nascent republic the freedom won by "Waghinston" and Franklin, with the generous support of France.

Finally, we note one of the hundreds of pamphlets (some of them verses) that Franklin acquired in France. This one—*Pericula Poëtica: Munus Amicis* ([Holland], 1783)—seems to have been hand-delivered by the author, the Dutch poet Jacob Henrik (Hendrik) Hoeufft, who signed it and inscribed on the verso of the half-title a 12-line dedication to Franklin in Latin verse. The dedication praises him as the ornament of the age, who, like Nestor, is venerable, wise in counsel, and eloquent.[5]

2. The enclosed ode is missing. Later in 1783 the *Mémoires secrets* announced his wife's death from a "maladie cruelle" that one does not contract in the cloister or in a state of celibacy, and described the comte as an "homme de beaucoup d'esprit, poëte libertin, & l'un des plus aimables roués qu'il soit possible de voir." In 1786 the *Mémoires secrets* reported on the publication of the comte's pamphlet, *Le Plus Court & le plus vrai des Mémoires*, and on his release from prison: Bachaumont, *Mémoires secrets*, XXIV, 101; XXXII, 141–2, 144–5, 167–8, 229–30; XXXIII, 111, 205–6.

3. Saunier (b. 1750) was a man of letters and a printer: Larousse; Quérard, *France littéraire*. His enclosure is missing.

4. The work is a march scored for five parts. The seven stanzas, annotated with explanatory marginalia, are primarily concerned with the French participation in the war, though BF and Washington are mentioned. BF's copy is at the Hist. Soc. of Pa.

5. Hoeufft (1756–1843) was a jurist and poet: A. J. van der Aa, *Biographisch Woordenboek der Nederlanden* . . . (7 vols., Haarlem, 1852–78; reprint, Amsterdam, 1969). The dedication is reprinted in Wolf and Hayes, *Library of*

Monsieur,   au Collège de lisieux ce 2. mars 1783.
C'eut été pour moi une Satisfaction bien douce de pouvoir
vous presenter mon ode Sur la paix.[6] Cétoit dans l'espérance de
jouir de Cet honneur, que, malgré une indisposition causée par
de longues veilles, j'ai fait le voyage de Passy. J'avois encore envie de vous communiquer quelques Strophes que le Censeur de
mon ouvrage m'a fait Supprimer, comme trop hardies, Selon lui;
mais qui, au jugement de plusieurs Sçavants à qui j'en ai fait part,
ne Sont pourtant que dans la plus èxacte vérité. Je vous les envoye cy-jointes; et je laisse à votre éxpérience à décider Si j'ai été
emporté trop loin par mon enthousiasme et mon admiration
pour un peuple dont votre prudence à Si heureusement défendu
les droits et rétabli la liberté. Dans le Supplément que je vous envoye, Monsieur, j'ai cru, pour ne point choquer votre modestie,
devoir omettre une Strophe qui vous regarde personnellement.
Mais en même tems j'ai cru pouvoir la joindre aux autres dans la
distribution que j'en ai faite aux gens d'esprit. La Supprimer entièrement, c'eut été manquer à ce que je dois au témoignage de
ma Conscience. Puisse ce foible hommage, que je rends à votre
mérite vous prouver avec qu'elle éstime et qu'elle vénération je
suis, Monsieur, Votre trés humble et trés Obéissant Serviteur
                                              RICHARD
                                    Etud. en philosophie

P.S. Comme je Suis à la dernière année de mes études, je prends
la liberté de Réclamer votre protection dans le cas ou vous pourriez me faire avoir quelque place, soit d'educateur, soit de sécré-
taire. Mais je désirerois, autant qu'il Seroit possible, avoir un
emploi qui me laissât quelques moments libres pour m'occuper
des belles-lettres qui sont ma passion favorite, et aux qu'elles je
me livrerois sans restriction, si le défaut de fortune ne me met-

---

Benjamin Franklin, p. 419. Twenty years later, when including the dedica-
tory verse in an anthology, the author dated it 1783 and introduced it with a
Latin phrase which translates as, "To Benjamin Franklin, as the author was
offering him his poems": J. H. Hoeufft, *Carmina* (Breda, 1805), p. 234.
Hoeufft also wrote a poem about balloons in 1783; this pamphlet was published in Paris, and BF's copy is at the Hist. Soc. of Pa.
  6. *Ode, à l'Occasion de la Paix dédiée au Roi* ([Paris, 1783]) is 11 pages long.
BF's copy is at the Hist. Soc. of Pa.

toit dans la nécessité de m'attacher à d'autres objets, et de Sacrifier mes gouts à mes besoins. Des témoignages avantageux de la part des Supérieurs d'un Collège où je Suis depuis près de dix ans en qualité de boursier, et conséquemment où je n'ai pu me maintenir que par une Conduite irréprochable; des Succès plus qu'ordinaires dans le Cours de mes études; et de l'ardeur pour le travail: voila, Monsieur, les Seuls titres que je puisse faire valoir, et les Seuls aussi qui puissent vous interresser./.

au lieu de la Strophe commençant par ces mots *la paix, l'aimable paix &c.* je continuois ainsi:
D'un Empire nouveau les colonnes naissantes
ont enfin soulevé ces chaines flétrissantes
que forgeoit des Tyrans la sourde ambition.
Ô douce liberté, viens rompre les entraves
de cent peuples èsclaves
sous le joug odieux des enfants d'Albion.
Oui, ces fers trop tendus se relachent, se brisent,
et du poids de leur chute écrasent et détruisent
le Thrône qu'élévoit un maitre redouté.
Tel un Chêne abattu sous les coups de la foudre
Voit Ses rameaux en poudre
couvrir de leurs dèbris le sol qui l'a porté.
Peuple Roi, peuple ésclave; ainsi dans ton délire
ivre du fol espoir d'un chimérique empire
Tu Prètendois regner sur ces nouveaux Climats:
mais en vain franchissant le vaste sein de l'onde
à la moitié du monde
Tes vaisseaux apportoient des fers ou le trépas.
Il est des dieux vengeurs, dont la lente justice
de fleurs couvre souvent les bords du prècipice.
Dans tes hardis desseins leur faveur t'a trompé:
par un cruel retour, renversant ta fortune
tu les vois de Neptune
briser entre tes mains le Trident usurpé.
Assez et trop longtems le Sceptre Britannique
Sous l'orgueil oppresseur d'une loi Tyrannique
à fait gémir les flots de l'ocean Surpris.
Va, tu n'entendras plus Amphytrite plaintive

de son onde captive
déplorer en tremblant l'injurieux mépris.
Aux rives de Boston, la fiére indépendance
à marqué dès-long-tems l'ecueil de ta Puissance.
Quitte de tes projets l'espoir audacieux;
s'il est vrai que des mers jadis tu fus l'arbitre
de Ce superbe titre
dépose pour toujours le faste ambitieux.
Partez, riches vaisseaux &c.

From Jean-Jacques Bachelier,[7] with William Temple Franklin's Note for a Reply ALS: American Philosophical Society

Monsieur   Paris 3. mars 1783

Il y a longtems que je désire vous faire mon compliment sur la paix qui vient d'etre Signée entre L'Europe Et L'amerique, J'ai même a ce Sujet des observations qui peuvent vous intéresser. Comme Made. Bachelier désire autant que moy, vous faire Son compliment, nous nous proposons de vous demander a diner le jour qui vous conviendra le mieux de Vendredy ou de samedy prochain.

J'attends L'honneur de votre réponse et suis avec Respect Monsieur Votre très humble et très obeissant Serviteur

BACHELIER

Directeur de l'Ecole Royale De Dessin rue des Cordeliers.

Notation in William Temple Franklin's hand: M. Franklin est bien faché que des Affaires et des Engagements l'empechent de recevoir a Diner Vendredy ou samedy Mr. et Me Bachellier.

Il a l'honneur de leur proposer Dimanche ou Mercredy de la semaine prochaine,—il desire beaucoup que l'un de ces deux

---

7. The painter and educator (XXIII, 619; *DBF*) whose last extant correspondence was in 1777. Bachelier founded the Ecole royale gratuite de dessein (presently the Ecole nationale supérieure des arts decoratifs) in 1766 to improve the quality of craftsmanship in France. In 1777 he had hoped to go to America to perform a similar service, that is, instruct young people in various manufactures: XXIV, 143.

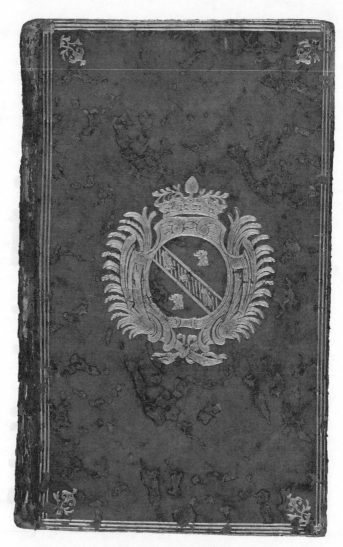

Franklin Coat of Arms

Jours puissent leur convenir, qu'il regrette d'avoir si longtems
èté privé de les voir.

Il attend leur descision pour l'un de ce deux Jours avec bien
de l'Impatience. M. Franklin le fils se reunis a M. son Pere pour
assurer Mr et Me. Bachellier de leur sincere et respectueux Attachement.

Passy le 5 Mars 1782[8]

Notation: Bachelier Paris 3 Mars 1783

From Gastellier[9]

ALS: American Philosophical Society

à montargis ce 3 mars 1783.

Monsieur et trés illustre Docteur

Recevés je vous supplie de nouveau mes actions de Graces
trés humbles de l'honneur que vous m'avés fait en recevant la
dédicace de mon foible ouvrage et surtout de la maniere beaucoup plus honnête que meritée avec la quelle vous avés daigné
l'accueillir.[1] Le souvenir d'un bienfait aussi précieux ne s'effa-
cera jamais de ma mémoire et je puis vous assurer que ma réconnoissance egale le profond respect avec le quel je suis Monsieur
votre trés humble trés obeissant serviteur   GASTELLIER

p.s. Trois exemplaires doivent accompagner la presente missive.
Celui qui est relié est destiné au président de la société de philadelphie et les deux autre au secretaire et à la société elle même.[2]

---

8. Bachelier answered WTF on March 6: they preferred Wednesday, March
12. In a postscript he asked whether BF would allow him to invite the chevalier de la Rigaudière, who had something interesting to tell him. For the
chevalier and his campaign to secure a free port in Saintonge see the headnote to the Jan. 31 letter from the Chamber of Commerce of Aunis.

9. This letter was forwarded by the marquis du Saillant, who inadvertently
opened it; see his letter below, March 14.

1. See the letters from Gastellier and Mirabeau, Feb. 9 and 13, above. BF's
response is unlocated.

2. BF's copy was bound in calf with his coat of arms tooled in gilt on the
front cover; see illustration, facing. An ink and wash drawing of his arms is
on the dedication leaf. The work was reviewed in the *Jour. de Paris* of March

From ——— Lacarre   ALS: Library of Congress

Monsieur   Isle d'Oleron le 3 Mars 1783
   Toute l'Europe a les yeux fixés Sur vous: Elle partage, avec les Etats-unis, Les vœux qu'ils font pour votre Conservation.
   Les Nouvelles publiques ont fait Mention que vous Etes ataqué de la Pierre:[3] J'ai Éprouvé la meme Incommodité, Et J'ai Jetté, depuis le 24 Juillet dernier, à l'aide d'une Tisane, dont Je Joins ici la Recette,[4] Environ 140 fragmens de pierres, dont quelques unes de la grosseur du Caffé Moka, Et d'autres Comme des Lentilles qui ont la forme de Champignons. J'entre dans Ce detail, Monsieur, pour vous Engager à faire usage de Cette Tisane: Si Elle ne produit pas Sur vous, le bon Effet que J'en ai Ressenti, dumoins Elle ne Saurait vous Nuire; J'en apprendrai le Succèz, avec la Satisfaction Et l'Interet, que Toute ame Honnête doit prendre à des Jours aussi pretieux que les votres./.
   Je Suis avec Respect Monsieur Votre Tres Humble & tres obeissant Serviteur./.   LACARRE
                    ancien Lit [Lieutenant] De roy

From ——— St. Clair[5]   ALS: American Philosophical Society

                    Paris March 3d. 1783
I am exceedingly mortified to trouble your Excellency upon this occasion but my necessity is really so pressing as urges me to it.

23, 1783, where Gastellier's novel approach to medicine as an art form (considering the patient overall, recognizing that many so-called remedies were ineffective, using conservative approaches) was heralded.
   3. BF's attack of the stone occurred in August, 1782, and he received numerous remedies thereafter: XXXVIII, 30–4, 39–42.
   4. The one-page prescription called for an infusion of wild carrot tops with the greens, with a pinch of pellitory. To be effective the carrots must be harvested in August and dried in the shade; pellitory grown in full sun is most efficacious. The patient could drink wine in moderation but should avoid strong beer as well as salty foods and every kind of meat stew.
   5. Formerly a lieutenant of marines on the *South Carolina,* who had left the ship after a disagreement with its captain. He had been imprisoned at Dunkirk in the summer of 1782 on what he claimed were false charges: XXXVII, 680–2; XXXVIII, 90–1.

In coming to Paris I entertained not the least doubt but your Excellency would have supported me in my application for a Dedomagement and I am very well convinced the Minister[6] would have ordered me at least part of my loss which I esteem at Seventy guineas besides the severity of it (which surpassed any thing of the Kind ever exhibited in that part of the Country the Chevalier de Sakl excepted) which is impayable however I would be content with any thing the Minister would order me. I would have wrot to your Excellency yesterday but really had not wherewith to buy paper till I sold off something this morning for third part value which was much wanted as I have not eat a bit of Dinner these two days: a friend of mine in Dunkerk failing to transmit me a trifle renders my situation exceedingly disagreable. I hope your Excellency will seriously consider my situation and put me in a way of returning to America. I remain with the most distinguished sentiments your Excellency's most humble & most obedient Servant   St Clair

Hotel de Lyon rue Jean St Denis Paris

Notation: St. Clair, Paris March 3. 1783.—

From August Friedrich Wilhelm Crome[7]

ALS: American Philosophical Society

Monsieur   Dessau. 4e. Mars 1783.

Pardonnés qu'un Homme etranger et inconnu de Vous, se mele dans la Foule de Ceux qui s'empressent depuis longtems à Vous temoigner, Monsieur, le profond respect et la parfaite veneration que Vous Vous etes aquise dans le Monde par la sage Vigi-

---

6. The marquis de Ségur, the minister responsible for French Flanders: XXXVII, 681n; XXXVIII, 91.

7. Crome (1753–1833) taught geography and history in Dessau between 1778 and 1783, and later became professor of statistics and public finance and administration (*Kameralwissenschaften*) at the University of Gießen. He published extensively on these subjects, and served as privy councilor to the court of Anhalt-Dessau, for which he undertook several diplomatic missions: *ADB*.

lance, et par la Constance inebranlable avec la quelle Vous avés travaillé si efficacement à briser les chaines d'un Peuple opprimé. Je suis persuadé, Venerable Viellard, que le même esprit de Sagesse et d'humanité Vous animera toujours du desir de rendre heureux les vastes Etats que Vous avés fondé; ensorte que l'empressement de ceux qui tachent d'y contribuer ne peut que Vous plaire. J'aspire Monsieur à la gloire de trouver une place parmi ces derniers, et je viens Vous prier de m'honorer de Vos sages Conseils sur la maniere dont je dois m'y prendre dans le dessein que j'ai de payer mon Tribut aux braves Americains. Je me propose de composer un Ouvrage qui contienne une Enumeration aussi complette qu'il me sera possible de toutes les productions du Pays *des Etats unis de l'Amerique,* relative aux besoins du Cultivateur, du Fabriquant, et du Commerçant; et cela topographiquement. Mon but est de renfermer dans cet Ouvrage non seulement une specification detaillée des productions actuelles de ce Pays, mais aussi de celles qu'il pourra un jour fournir au Commerce et aux Manufactures, soit en qualité ou en quantité. Le tout accompagné d'un Exposé de l'etat de leur Manufactures et de leur Commerce. Cet ouvrage sur l'etat œconomique de l'Amerique sera accompagné d'une Carte exacte dressée sur deux grandes feuilles jointes, gravée de la même maniere que *la Carte des productions de l'Europe,* que j'ai publiée il y a quelque tems, avec une explication abregée, et que j'ai l'honneur de Vous presenter[8] très humblement. Sans doute que l'Europe ne souhaite rien tant que d'aquerir une connaissance exacte d'un Pays ou l'on se presse de se rendre, et qui attire l'attention de tous les Commerçans. J'ose donc esperer, Monsieur, que cette entreprise

---

8. Crome undoubtedly enclosed his *Europens Produkte: Zum Gebrauch der Neuen Produkten-Karte von Europa* (Dessau, 1782). The book described the products, economies, and trade relations of various European countries and contained a two-page chart of their surface areas. Later in 1783 he published a slim volume entitled *Ueber die Größe, Volksmenge, Clima und Fruchtbarkeit des Nordamerikanischen Freystaats* (Dessau and Leipzig, 1783), but as he explained in the introduction, he had abandoned the plan for the work described in the present letter after learning that Christoph Daniel Ebeling was about to complete *Erdbeschreibung und Geschichte von Amerika* (7 vols., Hamburg, 1793–1816). There is no indication that BF provided Crome with advice or materials.

aura l'approbation du Pere de ces Etats; et dans cette esperance, je viens Vous prier de Vouloir bien m'honorer de Vos Avis à l'egard de cet Ouvrage, et de me communiquer toutes les relations que Vous jugerés convenables à mon but, ou de m'en indiquer les Sources, soit Cartes, ou livres; je tacherai de me les procurer à quelque prix que ce soit, puisque dans une telle entreprise on n'a jamais trop de Materiaux.

Je me propose de livrer cet Ouvrage en Français et en Allemand, et si Vous me faites la grace, Monsieur, de me pardonner la liberté que j'ose prendre, et de m'honorer d'une reponse favorable à mon projet, j'espere d'etre en etat de publier cet Ouvrage vers la fin de l'Automne.

Il n'est pas necessaire que je m'etende ici à Vous representer les Avantages qui peuvent resulter de cette entreprise pour le Commerce reciproque de l'Europe et des Etats unis. Vous les sentirés bien mieux que je ne pourrais vous les dire. Il me suffit de Vous prevenir sur le but que j'ai en Vue, et qui se rapporte tout à fait au Commerce; ensorte que je ne negligerai pas de parler des differentes branches de Commerce deja ouvertes ou qui peuvent s'ouvrir encore, et des places les plus avantageuses à cet Objet.

Agrées, Venerable Vieillard, les Vœux ardens que je fais pour la Conservation de Votre precieuse Vie, et le temoignage de la parfaite Veneration avec la quelle j'ai l'honneur d'etre Monsieur Votre très humble et très obeissant Serviteur.

A. F. W. CROME.
Professeur en Geo. et Statist.

Notation: Crome 4 Mars 1783.

The Swedish-American Treaty of Amity and Commerce, with Translation

(I) DS: National Archives,[9] Svenska Riksarkivet; copy: National Archives; incomplete press copy of DS: American Philosophical Society; (II) translation[1] and copy: National Archives

This treaty, negotiated by Franklin and the comte de Creutz, Swedish ambassador to the French court, was the first pact signed by the United States with a nation that was not already an ally in the War of Independence. Both parties recognized that its value was as much symbolic as commercial. King Gustavus III, who made an overture in April, 1782, as soon as Franklin began peace negotiations with Great Britain, wanted to be known as "the first Power not at war with England that had sought [an] Alliance" with America. Moreover, he requested that the treaty be negotiated with Franklin, whom he held in high esteem.[2] Congress, in response, conferred upon Franklin full powers and sent a draft treaty, instructing him not to let the possibly controversial Article 4 impede the process, since the "direct & essential object of the treaty is to obtain the Recognition of our Independency by another European power."[3] Franklin's papers provide scant information about the negotiations; he had promised to keep them confidential and had good reason to distrust the mail. Creutz, on the other hand, kept his monarch fully informed by means of secure couriers. We present here an account of events based largely on Creutz's dispatches and an examination of the treaty proposals provided by Congress and the Swedish court.[4]

9. In L'Air de Lamotte's hand. The official Swedish copy is in the hand of Creutz's secretary.

1. We are greatly indebted to Timothy Connelly of the National Historical Publications and Records Commission and Jane Fitzgerald of the National Archives for examining the DS and this translation, answering general questions, and verifying for us a list of words in the translation that were obscured in our photocopies. According to these experts the translation is in the hand of Charles Thomson, Secretary of the Continental Congress.

2. XXXVII, 204–5, 538.

3. XXXVIII, 151–3.

4. The editors wish to thank James Guffin and Laura Beardsley for providing us with copies of transcripts from the Amandus Johnson Collection at the Hist. Soc. of Pa., and Jan Brunius and Ingrid Eriksson Karth at the Svenska Riksarkivet in Stockholm for kindly sending copies of Creutz's dispatches and the draft treaties.

Traité d'Amitié et de Commerce conclu
entre Sa Majesté le Roi de Suède et les États Unis de
l'Amérique Septentrionale. ——

Le Roi de Suède des Goths et des Vandales &c. &c. &c.
Et les Treize États Unis de l'Amérique Septentrionale, sçavoir
New Hampshire, Massachusetts Bay, Rhode Island Connecticut,
New York, New Jersey, Pensylvanie, les Comtés de
New Castle, de Kent et de Sussex sur la Delaware, Maryland,
Virginie, Caroline Septentrionale, Caroline Meridionale et
Georgie, desirant d'établir d'une manière stable et
permanente les regles qui doivent être suivies relativement
à la Correspondance et au Commerce que les deux Parties
ont jugé necessaire de fixer entre leurs Pays, États et Sujets
respectifs, Sa Majesté et les États Unis ont cru ne
pouvoir mieux remplir ce but qu'en posant pour base
de leurs Arrangemens, l'Utilité et l'avantage reciproques
des Deux Nations, en évitant toutes les Preferences onereuses
qui sont ordinairement une Source de discussions, d'embarras
et de mécontentemens, et en laissant à chaque Partie
la Liberté de faire au Sujet du Commerce et de la
Navigation, les reglemens intérieurs qui seront à
Sa Convenance.

Dans

Creutz and Franklin began negotiations on December 18, 1782, as soon as Creutz received his instructions.[5] Franklin's instructions had arrived a month earlier, at which time Creutz had said that he could not begin discussions until the preliminary articles between England and America were signed.[6] Now that they had been signed, even though they were as yet provisional, the two men could compare the proposed treaties sent by their respective governments. Congress' proposal, adapted from a draft of the treaty with the Netherlands, consisted of 18 articles. Sweden's proposal contained 27 articles. It was, as Franklin had been told it would be, based on the Franco-American Treaty of Amity and Commerce, with a few additions taken from the recently concluded Dutch-American treaty.[7] Finding that the two proposals differed "in several points," Creutz sought further instructions from his court, informing Gustavus III that he would try to persuade Franklin to "accept unconditionally" the Swedish draft treaty. If Franklin "should insist on the admission of the articles in his draft which differ," Creutz would send a courier with Congress' draft for the king's consideration. Whichever congressional articles the king agreed to, they should be returned to Paris "worded in French, because the Treaty must be written in the two languages. Since I know English perfectly," he continued, "I shall examine the translation which Mr. Franklin makes very closely to see that it is exact. Moreover, the signatures will be under the French text." Creutz went on to describe Congress' Article 4, regarding Sweden's obligation to protect American ships, and the reciprocal Article 5, the two Congress predicted might be problematic. Not surprisingly, Creutz did forward a copy of the congressional draft to the Swedish court, doubtless at Franklin's request.[8]

5. XXXVIII, 446, 492n.

6. BF received his instructions and Congress' draft treaty by Nov. 14, when he so informed Creutz. Creutz's report on their conversation is quoted in Amandus Johnson, *Swedish Contributions to American Freedom, 1776–1783* (2 vols., Philadelphia, 1953–57), II, 575–6.

7. See XXXVI, 731, and Congress' draft treaty in *JCC*, XXIII, 610–21, where references to the Netherlands are crossed out and replaced by references to Sweden. The Dutch-American treaty is in *Adams Papers*, XIII, 348–81.

8. Creutz to Gustavus III, Dec. 19, 1782, translation in the Amandus Johnson Collection, Hist. Soc. of Pa. The copy of the congressional draft forwarded by Creutz is in the Svenska Riksarkivet.

Matters then stagnated as the diplomats waited for Sweden's response. It was not forthcoming. Creutz kept the king informed of the negotiations between England, France, and Spain, and reassured him on January 9 that he would "not take another step" with Franklin until the preliminary articles were published.[9] Finally, on January 23, three days after all the belligerents signed preliminary treaties and a cessation of hostilities was declared, Creutz reported that Franklin agreed to "accept the treaty exactly as it was drafted by Your Majesty." They would probably "proceed to the signing" by the following week.[1]

Creutz now felt that timing was critical. Franklin had begun to pressure him as soon as the armistice was signed on January 20; the American's eagerness to conclude a treaty had induced him to follow Congress' advice and not wait for Sweden's decision on the congressional articles that were not included in the Swedish draft. On Sunday, February 2, the British ratification of the Anglo-French preliminary treaty arrived at Versailles. Vergennes gave Creutz a copy that same day, which he immediately sent to Sweden.[2] On February 3 Vergennes exchanged ratifications with the British ambassador. With the British having announced that the Anglo-American preliminary articles granting independence to the United States would now take effect, Creutz believed that he had to "seize the moment" and conclude the treaty with Franklin. If he did not (as he explained to the king), he risked forfeiting Sweden's opportunity to be the first power to sign a treaty with the new nation. Portugal, he had learned, had already started negotiating with the United States, with England's knowledge. Franklin was "growing colder by the day." He could not afford to wait any longer.[3]

On February 5, at eleven o'clock in the morning, Franklin and Creutz signed the treaty in the Swedish ambassador's residence after exchanging powers. The text was identical to the draft sent by Sweden. "But as this Minister's instructions contained explicit orders to limit the treaty to 15 years," Creutz explained to the king, "we added a separate article to this effect, which can be ratified on its own." Franklin agreed to keep the treaty secret until it was ratified. So as not

9. Creutz to Gustavus III, Jan. 9, 1783 (Svenska Riksarkivet).

1. Creutz to Gustavus III, Jan. 23, 1783 (Svenska Riksarkivet).

2. Marianne Molander Beyer, ed., *Comte de Creutz: la Suède & les lumières, lettres de France d'un Ambassadeur à son Roi (1771–1783)* (Paris, 2006), p. 559.

3. Creutz to Gustavus III, Feb. 6, 1783 (Svenska Riksarkivet).

to "excite the attention of the other powers," Creutz decided that Captain d'Aminoff, a courier of the king's who would carry the treaty to Sweden, should disguise himself as a common traveler.[4]

That same day after dinner, Creutz received a dispatch from the king; by the time it was deciphered, it was nine o'clock at night. Its contents nearly plunged him into "despair": Gustavus had ordered him not to sign anything until after the Anglo-American preliminary treaty had been published in London. He was somewhat consoled by learning, from an accompanying dispatch from the president of the Chancellery, that the king's concerns about potential British retaliation would evaporate once the peace was concluded. Creutz assured the king that any "step backwards" with Franklin at this point would present "the most serious consequences and would serve only to compromise the interests of Your Majesty." He hit upon a plan that he doubted would work, but in fact it succeeded: he persuaded Franklin to agree to sign a new version of the treaty with the date left blank, to be filled in once the publication of the preliminary treaty arrived from London. Franklin, knowing that the treaty was already printed and expecting a copy to arrive in a matter of days, agreed to mollify Gustavus with this additional precaution. On February 8 the two ministers signed and sealed new, undated versions of the treaty and burned the previous ones.[5] L'Air de Lamotte had already made a copy of the February 5 treaty for Franklin, however, who kept at least a part of it. The section that survives is the final three pages: the last five articles, the date, and indications of the signatures and seals.[6]

For another week, with the undated treaty still in his office as he awaited news from London, Creutz continued to believe that the treaty was a secret to everyone but the American peace commissioners and Vergennes. He was wrong. On February 6 John Adams wrote the news to a member of Congress with no indication that discretion was required, and on the following day he sent word to Dumas that the treaty had been signed on February 5.[7] The British ambassador knew by February 9 that Franklin had "entirely finished & signed" the treaty with Sweden.[8] On February 14, after Adams' letter reached

4. *Ibid.* Congress had instructed BF to make the treaty for 12 years but gave him permission to extend it to 20 years if necessary: XXXVIII, 153.

5. Creutz to Gustavus III, Feb. 9, 1783 (Svenska Riksarkivet).

6. APS.

7. JA to Thomas McKean, Feb. 6, 1783; to Dumas, Feb. 7, 1783 (*Adams Papers,* XIV, 248–9, 251).

8. Fitzherbert to Grantham, Feb. 9, 1783, in Giunta, *Emerging Nation,* I, 765–6.

Holland, the *Gazette de Leyde* broadcast the news all over Europe. That same day, Creutz hosted a dinner for the Americans in honor of the accord.[9]

In the meantime, Gustavus had agreed to grant Congress the four articles not included in the Swedish draft, Articles 4, 5, 6, and 17. These were formulated into five separate articles (Congress' article 4 was split in two), which Creutz received on February 23. Although he informed Franklin that they had arrived, the Swedish ambassador stalled further negotiations out of fear that the debates then raging in Parliament might affect Britain's position on America. By the beginning of March even Vergennes was warning Creutz that he had better conclude the treaty, assuring him that America's position was stable and telling him of the other ambassadors who were openly making overtures to the Americans. That, coupled with Franklin's impatience and the unwelcome news that Creutz himself was being recalled to Sweden, contributed to his decision that he "could not postpone it any longer."[1]

On March 5, Creutz and Franklin agreed on the five separate articles and signed all the documents. Fearful of not signing on that day, but equally afraid of the king's displeasure if he once again signed prematurely, Creutz "persuaded Mr. Franklin to give the treaty the date of April 3, within which time everything should be settled that concerns the peacemaking and nothing should remain but the ratification." Creutz told the king that waiting for ratification was unnecessary, in any case. He chose the date of April 3 as the last day he was likely to be in Paris.[2]

The king's courier left Paris with the signed treaty on March 8.[3] The official text he carried, identical to its American counterpart published here, contained 27 articles drafted by Sweden, one unnumbered separate article added by Franklin on February 5, and five numbered separate articles supplied by Sweden at Franklin's request, reflecting everything else that Congress had sought.

---

9. JA to Jenings, Feb. 14, 1783 (*Adams Papers*, XIV, 260). JA was impressed with Creutz, whom he described as "a Man of Sense and Learning" with a vast library and a face pale enough to suggest that he used it.

1. Creutz to Gustavus III, Feb. 23, 27, March 8, 1783 (Svenska Riksarkivet). The king had named Creutz president of the Chancellory following Ulric Scheffer's retirement, though he knew Creutz would hate to leave Paris: Gustavus to Creutz, Feb. 5, 1783, in Gunnar von Proschwitz, ed., *Gustave III par ses lettres* (Stockholm and Paris, 1986), pp. 229–30.

2. Creutz to Gustavus III, March 8, 1783 (Svenska Riksarkivet).

3. Creutz to Gustavus III, March 9, 1783. (Svenska Riksarkivet; translation at the Hist. Soc. of Pa.).

Franklin finally informed Livingston on March 7 that the treaty was concluded and that he would send it at the first opportunity. He sent a duplicate on April 15, hoping that the first one had already been ratified. (Both letters are below.) When Congress did finally ratify the treaty on July 29, the members were struck by "a manifest impropriety" (in fact, two of them) in the preamble, which they insisted that Franklin amend: the name of the country and the name of one state were incorrect. The word "North" should be struck from "the United States of North America," they chided, and as for the three counties on the Delaware, "there is no such State in the union."[4] This preamble, supplied by Sweden, had been taken from the Franco-American commercial treaty signed by Franklin, Deane, and Lee in February, 1778. (The state's name was correctly listed in the preamble to the Franco-American treaty of alliance signed the same day.) In December, 1782, having just concluded the peace negotiations with England and with so much else on his mind, Franklin must not have bothered to scrutinize the preamble of the draft Creutz showed him. Thereafter, knowing that the text had not changed, he probably never read it again.

[April 3, <i>i.e.</i>, March 5, 1783]

I.

Traité d'Amitié et de Commerce conclu entre Sa Majesté le Roi de Suede et les Etats Unis de l'Amérique Septentrionale

Le Roi de Suede des Goths et des Vandales &c. &c. &c. Et les Treize Etats Unis de l'Amerique Septentrionale, sçavoir, New-Hampshire, Massachusetts Bay, Rhode Island, Connecticut, New-York, New-Jersey, Pensylvanie, les Comtés de New-Castle, de Kent et de Sussex sur la Delaware, Maryland, Virginie, Caroline Septentrionale, Caroline Meridionale et Georgie, desirant d'établir d'une maniere stable et permanente les regles qui devront être suivies relativement à la Correspondence et au

---

4. *JCC*, XXIV, 476–7; Boudinot to BF, Aug. 15, 1783 (Library of Congress). On Feb. 6, 1784, Baron Erik Magnus Staël von Holstein, the new Swedish minister plenipotentiary, wrote Gustavus that BF had informed him of the corrections: Hunter Miller, ed., *Treaties and Other International Acts of the United States of America* (8 vols., Washington, D.C., 1931–48), II, 149–50.

Commerce que les deux Parties ont jugé necessaire de fixer entre leurs Pays, États et Sujets respectifs, Sa Majesté et les Etats Unis ont cru ne pouvoir mieux remplir ce but qu'en posant pour base de leurs Arrangemens, l'Utilité et l'avantage reciproques des deux Nations, en évitant toutes les préferances onereuses qui sont ordinairement une Source de discussions, d'embarras et de mécontentements; et en laissant à chaque Partie la Liberté de faire au Sujet du Commerce et de la Navigation, les reglemens intériures qui seront à Sa Convenance.

Dans cette vue Sa Majesté le Roi de Suede a nommé et constitué pour son Plenipotentiaire le Comte Gustave Philippe de Creutz, son Ambassadeur Extraordinaire près sa Majesté très Chretienne et Chevalier Commandeur de ses ordres; et les Etats Unis ont de leur Coté pourvû de leurs Pleinpouvoirs le Sieur Benjamin Franklin leur Ministre Plenipotentiaire près Sa Majesté très Chretienne; les quels Plenipotentiaires, après avoir échangé leurs Pleinpouvoirs, et en consequence d'une mure deliberation ont arreté, conclu et signé les Articles Suivants.

Art. 1.

Il y aura une Paix ferme, inviolable et universelle, et une Amitié vraie et sincere entre le Roi de Suede, Ses Heritiers et Successeurs. et entre les Etats Unis de l'Amerique, ainsi qu'entre les Sujets de Sa Majesté et ceux des dits Etats, comme aussi entre les Pays, Isles, Villes et Places, situées sous la Jurisdiction du Roi et des dits Etats Unis, sans exception aucune de Personnes et de Lieux; les Conditions stipulées dans le présent Traité devant être perpetuelles et permanentes entre le Roi, ses Heritiers et Sucesseurs et les dits Etats Unis.

Art. 2d.

Le Roi et les Etats Unis s'engagent mutuellement à n'accorder par la Suite aucune faveur particuliere en fait de commerce et de Navigation à d'autres Nations; qui ne devienne aussitôt commune à l'autre Partie; et celle cy jouira de cette faveur gratuitement, si la Concession est gratuite; ou en accordant la même Compensation si la Concession est conditionelle.

Art. 3.

Les Sujets du Roi de Suede ne payeront dans les Ports, Havres, Rades, Contrées, Isles, Villes et Places des Etats Unis, ou dans aucun d'iceux [de ceux-ci], d'autres ni de plus grand Droits et impots de quelque nature qu'ils puissent être, que ceux que les Nations les plus favorisées sont ou seront tenues de payer; et ils jouiront de tous les Droits, Libertés, Privileges, Immunités et exemptions en fait de Negoce, Navigation et de Commerce dont jouissent ou jouiront les dites Nations, soit en passant d'un Port à l'autre des dits Etats, soit en y allant ou en revenant de quelque Partie ou pour quelque partie du monde que ce soit.

Art. 4.

Les Sujets et Habitans des dits Etats Unis ne payeront dans les Ports, Havres, Rades, Isles, Villes et Places de la Domination du Roi de Suède, d'autres ni de plus grands Droits ou impots, de quelque nature qu'ils puissent être, et quelque nom qu'ils puissent avoir, que ceux que les Nations les plus favorisées sont ou seront tenues de payer; et ils jouiront de tous les Droits, Libertés, Privileges, immunites et exemptions en fait de Negoce, Navigation et Commerce dont jouissent ou jouiront les dites Nations, soit en passant d'un Port à un autre de la Domination de sa dite Majesté, soit en y allant ou en revenant de quelque Partie du monde, ou pour quelque partie du monde que ce soit.

art. 5.

Il sera accordé une pleine, parfaite et entiere Liberté de Conscience aux habitants et Sujets de chaque Partie et personne ne sera molesté à l'égard de son Culte, moyennant qu'il se soumette, quant à la Demonstration publique aux Loix du Pays. De plus on permettra aux habitans et Sujets de chaque Partie, que decedent dans le Territoire de l'autre Partie, d'être enterrés dans les endroits convenables et décents qui seront assignés à cet effet, et les deux Puissances contractantes pourvoiront chacune dans sa Jurisdiction, à ce que les Sujets et habitans respectifs puissent obtenir les Certificats de mort, en cas qu'il soit requis de les livrer.

Art. 6.

Les Sujets des Parties contractantes pourront dans les Etats respectifs disposer librement de leur fonds et biens, soit par Testament, Donation ou autrement, en faveur de telles personnes que bon leur semblera, et leurs Heritiers dans quelque endroit où ils demeureront, pourront recevoir ces Sucessions, même ab intestato, soit en personne, soit par un procureur, sans qu'ils aient besoin d'obtenir des Lettres de Naturalization. Ces heritages, aussi bien que les Capitaux et fonds que les Sujets des deux Parties, en changeant de demeure, voudront faire sortir de l'endroit de leur Domicile, seront exemts de tout droits de Detraction, de la part du Gouvernement des deux Etats respectifs. Mais il est convenu en même tems, que le contenu de cet article ne derogera en aucune maniere aux ordonnances promulguées en Suède contre les Emigrations, ou qui pourront par la suite être promulguées, les quelles demeureront dans toute leur force et vigueur. Les Etats Unis, de leur côté, ou aucuns d'entre eux seront libres de statuer sur cette matiere telle Loi qu'ils jugeront à propos.

art. 7.

Il sera permis à tous et un chacun des Sujets et habitans du Royaume de Suede, ainsi qu'à ceux des Etats Unis de naviguer avec leurs Bâtimens en toute Sureté et Liberté et sans distinction de ceux à qui les Marchandises et leurs Chargemens appartiendront, de quelque port que ce soit. Il sera permis également aux Sujets et habitans des deux Etats de naviguer et de negocier avec leurs Vaisseaux et marchandises et de frequenter avec la même Liberté et Sureté, les Places Ports et havres des Puissances ennemies des deux Parties contractantes, ou de l'une d'elles, sans être aucunement inquietés ni troublés, et de faire le Commerce non seulement directement des Ports de l'Ennemi à un port neutre, mais encore d'un port ennemi à un autre port ennemi; soit qu'il se trouve sous la Jurisdiction d'un même ou des differents Princes. Et comme il est reçu par le present Traité, par rapport aux Navires et aux Marchandises, que les Vaisseaux libres rendront les marchandises libres, et que l'on regardera comme libre tout ce qui sera à Bord des Navires appartenants aux Sujets d'une ou de l'autre des Parties contractantes, quand même le Chargement ou partie d'icelui appartiendroit aux ennemis de l'une des deux, bien entendu néanmoins, que les marchandises de contrabande seront toujours exceptées; les quelles étant interceptées, il sera procedé conformement à l'esprit des articles suivants. Il est également convenu que cette même Liberté s'etendra aux personnes qui naviguent Sur un Vaisseau libre; de maniere que quoiqu'elles soient ennemies des deux Parties, ou de l'une d'elles, elles ne seront point tirées du Vaisseau libre, si ce n'est que ce fussent des gens de Guerre actuellement au Service des dits ennemis.

Art. 8.

Cette Liberté de Navigation et de Commerce s'étendra à toutes Sortes de marchandises, à la reserve seulement de celles qui sont exprimées dans l'article suivant et designées sous le nom de marchandises de Contrebande.

Art. 9.

On comprendre sous ce nom de marchandises de Contrabande ou defendues, les armes, Canons, Boulets, Arquebuses, Mousquets, Mortiers, Bombes, Petards, Grenades, Saucisses, Cercles poissés, Affuts, Fourchettes, Bandoulieres, poudre à canon, meches, Salpêtre, Souffre, Balles, Piques, Sabres, Epées, Morions, Casques, Cuirasses, Halbardes, Javelines, Pistolets et leurs Fourreaux, Baudriers, Bayonettes, Chevaux avec leurs Harnois et tous autres semblables genres, d'armes et d'instruments de guerre servant à l'usage des Troupes.

Art. 10

On ne mettra point au nombre des Marchandises defendues celles qui suivent sçavoir, toutes Sortes de draps et tous autres ouvrages de Manufactures de laine, de Lin, de Soye, de Cotton, et de toute autre matiere, tout genre d'habillement, avec les choses qui servent ordinairement à les faire; Or, Argent monnoyé ou non monnoyé, Etain, Fer, plomb, Cuivre, Laiton, Charbon à fourneau, bled, orge et toute autre Sorte de Grains et de legumes, la Nicotiane, vulgairement appellée Tabac, toutes Sortes d'aromates, Chaires Salées et fumées, Poissons salés, fromage et Beurre, Bierre, Huile, Vins, Sucres, Toutes sortes de Sels et de Provisions servant à la Nourriture et à la Subsistance des hommes; Tous genres de Coton, Chanvre, Lin, Poix tant liquide que Seche, Cordages, Cables, voiles, Toiles propres à faire des voiles, ancres et Parties d'Ancres quelles qu'elles puissent être, Mats de Navires, Planches, Madriers, Poutres et toute Sorte d'arbres et toutes autres choses necessaires pour construire ou pour radouber les Vaisseaux. On ne regardera pas non plus comme marchandises de Contrebande, celles qui n'auront pas pris la forme de quelque instrument ou attirail, servant à l'usage de la Guerre sur Terre ou sur mer, encore moins celles qui sont preparées ou travaillées pour tout autre usage. Toutes ces Choses seront censées Marchandises Libres de même que toutes celles qui ne sont point comprises et specialement designées dans l'article precedent, de Sorte qu'elles ne pourront sous aucune interpretation pretendue d'icelles être comprises sous les éffets prohibés ou de contrebande; au contraire elles pourront être librement transportées par les Sujets du Roi et des Etats Unis, même dans les lieux ennemis, excepté seulement dans les Places assiegées, bloquées ou investies; et pour telles, seront tenues uniquement les places entourées de prés par quelqu'une des Puissances Belligerantes.

Art. 11.

Afin d'écarter et de prevenir de part et d'autre toutes sortes de Discussions et de Discorde, il a été convenu que dans le cas où l'une des deux Parties se trouveroit engagée dans une Guerre, les Vaisseaux et Batimens appartenants aux Sujets ou habitans de l'autre devront être munis de Lettres de mer ou Passeports, exprimant le nom, la Proprieté et le Port du Navire, ainsi que le nom et la Demeure du maitre ou Commandant du dit Vaisseau, afin qu'il apparoisse par là que le dit Vaisseau appartient réellement et veritablement au Sujet de l'une ou de l'autre Partie. Ces Passeports qui seront dressés et expediés en due et bonne forme, devront également être renouvellés toutes les fois que le Vaisseau revient chez lui dans le Cours de l'an. Il est encore convenu que ces dits Vaisseaux chargés devront être pourvus non seulement de Lettres de mer, mais aussi de Certificats contenants les Details de la Cargaison, le lieu d'où le Vaisseau est parti, et celui de sa Destination, afin que l'on puisse connoitre s'ils ne portent

aucune des Marchandises defendues ou de Contrebande speci-
fiées dans l'article 9. du present Traité, lesquels Certificats seront
également expediés par les officiers du lieu d'où le Vaisseau sor-
tira.

Art. 12.

Quoique les vaisseaux de l'une et de l'autre Partie pourront
naviguer librement et avec toute Sureté, comme il est expliqué à
l'art. 7. ils seront néanmoins tenus, toutes les fois qu'on l'exigera,
d'exhiber tant en pleine Mer que dans les Ports, leurs passeports
et Certificats cy dessus mentionnés. Et n'ayant pas chargé des
Marchandises de Contrebande pour un port ennemi, ils pourront
librement et sans empechement poursuivre leur voyage vers le
lieu de leur Destination. Cependant on n'aura point le Droit de
demander l'exhibition des Papiers aux Navires Marchandes con-
voyé par des Vaisseaux de Guerre; mais on ajoutera foi à la parole de l'Officier commandant le Convoy.

Art. 13.

Si en produisant les dits Certificats il fut decouvert que le
Navire porte quelques uns de ces effets qui sont declarés prohibés et de Contrebande, et qui sont consignés pour un port ennemi, il ne sera cependant pas permis de rompre les Ecoutilles
des dits navires, ni d'ouvrir aucune Caisse, Coffre, malle, Ballot
et Tonneau, ou d'en deplacer ni d'en detourner la moindre partie des Marchandises, jusqu'à ce que la Cargaison ait été mise à
terre, en presence des officiers preposés à cet effet, et que l'inventaire en ait été fait. Encore ne sera t'il pas permis de vendre,
échanger ou aliener la Cargaison, ou quelque partie d'icelle,
avant qu'on aura procedé legalement au Sujet des marchandises
prohibées et qu'elles auront été declarées confiscables par Sentence; à la reserve neanmoins tant des navires même que des
autres marchandises qui y aurons été trouvées et qui, en vertu du
present Traité, doivent être censées libres; les quelles ne peuvent
être retenues sous pretexte qu'elles ont été chargées avec des
Marchandises defendues, et encore moins être confisquées
comme une prise Legitime. Et supposé que les dites Marchandises de Contrebande, ne faisant qu'une partie de la Charge, le
Patron du Navire agréat, consentit et offrit de les livrer au Vais-

seau qui les aura decouvertes; en ce cas celui cy, apres avoir reçu les Marchandises de bonne prise, sera tenu de laisser aller aussitôt le Batiment, et ne l'empechera en aucune maniere de poursuivre sa route vers le lieu de sa Destination. Tout Navire pris et amené dans un des Ports des Parties contractantes, sous pretexte de Contrebande, qui se trouve, par la visite faite n'être chargé que de marchandises declarées libres, L'armateur ou celui qui aura fait la prise, sera tenu de payer tous les fraix et dommages au Patron du Navire retenu injustement.

Art. 14.

On est également convenu que tout ce qui se trouvera chargé par les Sujets d'une des deux Parties dans un Vaisseau appartenant aux Ennemis de l'autre Partie, sera confisqué en entier, quoique ces effets ne soient pas au nombre de ceux declarés de contrebande, comme si ces effets appartenoient à l'Ennemi même, à l'exception néanmoins des effets et Marchandises qui auront été chargés sur des vaisseaux ennemis avant la Declaration de Guerre et même Six mois après la Declaration, après le quel Terme l'on ne sera pas censé d'avoir pu l'ignorer; les quelles marchandises ne seront en aucune maniere Sujettes à Confiscation, mais seront rendues en nature fidelement aux Proprietaires qui les reclameront ou feront reclamer avant la confiscation et vente; comme aussi leur provenu, si la reclamation ne pouvoit se faire que dans l'intervalle de huit mois après la vente, la quelle doit être publique, bien entendu néanmoins, que si les dites marchandises sont de Contrebande, il ne sera nullement permis de les transporter ensuite à aucun Port appartenant aux ennemis.

art. 15.

Et afin de pourvoir plus efficacement à la Sûreté des deux Parties contractantes, pour qu'il ne leur soit fait aucun prejudice par les Vaisseaux de Guerre de l'autre Partie ou par des armateurs particuliers, il sera fait defense à tous Capitanes et Commandants des Vaisseaux de Sa Mté. Suédoise et des Etats Unis, et tous leurs Sujets de faire aucun Dommage ou insulte à ceux de l'autre Partie; et au cas qu'ils y contreviennent, ayant été trouvés coupables, aprés l'examen fait par leur propre Juges, ils seront tenus de donner Satisfaction des tout dommage et interêt; et de les bonnifier sous peine et obligation de leurs Personnes et Biens.

Art. 16.

Pour cette cause chaque particulier voulant armer en course, sera obligé avant que de recevoir les patentes ou ses Commissions speciales de donner par devant un Juge competent, caution de Personnes solvables, chacun solidairement, pour une Somme suffisante afin de repondre de tous les dommages et Torts que l'Armateur, ses officiers, ou autres étant à Son Service, pourroient faire en leurs Courses, contre la teneur de present Traité et contre les Edits faits de part et d'autre en vertu du même Traité par le Roi de Suede et par les Etats Unis, même sous peine de revocation et Cassation des dites Patentes et Commissions speciales.

Art. 17.

Une des Parties contractantes étant en Guerre, et l'autre restant neutre, s'il arrivoit qu'un navire marchand de la Puissance neutre fut pris par l'ennemi de l'autre partie et repris ensuite par un vaisseau ou par un Armateur de la Puissance en Guerre; de même que les Navires et marchandises de quelle Nature qu'els puissent être lorsqu'elles auront été enlevées des mains de quelque Pirate ou Ecumeur de mer, elles seront emmenées dans quelque Port de l'un des deux Etats et seront remises à la Garde des officiers du dit Port, afin d'être rendus en entier à leur veritable Proprietaire, aussitot qu'il aura produit des preuves suffisantes de la propriété. Les Marchands, Patrons et proprietaires des Navires, Matelots, gens de toute Sorte, Vaisseaux et Batimens et en general aucunes marchandises ni aucuns effets de chacun des Alliés ou de leurs Sujets ne pourront être assujettis à aucun embargo, ni retenus dans aucun des Pays, Territoires, Isles, villes, Places, Ports, Rivages ou Domaines quelconques de l'autre allié, pour quelque expedition militaire, usage public ou particulier de qui que ce soit, par saisie, par force ou de quelque maniere semblable. D'autant moins serait'il permis aux Sujets de chacune des Parties de prendre ou enlever par force quelque chose aux Sujets de l'autre Partie, sans le consentement du proprietaire; ce qui néanmoins ne doit pas s'entendre des Saisies, Detentions et arrets qui se feront par ordre et autorité de la Justice et selon les voyes ordinaires pour dettes ou delits, au Sujet des quels il devra être procedé par voye de droit selon les formes de Justice.

Art. 18.

S'il arrivoit que les deux Parties contractantes fussent en même tems en guerre contre un ennemi commun, on observera de part et d'autre les Points suivans.

1°. Si les Batimens de l'une des deux Nations repris par les Armateurs de l'autre n'ont pas été au pouvoir de l'Ennemi au delà de 24 heures, ils seront restitués au premier proprietaire moyenant le Payement du Tiers de la Valeur du Batiment et de celle de la Cargaison. Si au contraire le vaisseau repris a été plus de 24 heures au Pouvoir de l'ennemi, il appartiendra en entier à celui qui l'aura repris.

2°. Dans le cas que dans l'intervalle de 24 heures un navire est repris par un Vaisseau de guerre de l'une des deux Parties, il sera rendu au premier Proprietaire, moyennant qu'il paye un Trentieme de la Valeur du Navire et de sa Cargaison, et le dixieme, s'il a été repris après les 24 heures, lesquelles sommes seront distribuées en guise de gratification aux Equipages des Vaisseaux qui l'auront repris.

3°. Les prises faites de la maniere susdite seront restituées aux proprietaires, après les preuves faites de la Proprieté, en donnant caution pour la part qui en revient à celui qui a tiré le navire des mains de l'ennemi.

4°. Les Vaisseaux de guerre et Armateurs des deux Nations seront reciproquement admis avec leurs prises, dans les Ports respectifs de chacune, mais ces Prises ne pourront y être dechargées ni vendues qu'après que la Legitimité de la Prise faite par des batimens Suedois aura été decidée selon les Loix et reglemens établis en Suede; tout comme celle des Prises faites par des Batimens Americains, sera jugée selon les Loix, et reglemens determinées par les Etats Unis de l'Amerique.

5°. Au Surplus il sera libre au Roi de Suede ainsi qu'aux Etats Unis de l'Amerique, de faire tels reglemens qu'ils jugeront necessaires relativement à la conduite que devront tenir leurs vaisseaux et armateurs respectifs à l'egard des Batimens qu'ils auront pris et conduits dans les Ports des deux Puissances.

Art: 19.

Les Vaisseaux de Guerre de sa Majesté Suedoise et ceux des Etats Unis, de même que ceux que leurs Sujets auront armés en guerre, pourront en toute Liberté conduire les Prises qu'ils auront faites sur leur ennemis dans les Ports ouverts en tems de Guerre aux autres Nations amies, sans que ces Prises, entrant dans les dits Ports, puissent être arrêtées ou saisies, ni que les officiers des lieux puissent prendre connaissance de la validité de dites Prises, les quelles pourront sortir et être conduites franchement et en toute Liberté aux lieux portés par les Commissions, dont les Capitaines des dits vaisseaux seront obligés de faire montre.

art. 20.

Au cas que quelque Vaisseau appartenant à l'un des deux Etats, ou à leurs Sujets, aura échoué, fait naufrage ou souffert quelque autre Dommage sur les Côtes ou sous la Domination de l'une des deux Parties, il sera donné toute aide et assistance aux Personnes naufragées ou qui se trouvent en danger, et il leur sera accordé des Passeports pour assurer leur retour dans leur Patrie. Les Navires et marchandises naufragées ou leur provenu, si ces effets eussent été vendue, etant reclamés dans l'an et Jour par les Proprietaires, ou leur ayant cause, seront restitués, en payant les fraix de Sauvement, conformement aux Loix et coutumes des deux Nations.

Art. 21.

Lors que les Sujets et habitans de l'une des deux Parties avec leurs vaisseaux soit publics, soit equipées en guerre, Soit particuliers, ou employés au Commerce, seront forcés par une Tempête, par la poursuite des Corsaires et des ennemis, ou par quelqu'autre necessité urgente de se retirer, et d'entrer dans quelqu'une des Rivieres, Bayes, rades ou Ports de l'une des deux Parties, ils seront reçus et traités avec humanité et honneteté, et jouiront de toute amitié, protection et assistance; et il leur sera permis de se pourvoir de rafraichissemens, de vivres et de toute

chose necessaires pour leur Subsistance, pour la reparation de
leurs vaisseaux et pour continuer leur voyage; le tout moyennant
un prix raisonnable; et ils ne seront retenus en aucune maniere,
ni empêchés de sortir des dits Ports ou Rades, mais pourront se
retirer et partir quand et comme il leur plaira sans aucun obstacle ni empéchement.

Art. 22.

Afin de favoriser d'autant plus le Commerce des deux côtés,
il est convenu que dans le cas où la guerre surviendroit entre les
deux Nations sus dites, ce qu'à Dieu ne plaise, il sera accordé
un tems de neuf mois apres la Declaration de Guerre, aux
marchands et Sujets respectifs de part et d'autre, pour pouvoir se
retirer avec leurs effets et meubles, les quels ils pourront transporter, ou faire vendre où ils voudront, sans qu'on y mette le
moindre obstacle, ni qu'on puisse arrêter les éffets et encore
moins les Personnes pendant les dits neuf mois; mais qu'au contraire on leur donnnera pour les vaisseaux et éffets qu'ils
voudront prendre avec eux des Passeports valables pour le tems
qu'il sera necessaire pour leur retour; mais s'il leur est enlevé
quelque chose, ou s'il leur a été fait quelqu'injure, durant le
Terme prescrit cy dessus, par l'une des Parties, leurs peuples et
Sujects, il leur sera donné à cet égard pleine et entiere Satisfaction. Ces Passeports susmentionnés serviront également de
Saufconduits contre toutes insultes ou prises que les Armateurs
pourront intenter de faire contre leurs personnes et leurs effets.

art. 23.

Aucun Sujet du Roi de Suede ne prendra de Commission ou
lettre de Marque pour armer quelque Vaisseau afin d'agir comme
Corsaire contre les Etats Unis de l'amerique, ou quelques uns
d'entre Eux, ou contre les Sujets, peuples ou habitans d'iceux,
ou contre la Proprieté des Habitans de ces Etats, de quelque
Prince ou Etat que ce soit, avec le quel ces dits Etats Unis seront
en Guerre. De même aucun Citoyen Sujet ou habitant des dits
Etats Unis et de quelqu'un d'entre eux ne demandera ni ac-
ceptera aucune Commission ou Lettre de marque afin d'armer
quelque Vaisseau pour courre sus aux Sujets de Sa Mté. Suedoise
ou quelqu'un d'entre eux ou leur proprieté, de quelque Prince

ou état que ce soit avec qui sa dite Majesté se trouvera en guerre. Et si quelqu'un de l'une ou de l'autre Nation prenoit de pareilles Commissions ou Lettres de marque, il sera puni comme Pirate.

Art. 24.

Les vaisseaux des Sujets ou Habitants d'une des deux Parties, abordant à quelque côte de la Dependance de l'autre, mais n'ayant point dessein d'entrer au Port, ou y étant entré ne desirant pas de decharger leur Cargaison, ou rompre leur Charge n'y seront point obligés, mais au contraire jouiront de toutes les Franchises et exemtions accordes par les Reglemens qui subsistent relativement à cet objet.

Art. 25.

Lors qu'un Vaisseau appartenant aux Sujets et Habitans de l'une des deux Parties, naviguant en pleine Mer, sera rencontré par un Vaisseau de Guerre ou Armateur de l'autre, le Dit vaisseau de Guerre ou Armateur, pour éviter tout desordre, se tiendra hors de la portée du Canon, mais pourra toutes fois envoyer sa Chaloupe à bord du Navire marchand et y faire entrer deux ou trois hommes, aux quels le maitre ou Commandant du dit Navire, montrera son Passeport qui constate la proprieté du Navire; et après que le dit Batiment aura exhibé le Passeport, il lui sera libre de continuer son Voyage; et il ne sera pas permis de le molester, ni de chercher en aucune maniere à lui donner la Chasse ou à le forcer de quitter la Course qu'il s'etoit proposé.

Art. 26.

Les deux Parties contractante se sont accordé mutuellement la Faculté de tenir dans leurs Ports respectifs des Consuls, Vice Consuls, Agents et Commissaires dont les functions seront reglées par une Convention particuliere.

Art. 27.

Le présent Traité sera ratifié de part et d'autre, et les Ratifications seront échangées dans l'Espace de huit mois, ou plus tôt si faire se peut; à compter du Jour de la signature. En foi de quoi les Plenipotentiaires respectifs ont signé les articles cy dessus, et y ont apposé le Cachet de leurs armes.

Fait à Paris le trois Avril L'an de grâce mil Sept cent, qua-
trevingt trois.

GUSTAV PHILIP COMTE DE CREUTZ   B FRANKLIN
[seal]   [seal]

Article separé.

Le Roi de Suède et les Etats Unis de l'Amerique Septentrionale sont convenus que le présent Traité aura son plein Effet
pendant l'espace de quinze ans consecutifs à compter du Jour de
sa Ratification; et les deux Parties contractantes se reservent la
faculté de le renouveller au bout de ce tems.

Fait à Paris le trois Avril, mil sept Cent quatre vingt trois.

GUSTAV PHILIP COMTE DE CREUTZ   B FRANKLIN
[seal]   [seal]

Articles separés.

Art: 1.

Sa Majesté Suedoise fera usage de tous les moyens qui sont
dans son pouvoir pour proteger et defendre les Vaisseaux et
Effets appartenans aux Citoyens ou Habitans des Etats Unis de
l'Amerique Septentrionale et à chacun d'iceux, qui seront dans
les Ports, Havres ou Rades ou dans les Mers près des Païs, Isles,
Contrées, Villes et Places de sa dite Majesté et fera tous ses
Efforts pour recouvrir et faire restituer aux Proprietaires legitimes tous les Vaisseaux et Effets qui leur seront pris dans
l'Etendue de sa Jurisdiction.

Art: 2.

De même les Etats Unis de l'Amerique Septentrionale prote-
geront et defendront les Vaisseaux et Effets, appartenans aux Sujets de sa Majesté Suedoise qui seront dans les Ports, Havres ou
Rades ou dans les Mers près des Païs, Isles, Contrées Villes et
Places des dits Etats, et feront tous leurs Efforts pour recouvrir
et faire restituer aux Proprietaires legitimes tous les Vaisseaux et
Effets qui leur seront pris dans l'Etendue de leur Jurisdiction.

Art: 3.

Si durant une Guerre Maritime à venir les deux Puissances
contractantes prennent le parti de rester neutres et d'observer

comme telles, la plus exacte Neutralité, alors on est convenu que s'il arrivoit que les Vaisseaux Marchands de l'une des Puissances, se trouvassent dans un Parage ou les Vaisseaux de Guerre de la même Nation ne fussent pas stationnés, ou bien s'ils se rencontrent en pleine Mer sans pouvoir avoir recours à leurs propres convois, dans ce cas le Commandant des Vaisseaux de Guerre de l'autre Puissance, s'il en est requis, doit de bonne foi et sincerement leur prêter les Secours dont ils pourront avoir besoin et en tel cas les Vaisseaux de Guerre et Fregates de l'une des Puissances serviront de Soutien et d'apui aux Vaisseaux Marchands de l'autre, bien entendu cependant que les Reclamans n'auroient fait aucun Commerce illicite ni contraires aux Principes de la Neutralité.

Art. 4.

Il est convenu et arrêté que tous les Marchands, Capitaines des Navires Marchands ou autres Sujets de sa Majesté Suedoise, auront l'entiere Liberté dans toutes les Places de la Domination ou Jurisdiction des Etats Unis de l'Amerique, de conduire eux mêmes leurs propres affaires, et d'employer qui il leur plaira pour les conduire, et qu'ils ne seront point obligés de se servir d'aucun Interprete ou Courtier, ni leur payer aucun honoraire à moins qu'ils ne s'en servent. En outre les Maitres des Navires ne seront point obligés, chargeant ou dechargeant leurs Navires, de se servir des Ouvriers qui peuvent être établis pour cet effet par l'autorité publique; mais ils seront entierement libres de charger ou de decharger eux mêmes leur Vaisseaux, et d'employer pour charger ou decharger ceux qu'ils croiront propres pour cet effet, sans payer aucuns Honoraires à titre de Salaire à aucune autre Personne que ce soit, et ils ne pourront être forcés de verser aucune espece de Marchandises dans d'autres Vaisseaux ou de les recevoir à leur bord et d'attendre pour être chargés, plus longtems qu'il ne leur plaira et tous et un chacun des Citoyens, Peuples et Habitans des Etats Unis de l'Amerique, auront et jouiront reciproquement des mêmes Privileges et Libertés dans touts les Places de la Jurisdiction du dit Royaume.

Art: 5.

Il est convenu que lorsque les Marchandises auront été chargées sur les Vaisseaux ou Bâtimens de l'une des deux Parties contractantes, elles ne pourront plus être assujetties à aucune Visite; toute Visite et Recherche devant être faite avant le Chargement, et les marchandises prohibées devant être arrêtées sur la Plage avant de pouvoir être embarquées, à moins qu'on ait des Indices manifestes ou des Preuves de Versement frauduleux de la part du Proprietaire du Navire ou de celui qui en a le Commandement. Dans ce cas seul il en sera responsable et soumis aux Loix du Païs où il se trouve. Dans aucun autre cas, ni les Sujets d'une des Parties contractantes se trouveront avec leurs Navires dans les Ports de l'autre, ni leurs Marchandises, ne pourront être arrêtés ou molestés pour cause de Contrebande, qu'ils auront voulu prendre à leur bord, ni aucune espece d'embargo mis sur leurs navires, les Sujets ou Citoyens de l'Etat ou ses marchandises sont declarées de Contrebande, ou dont la Sortie est defendue, et qui néanmoins auront vendu ou voulu vendre, et aliener les dites Marchandises, devant être les seuls qui seront duement punis pour une pareille Contravention.

Fait à Paris le trois Avril l'an de Grâce mil Sept cent quatre vingt trois.

GUSTAV PHILIP COMTE DE CREUTZ   B FRANKLIN
[seal]   [seal]

II.

A treaty of Amity and Commerce concluded between his Majesty the king of Sweden and the United States of North America

The King of Sweden, of the Goths and Vandals &c &c &c and the thirteen United States of North America, to wit, New hampshire, Massachusetts bay, Rhode island, Connecticut, New York, New Jersey, Pensylvania, The counties of New Castle, Kent and Sussex on Delaware, Maryland, Virginia, North Carolina, South Carolina and Georgia, desiring to establish in a stable and permanent manner the Rules which ought to be observed relative to the Correspondence and commerce which the two parties have judged necessary to establish between their respective countries, states and subjects His Majesty and the United States have thought that they could not better accomplish that end than by taking for a basis of their Arrangements the mutual interest and advantage of both nations thereby avoiding all those burthensome preferences, which are usually sources of debate, embarrassment and discontent, and by leaving each party at liberty to make respecting navigation & Commerce those interior regulations which shall be most convenient to itself.

With this view his Majesty the King of Sweden has nominated and Appointed for his plenipotentiary Count Gustavus Philip de Creutz, his Ambassador extraordinary to his Most Christian Majesty & Knight Commander of his Orders; and the United States on their part have fully empowered Benjamin Franklin their Minister plenipotentiary to his Most Christian Majesty; the said plenipotentiaries after exchanging their full powers and after mature deliberation in consequence thereof have agreed upon, concluded and signed the following Articles.—

Art. 1.

There shall be a firm inviolable and universal peace, and a true and sincere friendship between the King of Sweden, his heirs & successors, and the United States of America, and the subjects of his Majesty and those of the said States, and between the countries, islands, cities and Towns situated under the jurisdiction of the King and of the said United States, without any exception of persons or places, and the conditions agreed to in this present treaty shall be perpetual and permanent between the King his heirs & successors and the said United States.

Art. 2

The King and the United States engage mutually not to grant hereafter any particular favour to other nations in respect to Commerce & navigation, which shall not immediately become common to the other party, who shall enjoy the same favour freely, if the concession was freely made, or on allowing the same compensation, if the concession was conditional.—

Art. 3.

The subjects of the King of Sweden shall not pay in the ports, havens, roads, countries, islands, cities and towns of the United States, or in any of them, any other nor greater duties or imposts of what nature soever they may be, than those which the most favoured nations are, or shall be obliged to pay; and they shall enjoy all the rights, liberties, privileges, immunities & exemptions in trade Navigation & commerce which the said nations do or shall enjoy whether in passing from one port to another of the United States, or in going to or from the same from or to any part of the world whatever.

Art. 4.

The subjects and inhabitants of the said United States shall not pay in the ports, havens, roads, islands, cities and towns under the dominion of the king of Sweden any other or greater duties or imposts, of what nature so ever they may be, or by what name so ever called, than those which the most favoured nations are or shall be obliged to pay; and they shall enjoy all the rights, liberties, privileges, immunities and exemptions in trade, navigation and Commerce which the said nations do or shall enjoy whether in passing from one port to another of the dominion of his said Majesty or in going to or from the same from or to any part of the world whatever.

Art. 5.

There shall be granted a full perfect and entire liberty of Conscience to the inhabitants and subjects of each party, and no person shall be molested on Account of his worship, provided he submits, so far as regards the public demonstration of it, to the laws of the Country. Moreover liberty shall be granted, when any of the subjects or inhabitants of either party die in the territory of the other to bury them in convenient & decent places which shall be assigned for the purpose: And the two contracting parties will provide each in its jurisdiction that the subjects and inhabitants respectively may obtain certificates of the death in case the delivery of them is required.—

Art. 6.

The subjects of the contracting parties in the respective states may freely dispose of their goods and effects, either by testament donation or other wise in favour of such persons as they think proper; and their heirs in whatever place they shall reside, shall receive the succession even *ab intestato* either in person or by their attorney, without having occasion to take out letters of naturalization. These inheritances as well as the capitals & effects, which the subjects of the two parties, in changing their dwelling, shall be desirous of removing from the place of their abode, shall be exempted from all duty, called "*droit de detraction*" on the part of the government of the two states, respectively. But it is at the same time agreed that nothing contained in this article shall in any manner derogate from the Ordinances published in Sweden against emigrations or which may here after be published, which shall remain in full force and vigor. The United States on their part or any of them shall be at liberty to make, respecting this matter, such laws as they think proper.

Art. 7.

All and every [*of*] the subjects & inhabitants of the kingdom of Sweden, as well as those of the United States, shall be permitted to navigate with their vessels in all safety and freedom and without any regard to those to whom the merchandizes & cargoes may belong, from any port whatever. And the subjects and inhabitants of the two States shall likewise be permitted to sail & trade with their vessels and with the same liberty and safety to frequent the places, ports and havens of powers, enemies to both or either of the contracting parties, without being in any wise molested or troubled, and to carry on a commerce not only directly from the ports of an enemy to a neutral port, but even from one port of an Enemy to another port of an Enemy, whether it be under the jurisdiction of the same or of different princes. And as it is acknowledged by this treaty, with respect to ships & merchandizes, that free ships shall make free merchandizes and that every thing which shall be on board of ships belonging to subjects of the one or the other of the contracting parties shall be considered as free, even though the cargo or a part of it should belong to the enemies of one or both; it is nevertheless provided that Contraband goods shall always be excepted; which, being intercepted, shall be proceeded against according to the spirit of the following articles. It is likewise agreed that the same liberty be extended to persons who may be on board a free ship with this effect that although they be enemies to both or either of the parties they shall not be taken out of the free ship, unless they are soldiers in the actual service of the said enemies.

Art 8

This liberty of navigation & commerce shall extend to all kinds of merchandizes except those only which are expressed in the following article, and are distinguished by the name of Contraband Goods.

Art 9.

Under the name of Contraband or prohibited goods shall be Comprehended, Arms, great guns, cannon balls, Arquebuses, Musquets, mortars, bombs, petards, granadoes, Saucisses, pitch balls, carriages for Ordnance, Musquet rests, bandoliers, cannon powder, matches, Saltpetre, sulpher, bullets, pikes, Sabres, swords, morions, helmets, cuirasses, halbards, Javelins, pistols, and their holsters, belts, bayonets, horses with their harness and all other like kinds of arms and instruments of war for the use of troops.

Art 10.

These which follow shall not be reckoned in the number of prohibited goods, that is to say, all sorts of cloths, and all other manufactures of wool, flax, silk, cotton or any other materials, all kinds of wearing apparel together with the things of which they are commonly made; Gold, silver coined or uncoined, brass, iron, lead, copper, latten, coals, wheat, barley and all sorts of corn or pulse, tobacco, all kinds of spices, salted & smoked flesh, salted fish, cheese, butter, beer, oyl, wines, sugar, all sorts of salt and provisions which serve for the nourishment and sustenance of man; All kinds of coton, hemp, flax, tar, pitch, ropes, cables, sails, sail cloth, anchors and any parts of anchors, shipmasts, planks, boards, beams and all sorts of trees and other things proper for building or repairing ships; Nor shall any goods be considered as contraband, which have not been worked into the form of any instrument or thing for the purpose of war by land or by sea, much less such as have been prepared or wrought up for any other use. All which shall be reckoned free goods, as likewise all others which are not comprehended & particularly mentioned in the foregoing article, so that they shall not, by any pretended interpretation, be comprehended among prohibited or contraband goods. On the contrary they may be freely transported by the subjects of the king and of the United States even to places belonging to an enemy Such places only excepted as are besieged, blocked or invested, and those places only shall be considered as such, which are nearly surrounded by one of the belligerent powers.

Art. 11.

In order to avoid & prevent on both sides all disputes and discord, it is agreed that in case one of the parties shall be engaged in a war, the ships & vessels belonging to the subjects or inhabitants of the other shall be furnished with sea letters or passports, expressing the name, property and port of the vessel, and also the name & place of abode of the Master or Commander of the said vessel, in order that it may thereby appear that the said vessel realy & truly belongs to the subjects of the one or the other party. These passports which shall be drawn up in good & due form shall be renewed every time the Vessel returns home in the course of the year. It is also agreed that the said vessels when loaded shall be provided not only with sea letters but also with certificates containing a particular account of the cargo, the place from which the vessel sailed and that of her destination, in order that it may be known, whether they carry any of the prohibited or contraband merchandizes, mentioned in the 9 article of the present treaty; which certificates shall be made out by the officers of the place from which the vessel shall depart.

Art 12.

Although the vessels of the one and of the other party may navigate freely and with all safety as is explained in the 7 article, they shall nevertheless be bound at all times when required, to exhibit as well on the high sea as in port their passports & certificates above mentioned. And not having contraband Merchandize on board for an enemys port, they may freely and without hindrance pursue their voyage to the place of their destination. Nevertheless the exhibition of papers shall not be demanded of merchant ships under the convoy of Vessels of war; but credit shall be given to the word of the Officer commanding the Convoy.

Art 13.

If on producing the said certificates it be discovered that the vessel carries some of the goods which are declared to be prohibited or contraband & which are consigned to an enemy's port, it shall not however be lawful to break up the hatches of such ships, nor to open any chest, coffers, packs, casks or vessels, nor to remove or displace the smallest part of the merchandizes until the cargo has been landed in the presence of officers appointed for the purpose and until an inventory thereof has been taken. Nor shall it be lawful to sell, exchange, or alienate the cargo or any part thereof, until legal process shall have been had against the prohibited merchandizes and sentence shall have passed declaring them liable to confiscation, saving nevertheless as well the ships themselves as the other merchandizes which shall have been found therein, which by virtue of this present treaty are to be esteemed free, and which are not to be detained on pretence of their having been loaded with prohibited merchandize and much less confiscated as lawful prize. And in case the contraband merchandize be only a part of the Cargo and the master of the vessel agrees, consents & offers to deliver them to the vessel, that has discovered them, in that case the latter, after receiving the merchandizes which are good prize, shall immediately let the vessel go and shall not by any means hinder her from pursuing her voyage to the place of her destination. When a vessel is taken and brought into any of the ports of the contracting parties, if upon examination she be found to be loaded only with merchandizes declared to be free, the owner or he who has made the prize shall be bound to pay all costs & damages to the master of the vessel unjustly detained.

Art 14

It is likewise agreed that whatever shall be found to be laden by the subjects of either of the two contracting parties on a ship belonging to the enemies of the other party the whole effects, although not of the number of those declared Contraband, shall be confiscated as if they belonged to the enemy, excepting nevertheless such goods and merchandizes as were put on board before the declaration of war & even six months after the declaration after which term none shall be presumed to be ignorant of it, which merchandizes shall not in any manner be subject to confiscation, but shall be faithfully & specifically delivered to the owners who shall claim or cause them to be claimed before confiscation & sale, as also their proceeds if the claim be made within eight months & could not be made sooner after the sale, which is to be public: provided nevertheless that if the said merchandizes be Contraband it shall not be in any wise lawful to carry them afterward to a port belonging to the enemy.

Art. 15.

And that more effectual care may be taken for the security of the two contracting parties, that they suffer no prejudice by the men of war of the other party or by privateers all captains & commanders of ships of his Swedish Majesty and of the United States and all their subjects shall be forbidden to do any injury or damage to those of the other party, & if they act to the contrary, having been found guilty on examination by their proper judges they shall be bound to make satisfaction for all damages & the interest thereof & to make them good under pain & obligation of their persons and goods.

Art. 16.

For this cause, every individual who is desirous of fitting out a privateer shall before he receives letters patent or special commission be obliged to give bond with sufficient sureties, before a competent judge, for a sufficient sum, to answer all damages & wrongs which the owner of the privateer his officers or others in his employ may commit during the cruize, contrary to the tenor of this treaty, and contrary to the edicts published by either party, whether by the king of Sweden or by the United States in virtue of this same treaty and also under the penalty of having the said letters patent & special commission revoked and made void.

Art. 17.

One of the contracting parties being at war & the other remaining neuter if it should happen that a merchant ship of the neutral power be taken by the enemy of the other party and be afterwards retaken by a ship of war or privateer of the power at war, also ships & merchandizes of what nature soever they may be when recovered from a pirate or sea-rover, shall be brought into a port of one of the two powers & shall be committed to the custody of the officers of the said port, that they may be restored entire to the true proprietor as soon as he shall have produced full proof of the property. Merchants, masters & owners of ships, seamen, people of all sorts, Ships & Vessels & in general all merchandizes & effects of one of the allies or their subjects shall not be subject to any embargo nor detained in any of the countries, territories, islands, cities, towns, ports, rivers or domains whatever of the other ally on account of any military expedition or any public or private purpose whatever, by seizure, by force, or by any such manner, much less shall it be lawful for the subjects of one of the parties to seize or take any thing by force from the subjects of the other party without the consent of the owner. This however is not to be understood to comprehend seizures, detentions and arrests made by order and by the authority of justice & according to the ordinary course for debts or faults of the subject, for which process shall be had in the way of right according to the forms of Justice.

Art. 18.

If it should happen that the two contracting parties should be engaged in a war at the same time with a common enemy, the following points shall be observed on both sides

1. If the ships of one of the two Nations retaken by the privateers of the other have not been in the power of the enemy more than 24 hours, they shall be restored to the original owner on payment of one third of the value of the ship and cargo. If on the contrary the vessel retaken has been more than 24 hours in the power of the enemy, it shall belong wholly to him who has retaken it.

2. In case, during the interval of 24 hours, a vessel be retaken by a man of war of either of the two parties, it shall be restored to the original owner on payment of a thirtieth part of the value of the vessel and cargo, and a tenth part, if it has been retaken after the 24 hours, which sums shall be distributed as a gratifica-

tion among the crew of the men of war that shall have made the recapture.

3 The prizes made in manner above mentioned shall be restored to the owners after proof made of the property, upon giving security for the part coming to him who has recovered the vessel from the hands of the enemy.

4. The men of war and privateers of the two nations shall reciprocally be admitted with their prizes into each others ports; but the prizes shall not be unloaded or sold there until the legality of a prize made by Swedish ships shall have been determined according to the laws & regulations established in Sweden as also that of the prizes made by American vessels shall have been determined according to the laws & regulations established by the United States of America.

5 Moreover the King of Sweden and the United States of America shall be at liberty to make such regulations as they shall judge necessary respecting the conduct which their men of war & privateers respectively shall be bound to observe with regard to vessels which they shall take and carry into the ports of the two powers.

Art 19.

The ships of war of his Swedish Majesty and those of the United States, and also those which their subjects shall have armed for war may with all freedom conduct the prizes which they shall have made from their enemies into the ports which are open in time of war to other friendly nations, and the said prizes upon entering the said ports shall not be subject to arrest or seizure nor shall the officers of the places take cognizance of the validity of the said prizes which may depart and be conducted freely & with all liberty to the places pointed out in their Commissions, which the captains of the said vessels shall be obliged to shew.

Art 20.

In case any vessel belonging to either of the two States or to their subjects shall be stranded, shipwrecked or suffer any other damage on the coasts or under the dominion of either of the parties, all aid and assistance shall be given to the persons ship-wrecked or who may be in danger thereof and passports shall be granted to them to secure their return to their own Country. The ships and merchandizes wrecked or their proceeds if the effects have been sold, being claimed in a year & a day by the owners or their attorney shall be restored on their paying the costs of Salvage conformable to the laws and customs of the two Nations.

Art. 21

When the subjects and inhabitants of the two parties with their vessels whether they be public, and equipped for war or private or employed in Commerce shall be forced by tempest, by pursuit of privateers and of enemies or by any other urgent necessity, to retire and enter any of the rivers, bays, roads or ports of either of the two parties, they shall be received and treated with all humanity & politeness and they shall enjoy all friend-ship protection & assistance, and they shall be at liberty to supply themselves with refreshments, provisions & every thing necessary for their sustenance, for the repair of their vessels and for continuing their voyage, provided always that they pay a reasonable price; and they shall not in any manner be detained or hindered from sailing out of the said ports or roads but they may retire and depart when and as they please without any obstacle or hindrance.

Art 22

In order to favour Commerce on both sides as much as possible, it is agreed that in case a war should break out between the said two nations, which God forbid, the term of nine months after the declaration of war shall be allowed to the merchants and subjects respectively on one side and the other, in order that they may withdraw with their effects and moveables, which they shall be at liberty to carry off or to sell where they please without the least obstacle; nor shall any seize their effects & much less their persons during the said nine months, but on the contrary passports which shall be valid for a time necessary for their return shall be given them for their vessels and the effects which they shall be willing to carry with them. And if any thing is taken from them or if any injury is done to them by one of the parties their people & subjects during the term above prescribed, full and entire satisfaction shall be made to them on that account. The above mentioned passports shall also serve as a safe conduct against all insults or prizes which privateers may attempt against their persons and effects.

Art. 23.

No subject of the king of Sweden shall take a commission or letters of marque for arming any vessel to act as a privateer against the United States of America or any of them or against the subjects people or inhabitants of the said United States or any of them or against the property of the inhabitants of the said States from any prince or state whatever with whom the said United States shall be at war. Nor shall any citizen subject or inhabitant of the said United States or any of them apply for or take any commission or letters of marque for arming any vessel to cruize against the subjects of his Swedish Majesty or any of them or their property from any prince or State whatever with whom his said Majesty shall be at war. And if any person of either nation shall take such commissions or letters of marque he shall be punished as a pirate.

Art. 24

The Vessels of the subjects of either of the parties coming upon any Coast belonging to the other, but not willing to enter into port or being entered into port and not willing to unload their cargoes or to break bulk, shall not be obliged to do it, but on the contrary shall enjoy all the franchises and exemptions which are granted by the rules subsisting with respect to that Object.

Art. 25.

When a vessel belonging to the subjects & inhabitants of either of the parties sailing on the high Sea shall be met by a ship of war or privateer of the other, the said ship of war or privateer, to avoid all disorder shall remain out of Cannon shot, but may always send their boat to the merchant ship, and cause two or three men to go on board of her, to whom the master or commander of the said vessel shall exhibit his passport stating the property of the vessel and when the said vessel shall have exhibited her passport, she shall be at liberty to continue her voyage and it shall not be lawful to molest or search her in any manner, or to give her chase or force her to quit her intended Course.

Art 26

The two contracting parties grant mutually the liberty of having, each in the ports of the other, Consuls, vice Consuls, Agents and commissaries whose functions shall be regulated by a particular agreement.

Art 27.

The present treaty shall be ratified on both sides and the ratifications shall be exchanged in the space of eight months, or sooner if possible, counting from the day of the signature.

In faith whereof the respective plenipotentiaries have signed the above articles and have thereto affixed their seals.

Done at Paris the third day of April in the year of our Lord one thousand seven hundred and eighty three.

signed. GUSTAV PHILIP COMTE DE CREUTZ.   B. FRANKLIN
LS.   LS.

Separate Article

The king of Sweden and the United States of North America agree that the present treaty shall have its full effect for the space of fifteen years counting from the day of the ratification, and the two contracting parties reserve to themselves the liberty of renewing it at the end of that term.

Done at Paris the third of April in the year of our Lord One thousand seven hundred & eighty three

signed

GUSTAV PHILIP COMTE DE CREUTZ.   B. FRANKLIN

LS   LS.

Separate Articles

Art 1.

His Swedish Majesty shall use all the means in his power to protect & defend the vessels and effects belonging to citizens or inhabitants of the United States of North America and every of them, which shall be in the ports, havens roads or on the Seas near the countries, islands cities and towns of his said Majesty, and shall use his utmost endeavours to recover and restore to the right owners all such vessels and effects which shall be taken from them within his jurisdiction.

Art 2.

In like manner the United States of North America shall protect & defend the vessels and effects belonging to the subjects of his Swedish Majesty, which shall be in the ports, havens, or roads or on the seas near to the countries, islands cities and towns of the said states and shall use their utmost efforts to recover and restore to the right owners all such vessels and effects which shall be taken from them within their jurisdiction.

Art. 3.

If in any future war at sea the contracting powers resolve to remain neuter and as such to observe the strictest neutrality then it is Agreed that if the merchant ships of either party should happen to be in a part of the sea where the ships of war of the same nation are not stationed, or if they are met on the high sea, without being able to have recourse to their own convoys in that case the commander of the ships of war of the other party, if required, shall in good faith and sincerity give them all necessary assistance, and in such case the ships of war and frigates of either of the powers shall protect and support the merchant ships of the other, provided nevertheless, that the ships claiming assistance are not engaged in any illicit commerce contrary to the principle of the neutrality.

Art 4

It is agreed & concluded that all merchants, captains of merchant ships or other subjects of his Swedish Majesty shall have full liberty in all places under the dominion or jurisdiction of the United States of America to manage their own affairs and to employ in the management of them whomsoever they please; And they shall not be obliged to make use of any interpreter or broker nor to pay them any reward unless they make use of them. Moreover the masters of ships shall not be obliged, in loading or unloading their vessels to employ labourers appointed by public Authority for that purpose; but they shall be at full liberty, themselves to load or unload their vessels or to employ in loading or unloading them whomsoever they think proper without paying reward under the title of salary to any other person whatever, And they shall not be obliged to turn over any kind of merchandizes to other vessels nor to receive them on board their own nor to wait for their lading longer than they please, And all and every of the citizens people and inhabitants of the United States of America shall reciprocally have and enjoy the same privileges and liberties in all places under the jurisdiction of the said realm.

Art 5

It is agreed that when merchandizes shall have been put on board the ships or vessels of either of the contracting parties they shall not be subjected to any examination; but all examination and search must be before lading and the prohibited merchandizes must be stopped on the spot before they are embarked, unless there is full evidence or proof of fraudulent practice on the part of the owner of the ship or of him who has the command of her. In which case only he shall be responsible and subject to the laws of the country in which he may be. In all other cases neither the subjects of either of the contracting parties who shall be with their vessels in the ports of the other, nor their merchandizes shall be seized or molested on account of Contraband goods which they shall have wanted to take on board, nor shall any kind of embargo be laid on their ships, subjects or citizens of the State, whose merchandizes are declared contraband or the exportation of which is forbidden, those only who shall have sold or intended to sell or alienate, such merchandize, being liable to punishment for such contravention.

Done at Paris the third day of April in the year of our Lord one thousand seven hundred and eighty three signed

GUSTAV PHILIP COMTE DE CREUTZ.   B. FRANKLIN

LS   L.S.

Notation: Translation of Treaty with Sweden—

From Roze de Chantoiseau   ALS: American Philosophical Society

Monsieur   Ce 5 mars 1783.

Vous m'aviés fait esperer que vous me feriés part de vos sentimens et observations Sur Le Tresor National, ou Banque Gle. de credit public dont jai eu Lhonneur de vous adresser Le Plan il y a près d'un mois.[5]

Votre Silence, Monsieur, me donneroit Lieu de craindre que votre Santé ne Se soit trouvée alterée Si je n'avois bien plus de raisons d'apprehender que cet objet plus reflechi, n'ait pas repondû a Lidée avantageuse que Son Excellence m'avoit parû en avoir conçûe.

Je Sens bien que ce Plan est encore loin de La perfection qu'il est Susceptible d'atteindre, mais J'ose me flatter qu'a l'aide de vos Lumieres et de vos Conseils, Il sera au moins tel qu'il poura (Ainsi que je l'ai annoncé,) operer, non Seulement La liquidation des dettes d'un Etat,

Sans en dimminuer les revenus,
ny en aggraver Les Charges,

mais encore procurer deux cent, même trois cent pour cent de Benefice, à une partie des cooperateurs, cest a dire des *Endosseurs.* Vous m'entendés, cela Suffit.

Je suis en attendant lhonneur de votre reponse avec un tres profond respect Monsieur Votre tres humble et tres obeisst. serviteur   ROZE DE CHANTOISEAU

P.S. Je me Suis defait en votre Faveur de la feuille de Papier dont vous m'aviés fait Cadeau. J'ose me flatter que vous vous voudrés

---

5. Enclosed in his letter of Feb. 8.

bien la remplacer par une Autre et que vous ne douterés point que je ne la conserve comme un gage tres precieux./.

Notation: Roze de Chantoiseau, Paris 5 Mars. 1783

From St. Clair

ALS: American Philosophical Society

Paris March 5th. 1783

I had the honour to write to your Excellency two days ago by the post but as I have not been honoured with an answer I take the liberty once more to importunate you but not being possesed of three sols to pay the postage I find myself obliged to be the carrier of it. I have now no other party or choice left if your Excellency does not furnish me with the means of returning to America than to enlist as a private Soldier in the French service however humiliteting and degrading this must be to our service I cannot help if your Excellency will honour me with a few Lines I shall esteem it a particular favr.[6] I remain with the most sincer attachment your Exellency's most humble and most obedient Servant ST CLAIR

Addressed: To / His Excellency B. Franklin / Minister Plenipotentiary / of the United States / At / Passy

Notation: St. Clair, Paris March 5. 1783.

From Jonathan Shipley

ALS: American Philosophical Society

Dear Sir   Bolton Street March 5th 83

Having been just informd by your valuable Countryman Mr. Laurens that He had an opportunity of conveying a Letter to You[7] I could not refuse myself the pleasure of telling You that the unalterable friendship & affection all my Family feel for You

6. Through the intervention of JW and Thomas Barclay, St. Clair found lodging in Nantes and a passage "to Carolina": JW to Thomas Barclay, July 12, 1783 (Yale University Library); Account XXVII (XXXII, 4).

7. By Charles Storer, who carried Laurens' March 6 letter to BF, below.

has of late been very much quickend by the Hopes of seeing You again & very shortly. Indeed We look upon You as our great & general Benefactor without whose wisdom & abilities We might have waited much longer for the necessary blessing of Peace. For notwithstanding the opposition in the House of Commons, I hold it certain that there is not a Man in the Kingdom who is not glad to see an end of the War. The sole object of the Opposition was to ruin the Minister[8] & such was his Unpopularity that they succeeded. They carried a Majority against him for the best thing he ever did. I heartily wish all the World was of your opinion & mine as to the total inutility of War. But there seems to be a Sluggishness in human Nature which wants the pungency of arbitrary government or the sword & Fire of an Enemy to keep it awake. If such admonitions are really necessary, We have cause to be thankful for We have had our share of them: Many of us object to the Terms of Peace, which they think might have been more advantageous; but they are generally the Men who voted for the War. But bad as things are if We submit to our Situation & cultivate what is left to us we may perhaps gain more in private happiness than We have lost in Glory & Empire. How happy should I be to talk over these interesting Subjects with You. I have impartiality enough to acknowledge & submit to the Humiliation of this Country & rejoice with You in the Liberty & good Government & the growing Wealth & Happiness of America. Thus Happiness will last if You can but convince them that they will certainly destroy it by quarrelling amongst themselves. I would write more if I had time. We are full of fears & expectations but have no news. Mrs Shipley & her Daughters[9] desire to be most cordially rememberd to You.

Your ever faithful & affectionate   J St Asaph

Dr Franklin

---

8. Shelburne.
9. For the five Shipley daughters see XVIII, 199–202.

From the Abbé Georg Joseph Vogler[1]

ALS: American Philosophical Society

Monsieur   Paris le 5 du Mars 1783

J'ai eu l'honneur tant au Musée de Paris, dont je suis membre, qu'à Passi chez vous même, de vous expliquer quoîque bien faiblement ma Theorie nouvelle musicale ainsi que mon Instrument le *Tonometre* approuvè par l'academie des Sciences.[2]

Vous avez bien voulu m'accorder vos suffrages et encourager un auteur qui paroit pour la premiere fois en France. J'ose les rapeller dans ce moment pour ma pratique et je sèrais infiniment flatté si vous daigne honorer de votre presence un Opera que j'ai mise en Musique, et qu'on donnera bientôt aux Italiens intitulè *le Patriotisme*,[3] tandis que vous avez demontrè à l'Europe entier combien vous estimez le nom de Patriote. Et Vu les circonstances actuelles politiques en Amerique je prends la libertè de vous proposer un homme riche, et honête, Marchand à Majence et mon ami, qui desirerait d'être employè par le respectable Congrès comme un agent.

---

1. Vogler (1749–1814), a German composer, theorist, virtuosic performer, and inventor of musical instruments, had a varied and controversial career. He came to Paris in 1781 hoping to gain the approbation of the Académie des sciences for his theory of harmony; while there he performed frequently and was much admired by the queen. Later, in 1783, he removed to London and won the approbation of the Royal Society: Stanley Sadie, ed., *The New Grove Dictionary of Music and Musicians* (2nd ed., 29 vols., London, 2001); Michel Brenet, "L'Abbé Vogler à Paris en 1781–83," in *Archives Historiques, Artistiques et Littéraires* . . . (2 vols., Paris, 1889–91), II, 152. For a comprehensive study of his theory of music and an overview of his life see Floyd K. Grave and Margaret G. Grave, *In Praise of Harmony: the Teachings of Abbé Georg Joseph Vogler* (Lincoln, Nebr., and London, 1987).

2. The Academy approved his memoir on the theory of natural harmony in 1781. Essential to that theory were principles derived from his *tonomètre* (*tonmaass*), an instrument with eight strings all tuned to the same pitch, which afforded greater harmonic possibilities than the monochord; see Grave and Grave, *In Praise of Harmony,* pp. 17–20. The instrument is described and illustrated in Dr. Karl Emil von Schafhäutl, *Abt Georg Joseph Vogler* . . . (Augsburg, 1888), pp. 201–10.

3. The opera, evidently commissioned by Marie-Antoinette (who provided the text), was performed at Versailles on March 25. It celebrated the end of the fighting at Gibraltar: Brenet, "L'Abbé Vogler," pp. 151–2; *New Grove Dictionary*.

Il pourrait Servir pour tout ce qui regarde les lettres de Change, pour le commerce de Vin, qu'il exerce dejà long tems, et sur tout pour le Vin du *Rhin* et de *Mosèlle,* il servirait pour le manufactures de Verre dans la quelles il a la plus grande intelligence ayant même l'Entreprise du Verre pour tout l'Electorat de Majence.

Il s'offre dans les Etats du Nord-Amerique ou il y a des grandes forêts, d'etablir des manufactures et tout ce qu'il y appartient, de faire un depôt de Vins du Rhin &c. tel qu'il se trouve à Hambourg et de meriter votre Satisfaction partout. Son nom et adresse est Jacques Groeser Marchand à Majence.

Tous ces qui le connaissent pourront toujours repondre pour lui, mais je serais, on ne peut, plus reconnaissant si à ma recomendation vous daignerez accepter un homme, qui plus par son attachement aux vrais patriotes que par l'interêt desire vous Servir et être utile. En attendant votre reponse j'ai l'honneur d'être Monsieur votre tres humble et tres obeissant Serviteur

> ABBÈ VOGLER
> Conseiller Eccl. et maitre de Chapelle
> de S.A.S. Mgr. Elect. Palatin.

ruë Croix des petits champs maison d'un Peruquier à cotè du Cloitre St. Honorè.

Notation: Abbè Vogler Paris 5 Mars 1783

From Jonathan Williams, Jr.

ALS: American Philosophical Society; copy: Yale University Library

Dear & hond Sir.   Nantes March 5. 1783

The King has published an Arrêt suspendending the Payment of all Bills drawn by the Marine in America 12 months after the just time of their becoming due[4] and I have 184. thousand Livres

---

4. This *arrêt de conseil* resulted from the rivalry between Joly de Fleury, finance minister, and Castries, minister of the marine, whom Joly accused of fiscal irresponsibility. Joly calculated that in addition to spending a disproportionate amount of the treasury, Castries had also issued some 50 million *l.t.* in unregistered letters of exchange to finance military operations in the

in that Situation. These Bills belong to a number of Individuals who are here & the Returns are Shipped, I have already paid the greater part & must pay the Remainder, or keep the Bodies of these People for they have nothing but themselves and the Bills to pay with. You will readily conceive how hard it is for me to be the Victim of my Confidence in these Bills which I never before had any Reason to doubt. But the Arrêt expresses only Bills drawn from India & America (meaning by the Latter I suppose their Colonies which are always called *Amerique*) and no mention of the *United States.* I am therefore in hopes the Arrêt was not meant to apply to us; But the Treasurer[5] takes upon him to suppose so for although these Bills were presented a month ago (some more) they are among the Suspended.— I beg to intreat you Sir to endeavour to save me from this cruel Stroke, the Bills may as well be annihilated, as Suspended for a Year for I must have this money some how or other in a very short Time. I inclose a Letter to the Minister on the Subject, I left it unaddressed because I do not know whether it should go to the Marquis de Castries or M. de Fleury, you are the best Judge of the Propriety, and I beseech you to send it with your Support & Reccommendation:[6] I think if they can pay anything, they will pay these Bills after your Representation of the Matter, in which I beg you not to delay a moment, I am Sorry to be so troublesome to you,

---

colonies. He persuaded the king to issue this *arrêt* on Feb. 23, which suspended payment on the letters for one year and promised 5 percent interest. The *arrêt* was printed above Castries' signature, though Castries refused to sign: John Hardman, *French Politics, 1774–1789: from the Accession of Louis XVI to the Fall of the Bastille* (London and New York, 1995), pp. 65–6; François-André Isambert et al., *Recueil général des anciennes lois françaises* (29 vols., Paris, 1821–33), XXVII, 256.

5. The bills JW held were drawn on Charles-Simon Boutin (1719–1794) for the expenses of the French navy in America: JW to John Williams, March 1, 1783, and to Alexander John Alexander, March 21, 1783 (Yale University Library); Michel Bruguière, *Gestionnaires et profiteurs de la révolution: l'administration des finances françaises de Louis XVI à Bonaparte* ([Paris], 1986), p. 236. Boutin was one of two alternating treasurer generals of the navy; the other was Baudard de Saint James (XXXIII, 325n).

6. BF evidently forwarded JW's letter to Joly de Fleury on March 9 (see Joly to BF, March 15), and on the same date informed JW of the fact (see JW to BF, March 23). Both of BF's March 9 letters are unlocated.

but it is for me a very Serious Affair and I trust you will kindly give me all the Support in your Power to obtain Redress. I need not repeat all particulars because you will See them by reading the Letter to the Minister.

I once more beg your kind protection & an answer as soon as possible.

I am as ever most dutifully & affectionately Yours.

JONA WILLIAMS J

Addressed: A Son Excellence / Monsieur Franklin / en son Hotel / a / Passy / pres Paris

Notation: Jona. Williams March 5. 1783.

Benjamin Vaughan to William Temple Franklin

ALS: American Philosophical Society

My dear sir, London, March 5th:, 1783.

Mrs: Vaughan has ordered your glasses,[7] and we will engage Major White or some earlier passenger, to take care of them as far as Calais. Major White has for some time past had your damping cases from Woodmason,[8] and other articles; so that no censure will fix upon myself for delay. The gout has lately seized him, but I think he will soon be getting abroad again; but perhaps not to embark for Calais, as I conceive the provisional act respecting the American trade will offer him business enough here on the spot.[9]

7. See Vaughan to BF, Feb. 25.

8. These must be the damping boxes Woodmason offered for sale in 1781; see XXXV, 575, where we said that we had not found evidence of BF's having ordered them.

9. White's two purposes in going to London (see JW to BF, Jan. 25) had evaporated: the British passports he and JW sought for their ships were no longer necessary, and recovering the *Trio* seemed hopeless. (JW, frustrated over the tangle of legal proceedings, told White on March 13 to "let the Trio go to the Devil": Yale University Library.) He remained in England to explore further commercial opportunities. On March 5 he wrote WTF asking whether British goods would be received in America before a general commercial treaty was passed, and on April 15 he wrote again asking if BF or one

You have seen the hurly burly of ministers. I am very glad to find Lord Shelburne has been composed when I have seen him, as to every possible species of event, as he knows his reputation is safe;—and what else is there he has to care for, besides his reputation?— I am in great hopes, that whoever is minister, and however the peace may have been abused, that not only the terms but the *principles* of it will be abided by; so much is the benefit resulting from a liberal man's conversation with a certain personage,[1] and a daring manly conduct respecting the public.— If you ask what has been the occasion of this political bustle, I will tell you a part of it. Too many of the *great* stood excluded from ministry; this occasioned faction without, and opinion of infirmity within; which made real infirmity, because those who were within, looked for change & made friends without. The peace was made the handle; because that opportunity missed, the occasions of routing out a ministry became less certain and frequent. Sensible men seem to have little objection to the peace, though it has never yet been sensibly explained. The only articles they touch upon, are in the *American* treaty; namely the Refugees before all the rest, and the back lands, as being given, together with the fishery, without a compensation.— You certainly by making so hard a peace, have lost the man who had most boldness, most system, and most regard of future times in him. I hope he will leave some traces of his policy & character behind him, that we may less miss him.— I am pleased at one thing, which is, that he appears to fill every gazette with marks of attention to his friends. He does not seem to me to think that he has owed much to the Governor, your father, as the Refugees

---

of the other American commissioners could provide papers for an American-owned ship purchased in Britain. In that second letter White also told WTF that he had dined with WF, who asked after both WTF and BF: White to WTF, March 5, 1783 (APS); White to WTF, April 15, 1783 (University of Pa. Library). He entrusted his April 15 letter, along with packages for WTF and others, to a certain MacIntosh, who had them delivered to Passy on April 22 with a letter asking WTF to forward them all. APS. White was back in Boston by early August, and failed to reply to JW's increasingly agitated letters: JW to White, Oct. 25 and Nov. 18, 1783, and Jan. 14, 1784 (Yale University Library).

1. Possibly George III had reassured Shelburne on this point.

were made the Mill Stone to sink him. He desired something to be proposed by *our* family for their interest and consulted Mr Manning;[2] but they declined the offer of several West India places, my father having but one view for his family, North America, (whither he will set sail in all next month, or the month of May, his houshold furniture, books &c being all packed up & ready for shipping, & his house in the country offered to any one who will take it.)

I must not forget to tell you, that one objection made to the minister is, that he attempted to govern the country like Mr Pitt.[3] Be it so, and will it not then help to explain who made the American treaty, as now concluded, upon the principles on which we *know* it was concluded?— On that ground it becomes you all to do this person justice; for there is no one who is not shocked at him for the *supposed* dereliction of the refugees. I should be hurt among the rest, provided I thought the refugee article really waste paper.— On the other hand, if you on your side, wish to *regain* every Englishman, you cannot find a surer basis on which to build a family reconciliation & solid RESPECT, than by behaving handsomely to the better behaved & more innocent people among the refugees.

I have not much to say for the times; but I assure you that many Englishmen are as much shocked with them, as you Americans can be. The greater part of the Rockinghams are warm & weak men, who all hang together; & of course they make very proper materials for knaves to work upon, and knaves have not been wanting, that were both noisy & needy. Hence at one moment they abuse a man for not conceding to America & at another moment for conceding; at one moment they charge him with meaning to join Lord North, & the next moment join him themselves; at one moment they say no peace can be too bad, because they conjecture that the minister meant war, but when they find he accomplishes peace, then they call a very decent & as-

2. Vaughan's father-in-law, William Manning: xxx, 503n.

3. William Pitt, the first Earl of Chatham. The criticism that Shelburne's administration relied upon the electorate rather than Commons was leveled by Earl Temple (xxxvii, 299n): John Norris, *Shelburne and Reform* (London and New York, 1963), p. 264.

suredly a very wise peace, an execrable one; at one moment they are all for reform, because it is popular, & at the next moment they object to a retrenching custom-house bill as changing the commercial policy of the land, only because the minister proposes it. If they have the proposing however of things themselves, they may then no longer impede the public good; but while they remain an opposition, *if we have a good minister,* they must necessarily be an absurd peevish & hateful opposition.

I am, my dear sir, yours ever most faithfully & affecty

BENJN VAUGHAN

Endorsed: B. Vaughan 5th March 1783

To John Coakley Lettsom

Reprinted from Thomas Joseph Pettigrew, ed., *Memoirs of the Life and Writings of the Late John Coakley Lettsom* . . . (3 vols., London, 1817), I, 171-2 of second pagination.

Dear Sir, Passy, March 6 [or 17],[4] 1783.

I received your favour of September last.[5] It found me labouring under a painful disorder, which continued long, and put me much behind-hand in my correspondence. I thank you for the

4. The date ascribed by Lettsom when he published an extract of this letter (a condensed version of the second paragraph) in *Some Account of the Late John Fothergill* . . . (London, 1783), pp. clxvii–clxviii.

5. The most recent surviving letter from Lettsom was written on Sept. 13, 1781 (XXXV, 478–9). The present letter seems to be answering it in many respects, including BF's allusion to the publications Lettsom had sent and his desire to subscribe to the multi-volume *Works of John Fothergill, M.D.* . . . . In the fall of 1782 Lettsom (at the urging of Fothergill's friends) was preparing to publish his account of Fothergill's life separately, in advance of the *Works*. David Barclay was reviewing that MS when he wrote BF about the project in December, 1782; BF replied early in January: XXXVIII, 508–10, 564–5. Lettsom wrote the introduction on May 1, 1783; *Some Account of the Late John Fothergill* was published by July, when it was reviewed in the *Gent. Mag.* The review focused on previously unpublished material, quoting the letter BF wrote Barclay upon learning of Fothergill's death (XXXIV, 366): *Gent. Mag.,* LIII (1783), 603–4.

valuable publications that accompanied it, particularly those of your own composition, which I read with pleasure.[6]

Our late excellent friend was always proposing something for the good of mankind. You will find instances of this kind in one of his letters which I inclose, the only one I can at present lay my hand on. I have some very valuable ones in America, if they are not lost in the late confusions. You will be so good as to return this to me, after having extracted from it what you may think proper.[7] Just before I left England, he, in conjunction with Mr. Barclay and myself, laboured hard to prevent the coming war. But our endeavours were fruitless. This transaction is alluded to in the paragraph that begins at the bottom of the first page.[8] If we may estimate the goodness of a man by his disposition to do good, and his constant endeavours and success in doing it, I can hardly conceive that a better man has ever existed.

I desire to be considered as a subscriber, if there is a subscription, for two sets of his Works, which I will pay for on demand.

With great esteem, I am, Sir, Your most obedient and most humble servant, B. FRANKLIN.

From the Conde de Aranda AL: American Philosophical Society

a Paris ce 6 Mars 1783.
L'ambassadeur d'Espagne ne pouvait point oublier l'invitation de Mr. Franklin pour samedi,[9] il desirait meme le moment d'y concurrir avec la plus grande satisfaction.

6. See XXXV, 478–9. Lettsom may also have enclosed a copy of his own *History of the Origin of Medicine* (London, 1778), which BF owned at the end of his life: Wolf and Hayes, *Library of Benjamin Franklin*, p. 500.

7. BF enclosed Fothergill's letter of Oct. 25, 1780 (XXXIII, 458–61), which Lettsom paraphrased in a footnote to the extract he published of the present letter: *Some Account of the Late John Fothergill*, p. clxviiin.

8. The paragraph beginning with "Much horrible mischief . . . ": XXXIII, 459.

9. March 8. Among those attending the dinner at Passy were Ambassador Aranda, JA, Jay, Chastellux, Morellet, and Rochambeau: Butterfield, *John*

Mr. le chevr. del Campo profitera egalement de ses bontès.[1] A l'egard du jeune Mr. Campos[2] s'il etait de retour pour ce jourla, puisqu'il est atendu d'un jour a l'autre il sera bien flatè du souvenir dont on l'honore, et il en profitera.

L'ambasr. se fera un plaisir de faire conoitre les intentions polies de Mr. Franklin a Mr. le vicomte de la Herreria,[3] qui etoit aussi l'autre jour chez Mr. Jay: et en atendant il a l'honeur de renouveller son parfait atachement a Mr. Franklin.

Notation: D'Arrandir Paris 6 Mars 1783

From William Hodgson

ALS: American Philosophical Society

Dear sir   London 6th Mar: 1783

I wrote you a few days ago[4] on the Subject of our Ship to America craving your Advice & Assistance wh. I hope you will be so obliging as to favor me with a speedy Answer— I now inclose you the Draft of a Bill now in the House & which no doubt will pass into a Law, for restoring Trade betwixt this Country & America[5] it is formed upon liberal principles & will I have no

---

Adams Diary, III, 110. Morellet wrote a note to WTF on "jeudi" (March 6) explaining that he and Chastellux would come together, but that Marmontel was unable to attend. APS.

1. Del Campo, who had arrived in Paris around March 3, was en route to his post as minister plenipotentiary in Britain. He was in London by March 21 and presented his credentials three days later: *Morning Chronicle, and London Advertiser,* March 15; Didier Ozanam, *Les Diplomates espagnols du XVIIIe siècle: Introduction et répertoire biographique (1700–1808)* (Madrid and Bordeaux, 1998), p. 205.

2. Clemente de Campos y Sahún (1756–1834), who was attached to Aranda's embassy: Ozanam, *Les Diplomates espagnols,* pp. 206–7.

3. For whom see Mme de Lafreté to BF, Jan. 30. Jay had known him and his wife since the previous December: Morris, *Jay: Peace,* pp. 447–8.

4. Above, Feb. 25.

5. While he was still prime minister, Shelburne had John Pownall (XIV, 74n) draft the so-called American Intercourse Bill in order to regulate British commerce with the United States until a definitive commercial treaty was signed. According to its provisions, American produce in British ports would be treated as if it were British, and American shipping could carry both exports from the British West Indies and American produce to the British West

doubt produce the desired effect— I likewise inclose you a Letter from the Earl of Buchan which I recd from Mr Strahan.[6] Mr Jones has got the appointment of one of the Judges in Bengal— a place of very great Emolument—[7] I requested some Time ago the favor of Mr W. Franklin to make an Enquiry for me at Mr de Castries Office[8] I fear it escaped his Memory— No Ministry as yet formed— I am Dr sir Yours most sincerely

WILLIAM HODGSON

N.B. The Prisoners are at last, all ordered away to France[9]

His Excellency B. Franklin Esqr

From Henry Laurens

ALS: Library of Congress; incomplete copy: South Carolina Historical Society

Sir.   London 6th. March 1783.
Hitherto, since my arrival on this side of the Channel I have had nothing worth your attention, to offer, indeed five or six last days excepted I had been confined at Bath.

Indies. On March 3, with the ministry still in disarray (see the headnote to Hodgson's Feb. 25 letter), William Pitt introduced the bill into the House of Commons. It was severely criticized in debate on March 7 before being referred to committee: Harlow, *Second British Empire*, 1, 448–54; Cobbett, *Parliamentary History*, XXIII, 602–15; C. R. Ritcheson, "The Earl of Shelburne and Peace with America, 1782–1783: Vision and Reality," *International History Review*, V (1983), 341n; John Ehrman, *The Younger Pitt* (3 vols., New York and Stanford, Calif., 1969–96), 1, 96–7.

6. Probably Buchan to BF, Feb. 18.

7. On March 4 William Jones was appointed judge of the high court of Calcutta; two weeks later he was knighted. Garland Cannon, *The Life and Mind of Oriental Jones: Sir William Jones, the Father of Modern Linguistics* (Cambridge, New York, and Port Chester, N.Y., 1990), pp. 191–2.

8. His inquiry concerned the freighting of the ship *Weeren Frienden* at Lorient: Hodgson to WTF, Jan. 24, 1783 (APS).

9. The order was issued on March 3. A month earlier there still were more than 300 American prisoners in England, including 272 at Mill and Forton prisons: Sheldon S. Cohen, *Yankee Sailors in British Gaols: Prisoners of War at Forton and Mill, 1777–1783* (Newark, Del., and London, 1995), pp. 205–6.

Mr. Oswald said to me yesterday, he was going to the proper place for learning, whether he should be soon, or when required to attend upon the business of a Definitive Treaty & promised to acquaint me with the result of his inquiry. I have not since heard from him. While I am here I find employment. I have upon proper occasions offered my sentiments upon the Lamentations over the good people called Loyalists & if appearances are to be trusted I have afforded consolation to some folks.[1]

An active M P. said to me this Morning, he had thoughts of impeaching Lord Shelburne for Sins of omission & was proceeding to make special enquiries, which I took the liberty of interrupting by an observation that these were things out of our line.— He went on, "do you know that Lord Shelburne declared to the House of Lords, the Provisional Treaty was obtained from the American Ministers without the concurrence or participation of the Court of France, that the Court was not pleased & consequently would not hereafter be so friendly to the United States, I am afraid added our friend of ill consequences, I suspect every thing & shall suspect till the Troops are entirely withdrawn from your Country." I replied don't be anxios Sir, You talked just now of an impeachment, admit the Case to be as Lord Shelburne has stated, which I do not admit, say to Lord Shelburne & from me if you please, that John Adams. Benja. Franklin, John Jay & poor Henry Laurens, may be impeached & hanged for aught I know but the United States will not be hurt nor the friendship of the Court of France shaken by the infidelity of those fellows. For my own part I am no more afraid of being hanged than I was in your Tower of London. Our friend was pleased with the explanation & I presume Lord S. will hear of it. With respect to your Troops at New York, I appeal to you Sir, If there was a Serjeant's Guard in your House, would you proceed on business 'till they were effectually removed? No.

I send by the hands of Mr. Storer for the use of the Commissioners at Paris, The Bill for the Provisional Establishment of

---

1. Laurens, like BF, distinguished between "true Loyalists"—American patriots—and those who called themselves Loyalists. For an example of Laurens' words of "consolation" for the opportunists who now lamented the loss of the spoils they expected see *Laurens Papers*, XVI, 135.

Commerce between Great Britain & the United States.[2] My opinion has been often asked; I say, it may very well suit the purpose of one party, but there ought to be two to a bargain. But are we not very liberal in opening the Trade upon such terms? Undoubtedly—you want to purchase Rice & other Provisions for home consumpt & for the West Indies, you are desiros of selling your Woolen & Iron Wares—you are liberal. But we cannot profit of your bounty, while the Serjeant's Guard is in the House.— Don't be uneasy the Troops will be removed as speedily as possible—suspend then your beneficent Acts until they are removed. Possibly America may ask, When you were accustomed to send Troops to that Country, were you puzzled to find Transport Ships for the purpose?

I have found it necessary to say to Mr. Adams, Doctor Franklin is possessed of another anonymos Letter with the Bruxelles mark on it & I am *now* confirmed in my "Belief" of the Author of both. I wish Mr. Adams may communicate all that I have further said on this occasion.[3]

Mr. Storer will deliver you a Packet containing a third Edition of Mr. Days Tract with additions & amendments.[4]

I beg my Compliments to your Grandson & that you will be assured I am with the most sincere & affectionate Regard Sir Your Obliged & Obedient servant   HENRY LAURENS

the good Bp. of St Asaph is just gone from me, His Lordship made the most cordial enquiries respecting your health & said he would soon write to you, that Mrs. Shipley & all the family longed to see you. the Bishop has sent a Letter which will be under Cover with this.[5]

His Excellcy. Benja. Franklin Esquire Paris.

---

2. The American Intercourse Bill, whose full title was "A Bill for the Provisional Establishment and Regulation of Trade and Intercourse between the Subjects of Great Britain and those of the United States of North America."

3. Laurens to JA, March 6: *Laurens Papers*, XVI, 157–60. Laurens suspected Edmund Jenings of writing inflammatory anonymous letters which had come into JA's possession: XXXVI, 499.

4. Thomas Day, *Reflections upon the Present State of England, and the Independence of America* (3rd ed., rev., London, 1783).

5. Jonathan Shipley's letter of March 5, above.

From Laval & Wilfelsheim[6]   ALS: American Philosophical Society

Monsieur   a paris ce 6 Mars 1783

Il y a 15. Jours que nous avons remis a Monsieur Grand le pere une Lettre pour votre Excellence qui nous est venue de Bremen.[7]

L'Amy pense qu'elle ne nous est pas parvenue, & nous en demande des Nouvelles. Nous supplions votre Excellence, de nous rendre le Service, & de daigner y faire une Reponse, le Courrier part deman.

Nous avons l'honneur d'etre avec Respect, Monsieur de Votre Excellence, les trés humbles & trés obeissans Serviteurs

LAVAL & WILFELSHEIM
Banqrs. rue du mail

A S.E.M. franklin Ambassadeur des Etats unis de lAmerique Septe.

Notation: Laval & Wilfelcheim Paris 6. Mars 1783.

To Robert R. Livingston   ALS and transcript: National Archives

Sir,   Passy, March 7. 1783.

I but this moment hear of this Opportunity, by which I can only send you a Line to acquaint you, that I have concluded the Treaty with Sweden, which was signed on Wednesday last.[8] You will have a Copy by the first good Opportunity. It differs very little from the Plan sent me,—in nothing material.— The English Court is in Confusion by another Change of Ministry; Lord Shelburne & his Friends having resigned; but it is not yet certainly known who will succeed; tho' Lord North & Mr Fox are talk'd of as two, they being reconcil'd!![9] cannot add but that I am, with great Esteem Sir, Your most obedient humble Servt

B FRANKLIN

6. Jean-François Laval and Jean-Henri (Henry) Wilfelsheim were the principals of this Paris banking firm: Lüthy, *Banque protestante*, II, 695n.

7. From Delius, Feb. 7.

8. Published above, under [March 5].

9. See Hodgson to BF, Feb. 25.

P.S. The Change in the Ministry is not suppos'd of any Importance respecting our Definitive Treaty, which must conform to the Preliminaries: But we shall see!

R R. Livingston Esqr

Notation: Letter March 7. 1783 B. Franklin Recvd July 16. 1783

To Robert Morris

Press copy of LS:[1] New Hampshire Historical Society

Dear Sir,   Passy, March 7th. 1783.

With this I send you a Copy of the last Contract I made with this Court respecting the late Loan of Six Millions, the Terms of the Loan and the Times of Repayment.[2] It was impossible for me to obtain more, and indeed, considering the State of Finances and Expences here, I wonder I have obtained so much. You will see by the inclosed Gazette, that the Government is obliged to stop Payment for a Year of its own Bills of Exchange drawn in America and the East Indies;[3] yet it has advanced Six Millions to save the Credit of ours. You will I am sure do all in your Power to avoid drawing beyond your Funds here for I am absolutely assured that no farther Aid for this Year is to be expected; and it will not be strange that they should suffer your Bills to take the same Fate with their own. You will also see in the Contract fresh Marks of the King's Goodness towards us in giving so long a Term for Payment, & forgiving the first Years Interest. I hope the Ravings of a certain mischevous Madman here against

1. In WTF's hand.
2. Morris provided Congress with an extract of this letter and a copy of the Feb. 25 contract (published above). Congress referred it to a committee consisting of delegates James Madison, James Wilson, and Stephen Higginson; upon their recommendation Congress ratified the contract on Oct. 31: *JCC,* XXIV, 422n; XXV, 773–8.
3. For which see JW's letter of March 5 and Joly de Fleury's of March 15. News that payments had been stopped reached the United States in April: *Morris Papers,* VII, 510–11n.

France and its Ministers, which I hear of every Day,[4] will not be regarded in America, so as to diminish in the least the happy Union that has hitherto subsisted between the two Nations; and which is indeed the solid Foundation of our present Importance in Europe. With great Esteem, I am ever Dear Sir, Your most obedient and most humble Servant   B Franklin

Honble R. Morris Esqr. &ca &ca &

From Antonio Francesco Salucci & fils

ALS: American Philosophical Society

Votre Excellence   Livourne ce 7. Mars 1783
L'heureuse conclusion de la Paix, et l'Indipendence des treize Provinces Americaines, par la quelle ces Peuples fortunes ont à Votre Excellence des obligations Majeures, offrent à la Toscanne l'occasion, depuis si long tems desirée, d'entamer un Commerce des plus ètendus, et de former des Liaisons capables d'apporter le plus grand avantage aux deux Nations.

La Situation favorable de notre Port, eu egard aux autres qui Sont dans la Mediterranée, la bonne et parfaite qualité des nos Produits qui formoient autrefois une branche bien importante de négociation entre La Toscanne, et L'Angleterre, qui par Ses ex-

---

4. BF named JA as the source of these "ravings" in his letter to Laurens of March 20. JA had expressed these views to Benjamin Vaughan on Jan. 12; Vaughan described them in detail in his letter to Shelburne of the same date: Butterfield, *John Adams Diary*, III, 103–6; Charles C. Smith, ed., "Letters of Benjamin Vaughan," Mass. Hist. Soc. *Proc.*, 2nd ser., XVII (1903), 432–5, where most of Vaughan's letter is published. In the unpublished portion, Vaughan characterized JA as being "no less a decided enemy to Dr. Franklin than to M. de Vergennes; & attributes to these gentlemen jointly, every hostile measure that any persons whatever conceive against him; nay he even attributes to them every pasquinade in the newspapers. I believe his enmity to Dr. Franklin is however the most difficult to stiffle of the two" (APS). JA's "prejudice against the French Court" and "venom against Doctr. Franklin" already had caused comment in America: Madison to Jefferson, Feb. 11, 1783 (*Jefferson Papers*, VI, 235). JA was suspicious that the French and BF wanted to keep him from returning to America where he might cause them mischief: JA to Abigail Adams, April 16, 1783 (*Adams Correspondence*, V, 126).

peditions a l'Amerique Septentrionale en tiroit des tres grands avantages, et la facilité avec laquelle l'on traite toute Sorte d'Affaires dans notre Port Franc, Sont autant de raisons qui Nous donnent les plus grands espoirs Sur la future prosperité de ce Nouveau Commerce.

C'est pourquoi nous allons disposer, et expedier à Philadelphie le plus promptement qu'il nous sera possible deux Navires de notre propritè avec Pavillon Toscan, ce qui arrivera d'abord qu'ils Seront de retour des voyages auquels nous les avions destinès précédement. Rien ne manque à cet Objet ayant deja promptes leurs Cargaisons.

Pendant que nous nous faisons un devoir de prevenir Votre Excellence de notre résolution de la quelle nous attendons un Succès heureux qui nous dèdommage du Malheur essuyé dans notre premiere expedition au Nord-Amèrique du Navire La Prosperité Cape [capitaine] Bettoja, pour laquelle Votre Excellence eut aussi la bonté dans l'Annèe 1779, de nous honnorer de Sa gracieuse approbation,[5] nous prenons la liberté de la prier a prendre en consideration ces Nouvelles dispositions de notre part, et d'honnorer notre Maison de Son valable appuy auprès du Ministere Americain afin que la Nation Toscanne non Seulement reçoive le même gracieux accueil des autres Nations qui l'encourage après notre exemple à entreprendre avec ces Pays-là des relations toujours plus ètendues, mais aussi pour étre particulierement honnorès des Commissions des Ses Etats, lesquels tôt, ou tard auront des Connexions agréables avec le Notre.

Que Votre Excellence Daigne accepter les plus humbles, et Respectueux homages de felicitation, et de respect, tandis que nous Sommes avec la plus haute Consideration, De Votre Excellence Les Tres humbles et Tres Obeissants Serviteurs

ANTE FRANS SALUCCI & FILS

Monsieur Benjamin Francklin Ministre Plenipotentiaire des 13. Etats Unis a la Cour de Paris/.

5. For BF's encouragement of the venture and the capture of the *Prosperité* (*Prosperità*) see XXIX, 156; XXX, 15–16.

From Tourton & Ravel[6]

LS: American Philosophical Society

Monsieur   Paris 7 mars 1783

Mr. Leveillard nous ayant dit que vous seriés fort aise que M. Schutze de Berlin s'addressat a Mr. Bache pour les affaires qu'il pourroit avoir a Philadelphie nous avons lhonneur de vous addresser ci joint la lettre que le d. [dit] sr. fred: Gme: Schutze nous envoye pour le d. mr. Bache et nous vous prions de recommander a celui ci les interets de m. Schutze, qui est un négotiant riche et solide; nous le connoissons depuis longtemps et nous sommes persuadés que m. Bache Sera très content de sa correspondance, nous profitons de cette occasion pour vous assurer de la parfaite Consideration avec laquelle nous avons lhonneur d'etre Monsieur Vos très humbles et très obeissans serviteurs

TOURTON ET RAVEL

Notation: Tourton & Ravel,— Paris 7 Mars 1783.

From Félix Vicq d'Azyr

LS: American Philosophical Society

Monsieur   ce 7 mars 1783.

La societé Rle. [royale] de medecine m'a chargé de Vous envoier les Billets cy joints pour sa séance publique qui aura lieu Mardi prochain;[7] elle Vous invite à cette assemblée. Nous n'avons point eû lhonneur de Vous posséder dans la derniere, ce qui redouble aujourd'hui nos desirs et nos instances.

La société s'est empressée de Contracter une association de

6. At the end of 1782 Louis Tourton dissolved the firm of Tourton & Baur (Baur was long deceased) and on Jan. 1, 1783, formed a partnership with his nephew Pierre-Antoine Ravel. Also in January Tourton received *lettres de noblesse*, a sign of royal protection accorded to those who had distinguished themselves in commerce: Lüthy, *Banque protestante*, II, 173–4; Jean Bouchary, *Les Manieurs d'argent à Paris à la fin du XVIIIe siècle* (3 vols., Paris, 1939–43), III, 59–60, 259–60.

7. One of the tickets remains among BF's papers: the March 11 meeting was called for 4:30 in the afternoon *"très-précises"* (University of Pa. Library). Prizes were distributed for the best answers to medical questions posed at previous meetings, and new questions were announced. An extensive report appeared in the *Jour. de Paris*, issues of March 12 and 14.

Correspondance avec le Collège de Médecine de Boston; et le Diplome en a été Remis à M. Adams.[8] Nous avons été flattés de Nous lier intimement avec les savans d'un pays que Vous avez si honorablement et si utilement servi.

    Je suis avec Respect Monsieur Votre trés humble et très obeissant serviteur   VICQ DAZYR

M franklin

Notation: Vic-d'azir, 7 Mars 1783.

From ———— Viau and ———— Vineau

LS: American Philosophical Society

Monsieur   A Nantes le 8 Mars 1783.

    Nous eumes L'honneur D'écrire, à Mr le Commissaire de L'Orient,[9] le mois dernier au Sujet de nos Intérêts dans la frégatte la pallas, et voici sa réponse Môt pour Môt;

    La frégatte la pallas a été armé pour compte Des Américains, et la répartition des prises faitte par cette frégatte, n'a point eû Lieu Jusqu'à présent. C'est à leur Agent à paris, qu'il faut S'adresser pour en obténir le paÿment, parce quil est à présumer, qu'ils n'en Séront point remise à L'Orient.[1]

    Il nous renvoÿ, comme vous voyez à vous Monsieur, nous espérons que vous aurez pitié, De deux pauvres Malheureuses femmes, qui Languissent Depuis un Si long tems après leur dûe, et que vous aurez la bonté de nous donner une réponce Satis-

---

8. JA had proposed the correspondence to the Société and other medical institutions at the request of the newly formed Massachusetts Medical Society: Butterfield, *John Adams Diary*, III, 97–8; *Adams Papers*, XIV, 142–4, 232–4.

9. Clouet (XXXVI, 629n).

1. The writers were misinformed; the former French privateer was leased by the French naval ministry in 1779, although it was part of John Paul Jones's squadron. In late 1781 the responsibility for paying prize shares, formerly in Chaumont's hands, had been transferred to the naval ministry: XXIX, 493; Thomas Schaeper, *France and America in the Revolutionary Era: the Life of Jacques-Donatien Leray de Chaumont, 1725–1803* (Providence, R.I., and Oxford, 1995), pp. 233–5, 243, 270–1, 275–9.

faisante, en nous faisant faire Remise de nos fonds sans plus Tarder. Et nous Sommes Monsieur avec le plus Soumis respect Vos tres humbles Servantes   FEMMES VIAU ET VINEAU

Demeurant a La Saulzain Proche L'isle feydeau a Nantes./.

Monsieur A Paris

Addressed: A Monseigneur / Monseigneur Franselin en Son / hôtel à passi / près paris

Notation: Viau & Vinau les Femmes—Nantes le 8 Mars 1783.

To William Hodgson   ALS: Privately owned

Dear Sir,   Passy, March 9 1783.

Your Favour of the 25th past, is but just come to hand. I think with you, that the making you pay 23£ for our Passport is a shameful Imposition. Your Secretaries had 200 of us; in exchange for as many of theirs indeed; but we had no Occasion for a quarter of the Number; and those that were wanted we gave away gratis. There is no bounds to the Avidity of Officers in old corrupt Governments.

Your Reasoning is right that there is no Occasion generally for an express Treaty to enable Subjects of different States in Amity to trade with each other. But in the present Case you know you have Acts of Parliament forbidding you to trade with us;[2] and our People have Acts of Congress forbidding all Commerce with yours.[3] It does not seem clear that a Treaty of Peace necessarily repeals these Acts. A late Act of Parliament impowering the King to suspend them[4] implys that otherwise they would continue in force till repeal'd; and they are not as yet either repeal'd or suspended. It is probable that when it shall be known in America that they are repeal'd, similar Repeals will take place there. Till then I should imagine English Goods

2. These included the Boston Port Act of 1774 (XXI, 152n) and the Prohibitory Act of 1775 (XXII, 268n).
3. By the ordinance of March 27, 1781: *JCC*, XIX, 314–16.
4. The Enabling Act: XXXVI, 688n.

W<small>E</small>, JOHN ADAMS, BENJAMIN FRANKLIN AND JOHN JAY, <small>THREE OF THE</small> M<small>INISTERS</small> P<small>LENIPOTENTIARY</small> <small>OF THE</small> U<small>NITED</small> S<small>TATES OF</small> A<small>MERICA</small>, for making Peace with Great Britain, TO ALL Captains or Commanders of ships of War privateers or armed Vessels belonging to the said States or to either of them, or to any of the Citizens of the same AND TO ALL others whom these Presents may concern, SEND GREETING.

WHEREAS Peace and Amity is agreed upon between the said United States and his Britannic Majesty, and a suspension of Hostilities to take Place at different Periods in different Places hath also been agreed upon by their respective Plenipotentiaries. AND WHEREAS it hath been further agreed by the said Plenipotentiaries, to exchange Passports for merchant Vessels, to the end that such as shall be provided with them, shall be exempted from Capture altho' found in Latitudes at a time prior to the taking Place of the said suspension of Hostilities therein. NOW THEREFORE KNOW YE that free Passport, Licence and Permission is hereby given to the

commander now lying at the Port of _____

and bound from thence to

AND WE do earnestly enjoin upon and recommend to you to let and suffer the said Vessel to pass unmolested to her destined Port, and if need be, to afford her all such succour and Aid as Circumstances and Humanity may require.

GIVEN under our Hands and Seals at Paris on the

Day of _____ in the year of Our Lord 1783.

GRATIS.

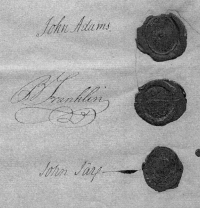

John Adams.

B. Franklin.

John Jay.

Passport for British Ships

landed there may be subject to Confiscation.⁵ But if your Ship only arrives in Port, & remains without breaking Bulk till the Commerce is legally opened, or a Permission to land and Store them obtained, I should suppose they would be safe, tho' I have not the Law before me, & therefore cannot speak positively. It is probable your Parliament will immediately take off the Restraints on your Part, and your sending the Act made for that purpose in the same Ship with your Goods, may facilitate & expedite the taking them off on our part. I inclose a Recommendatory Letter to our Minister for foreign Affairs, which I hope if there should be Occasion may be of Service.⁶ But no Passport from me would secure your Goods against the Operation of positive Laws still remaining in Force.

I lament the Distraction in your publick Counsels; it lowers the Nation in the general Esteem of Europe, and gives a degree of Uncertainty & Hazard to all propos'd Connections with it. I am, with great & sincere Esteem, Dear Sir, Your most obedient & most humble Servant   B Franklin

P.S. You have been assured from time to time ever since October last, that Transports would be provided to send away hither the Prisoners that are enforc'd in England to be exchanged. In faith of this, I have as you know, discharged a Number of Officers: But I see yet no Sign of Performance, and I lately hear that those in Mill Prison suffer much, being destitute of Cloathing many having neither Shirts nor Shoes.⁷ If they had been sent to me when it was propos'd, I could have sent them home distributed in various Vessels who are now gone; and at present I know not what to do with them if they come here, all our Ships now here or expected being over-mann'd for Peace-time. I must therefore beg you to finish the good Work you have been so long engag'd

5. This did not happen. Within weeks of the official end of hostilities on April 11, British goods began reaching American ports, and by June more ships were arriving in Philadelphia from Britain than from all the other northern European states combined: Richard Buel, Jr., *In Irons: Britain's Naval Supremacy and the American Revolutionary Economy* (New Haven and London, 1998), pp. 245–6.
6. Not found.
7. See Jacob Smith to BF, Jan. 24, above.

in, and obtain if possible the Liberty of those good People; and if the Government will not provide for sending them home, that you would hire a Ship for that purpose on our Account, & send them to America directly from England, the Expence of which I will provide for & pay punctually: But get it done by Government if you can.— B F.

[*In William Temple Franklin's hand:*][8] Mr W. T. Franklin has done every thing in his Power to obtain the Information Mr Hodgson desired of him,—but without Success: notwithstanding he has applied both in the Offices here, but also in the Ports.

To Vergennes

LS:[9] Archives du Ministère des affaires étrangères; AL (draft): American Philosophical Society

Sir, Passy, March 9. 1783.

Mr. Barclay, our Consul general, waits upon your Excellency with a Complaint of a gross affront and Injury offered to the Congress of the United States at L'Orient, by some English Merchants residing at Bourdeaux, to which I beg your Excellency's Attention, and that you would order such Measures to be taken for Redress as the Nature of the Case will appear to require.[1] I am, with great Respect Sir, Your Excellency's most obedient & most humble Servant B FRANKLIN

M. le Comte de Vergennes.

8. In answer to Hodgson's reminder in his letter to BF, March 6. JW attempted to obtain information from Lorient for Hodgson but was unsuccessful: JW to WTF, Jan. 21 and 23, 1783 (both at the APS).

9. In L'Air de Lamotte's hand.

1. The merchants were Forster frères, who attached the proceeds from the recent sale arranged by Barclay of prizes made by the *Alliance*. They claimed damages from the 1779 capture of their ship *Three Friends* by the *Alliance* while it was under the command of Pierre Landais: XXX, 12, 173–4; Forster frères to Louis XVI, [June, 1783] (National Archives); William B. Clark, *Gallant John Barry, 1745–1803: the Story of a Naval Hero of Two Wars* (New York, 1938), pp. 277, 285. On March 12, Vergennes sent the present letter and supporting documentation (probably provided by Barclay) to Castries, asking that the *saisie* be lifted. AAE.

From John Bourne   ALS: University of Pennsylvania Library

Sir   Newington Butts March 9th 1783 London
    The esteem I have for America, permit me to lay before you,
a few Remarks, which if they meet with your aprobation, the
End will be answer'd, as America is become a new State, beware
of Taxes Tax not her Land, let the Land and People be Free, encourage Agriculture do not Increase your Shipping too fast that
may bring opulence to Individuals but Pride & Luxery to the State
beware of Titles, they will divide the People, Build few Arm'd
Ships, by increasing, will bring a Clog to the State the Coast
wants no Guard all Urope will desire to Trade with America, &
as She has Contracted debts by the Warr, particularly with
France, viz
    Every Vessel Trading to America to pay 1 s per Ton
    (except France, to be free for such a Term, or any other
    Mode)
will be no hinderance to Trade, nor felt by any Nation.
    Every Proprietor of Land in America to be limited, let there
be no Monoply while the Lands are low the State will Increase,
& become Powerfull
    Let there be no Lawyers or professers of Law in the Country
under pain of Death &c
    Let there be two Courts of Justice in each Province, an upper
and an inferor one consisting of 12 Men each; all complaints
made to the Inferior Court, to examine upon the spot where the
complaint was said, and reported to the upper Court upon Oath,
their determination final, if any of the lower Court be Convicted
of any misdemeaner shall be for ever excluded holding any Public place, and suffer sever penalty, the Courts to be chosen every
year & to Sit every Month all fees to be limited I am Sir your most
Obedt. & Humble Servant   JOHN BOURNE

Addressed: To / Benjn, Franklin Esqre, / at Paris

From François de Launey de Fresney[2]

LS:[3] Archives du Ministère des affaires étrangères; copy: American Philosophical Society

Monsieur,   A Laval 9. Mars 1783.

Les fournitures très-conséquentes qui m'ont été confiées pendant toute la Guerre pour le Service de la Marine du Roi,[4] ne m'ont point distrait des expéditions particuliéres pour les différentes maisons Amériquaines, vos compatriotes, établies à Nantes et L'Orient; j'ai joui jusqu'à ce moment de Leur pleine confiance pour des affaires majeures: l'événement de La Paix semble devoir changer la face des choses, et porter un préjudice notable aux fabriques de france, essentiellement à la nôtre, dont l'espèce de toile analogue à celle d'Irlande, avait procuré un débouché marquant pour les Etats-unis, et donné à l'industrie un principe d'activité et de soin qui nous aurait mis dans le cas de n'en point craindre La rivalité; mais un obstacle absolu va détourner les spéculations de nos alliés, si nous ne les captivons en entier par la Libre admission des Tabacs de Leur Continent, ainsi que le fait La Hollande &a.; Cependant La france est le seul Royaume qui consomme 25000. Boucauts de Tabac par an: il est évident que quand bien même on mettrait un droit très-fort sur cette feuille que la branche de commerce qui en résulte serait seule capable de nous attirer La préférence sur les autres Pays. Tous nos Met-

2. François de Launey (Delauney) de Fresney (1729–1799) was an important textile manufacturer, merchant, and local public official. He was the first to manufacture sailcloth in Laval, and was granted *lettres de noblesse:* Henri Sée, "Le Commerce des toiles de Laval à la fin de l'ancien régime et pendant la Révolution," Commission Historique et Archéologique de la Mayenne *Bulletin*, 2nd ser., XLIII (1927), 38n; Louis Bergeron and Guy Chaussinand-Nogaret, eds., *Grands notables du Premier Empire: notices de biographie sociale* (28 vols. to date, Paris, 1978–), XIV, 78–9; A. Angot, *Dictionnaire historique, topographique et biographique de la Mayenne* (4 vols., n.p., 1903–09; reprint, Mayenne, 1990), II, 22.

3. According to the docketing, this was forwarded to Vergennes with BF's letter of March 16. The copy listed here is the one BF retained, marked by him "Copie" and made by L'Air de Lamotte.

4. He was selected to supply the Royal Navy in Brest, Lorient, and Rochefort in 1779: Henri Sée, "Note sur l'industrie textile de la Mayenne dans la première moitié du XIXe siècle," Commission Historique et Archéologique de la Mayenne *Bulletin*, 2nd ser., XLIII (1927), 220n.

tiers & ouvriers sont montés pour entretenir ce Commerce important; la privation y portera un préjudice des plus sensible: Laval Sera une des fabriques qui souffrira davantage, et en mon particulier j'éprouve déja un tort notable par les ordres qui ont été retirés ou supprimés entre mes mains de la part des maisons les plus accréditées du Continent Amériquain.[5]

Comme au Ministre Sur qui toute l'Europe a les yeux fixés, par ses qualités Justes et équitables, J'ose vous adresser, Monsieur, La verité de mes représentations, pour les faire valoir auprès des Ministres du Roi. Ce n'est point l'intérêt privé qui me fait agir, Dieu m'aïant mis dans une position à ne rien désirer, mais le bien général de ma Patrie. J'espére aussi que loin d'improuver mes démarches vous aurés la bonté d'y donner l'attention et l'autorité qui dépendront de vous.

Je suis avec respect, Monsieur, Votre très hûmble & très obéïssant Serviteur./.   FRANÇOIS DE LAUNEY

Monsieur Francklin, à Paris./

From Graf von Schönfeld[6]

ALS: Library of Congress

Monsieur   Paris ce 9. Mars 1783
 Permettés Monsieur, que j'aie l'honneur de Vous adresser le Sr: Bidermann Conseiller de la Cour de Saxe. Il desire infiniment

5. The monopolistic practices of the Farmers General relating to American tobacco sold in France resulted in a shortage of tobacco for the year 1783. The French government received a number of complaints beginning in early March: Price, *France and the Chesapeake*, II, 737, 740–1; Frederick L. Nussbaum, "American Tobacco and French Politics, 1783–1789," *Political Science Quarterly*, XL (1925), 498–500.

6. Minister plenipotentiary at the French court of the Elector of Saxony from 1778 to 1785: XXVI, 171; *Repertorium der diplomatischen Vertreter*, III, 374. On Aug. 8, 1782, he announced to his government BF's promise to help establish commercial relations between the United States and Saxony once peace was established. Shortly after the signing of the preliminary peace agreement on Jan. 20, BF asked Schönfeld for a list of Saxon manufactures. In a March 28 dispatch, Schönfeld reported providing BF with such a list and obtaining in exchange the names of RB and Jonathan Williams, Sr., as "les

d'avoir celui de Vous faire sa cour, et de Vous consulter sur l'intention où il seroit d'établir quelques branches de Commerce entre l'Amerique Septentrionale et la Saxe.[7] Comme ce Sont également les Sentimens de ma Cour, ainsi que j'ai eu l'honneur de Vous en parler Monsieur, dès le premier moment de Votre arrivée dans ce pays,[8] j'ose me flatter que Vous voudrés bien l'accueillir avec bonté et lui faire éprouver le Secours de Vos lumieres et de Votre protection.

Je Saisis cette occasion Monsieur, pour Vous renouveller l'assurance des Sentimens respectueux avec les quels j'ai l'honneur d'être Monsieur, Votre très hûmble et très obeïssant Serviteur

DE SCHÖNFELD.

From the Société Royale de Médecine

Printed invitation with MS insertions: American Philosophical Society

M [before March 10, 1783]

Vous êtes invité à assister à plusieurs expériences qu'on va faire en présence de MM. les Commissaires nommés par la Société Royale de Médecine.

1°. A celle d'un Vêtement qui peut rétablir la transpiration supprimée, en provoquer une abondante, & qui par-là peut obvier à bien des infirmités.

2°. A celle d'un autre Vêtement hermétiquement fermé, par

---

deux maisons les plus solides" of Philadelphia and Boston: William E. Lingelbach, "Saxon-American Relations, 1778–1828," *American Hist. Rev.*, XVII (1911–12), 520–1. Among BF's papers at the APS is an undated, seven-page memoir extolling Saxony and the port of Hamburg, listing the chief Saxon exports, and discussing the potential market for American rice, tobacco, indigo, and furs.

7. BF did meet with him. On March 11 Ehrenhold Fredric Biedermann wrote BF from Paris, explaining that he had been given the present letter of introduction and requesting an appointment. On March 24 he sent a note reminding BF that he had promised letters of recommendation to some solid commercial houses in Philadelphia and Boston. APS.

8. His discussions with BF were unofficial, however, until the war was over: Horst Dippel, *Germany and the American Revolution, 1770–1800* . . . , trans. Bernhard A. Uhlendorf (Chapel Hill, N.C., 1977), p. 39n.

le moyen duquel on peut, sans risque, travailler à des compositions dangereuses, & aller également dans des lieux infects, comme Latrines, &c.

3°. A celle d'un Habillement qui a diverses propriétés, entr'autres celle de faire surnager l'homme & de l'aider à en sauver un autre, & cela dans le temps même que l'eau est excessivement froide & plus dangereuse, &c.

4°. A diverses autres Expériences, qui ont pour but de prouver qu'un homme, qui ne sait pas nager, peut lui-même, sans aucun risque, sauver une personne qui se noie. Ces Expériences, dont l'Auteur est M. LE ROUX*, se feront le *10 de Mars*, de cette année 1783, à *4*. heures précises, aux Bains Chinois, à la pointe de l'Isle Saint-Louis. On entrera avec la présente.[9]

---

* Il est encore l'Auteur du Mémoire & du Plan d'une Ecole ou Académie de Natation, que l'on trouve imprimés & gravés chez Lami, Libraire, quai des Augustins, & pour lesquels Ouvrages il a reçu une gratification du Magistrat qui préside le Corps Municipal de la Ville de Paris.[1]

Addressed: a Monsieur / Monsieur Le Docteur / Franklin / à Passi/. / Expérience de MM. De la / Société Royale de Medecine

9. Charles (C.-J.) Le Roux, whom BF knew because of his interest in education (XXVI, 440; XXVIII, 568, 609–10), was in the 1780s being called "physicien en l'Université de Paris" and working on various projects useful to the preservation of mankind: Jean Sgard, ed., *Dictionnaire des journalistes* (2 vols., Oxford, 1999), II, 634–5. At the Society's meeting of April 25 the commissioners made their report and Le Roux's impermeable fabrics were granted approval and deemed superior to the waxed fabrics already available. His secret substance guarded against water and wind, and garments made from treated fabrics were being called "healthful": *Mercure de France*, May 31, pp. 229–30; *Jour. politique de Bruxelles*, June 7, pp. 36–7; July 19, pp. 133–4.

1. The plan of his swimming school and descriptions of his diving suits were included in the supplement to the 4th edition of Melchisédech Thévenot's *L'Art de nager* (Paris, 1781): Quérard, *France littéraire*.

From Lafreté ALS: American Philosophical Society

Paris le 10. mars 1783.
M. Gallard de Bayonne, dont je vous ai déja parlé mon cher Papa a des affaires interressantes à traitter avec vous. Cest un homme très instruit et un de mes bons amis j'espere que vous voudréz bien le recevoir avec bonté, et qu'il S'appercevra que vous avéz un peu d'amitié pour nous. Ma petite femme est à peu près dans le meme Etat. Vous lui avéz promis de venir diner avec nous, nous vous attendons, et vous assurons tous deux, mon cher Papa de Notre tendre, et Respectueux attachement. LAFRETÉ

From Richard Price ALS: Yale University Library

My Dear Friend   Newington-Green Mch. 10th: 1783
  This letter will be deliver'd to you by Mr *Redford*,[2] a Gentleman for whom I have a great regard and who has my best wishes. He is going to Settle for life in one of the thirteen united States; and he has already Sent thither a part of his fortune. May I take the liberty to request your notice of him? Any assistance or information which you may be pleased to give him will be bestowed on a worthy man and a warm friend to universal liberty, who is well qualified to make an useful member of the united States. Indeed I can Scarcely wish them better, than that they may be filled with men of his character, abilities and principles.— He has been in business about five years; but having in his education contracted habits wch: render him more disposed to litterary than mercantile persuits, he does not intend to engage in commerce but to purchase an estate in order to turn it to the best account that the customs of the country will allow. He has been for some time a member of the Club of whigs at the London-Coffee-House, who will be always proud of having had you for a member. The motives wch: have determined Mr Redford to Settle with his property in America, are his zeal for liberty, his high opinion of the American Governmts:, and his desire to

2. Archibald Redford: XXXVIII, 320n.

Share in the blessings and happiness of a rising country. I have given him a general testimonial which he will Shew you. Would it be too much to beg that you would by a line at the bottom attest that it is my hand-writing?

Mr Redford is likely to be followed by many more emigrants from hence and from Ireland. He will inform you, particularly, of a body of people in Ireland who have resolved to remove to America, and commissioned Mr Noble, a major of the Irish armed volunteers, to go before them in order to engage a tract of land for them. Mr Redford is to assist in transacting this business, and will think himself obliged to you for your advice.[3]

Permit me to congratulate you on the late Peace, and on the Revolution in favour of liberty which has taken place by the establishmt: of the independence of America. I cannot express to you the Satisfaction this has given me. I have wished to live to See this issue of the contest with America; and I am thankful that I have Seen it. The world owes it partly to you; and may Heaven heap its blessings upon you, comfort you in the evening of life, and make you completely happy beyond the grave.

You probably well know what a detestable coalition of parties has lately taken place among us. Never Surely was there an in-

---

3. For Arthur Noble see also Brocklesby's letter of March 12, below. BF was given a copy of the petition Noble had received from "78 Persons [signing] for themselves & their families—making in the whole about 450 persons" including 60 armed and trained volunteers. They listed their grievances as tenants and entreated Noble to purchase a tract of land in America which they would lease from him on whatever terms he specified: Seventy-Eight Persons to Arthur Noble, undated, APS.

Noble arrived in Philadelphia in mid-October carrying an enthusiastic letter of recommendation from BF to Robert Morris (now missing); Morris, in turn, recommended him to George Washington and Robert Livingston. In 1787 the N.Y. Assembly granted Noble the patents of Arthurborough and Nobleborough in the present-day counties of Hamilton and Herkimer. There he settled about one hundred families, built a sawmill, and began producing maple sugar, which they hoped would supply the entire country. The enterprise had failed by 1792: *Morris Papers*, VIII, 647, 833; Harold C. Syrett *et al.*, eds., *The Papers of Alexander Hamilton* (27 vols., New York, 1961–87), IV, 66–7; J. H. French, *Gazetteer of the State of New York* ... (Syracuse, N.Y., 1860), pp. 337, 339, 342; George A. Hardin, ed., *History of Herkimer County, New York* (Syracuse, N.Y., 1893), p. 450; *Jefferson Papers*, XX, 343–4.

stance of Such proffligate conduct. Mr Fox, the pretended friend of the country, united to Ld North, the destroyer of the country— The *Rockingham* party, a body of men who would be thought zealous whigs, united to Tories and the friends of despotism, to oppose and censure a peace which has Saved the kingdom— I hope foreigners See this in its true light; as, merely, a Struggle of ambitious and disappointed men to get into power. May the united States take care to guard agst: the danger and misery of Such factions.

Relying on the indulgence and candour wch: I have always experienced from you, I am, with the greatest affection and respect, ever yours   RICHD: PRICE

Many of your Friends are flattering themselves with the hope of Seeing you soon in *England*. If not improper, deliver my respects to Mr Adams.

To Philip Mazzei   Transcript:[4] American Philosophical Society

March [11],[5] 1783

According to Mr Mazzei's Request, Dr. Franklin has the honour to inform him that there is no Court at Versailles on Tuesday next, consequently that he shall not be there.—[6]

Dr. Franklin desires the honour of Mr & Mrs Mazzei's[7] Company at Dinner on Wednesday the 12th Inst.—at ½ pst 2

---

4. Made in 1952 from a private collection in Geneva.

5. Mazzei wrote in his autobiography that this note invited him to dine the following day: Philip Mazzei, *My Life and Wanderings*, trans. S. Eugene Scalia, ed. Margherita Marchione (Morristown, N.J., 1980), p. 271.

6. BF had agreed to present Mazzei at court. When he did so the following Tuesday, he was surprised to learn that Mazzei had already been introduced to Vergennes: Mazzei, *My Life and Wanderings*, pp. 270–1, 305.

7. Marie Hautefeuille Martin Mazzei had already left Paris: Mazzei, *My Life and Wanderings*, pp. 19, 410, 429.

From Benjamin Vaughan

ALS: American Philosophical Society

My dearest sir,   London, March 11, 1783.

There seems still an indecision in public affairs, as far as relates to ministry, but every body is glad to stand upon the clear ground of a peace; so that you need not fear that your treaty will be shaken.

I find every plan I had heard spoken of, was in a great state of ripeness, when I arrived in London; and the grandest ideas prevailing about free trade, free will, and the nonsense of force. In short I saw few things to mend; and it did not appear to me that any thing was repented of. To say the truth however, England wanted & still wants the *data*, by which to judge of the American peace, & the motives & merits of those who concluded it. I can only tell you that we were both right in singling out the only man, who had head & *courage* enough to execute and even force the business.[8] In a year more he would have completed it, as far as depended upon him; that is, had he canvassed his people like Ld. North, & still more had he paid them; because having survived the crisis, people would have been less resolute against the rest of his proceedings, from obvious reasons.

We are still in the dark about the impression this revolution has made at Paris.

I am myself very indifferent about persons, and I hope we all are so; and therefore if you find the new people, (if there are to be such,) tending to liberality, you must be content with them instead of better ones, and if we cannot get good sense at the hands of its real authors, we must be content with it at second hand. But I assure you that the surest means of raising up & continuing good sense here, is by using generous national language from Paris, and exhibiting lenient relenting measures towards refugee property in America. The moment we are convinced that you will meet us, & still more advance to us, you will find few things not forgot by England, stubborn as her pride is, & much as is gone from her.

It is true we were *all* losers by the late convulsion, because at

---

8. Shelburne.

a critical *moment,* it cut short that intercourse which experience tells us has of all others been most succesful with the Royal mind.

I trouble you with one more person to patronize; Mr Archibald Redford.[9] He is a citizen of the world in all senses, but most so in his philanthropy. He is going to settle in America, & goes by France having business at Nantes. The way being now open from England, you will have little trouble of this kind in future, especially as our family set sail in less than two months. I am, my dearest sir, Your ever devoted, grateful, & respectful

BENJN VAUGHAN.

In haste.

From Richard Brocklesby[1]   ALS: American Philosophical Society

London 12th March 1783

I beg leave to congratulate my ever respectable & honored friend on the events of late establishd between Great Britain & America, which naturally tend to restore both parties to their mutual good humor, & that common confidence in each other, wch the late fatal & ingloriously *unnatural* Contest had unhappily for this Country at least interrupted a deplorable Series of Years.

This letter will be put into your Excellencys hands by a Mr Redford, who is commissioned by Arthur Noble Esqr.[2] a Major in the Irish Volunteers a Man of solid property of his own, to commence a correspondence wth your Excellency upon a Subject of national Importance. What remains for me to say is that I know Mr Noble to be a man of strict honour & I believe him to be a Gentleman of substantial Property in Ireland & should have no difficulty to trust him to the extent of 5,000£ property on his own account. On this account I recommend to your Excellency Mr Noble as fully meriting the Consideration & sagacity of Dr Franklin or the American Lycurgus. Mr Radford is I am told charged wth a letter from Dr Price confirming what is

9. Whom Price had recommended the previous day, above.
1. A physician and fellow of the Royal Society: XXX, 572n.
2. For whom see Price to BF, March 10.

here said concerning Mr Noble & that the result may fully answer the expectations of all concerned is the earnest wish of Dr
Sr. Your most Obliged & most faithful Hle & Obedt. Servt

RICHARD BROCKLESBY

To His Excellency Benjamin Franklin Esqr.

From David Hartley   Copy:[3] Massachusetts Historical Society

My dear Friend,   London March 12. 1783.
    It is a long while since I have heard from you or indeed since
I writ to you.[4] I heartily congratulate you upon those pacific
events which have already happened and wish to see all other
final Steps of Conciliation succeed speedily. I send you Copies
of two Papers which I have already communicated to Mr. Laurens the one called conciliatory Propositions in March 1783; the
other a Sketch of a provisional Treaty of Commerce for opening the Ports between Great Britain and the United States of
America without Delay, to each of which is prefixed a short State
of the Argument on each head.
    As for the News of this Country you have doubtless heard
that Ld. Shelburn's Administration has for some time been considered as at an End, altho' no other has been as yet substituted
in the Place of it. It was understood yesterday, and I believe with
good Foundation, that what is now called the Portland Party
have been applied to, and they are considered as the Party most
likely to succeed. As far as my wishes go such an event wd. be
most satisfactory to me. I have known the D. of Portland for
many Years and by Experience, I know him to be a Noble Man
of the strictest honor and of the soundest Whig Principles, sincere and explicit in every thought and Transaction, manly in his
Judgement and firm in his Conduct. The Kingdom of Ireland of
wch. he was lately Ld. Lieutenant bears unanimous testimony to

3. In the hand of L'Air de Lamotte, with corrections by WTF.
4. Except for the brief letter of introduction Hartley wrote on Feb. 4,
above, his last exchange of letters with BF was the previous November:
XXXVIII, 325–6, 371.

this Character of him. The Cavendish Family (a good whig Name) Mr. Fox, Ld. Fitz William &c. &c. form the core of his System and connexions.[5] I most earnestly wish to see a firm Administration upon a whig foundation which I should consider as a solid Basis on the Part of this Country for a perpetual Correspondence of Amity & conciliation with America. I am very anxious to hear of your health. God bless you.

Ever Your most affecte. G. B.

Conciliatory Propositions March 1783.

Terms of Peace having been agreed upon between Great Britain and France on 20. Jan. 1783 There need not be any farther Delay in proceeding to conclude the proposed Treaty between G. B. and the United States of America upon the Basis of the provisional Articles of the 30th. of November 1782.[6]

It is to be observed that none of the Articles of the provisional Treaty are to take effect untill the Conclusion of the definitive Treaty with America. At which time likewise all Places in the American States in possession of the British arms are to be evacuated, and the British Army withdrawn from the United States (by Art. 7). If therefore it should be wished on the Part of G. Bn. to bring forward the 5th. Article respecting the Loyalists before the Conclusion of the definitive Treaty with Amera. The Bayonet shd. be withdrawn from the American Breast by the voluntary removal of the British Troops with all convenient Dispatch. This Condition of the Removal of the Troops is likewise necessary before any provisional Terms of Commerce with America can take place.

5. William Henry Cavendish-Bentinck, Duke of Portland (XXXVII, 125n), had aided Hartley in 1768 in his first campaign for the House of Commons. He served as Lord Lieutenant of Ireland during the Rockingham government, but resigned in sympathy with Fox when Shelburne took office. He became prime minister when the new government was formed in April, 1783, and Fox and North served in his cabinet. Portland was married to Lady Dorothy Cavendish, the niece of Lord John Cavendish, the former Chancellor of the Exchequer: *ODNB*, under Bentinck and John Cavendish; Namier and Brooke, *House of Commons*, II, 203–5, 592. William Wentworth, Earl Fitzwilliam (*ODNB*, under Fitzwilliam), was a wealthy friend of Fox.

6. XXXVIII, 382–8.

By the 6th. Article of the provisional Treaty all future Confiscations in America are precluded altho the Prosecutions at present subsisting are not to be stopped before the definitive Treaty. But if the substantial Pledge of returning Amity on the part of G. B. viz the removal of the Troops shd. be voluntarily anticipated, it would be but seasonable that all Propositions shd. be immediately abated on the part of America, and to facilitate the removal of the Troops the Loyalists may be permitted to remain in Safety & unmolested (if they chuse to remain) from the period of removing the Troops untill 12 Months after the definitive Treaty.

There is another Article of the provisional Treaty the delay of which is much to be lamented viz the mutual release of Prisoners of War on both Sides.[7] As this is an Article of Reciprocity, both Sides from principles of Humanity are equally interested to bring it forward into effect speedily; that those unhappy Captives may not alone suffer the Miseries of War in the time of Peace.

Upon these Considerations the following Supplemental Terms of Treaty between G. Bn. and the United States are proposed.

1. That the British Troops shall be withdrawn with all convenient speed.

2. That the Commissioners on both Sides do proceed to the Conclusion of the Definitive Treaty.

3. That the Commrs. do speedily negociate a provisional Convention of Commerce (hereunto annexed) to take Place immediately. The Terms of this temporary Convention not to be pleaded on either Side in the Negociation of a final and perpetual Treaty of Commerce between G. B. & the United States.

4. That the Commrs. do negotiate a perpetual Treaty of Commerce.

5. That all Prosecutions of the Loyalists in Ama. be immediately abated and that they be permitted to remain until 12. Months after the definitive Treaty unmolested in their Endeavours to obtain Restitution of their Estates.

6. That all Prisoners on both Sides be immediately released.

7. This is part of Article 7: XXXVIII, 386.

7. That Intercourse of Amity and Commerce do immediately take Place between Great Britain & the United States of America.

Sketch of a provisional Treaty of Commerce.

As soon as Preliminaries of Peace are signed with any independent State such as Spain France & Holland the Course of mutual Commerce emerges upon the same Terms and Conditions as were existing antecedent to the War the New Duties imposed during the War excepted. The Case between Great Britain and America from a dependent Nation before the War emerges an independent Nation after the War. The Basis therefore of Provisional Treaty between G. B. & the United States would be simply to arrange such Points as would emerge after the War impracticable and discordant to the newly-established Independence of the American States and to leave all others as much as possible untouched. For Instance that all instrumental Regulations such as Papers Bonds, Certificates Oaths, and all other Documents should be between G. B. and the United States upon the same footing and no other than as between G. B. and any other independant Nation, but that all Duties, draw-backs Bounties, Rights, Privileges and all pecuniary Considerations should emerge into Action and effect as before. I say emerge as before not stipulated for any fixed Term, because I am speaking of a provisional Treaty not of a Provisional *Bill* of Commerce for a specified Period. By this Means all Difficulties which otherwise would be accumulated & obstruct a temporary & provisional Act are avoided *in Limine*.[8] The Ports will be immediately & mutually opened upon specified and known Conditions. If the Legislature of either Country think proper to introduce on its own Part any New-Conditions or Regulation even previous to the intended Treaty of Commerce that will not shut the Ports again generally but only operate *pro tanto* according to the Case; on which side soever any novel Condition shou'd arise the other will likewise be at Liberty to make any corresponding Regulations as between Independent Nations. The Great Object is to

8. At the very outset.

open the Ports between Great Britain and the United States immediately upon the Signature of Preliminaries of Peace as between France & G. B. By the Proposition above stated G. B. and France & G. B. & the United States, respectively on the Subject of Intercourse of Commerce, would emerge again after the War, into Situations relatively Similar to their Situation before the War.

The Crown of G: B. is enabled by the conciliatory Act of 1782 to repeal, annull, make void or suspend for any time or times the Operation & Effect of any Act of Parliament or any clause Provision, Matter or thing therein contained relating to the Colonies or Plantations now become the United States of America; and therefore the Crown is not only competent to conclude but likewise to carry into effect any provisional Treaty of Commerce with America.[1] The first Foundation must be laid in the total repeal of the Prohibitory Act of Decr. 1775,[2] not only as prohibiting Commerce between Great Britain and the United States, but as the Corner Stone of the War by giving up universally all American Property at Sea to military Plunder without any Redress to be obtained by Law in any British Court of Admiralty. After this all Obstructions from the Act of Navigation and other Acts regulating the Commerce of the States of America (formerly dependant upon G. B.) may be removed.— Instructions may be sent to the Commissioners of the Customs to dispence with Bonds Certificates &ca. which by the old Laws are required to be discharged or attested by supposed Governors naval or Custom House officers in America. The Questions of Drawbacks Bounties &a after opening the Ports, may remain free Points of Discussion & Regulation as between States having no commercial Treaty subsisting between them. As the Crown is competent to open an Intercourse of Commerce with America by Treaty, this mode is preferable to any Act of Parliament

---

1. Hartley is referring to the Enabling Act (XXXVI, 688n).

2. For which see XXII, 268n. In April Parliament took under consideration a bill to repeal it as well as other legislation; see our annotation of Laurens to BF, April 4.

which may only be a Jealous & suspicious Convention *ex parte*.[3] This Mode by Treaty avoids the accumulated Difficulties which might otherwise obstruct the first opening of the Ports by Act of Parlt. and above all it secures an alternate Binding Part of the Bargain which no act of Parliament can do.

Breviate of the Treaty viz Provisional for Intercourse & Commerce between G. B. & the United States of America.

1st. That all Ports shall be mutually open for Intercourse and Commerce.

2. And therefore the King of Great Britain agrees for the Repeal of the prohibitory Acts viz 16 Geo. 3d Chapt. 5th. &ca. the K. of Great Britain likewise agrees by Instructions according to the Laws of G. B. to his Commissioners of Customs, & other officers to remove all obstructions to American Ships either entering inwards or clearing outwards which may arise from any Acts of Parlt. heretofore regulating the Commerce of the American States, under the Description of British Colonies and Plantations, so as to accomodate every Circumstance to the reception of their Ships as the Ships of Independent States.

3d. All Duties, Drawbacks, Bounties, Rights, Privileges and all other money-Considerations shall remain respecting the United States of America, upon the same footing as they now remain respecting the Province of Nova Scotia in America, or as if the aforesaid States had remained dependent upon Great Britain. All this subject to Regulations or Alterations by any future Acts of the Parlt. of G. B.

4th. On the Part of the States of America it is agreed that all Laws prohibiting the Commerce with G. B. shall be repealed.

5th. Agreed upon the same Part that all Ships & Marchandizes of the British Dominions shall be admitted upon the same terms as before the War, except any Imports laid during the War. All this subject to future Regulations or Alterations by the Legislaturs of American States respectively.

6th. The Principles & Spirit of this Treaty to be supported on ei-

---

3. From one side only.

ther Side by any necessary supplemental Arrangements No tacit Compliance on the Part of America in any subordinate Points to be argued at any time hereafter to the Prejudice of their Independence.——

Notations: [*by William Temple Franklin*] Copy of a Letter from D. Hartley Esqr to B: Franklin Esqr / [*by John Adams*] Mr Hartley's Letter to Dr Franklin March 12. 1783.

From Richard Bache   ALS: Historical Society of Pennsylvania

Dear & Hond: Sir   Philadelphia March 13th: 1783.

Yesterday Captain Barney brought me your much esteemed Favor of 26th: Decr.——[4] I hope we shall not be long 'till we hear that Peace is concluded on, it is an Event much wished for here, except by a few self-interested Individuals—— Should you upon a Peace determine upon returning to your native Country; my inclination would lead me to pay a visit to France, where perhaps I might form some valuable commercial connections, and after this was done, accompany you home, when I should have an opportunity of further testifying that Duty & affection which I hold towards you——

As this Vessel is just upon the Wing, I have only time to add, that we are perfectly well, and join in sincere Love to yourself Temple & Ben; I have wrote a few Lines to the latter, which please to forward to him.

Inclosed is 5th. Bill of a Sett already sent you——[5] I am ever Dear Sir Your affecte. son   RICH. BACHE

You will receive the Newspapers herewith, should be glad if Temple would send me some Englishpapers from time to time—— Miss Beckwith has done us the favor to stay at our house, 'till she fixes herself; she has taken Mount Airy, where she intends keeping a boarding School, & will go there soon——

---

4. An extract of which appears in XXXVIII, 503. Joshua Barney, captain of the *General Washington*, had just arrived in Philadelphia: XXXVIII, 560n.

5. See RB's note on the first of SB's Jan. 24 letters.

Addressed: The Honble. / Dr. Franklin / Passy. / Per Capt Truxton[6]

From John Calder[7]

ALS: American Philosophical Society

Dear Sir St(?) Chads Row No. 18. March 13. 1783

I chearfully embrace this opportunity of writing to you, the rather, as the paper I write upon is to be the cover of a letter from a worthy old friend of yours & mine,[8] who does not rejoice more sincerely or heartily than I do, in the honours & merit you have acquired by the services you have done to your country & the world. For the conveyance of this I am indebted to my friend Lieutenant General Melvill,[9] who though he had not the felicity of enjoying so much of your company here, as 'Twas my good fortune to do, has nevertheless, in these late trying times of friendship & principles, uniformly thought & spoke of you with the esteem & affection of your particular friends. Uniting as he does so happily, the Gentleman & the Scholar, I think he is certain of being favoured with your countenance & advice both

6. Thomas Truxtun, most recently captain of the *Commerce,* was establishing a Philadelphia-based merchant firm. He sailed to London in June, 1783, to bring back British goods: Eugene S. Ferguson, *Truxtun of the* Constellation: *the Life of Commodore Thomas Truxtun, U.S. Navy, 1755–1822* (2nd ed., Baltimore, 2000), pp. 48–50.

7. This is the first extant letter between BF and the Rev. John Calder (1733–1815), who was by turns a librarian, clergyman, editor, and author: *ODNB.* The two men must have met through the Club of Honest Whigs, which Calder joined *c.* 1772: XIX, 310–11n; Verner W. Crane, "The Club of Honest Whigs: Friends of Science and Liberty," *W&MQ,* 3rd ser., XXIII (1966), 219, 221.

8. John Whitehurst; his letter to BF of the same date is below.

9. Lt. Gen. Robert Melville (1723–1809), a classical scholar and member of the Royal Societies of London and Edinburgh, served as governor-general of Grenada and its dependent islands of Dominica, St. Vincent, Tobago, and the Grenadines from 1764 to 1771. He traveled in Europe between 1774 and 1776, returning to England at the outbreak of the war. He was promoted to lieutenant-general in 1777 though he never saw active duty: *ODNB;* John Nichols, *Illustrations of the Literary History of the Eighteenth Century . . .* (8 vols., London, 1817–58), IV, 833–4n.

upon his own account, & on the score of his errand. He is appointed, very wisely in the general opinion of those who know him as I do, Negotiator in behalf of himself & his fellow sufferers in Tobago, the scape-goats of their country, who as men & protestants, cannot help feeling as they do, at being transferred with the Island, without any stipulation in favour of their rights & properties.[1]

I now enter unwillingly on a subject so insignificant, but I must necessarily say something of myself, as an apology for what it might else be impertinent in me to mention. On the dissolution of the Religious Society of which Mr. Radcliffe & I were the Ministers,[2] which happened soon after you left England, I declined the stated exercise of the profession to wc I was educated, & have ever since been a private Member of the Church of Unitarian Christians in Essex Street at the opening of which you was present.[3] There only I sometimes officiate occasionally as Minister & never but when necessity requires it. In the mean while, in a comfortable retirement about a mile from town, my books have been my principal companions, & the culture of a garden my chief amusement. Here I have for some years inwardly cherished the hopes of seeing you again, & endeavoured to save all I can, to transport me & my companions to Pennsylvania, where whether I accompany them or not, I mean they shall be ultimately deposited in the Library of which you was the founder.[4] Turned as I am the meridian of life, being but a year younger than your very good friends & mine Dr Priestley & Mr Lee[5] & urged by no grievous necessities nor un-

1. Britain had ceded Tobago to the French in the preliminary peace agreement of Jan. 20. Melville helped negotiate the annulment of the *droit d'aubaine* for the British settlers remaining on the island: Nichols, *Literary History of the Eighteenth Century*, IV, 833n.
2. Ebenezer Radcliffe (XIV, 219n) was minister of the Presbyterian congregation in Aldgate, London, which was dissolved in 1774: XIX, 310–11n.
3. XXI, 195–7.
4. Calder's dream of emigrating was never realized. He died in London in 1815 and his library was sold at auction: *Gent. Mag.*, LXXXV (1815), 564; *A Catalogue of the Entire and Select Library of the Late Rev. John Calder ... Which Will Be Sold by Auction, etc.* (London, 1816).
5. Priestley and John Lee were born within a week of each other in March,

favourable prospects here, perhaps even the friends I mention will condemn my resolutions. But with such undisclosed views I have long secretly sighed for a sight of the American Constitutions & have been within these few days in possession of my wishes.[6]

I concern myself chiefly with the Constitution of the state in which my views terminate, & I rejoice that it has in all respects the preheminence. In its Council of Censors there is a resource for the removal of the objection, for I have but one, & therefore after what I have said, I know you will forgive my taking the liberty of mentioning it, in the way of query.

Is the last clause of the Declaration in Sect. 10 of Chap. II[7] reconcileable to the clause in the 2d Article of the Declaration of Rights[8] which says, "Nor can any man who acknowledges the Being of a God be justly deprived of any civil right as a Citizen on account of his religious sentiments, or peculiar mode of religious worship." I cannot think that the State of Pennsylvania would have even endangered its welfare by admitting freely & universally to a denizonship in it, "all foreigners of good character"[9] Christians or no Christians.

1733 (*ODNB*); the latter defended BF at his hearing in the Cockpit: XV, 255; XXI, 38n, 90.

6. An edition of the thirteen state constitutions had been published by order of Congress in 1781: XXXVIII, 216n. The first of several London reprints appeared in 1782.

7. The Pa. constitution consisted of a preamble, a declaration of rights (Chapter I), and a plan of government (Chapter II). Calder is here referring to the religious test required of all representatives in the General Assembly, in addition to an oath of allegiance: "I do believe in one God, the creator and governor of the universe, the rewarder of the good and the punisher of the wicked. And I do acknowledge the scriptures of the Old and New Testatment to be given by divine inspiration." *The Constitutions of the Several Independent States of America . . .* (Philadelphia, 1781), pp. 91–2.

8. *Ibid.*, p. 87.

9. Section 42 stipulates: "Every foreigner of good character, who comes to settle in this state, having first taken an oath or affirmation of allegiance to the same, may purchase, or by other just means acquire, hold, and transfer land or other real estate; and after one year's residence, shall be deemed a free denizen thereof, and intitled to all the rights of a natural born subject of this state, except that he shall not be capable of being elected a representative, until after two years residence." *Ibid.*, p. 100.

But passing from this, there are Christians & sincere worthy Christians, who after all their pains to make up their minds on the subject of the divine inspiration of the *Old Testament* especially, must express themselves as our friend Mr Lee did on another subject, when he said 'I have been a great part of my life, endeavouring to understand it, but I cannot yet tell you what a Libel is.' If the State of Pennsylvania wishes to grant citizenship to all foreigners of good character who are Christians, why establish a declaration which some Christian foreigners of good character must object to?[1] Is it an incredible thing that a man be really a Christian, who is not yet a Jew? Or is it indispensibly requisite that a man must first be a Jew before he can be qualified to be a good Denizon of the State of Pensylvania? May not the friends of Christianity have connected it injudiciously, & injured its cause by connecting it more closely wt Judaism than its Author & first publishers did?

Are not the Evidences of Christianity & the evidences of Judaism distinct? Why then complicate them with each other so oddly, as that they must necessarily stand or fall together? I needed not to have said so much to you who think & to those who do not think it is not necessary to say any thing.

It is very immaterial whether I have or have not a personal reason for touching on this point; for if I ever cross the Atlantic, I shall come with a settled purpose of never being a Religious Teacher of any denomination whatsoever; but as a private individual, purposing to employ myself in some humbler station more usefully, I could wish for equal freedom for my own & every other man's religious opinions. I ought to apologize for the length & freedom of this letter, when I consider your greatness & the importance of your time, but I know your goodness, & rely for my pardon on your belief of my being in all essential

1. The religious test in Section 10 only applied to members of the General Assembly. The oath of allegiance taken by "all foreigners of good character" was the same as that prescribed for officers of the state in Section 40, affirming loyalty to the commonwealth of Pennsylvania and to the constitution: *ibid.*, p. 100. While the oath changed several times during the war, it never contained a religious component: Douglas M. Arnold, *A Republican Revolution: Ideology and Politics in Pennsylvania, 1776–1790* (New York and London, 1989), pp. 106–8.

respects no worse than when you left me in the honoured circle of your acquaintances.[2] I cannot yet conclude without congratulating you, on the accomplishment of your character & on the conclusion of a war wc considering its origin & conduct has happily terminated in the only way that could have prevented many of your friends from becoming Sceptics or Atheists. I am wt the highest esteem reverence & affection Dr Sir Your's &c

JOHN CALDER

Notation: Calder 13 March 1783

From Jonathan Nesbitt

AL: American Philosophical Society

Thursday March 13: 1783

Mr: Nesbitt's most respectful Compliments wait on Doctor Franklin, & requests that he will grant a Pasport for a Gentleman (a Mr. Bacon)[3] who goes for England tomorrow. If Dr. Franklin has any Commands for England, Mr Bacon may be depended upon.

From John Whitehurst,[4] with a Note by John Calder

ALS: American Philosophical Society

Sir   London 13 March 1783
   Please to accept My Sincere congratulations for the Restoration of *Peace,* and the *Natural rights of Mankind,* in *America.*

---

2. The Club of Honest Whigs.
3. Possibly the Bacon who received a passport the previous June: XXXVI, 379.
4. The Derbyshire maker of clocks and scientific instruments: IX, 42n; Maxwell Craven, *John Whitehurst of Derby: Clockmaker and Scientist, 1713–88* (Mayfield, Eng., and Summit, N.J.). In March, 1779, Whitehurst sent BF a copy of his recently published treatise on geology (XXXII, 379–80n); BF's copy is at the APS. Though he says here that he shipped BF items in a "clock-case," neither we nor his biographer Maxwell Craven (who was kind enough to check his records for us) have found any trace of them.

That all the Provinces may be Settled and Governed by Laws calculated for the Mutual benefit of every individual is the Ardent wish of Sir Your Most Obedient Servt   J WHITEHURST

Pray did the things contained in the bottom of the Clock-Case come Safe to hand?

Addressed: Docr. Franklin

[*In the hand of John Calder:*] Seeing some blank paper here, I make a Siezure of it to tell you that long as you may think my letter,[5] I did great violence to myself in not making it longer. Impute it to the habits in which I have been bred, that I cannot prevail on myself to part with this paper without observing that when we leave providence out of the consideration, we see only the dark side of History.

God bless you & preserve you.

From Henrietta Maria Colden

ALS: American Philosophical Society

Sir   Douglas. in the Isle of Man. March 14th. 1783.

After congratulating your Excellency, on having established the United States of America on the Basis of Civil, Religious and Commercial Liberty; permit me to Sollicit your Protection of my Infant Sons, Natives of New York, who owe their Allegiance to the New Republick.— After the Death of my Husband Richard Nicholls Colden (eldest Son of Mr Alexander Colden) who died of a Fever at New-York in 1777 finding myself destitute and helpless in a Country filled with Foreign Troops, I came over with my two Children in 1778 to my Father in this Island, where we have resided ever since, nor have we received any Pension or Support from the British Government.—[6] Hence it happens,

---

5. Of this date, above. This note was written on the verso of the address sheet.

6. While serving with the 42nd Royal Highlanders, Richard Nicholls Colden (XIV, 137n; XXI, 10n), the son of Alexander Colden (VI, 113n) and

that we fall under the Description of Persons resident in Great Britain, whose Rights and Properties, in America, are secured to them, by the late Treaty of Peace. However, I have such confidence, in the Justice of Congress and the Governments of the Confederate Provinces, that I cannot suppose my Infants (tho' no such Provision had been made in that Treaty) would meet with any difficulty, in being admitted to the natural Rights and Priviledges, of Subjects and Citizens in their Native Country.— None of their Progenitors took any Part, in the late War, (all of them having Died, either before, or soon after its commencement) and being Men of Humane and pacific dispositions, they extended their good Offices alike, to all their suffering Neighbours, and lived and died in Amity with all Men. From them therefore, my Sons inherit, no party Hatred, or spirit of Dissension, and I engage that they will demean themselves, as Faithful and Dutiful Subjects of the Government of their Province as a Member of the United States.

Nevertheless, I am truly sensible, that as Things are at present situated, it is necessary we should have some Friend, to Patronize our Interests, and I have presumed from the Acquaintance that long subsisted, between your Excellency and my Husband's Family, to entreat your Good Offices, in this Matter, that your Excellency, would be pleased to lay our Case before Congress, and desire that august Body, to use their Influence with the Provincial Government of New York, on behoof of myself and my Infants— All we Sollicit, is to be received under the Protection of that Government and to possess our Rights of Inheritance within its Jurisdiction, on the same Footing with its other Subjects on which Footing, as Innocent and unobnoxious Persons, we should undoubtedly have stood, had we not been compelled to leave our Country, by the distresses and calamities of Civil War.—

---

grandson of Cadwallader Colden (II, 386n), married Henrietta Maria Bethune, a native of the Isle of Man. They had two childen, Alexander and Cadwallader, the latter of whom became editor of the *U.S. Sporting Magazine* in 1835: Edwin R. Purple, *Genealogical Notes of the Colden Family in America* (New York, 1873), pp. 12–13. We have found no response to this letter.

I rely on your Excellency's known Benevolence to pardon this Application from a Mother, anxious for the Interests of her Children, and whose Situation precludes her, from any other Mode of addressing herself to your Excellency.

I have the Honor to be, with great Respect, Your Excellency's, most Obedient & very humble Servant

HENRIETTA MARIA COLDEN.

His Excellency, Benjamin Franklin.—

From Dumas

ALS: Library of Congress; AL (draft): Algemeen Rijksarchief

Monsieur,   Lahaie 14e. Mars 1783.

J'ai reçu des mains de Mrs Wheelock la Lettre dont il vous a plu m'honorer;[7] avec la juste sensibilité que j'aurai toujours pour toutes les marques que vous voulez bien me donner de votre précieux souvenir. Il y a effectivement trop longtemps que nous ne nous étions donné signe de vie, & que nous n'avons qu'indirectement des nouvelles l'un de l'autre: car vous avez eu sans doute connoissance de l'une ou l'autre des fréquentes Lettres que j'ai écrites officiellement à Mr. Adams touchant les affaires de ce pays. Cette correspondance, celle de l'Amérique, & l'interne de ces provinces, avec des maladies presque continues depuis 3 mois, m'ont absorbé depuis bien du temps.

Mrs. Wheelock ont suivi mes conseils ici & à Leide, & s'en sont trouvés bien. Je les leur ai donnés pour Amsterdam aussi; & j'attends qu'ils m'apprennent quelque chose de leurs succès, pour lesquels il y avoit bonne apparence quand nous nous sommes quittés à Leide, jusqu'où je les avois accompagnés. En attendant je leur ai préparé d'autres succès ailleurs, mais qui dependent de celui qu'ils auront à Amsterdam.

J'ai vu avec plaisir la description d'une Médaille, que, selon les Gazettes, vous avez fait frapper, Monsieur, à Paris: *l'Enfant*

7. Above, Feb. 17.

Hercule étouffant des Serpens;[8] & je serois bien aise de pouvoir m'en procurer une par occasion. J'espere d'apprendre surtout, que Vous êtes entierement rétabli, & à même de pouvoir jouir des fruits de la paix si glorieuse pour les Etats-Unis. Puisse-t-elle leur être aussi salutaire, qu'elle fait honneur aux Plénipotentiaires qui l'ont conclue. On m'a fait confidence de quelques changemens imprévus au département des affaires étrangeres à Philadelphie;[9] comme aussi du Ministre qui ira à Londres de la part des Etats-Unis.[1] Je ne serois pas faché de savoir ce qui en est: mais crainte de montrer une curiosité peut-être indiscrete, j'aime mieux réprimer la mienne.

Je suis avec le respectueux attachement qui vous est voué pour toujours, Monsieur, De V. Exce. le très humble & très obéissant serviteur   DUMAS

A Son Exce. Mr. Franklin Min. Plenipo: des E.U.

Addressed: Grand / à Son Excellence / Monsieur B. Franklin, Esqr. / Ministre Plenipo: des Etats / Unis, / Passy./.

---

8. Dumas must have seen the article about the *Libertas Americana* medal in the March 11 *Gaz. de Leyde,* sup., which focused on the side portraying the infant Hercules; see the headnote to Franklin and Morellet's "Explanation of a Medal," [c. May 5]. The first newspaper to carry the story seems to have been the *Gaz. des Deux-Ponts,* which published an imperfect description of the design on March 4; a second article, which resembled the one in the *Gaz. de Leyde,* appeared on March 11: Lester C. Olson, *Benjamin Franklin's Vision of American Community: a Study in Rhetorical Iconology* (Columbia, S.C., 2004), pp. 158–9.

9. Apparently a reference to Livingston's impending resignation (for which see XXXVIII, 405–6n).

1. Negotiations for a commercial treaty were conducted in Paris, however. A minister to the court of St. James's was not selected until Feb. 24, 1785, when JA was chosen: *JCC,* XXVIII, 98.

From the Marquis du Saillant et de Saint-Viance[2]

ALS: American Philosophical Society

Monsieur   paris le 14. mars 1783.
Je viens De Comettre unne Etourderie Dont je vous prie De
Recevoir mes Excuses. Mr. gatellier ma Envoyé trois Exemplaires De son ouvrage pour vous Les faire passer, jay Cru que
La Lettre qui Etoit De Dans Etoit pour moy,[3] & dans Cette idee
je Lay ouvertte, jespere que vous voudres bien avoir De Lindul-
gence pour unne fautte involontaire je vous Le Demande Et Detre persuadé Du Respect avec Lequel je Suis Monsieur Votre tres
humble & tres obeissant Serviteur   Le Mquis Du Saillant

From Dom ——— Gauthey[4]

ALS: American Philosophical Society

Monsieur,   Paris le 14 Mars 1783
Vous avez eu sansdoutte la complaisance de lire le prospectus
sur la propagation du son dans des tuyaux que Monsieur Du-
fourni de Villers, eut la bonté de vous remettre au Musée le 6 du
présent,[5] et j'aime à croire que le projet d'une Experience de

2. The marquis du Saillant (1740–1815) was married to the marquis de
Mirabeau's daughter: *DBF*, under Lasteyrie; Barbara Luttrell, *Mirabeau*
(New York, London, and Toronto, 1990), pp. 24, 291.

3. Gastellier to BF, March 3.

4. A Cistercian monk (sometimes confused with the engineer Emiland-
Marie) who, in the spring of 1782, submitted to the Academy of Sciences a
proposal for how to communicate quickly and confidentially over long distances by means of lengths of pipe, of the kind used to transport water for
the pumps at Chaillot. Condorcet and the comte de Milly witnessed a demonstration of the first method and issued a highly favorable report, which kept
the details secret. An examination of the second method was postponed until Gauthey could finance the experiment, which he tried to do through a subscription (the subject of the present letter): [Ignace-Urbain-Jean] Chappe,
Histoire de la télégraphie (Paris, 1824), pp. xx, 226–9; *Jour. de Paris* for June
20, 1782.

5. Dufourny de Villiers (who wrote on March 29, below) evidently attended the March 6 celebration in honor of the peace; see Court de Gébelin
to the APS, March 15, below.

cette nature, quelqu'en soit l'issüe, n'a put manquer d'interesser un vrai savant, puis qu'elle tend à fixer nos connoissances assez vagues dans cette partie.

Vôtre zele et vôtre amour pour les sciences, que vôtre rare et vaste genie cultive avec autant de succes et font marcher avec autant de rapidité, me sont un sure garand que vous excuserez la liberté que je me donne de vous écrire pour vous prier de me communiquer vos reflexions et vos lumieres à ce sujet.

J'ose même vous demander vôtre suffrage et la permission de pouvoir embelir ma Liste de vôtre nom, si vous jugez que Cette entreprise mérite des Coopérateurs.[6] Ce suffrage est d'un trop grand poids et d'une trop grande authorité pour ne pas l'ambitionner avec ardeur et n'en pas sentir tout l'avantage: et j'ai cru pouvoir me flatter que vous daigneriez acceüillir au moins mes éfforts; puisse le Succès réalisant mes Esperance, justifier cet acceuil, et me fournir des occasions plus particulieres de vous présenter mon hommage et vous faire agrèer le profond Respect et la plus haute Estime avec les quels jay l'honneur d'Etre Monsieur Votre tres humble et tres obeissant serviteur   D Gauthey

adresse Chez Monsieur Gardeur sculpteur[7] cloitre st jacques l'hopital rue mauconseil a paris

Notation: Gauthey 14 Mars 1783.

6. BF obliged; his name appears near the end of the four-page list of distinguished subscribers that Gauthey included in his printed prospectus, *Expérience sur la propagation du son et de la voix dans les tuyaux prolongés a une grande distance, nouveau moyen d'établir & d'obtenir une correspondance très-rapide entre les lieux fort éloignés,* which was announced and summarized in the *Jour. de Paris* on May 13, 1783. Gauthey explained in general terms the acoustic properties of long pipes, which allowed sound to travel with perfect clarity and even amplification. For vast distances he proposed a relay system with men stationed between pipes, receiving and passing along messages; in this way, a message could travel 300 leagues in an hour. Gauthey's subscription fell short of what was required, and his methods remained untested in his lifetime. Two copies of his printed prospectus are among BF's pamphlets at the Hist. Soc. of Pa. His proposals are summarized in Chappe, *Histoire de la télégraphie,* pp. 66–71.

7. Jean-Nicolas Gardeur: XXVI, 198n.

From the Comte de Sarsfield AL: American Philosophical Society

Vendredi 14 mars 1783

Mr De Sarsfield a lhonneur de faire bien des Complimens a Monsieur franklin Et le prie d'avoir la bonté de luy envoyer la lettre de recommandation qu'il a eu celle de lui promettre En faveur De lady Juliana Penn dont un des fils va passer En pensilvanie.[8]

Addressed: hotel de sarsfield} a Monsieur / Monsieur franklin ministre / plenipotentiaire des Etats / unis d'Amerique / A Passy.

From Peter Boillat[9] *et al.* ALS: American Philosophical Society

St Malos the 15th March 1783

Very Honourable Dr Franklin, at the Court of France

I Peter Boillat, Represents to your excellency the Circumstance in which I find myself with four Other Americans, I was Capt and have Served with honour during the War, in the Service of Congress, where I have been Severely Wounded, I have Served ever with Zeal my Country, And took the Command of the Privateer Called the Lawrens of Twelve Guns, I was taken by a King's Sloop of War Called the Germaine,[1] on Our Coast of America, and was plundered entirely, plundered of all my Effects and put in Prison on board the Old Jersey, from whence I made my escape on board a french Transport which brought me to St Malos about Three Months and a half ago, without

8. For Lady Juliana Penn, her family, and her attempt to reclaim family property in Pennsylvania see XXXVIII, 343–4, 464n. Her son John arrived in Paris on Jan. 31 and went immediately to visit the American commissioners: Howard M. Jenkins, "The Family of William Penn," *PMHB*, XXI (1897), 424. BF recommended him to John Dickinson in a letter of March 23, below.

9. Boillat swore allegiance to the state of South Carolina on or before May 16, 1778: Robert B. Simons, comp., "Regimental Book of Captain James Bentham, 1778–1780," *S.C. Hist. Mag.*, LIII (1952), 104.

1. Probably the armed ship *Germaine*, purchased in 1779 and taken by the French in 1781: David Lyon, *The Sailing Navy List: All the Ships of the Royal Navy Built, Purchased and Captured, 1688–1860* (London, 1993), p. 231.

money or Cloathing, here I found a poor Irish man married in
the Country who Gave me Boarding and lodging to this day,
without finding a passage to return home, with four American
Seamen which are here in the same Situation with me, One of
which was Severely Wounded By a musket Ball in his Right
Legg. I hope that your Excellency would be so kind as Allow us
Forty Guineas to pay Our Debts and for Cloathing.

We pray your Excellency also, would send us an Order to be
recieved on board the Ship Pacifique, which is bound to Boston,
to put in at Cadis.[2] We will ever Owe to your Excellency the
most Sensible Acknowledgements, for having deliver'd us from
the Distress which the fortune of War has brought us to

PETER BOILLAT.
JOHN RUSSELL
LEVY SMITH
SAMUEL NAP
NATHANIEL TRUNDY

Very Honourable Dr Franklin

Notation: Boillat 15 March 1783

From William Carmichael

ALS: Library of Congress

Dear Sir   Madrid 15 March 1783

I had the honor to receive, altho Somewhat Late the Communications you made to me of the Treaty signed the 30th of
Novr. with G. Britain.[3] Your Letter remained more than three
weeks in the hands of this Ministry, If I may be Allowed to Judge
from its Date & Delivery. I am Infinitely sensible for the Communication which you did me the honor to make of this Important event & the more so as I had a right to expect it from
Others who have not given me the least Information on the Subject— I should have answered your Letters Immediately If I

2. In the margin Boillat added, "The Ship Pacifique will sail the latter end
of this Month."
3. Not found. On Feb. 4 Carmichael wrote WTF to thank him for sending
news of the preliminary agreement (APS).

could have made return adequate to the Communication which You did me the honor to make me; But our Affairs here were for so long a time in such an uncertain Situation that I dared not venture to predict their Issue & at all Events I expected to receive advice & not to be Obliged to demand it— The Marquis de la Fayette will have informed you of the Situation of affairs here—[4] I did not write your Excy by him, because I was convinced that he could give you much better Information vivâ voce, than I could do by Letter— I wished to have sent by him an Acct of Money Transactions here, I reserve it for the Ct. D Estaing.[5] I hope you will find that it will be satisfactory— I have recd Letters from Mr Livingston Informing me that he had remitted Bills for my Salary for one half year & That these Bills were sent to your Excy;[6] I have drawn in that Interval for near a years Salary, but still the Public is in arrears to me.[7] I hoped that Mr Jay would have settled his Accts with your Excy & in that case you would have seen that there was still a considerable defect in my favor— By the next post I shall have the honor to transmit my public & private Accts— The Sums due here are not considerable & that Circumstance renders their payment the more necessary to establish our credit on a permanent footing— The Baron Le Fort[8] will have the honor to present to your Excy this Letter. It

4. Lafayette arrived in Paris on March 12: *Gaᶎ. de Leyde*, March 21. While in Spain he had gone to Madrid to advise Carmichael and urged the Spanish court to cultivate friendship with America: Idzerda, *Lafayette Papers*, v, 86, 94, 106.

5. The French contingent of d'Estaing's fleet at Cadiz departed for Brest and Toulon in mid-March and arrived in the two harbors on March 31 and in early April, respectively: *Courier de l'Europe*, XIII (1783), 249; Idzerda, *Lafayette Papers*, v, 433. According to Carmichael, d'Estaing was still in Spain in early April, so he apparently traveled to France on his own: Carmichael to WTF, April 10, 1783 (APS).

6. Livingston to Carmichael, July 6 and Sept. 12, 1782: Wharton, *Diplomatic Correspondence*, v, 597–8, 725–6.

7. Account XXVII (XXXII, 4) shows that Grand paid in January Carmichael's bills of Sept. 23 and Oct. 1, 1782. They totalled just over half his annual salary of £1,000 sterling (XXX, 543), approximately 24,000 *l.t.*

8. Probably Frédéric-Antoine-Henry (Henri), baron Le Fort (1754–1792), who served as a French army captain during the sieges of Minorca and Gibraltar: Six, *Dictionnaire biographique;* Albert de Montet, *Dictionnaire biographique des Genevois et des Vaudois . . .* (2 vols., Lausanne, 1877–78).

was a request on his part that I could not refuse when Seconded by his Uncle the Baron de Falkenhain[9] who commanded the French troops at Minorca & Gibraltar. I am Obliged to write This Letter with much precipitation, & I have neither the head or hand so much at my disposition as I could wish when I have the honor to Address one whose good opinion I have so much at heart. I pray your Exy to think well of me untill at least you have convincing proofs to the Contrary. Your long Silence & your last Laconic Letter[1] gave me the bile for a much longer Time than I Dare to tell you. My heart has always loved and honored you & I hope that you will respect its feelings, altho you may have little regard for the head which is not in the Case to follow as it ought to do, its Impulse— On Monday or Thursday I shall have the honor to write to your Exy such sentiments as I expect will be inspected by this Court— I hope Mr Jay will soon decide what he means to do, for until I know his decision I shal not act in one manner or another.

I have the honor to be with great respect Your Excys. Most Obliged & Humble Sert   Wm. Carmichael

His Excy. Benjamin Franklin—

From Jean-François Joly de Fleury de La Valette

LS: American Philosophical Society

Paris le 15. Mars 1783.

J'ai reçu, Monsieur, la lettre que Votre Excellence m'a fait l'honneur de m'écrire le 9. de ce mois[2] avec l'état des Lettres de change tirées de l'Inde et de l'Amérique, pour le service de la Marine qui appartiennent aux Américains et dont le paiement est reculé d'une année, en vertu de l'arrêt du Conseil du Roi du 26. fevrier

---

9. Charles-Gustave de Falkenhayn (b. 1724), an Alsatian who commanded the eight French battalions that helped the Spanish army capture Minorca in 1781: *DBF*.

1. Missing.

2. BF's letter (missing) forwarded one from JW; see JW to BF, March 5, for the background to this response.

dernier.[3] S'il étoit possible de faire une seule exception aux dispositions de ces arrêts, ce seroit certainement en faveur des américains; mais elle tireroit à de trop grandes conséquences, pour écouter le desir que j'aurois de vous satisfaire à cet égard. Soyéz, je vous prie, Monsieur, persuadé de tout mon regret. Au surplus Votre Excellence doit remarquer que la condition des intérêts à 5% payés pour l'année de retard, et l'attention qu'on a eue de ne point dénaturer le titre, lui conserveront nécessairement Son activité et sa valeur, toutes les fois que, dans ce moment-ci, l'on ne précipitera pas la négociation. J'ajoute à cette observation l'assurance positive que ces lettres de change Seront exactement payées à l'échéance déterminée par l'arrêt du Conseil.

J'ai l'honneur d'être avec un Sincère attachement Monsieur, Votre très-humble et trés-obéissant Serviteur. JOLY DE FLEURY

M Francklin.

Notation: Joly de Fleury, Paris 15 Mars 1783.

From Benjamin Vaughan ALS: American Philosophical Society

My dearest sir, London, March 15, 1783.

A very respectable planter of Antigua writes to desire of Mr Manning, "as a particular favor, that he would procure for his son a letter to Dr Franklin, as he is desirous he should know one of the first characters this age has produced."

The young gentleman, Mr Mackinnen, who presents you with

3. Joly de Fleury, the author of the *arrêt du conseil,* misremembered its date, which was Feb. 23. The king's approval of the *arrêt* was a humiliating defeat for Castries, who was responsible for the French colonies. At the same time Louis also promoted Vergennes, another rival of Castries (see the annotation of the contract signed by Vergennes and BF on Feb. 25, above). In revenge against Joly de Fleury, Castries refused to cooperate with him, prompting Joly's resignation on March 29: Munro Price, *Preserving the Monarchy: the Comte de Vergennes, 1774–1787* (Cambridge, New York, and Oakleigh, Australia, 1995), pp. 73–84; John Hardman, *French Politics, 1774–1789: from the Accession of Louis XVI to the Fall of the Bastille* (London and New York, 1995), pp. 64–6; *Courier de l'Europe,* XIII (1783), 146, 217.

this letter is the person alluded to,[4] and though he is unfortunate enough to be obliged to travel for his health, I conceive that he will find some alleviation in having had the pleasure of being introduced to you in the course of his journey. I have not the pleasure of knowing Mr Mackinnen Junr:, but I believe that I need not use many words to induce you to shew civilities to a connection for which my father in law, Mr Manning, expresses his esteem & his wishes to be useful.

I am, my dearest sir, with the deepest respect, your ever devoted, grateful, and affectionate, BENJN: VAUGHAN

Antoine Court de Gébelin to the American Philosophical Society: Extract[5]

Extracted from ALS: American Philosophical Society

Au musée de Paris Rue Dauphine[6] 15e. Mars 1783
Le 6. de ce mois, notre Societé litteraire connue sous le nom de *Musée de Paris* a donnè une brillante fete pour la paix: le Dr Franklin l'honora de sa presence: il y avoit l'élite des Academies,

4. William Mackinnen, Jr. (1760–1794), was the son of William Mackinnen (1732–1809), a member of the Antiguan Council: Vere Langford Oliver, *The History of the Island of Antigua: One of the Leeward Caribees in the West Indies, from the First Settlement in 1635 to the Present Time* (3 vols., London, 1894–99), II, 226, 228–9. He sent this letter to Passy on April 9; see his letter of that date.

5. This letter, addressed to the secretary of "la Societé Litteraire des Etats-Unis," begins by recalling an earlier letter (which he fears may have been lost) thanking the Society for making him a member. Now that the peace is declared, he writes again giving news of his Musée de Paris, proposing that the two societies form an affiliation, and announcing that his two-year term as president is over (he is now Inspector General). He also promises to send volumes of his *Monde Primitif* by various messengers, including BF. The letter was read at the Sept. 26 meeting of the APS: *Early Proceedings of the American Philosophical Society . . . from the manuscript minutes of its meetings from 1744 to 1838* (Philadelphia, 1884), p. 118. We excerpt here the paragraph describing BF's attendance at a Musée celebration.

6. The Musée had recently moved to new quarters. The elaborate inaugural session on Nov. 21, 1782, is described in Bachaumont, *Mémoires secrets*, XXI, 203, 219–21.

des Ambassadeurs, de Paris: 400. Dames plus brillantes les unes que les autres: les lectures en vers & en prose commencerent un peu après 5 heur. Le Concert entre 7. & 8. L'Orchestre etoit superieurement composè. Sur les 10h. & demi, on porta la Santé des Etats-Unis & Celle de Votre Societè litteraire— M. le Dr Franklin y repondit d'une maniere qui excita la plus vive sensation.[7]

To Vergennes   LS:[8] Archives du Ministère des affaires étrangères

Sir,   Passy, March 16. 1783.

I received the Letter your Excellency did me the honour of writing to me respecting the Means of promoting the Commerce between France and America.[9] Not being myself well acquainted with the State of that Commerce, I have endeavoured by Conversation with some of our Merchants to obtain Information. They complain in general of the Embarrassments it suf-

7. According to the published accounts (which did not record BF's toast) this public meeting was the most solemn that the Musée had organized to date. It was a celebration of the peace and, consequently, of "la naissance de la nouvelle république des Etats-Unis" represented by BF. His entrance at five o'clock was greeted with sustained applause. After the many speeches and verses, a bust of BF by Houdon was unveiled to great acclaim; the resemblance, which the assembled were in a position to verify, was extraordinary. M. Vieilh read a verse composed for the bust. (This was undoubtedly the young Jacques-François-Marie Vieilh de Boisjolin: *Nouvelle biographie*.) The concert, which ended with a piece by Bach, was described as brilliant, and the ensuing supper was sponsored by Court de Gébelin. Then, in "un aimable délire," BF allowed himself to be crowned with laurel and myrtle: Bachaumont, *Mémoires secrets*, XXII, 134–5; *Mercure de France (Jour. politique de Bruxelles)* for March 22, 1783.

The bust of BF, assumed to be one of the plaster casts the sculptor distributed, has not been located. Houdon gave four of them to BF. WTF lent one to the Salon de la Correspondance in February, 1783, for their exhibition of famous men: Sellers, *Franklin in Portraiture*, pp. 306–9; Anne L. Poulet *et al.*, *Jean-Antoine Houdon: Sculptor of the Enlightenment* (Washington, D.C., Chicago, and London, 2003), p. 250.

8. In the hand of L'Air de Lamotte; BF added the last six words of the complimentary close.

9. Above, Feb. 27.

fers by the numerous internal Demands of Duties, Searches, &c. that it is subjected to in this Country. Whether these can be well removed, and the System changed, I will not presume to say. The inclosed Letters may however inform your Excellency of some of the Circumstances,[1] and probably Mr. Barclay, our Consul, may furnish others. In general I would only observe, that Commerce, consisting in a mutual Exchange of the Necessaries and Conveniences of Life, the more free and unrestrained it is, the more it flourishes; and the happier are all the Nations concerned in it.[2] Most of the Restraints put upon it in different Countries seem to have been the Projects of Particulars for their private Interest, under Pretence of pu[blic?] Good. Your Excellency has no doubt seen the Bill now under Consideration in the British Parliament respecting their Trade with America,[3] and will consider how far it may be practicable to give Facilities to the future Trade between America and your Sugar Islands, as well as with France, similar to those which seem now to be projected by England. I myself wish most earnestly that France may reap speedily those great Advantages from the American Commerce which She has so well merited by her generous Aids in freeing it from its former Monopoly; and every thing in my Power to promote that desired End may be depended on. With great Respect, I am, Sir, Your Excellency's most obedient and most humble Ser.   B FRANKLIN

M. le Comte de Vergennes.

Endorsed: M de R

1. BF enclosed JW's memoir of June, 1782 (XXXVII, 484–90), and the March 9 letter he had just received from Launey (above). Vergennes forwarded BF's letter and its enclosures to Joly de Fleury on March 23. Joly replied on March 25: he believed that most of the problems cited by JW would cease once the Americans received a free port; the one remaining issue would be how to collect and remit duties on tobacco. JW's suggestion that duties be collected according to the British system was unworkable in France, because of its size. Deciding on the free port should be a priority; Joly argued for anywhere but Bayonne: Joly de Fleury to Vergennes, March 25, 1783, AAE.

2. A view long held by BF; see, for example, XI, 182.

3. The American Intercourse Bill.

From William Bache[4] ALS: American Philosophical Society

Dear Grandpapa   Philadelphia March the 16 1783

I embrace this opportunity of letting you know that Papa is going to Passy to wait upon you home to Philadelphia;[5] My Sister is going to boarding School to Miss Beckwith; there is a refugee Rowgally[6] taken and brought in here. Bob[7] says he is very glad to hear that you are in A good State of health. There are two French Frigates going out to Fight two British ones.[8] I am going to latin School two morrow. I hope that Beny can read My letter. I See that he can write English, my Sister wants some Babys some Gloves & some Shoes & a little Sofa too for her & her Baby. Please to lett me know if Benny is well. My Sister Deborah speaks a little Bad English. I must not say Scotch for fear of affending Beny. She Calls baby barbie & many Comical words. My Mama has wrote you A letter, my Papa & mama received Bennys Pictures,[9] the People talk of Peace we had A dog named Juno but She is lost, Carlo is alive, but Pompy is Dead, we have A dog that is Juno's Sister her name is Fanny, She is Papa's favourite dog, that he takes ahunting with him. She is of the same breed as carlo, Betsy Louis Deborah & my Self are very well & they Send their love to you.

I am your most affectionate Grand Child   WILLIAM BACHE

Addressed: To / Benjamin / Franklin Esqr.

---

4. BF's nine-year-old grandson. This is his only extant letter. BF read it to SB's friend Dorcas Montgomery: Montgomery to SB, July 26, 1783 (APS).

5. RB had proposed this idea in his March 13 letter, above.

6. A row galley (*i.e.*, one propelled only by rowing).

7. RB's slave, whom BF, in his will, requested be manumitted: XXVII, 605n.

8. On March 16 the *Danaé* and *Gloire* descended the Delaware, planning to sail free of British ships and cruise off Bermuda. They encountered the *Triomphe*, another French ship, which sailed upriver with news that the preliminaries of peace had been signed: Amblard-Marie-Raymond-Amédée, vicomte de Noailles, *Marins et soldats français en Amérique pendant la guerre de l'indépendance des États-Unis (1778–1783)* (2nd ed., Paris, 1903), pp. 338–9.

9. BFB's drawings included a profile sketch of BF: XXXVIII, 186, 556.

To the Earl of Buchan

ALS: Yale University Library; press copy of ALS: Library of Congress; copy: Massachusetts Historical Society

My Lord,   Passy, March 17. 1783—

I received the Letter your Lordship did me the honour of writing to me the 18th past, and am oblig'd by your kind Congratulations on the Return of Peace, which I hope will be lasting.

With regard to the Terms on which Lands may be acquired in America, & the Manner of beginning new Settlements on them, I cannot give better Information than may be found in a Book lately printed at London, under some such Title as *Letters from a Pensilvanian Farmer,* by Hector St. John.[1] The only Encouragements we hold out to Strangers, are a good Climate, fertile Soil, wholesome Air, & Water, plenty of Provisions & Fuel, good Pay for Labour, kind Neighbours, good Laws, Liberty, & a hearty Welcome. The rest depends on a Man's own Industry & Virtue. Lands are cheap, but they must be bought. All Settlements are undertaken at private Expence: The Publick contributes nothing but Defence and Justice.— I should not however expect much Emigration from a Country so much drain'd of Men as yours must have been by the late War; since the more have left it, the more Room & the more Encouragement remains for those who staid at home. But this you can best judge of; and I have long observed of your People, that their Sobriety, Frugality, Industry & Honesty, seldom fail of Success in America, and of procuring them a good Establishment among us.

I do not recollect the Circumstance you are pleas'd to mention of my having sav'd a Citizen at St. Andrews, by giving a Turn to his Disorder; and I am curious to know what the Disorder was, and what the Advice I gave which prov'd so salutary.—[2]

1. St. John de Crèvecœur, *Letters from an American Farmer* (London, 1782).

2. On the copy at the Mass. Hist. Soc., an asterisk inserted here points to the following note, identified as being by the Earl of Buchan, which may have been excerpted from a now-missing reply: "It was a Fever in which Lord Buchan then Lord Cardross lay sick at St. Andrews, & the advice was to ab-

346

With great Regard I have the honour to be, My Lord, Your Lordship's most obedient & most humble Servant

B. FRANKLIN

Rt. honble Earl of Buchan

To William Jones   ALS: Yale University Library

Dear Friend,   Passy, March 17. 1783

I duly received your obliging Letter of Nov. 15:[3] You will have since learnt how much I was then and have been continually engag'd in public Affairs, and your Goodness will excuse my not having answered sooner. You announc'd your intended Marriage with my much respected Friend Miss Anna Maria, which I assure you gave me great Pleasure, as I cannot conceive a Match more likely to be happy, from the amiable Qualities each of you possess so plentifully. You mention its taking place as soon as a prudent Attention to worldly Interests would permit. I just now learn from Mr Hodgson, that you are appointed to an honourable & profitable Place in the Indies;[4] so I expect now soon to hear of the Wedding, and to receive the Profile.[5] With the good Bishop's Permission I will join my Blessing with his; adding my Wishes that you may return from that corrupting Country with a great deal of Money honestly acquir'd, and with full as much Virtue as you carry out with you.

---

stain from an immense Blister of Spanish flies which Dr. Thomas Simson, brother to the celebrated Mathematician at Glasgow, proposed according to the old System of the Æsculapian Man-killing Monarchs to lay upon the Back of the said Lord Cardross. This Dr. Franklin dissuaded his Father from permitting to be applied." A shorter version of this note appeared as a footnote when the present letter was published in the *Gent. Mag.*, LXIV (1794), 587. Dr. Simson, who was then Chandos professor of medicine and anatomy at the University of St. Andrews, had been one of the signers of BF's honorary doctorate from that university: VIII, 278, 280; *ODNB*.

3. XXXVIII, 310–12.

4. See Hodgson to BF, March 6.

5. See Jones's Nov. 15 letter cited above. He and Anna Maria Shipley were married on April 8: Garland Cannon, *The Life and Mind of Oriental Jones: Sir William Jones, the Father of Modern Linguistics* (Cambridge, New York, and Port Chester, N.Y., 1990), p. 193.

The Engraving of my Medal, which you know was projected before the Peace, is but just finished. None are yet struck in hard Metal, but will be in a few Days: In the mean time having this good Opportunity by Mr Penn,[6] I send you one of the *Epreuves.* You will see that I have profited of some of your Ideas, and adopted the Mottos you were so kind as to furnish.[7]

I am at present quite recover'd from my late Illness, and flatter my self that I may in the ensuing Summer be able to undertake the Trip to England, for the Pleasure of seeing once more my dear Friends there, among whom the Bishop & his Family stand foremost in my Estimation & Affection.

I thank you much for your good Wishes respecting me. Mine for your Welfare & Prosperity are not less earnest and sincere; being with great Truth, Dear Sir, Your affectionate Friend & most obedient Servant.   B FRANKLIN

Please to present my Respects to the Club.[8] I always remember with Pleasure the agreable Hours I had the Happiness of Spending with them.—

W Jones, Esqr

Notations in different hands: From Benj. Franklin / Franklin March 1783

To Jonathan Shipley

ALS: Yale University Library; copy: Library of Congress

Passy, March 17. 83.

I received with great Pleasure my dear & respected Friend's Letter of the 5th Instt. as it inform'd me of the Welfare of a Family I so much esteem & love.

The Clamor against the Peace in your Parliament would

6. John Penn; see his letter of March 24.
7. For the mottos see the annotation of Brongniart to BF, Jan. 23.
8. The Club of Thirteen: XXXV, 46n; Verner W. Crane, "The Club of Honest Whigs: Friends of Science and Liberty," *W&MQ*, 3rd ser., XXIII (1966), 223n.

alarm me for its Duration, if I were not of Opinion with you, that the Attack is rather against the Minister. I am confident none of the Opposition would have made a better Peace for England if they had been in his Place; at least I am sure that Lord Stormont, who seems loudest in Railing at it, is not the Man that could have mended it.[9] My Reasons I will give you when I shall have what I hope to have, the great Happiness of seeing you once more, and conversing with you. They talk much of there being no Reciprocity in our Treaty: They think nothing then of our passing over in Silence the Atrocities committed by their Troops, and demanding no Satisfaction for their wanton Burnings & Devastations of our fair Towns and Countries.[1] They have heretofore confest the War to be unjust, and nothing is plainer in Reasoning than that the Mischiefs done in an unjust War should be repaired. Can Englishmen be so partial to themselves, as to imagine they have a right to plunder & destroy as much as they please, and then without satisfying for the Injuries they have done, to have Peace on equal Terms? We were favourable, & did not demand what Justice entitled us to. We shall probably be blam'd for it by our Constituents: And I still think it would be the Interest of England voluntarily to offer Reparation of those Injuries, & effect it as much as may be in her Power. But this is an Interest she will never see.—

Let us now forgive and forget. Let each Country seek its Advancement in its own internal Advantages of Arts & Agriculture, not in retarding or preventing the Prosperity of the other. America will, with God's Blessing, become a great & happy Country; and England, if she has at length gain'd Wisdom, will have gain'd something more valuable, & more essential to her Prosperity, than all she has lost; and will still be a great and respectable Nation.— Her great Disease at present is the Number

9. David Murray, Viscount Stormont, was the British minister to the French court during BF's first year in Paris, and subsequently became secretary of state for the northern department: XXXVI, 260n. On Feb. 17 he spoke at length against the American treaty in the House of Lords: Cobbett, *Parliamentary History*, XXIII, 396–402.

1. During the final discussions before the preliminary peace agreement, BF raised the issue of British atrocities in response to the British negotiators having proposed American compensation for the Loyalists: XXXVIII, 375–7.

& enormous Salaries & Emoluments of Office.[2] Avarice & Ambition are strong Passions, and separately act with great Force on the human Mind; but when both are united and may be gratified in the same Object, their Violence is almost irresistable, and they hurry Men headlong into Factions and Contentions destructive of all good Government. As long therefore as these great Emoluments subsist, your Parliament will be a stormy Sea, and your public Counsels confounded by private Interests. But it requires much Public Spirit and Virtue to abolish them! more perhaps than can now be found in a Nation so long corrupted.

Please to present my affectionate Respects to Mrs Shipley and all my young Friends, whom I long to see once more before I die. I hope soon to congratulate you on the Marriages that I hear are in Contemplation.[3] Every thing interests me that regards the Happiness of your Family; being ever, with the sincerest Esteem & Affection, My dear Sir, Your most obedient & most humble Servant   B FRANKLIN

Lord Bp. of St. Asaph

From the Chevalier Du Bouchet[4]

AL: American Philosophical Society

paris. March. 17th. 1783.

Colonel DuBouchet, Deputy adjutant General to the french army in america, has the honor to present his Best Respects to his excellency doctor franklin. He is Very sorry to have Been hindered By Business to Wait upon his excellency, and to Give him the agreable information of the perfect state of health of all

2. A point BF had made earlier: XXXV, 499–500; XXXVIII, 597n. The British government had been criticized in similar terms for more than half a century: Bernard Bailyn, *The Ideological Origins of the American Revolution* (Cambridge, Mass., 1967), pp. 48–50.

3. In the letter immediately above BF congratulated William Jones on his engagement to Bishop Shipley's daughter Anna Maria. Jones's letter to him had also announced the engagement of Anna Maria's sister Georgiana: XXXVIII, 310–12.

4. For whom see XXVI, 609n.

his relations and friends in philadelphia; he Left them the 3d. of january Last; and Was desired By Mrs. Beach to assure him, that she and her husband and family Were Very Well at that time— Colonel duBouchet Would Be extreamly happy to Know, When he could (Without disturbance) Wait upon his Excellency, and introduce to him, Major General Beville quarter-Master-General of the army, one of his friends—[5] The colonel is in hopes that his excellency has not forgot, that he is the Lt. colonel of the american Rifflemen, Who, on his Return to france after the surrender of Burgoigne, had the honour to see him at passy, he is Very Confident that he Will not experience his politeness Less, after the taken of a second British army, having had the Good Luck to Be also at yorktown, under the Command of count Rochambeau—[6] His excellency is desired to send the colonel an answer. Gel. Beville and himself Being Waiting for.[7]

5. Pierre-François "de" Béville (b. 1721), Rochambeau's *maréchal général des logis*, was promoted to *maréchal de camp* on Dec. 5, 1781. He returned to France with Rochambeau aboard the frigate *Emeraude*, arriving at St. Nazaire on Feb. 10: Bodinier, *Dictionnaire;* Rice and Brown, eds., *Rochambeau's Army*, I, 84n.

6. Du Bouchet distinguished himself in both battles. He served as a rifleman under Daniel Morgan and was breveted major for gallantry in action. He later was an *aide major-général* on Rochambeau's staff: Morris Bishop, "A French Volunteer," *American Heritage*, XVII, no. 5 (August, 1966), 104–7; Rice and Brown, eds., *Rochambeau's Army*, I, 266n, 337. BF later presented Du Bouchet with a silver *Libertas Americana* medal, complimenting him on being the only Frenchman to have fought at both the Battles of Saratoga and Yorktown: Denis-Jean-Florimond Langlois de Mautheville, chevalier du Bouchet, "Journal d'un emigré" (MS; 3 vols., Cornell University Library), I, 245–9.

7. We have no record of an answer. His last extant communication was a letter to WTF dated only "Vendredi, au Soir," probably written at the end of July: he had been out of town for a long while, had been promoted to lt. col. in the French army, and now sought BF's certification of the accuracy of a French translation of testimonials written on his behalf by Congress, Gen. Gates, and Gen. Washington. Du Bouchet evidently dropped off the translation on Aug. 1 (what appears to be a cover sheet is dated "Monday 6 o'clock"), and BF signed an attestation written by L'Air de Lamotte on Aug. 6, 1783. (These three documents are at the APS.) Du Bouchet's promotion came on June 13; for his subsequent career see Bodinier, *Dictionnaire*, under Langlois; Samuel F. Scott, *From Yorktown to Valmy: the Transformation of the French Army in an Age of Revolution* (Niwot, Colo., 1998), p. 157.

hôtel du parc Royal. Rüe Du colombier. f. B. st. Germain.

his excellency doctor francklin.

Addressed: a son excellence / Monsieur Le Docteur franklin. / Ministre plenipotentiaire Des / etats unis De L'amerique. / à passy.

Notation: Du Bouchet Paris March 17th. 1783

From Henry Laurens

LS: Library of Congress; copy: South Carolina Historical Society

Sir,   London 17th March 1783.

I beg leave to refer to my letter of the 6th Instant by the hands of Mr. Storer—to speak in the current stile, Government is still a float. In the moment when it was thought an Administration would be formed, the prospects of the Coalition have been dashed—[8] The K. it seems has been the stipulator, insisted upon keeping the Lord Chancellor and introducing Lord Stormont and His M. immediately went out of Town.[9] The Duke of Portland will not submit to recieve materials into the foundation which may endanger the Fabric. On one side Chagrin on the other Sneering, is visible, on our part We keep Lent, I cannot hide from myself the mortification which I suffer. Not a step taken towards a Definitive Treaty and establishing the important " *Then*"— The Bill of which I sent my Colleagues a Copy by Mr. Storer is annihilated and another, called an Amendment, introduced. A Copy of this for their use, You will recieve under the present Cover, You will read my idea of its merit in three words interlined in the Title. I am persuaded it will be torn to pieces to day—[1] I hold the language steadily. "Make what Acts you please

8. The coalition of the Duke of Portland, Lord North, and Charles James Fox; see the headnote to William Hodgson to BF, Feb. 25.

9. Lord Chancellor Thurlow and Viscount Stormont refused to join a new government under the king's stipulation that the ministry be headed by North rather than Portland: Alan Valentine, *Lord North* (2 vols., Norman, Okla., 1967), II, 360–1; Fortescue, *Correspondence of George Third*, VI, 280.

1. The enclosure is missing. The American Intercourse Bill was "mauled

for opening Commerce, however suitable to the purposes of Great Britain or speciously conducive to the mutual interests of Great Britain and the United States, I think there cannot be, I hope there will not be, an intercourse permitted on our part until a Definitive Treaty is concluded and the British troops completely withdrawn from our Territories."

I lately saw in a Morning Chronicle a Publication of Mr Adams's first Commission for making a Treaty of Commerce with Great Britain and of the revocation of that Commission,[2] I know but of one Man in this Kingdom capable of giving such intelligence, I wish he may not be possessed of more important Documents. Shall I request you Sir to inform me if it be not improper, whether there is at this time a subsisting Commission for entering into such a Treaty.

Mr. Redford[3] the Gentleman who will do me the honor of presenting this Letter will also deliver you "A State of Facts" a Recriminatory Libel calculated for shewing there are other bad Men besides the Hero of "The Defence of the Earl of Shelburne"—[4] Be it among you blind harpers. My Daughter has reproached me for having omitted in my last her best respects to Doctor Franklin and hearty thanks for his very polite attention to her while she was at Paris. The young Lady and her Brother[5] join in the most respectful salutes to yourself & Mr Franklin with Sir Your obliged & Most Obedient servant   HENRY LAURENS,

P.S. I have packed up a few of the latest News papers and put them into the hands of Mr. Redford for your use.

---

beyond recognition" at the committee stage. Opponents like William Eden attacked it as a threat to the Navigation Acts, British security, and the sovereignty of the state: Harlow, *Second British Empire*, I, 451–8.

2. The March 11 issue of the *Morning Chronicle, and London Advertiser* printed JA's commission to negotiate a commercial treaty with Great Britain and its July 12, 1781, revocation (*JCC*, XV, 1117; XX, 746).

3. Archibald Redford, whom Richard Price introduced in a letter of March 10, above.

4. *A State of Facts: or a Sketch of the Character and Political Conduct of the Right Hon. Charles Fox* (London, 1783) was written to counter [Dennis O'Bryen], *A Defence of the Right Honorable the Earl of Shelburne, from the Reproaches of His Numerous Enemies* (London, 1782).

5. Martha and Henry, Jr.

His Excellency Benjamin Franklin Esquire. at Paris.

Endorsed: Mr Laurens March 17. 1783

From Louis-Marie Marion de La Brillantais[6]

ʟs: American Philosophical Society

Monseigneur.   St. Malo. Le 17 Mars 1783.

Nous avons l'honneur de vous remettre Ci-jointe une requête qu'adressent à votre excellence d'infortunés Americains,[7] victimes de la guerre. Leur objet est de repasser dans leur patrie Sur le Navire Le Pacifique que nous venons d'armer dans Notre port, pour l'amérique Septentrionale. Nous Sommes bien fachés que leurs blessures et le Complettement de Notre équipage ne nous permettent pas de les Employer dans le voyage pour Leur procurer gratuitement Le passage; L'humanité nous ferait un devoir de donner à ces infortunés la Consolation de revoir leur païs. Malheureusement nous sommes forcés de ne les prendre que comme passagers; nous en faisons l'offre à Votre excellence et la prions de nous honorer d'une prompte réponse, parceque le Navire est prêt à faire voile.

Nous Sommes avec respect Monseigneur Vos très Humbles Et très obéissants serviteurs

MARION DE BRILLANTAIS MARION FRERES

a Son Excellence Le Très honorable Dr. Franklin Ministre des Etats-unis de L'amérique

---

6. Writing, as he says, on behalf of Marion frères, a firm that probably descended from the one founded in the seventeenth century by André Marion, sieur du Fresne: André Lespagnol, *Messieurs de Saint-Malo: une élite négociante au temps de Louis XIV* (2 vols., Rennes, 1997), ɪɪ, 856. This brother (b. 1743) was an architect as well as a merchant, and a member of the Saint-Malo masonic lodge La Triple Essence: Le Bihan, *Francs-maçons parisiens*, p. 341.

7. From Peter Boillat *et al.*, March 15, above.

From Antoine-Alexis-François Cadet de Vaux

ALS: American Philosophical Society

Monsieur,   ce 19 Mars 1783

J'ai passé hier trois heures avec M. Robillard, chevalier de l'ordre du Roi, chirurgien majeur de l'armée francaise en Amérique.[8] Il a Vu votre hémisphere en homme Instruit et me parait avoir rapporté de ce pays là des observations faites pour intéresser le lègislateur du nouveau monde. J'ai présumé que vous le Verriés utilement et Je lui ai proposé de le conduire chès vous, monsieur, un jour de la Semaine prochaine que vous voudriés bien m'Indiquer. M. Robillard a Surtout porte Ses remarques Sur la constitution physique et Sur les choses qui, dans certaines provinces de l'Ameriquè contribuent à l'altérer.

Vous vous doutés bien, Monsieur, que M. Parmentier et moi avons du l'Interroger Sur l'Etat de la boulangerie et nous avons appris, avec quelqu'Etonnement, que les americains en Etaient encore pour la majeure partie au pain azyme. Cet objet Etant digne de Votre attention, Je vous demande la permission d'en conférer avec vous, conjointement avec M. Parmentier, que J'aurai l'honneur de vous prèsenter, le Jour que J'accompagnerai M. Robillard. Le comité de l'Ecole de Boulangerie[9] pourrait entretenir une correspondance avec la Société de Philadelphie Sur les objets d'œconomie Rurale; trop heureux Si ces marques de mon Zele vous Sont agréables.

---

8. Fiacre Robillard (b. 1733), who had been *chirurgien major* at the military hospital at Metz, served as chief surgeon with Rochambeau's army in America. He was made a chevalier of the *ordre de Saint-Michel* and awarded a pension in consideration of his services in America; the University of Pa. awarded him an honorary degree: Marquis de Chastellux, *Travels in North America in the Years 1780, 1781 and 1782*, ed. and trans. Howard C. Rice, Jr. (2 vols., Chapel Hill, N.C., 1963), I, 310; II, 613; Rice and Brown, eds., *Rochambeau's Army*, I, 317; Maurice Bouvet, *Le Service de santé français pendant la guerre d'indépendance des Etats-Unis, 1777–1782* (Paris, 1933), pp. 103, 109.

9. Parmentier and Cadet de Vaux had opened the school two years before: XXXII, 482–3.

Je Suis avec un respect profond Monsieur, Votre très humble et très obéissant Serviteur

CADET DE VAUX
Censeur Royal, Rue des Gravilliers

Notation: Cadet de Vaux Paris 19 Mars 1783

From Sir Edward Newenham

ALS: Historical Society of Pennsylvania

Dear Sir   Leghorn 19 March 1783—
Now that the long wished-for point is finaly Obtained by the Spirit of the United States, in whose cause I have always been warm & never varied, I must Again in the most EARNEST MANNER press your Excellency to *have* Mr John Christopher Hornbostel appointed Consul for those states at Marsailles;[1] he justly merits it to my own Knowledge and I think I have some Claim for that favor, for I never Changed in all the Vicissitudes of the Affairs of that now happy Continent—
I hoped for the Honor of a Letter in Answer to my former ones,[2] but flatter myself that, the Answer to this, will be his Appointment; for which I shall return my personal & Gratefull thanks before I leave the Continent—
At present I shall not presume to take up your time with a long Letter, but request you & your Son will accept of the Sincerest Respects of Lady Newenham, my Son & Daughter—
I have the Honor to be, Dear Sir, with Evry sentiment of respect your Excellencys most obliged & most obt: Humble Sert
EDWD NEWENHAM

PS— I shall remain here untill I receive the honor of yr Excellencys Answer Pray, is the Marquiss La Fayette in France?

---

1. Hornbostel (XXVI, 212) and Newenham had made this request three times: XXXVIII, 306–7.
2. XXXVIII, 187–8, 301–2, 302–4, 306–7.

From Patience Wright   ALS: American Philosophical Society

Ever honred Sir   Merch 19th 1783
    With the pleasing prospect of peace I Expected To See you
arive in London with Public Entry and all my Romantick Ideas
fullfilld this Winter.— But to My Mortification another Year
longer before Bag and Bagage is Exported to *Hannover*—[3] We
are Framing *parliment* Laws for traid and other Delays To Fill
up the History of this Kings Reign— The honour the American
heros have Compleated by this peace, has given me new Spirits
health, and Money is to Come of Course: and I now no longer
the old Mad Woman but Madam Wright or "the Ingenous Mrs
Wright from America who told us TRUTH"— Now I have a feild
for my Politicall genis Joynd with My Wax Work which will do
me Some Credit if I Keep Within proper bounds— Experienc
that Exelent School Master has taught me to folow Reason and
let the World do as they please— I dont give up My hope of Seeing You in London in a very Short time— This day a Comitte
of Membrs of Parlmt Intend Calling out for Comitte of Safty—
which if it takes Place it will astonish the Junto,[4] and Restore the
lost honour of that house— May you live to Enjoy all the Blessing of health peace and Liberty is the hearty prayr of Dear Sir
your faithfull Friend   P. WRIGHT

Mrs Stephensons Death together with My Son Jos Wrights being Cast away on bord the Ship Argo Nere Boston from Nantz
& The Cold Winter—old age and Some other things has Save'd
you Meny a long letter but as my philosophy, my health; All
Joyne in the grand object of hapiness I am determand to Write
to Doctr Franklin and Enjoy the pleasing hope that he is not unwilling (at Sometimes) to See a letter from Mrs Wright

    I Wrote to M: Wm Franklin and Infirmd him that govonor
Franklin was Rathr unwell but now he is Recoverd and is
apointed by his Contrymen to assist in application in their behalf
&ce he lodges in Suffolk Street a few doars from me I Calld on
him but have not Seen him

3. For this and other matters see her earlier letter, Feb. 22.
4. Either the coalition ministry or, in particular, Fox, North, and their supporters.

Addressed: Exclncy Doctr B. Franklin Esqr / a Passy / prés Paris

Notation: Wright 19 Mars 1783.

To Henry Laurens

ALS: Princeton University Library

Sir, Passy, March 20. 1783

I received your Favour of the 6th Instant, with a Copy of the Bill for the provisional Establishment of Commerce, & Mr Day's Tract. I am much oblig'd by your kind Attention in sending them.

I am glad you happen to be on the Spot to say what ought to be said respecting the pretended Loyalists. Setting them in their true Light must be of great Service. The World had never seen a more universally Loyal People than the Americans who were *forc'd* by the mad Measures of the Ministry to take up Arms in Defence of their Rights. They did it with Reluctance. They were truly Loyalists. Very few if any of these Pretenders had any such Principle, or any Principle but that of taking care of themselves by securing Safety with a Chance of Emolument & Plunder. They fancied the King's Side would prove the strongest. Could they have foreseen our Success, they would never have oppos'd us, nor would England have been dunn'd with their Claims of Recompense for their Loyalty!

The Bill for establishing Commerce, is, I hear, to be new modeled: I shall be glad to be inform'd of the Alterations as soon as possible. I do not like the Delay of the definitive Treaty by the Detention so long of Mr Oswald, nor the Delay of Evacuating New York. If these Delays are lengthen'd much more, I shall suspect an Intention of renewing the Quarrel. I hope you will not fail to come with Mr Oswald if he returns hither, or with whoever shall come in his Place.

Mr Adams has communicated nothing to me on the Subject of the anonymous Letters. I hear frequently of his Ravings against M de Vergennes & me whom he suspects of Plots against him which have no Existence but in his own troubled Imagination. I take no Notice, & we are civil when we meet. In removing my

Papers I have found a second of those Letters with the Bruxelles Mark also, but dated at Ghent 8 May 1782.[5]

There is now a Talk of employing the Mediators[6] at the definitive Treaty. I do not know why nor what they are to mediate the important Points being settled.

We have no News here yet of the Reception of the Preliminaries in America; nor any Letters later than the Beginning of January.

The Court of Spain has agreed to the Boundaries, or at least express'd its Acquiesience in those establish'd by England & America:[7] so that we shall be free from the Difficulty expected from that Quarter.

My Grandson is sensible of the Honour done him by your kind Remembrance, and presents his respectful Compliments with mine. We join also in Compliments to your amiable Son and Daughter.

With sincere Esteem and Affection, I am, Sir, Your most obedient & most humble Servant   B FRANKLIN

Notation: B. Franklin 20th March 1783 Reced. 31st. Ansd 4th April.

From John Bourne   ALS: Historical Society of Pennsylvania

Sir   March 20th. 1783
    Indulge me with this and I shall trouble no more.[8]
    Establish no priest craft in the Land. Curtail the power of Ex-

---

5. XXXVII, 289–91. For the first anonymous letter see XXXVI, 499–501.

6. The Austrians and Russians: XXXIV, 350n.

7. As Floridablanca had informed Lafayette: Idzerda, *Lafayette Papers*, V, 101–7; *Laurens Papers*, XVI, 168n.

8. He was as good as his word. He did, however, send communications to JA and Laurens, and in May asked Patience Wright to forward his opinions to Congress. He claimed to be of noble birth: Bourne to Congress, May 10, 1783; Patience Wright to the Pa. Delegates, May 29, 1783 (both at the National Archives); Charles Coleman Sellers, *Patience Wright: American Artist and Spy in George III's London* (Middletown, Conn., 1976), p. 216.

ecutors viz a person Dies posess'd of Effects, left in the hands of Executors; let there be two Courts, an upper and a lower the lower Court to take Cognozience, & the Will to be Register'd, the Executor with an examiner to give in a just Acct, upon Oath, and upon Confiscation of Effects (Death) with satisfaction if the Executor is posess'd of so much, the lower Court to be Accountable to the upper any One belonging to either Court committing any defraud, severe punishment & penalty, and excluded from ever holding a place under Goverrment the expences to be settld by Goverment according to value.

Suppose America a Commonwealth suffer no Candidate to solicit Votes under great penalties, or any one for him, the Candidates may send their names to a Committey appointed for that purpose, printed Copies sent to every Province, the Voters to signe their names, every Man to have equal Vote, the time of Voteing limited when fill'd up, that sent to the Committey to publish the choice of the greatest number of Voters, the Candidite to have nothing to do in it or be present at any time of meeting or any one for him, (to be chosen annually).

I beg Sir you will please to excuse the rudeness, it's only from that sincere wish for the welfare of that dear Country where I shou'd be happy to spend my days and I hope that Almighty hand that brot you thro', will direct your Councils and that you may be all directed to believe that; that Almighty Power Governs the Universe, and that he may power his choisest blessing on you and make you a happy People is the desire of Sir your most Obedient and humble Servant   JNO BOURNE

From Luigi Pio[9]

AL: American Philosophical Society

Ce 20. mars 1783. Hôtel Montmorency
chaussée d'Antin. /.

Mr. de Pio a L'honneur de renouveller Les assurances de son respect à Monsieur Franklin, Ministre Plenipotentiaire des Etatsunis de l'amerique Septentrionale, et de lui dire, qu'il tient à sa

9. The chargé d'affaires of the Kingdom of the Two Sicilies: xxxviii, 38n.

disposition douze Exemplaires de l'ouvrage de Mr. le chevr. Filangieri de Naples, qui a pour titre "Science de La Legislation"[1] Mr. de Pio attend les ordres de Mr. Franklin pour les lui faire tenir de la façon qu'il jugera convenable.

Mr. de Pio ose demander à Mr. Franklin, si la nouvelle Medaille qu'il vient de faire frapper ici pour sa République[2] est deja achevée et si Mr. de Pio seroit assez heureux pour pouvoir en avoir une.

Notation: Pio 20 Mars 1783 A Paris

To Richard Bache[3]   LS: Robert J. Walker III, Jupiter, Florida (1969)

Dear Son,   Passy, 21. Mar. 1783.

The Bearer Mr John Darby, of excellent Character & Connections in England, and in very capital Business, goes over with a View of Visiting America; & may perhaps finally settle there.— I beg you will do every thing in you Power to render his stay as agreable as possible, by shewing him every Civility and Attention and by affording him your Counsels if he should stand in need of them. In doing of which, you'll oblige much Your ever affectionate Father.   B FRANKLIN

R. Bache Esqr.

Addressed: R. Bache Esqr / merchant / at Philadelphia

1. See XXXVIII, 37–9, 317–18, 571–3.
2. The *Libertas Americana* medal.
3. Written at the request of Benjamin Vaughan; see Vaughan to BF, Feb. 25.

To Benjamin Vaughan

Reprinted from William Temple Franklin, ed., *Memoirs of the Life and Writings of Benjamin Franklin* . . . (3 vols., 4to, London, 1817-18), II, 227-8.

Dear Sir,   Passy, March 1784 [*i.e., c.* March 21, 1783][4]

You mention that I may now see verified all you said about binding down England to so hard a peace. I suppose you do not mean by the American treaty; for we were exceeding favourable in not insisting on the reparations so justly due for the wanton burnings of our fine towns and devastations of our plantations in a war now universally allowed to have been originally unjust. I may add that you will also see verified all I said about the article respecting the royalists,[5] that it will occasion more mischief than it was intended to remedy, and that it would have been better to have omitted all mention of them. England might have rewarded them according to their merits at no very great expence. After the harms they had done to us, it was imprudent to insist on our doing them good.

I am sorry for the overturn you mention of those beneficial systems of commerce that would have been exemplary to mankind. The making England entirely a free port would have been the wisest step ever taken for its advantage.

I wish much to see what you say a respectable friend of mine has undertaken to write respecting the peace. It is a pity it has been delayed. If it had appeared earlier it might have prevented much mischief, by securing our friends in their situations; for we know not who will succeed them, nor what credit they will hold.

---

4. The year assigned by WTF is obviously an error, as the present letter is a response to Vaughan's of Feb. 25, above. The enclosures mentioned in the last paragraph were most likely the recommendations Vaughan requested for Grigby and Darby. The latter, written to RB, is immediately above. The former is unlocated, but BF wrote David Hartley on March 23 that he sent it to Vaughan "the other day." Vaughan forwarded either the original of the present letter or a copy to Shelburne on March 30; a typescript of his covering letter is at the APS.

5. Article 5 of the preliminary articles (XXXVIII, 385-6), a compromise that followed weeks of dispute. For the earlier proposals and debate see XXXVIII, 324, 370n, 375-7.

By my doubts of the propriety of my going soon to London, I meant no reflection on my friends or yours. If I had any call there besides the pleasure of seeing those I love, I should have no doubts. If I live to arrive there I shall certainly embrace your kind invitation, and take up my abode with you. Make my compliments and respects acceptable to Mrs. Vaughan.

I know not what foundation there can be for saying that I abuse England as much as before the peace. I am not apt, I think, to be abusive: of the two I had rather be abused.

Inclosed are the letters you desire. I wish to hear from you more frequently, and to have through you such new pamphlets as you may think worth my reading. I am ever, my dear friend, yours most affectionately, B. FRANKLIN.

Franklin's Answers to Five Questions about Trade[6]

Retranslation: reprinted from Nina N. Bashkina *et al.*, eds., *The United States and Russia: the Beginning of Relations, 1765–1815* ([Washington, D.C., 1980]), p. 179.[7]

[on or before March 21, 1783]

Question 1: Are all the nations of Europe, including those of the North, allowed to trade freely and safely with the United States of North America, to land on their coast, to frequent their ports, harbors, etc.?

Answer: Yes.

Question 2: Is the importation of certain goods prohibited or forbidden? And what are these prohibited goods?

Answer: All kinds of English goods.[8]

---

6. On March 21, 1783, Prince Ivan Bariatinskii, the Russian minister at the French court, sent to Empress Catherine II a copy (entirely in French) of these questions and BF's answers, explaining that the queries were posed to BF by a fellow minister and that BF "made replies in his own hand": Nina N. Bashkina *et al.*, eds., *The United States and Russia: the Beginning of Relations, 1765–1815* ([Washington, D.C., 1980]), p. 179n.

7. Translated from the French copy, described above, at the Arkhiv vneshnei politiki Rossii, Moscow. We assume that BF penned his remarks in English on the now-missing original.

8. See BF to Hodgson, March 9.

Question 3: Are foreign vessels allowed to carry all American products, or are some goods excepted?

Answer: There are no exceptions.

Question 4: Is there an already-established and well-known tariff? What are the import and export duties imposed on ships and their cargo? Are all nations in this matter treated equally or do some particular nations enjoy certain exceptions or privileges?

Answer: There are no such duties. Nations are all treated equally, except for the English, who will not be able to come into the ports of the United States until Congress has revoked certain prohibitory measures.

And finally, question 5: What are the most wanted goods in North America, and in what port can they best be sold?

Answer: Everything relating to men's and women's clothing. In Philadelphia or in Boston.

From James Moylan

ALS: American Philosophical Society

Honor'd Sir   L'Orient 21st. March 1783

Your Dispatches for the Ministers of Foreign affairs & Finances have come safe to my hands,[1] and agreeable to your directions I have deliver'd them to the Captain of the Frigate bound to America,[2] who promised to take particular care of them.

With the utmost respect I have the honor to be Honor'd Sir Your most obedt. & most hle Servt   JAMES MOYLAN

---

1. Doubtless those of March 7, above.

2. Probably the *Active*, which arrived at Chester, Pa., before the end of April. She was the last French frigate to reach the Delaware before the evacuation of French forces: Amblard-Marie-Raymond-Amédée, vicomte de Noailles, *Marins et soldats français en Amérique pendant la guerre de l'indépendance des Etats-Unis (1778–1783)* (2nd ed., Paris, 1903), p. 339. For her captain, Edouard-Charles-Victurnien Colbert, comte de Maulevrier (1758–1820), a nephew of d'Estaing, see the *DBF*, under Colbert; Rice and Brown, eds., *Rochambeau's Army*, I, 294.

The Honble B. Franklin Esqr. Minister plenepotentiary of the united States of America &ce. &ce.—

Addressed: A Monsieur / Monsieur Franklin / Ministre plainé-potentiaire des / Etats Unis de l'Amerique / a Passy / près Paris

Notation: J. Moylan 21 March 1783

From Patience Wright   ALS: American Philosophical Society

Honoured Sir   London March 21th 1783
  By the Desire of Some of the honest membrs in Parliment this Inclosd proposals for a very useful paper (which is much wanted at this time)—the news papers are So undr the Direction of the Party of george—that no truth Comes out to inform the People—the people grone undr the tyrant and by assistance from America will through Such useful papers open the way to truth— Mr Martain Mr Evins and Councellor Lafft[3] with othrs have Set forward This Weekly paper and by *Franks* and by *Friends* it will find its way through all Ranks of men— Major Labilliere Still is on his Hunt after the Enemis of truth as a Christian Solder he Sends his love and Enjoys the prospect when you arive— Inclosd is a note I wrote to you[4] per a friend who delayd his going— The Barer Young MccKenning is to Set out tomorrow only waits Ld Surrys Motion in the house Lords Respecting Chussing a Minister.[5]
  I am now in Fashon several noblemen this day Calld at my

3. James Martin, who represented Tewkesbury in the House of Commons, was an opponent of the Fox-North coalition: Namier and Brooke, *House of Commons,* III, 113–14. Thomas Evans was a bookseller and publisher, while Capel Lofft was a writer and founding member of the Society for Constitutional Information: *ODNB.*
  4. Above, March 19.
  5. The bearer was William Mackinnen, Jr., whom Benjamin Vaughan had introduced to BF in a letter of March 15, above. Charles Howard, Earl of Surrey (for whom see Samuel Vaughan, Jr.,'s Feb. 14 letter), seconded a motion in the House of Commons on March 24 to send an address to the king requesting a new administration: Namier and Brooke, *House of Commons,* II, 645; Cobbett, *Parliamentary History,* XXIII, 686–7.

house and I find a total *Eclieptes* or darkness has Sezd on Pharoh—[6]

Pray help the Industorous honest hearted week English— Pity the people and Send this Rebel to Power over to Some Place where his Mischevous Consort or Party can no longer destroy the peace and Hapiness of Mankind—

The Honourabl Part the french Court has acted and the Light from America has now opend the Eyes of England—they only want your help to Set wisdom at Work—which will bring Peace and hapyness to us again— I beg you for god's Sake for the Sake of Reason Concience Honour and the good of all Men write to the Membrs Parliment or City Membrs Direct them to actt Honest to the Articles of Peace. My daughter[7] Joynes me in most Respectful Complnts to your grand Son Wm Franklin to Madam Elvisious and others Who Know my princepls I am Dear Sir your most faithful friend and very humble svt

PATIENCE WRIGHT

great talk of a Comitte of Safty &c. the men who is talkd of are Sir Cecil Wray Mr Martin Mr Powis Mr Eliott or Eliss[8] 5 in Numbr if No Choice this day is Made by the King the People PROCEED—

All your old friends in England Rejoyce in the hope of Seeing you once more amongst them and thousands Famalys Ready to Set out for America applications are making Evry day for Passages or Information Concerning the Voyge and for owners of Land and the meckanicks traids men merchts all Sorts openly declare England is Ruind they will go to Americca—this is thought one of the Reasons Why No minister and So long as no Ministers no Emigrations to America &cc Kings Politicks—

6. George III.
7. Probably Phoebe Wright Hoppner, with whom she was living.
8. Sir Cecil Wray, James Martin (above), Thomas Powys, Edward Eliot, and Welbore Ellis (XIII, 145n) were members of the House of Commons: Namier and Brooke, *House of Commons*, II, 390, 397–400; III, 113–14, 320–2, 663–5.

Addressed: For / His Exelency / B. Franklin Esqr / Paris

Notation: Wright 21 Mars 1783

From Vergennes: Three Letters

(I) LS: American Philosophical Society; draft: Archives du Ministère des affaires étrangères; (II) LS: Library of Congress; draft: Archives du Ministère des affaires étrangères; (III) draft: Archives du Ministère des affaires étrangères

I.

à Versles. le 22. Mars 1783.

J'ai l'honneur de vous envoÿer, Monsieur, Copie de la réponse que j'ai reçue de Mr. le Mis. [Marquis] de Castries relativemt. à la Saisie faite sur les déniers provenants de l'armemt. de la frégate Américaine l'*Alliance.*[9] Cette réponse du Ministre de la Marine ne vous laissera, Monsieur rien à désirer sur les ordres qui ont été donnés pour redresser le procédé irrégulier qui a fait le Sujet de vos plaintes.

J'ai l'honneur d'être très sincérement, Monsieur votre très humble et très obéissant Serviteur./.   DE VERGENNES

M. franklin./.

II.

à Versles. le 22. Mars 1783.

J'ai l'honneur, Monsieur, de vous envoyer copie d'une lettre que j'ai reçüe de Mr. le Mis. de Ségur et de l'état qui y est joint d'effets d'artillerie appartenants au Roi, qui Sont restés à Baltimore.[1]

9. See BF to Vergennes, March 9, where Vergennes' letter to Castries is described. Castries' answer, dated March 14 (filed with the present letter), said that he had informed Forster frères of the impropriety of their actions and ordered them to lift the attachment immediately. The firm complied, but lodged an appeal in April: Barclay to Vergennes, April 11, 1783, AAE.

1. Both enclosures are at the Library of Congress. Minister of War Ségur's letter, dated March 3, says that Castries has informed him that several of the ships dispatched to bring back Rochambeau's troops and stores are out of service. Because the artillery stores are the heaviest items, Castries suggests

Vous verrés, Monsieur, par la lettre de ce Ministre qu'il propose aux Etats Unis d'en faire l'acquisition conformémt. aux différens prix indiqués sur chacun des articles dont il s'agit. Je vous prie de me faire connoître ce que vous pensez de cette proposition, et de me mettre, le plustôt qu'il vous Sera possible, en état de répondre à Mr. le Mis. de Segur.

J'ai l'honneur d'être Très Sincérement, Monsieur votre très humble et très obéissant Serviteur./. De Vergennes

M. franklin.

III.

A Versles. le 22. Mars 1783.

M. le Cte. de Mercy m'a adressé, M. les pieces que j'ai l'honneur de vous envoyer ci joint en original. Elles concernent la proprieté du navire Den Eersten et de Sa cargaison dont le Corsaire Americain Le Darby S'est emparé.[2] Je vous prie, M. de vouloir bien examiner ces pieces, et Si elles ne vous laissent aucun doute Sur la legitimité de la reclamation dont il S'agit, je Suis bien persuadé que vous ne differerez pas a me mettre à portée de faire une reponse Satisfaisante à M. le Cte. de Mercy.

M. franklin

---

that they be sold to the United States. The inventory of artillery supplies at Baltimore lists cannon balls, shells, and other items by number, weight, and value, totalling just over 425,836 *l.t.* This idea was not adopted. Most of the soldiers and equipment sailed in May, and when the last French ship departed Baltimore in October, some supplies were left with the chevalier Charles-François d'Annemours, the resident French consul, to sell: Rice and Brown, eds., *Rochambeau's Army*, II, 181; Amblard-Marie-Raymond-Amédée, vicomte de Noailles, *Marins et soldats français en Amérique pendant la guerre de l'indépendance des Etats-Unis (1778–1783)* (2nd ed., Paris, 1903), pp. 339–41.

2. The now-missing enclosures from Mercy-Argenteau, the Austrian and Imperial ambassador (XXXV, 549n), apparently dealt with the same subject as a memoir sent to BF by Vergennes on Jan. 18, 1782 (XXXVI, 446–7): the capture of the ship *Den Eersten* from Ostend (in the Austrian Netherlands) by the privateer *Hope,* Capt. Daniel Darby.

To John Dickinson

LS:[3] Historical Society of Pennsylvania; copy and press copy of LS: Library of Congress

Sir,   Passy, March 23d. 1783.

Permit me to congratulate your Excellency on your Advancement to the Presidency of Pennsylvania,[4] wherein I hope you may find Opportunities of doing much good to your Country, the only Consideration that can make an elevated Situation agreable to a reasonable Mind.

Mr Penn, Son of our late Proprietary, purposes going over shortly, and will do me the honour of delivering this Line to you.[5] He appears to me, in the short Acquaintance I have had with him, to be an amiable young Gentleman of a promising valuable Character, and if any Recommendations of mine to your Civilities and Friendship could be thought necessary, he should have them fully. But I confine myself here to what regards the Family in general. They think the late Act of Assembly respecting their Lands has done them great Injustice. Not being in the Country when it was made, and being unacquainted with the Reasonings upon which it was founded, I have been only able to say, that I did not believe any Injustice was intended, and that the offer'd Compensation had been supposed an equitable one. I have not heard that the Family was considered as delinquent in the Affair of the Revolution: but as I find it is imagined that some Suspicions of their being unfavourable to it have perhaps prejudiced the Assembly against them, and that the Warmth of the Times has produced a harder Treatment of their Interests than would otherwise have been thought of, I would beg leave to mention it to your Excellency's Consideration, whether it would not be reputable for the Province in the cooler Season of Peace,

---

3. In WTF's hand, except for the portion of the complimentary close after "Excellency's," which is in BF's hand.

4. On Nov. 7, 1782, Dickinson, a conservative in Pa. politics, was elected president of the Pa. Supreme Executive Council: Robert L. Brunhouse, *The Counter-Revolution in Pennsylvania, 1776–1790* (Harrisburg, 1942), p. 123.

5. Sarsfield reminded BF of his promise to write this recommendation on March 14, above. John Jay had already written Dickinson and Robert Morris on Penn's behalf: Morris, *Jay: Peace*, pp. 497–8; *Morris Papers*, VII, 548–9.

to reconsider that Act, and if the Allowance made to the Family should be found inadequate, to regulate it according to Equity: Since it becomes a Virgin State,[6] to be particularly careful of its Reputation and to guard itself not only against committing Injustice, but against even the Suspicion of it.

With great Esteem & Respect I have the honour to be, Sir, Your Excellency's most obedient & most humble Servant

B FRANKLIN

His Excellency John Dickenson Esqr, President of the State of Pennsylvania.

To David Hartley

Reprinted from William Temple Franklin, ed., *Memoirs of the Life and Writings of Benjamin Franklin* . . . (3 vols., 4to, London, 1817–18), II, 428.

Dear Sir,   Passy, March 23, 1783.

I received the letter you did me the honour of writing to me requesting a recommendation to America of Mr. Joshua Grigby.[7] I have accordingly written one; and having an opportunity the other day, I sent it under cover to Mr. Benjamin Vaughan.[8] The general proclamations you wished for, suspending or rather putting an end to hostilities, are now published;[9] so that your "heart is at rest," and mine with it. You may depend on my joining my hearty endeavours with yours, in "cultivating conciliatory principles between our two countries," and I may venture to assure you, that if your bill for a provisional establishment of the commerce had passed as at first proposed,[1] a stipulation on our part in the definitive treaty to allow reciprocal and equal advantages and privileges to your subjects, would have

6. A favorite way of his of referring to the United States; see, for example, XXIII, 511.

7. On Feb. 4, above.

8. [*C.* March 21], above.

9. By the American peace commissioners themselves; see their declaration of Feb. 20.

1. *I.e.*, the ill-fated American Intercourse Bill.

been readily agreed to. With great and sincere esteem, I am ever, &c.   B. FRANKLIN.

To Benjamin Vaughan   ALS: American Philosophical Society

My dear Friend,   Passy, March 23. 1783.

I wrote to you a few Days since by Mr Williams,[2] but I omitted some Newspapers which I had intended to send by him: I now inclose them. They contain sundry Articles relating to the Barbarities exercis'd by the British in America; and as you had borrow'd of me a Paper containing an Account of those committed by Lord Cornwallis, and thought there might be some Use in showing it in England, I send you these for the same Purpose. Perhaps it would not be amiss to publish them, that considering such Provocations, some Value may be set upon our Moderation, in not demanding Reparation for the wanton Devastations made of our fine Towns and Plantations, & that thence it may appear that there is more Reciprocity in our Treaty than our Enemies have been pleas'd to find in it. I thank you much for the Castor Oil, but wish to learn from you the Use & Virtues of it, & the Quantity & manner of taking the Doses. Please to present my Respects to your good Father, and acquaint him that a Letter which your Brother mentions to me, never came to hand. I am ever, my dear Friend, Yours most affectionately

                                                                                    B FRANKLIN

B. Vaughan Esqr

Endorsed: Passy March 23. 1783

2. BF's letter of [*c.* March 21] was carried by Jonathan Williams, Sr.

From Charles-Louis-François Fossé[3]

ALS: American Philosophical Society

Monsieur!   à caën le 23. mars 1783.

J'ay prié Monsieur Déshoteux de Vous remettre un Exemplaire de Mon Essai Sur l'attaque et la deffense des petits postes. Ce n'est qu'après avoir Surmontée bien des dificultees que je suis parvenus à Former des artistes capables déxécuter ce genre de gravure utile aux militaires. Il procure plus de clartée dans les déscriptions, et létude en devient plus amusante aux jeunes officiers pour lesquels cet ouvrage est fait; c'est un chainon qui lie la petite et la grande tactique.[4]

Il peut Vous ressouvenir Monsieur que dans un Voyage que je Fis à paris il y à deux ans Vous eutes la complaisance de me déveloper le méchanisme de vos cheminées Economiques,[5] elles Seroient d'une grande utilitée en France, Si elles étoient faites par des ouvriers inteligents et conduites par des gens raisonnables, mais la plus part les gouvernent mal en y faisant trop de feu, Je m'en Suis bien trouvé.

Je Vous prie de recevoir mon Essai comme une reconnoissance que je Vous doit, Je me croirez heureux s'il peut meriter Votre suffrage, et s'il devient utile à Vos compatriotes.

---

3. Fossé (1734–1812) was an officer in the regiment d'Infanterie du Roi, who eventually rose to the rank of lieutenant-colonel (1793). In 1769 he was put in charge of the regiment's training school for officers, and he wrote several books intended as instruction manuals: *DBF*.

4. *Idées d'un militaire pour la disposition des troupes confiées aux jeunes officers dans la défense et l'attaque des petits postes*, printed by Didot l'aîné (Paris, 1783), was a treatise magnificently illustrated with color plans drawn by Fossé and engraved by Louis-Marin Bonnet, using his pioneering method of color aquatint and stipple engraving. The work was in two sections, both of which were keyed to the plates. The first was a manual on tactics, as the title suggests; the second was an equally detailed treatise on how to draw and color field maps. For Bonnet's description of his labor-intensive technique, which he invented in 1769, see Victor I. Carlson and John W. Ittmann, *Regency to Empire: French Printmaking, 1715–1814* (Minneapolis, 1984), pp. 194–6; see also Jane Turner, ed., *Dictionary of Art* (34 vols., New York, 1996); Jacques Hérold, comp., *Louis-Marin Bonnet (1736–1793): Catalogue de l'œuvre gravé* (Paris, 1935), pp. 14–28.

5. BF evidently also gave him an engraving of his stove: Fossé to BF, June 27, 1785 (Hist. Soc. of Pa.). For that engraving see XXVII, 507n.

Daignez agréer les sentimens respectueux avec lesqu'els J'ay lhonneur dêtre. Monsieur Votre très humble et très obeïssant Serviteur FOSSÉ

officier au regt. du Roy.

J'aurez l'honneur de Vous faire passer dans le courrant de mai, une feuille a la place de l'epitre et sur laquelle Sera les armes de Monsieur Le duc du chatellet, elle seront gravés aussi en couleurs.[6]

Il seroit bon de ne faire relier cet ouvrage qu'après lété parcqu'il pourroit maculer sous le marteau du relieur.

From Le Roy ALS: American Philosophical Society

ruë de Seine ce 23 Mars [1783]

Permettez vous Mon Illustre Docteur que Je profite de L Occasion du Voyage de Me. [Madame] Le Roy à Passy pour vous Solliciter de nouveau en faveur de la personne de Bayonne qui désire d'avoir l'honneur d'être Le Consul de Messieurs Les Amèricains dans cette Ville et dont j'ai eu Lhonneur de vous envoyer le mémoire qui m'a èté fortement recommandé comme Je vous l'ai marqué par un homme auquel Je suis fort attaché (M Le Comte d'Ornano).[7] J'aurois bien voulu pouvoir accompagner Me. Le Roy à Passy mais J'ai un malheureux engagement qui m'en empêche. Je ne vous dis rien pour M. Martin il aura un meilleur Avocat que moi auprès de Vous puisque Me. sa femme compte avoir lhonneur de vous voir avec Me. Le Roy avec un bon nombre d'exemplaires de son memoire Sur le Commerce d'importation et d'exportation du port de Sette, traduit en Anglois.[8] Je joins dans ce pacquet cette Lettre Mon Illustre Docteur

6. The volume was dedicated to the duc du Châtelet, colonel of the regiment (*Etat militaire* for 1783, p. 176). Bonnet engraved his arms, in color, above the text that Didot printed.

7. Le Roy's cover letter of March 9 and the memorial from Bérian frères of Bayonne are summarized in the headnote on consulship seekers, above, attached to the Jan. 28 letter from Pitot Duhellés.

8. The six-page memoir, one example of which has survived among BF's papers, is from C. Barthélemy Martin fils aîné, who had been applying for

que je vous Serai infiniment obligé Si vous voulez bien faire passer à Son adresse en Amèrique.

Jai eté dèsolé toute cette Semaine de n'avoir pu aller dejeuner avec vous comme je me le proposois mais Je compte que cellecy ne se passera pas de même.

Recevez Mon Illustre Docteur les sincères assurrances de tous les sentimens distingués d'attachement que Je vous ai vouès pour la Vie   LE ROY

PS Je vous porterai votre papier au premier Jour

Notation: Le Roy

From Jonathan Williams, Jr.

ALS: American Philosophical Society; copy: Yale University Library

Dear & Hond Sir.   Nantes March 23. 1783.

I recd your Favour of the 9 Inst[9] some days since, and beg your Pardon for the delay of my Answer which the hurry of Business has occasioned. I thank you for espousing my Cause with Mr de Fleury, but I find the minister will not grant the Exception requested.[1]

The packet[2] was sent by our admiralty without my knowledge, they never consult me on these occasions, but it is not just you should pay the Postage I will therefore give you credit for it

---

the consulship at Sète since February, 1782: XXXVI, 304. It is entitled "Memorial on the Trade of the Sea Port of Sette, in the Province of Languedoc." Hist. Soc. of Pa.

Another memoir from Martin, in French, three pages long, and dated only 1783 (APS), concerns aspects of the tobacco trade that ought to be addressed in a treaty of commerce. The importance of this trade to both countries underscores the need for Americans to have an agent familiar with the local laws and resources. Martin asks to be appointed consul at Sète to represent American commercial interests.

9. Missing. It was in response to JW's letter of March 5, and evidently informed JW that his letter to Joly de Fleury was being forwarded.

1. Joly de Fleury explained as much to BF in his letter of March 15, above.

2. Perhaps the proceedings of the admiralty forwarded by Perret on Feb. 14, above.

& charge the prizes.— The two Cheezes advised from Orleans are not from me unless sent a long time ago as I do not remember sending any lately. I sent to Orleans in January a variety of Articles as follow.[3]

J Jay		a pipe Madeira.	for Mr Jay.
MW		an Anchor do.	for Mrs Williams
BF	N 1.	a do of old jamaica Rum	for yourself.
do.	2	a Bl of Sugar	do.
do.	3	a Case of 80 Bottles of Porter.	do.
MM		a do.	Mrs Montgommery
MR		a do.	Mr Ridley
J Jay		a do.	Mr Jay.

It may be that two Cheezes were added & a note omitted to be taken, but I cannot at present tell. If you find them good the better way is to eat them & leave the matter to be settled when the Owner appears, as they may otherwise in the mean time be spoiled.

I thank you for your kind Attention to my Father & Mrs Williams and am as ever most dutifully & Affectionately Yours.

JONA WILLIAMS J

His Excellency Doctor Franklin.

Addressed: A Son Excellence / Mr Franklin / en son Hotel / a / Passy / pres Paris

Notation: Jona. Williams March 23. 1783.

From the Duc de La Rochefoucauld

AL: American Philosophical Society

Lundi matin [March 24, 1783]

Le Duc de la Rochefoucauld a l'honneur d'envoyer à Monsieur franklyn le projet de lettre convenue hier: peut être y manquera-

---

3. WTF had given JW this order in December. It was sent care of Fleury & Demadières in Orléans, who forwarded the items to Passy on Feb. 14: Gurdon Mumford to WTF, Dec. 17, 1782; JW to WTF, Jan. 21, 1783; Fleury & Demadières to WTF, Feb. 17, 1783 (all at the APS).

t-il quelquechose pour la forme, mais Monsieur franklyn la corrigera.[4] Il Sera bon qu'il la remette lui même demain à M. le Cte. de Vergennes, ou du moins qu'il lui en parle pour accélérer l'expedition.

Le Duc de la Rochefoucauld a l'honneur d'y joindre Sa recommandation pour la place de Consul des Etats-Unis à fecamp,[5] et de faire mille complimens à Monsieur franklyn

Notations in different hands: Le Duc de La Rochefoucauld. / Mar. 24. 1783

To Vergennes

LS:[6]Archives du Ministère des affaires étrangères; draft:[7] American Philosophical Society

Passy ce 24 mars 1783

Je desirerois, Monsieur le Comte, faire imprimer la Traduction du Livre des Constitutions des Etats-Unis de l'Amerique publié en 1781 à Philadephie par Ordre du Congrès Général;[8] plusieurs de ces Constitutions ont dèja paru dans le Journal des Affaires de l'Angleterre et de l'Amerique, d'autres ont déja paru ailleurs, mais il n'en existe pas encore de Traduction complette, celle dont

4. BF adopted the text as written; it is the letter to Vergennes, immediately below.

5. He must have enclosed the undated petition from Jacques-Laurent Berigny (Hist. Soc. of Pa.) requesting a consulship or vice-consulship in Fécamp. (A notation on that petition indicates that La Rochefoucauld recommended Berigny to BF on March 23.) Berigny's qualifications seem to be that his father, with whom he resides, is the principal merchant/outfitter of Fécamp, and the only merchant there with the resources to assist foreign ships. Berigny also points out that, having spent much of his youth in England, he has a great facility in English (though he writes this appeal in French). He offers to serve with zeal, and for the honor of being useful to his nation.

6. In the hand of L'Air de Lamotte.

7. Provided by La Rochefoucauld, under cover of the letter immediately above.

8. *The Constitutions of the Several Independent States of America . . .* (Philadelphia, 1781): XXXVIII, 216–17n.

j'ai l'honneur de parler à votre Excellence, qui formera un Volume in octavo, renferme les diverses Constitutions des Etats-Unis, leur Traité avec la France, et ne contient aucunes matieres étrangeres; J'ai pris pour cet objet des arrangemens avec le Sr. Pierres qui est prêt à commencer l'Impression, J'esper que Votre Excellence voudra bien donner son Agrément à cette Publication.[9]

Le Sr. Pierres a besoin d'une Permission de M. le Garde des Sceaux[1] pour imprimer et pour debiter ensuite cet Ouvrage, lorsqu'il m'aura livré le Nombre d'Exemplaires convenu; comme J'aurois lieu de souhaiter que cette Traduction pût paroître sous peu de tems, je serai très obligé à votre Excellence si elle veut bien engager M. le Garde de Sceaux à faire expedier promptement son ordre et même dans le Cas où les Formalités requises pour cette Expédition exigeroient un certain tems, de l'engager à autoriser par une Lettre le Sr. Pierre à commencer l'Impression.

9. In 1777, as various state constitutions were ratified and their texts became available in France, they were translated by La Rochefoucauld with BF's assistance and published in the *Affaires de l'Angleterre et de l'Amérique;* see XXIII, 480–1, and BF's correspondence with La Rochefoucauld in vols. 23–25. The first edition of all thirteen constitutions and other founding documents of the country, including the 1778 Franco-American treaties, was published by order of Congress in 1781; see above. By June of the following year, a London reprint of the Philadelphia edition was "printed for J. Stockdale in Picadilly and sold by J. Walker." (The editor's advertisement is dated June 15, 1782.) We have no record of when BF obtained one of these volumes, but La Rochefoucauld was translating the post-1777 constitutions by October, 1782: XXXVIII, 216–17. There is no reason to believe that BF did not review those translations, just as he had the earlier ones. The French edition printed by Pierres—*Constitutions des treize Etats-Unis de l'Amérique* (Paris, 1783)—would ultimately include the other founding documents published in the 1781 edition, the Dutch-American Treaty of Amity and Commerce of Oct. 8, 1782, and the Swedish-American Treaty of Amity and Commerce dated April 3 (published above under [March 5]). See also Gilbert Chinard, "Notes on the French Translations of the 'Form of Government or Constitutions of the Several United States' 1778 and 1783," APS *Yearbook* for 1943, pp. 97–106.

1. Armand-Thomas Hue de Miromesnil: XXXV, 258n; Michel Antoine, *Le Gouvernement et l'administration sous Louis XV: Dictionnaire biographique* (Paris, 1978), p. 130.

J'ai l'honneur d'être avec une respectueuse Consideration, de Votre Excellence, Le très humble et très obeissant Serviteur

B Franklin

[Son] Exce. le Comte de Vergennes.

Endorsements: Envoyé copie à M. le Garde des Sceaux le 30. Mars 1783. / M. franklin / M. de R [Rayneval]

From Herman Heyman's Sons

ls:[2] American Philosophical Society

Sir   Bremen the 24 March 1783

We are under great Obligation to your Excelency to honour us with an answer on our Letter by your Excelency much esteemed favor of the 10th Curt.,[3] by which we perceive with great Satisfaction that our new establishing House in Nord America may expect the best reception there, and that no Recommandation to the Government to Protect it, is necessary. We find us however much Obliged & indebted to your Excelency, for the Kindness you have for us, to favour us with two Letters of Introduction, one for Boston & the other for Philadelphia,[4] and we have no doubt or they will be of the greatest Influence & Assistance to our Mr A Delius; as our Vessell departed two Days before the Reception of yr Excelencys Esteemed Letter, we forwarded them by way of London, and Send Coppy by way of France & Hamburg and took the Liberty to address them to Rd Bache Esqr. at Philadelphia.

One of our Vessells Call'd Batavia, on which master John Huesman of 280 tuns, which lays now at Bordeaux is going for our account Empty to Charlestown, he takes ready money on board & has Orders to purchase a Cargo of Rice & to bring it to

2. In the hand of Heinrich Talla.

3. BF's now-missing response, drafted on their earlier letter of Feb. 17, was probably prompted by the March 6 reminder he received from Laval & Wilfelsheim.

4. To RB and Jonathan Williams, Sr.; see BF's note for a reply on the firm's Feb. 17 letter.

our Port; it will depart in about 3 Weeks time from Bordeaux; in case your Excelency should have any commands or some things to send along with it, you please to address such to Mess Boyer Metzler & Zimmerman,[5] & we have given to these Gent as likewise to our Captain by this Mail the Necessary Instructions, to be at your Excelencys Commands.

We wish nothing more then that yr Excelency would resolve to pay a Visit to this port; when we should endeavour to Convince you of the high Esteem which we bear for your Excelency, & to be of some service to you, if however you should find such likewise at any other occasions, we beg to command us freely, as we shall think us happy to be to some Use to your Excelency, and to give you a proof of our most Sincere Attatchment; with which we have the Honour to Remain & to Subscribe ourself with utmost Regard Sir Your most Obedt & humbl Servts.

HERMAN HEYMANS SONS

To His Excelency B Francklin Esqr.

From John Penn   AL: Historical Society of Pennsylvania

Hotel d'Espagne March 24th:— 83.
Mr. Penn presents his Compts: to Mr. Franklin & has sent his Servt: for the Letters He did Him the honor to promise him. He means to leave Paris as soon as the Bearer returns.—[6]

5. The firm of Pierre-Boyer-Metzler et Zimmermann was one of Bordeaux's eight biggest mercantile houses: Paul Butel, *Les Négociants bordelais: l'Europe et les Îles au XVIIIe siècle* (Paris, 1974), p. 287.
6. The letters included BF's recommendation of Penn to John Dickinson, March 23, above; as Penn was first traveling to England, he also carried BF's personal letters to friends there, including William Jones and Benjamin Vaughan. In June Penn sailed from Falmouth to New York. He resided in Philadelphia for five years but failed to win additional compensation for his family from the state government: Lorret Treese, *The Storm Gathering: the Penn Family and the American Revolution* (University Park, Pa., 1992), pp. 196–7.

Robert R. Livingston to the American Peace Commissioners

Two copies:[7] Massachusetts Historical Society; AL (draft): New York Public Library; transcript: National Archives

On the morning of March 12 Congress learned from the hand of Joshua Barney, captain of the packet *General Washington*, that the American peace commissioners had signed conditional preliminary articles with Great Britain on November 30, 1782. In addition to delivering the provisional peace agreement itself, Barney also presented Congress with a wealth of explanatory material from the commissioners including Franklin's letters of December 4, December 5[–14], and December 24[–25]; the commissioners' joint letter of December 14; and Franklin's journal of the peace negotiations.[8]

Congress' elation at the terms of the agreement was tempered, as Livingston writes here, by distress at learning that the commissioners had settled the agreement without consultation with the French, and that they had agreed to a secret and, in Congress' view, dangerous separate article concerning the boundary with West Florida that they had deliberately withheld from Vergennes.[9] The delegates spent the next two weeks vigorously debating whether the American commissioners had disobeyed their instructions, whether they ought to be censured, and what Congress should communicate to the French minister in Philadelphia. As James Madison wrote, "the dilemma to which Congress are reduced is infinitely perplexing." To collude in the secrecy

7. We print from the one in the hand of John Thaxter, Jr., and retained by JA. According to the transcript two versions of this letter were sent to France, one on the *Hope* and the other on the *General Washington*. We have silently corrected several minor copying errors, based on comparisons with the draft, transcript, and the other copy.

8. All the letters are published above; for the journal see XXXVII, 291–346. Barney also carried BF's letters to Robert Morris of Dec. 14 and 23; letters to Congress from the other peace commissioners; and journals kept by JA and Jay: William T. Hutchinson *et al.*, eds., *The Papers of James Madison*, First Series (17 vols., Chicago, London, and Charlottesville, 1962–91), VI, 330n; Butterfield, *John Adams Diary*, III, 41–3n. In addition, he transported 600,000 *l.t.* in specie from the French court. His voyage took nearly two months: XXXVIII, 56n.

9. The separate article (XXXVIII, 388), kept secret from France because of its alliance with Spain, granted more generous borders to West Florida if it were assigned to Britain at the general peace than if it were assigned to Spain; see below.

and risk, irreparably alienating France before that country had signed its own treaty with Britain, struck Congress as a grave issue of national security as well as a matter of national honor. Livingston submitted his views in a letter of March 18; Congress' debate over his recommendations dominated the session of Saturday, March 22. The following Monday, March 24, they received news that the Anglo-French preliminary treaty had been signed on January 20, thereby eliminating the conditional nature of the Anglo-American agreement. The debate over what to tell the American commissioners evaporated.[1] Livingston, eager to respond to the commissioners, wrote the present letter without Congress' agreement on what it should include, choosing instead to enclose evidence of the discussions.

One of James Madison's first reactions to the dispatches brought by Barney was admiration for Franklin. Writing to Edmund Randolph on March 12, Madison described the preliminary articles and then added: "Franklin's correspondence on this occasion denotes a vigor of intellect, which is astonishing at his age. A letter to the British Minister on the case of the Tories in particular is remarkable for strength of reasoning, of sentiment & of expression." (He was referring to Franklin's November 26, 1782, letter to Richard Oswald, which Jay had forwarded.)[2] Madison went on to describe Franklin's poignant request to be relieved of his duties, "being in his 78th year."[3] Randolph answered that Madison's letter was an antidote to one he had just received from Arthur Lee, criticizing Franklin for having kept Congress "utterly in the dark as to the progress of the negotiations at Paris," and insinuating that this would have grave consequences.[4] Madison replied: "The extract from [Lee]'s letter recited in yours astonished me more than it could do you, because I must be more sensible of its contrast to truth. High as my opinion of the object of it was, the judgment & acuteness & patriotism displayed in the last despatches from him, have really enhanced it. So far are they in particular from studiously leaving us in the dark, that some of them are of as late date as any, if not later than those from several & perhaps as voluminous as all the rest put together."[5]

1. For the Congressional debate and Madison's views see *JCC*, XXIV, 193–4; Hutchinson, *Papers of James Madison*, VI, 328–33, 351–2, 355–69, 375–8.
2. See XXXVIII, 350n.
3. Hutchinson, *Papers of James Madison*, VI, 340–1.
4. *Ibid.*, p. 380.
5. *Ibid.*, p. 430.

Gentlemen,   Philadelphia 25th. March 1783.

I am now to acknowledge the favor of your joint Letter by the Washington, together with a Copy of the preliminary Articles— Both were laid before Congress— The Articles have met their warmest approbation, and have been generally seen by the People in the most favorable point of view.

The steadiness manifested in not treating without an express acknowledgment of your Independence previous to a Treaty, is approved; and it is not doubted but it accelerated that declaration. The Boundaries are as extensive as we have a right to expect, and we have nothing to complain of with respect to the Fisheries— My Sentiments as to English Debts you have in a former Letter, no honest Man could wish to withhold them.[6] A little forbearance in British Creditors till People have recovered in part the losses sustained by the war will be necessary to render this Article palatable, and indeed to secure more effectually the Debt. The Article relative to the Loyalists[7] is not quite so accurately expressed as I could wish it to have been. What, for instance, is intended by *real British Subjects?* It is clear to me that it will operate nothing in their favor in any State in the Union; but as you made no secret of this to the British Commissioners, they will have nothing to charge you with, and indeed the whole Clause seems rather to have been inserted to appease the clamours of these poor Wretches, than to satisfy their wants. Britain would have discovered more candour & magnanimity in paying to them three months expence of the war establishment which would have been an ample compensation for all their losses, and left no germ of dissatisfaction to bud and blow, and ripen into discontents here—another Administration may think the noncompliance of the Legislatures with the Recommendations of Congress on this subject a sufficient cause for giving themselves and us new trouble—[8] You however were perfectly right in

6. XXXVIII, 554.

7. Article 5: XXXVIII, 385–6.

8. A prescient observation, as the British government used non-compliance as an excuse for not evacuating western posts within the boundaries of the United States: Charles R. Ritcheson, *Aftermath of Revolution: British Policy Toward the United States, 1783–1795* (Dallas, 1969), pp. 49–87.

agreeing to the Article—the folly was theirs, who did not either insist upon more, or give up this.

But, Gentlemen, tho' the issue of your Treaty has been successful, tho' I am satisfied that we are much indebted to your firmness and perseverance, to your accurate knowledge of our situation, and of our wants for this success; yet I feel no little pain at the distrust manifested in the management of it, particularly in signing the Treaty without communicating it to the Court of Versailles till after the Signature, and in concealing the seperate Article from it even when signed. I have examined with the most minute attention all the reasons assigned in your several Letters to justify these Suspicions. I confess they do not appear to strike me so forcibly as they have done you, and it gives me pain that the Character for Candour and Fidelity to its Engagements, which should always characterize a great People should have been impeached thereby. The concealment was in my opinion absolutely unnecessary. For had the Court of France disapproved the terms you had made after they had been agreed upon, they could not have acted so absurdly as to counteract you at that late day, and thereby put themselves in the power of an Enemy, who would certainly betray them, and perhaps justify you in making terms for yourselves.

The secret Article is no otherwise important, than as it carries in it the Seeds of Enmity to the Court of Spain, and shews a marked preference for an open Enemy.

It would in my opinion have been much better to have fixed on the same Boundaries for West Florida into whatever hands it fell without shewing any preference, or rendering concealment necessary—since all the Arguments in favor of the Cession to England would then have operated with equal force, and nothing have been lost by it, for there can be no doubt, that whether Florida shall at the close of the War be ceded to England or to Spain, it will be ceded as *it was held* by Britain.[9] The seperate Ar-

9. Great Britain was awarded East Florida and West Florida (formerly part of French Louisiana) by the Treaty of Paris of 1763. In 1764 the British raised the northern boundary of West Florida to include Natchez, thereby diminishing Georgia: Lawrence H. Gipson, *The British Empire Before the American Revolution* (15 vols., Caldwell, Idaho, and New York, 1936–70), IX,

ticle is not I suppose by this time a Secret in Europe, it can hardly be considered as such in America. The Treaty was sent out to the General with this Article annexed by Sir Guy Carleton, without the smallest injunction of Secrecy[1]—so that I dare say it has been pretty generally read at Head Quarters. Congress still conceal it here. I feel for the Embarrassment explanations on this subject must subject you to, when this Secret is known to your Allies.

I intended to have submitted this Letter to Congress, but I find that there is not the least prospect of obtaining any decision upon it in time to send by this conveyance, if at all. I leave you to collect their Sentiments as far as I know them from the following state of their proceedings. After your joint and seperate Letters, & the Journals had been submitted to them by me, and had been read, they were referred back to me to report, when I wrote them the inclosed Letter No. 1.— When the Letter was taken into consideration, the following Motions No. 2. 3. 4. were made and debated a whole day. After which the Letter and Motions were committed, and a Report brought in No. 5.[2] This was under con-

---

203. Spain captured West Florida between 1779 and 1781. The southern boundary of the United States established in Article 2 of the provisional treaty recognized the 1763 border of West Florida, but the separate article assigned the 1764 border in the event that Great Britain recovered West Florida in the negotiations with Spain: XXXVIII, 383–4, 388. The provisional British-Spanish treaty of Jan. 20, 1783, awarded both Floridas to Spain, but did not specify the borders: *Courier de l'Europe*, XIII (1783), 68. Spain claimed the full extent of the territory it occupied, *i.e.*, the 1764 border. See Samuel F. Bemis, *Pinckney's Treaty: a Study of America's Advantage from Europe's Distress, 1783–1800* (Baltimore, 1926), pp. 48–50.

1. As George Washington informed Congress on March 21, the British commanders in North America, Lt. Gen. Guy Carleton and Rear Adm. Robert Digby, sent him a copy of the treaty. Their covering letter was dated March 19: Fitzpatrick, *Writings of Washington*, XXVI, 249; K. G. Davies, ed., *Documents of the American Revolution, 1770–1783 (Colonial Office Series)* (21 vols., Shannon, Ire., 1972–81), XIX, 384.

2. The other copy includes a general list of these enclosures. Livingston's letter to the President of Congress was dated March 18 (Wharton, *Diplomatic Correspondence*, VI, 313–16). For the three motions, made the following day by Richard Peters, Hugh Williamson, and Alexander Hamilton, see *JCC*, XXIV, 193–4; Hutchinson, *Papers of James Madison*, VI, 359–62. The report of the committee appointed to consider all of the above, delivered on March 21, recommended that the commissioners be thanked, that they should

sideration two days, when the arrival of a Vessel from Cadiz with Letters from the Count d'Estaing & the Marquis de la Fayette, containing Accounts that preliminaries were signed, induced many Members to think it would be improper to proceed in the Report, and in that state it remains without any express decision. From this you will draw your own inferences. I make no Apology for the part I have taken in this business. I am satisfied you will readily acquit me for having discharged what I concieved my duty upon such a view of things as you presented to me. In declaring my Sentiments freely, I invite you to treat me with equal Candour in your Letters; and in sending original papers I guard against misrepresentations that might give you pain. Upon the whole I have the pleasure of assuring you, that the Services you have rendered your Country in bringing this business to a happy issue are very gratefully recieved by them, however we may differ in Sentiment about the mode of doing it. I am sorry that the extreme negligence of the different States has prevented, and will probably long prevent my being able to send you a State of the injury done to real property, and the Number of Slaves destroyed and carried off by the British Troops and their Allies—[3] Tho' no pains have been or shall be wanting on my part to urge them to it.

I have the honor to be, Gentlemen, with great Respect & Esteem, your most obedient hble Servant. ROBT. R. LIVINGSTON.

No. 1. 2plicate.

Honable John Adams, Benja. Franklin John Jay & Henry Laurens Esquires

Copy

Notation by John Adams: Mr Livingstone. 25. March 1783. to The Ministers for Peace.

---

communicate the secret article to the French court in a tactful manner, and that Livingston should inform them that Congress wished they had communicated the Preliminary Articles to France before signing. This was inconclusively debated on March 22: Hutchinson, *Papers of James Madison*, VI, 375–6, 378n.

3. Information that Congress directed Livingston to compile: XXXVIII, 102n.

From Caffiéri

ALS: American Philosophical Society

Monsieur   Paris ce 25 mars 1783

Je vien D'aprendre par Des vois indirect que Les Etats unis de L'amerique etoient dans Lintentions de faire Elevé une Statue a La Gloire Du Roy,[4] Si La chose est vraie, il Sauroit tres flateure pour moi D'Etres chargé de L'execution de Se monument. Je vous prie Monsieur Dans cette occasion et Dans touts autre de vouloire bien vous Resouvenire de moy et D'etre persuader de mon Zele et de ma Reconnoissance.

Jay Lhonneur D'etre avec Respect Monsieur Votre tres humble Et tres obeïssant Serviteur   CAFFIERI

---

4. This rumor was initially published in the *Courier de l'Europe* in mid-February; see the baron d'Haxthausen's letter of Feb. 26. A new report was published in that same paper on March 18, based on news from Paris dated March 4, linking the proposed statue with the *Libertas Americana* medal and quoting a 14-line Latin inscription which was said to have been selected for it. The inscription, given also in French translation, praised the Supreme Being for granting this hard-won liberty, extolled the generosity of Louis XVI, and offered the eternal gratitude of the United States: *Courier de l'Europe,* XIII (1783), 122, 170–1. On March 19 this story was reprinted, with slight variations, in both Métra's *Correspondance secrète* (XIV, 194) and in Bachaumont, *Mémoires secrets* (XXII, 155), the latter of which reproduced the Latin inscription.

This inscription was criticized in a letter, evidently sent to BF from Italy, that only survives in a curious, truncated copy in BF's hand. The author had read about the statue in a news story from Paris; he finds the inscription (which he quotes) "verbose, if not lapidary" and in poor Latin. BF's copy is in flawed Italian and trails off before the complimentary close and signature (APS). We speculate that it is an Italian exercise that BF created for himself, in preparation for his anticipated journey to Italy. He may have translated the now-missing original into English, and then produced this re-translation. The text is reprinted in Antonio Pace, *Benjamin Franklin and Italy* (Philadelphia, 1958), p. [367], and described on p. 9.

From the Marquis de Condorcet

ALS: Historical Society of Pennsylvania[5]

Mon cher et illustre Confrere,   A Paris ce 25 Mars 1783.
Permettez-moi de vous recommander Le mémoire que vous trouverez joint a cette Lettre. Il a pour objet une place de consul des treize états-unis pour le port de Cette. Je desirerais beaucoup obliger les négotians qui vous l'adressent et qui Sont d'anciens amis des américains.

Vous Connaissez, mon cher et illustre Confrere, ma veneration mon respect et mon tendre attachement,

LE MIS. DE CONDORCET

From Peter Paul von Giusti[6] ALS: American Philosophical Society

Monsieur   A Milan ce 25. Mars 1783.
L'heureux Accomplissement d'une Revolution interessante pour le Bien étre général des Nations, qui forme à coûp sûr L'Epoque plus remarquable du XVIIIme. siècle, et dont Vous avez jettè, Monsieur, les fondements immortels: suffiroient pour Vous attirer l'admiration et la réconnoissance des Peuples et des Philosophes. Mais Lorsqu'à de si puissants motifs se joint le titre d'un dévouement particulier, de la connoissance personnelle, et de plusieurs marques de bontè et d'Amitiè dont on a ètè honorè de Votre part, comme il m'est arrivè l'Ete de 1781. à Paris,[7] lorsque j'y ai passè de retour de ma Commission de Chargè d'Affaires de L'Empereur à la Cour d'Espagne; il est trés-naturel de s'interesser avec autant plus d'ènergie à ce grand Evenement, et de prendre une part plus intime à la gloire qui Vous en revient,

---

5. This letter is bound with an unrelated pamphlet, *Discours aux Américains*, which the Hist. Soc. of Pa. attributes to Condorcet.

6. A diplomat whom Carmichael and Jay had introduced to BF (XXXIV, 405–6, 547, 553, 564–5). For his career after returning to Italy see the *Dizionario biografico degli Italiani* (69 vols. to date, Rome, 1960–), under Luigi Giusti.

7. BF saw the baron often in 1781 and praised him to Carmichael: XXXV, 398, 485.

et qui garantit à Votre Nom une célebritè aussi solide qu'éter-
nelle. Agréez donc Monsieur mes compliments trés humbles à ce
sujet, et daignez me continuer les sentiments flatteurs dont Vous
m'avez honorè, en Vous persuadant, que rien ne sçauroit égaler
ceux du dévouement sans bornes et de la parfaite consideration,
avec laquelle je suis Monsieur Votre trés humble et trés-obéissant
Serviteur   LE B DE GIUSTI

Mr. de Franklin Ministre Plénipe. des Etats d'Amerque. à la Cour
de France

Notation: De Giust 27 May 1783.

From William Hodgson   ALS: American Philosophical Society

Dear sir   London 25 March 1783
    I reced your kind favor of the 9th & have to return you many
thanks for your advice relative to our Ship to which shall strictly
conform Mr Vaughan & myself think ourselves very particularly obliged for your Recommendatory Letter to Mr Livingstone— I sent you a copy of the first draft of the intended Bill
for opening a Trade to America,[8] I thought it wou'd have met
with little or no Opposition, I was grosly mistaken, we have no
Ministry & every man vents his Crudities relative to American
Commerce & wishes to be a Legislator, the Bill is no more what
it was, as to form & yet Substantially the main points remain, viz
the Americans to go freely to the Islands to carry their own produce, to bring every thing here, their own produce, to be entituled to all Bountys & Draw backs on goods outward, no Bounty
inward, upon any sort of goods is intended to be continued— In
short that with respect to the intermediate Trade in Europe, the
Americans to be upon the same Footing with other Powers, Our
Navigation act you know will not Suffer the Ship of any Country to bring into Gt Brittain other than goods the growth of the
Country to which the Vessell belongs, this Regulation I understand is meant to be adhered to. There never was a Time when
it wou'd be more usefull for you to favor me with your digested

8. On March 6, above.

plan & System for regulating the Commercial Intercourse betwixt the two Countrys, I cannot tell who will be Ministers there never was before such an Interregnum such a compleat Chaos in publick Affairs, I have done every thing in my power to adopt your Ideas relative to the Prisoners—those from Plymo. [Plymouth] were gone prior to the Reception of your Letter,[9] I waited upon the Duke of Portland to whom the premiership was generally given his Grace assured me of his readiness to do what you desired if it rested with him to advise—but assured me at the Same Time he was no Minister (this was Sunday)[1] I waited upon Ld. Shelburne, who said he had been very ill treated for his Liberality to America & he cou'd do nothing in the Affair—at the Same Time his Lordship said he considered Congress as having broken their faith in the last agreement which he had ordered to be made with me, for they had not returned a Single Man,[2] what excuses they set up he knew not but he said nothing in his Opinion coud justify such breach of faith— I waited upon the Commissioners of Sick & Hurt to know if they wou'd postpone the Embarkation of the Men from Forton untill the New Ministry were appointed they told me it was out of their power for they believed they were allready sailed, I hope you will believe I have done every thing in my Power to carry your Views into execution & am sorry I have not been more Succesfull—the House of Commons last night agreed to address his Majy to form an Administration—[3] as yet I do not know his Majestys Answer if I learn it before the Time for sending this to post I will acquaint you with it— Mr Justice Jones[4] has been knighted I am most truly Dr sr your most Obliged Friend & Hble Servant

WILLIAM HODGSON

9. They sailed for Morlaix on or about March 14, which was 11 days after the Admiralty issued orders for the immediate and complete exchange of all American prisoners in Great Britain: Sheldon S. Cohen, *Yankee Sailors in British Gaols: Prisoners of War at Forton and Mill, 1777–1783* (Newark, Del., and London, 1995), pp. 205–6.

1. March 23.

2. See XXXVIII, 441.

3. Cobbett, *Parliamentary History,* XXIII, 660–687; Fortescue, *Correspondence of George Third,* VI, 308–9.

4. William Jones.

I believe that young Mr Pitt has accepted the premiership,[5] C.F. [Charles Fox] Ld. Norths' Coalition therefore proves abortive

Addressed: To / His Excellency / Benj. Franklin Esqr

Endorsed: answerd

From John MacMahon ALS: American Philosophical Society

Dear and Honourable sir   March the 25th: 1783
    The Lady who intends to wait upon you with this letter is Daughter to an Irish Gentleman Sir Walter Rutledge, and married to a French Officer M. le Chevalier D'Herbigny.[6] She is related to Mr. Rutledge of America,[7] who was, I think and perhaps is still in Congress. She wants to obtain a favour that depends upon M. le Comte De Vergennes, and begged me to introduce her to you to obtain a recommendation to the Minister. If you can render her that good Office, as a Relation to a Member of Congress, it will be rendring an essential Service to a Lady of real merit, and a very great obligation conferred upon Dear and Honourable sir your most humble and obedient Servant

J. Mac Mahon
MD. P.

Addressed: To / The Honourable Dr Benjamin / Franklin Minister Plenipotentiary / to the united states of North America / at Passy

Notation: Mac Mahon 25 Mars 1783.

5. On March 25 Pitt again declined the king's offer: Fortescue, *Correspondence of George Third*, VI, 311.
6. Marie-Julie Rutledge d'Herbigny, whose March 26 letter is below, was the daughter of a Dunkirk merchant and banker. Her husband was Nicolas-Remi Favart d'Herbigny (Nicolas-Rémy de Favart), a captain and engineer in the French army who received the title Chevalier de Saint-Louis in 1781: *DBF*, under Favart d'Herbigny; Anne Blanchard, *Dictionnaire des ingénieurs militaires 1691–1791* (Montpellier, 1981), pp. 274–5; Richard Hayes, *Biographical Dictionary of Irishmen in France* (Dublin, 1949), pp. 280–1.
7. John Rutledge of South Carolina (XXVII, 67), who had been a member of the First and Second Continental Congresses and governor of South Carolina, and from 1782 to 1784 served as a member of Congress: *ANB*.

From Jules-François de Cotte[8]

ALS: American Philosophical Society

a Paris le 26 Mars 1783

M. Dupré m'a remis, Monsieur, la lettre que vous m'avez fait Lhonneur de m'ecrire, en aportant les coins que vous luy aves fait graver.[9] Ils ont eté essaiés et pouront servir a fraper non seulement les Medailles que vous desires avoir en ce moment, mais meme un plus grand nombre, si vous en aves besoin. Les 2 d'or, 20 d'Argent et 20 de bronze, que vous aves demandé, seront demain en Etat d'etre livrées a la personne que vous chargeres de les retirer des mains du S. Roger principal Commis de la Monnoye des Medailles.[1]

J'ay lhonneur detre avec les sentimens distingués dus a vos vertus, a vos talens et a votre Caractere, Monsieur, votre tres humble et tres Obeissant serviteur   DECOTTE

Je crois devoir vous avertir, qu'on vient d'aporter a la Monnoye des Medailles, un lingot d'une matiere imitante l'argent, pour essayer si elle seroit propre a la fabrication des Jettons ou de la Monnoye; a l'épreuve la matiere est si cassante qu'elle ne paroit propre a rien en ce genre, et celui qui la aporté a dit l'avoir recu de Nantes et comme etant destinée a une speculation de comerce, pour les Etats unis de lAmerique. Peut etre est ce une fausse indication, mais il est toujours bon je crois que vous en soies prevenu.

M. franklin

Notation: Necotte Paris 26 Mars 1783

---

8. *Directeur et contrôleur de la monnaie des médailles* from 1767 to 1803: Fernand Mazerolle, *L'Hôtel des Monnaies* (Paris, 1907), pp. 40–1.

9. BF's letter has not been found. Augustin Dupré engraved the dies for the *Libertas Americana* medal.

1. De Cotte received 1,046 *l.t.* 1 *s.* 3 *d.* on April 1 "for the Metal & Striking 2 Gold, 20 Silver & 20 Copper Medals." Payment for subsequent medals was made to Roger. On April 30 Roger received 581 *l.t.* 18 *s.* 5 *d.* "for 20 Silver & 100 Copper Medals"; on July 2 he received 450 *l.t.* 1 *s.* 9 *d.* "for Silver & Copper Medals": Account XXVII (XXXII, 4).

From Marie-Julie Rutledge d'Herbigny[2]

LS: American Philosophical Society

Son excellence   a paris ce 26 mars 1783.

Mon grand pere jacques Rutledge quitta l'irlande vue son attachement pour la maison de Stuart, mon pere Sir Walter Rutledge fut victime du meme Zele il arma à ses frais l'élizabet qui escorta le prince et la fortune de ma mere fut inglobé par une Suite de ce desastre.[3]

Les droits d'un frere d'un premier lit acheverent notre ruine[4] il m'estoit resté pour toute resource une Somme de dix mil livres que jai placé Sur mr le prince de guémené.[5] Vous en connoissez les Suites.

Depuis le temp que nous Sommes en france la plus grande partie de ma famille a été attaché au Service il me reste un frere paralitéque a ma charge ainsi q'une mere dans la Situation que je viens de rendre et un autre frere chanoine de Reims dont le peu de revenu ne peut suffire a nos charges.

Je Suis femme d'un militaire qui Sert avec Zele et j'ai un enfant.

Mr. lecomte de maurepas qui connoissoit ma Situation et les particularitez cydessus estoit a la veille de sy interesser fortement alors que j'ai eu le malheur de le perdre.[6]

2. Whom John MacMahon introduced in his letter of March 25; see the annotation there for her immediate family.

3. Her grandfather James Rutledge, an Irish Jacobite, followed James II to France in 1691. Her father had chartered the *Élisabeth*, 64, from the Ministry of Marine to accompany Prince Charles Edward Stuart to Scotland in 1745: Richard Hayes, *Biographical Dictionary of Irishmen in France* (Dublin, 1949), pp. 280–1; John S. Gibson, *Ships of the '45: the Rescue of the Young Pretender* (London, 1967), pp. 8–9.

4. For the inheritance dispute with her brother James (xxv, 501n) see the *DNB*, under James Rutledge; Raymond Las Vergnas, *Le Chevalier Rutlidge "Gentilhomme Anglais" 1742–1794* (Paris, 1932), p. 26.

5. Probably Henri-Louis-Marie de Rohan, prince de Guemené (1745–1808), who had declared bankruptcy in 1782: *Nouvelle biographie*, XLII, 536–7; Michel Gaudart de Soulages Hubert Lamant, *Dictionnaire des Francs-Maçons français* (Paris, 1995), pp. 785–6; Tourneux, *Correspondance littéraire*, XIII, 191, 218.

6. The comte de Maurepas died in November, 1781: XXII, 453n; XXXVI, 76n.

Je Sollicite dans le moment les bontez de monsieur le comte de vergennes pour obtenir des graces du Roÿ soit Sur le tresor Royal Soit sur le fonds des ecossois en un mot une pension qui me rende lexistence et qui me mette a meme de Soutenir ma famille.

Lhonneur que j'ai dappartenir a un des membres de votre congrez, et d'estre peuetre la Seul en france dans ce cas me fait esperer dobtenir votre confiance et votre appuy a ce titre ainsi quaupres de Mr. le comte de vergennes.

Je joins icy le memoire que ce ministre a deja bien voulu acceuillir et que je vous prie de lui representer appostillié par vous. Si vous daignez m'accorder votre appuy j'ose tout esperer.[7]

Je Suis avec Respect de votre excellence votre tres humble et tres obeissante Servante   RUTLEDGE DHERBIGNY

chez monsieur bart[8] chef descadre
ancien gouverneur de St. domingue
rue St. anne

Notation: Rutledge D'Herbigny Paris 26. Mars 1783.

From Robert R. Livingston

LS and L:[9] University of Pennsylvania Library; AL (draft): New-York Historical Society; transcript: National Archives

Sir   Philadelphia 26th March 1783

I need hardly tell you that the intelligence brought by the Washington diffused general pleasure here—[1] We had long been in suspense with respect to the negotiations, & had received no other lights on that subject than those the speech of his Britan-

---

7. The enclosure is missing. On May 20, 1783, she wrote again to thank BF for his help (APS).

8. Philippe-François Bart: *DBF.*

9. According to the transcript the LS was sent by the ship *Hope*, and the L (marked duplicate) by the packet *General Washington.*

1. See Livingston to the American Peace Commissioners, March 25.

nic Majesty & Mr Townshend's Letters threw upon it—[2] These were by no means Sufficient to dissipate all our apprehensions— The terms you have obtained for us comprize most of the objects we wish for— I am sorry however that you found it necessary to act with reserve & to conceal your measures from the Court of France. I am fearful that you will not be able to produce Such facts as will justify this Conduct to the world, or free us from the charge of ingratitude to a friend who has treated us not only justly but generously— But this is a disagreeable subject, & I refer you for my Sentiments and those of Congress to my Letter in answer to the joint Letters from our Ministers— I am sorry that the commercial Article is struck out[3]—it would have been very important to us to have got footing at least in the British West Indies, as a means of compelling France to pursue her true interest & ours by opening her ports also to us.

We have just learned by a Vessel from Cadiz that the preliminary Articles for a general peace were signed the 20th[4]—the abstract of the Treaty sent me by the Marquis de la Fayette[5] does the highest honor to the moderation & wisdom of France— Never has she terminated a war with more glory; & in gaining nothing but that trophy of victory Tobago, She has established a character which confirms her friends, disarms her enemies, & obtains a reputation that is of more value than any territorial acquisition she could make— We have been in great distress with respect to our Army—pains were taken to inflame their minds & make them uneasy at the idea of a peace which left them without support— Inflammatory papers were dispersed in camp,

2. The Feb. 19 issue of the *Pa. Gaz.* printed an extract of a Dec. 3 letter from Secretary of State Townshend to the Lord Mayor of London which said that a preliminary agreement had been signed; it also printed George III's Dec. 5 address to Parliament which hinted at it.

3. Part of Article 4 of the first draft peace treaty: XXXVIII, 193–4.

4. The news was brought to La Luzerne by the cutter *Triomphe*, which had sailed from Cadiz in mid-February. La Luzerne promptly informed Congress, and Livingston then informed the British commanders Carleton and Digby: *Morris Papers*, VII, 622; *JCC*, XXIV, 210–11; Wharton, *Diplomatic Correspondence*, VI, 337; *Pa. Gaz.*, issues of March 26 and April 2.

5. Presumably an enclosure to the Feb. 5 letter Lafayette wrote Livingston from Cadiz: Idzerda, *Lafayette Papers*, V, 86–8.

calling them together to determine upon some mad action. The General interposed, posponed the meeting to a future day on which he met with them, made them an address that will do him more honour than his victories— After which they passed several resolves becoming a patriot army.[6] Congress are seriously engaged in endeavouring to do them Justice— I am in great hopes that we shall shortly be brought back to such a situation as to be enabled to enjoy the blessings you have laid the foundation of.

I received from Mr T. Franklin the papers relative to the Portuguese Vessel which I have caused to be laid before the Court of appeals, where the cause is now depending, the cargo having been condemned, & the yacht acquitted at Boston—[7] I doubt not but full justice will be done to the proprietors on the rehearing— You know So much of our Constitution as to see that it is impossible to interfere farther in these matters than by putting the evidence in a proper train to be examined— I have had the proceedings in the case of the Brigantine Providence, transmitted me from Boston, with a full state of the evidence which I have examined—[8] The cargo is condemned & the Vessel acquitted— An allowance for freight having been made by the Court— The

6. The first inflammatory address concerning their pay was distributed among the officers at the camp of Newburgh, N.Y., on March 10. An address to the officers by George Washington five days later caused them to moderate their demands on Congress: *Morris Papers*, VII, 579–80, 592–3n; Richard H. Kohn, *Eagle and Sword: the Federalists and the Creation of the Military Establishment in America, 1783–1802* (New York and London, 1975), pp. 17–39; C. Edward Skeen, *John Armstrong, Jr., 1758–1843: a Biography* (Syracuse, 1981), pp. 8–17.

7. XXXVIII, 185. The case concerned the schooner *Nossa Senhora da Soledade Saõ Miguel é Almas*, captured by the privateer *Sally* in October, 1781. A jury returned the ship to her master, Vincenti Doo, but not the cargo. Both parties appealed the verdict. In May, 1783, the Court of Appeals found on behalf of Doo: Henry J. Bourguignon, *The First Federal Court: the Federal Appellate Prize Court of the American Revolution, 1775–1787* (Philadelphia, 1977), pp. 230–1.

8. A Danish vessel captured by an American privateer; see XXXVII, 204n, 538. The cargo was the property of Richard Vaux (XXXVII, 632n): James Farley, "The Ill-Fated Voyage of the *Providentia*: Richard Vaux, Loyalist Merchant, and the Trans-Atlantic Mercantile World in the Late Eighteenth Century," *Pa. History*, LXII (1995), 364–72.

evidence does not admit a doubt of the justice of this decree. Should the court of Denmark not be satisfied with this account, I will cause a copy of the proceedings to be transmitted you for their satisfaction— I hope this mark of attention to them will induce them to acknowledge the injustice they have done us in the detention of our prizes—[9] This object should not be lost sight of— I thank you for your present of Mr d'Auberteuil's essay & shall dispose of the copies he has sent in the way you recommend,[1] tho' I think the best answer you can give him will be the boy's reply to Pope's *God mend me*—[2] I could hardly have believed it possible that so many errors & falshoods that would shock the strongest faith on this side the water could be received as orthodox on the other— I remit bills for the salaries of our Ministers—it is impossible that I can adjust their accounts here—you must settle with them & they repay you out of the drafts I have made in their favor when they have been overpaid— Congress have in pursuance of your sentiment in your Letter of October passed the enclosed resolve so that on the quarter's salary due in April there will be a deduction of all you gained by the course of exchange & the payments will be reduced to par, at which rate they will always be paid in future.[3] The deduction amounts on your salary to eight thousand three hundred & thirty six livres as will appear from the account that will be stated by Mr Morris— I shall pay your bills into the hands

9. Prizes sent into Bergen, which the Danish government had returned to Britain, thereby provoking a protest by BF: XXXI, 261–5.

1. Michel-René Hilliard d'Auberteuil, *Essais historiques et politiques sur les Anglo-Américains:* XXXVIII, 415–16.

2. In 1787 James Wilson told the anecdote to the Pa. ratifying convention. One evening, a boy who was lighting the way of the physically deformed poet Alexander Pope leaped over a gutter causing Pope to exclaim "God mend me." The boy replied, "God mend you! he would sooner make half-a-dozen new ones." Philip B. Kurland and Ralph Lerner, eds., *The Founders' Constitution* (5 vols., Chicago and London, 1987), I, 202.

3. Upon BF's suggestion (XXXVIII, 222), Congress resolved on March 7 to fix the salaries of its ministers and other officers in Europe at an exchange rate of 4 s. 6 p. per (specie) dollar, the money to be paid in bills of exchange at a rate of 5 *l.t.* 5 s. per dollar: *JCC*, XXIV, 175–6. BF's salary was £2,500 or about $11,111 per year: *Morris Papers*, V, 127.

of Mr Robert Morris whom you have constituted your Agent—[4] The bills for the other Gentlemen who may not be with you are committed to your care, as the bills are drawn in their favour, they can only be paid on their endorsement.

Congress will, I believe, agree very reluctantly to let you quit their service[5]—the subject, together with Mr Adams's & Mr Laurens's resignation is under the consideration of a committee[6] if they report before this Vessel sails you shall know their determination.

On the arrival of the Triumph from Cadiz which brought orders for recalling the cruizers of His Britannic Majesty—Congress passed the enclosed resolution[7] which I transmitted with the intelligence we had received to Carleton & Digby— I sent my Secretary with my Letters & expect him back this evening— I am anxious to know how the first messenger of peace has been received by them as well as to discover thro' him what steps they propose to take for the evacuation— I ought to thank you for your Journal[8] before I conclude—the perusal of it afforded me great pleasure—I must pray you to continue it. I much wish to have every step which led to so interesting an event as this treaty which established our independence— And tho' both Mr Jay & Mr Adams are minute in their Journals,[9] for which I am much obliged to them—Yet new light may be thrown on the subject

4. XXXVII, 738.

5. On Dec. 14, 1782, BF had renewed his request to be relieved of his diplomatic responsibilities: XXXVIII, 416–17.

6. According to the *JCC*, that committee was only charged with considering the resignation requests of JA and Laurens; it recommended on April 1 that they be accepted: *JCC*, XXIV, 225–7. BF's request must also have been under consideration (Boudinot mentioned it in a letter of April 1: Smith, *Letters*, XX, 126), but Congress postponed making a decision. Livingston told JA on April 14 and BF on May 31 that a decision had not yet been reached: *Adams Papers*, XIV, 409; Wharton, *Diplomatic Correspondence*, VI, 459.

7. To "recall all armed vessels cruizing under commissions from the United States of America": *JCC*, XXIV, 210–11.

8. Which BF enclosed in his letter of Dec. 5[–14]: XXXVIII, 412.

9. Jay's journal of the negotiations was a lengthy Nov. 17 letter to Livingston: Wharton, *Diplomatic Correspondence*, VI, 11–49. For JA's journal see our annotation of Livingston to the American Peace Commissioners, March 25.

by you who having been longer acquainted with the Courts of London & Versailles have the means of more information relative to their principles & measures.

I have the honor to be sir With great respect & esteem Your most obedient and most humble servant ROBT R LIVINGSTON

Honble. Benjamin Franklin, Esquire

No. 26

From Lotbinière

ALS: American Philosophical Society

paris, petit hôtel de Lordat Rue de Bourgogne près la place du palais bourbon, le 26 mars 1783.—

Monsieur

J'ai l'honneur de vous informer que Mr. de Rayneval m'a marqué dans Sa lettre du 24, que M. le Comte de Vergennes devoit vous remettre, le premier jour que vous vous rendriez a la Cour, un Mémoire au Sujet de mes deux Seigneuries a la tête du lac Champlain.[1] Quelque décidé que je fusse a attendre Cette justice des seuls mouvemens de Votre Excellence auprès des Etats-unis de l'Amérique, il m'a Eté aisé de sentir, lorsque j'ai Eu l'honneur de la voir a Ce Sujet, que je la mettrois beaucoup plus a son aise Sur les Services que je la voyois toute portée a me rendre, par une pareille démarche de la part du gouvernement françois.

Au moyen du Memoire Ministèriel qui doit vous Etre remis au premier instant, S'il ne l'a pas desja Eté, les papiers que j'avois Eu l'honneur de vous laisser, Monsieur, pour vous mettre particulierement au fait de la chose vous deviennent totalement inutiles, Et je vous serai infiniment obligé de vouloir bien me les renvoyer sous Couvert fermé de Votre Cachet, Etant la minute même de la majeure partie de mon travail a ce sujet.

J'ai l'honneur d'Étre avec beaucoup de Respect Monsieur Vôtre tres humble Et tres obeissant serviteur LOTBINIERE.

P.S. Si Votre Excellence a la bonté de m'indiquer un jour Et l'heure a laquelle je pourrois sans indiscretion me rendre a son

1. See Lotbinière's letters of Feb. 2 and 8.

hôtel j'aurois l'honneur de m'y présenter.—CL.—oserois-je la supplier de Vouloir Exprimer pour moi a Monsr. son fils, les choses les plus particulieres Et les plus gracieuses.

Notation: Lotbiniere 26 Mars 1783.

From Francis Hopkinson   ALS: American Philosophical Society

My ever dear Friend   [March 27, 1783]

To be noticed by the *Great* is an Honour but to enjoy the Friendship of the *Good* is more than Honour—it is Happiness. I was much gratified by your kind Letter per Capt. Barney, & thank you for the *Premiere Livraison* of the *Encyclopédie.*[2] But you have not informed me in what Manner I shall make Payment for them. The Sum total is larger than I could have ventur'd on at Once; but as the Publications will be in annual Portions, I suppose the Payments will be so too:—which will bring the Matter within the Compass of my Abilities: But I wish to know what is expected from the Subscribers.—

A Vessel arrived here a few Days ago Express from Cadis, with Letters from the Marquis Fayette announcing *Peace* to all the World. This has diffused general Joy thro' this suffering Country. Yet there are some who, tho' they cannot be sorry for it with a good Grace, are nevertheless sorry. I mean those who have large Quantities of Goods on hand at *War* Prices. But if it should never rain till it suited every Individual's Convenience the whole World would blow away in Dust. The Terms for America are unexceptionable. The boundary Lines of the United States, liberal & permanent. I have heard no Objections— Even long-sighted Politicians of the Grumbletonian Fraternity seem satisfied.

Blessings, like Misfortunes seldom come unaccompanied. I am told you intend to return & spend the Remainder of your Days at home. This will be a most agreeable Gratification to your Friends—to none more than me— America gave you Breath, you have repaid the Obligation by being so principally

2. XXXVIII, 490.

instrumental in giving her Peace, Liberty & Independence. Individuals will readily acknowledge how much the Public is indebted to you for your important Services; how far the Public will be found grateful is a Problem. The least I think that can be expected is that you may enjoy the Remainder of your Days in Ease & Honour.— The Official Dispatches respecting the Peace are look'd for every Day, and great Pageantry's are preparing for the joyful Proclamation.—

You flatter my Vanity by approving of my Piece respecting the Trees— The Law was repealed & the Innocents saved from Slaughter.[3]

I amused myself one snowy Day with devising a new Game at Cards. I enclose you a Copy of the Rules printed on the wrapping Paper of each Pack, & also a Couple of the Cards as a Sample. They are not so well executed as I could wish, but may serve for a first Essay. My Object was to make my Children dextrous & critical in spelling, & to give them a Knowledge of the Use of Letters in the Formation of Words. These Cards are getting into great Vogue.

My good Mother[4] is well, & retains a most respectful & affectionate Regard for you, whom she considers as almost the only one of her Husband's friends, who has extended any Regard to his Family.—

I have written many Letters to you, which I fear have miscarried. One in particular I am anxious about, in which I gave you a narritive at length of a most unhappy Circumstance—no less than a Combination to ruin me forever by some whom from my Youth up I had esteemed as my most confidential friends, & on whom I had without Remission conferr'd such Acts of Kindness as I was capable of.—[5] You are no Stranger to the Feelings that must occur on such an Occasion.—

Adieu & be assured I am ever Your faithful & affectionate

FR HOPKINSON

Addressed: To the Honourable / Doctor Franklin / at / Passey

3. See XXXVIII, 229–30, 490.
4. Mary Johnson Hopkinson, the widow of Thomas Hopkinson: XII, 124–5n.
5. See XXXVI, 172–5.

Endorsed: Not dated, but suppos'd to be about the 27th March 83

Notation: F. Hopkinson 27 March 1783

To Lotbinière   LS:[6] American Philosophical Society

Passy ce 28 Mars 1783

J'ai reçu, Monsieur la Lettre que vous m'avez fait l'honneur de m'écrire le 26 de ce mois. Je vous renvoye cy joint les Papiers que vous m'avez laissés. Je suis tous les Matins chèz moi Jus qu'à onze heures, excepté les mardis, et Je vous verrai avec plaisir Si vous m'honorez d'une Visite.

J'ai l'honneur d'être très parfaitement, Monsieur votre très humble et très obeissant Serviteur./.   B Franklin

[*In Franklin's hand:*] M. de V. [Vergennes] ne m'a pas parlé encore de votre Affaire, mais je ferai tout ce que je peux.[7]

Mr. Lotbiniere

To Matthew Ridley

LS:[8] Archives du Ministère des affaires étrangères

Sir,   Passy, 28 March 1783

I have read the Letter from Monsieur de Rayneval to you of the 20th. instant, wherein he thinks that the Representation of Mr. Putnam's Case as stated by a Resolve of Congress of Septr 4. 1780,[9] ought to be from me. The Multiplicity of Affairs in which I was engaged when Mr. Putnam was at Paris made me wish that some American Gentleman would undertake this Business. The Choice he made of you was quite agreable to me; and

6. In L'Air de Lamotte's hand, except for the noted addition by BF. As it remains among BF's papers, it may have been unsent or a retained copy.

7. BF forwarded Lotbinière's memoir to Charles Thomson on Sept. 13.

8. In the hand of L'Air de Lamotte. BF added the complimentary close before signing.

9. *I.e.,* 1779.

it is my Desire that you should pursue the Reclamation.[1] Other more weighty Objects on my Mind at this Time, would render it very difficult for me to give the Attention necessary to the one in Question. And therefore I flatter myself that upon your producing this Letter to Comte de Vergennes no Difficulty will be made to your obtaining the Information you may Want & such Justice as the Nature of the Affair requires.

With great Esteem, I have the honor to be Sir, Your most obedient & most humble Servant   B FRANKLIN

Mr. Ridley.

From Gaspard-Bonaventure-Timothée Ferry:[2] Résumé

ALS: American Philosophical Society

⟨Marseille, March 28, 1783, in French: You will probably be surprised that a young man barely 20 years old, a runt in the field of physics, would take the liberty of writing to you. I am motivated by the spirit of emulation, which obliges great men to enlighten those who ask for instruction. My teacher, père Aubert, favors

1. Benjamin Putnam had long been seeking resolution on two claims. This one, from 1779, concerned an English sloop he commandeered in Antigua and sailed to Guadeloupe, where it was confiscated by the French authorities and returned to its owners. Congress resolved on Sept. 4, 1779, to protest the case to the French minister, Conrad-Alexandre Gérard. BF attempted to pursue this matter with Gérard in 1781, to no avail: XXXIV, 370; XXXV, 78, 477. In December, 1782, Putnam (visiting Paris) engaged Matthew Ridley to pursue his claims, but begged BF to intercede in the matter of the sloop and forward the congressional resolution to the French ministry; he also asked WTF to make sure BF did so: XXXVIII, 512–13; Putnam to WTF, [Jan.] 7, 1783 (APS).

On April 3 Ridley sent the present letter to Rayneval, asking him to forward it to Vergennes with several enclosures: his own memorial to Vergennes of the same date, a statement by Putnam, and a copy of the congressional resolution. AAE.

2. This 18-page critique of BF's theory, written when Ferry was enrolled in a collège run by Oratorians, is full of flattery and false modesty. At the end of 1783 he wrote a shorter set of observations on the abbé Nollet's electrometer, which was published in the Jour. de physique, XXIV (1784), 315–18. Ferry became a professor of experimental physics and also published works of poetry: Quérard, France littéraire.

your view of the Leyden jar over that of the abbé Nollet. While I was initially skeptical, I eventually came to the same opinion. Still, while I regard your theory of attraction and repulsion as one of the most beautiful discoveries, I have the audacity to claim that it is not supported by physical explanations.[3] I base this assertion on what appears starting on page 208 of d'Alibard's 1756 translation of your letters. [Ferry summarizes and quotes at length passages about the nature of glass and how it receives and repels electrical fluid.][4] I confess that I never liked abstract ideas in physics, including the terms attraction and repulsion. M. Nollet demanded that you explain your theory on the basis of some solid reason derived from the nature of the bodies. I now offer such an explanation: glass itself is elastic, even in the middle layer where the pores are smallest. The Leyden shock results from the elastic spring of the inner surface of the glass, which is bursting with electrical fluid. Moreover, the elasticity of glass can also explain the central mystery of the Leyden jar: why one cannot charge it when the jar is insulated. If the jar is insulated, the outer surface must retain its electrical fluid. Therefore, it does not allow the inner surface to expand and take in a quantity of excess electrical fluid. The elasticity also explains why the jar works better when filled with hot water than with cold (hot water dilates the pores of the glass) and why thin glass works better than thick glass (thin glass is more elastic).

If you deign to honor me with a response, please give the reply to the person who delivered the present letter.[5] And, because

3. Though Ferry proclaims his own audacity, his response was typical of many French scientists' reaction to BF's theory of electrical action, namely that BF did not offer "physical causes" for attraction and repulsion, or, indeed, for any electrical effect. For a detailed analysis of the differences between BF's and Nollet's electrical theories see Jessica Riskin, *Science in the Age of Sensibility: the Sentimental Empiricists of the French Enlightenment* (Chicago, 2002), pp. 68–103, and J. L. Heilbron, *Electricity in the 17th and 18th Centuries* (Berkeley, Los Angeles, and London, 1979). We are indebted to Prof. Riskin for her help in summarizing Ferry's argument.

4. Benjamin Franklin, *Expériences et observations sur l'électricité faites a Philadelphie en Amérique . . .*, trans. Thomas-François Dalibard (2nd ed., 2 vols., Paris, 1756), I, 208–11. For the original passage see IV, 28–9.

5. Ferry gives his address as "Ferry fils, rue de la Roquette près l'oratoire."

someone who knows I wrote to you might try to send me a false reply, please put on the address sheet this distinctive mark [an infinity symbol].⟩

From Ginette frères & Luc Laugier

ALS: American Philosophical Society

Monsieur   Marseille Le 28 mars 1783./.

Nous prenons La Liberté d'envoyer à Votre Excellence, La Copie d'un acte fait au bourg St pierre isle de La Martinique par des officiers du brigantin Les marie-therese Commandé par Le Capitaine pierre fremont qui, etant parti dudit port pour Venir à Marseille, fut pris par un Corsaire anglais Le Sept decembre dernier[6] et repris Six heures après par la fregatte La hague Commandée par Monsieur Manley,[7] appartenant aux Etats unis de L'amerique; Cette reprise a été envoyée à Boston.

Nos Correspondans de la Martinique n'ont point perdu de tems pour envoyer à Boston à Mr. Le Consul de france, l'extrait de la declaration dont nous envoyons Copie à Votre Excellence.[8] Quoique nous Soyons Convaincûs que Le Congrès aura eu egard aux reclamations justes de Monsieur Le Consul, nous

---

The person who delivered the letter, a M. Parraud, wrote on June 8 to remind BF of his promise to reply. APS.

6. Enclosed was an extract of the Dec. 12, 1782, testimony by two officers of the *Marie-Thérèse*, stating that the ship sailed from St. Pierre on Dec. 5, 1782, and was captured by the *Quaker* of Antigua three days later. The officers were Etienne Alliés, second captain, and Antoine Perrault, lieutenant; the statement was attested by Jean Amans Astory, *conseiller du roi* and acting *lieutenant général* of the admiralty of St. Pierre.

7. John Manley, currently captain of the Continental frigate *Hague:* XXXI, 418–19n; *Morris Papers,* VI, 154–5.

8. Also enclosed with the present letter was a copy of a Dec. 26, 1782, joint letter from the governor of Martinique (the marquis de Bouillé: XXIV, 60n) and the *intendant de la marine* (Peynier: XXVIII, 350n) to the French consul at Boston (Philippe-André-Joseph de Létombe: XXXVI, 540n), requesting that he forward to Congress a mémoire from representatives of the ship's owners.

avons Crû devoir faire part a Votre Excellence de cet evenement et des demarches qui doivent deja avoir été faites.

Nous esperons que Votre Excellence Voudra bien appuyer notre demande et faire ensorte que la restitution de ce Brigantin ne Souffre pas de delay, Comme ayant été repris dans un terme que les loix de l'amerique et de toutes les Nations Maritimes determinent pour que La recousse retourne à Ses premiers propriétaires Sous une gratification oû portion indiquée par ces mêmes loix;[9] l'amour de la justice qui Caracterise le Congrés, ne nous Laisse aucun doute Sur La promte decision de cette affaire, Surtout appuyée et reccommandée par Votre Excellence.

Nous Sommes avec Respect de Votre Excellence Les très humbles et très obeissants Serviteurs[1]

GINETTE FRERES ET LUC LAUGIER

JAQUES SEIMANDY chargè des pouvoirs des assureurs de Marseille

Notation: Ginette freres & Luc Langier, 28 Mars 1783

From James Hunter, Jr.[2]   ALS: American Philosophical Society

Sir   Richmond Virginia. 28 March 83

Mrs. Strange desires me to continue the Liberty of addressing Her to your Care, and I pray your Excuses for the Trouble.

I am most respectfully Sir Your mo Ob Sert. JAMES HUNTER

9. According to the American law passed on Dec. 4, 1781, if a prize was retaken in less than 24 hours after its capture, restitution would be made to the original owners upon the payment of ⅓ of its salvage value: *JCC,* XXI, 1156. Létombe reported to Castries on Oct. 6, 1784, that the prize had been sold and that he was drawing on Treasurer General Boutin for a sum to be remitted to Ginette frères & Luc Laugier: Abraham P. Nasatir and Gary E. Monell, *French Consuls in the United States* . . . (Washington, D.C., 1967), p. 30.

1. The firm wrote again on May 15, 1783: since writing their last letter they have learned that the *Marie-Thérèse* arrived in Boston and that the French consul has taken the necessary steps. They ask again that BF intervene to see that justice is done. APS.

2. The Virginian whose wife was Isabella Strange's cousin: XXXV, 394; XXXVII, 690.

From Georges-René Pléville Le Pelley[3]

ALS: American Philosophical Society

Monsieur   Marseille Le 28e. mars 1783

J'ose joindre ma Supplique a celle des Negotiants cy joint[4] pour La remise du Brigantin Les marie therese Capn. fremond, Sur Lequel Le Sr. Luc Laugier mon gendre avoit une Bonne partie de Sa fortune. Mon seul titre auprès de vous Monsieur est La connoissance de vos Bontés; je Suis un des premiers françois qui ont couru au Secours de Votre patrie; j'etois Lieutenant Sur Le Languedoc avec Mr. DEstaing: qui m'ayant chargé de Lintendance de Lescadre a Boston: Se trouvoi assommé par une Rixe d'anglais desertee de Prison avec Le chv. De St. Sauveur mon adjoint qui perit et fut inhumé dans cette ville.[5]

Je Suis avec respect Monsieur Votre très humble et tres obeissant Serviteur   PLEVILLE LEPELLEY

Capn de vsau et de Port, Commandant

---

3. Pléville Le Pelley (1726–1805), *capitaine de vaisseau,* retired from active service in 1789. He returned in 1796 to become *chef de division,* vice-admiral, and, for nine months, naval minister: Christian de La Jonquière, *Les Marins français sous Louis XVI: Guerre d'indépendance américaine* (Issy-les-Moulineaux, France, 1996), p. 237; Jacques Aman, *Les Officiers bleus dans la marine française au XVIIIe siècle* (Genève, 1976), p. 193; Six, *Dictionnaire biographique.*

4. Ginette frères & Luc Laugier to BF, March 28, above.

5. Saint-Sauveur had served as *lieutenant de vaisseau* on the *Tonnant,* part of d'Estaing's squadron, in 1778. On Sept. 8 of that year, a group of American sailors in Boston demanded bread from one of the squadron's bakeries; when it was refused, they attacked the bakehouse. Saint-Sauveur and Pléville Le Pelley were both beaten, and the former died as a result of his wounds: Ministère des Affaires Etrangères, *Les Combatants français de la guerre américaine, 1778–1783* (Paris, 1903), p. 18; Charles W. Akers, *The Divine Politician: Samuel Cooper and the American Revolution in Boston* (Boston, 1982), p. 266.

From Pieter Buyck[6]   LS: American Philosophical Society

Son Excellence   Gand 29 mars 1783
    J'ai L'honneur de Vous Confirmer ma dernre. du 17. feve.[7]
Sur la quelle Je me flattois de me Voir favorisé de Votre reponse,
mais a mon deplaisir Je m'en trouve frustré Jusqu'a ce moment.
Puisque Je trouve que Le plus long terme, que m'a fixé monsr.
Wm. Bell[8] de Recevoir de Son Excellence La Remise des ƒ.
6888..10..8 de change, est Échu aux environs d'un mois, Je
prends de nouveau la liberté de Vous Supplier de Vouloir daigner
m'honnorer de Votre chere reponse & me mander a quel term Je
puis m'en prevaloir Sur Vous, ayant besoin des gros fonds pour
des considrables achats de toilles Ecruës que Je dois faire.
    J'ai L'honneur d'Etre avec un devouëment Le plus Res-
pectueux De Son Excellence Le plus he. & plus obt. Serviteur
                                              Pr. Bûyck

Son Excellence. Doctor frankelyn A Paris

Addressed: A Son Excellence / Doctor frankelyn / ministre general des Etats unis / d'amerique en france / À Paris

Notation: Buyck 29 Mars 1783.

From Louis-Pierre Dufourny de Villiers
                          ALS: American Philosophical Society

Votre Excellence   Paris le 29. Mars 1783
    L'Attraction qu'opére entre les hommes, la conformité de
sentiments et de désirs, est sans doutte la cause qui me fait ren-
contrer ceux d'entre les François, qui sont les plus estimables,
par leur attachement pour les Etats unis, par le zêle et les talens
qu'ils ont montrés à leur serviçe, et par la vénération qu'ils ont

6. A Ghent textile merchant who had been involved a year earlier with
Barclay's efforts to exchange British goods for those of Holland or Germany
so they could be sent to America: XXXIV, 365n; XXXVI, 574; XXXVII, 42, 135.
    7. Not found.
    8. A Philadelphia merchant who had secured a pass from BF the previous
summer to travel to Ostend, from whence he sailed to Philadelphia: XXXVI,
380; XXXVII, 644n; XXXVIII, 109.

pour votre personne. C'est à tous ces titres que je dois la demande que me fait, Monsieur De Quernay, chevalier de Saint Louis, Colonel dans le corps du Génie, lequel a commandé en chef le siège d'York-town, de sollicitter l'honneur de vous présenter ses respects.[9] Il me conviendroit peu, de relever à vos yeux l'importance de ses services, elle vous est mieux connüe qu'a moy, et leur prix est fixé par la prise de larmée de Cornwalis, et par l'influence que ce grand événnement a eu sur l'Indépendance et sur la Paix. Si cet officier ne peut vous donner aucuns détails qui auroient échappés à vos correspondants, il vous rapellera du moins, avec le plus vif intérêt, des souvenirs toujours chers; et il trouvera dans l'aceuil que vous luy ferez, une grande partie de la récompense qui est due à sa bravoure, à son dévouement, et à ses talens. Je suis jaloux, je vous l'avoue, de la bonne fortune de ceux qui même sans avoir lhonneur de vous connoitre, ont cependant eu l'ocasion de bien méritter de vous et de votre Patrie, tandis que moy qui ai eu l'avantage d'être admis aupres de vous, les mains vuides d'oeuvres et le coeur plein de zèle et du plus sinçére attachement, je suis encor réduit aux expressions verbales du plus profond respect. Je suis De Votre Excellence Le tres humble et le tres obeissant serviteur

DUFOURNY DE VILLIERS
Au petit hotel de Clugny rue des Mathurins

Notation: Du Fourny de Villiers Paris 29 Mars 1783

From Robert Strange   ALS: American Philosophical Society

Sir   Hotel d'Espagne rue Guenegaud 29th. March 1783
    A succession of hurry and business for some months past have prevented me the honour of paying my respects to you, or even

---

9. Guillaume Querenet de La Combe (1731–1788), who accompanied Rochambeau to Newport, commanded the contingent of French engineers at Yorktown, and became a member of the Society of the Cincinnati: Rice and Brown, eds., *Rochambeau's Army,* I, 71, 150, 319; II, 116n, 158; Anne Blanchard, *Dictionnaire des ingénieurs militaires 1691–1791* (Montpellier, 1981), p. 616; Asa B. Gardiner, *The Order of the Cincinnati in France . . .* (n.p., 1905), p. 105.

D^R. FRANKLIN requests the honour
of M^r. *Fox's*
Company at Dinner on *Sunday* the *30 th Instant.*

Paſſy, *March* 178*3*. —

The favour of an Anſwer is deſired,

Printed Invitation to Dinner

congratulating you upon the success of your late glorious and indefatical labours, in having accomplished the independancy of your country—[1] May health and every other blissing yet prolong your days to witness its rising grandour. I had a few weeks since a letter from Mrs. Strange wherein she mention'd her having had a visit of your Son—[2] I long much on his fathers account to pay my respects to him, which I shall certainly do soon after my arrival in London— My health is but at present indifferent which accelerates my leaving Paris, I must therefor in this manner ask your commands as I shall set out about thursday next. I take the liberty of committing to your care the inclosed letters, and am most respectfully Sir Your obedt. humb. Servt.

ROBT STRANGE

To George Fox[3]

Printed invitation with MS insertions:[4] University of Pennsylvania Library

[before March 30, 1783]

DR. FRANKLIN requests the honour of Mr. *Fox's* Company at Dinner on *Sunday* the *30th Inst.*

Passy, *March 1783.*

The favour of an Answer is desired.

Addressed: A Monsieur / Monsieur Fox / Hotel de Montgomery / Rue du Collombier.—

1. Strange, now *graveur du roi,* had just issued his celebrated engraving of Van Dyck's portrait of Charles I, owned by the French royal family. (He announced on Jan. 17 that it would be available in ten days, but it evidently took longer than anticipated.) On April 4 it was announced that he would engrave Van Dyck's portrait of Charles' wife, Henrietta Maria of France, which was in the British royal collection. These engravings were exhibited at the Salons of 1783 and 1785, respectively; Strange was presented to the king and queen of France in 1784, and was knighted three years later: *Jour. de Paris,* issues of Jan. 17, March 28, and April 4, 1783; *ODNB; Collection des livrets des anciennes expositions* (42 vols., Paris, 1673–1880), XXXII, 57; XXXIII, 53.
2. Isabella Strange had remained in London; see XXXVI, 627.
3. WTF's friend, who would soon leave for America: XXXII, 313n; XXXVIII, 474n.
4. Printed at Passy. WTF filled out the form and addressed it.

From Benjamin Franklin Bache

ALS: American Philosophical Society

Dear Grandpappa.   Geneva March. the 30 1783—
After a long Weariness caus'd by not receiving Letters from any of my freinds. I write you to engage you or My Cousin to write me the state of your health. I have heard from Johonnot that our Good General Washington intend's coming to France. I heard also from the Same that you have made medals for the Liberty of my Dear Country having Said Before Mr Marignac that I intended to ask one for Johonnot and one for me I thought it would Please him to have one. You would do me an extrem Pleasure to send me 3 One for Mr Marignac an other for Johonnot and an other for me.

I begin to paint and I Send you my first Landscape for to Judge of it.

I expect in the first letter I schall recieve your consent of my having a gold watch as I asked it in my last letter.[5]

Excuse the Schortness of this But as I am a going to dine to Mr Pigott's with my friend Johonnot who presents his respects to you as well as Mr and Me Marignac My Compliments to My Cousin and Beleive me for ever Your Most Dutiful and Obedient Grandson   B. Franklin Bache

NB. In your last letter you Mention'd your having sent Some English Books[6] as I have not receiv'd any other than the spectator the fables the speaker and an other little book,[7] I desire yo Would be so good as to tell me what Books and By whom You sent them.

---

5. Jan. 30, above, his second-to-last letter.

6. XXXVIII, 557.

7. BFB had requested and received the *Fables* of Phaedrus during his first year in Geneva: XXIX, 348; XXX, 587. BF sent *The Spectator* in 1781: XXXV, 367. BFB alluded to a work in an October, 1782, letter to BF that we speculated was *The Speaker*, a miscellany compiled by William Enfield: XXXVIII, 186. The unnamed work listed here is probably Henry Fielding's *Joseph Andrews*, which BFB mentioned in another October letter to BF: XXXVIII, 169.

From Giuseppe Bartoli[8]   ALS: American Philosophical Society

Monsieur   Paris, rue Cadet, ce 30 Mars 1783
    La derniere fois que j'ai eu l'honneur de Vous rendre visite, je
vous ai mis sous les yeux le papier même de la Traduction Angloise, que l'Antiquaire de S.M. Britannique avoit faite, en 1775,
de mes Vers Italiens qui furent imprimés à Londres: dans lesquels
alors j'ai prédit le succès qu'eut la Guerre declarée, ces jours-là,
par le Roi d'Angleterre, contre l'Amerique. Vous eutes, Monsieur, la bonté de me permettre de Vous en faire tenir une Copie,
avec l'Original Italien.[9]
    Mais cette Traduction étant peu fidelle dans les autres parties
qui n'ont point de rapport avec ma prédiction, j'ai cru devoir y
ajouter non seulement une Traduction Francoise de Mlle.
Leclerc, mais un autre en Anglois, que M. L'Heritier, Avocat au
Parlement de Paris, a eu la complaisance de faire, le plus exactement possible, pour un François.[1]
    Il se rend lui même à Passy pour avoir l'honneur, Monsieur,
de Vous présenter, avec ma lettre, ces quatre Piéces, et contempler de près le grand Philosophe et Ministre, admiré de Toutes
les Nations.
    Mr. L'Heritier joint à ses connoissances scientifiques l'avan-

8. Bartoli (1717–1788) was professor of literature and eloquence at the
University of Turin and antiquary to the king of Sardinia: Antonio Pace,
Benjamin Franklin and Italy (Philadelphia, 1958), p. 239; *Dizionario biografico
degli Italiani* (69 vols. to date, Rome, 1960–).
    9. Bartoli had written four sonnets glorifying the British which were trans-
lated into English at the king's request: Pace, *Benjamin Franklin and Italy*,
p. 239. We have found no record of this previous meeting.
    1. The two-page enclosure, in L'Héritier's hand, concerns the sonnet writ-
ten on the occasion of a regatta, ball, and supper held when George III submitted to Parliament the "Bill against America" (presumably the Prohibitory
Act, introduced on Nov. 20, 1775: XXII, 268n). In addition to the new translations Bartoli mentions, the enclosure provides the original verse in Italian
and the 1775 English translation by "Mr. Matthews Keeper of the Cabinet of
the King of England's Medals." Although the new English translation does
nothing to tone down the poet's ardent Anglophilia, BF reciprocated to this
strangely ill-timed gift by sending Bartoli a copy of the *Libertas Americana*
medal; see Bartoli to BF, April 11. The sonnet was later published in Giuseppe
Bartoli, *Sonetti di Giuseppe Bartoli . . .*, ed. Pier-Alessandro Paravia (Padua,
1818), p. 27.

tage de posseder l'Anglois, l'Allemand, l'Italien, l'Espagnol, sans parler du Latin et du Grec. Toutes ces considerations, Monsieur, m'ont déterminé à Lui ceder aujourd'hui la satisfaction, et l'honneur, d'être en personne à Vous assurer du profond respect avec lequel je suis Monsieur votre très-humble, et tres-obeissant Serviteur[2]   BARTOLI.

Notation: Bartoly 30 Mars 1783

From David Hartley: Letter and Two Memoranda[3]

(I) Copy: Massachusetts Historical Society; (II) copies: Massachusetts Historical Society, Public Record Office; (III) copy: Massachusetts Historical Society

I.

My dear Friend.   March 31. 1783. London.

I send you a Paper entitled *Supplemental Treaty,* the Substance of which I sent you some time ago, as I read it, in part of a Speech

2. L'Héritier, emboldened by the warm reception he received, sent BF a letter (undated) explaining his circumstances. He is 25 years old and has no chance of advancement under the regulations imposed by the order of *avocats.* He feels obliged to quit his profession but, with only the "vain et sterile" title of Master of Arts, has limited options. The Bureau of Foreign Affairs is a possibility, and he requests BF's recommendation to Vergennes (APS). BF also received at some time a curious demonstration of L'Héritier's linguistic skills: a one-sentence definition of *calumny* in the six languages Bartoli mentions in the present letter, plus Dutch and French, followed by a rendering in Latin verse. BF endorsed it "M. Heritier's 8 Languages." APS.

3. Though Hartley's originals have not survived, there is a copy by L'Air de Lamotte of the letter and second enclosure (document III), written continuously, among JA's papers. We have added to those the text of the "Supplemental Treaty," document II, from the version Hartley gave the American peace commissioners at their meeting on April 27. (It is in the hand of his secretary, George Hammond.) At that meeting, Hartley also gave them a memorandum about the "Supplemental Treaty," which we publish under the date [before April 27]. WTF published the letter and enclosures in *Memoirs,* II, 428–31. We have silently corrected two spelling mistakes made by L'Air de Lamotte.

in the H. of Commons.[4] I have given a Copy of it to M. L [Laurens], as the Grounds upon which my Friend the D. of P: wd: have wished that any Administration in wch. he might have taken a Part should have treated with the American Ministers. All Negociations for the Formation of a Ministry in concert with the D. of P. are at an End.[5]

The 10th. Article which is supposed to be refered to the definitive Treaty, is a Renewal of the same Proposition wch. I moved in Parlt. some Years ago, viz on the 9th. of April 1778.[6] I see nothing inconsistent with that Proposition either in the Declaration of Independence or in the Treaty with France, let it therefore remain, & emerge after the War as a point untouch't by the War. I assure you my Consent shd. not be wanting to extend this Principle between all the Nations upon Earth. I know full well that those Nations to wch. you and I are bound by birth and Consanguinity wd. reap the earliest fruits from it. *Owing no man hate & envying no man's hapiness,*[7] I should rejoice in the Lot of my own Country, and on her Part say to America, *nos duo turba Sumus.*[8] I send you likewise enclosed with this some Sentiments respecting the Principles of some late Negociations drawn up in the Shape of Parliamentary Motions by my Brother,[9] who joins

4. See Hartley's letter of March 12. His speech in the House of Commons was on March 11: Cobbett, *Parliamentary History*, XXIII, 640.

5. Hartley was proven wrong the following evening, April 1, when the king consented to the terms presented by the Duke of Portland for forming a government: Fortescue, *Correspondence of George Third*, VI, 328–9; Lord John Russell, ed., *Memorials and Correspondence of Charles James Fox* (2 vols., Philadelphia, 1853), II, 64. According to one of Hartley's friends, Portland initially proposed him for the Board of Treasury, but when this proved to be problematic, Hartley offered to go to the United States as plenipotentiary. Portland and Fox were delighted, and after meeting with the king, appointed him instead to negotiate the treaty with the American commissioners: Richard Warner, *Literary Recollections* . . . (2 vols., London, 1830), II, 223n.

6. Cobbett, *Parliamentary History*, XIX, 1069–78.

7. "Owe no man hate, envy no man's happiness": *As You Like It*, Act III, Scene ii, line 74.

8. Nos duo turba sumus; possedit cetera pontus (we two are all the population; the sea has claimed the rest): Ovid, *Metamorphoses*, book 1, line 355, trans. D. E. Hill (Warminster, Eng., and Oak Park, Ill., 1985), pp. 26–7.

9. Winchcombe Henry Hartley represented Berkshire: Namier and Brooke, *House of Commons*, II, 594.

with me in sincerest Good wishes to you for health & Happiness, and for the Peace of our respective Countries and of Mankind.
Your ever affecte. D. H.

II.

Supplemental Treaty between Great Britain and the United States of North America

1. That the British Forces be withdrawn from the united States with all Convenient Speed.
2. That all further prosecutions of the Loyalists in America be immediately Abated, and that they be permitted to remain untill 12 Months after the definitive treaty with America, in safety And unmolested in their endeavours to obtain restitution of their Estates.
3. That all the ports shall be mutually opened for intercourse & Commerce between G. Bn. & the united States.
4. Agreed on the part of Great Britain that all prohibitory Acts shall be repealed, and that all obstructions to American Ships either entering inwards or clearing outwards shall be removed which may arise from any Acts of Parliament heretofore regulating the Commerce of the American States under the Description of British Colonies & Plantations so as to accommodate every circumstance to the reception of their Ships as the Ships of Independent States.
5. Agreed on the part of G. Bn. that all duties rights privileges & all pecuniary consideration shall remain respecting the united States of America upon the same footing as they now remain respecting the Province of Nova Scotia, or as if the aforesaid States had remained dependent upon Great Britain. All this Subject to Regulations or alterations by future Acts of the Parliament of Great Britain.
6. On the part of the States of America it is agreed that all Laws prohibiting the Commerce with G. Bn. shall be repealed.
7. Agreed on the part of the American States that all Ships and Merchandize of the British Dominions shall be admitted upon the same terms as before the War. All this Subject to future regulations or alterations by legislatures of the American States respectively.

8. That all Prisoners on both sides be immediately released.

9. The principles & Spirit of this treaty to be supported on either side by any necessary Supplemental arrangements. No tacit compliance on the part of the American States in any subordinate points to be urged at any time hereafter in derogation of their independence.

Seperate Article to be referred to the definitive treaty

10. Neither shall the independence of the united States be considered any further than as Independence absolute & unlimited in Matters of Government as well as Commerce; not into Alienation; And therefore the Subjects of his Britannick Majesty & the citizens of the united States shall mutually be considered as Natural born Subjects, & enjoy all rights & privileges as such, in the respective Dominions and territories, in the Manner heretofore accustomed.

[*In David Hartley's hand:*] Supplemental Treaty

Notation by John Adams: Project of Mr Hartley

III.

1st. That it is the Opinion of this House, that whenever Great Britain thought proper to acknowledge the Independence of America the Mode of putting it into Effect most honorably for this Country would have been to have made the Declaration of Independence previous to the Commencement of any Treaty with any other Power.—

2d. That a Deviation from this Line of Conduct has the effect of appearing to grant the Independence of America solely to the Demands of the House of Bourbon, and not, as was the real State of the Case, from a Change in the Sentiments of this Country, as to the object and Continuance of the American War.

3d. That when this House, by its Vote against the further Prosecution of offensive War in America, had Given up the Point of Contest and adopted a conciliatory Disposition, the pursuing those Principles by an immediate and liberal Negociation, upon the Basis of Independence, at the same time expressing a Readiness to conclude a general Peace with the Allies of America upon

honorable Terms, Would have been the most likely Way to promote a mutual and beneficial Intercourse between the two Countries—to establish Peace upon a firm Foundation, & would have
prevented the House of Bourbon from having a Right to claim
any farther Obligations from America, as the assisters of their
Independence.

4th. That the Minister who advised the late Negociations for
Peace has neglected to make use of the Advantages which the
Determination of the House put him in Possession of, That, by
his Delay in authorising Persons properly to negociate with the
American Commissioners, he has shown a Reluctance to acting
upon the liberal Principles of granting Independence to America as the Determination of Great Britain upon mature Consideration of the Question, and has by such Methods given Advantages to the Enemies of this Country to promote and confirm
that Commerce & Connexion between the United States of
America & themselves, which during the Contest have been
turned from their natural Channel with this Country & which
this Peace so concluded has not yet contributed to Restore.—

Notations by John Adams: Copy Mr Hartley's Letter to Dr
Franklin 31. March 1783. / Mr Hartley to Dr. F. 31. March 1783.

From Morellet   AL: American Philosophical Society

lundi. [March 31, 1783][1]
Voilà mon cher et respectable ami l'explication de vôtre medaille. Je crois avoir rempli vôtre objet qui etoit à ce que vôtre
fils m'a dit non pas d'annoncer vôtre liberté votre existence politique comme entierement et completement etablies mais simple-

1. The day Morellet replied to the March 23 letter he received from his
friend Shelburne. Shelburne had informed him of his campaign to persuade
Vergennes to "promote you to some Benefice or some Abbaye," in recognition of Morellet's contribution to the peace settlement. One of the people
Shelburne had solicited was Gérard de Rayneval, Vergennes' *premier commis.* In the present letter Morellet asks BF to sound out Rayneval about an approach to Vergennes, undoubtedly on the same subject. Morellet himself met
with Rayneval on April 1 at Versailles, and wrote to Shelburne immediately
afterwards: Medlin, *Morellet,* I, 484n; see also pp. 479–80, 480–5.

ment *les evenemens designès dans la medaille.*[2] Je ne vous verrai pas d'icy à quelques jours si vous alles à versailles ne m'oublies pas auprès de mr. de reyneval et demandès lui sil approuveroit que vous parlassies à mr. de vergennes lui même de l'interet que vous mettes à moi. Je vous salüe et je vous embrasse de tout mon cœur sans préjudice du respect que vous m'aves inspiré.

From the Burgomasters and Senators of Hamburg

ALS: American Philosophical Society

Monsieur, [April 1, 1783]

COMME les Provinces unies de l'Amerique Septentrionale doivent principalement au merite distingué de VOTRE EXCEL-LENCE l'indépendance et la souveraineté, dont ils jouissent aujourd'hui, en vertu du traité, conclu avec SA MAJESTÉ BRITAN-NIQUE, nous prenons la liberté de feliciter VOTRE EXCELLENCE de voir couronné SON ouvrage.

NOUS avons addressé à cette même occasion à L'ILLUSTRE CONGRÈS la lettre de felicitation ci-jointe et LUI avons demandé l'honneur de SES bonnes graces.[3]

NOUS supplions VOTRE EXCELLENCE de vouloir bien employer SES bons offices et SA puissante entremise auprès de L'IL-LUSTRE CONGRÈS, pour nous honorer de Son affection et pour faciliter à nos negocians la liberté de former avec les habitans des ILLUSTRES ETÂTS NORD-AMERICAINS des liaisons de commerce, utiles de part et d'autre.[4]

NOTRE reconnoissance de cette faveur égalera la haute con-

2. The *Libertas Americana* medal had just been struck: de Cotte to BF, March 26. Morellet's enclosure has not been found. BF must have solicited it to accompany the medals that he would present at court on Tuesday, April 8. The text, or a revision of it, was later paired with an English version and given to the printer Philippe-Denis Pierres, who produced a dual-language pamphlet: "Explanation of a Medal," [*c.* May 5], below.

3. This March 29 letter detailing the trade advantages of Hamburg is published in Giunta, *Emerging Nation,* II, 77–9.

4. Owing to conflicts with its neighboring port cities Hamburg did not become a center of American commerce until the mid-1790s: Horst Dippel, *Germany and the American Revolution, 1770–1800* . . . , trans. Bernhard A. Uhlendorf (Chapel Hill, N.C., 1977), pp. 233, 272.

sidération, due à VOTRE profond scavoir et à Vos vastes lumières politiques.

AGRÉEZ, nous Vous en prions, les assurances du parfait respect, avec lequel nous avons l'honneur d'étre, Monsieur, de VOTRE EXCELLENCE, les très humbles & trés obeissants Serviteurs. LES BOURGUEMAITRES ET SENATEURS DE LA REPUBLIQUE DE HAMBOURG.

Donné sous le Sceau de notre Ville le 1r. Avril 1783.

From François-Félix Nogaret

ALS: American Philosophical Society

Très Respectable   Vlles. Le 1er avril 1783
    Puis-je, sans indiscretion, me mettre sur les Rangs, et esperer que vous me ferez la faveur de me donner une de vos ingenieuses médailles?[5]
    J'ai des remercimens à vous faire. M. Le Mis. de Serrent à qui vous avez eu la bonté d'ecrire pour moi L'an passé, pour une place de Bibliothécaire,[6] se Souvient très fort de votre puissante recommandation: il a dit ces jours passés à quelqu'un, que, dans un tems ou dans un autre; il se ferait un devoir de repondre à la bonne opinion que lui avaient donnée de moi Messieurs franklin et Buffon. J'entends dire que vous vous disposés à quitter notre beau païs pour retourner dans votre Patrie. Vous couronneriez L'oeuvre, et vous Seriez Sûr de laisser un heureux de plus, Si, avant de partir, vous ecriviez à M. Le Mis. de Serrent ces Seuls mots:
    "Je Sçais, Monsr. que vous voulez bien penser à M. felix-nogaret que je vous ai recommandé: je vous en remercie, et vous prie avant mon départ de lui continuer cet interet à Son avancement."
    Pardon mille fois, très respectable. Je comptais jouir de la faveur de vous voir au Musée[7] où j'avais un morceau à Lire. Ma

5. The *Libertas Americana* medal.
6. See XXXVII, 233–4.
7. The Musée de Paris held meetings the first Thursday of every month:

santé derangée ne me la pas permis. J'invoque, en ma faveur, et votre utile amitié et Les droits que me donne le grand Architecte sur un coeur comme le vôtre.

J'ai la faveur d'etre—Très Respectable votre très humble et très obeissant Serviteur   F.˙. FELIX-NOGARET

Made. nogaret vous assûre de Ses respectueuses civilitès, nous vous prions L'un et l'autre de ne pas nous oublier auprès de Monsieur votre fils.

Endorsed:[8] M. Drouet Cul de Sac Notre Dame des Champs—

Notation: Flix Nogaret 1er. avl. 1783

From [Jean-Antoine?] Salva[9]

Copy[1] and transcript: National Archives

Monsieur,   [April 1, 1783]
Le Danger éminent où se sont trouvés les Navires de votre Nation partis en mars dernier de Marseille qui ne doivent leur Salut qu'au Dieu des mers, semble devoir m'enhardir à vous le faire observer.

Des Ennemis cachés (que Je connois) ayant fait donner avis à cette Regence de ce Depart, il partit de suite 9. Corsaires pour les aller attendre sur le Cap de Palos, il est a presumer que les Americains ont passé le Detroit.

Alger est fecond en detours, et la Politique de certaines Puis-

---

Louis Amiable, "Les Origines maçonniques du Musée de Paris et du Lycée," *La Révolution Française*, XXXI (July-December, 1896), 489.

8. This note, jotted in a corner of the first page, might have been written when Droüet appeared in person. (His last extant letter was written on Jan. 28, 1783; it is summarized in annotation to his first letter: XXVI, 686–8.) On the verso of the second page BF sketched a circle between two wedges.

9. This native of Languedoc, captured by Algerian corsairs, was working off his ransom at the French consulate: Archives nationales, *Correspondance des consuls de France à Alger, 1642–1792* (Paris, 2001), pp. 721, 725, 727.

1. In L'Air de Lamotte's hand, and enclosed in BF to Livingston, July 22, 1783. An English translation of this document (National Archives) is published in Giunta, *Emerging Nation,* II, 79–80.

sances de l'Europe ne se restraint pas à payer Tribut pour Jouir de la paix, elles se servent de ces Harpies humaines pour être l'Epouvantail des Nations belligerentes, desquelles ils enchainent le Commerce au char de la piraterie Algerienne.[2] On en a vu l'exemple, lorsque Sa Maj. Imperiale voulant affranchir son Pavillon, se servit du Firman de la sublime Porte,[3] qu'on fit attaquer 5. prises conduites en ce Port en 1781. dont 4 en lest furent rendues en fevr. 1782. sur la Reclamation d'un Capigi Bachi de la porte, et de M. Timoni Agent imperial[4] qui fut expulsé, et duquel Je suis le Correspondant ayant été son Secretaire à cette occasion, et ayant revélé à S.A. Mgr. le Prince Kaunitz Rietberg Ministre en Cour de Vienne,[5] des horreurs et des Attentats qui fussent restés dans l'Impunité, s'il n'eut été ma plume.

L'Humanité seule m'engage, Monsr., à vous donner cet avis, Je vous prie de vouloir le garder sous le Secret, Votre Prudence operera à cette occasion ce qui sera nécessaire.

J'ai l'honneur de vous offrir tous les Renseignements sur cette Échelle, Je me flatte d'y reussir. Je crois d'en partir en May ou Juin prochain pr. Marseille et quiter ces Barbares Cores. [Corsaires].

J'ai l'honneur d'être avec un profond Respect, Monsr., Votre &c. (signé) SALVA.

Adresse à Mrs. Pre. Siau & Co. Negts. à Marseille. Pre. [Première] Enveloppe sans écrire à ces messieurs. La Seconde à Salva à Alger.

2. The fleet of Algiers had declined from 75 corsairs at the beginning of the seventeenth century to less than 20 by the second half of the eighteenth century. Piracy, a state monopoly, still posed a considerable threat, however, even while Algiers and Spain were at war from 1770 to 1785: Jamil M. Abun-Nasr, *A History of the Maghrib in the Islamic Period* (Cambridge, Eng., 1987), pp. 165–6.

3. A firman was a decree from the Sublime Porte, the government of the Ottoman Empire and the nominal ruler of Algiers; for the tenuous relationship between the dey of Algiers and the sultan in Istanbul see John B. Wolf, *The Barbary Coast: Algiers under the Turks, 1500 to 1830* (New York, 1979), pp. 290–1.

4. Louis Timoni was agent of the Holy Roman Empire in Algiers from Feb. 2 to March 26, 1782: *Repertorium der diplomatischen Vertreter*, III, 62.

5. XXXIV, 565n.

Forces maritimes d'Alger.
au pr. Avril 1783.

1. Caravelle Servant d'Amiral de 42. Canons, hors de service.

1. Barque	26.
1. ditto	32
1. ditto	30
1. ditto	22.
1. ditto	24.
1. Chebeck	34.
1. ditto	24.
1. ditto	18.
1. ditto	18.
3. demi-Galeres	4.
3. Galiotes	4
2. ditto	2.

18. Corsaires

Copie d'une Lettre de M. Salva à M. Franklin, datée d'Alger le 1er. Avril 1783.—

Notation by William Temple Franklin: Letter from Algier

From the Comtesse d'Houdetot

LS: American Philosophical Society

Mercredy 2. Avril 1783.

Monsieur De Crevecœur Est fort En peine Mon Cher Docteur D'une Reponse qu'il attend De Vous au Sujet De L'affaire dont il Vous a parlé Chez Vous Dernierement; Comme il Est Chargé D'En Rendre Compte a Monsieur De Castries, il Est important qu'il Recoive Cette Reponse,[6] Et il a Crû que je pouvais Con-

---

6. Crèvecœur had been commissioned by Castries to provide a detailed report, or series of reports, on the United States, including geography, population, culture, industries, etc. He evidently worked on the project for seven weeks; the result so pleased Castries and the king that in June he was given

tribuer a L'accellerer. L'Estime que je fais De Sa personne Et L'Extreme interest que je prend a Luy, ne M'ont pas permis De Le Refuser; Sentant tres Bien L'Embaras ou Le Deffaut De Reponse le Mettrait avec Monsieur De Castries avec qui il a Rendez-vous Vendredy tant pour Cette affaire que pour D'autres qui Luy Sont particulieres. J'Espere toujours Mon Cher Docteur avoir Le plaisir de Vous Voir jeudy a huit heures.[7] Vous Scavés Combien je mets De prix a Ce Rendez-vous.

LA CTESSE DHOUDETOT

Voulés Vous Bien M'Envoyer par Le Comissionnaire Un Manchon que j'ay Laisse Chez Vous.

From Jean-Louis Giraud Soulavie[8]

AL: Dartmouth College Library

Monsieur   Paris ce 2 avril 1783
Vous faites bien de L'honneur a mes faibles Travaux, non seulement en agreant L'hommage que je j'en ai fait au Liberateur de l'amerique, Mais en Voulant bien faire passer Sous Vos auxpices un exemplaire à La bibliotheque De philadelphie qui Vous doit Son existence est a Celle de lacademie de la meme ville qui vous doit Sa gloire.[9] Daignés recevoir mes remercimens pour le

---

his choice of consular posts in America. The report has never been located and its date is unknown. A fragment of a memorandum survives, c. March 10, 1783, in which Crèvecœur discussed New York commerce and recommended the establishment of a packet boat service: Julia P. Mitchell, *St. Jean de Crèvecoeur* (New York, 1916), pp. 79–80, 177–8; Robert de Crèvecœur, *Saint John de Crèvecoeur: sa vie et ses ouvrages (1735–1815)* (Paris, 1883), pp. 77–9; Howard C. Rice, *Le Cultivateur américain: étude sur l'œuvre de Saint John de Crèvecœur* (Paris, 1933), p. 22n. We assume that he is here asking BF to review his draft proposal for that service. The proposal has not been found, but BF's response to it is below, [after April 2].

7. One of her musical evenings; see her earlier invitation to BF of Feb. 4.
8. This is the last extant letter from the naturalist, with whom BF discussed geology and whose *Histoire naturelle de la France méridionale* was nearing completion: XXXV, 354–61; XXXVII, 384–5; XXXVIII, 123–7, 239–41. Vol. 6 had just been published; it was announced for sale in the March 23 issue of the *Jour. de Paris.*
9. BF forwarded sets of Soulavie's works to both the Library Company of

service que vous Voulés bien me rendre en maccordant Votre
protection auprès de la societé De philadelphie dont je ne suis pas
digne d'etre l'assossié; mais pour laquelle je suis penetré de Veneration.[1]
    Je suis avec un profond Respect Monsieur Votre Très-humble
& très obeissant serviteur   L'ABBÉ SOULAVIE

From Jonathan Williams, Jr.   Copy: Yale University Library

Dr & Hond Sir   L'Orient April 2d. 1783
    Mr A. J. Alexander will shew you a letter relative to some Ar-
rests placed in the hands of Williams Moore & Co to stop Mon-
eys Mr Alexander was to pay Messrs Barclay & Moylan through
them— The Letter & papers it incloses will inform you fully—
I have therefore only to beg you will believe my refusal proceeds
only from a fear of future ill Consequences and as the matter is
wholy in Mr Alexanders name he is the proper person to act in
it— I refer you to my Uncle for further particulars.[2]
    It is reported here that Governement intend to make Port

Philadelphia and the APS. The former recorded the gift on Nov. 11 (unpublished minutes), the latter on Sept. 26 (*Early Proceedings of the American
Philosophical Society . . . compiled . . . from the Manuscript Minutes of its
Meetings from 1744 to 1838* [Philadelphia, 1884], p. 118). One of Soulavie's
letters of presentation survives, written on April 2 and perhaps enclosed with
the present letter. He does not name the institution, but refers to his gift as
being sent under the auspices of "Votre immortel fondateur." Hist. Soc. of
Pa.

    1. At BF's suggestion, Soulavie was elected to membership in the APS in
1786: BF's "List of Persons to be Recommended for Members of P. Society"
(undated, Library of Congress); APS membership records.

    2. Alexander John Alexander was the uncle of JW's wife. On March 21 JW
notified him that creditors of the United States had served Williams, Moore
& Co. with a stop payment order, in consequence of Forster frères' attachment of the proceeds of the prizes captured by the *Alliance* in the fall of 1782.
Alexander had purchased sugar through Williams, Moore & Co. at a sale of
the prizes' cargo, but was prevented from making payment by the attachment. XXXVIII, 232–3; JW to A. J. Alexander, March 21, 1783 (Yale University Library); William B. Clark, *Gallant John Barry, 1745–1803: the Story of
a Naval Hero of Two Wars* (New York, 1938), pp. 276–7, 313, 317.

Louis a free port.[3] I shall be obliged for what information you can consistantly give on this matter as it is of serious Consequence to my house here— Port Louis has hitherto been a Small Garrison of no more Commerce than its own Consumption, to make it a port of trade will require some Undoing and a great deal of doing— Military and Commercial Conveniences are very opposite, Forts should therefore be turned into Quays and Soldiery and Idleness must give place to Artisans & Industry as nothing can be produced without time so I think *that* the only thing necessary to make Port Louis a good Port; the same may be said of Painboeuf with this difference that there is nothing to undo there, and not near so much to do. For my own part I think a free trade with America Should not be Confined to one port, so far as relates to exportation all France is a great Shop and the more Encouragement she gives her Customers, by selling Cheap and exporting with facility the more she will Sell and as the nature of her productions are Fabrications the more Industry will be brought forth, her Capital turned often & her riches will increase.

It is not on the narrow Scale of immediate profit that the Commercial Interests of the nation should be managed by setting out on liberal Principles, Commerce will manage her own Affairs better than all the Regulations in the World, in short as you observe in one of your Notes to a little english Book *laisser nous faire* is the least thing Governement can do,[4] So far as a place of deposit may be requisite a free port for importations will be advantageous but this should be for the productions of all the World that the Americans may find every thing by coming to France. I hear that Government mean to encourage the Importation of Teas, so as that Article may be afforded Cheaper than from any other Nation, this is a good Idea for as it is a very Saleable Article it will Serve to bring Customers who will always buy Something else at same time.

3. Many municipalities wished to be named free ports; see the Chamber of Commerce of Aunis to BF, Jan. 31.

4. See BF's notes in George Whatley's *Principles of Trade, Fredom and Protection Are Its Best Suport* . . . (London, 1774), a copy of which he gave to JW: XXI, 175.

I do not mean to trouble you by giving me all the details I ask but I shall be much obliged if you will desire Billy to favour me with a full and Circumstantial letter on the Subject it will be an addition to the many kind attentions he has shewn and will highly oblige me. My Love to him I am as ever &c

P.S. Finding a Cartel here I have sent for all the Prisoners which are in Nantes to come hither to embark[5] the Expence I suppose will fall on me but I hope the publick will reimburse me and I shall send the accot accordingly.

His Excellency Doctor Franklin Passy

To Michel-Guillaume St. John de Crèvecœur

AL (draft): Library of Congress

Sir, [after April 2, 1783][6]
I have perused the foregoing Memoir, and having formerly had some Share in the Management of the Pacquet Boats between England and America,[7] I am enabled to furnish you with some small Remarks.—

The Project is good, & if carried into Execution will certainly be very useful to Merchants immediately, and profitable to the Revenue of the Post Office at least after some time; because not only Commerce increases Correspondence, but Facility of Correspondence increases Commerce, & they go on mutually augmenting each other.

5. For the prisoner exchange see Bondfield's and Hodgson's letters of Jan. 26, above.
6. Dated on the basis of the comtesse d'Houdetot's letter of that date, which we believe elicited this one. Our annotation there provides background on Crèvecœur's proposal for a packet boat service, the subject of this response.
7. Service between New York and Falmouth began in 1756 and was administered by the British Post Office: Julia P. Mitchell, *St. Jean de Crèvecoeur* (New York, 1916), p. 178n; Kenneth Ellis, *The Post Office in the Eighteenth Century: a Study in Administrative History* (London, New York, and Toronto, 1958), pp. 34–7. BF, who was appointed joint deputy postmaster general of North America in 1753, was involved with the service during the time when he was residing in America (1756–57 and 1762–64).

Four Packet Boats were at first thought sufficient between Falmouth and New York, so as dispatch one regularly the first Wednesday in every Month. But by Experience it was found that a fifth was necessary; as without it, the Regularity was sometimes broken by Accidents of Wind & Weather, & the Merchants disappointed & their Affairs deranged, a Matter of great Consequence in Commerce.— A fifth Packet was accordingly added.[8]

It is probable, as you observe, that the English will keep up their Packets. In which Case I should think it adviseable to order the Dispatch of the French Packets in the intermediate times, that is on the third Wednesdays. This would give the Merchants of Europe & America Opportunities of Writing every Fortnight. And the English who had miss'd Writing by their own Packet of the first Wednesday, or have new Matter to write which they wish to send before the next Month, will forward their Letters by the Post to France to go by the French Packet, & *vice versa*, which will encrease the Inland Postage of both Nations.—

As these Vessels are not to be laden with Goods, their Holds may, without Inconvenience, be divided into separate Apartments after the Chinese Manner, and each of those Apartments caulked tight so as to keep out Water. In which Case if a Leak should happen in one Apartment, that only would be affected by it, & the others would be free; so that the Ship would not be so subject as others to founder & sink at Sea. This being known would be a great Encouragement to Passengers.[9]

I send you a Copy of a Chart of the Gulph Stream which is little known by European Navigators, and yet of great Consequence; since in going to America they often get into that Stream and unknowingly stem it, whereby the Ship is much retarded & the Voyage lengthened enormously.— The directions being imperfectly translated and expressed in French, I have put them more correctly in English.[1]

---

8. The French service began with six ships: Robert de Crèvecœur, *Saint John de Crèvecoeur, sa vie et ses ouvrages (1735–1813)* (Paris, 1883), p. 312.

9. BF would later discuss this "well-known practice of the Chinese" in his "Maritime Observations": Smyth, *Writings*, IX, 381.

1. See the illustration on the facing page. This chart is Le Rouge's copy of the Gulf Stream chart that BF had caused to be engraved in London *c.* 1769,

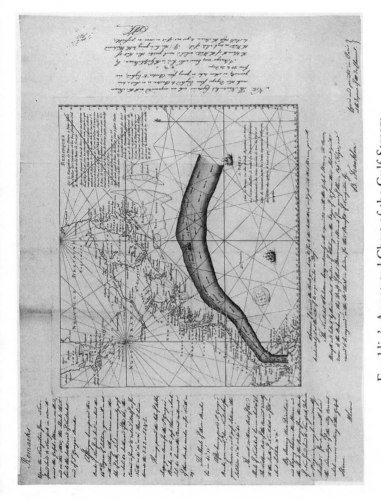

Franklin's Annotated Chart of the Gulf Stream

I have the honour to be &c

M. St. Jean de Crevecoeur

From Samuel Vaughan, Jr. ALS: American Philosophical Society

Dear Sir,   Paris, 3 April, 1783.

I should be much obliged if you could with convenience lend me three hundred Livres Tournois, for which, I have the honor to inclose you a Bill on my Brother William.[2]

With respect to the 600 Livres you was so good as to advance on my note the 26 Feby: last,[3] I have written to my Brother Ben; who says, that he has a demand upon you, for about £30, on account of money expended in pamphlets & glass, or advanced to Mrs Stewart;[4] & that he will shortly take the liberty of troubling

for use by the British postal service. (We published the Le Rouge chart in XXXIII, facing p. 298, and discussed it there.) The sailing directions BF here crossed out were translated from the directions engraved on the original, written by Capt. Timothy Folger (XV, 246–8). BF's revisions do not so much correct Le Rouge's French as improve upon the original directions, making them comprehensible to any navigator sailing into New England for the first time and unfamiliar with the Gulf Stream and the dangerous shoals south of Georges Bank and Nantucket. BF's "Remarks" were written in the left and bottom margin by L'Air de Lamotte, who also signed BF's name. In the right margin, BF himself added a "Note" about how long it takes experienced Nantucket captains to make the eastward and westward voyages, and how a "Stranger" can tell if he is in the Gulf Stream by feeling the warmth of the water. BF had these marginalia copied on several of the Le Rouge charts, one of which he presented to the APS for publication along with his "Maritime Observations." For the text of his marginalia see Smyth, *Writings*, IX, 405–6. For a full discussion of this chart and its significance see Ellen R. Cohn, "Benjamin Franklin, Georges-Louis Le Rouge and the Franklin/Folger Chart of the Gulf Stream," *Imago Mundi*, LII (2000), 124–5, 128–42.

2. BF advanced him this sum the same day. He advanced another 1,000 *l.t.* on May 1: Account XVII (XXVI, 3).

3. Recorded on Feb. 27: Account XVII.

4. Margaret Stewart (XXIII, 302n) had appealed to BF for financial help in January and April of 1782: XXXVI, 410; XXXVII, 229–30. On March 8, 1783, Benjamin Vaughan loaned her 12 guineas on BF's account, which she promised to either repay in one month's time or send 12 copies of her brother's publication *The Senator's Remembrancer*. (Her receipt is at the APS.) She

you with the particulars: It should, therefore, seem more proper to leave this debt unsettled, till the above particulars are received. With the utmost respect I remain, Dear Sir, Your very obliged & humble servt., SAMUEL VAUGHAN JUNR.

Addressed: A Son Excellence / Monsieur Franklin, / Ministre Plenipotentiare des Etats Unis &c, / a Passy, / pres de Paris.

From Jonathan Williams, Sr.

ALS: American Philosophical Society

Hond sr   London apl. 3d. 1783

After a plesent Journey with a very agreeable Compainion (Mr Martin)[5] I ariv'd Safe to this great City have taken lodgings in the Strand at John Reads No 394 Opposite Cecil street. If you or Mr Wm.[6] Should have any Commands I Should be glad to Receive & Execute them. I have seen Messrs Vaughan Hodgson & Mr Laurence[7] have Recd great Civilities from those Gentm. in Consequence of your kind Recommendations for Which I am much Obligd to you, doubtless you will have heard of the Settlement of the new ministry the Duke of Portland the first Lord of the Treasury Lord North & Mr Fox is in[8] & I am told the Whol is Settled we may now expect the Definitve treaty will be finish'd & the Trade opened tho' I Cant think it possible untill all the Kings troops are taken from America & New York free'd & that I am told is a Werk of time Some months at Least.

I Went yesterday to Kensington inquird after Mrs Hewson &

---

eventually gave Vaughan the 12 copies, though in her only other letter to BF, written five years later, she did not know whether he received them: Stewart to BF, Aug. 3, 1788, APS.

5. Williams and James Martin left Paris early on the morning of March 22: Martin to JA, March 22, 1783 (Mass. Hist. Soc.).

6. WTF.

7. Williams probably carried BF's March 20 letter to Henry Laurens, and his letter to Benjamin Vaughan of [c. March 21].

8. Portland's ministry (with North as home secretary and Fox as foreign secretary) took office on April 2: E. B. Fryde et al., eds., *Handbook of British Chronology* (3rd ed., London, 1986), pp. 114, 121, 123.

found that Mrs. Stivenson was dead & She Moved into the Coun-
try—[9] there is no new abrigment of the Comm Prayer Book[1] an
Atempt was made but did not Succed.— My Love to all you
Love & belive me ever Your Dutyful Nephew

JONA WILLIAMS

Addressed: His Excellency Benjamin Franklin Esqr / Passy near
/ Paris

To John Ewing[2] LS:[3] University of Pittsburgh Library

Revd. Sir, Passy, April 4. 1783
   This Line will be put into your Hands by Mr. Redford from
Ireland, who goes to America, with Views of settling there.[4] He
is strongly recommended to me by several of my Friends, as a
Gentleman of excellent Character, for his Principles, his Knowledge and Abilities, such as must render him an useful Citizen of
America. I beg leave to request for him your Civilities, and the
Advice that as a Stranger he may occasionally require; in which
you will much oblige me, who from the short Acquaintance I
have had with him, feel myself much interested in his Favour,
and heartily wish that our Country may be agreable to him. With
great Esteem, I have the honour to be, Sir, Your most obedient
& most humble Servant B FRANKLIN

Revd. Mr. Ewing.

---

9. Mary Hewson had moved to Kensington for her mother's sake, but returned to Cheam after her mother's death: XXXVII, 260; XXXVIII, 578–9; BF to
Hewson, April 26, below.
   1. For BF's earlier collaboration with Baron Le Despencer on the *Abridge-
ment of the Book of Common Prayer . . .* (London, 1773) see XX, 343–52.
   2. A pastor in Philadelphia: XI, 526n; XVII, 11n.
   3. In L'Air de Lamotte's hand, except for the complimentary close, which
was written by BF.
   4. Archibald Redford was introduced to BF by Richard Price and Benjamin
Vaughan; their letters are above, March 10 and 11.

To Benjamin Rush

LS:[5] Yale University Library

Dear Friend,   Passy, April 4. 1783

I take the Liberty of introducing to your Acquaintance the Bearer Mr. Redford, because I am persuaded that I shall therein do you a Pleasure. His Character you will find in an enclos'd Letter to me from Dr. Price.[6] I hope his Reception in our Country will be such as to make it agreable to him and induce him to settle among us; as from the short Acquaintance I have had with him, I am of Opinion he will prove a valuable Member of Society.[7] With great Esteem & best Wishes for your Prosperity, I am ever, my Dear Friend, Yours most affectionately

Endorsed: B: Franklin April 4th. 1783[8]

From Henry Laurens

LS: Library of Congress; copy: South Carolina Historical Society

Sir,   London 4th April 1783.

I had the honor of recieving your letter of the 20th. Ulto. on the 31st.

It affords me great satisfaction to recieve your favorable sentiments respecting my transient Residence on this Spot, I might have selected a place more agreeable to my health and tranquility and less expensive to my pocket. I have not been quite idle nor quite unsuccessful in my Endeavours to promote the honor and interest of our Country.

I have displayed the error of calling Men [*loyal*],[9] whose fears or whose Avarice prompted some of them to act on both sides, restrained others to a mean and shuffling Neutrality, others again

5. In L'Air de Lamotte's hand. The signature has been cut off; only the top portion is visible.

6. Price to BF, March 10.

7. Redford arrived in Philadelphia some time before Sept. 25: *Morris Papers*, VIII, 546.

8. Rush also received a letter from BF dated Feb. 14, 1783. The text is missing; all that survives is an address sheet on which BF indicated that it would be sent by Capt. All, and Rush noted the date. Hist. Soc. of Pa.

9. This word is supplied from Laurens' letterbook copy.

who by maliciously blowing a Spark, which but for them might have been happily extinguished, have involved this Kingdom in Disgrace and almost Ruin.

Mr Pitt told the House of Commons, the Commissioners at Paris were well pleased with the outlines of the Provisional Bill,[1] the one in London smiled at the Report, and said he could trust his Colleagues; it was pretty notorious that he had been on the reserve save now and then dropping a cautionary Hint to beware of the old Error of legislating for the United States. My Opinion had been often asked, but for the most obvious Reasons I declined an interference. At length I framed an American Bill for regulating Commerce with great Britain, and held it up to the proper Characters as a Mirror, from that time, the 22d March their own Bill which was to have been finished on the 23d. has slept with very little interruption. You will recieve a Copy of the American Bill enclosed which I presented as coming by an expeditious Courier in five Days.[2]

Government as 'tis called is again restored to Great Britain an administration is formed— An Administration which presents to me a prospect of doing Business with us immediately & effectually.[3] I shall know more of this Matter before I Seal, meaning presently to pay Compliments of Congratulation.[4]

1. This refers to Pitt's March 17 remarks on the American Intercourse Bill: *Laurens Papers*, XVI, 174n.

2. The text is published in *Laurens Papers*, XVI, 177–9.

3. Laurens' optimism was misplaced. Portland's new government (with North as home secretary and Fox as foreign secretary) assumed office on April 2. Six days later the cabinet decided to open negotiations for establishing trade relations with the United States on an equal footing. It insisted, however, that care be taken "to restrain American Ships from bringing any goods but of their own produce either to Great Britain or to the British West Indies, and that British Ships trading from America to Europe & vice-versâ shall touch at some port of Great Britain." On April 9 Fox moved that the Commons suspend consideration of the American Intercourse Bill until after the signing of the final peace treaty. He proposed instead to repeal the Prohibitory Act and remove other obstacles to the resumption of trade, such as the requirement that ships arriving from American ports present bonds and certificates. Cobbett, *Parliamentary History*, XXIII, 723–30; Fortescue, *Correspondence of George Third*, VI, 331, 348–9; Harlow, *Second British Empire*, I, 458–60; see also the annotation of William Hodgson's letter of April 18.

4. Hartley had arranged for Laurens to call on Fox on April 4 and on Port-

The acquiescence of Spain in the Boundary lines is excellent, tho' I believe very mortifying to some folks here, who I have every reason to believe harboured intentions of renewing the Quarrel.

I am as much at a loss as you are, to know what Employment can be found for Mediators, probably tis only "Talk," but if they come, We must meet them; our Ground is fair.

I have now transmitted to Mr Adams such proofs of Mr. Jenings's dishonor as will certainly induce our Colleague to think him a very unfit person for a confidential friend in the Business of the United States.[5]

My Son and Daughter desire to join with me in respectful Compliments and every good Wish to yourself & Mr. Franklin. We shall prepare to morrow for paying a Visit to Passy. I fancy Mr. Oswald will not be of our party a letter which I herewith forward from our friend Mr Hartley will probably clear up that point.[6]

I have the Honor to be With the most affectionate Esteem & Regard sir, your obedient and very humble servant,

HENRY LAURENS,

ps. I have had a Conference with Mr. Fox—reserving neither to Commit nor pledge myself for any opinion I might give. Mr. Fox discoverd a disposition to proceed to business with us with Liberality & effect, I urged the necessity of concluding the definitive Treaty & withdrawing the British Forces from the United States, without delay— In answer to supposed difficulties in obtaining Transport Ships, I proposed the Troops to be removed to Long or Staten Island—& added, that we might not insist upon Hostages for their peaceable behavior & final removal, tho'

---

land on April 5: Hartley to Laurens, April 3 and 4, 1783 (University of S.C. Library).

5. On March 6 Laurens sent JA a paper concerning "Jenings's misconduct," which did not produce the desired effect; JA's response of March 12 was noncommittal: *Laurens Papers*, XVI, 157–61. In a letter to JA of March 26[–April 4] Laurens reiterated his charges against Jenings: *Adams Papers*, XIV, 365–7.

6. We have not located the letter. Fox informed Laurens on April 5 that Hartley was replacing Oswald: Oswald to Caleb Whitefoord, April 5, 1783, in W. A. S. Hewins, ed., *The Whitefoord Papers* ... (Oxford, 1898), p. 185.

some powers would. That the State of New York ought immediately to be put in possession of the City & Port— Upon the whole the Secretary of State asked if he might Report, "that I believed there was a disposition & powers on the part of the American Commissioners to open an intercourse & Commerce of terms of reciprocity without delay—" I assented as my belief & opinion— I hope for the honor of saluting you within ten days.— Be pleased Sir to communicate this PS. to Mr. Adams & Mr Jay.   H L.

His Excellency Doctor Franklin Passy,

From Jean-Baptiste Réveillon[7]

D: American Philosophical Society

[on or before April 4, 1783][8]

Mémoire Pour Le Sr Réveillon

Quelques fabriques de Papiers peints et tontisses les plus considérables de celles qui sont établies en france ont conçu, depuis la paix, le projet de faire passer en Amérique quelques Envois de

7. This is the only extant communication from Réveillon (1725–1811), one of the most important papermakers in eighteenth-century France. He produced wallpapers at a manufactory in the faubourg Saint-Antoine and owned a paper mill in Courtalin-en-Brie, outside Paris. On Jan. 22 he had presented samples of his Courtalin papers to the Académie des sciences, including *papier vélin* (wove paper), which he claimed was the first manufactured in France. Both Anisson and Philippe-Denis Pierres had admired it, he wrote, and Pierres had requested the first ream. (Académie des sciences, *Procès-verbaux*, Jan. 22, 1783, and accompanying memoir.) Réveillon's wallpaper manufactory and paper mill were designated royal manufactories in July and December, 1783, respectively; in 1789 his house was destroyed and he was imprisoned during what came to be known as the Réveillon riots: Leonard N. Rosenband, "Jean-Baptiste Réveillon: a Man on the Make in Old Regime France," *French Hist. Studies*, XX (1997), 481–510.

8. Among BF's papers at the APS is a letter from a M. Guérin to an unnamed female cousin, dated April 4, 1783, asking her to give Réveillon's memoir to BF and "inspire his interest" in it. Guérin was sure that BF knew of Réveillon's paper manufactory.

leurs marchandises. Les unes, en les adressant directement dans le pays à des maisons de commerce, à l'effet de vendre pour leur compte, les autres en vendant ici à des Spéculateurs connus qui ont fait entrer cet article dans leurs Spéculations avec le pays américain.

Le Sr R. qui tient aujourdhuy la manufacture la plus considérable dans ce genre de fabrique, et dont les papiers sont, sans contredit, les plus soigneusement fabriqués, ne peut pas voir ses concurrens donner cette extension à leur commerce, sans songer à faire marcher le sien d'un pas égal.

En conséquence il desireroit de deux choses. l'une. Où la recommandation de Monsieur Francklin auprès des Spéculateurs connus qui font ici le commerce avec le pays américain, à l'effet de vendre ses papiers à ceux qui jugeroient convenable de faire entrer cet article dans leurs spéculations. où les instructions nécessaires pour faire passer directement ses papiers à des maisons établies sur le lieu, qui les vendroient pour son compte, avec des recommandations pour les personnes auxquelles on pourroit les adresser.

De ces deux partis le Sr Reveillon préféreroit toujours le premier, même avec beaucoup moins d'avantage, attendu la longueur qu'entraîne ces sortes de spéculations, quand on les fait directement, l'embarras des retours, et les suites d'affaires qu'ils occasionnent, lesquelles deviennent étrangeres aux objets dont le sr. Reveillon est entièrement occupé, et dont il ne peut être distrait sans beaucoup d'inconvenient./.

From Vergennes

LS: American Philosophical Society; draft: Archives du Ministère des affaires étrangères

à Versles. le 5. Mars [*i.e.*, April][9] 1783.

J'ai communiqué, Monsieur, à Mr. le Garde des Sceaux la demande que vous avez faite pour publier par la voye de l'impres-

9. The month is correct on the draft and was corrected in pencil to "April" on the LS, presumably by someone in BF's office. This letter is a response to BF's of March 24.

sion la traduction du livre des *constitutions des Etats-unis de l'amque. Sepale.* Mr. le Garde des Sceaux vient, Monsieur, de me répondre qu'il avoit autorisé le Sr. Pierres Imprimeur à commencer l'impression de cet ouvrage, à condition d'envoyer les feuilles d'impression à fûr et mesure qu'elles sortiront de Ses presses à Mr. de Neville[1] Directeur Général de la librairie afin que ce Magistrat en confie l'examen à un censeur. Cette derniere formalité est, Monsieur, indispensable pour se conformer aux réglements relatifs à la librairie.[2]

J'ai l'honneur d'être très sincérement, Monsieur, votre très humble et très obéissant Serviteur./. De Vergennes

Mr. franklin./.

1. François-Cl.-Michel-Benoît Le Camus de Néville: Robert Darnton, *The Business of Enlightenment: a Publishing History of the* Encyclopédie, *1775–1800* (Cambridge, Mass., and London, 1979), pp. 65, 72, 537–8; Léon-Noël Berthe, *Dictionnaire des correspondants de l'Académie d'Arras au temps de Robespierre* (Arras, 1969), p. 164.
2. Vergennes had forwarded BF's request to Miromesnil on March 30, and the *garde des sceaux* replied on April 1. (Both letters are at the AAE.) Miromesnil told Vergennes that he would allow this unusual procedure because of Vergennes' request that the publication process be expedited, as BF wished. Normally, Miromesnil would not authorize the printing of a manuscript until after he had sent it to the royal censor. He added that he was recommending to Néville that he tell the censor to examine the sheets with "le plus de Célérité possible."

To François-Marie-des-Neiges-Emmanuel (Emanuel) de Rohan-Poulduc (Polduc)[3]

Copy[4] and transcript: National Archives

Monseigneur, [April 6, 1783]

J'ai l'honneur d'adresser à votre Altesse Eminentissime la Medaille que Je viens de faire frapper:[5] C'est, Monseigneur, un Hommage de Reconnoissance du à l'Intérêt que vous avez pris à notre Cause, et nous ne le devons pas moins à vos Vertus et à la Sagesse du Gouvernement de votre Altesse Eminentissime.

Permettez, Monseigneur, que Je demande votre Protection pour ceux de nos Citoyens que les Circonstances pourront amener dans Vos Ports.[6] J'espere que votre altesse Eminentissime voudra bien la leur accorder et recevoir avec bonté l'assurance du profond Respect avec lequel Je suis, Monseigneur, de votre altesse Eminentissime Le tres humble et tres obeissant Serviteur. (signed) B. FRANKLIN

Copie d'une Lettre de M. B. Franklin à Son altesse Eminentissime, Monseigneur le Grand maitre de Malte, datée de Passy le 6. Avril 1783.

[*In William Temple Franklin's hand:*] To the Gd. Master of Malta

---

3. Rohan (1725–1797), a member of an illustrious family, was the first French grand master of the Knights of Malta since 1697. Elected in November, 1775, he served until his death: *Dictionnaire de la noblesse*, XVII, 538; Michael Galea, *Grand Master Emanuel de Rohan, 1775–1797* (Valletta, Malta, 1996); Whitworth Porter, *A History of the Knights of Malta* . . . (rev. ed., London, 1883), pp. 639–46.

4. In L'Air de Lamotte's hand and enclosed with BF's July 22, 1783, letter to Livingston. For an English translation see Wharton, *Diplomatic Correspondence*, VI, 361.

5. The *Libertas Americana* medal.

6. American commerce needed protection from the Barbary states; see Salva to BF, April 1. The Knights of Malta continued to maintain a fleet of four galleys: Jan Glete, *Navies and Nations: Warships, Navies and State Building in Europe and America, 1500–1860* (2 vols., Stockholm, 1993), II, 515–16.

From Samuel Vaughan, Jr., with Franklin's Note
for a Reply   ALS: American Philosophical Society

Dear Sir,   Paris 6 March [*i.e.*, April], 1783.[7]

I hope you will have the goodness to excuse my not communicating in person the following extract of a letter from my Brother Ben, which I should do with a great deal of pleasure, was it not entirely out of my power from the Business I have at present; &, as the latter part should be communicated early.

"Tell Dr Franklin, with my most affectionate respects, that I thank him for his letter,[8] & shall observe to write him by every safe opportunity. I have ordered one of Mr Nairne's patent machines to be put up for him, which I beg his acceptance of, & intend sending him by the same opportunity, together with his 4to bible.—[9] Mr Williams[1] may depend upon every attention from me.— I thank the Doctor for his letters for my friends going to America."

"At the same time that you say these things to Dr Franklin, mention to him the Death of Dr Hunter;[2] & the propriety of bringing Dr Priestley forward again, for the vacant seat in the Academy of Sciences."[3]

By a letter antecedent to the above, my Brother Ben begs I will

7. The month must be April, given the date of Hunter's death and the visit to Hoffmann; see our annotation below.

8. Above, [*c.* March 21].

9. Nairne's "patent electrical machine," which received its patent in February, 1782, was an improvement on his earlier versions: xx, 433–4n; W. D. Hackman, "The Design of the Triboelectric Generators of Martinus van Marum, F.R.S. A Case History of the Interaction between England and Holland in the Field of Instrument Design in the Eighteenth Century," *Notes and Records of the Royal Society of London*, XXVI (1971), 178n. It and the Bible were included in the shipment of goods that Vaughan sent in June; see the annotation of Benjamin Vaughan to BF, Feb. 25.

1. Jonathan Williams, Sr.

2. Dr. William Hunter, the famous anatomist (XVIII, 192), died on March 30: *ODNB*.

3. BF recommended Priestley to the Academy of Sciences at Paris on more than one occasion, but it was not until February, 1784, that he finally became an *associé étranger:* BF to Richard Price, Aug. 16, 1784 (Smyth, *Writings*, IX, 255); Institut de France, *Index biographique des membres et correspondants de l'Académie des sciences de 1666 à 1939* (Paris, 1939), p. 375.

request, your honoring Mr John Darby & Mr Grigby with some introductory letters for America.[4] Their views are I *believe* commercial. Mr John Darby is established in London in the Irish linen trade; is our relation & intimate friend, & about whom the family most particularly interest themselves. Your friend Mr Jackson[5] is giving him letters of the strongest kind.— The above two gentlemen will, in all likelihood, travel together.

I had the pleasure of seeing the Duke of Chaulnes on Friday; but being indisposed, he cannot promise any particular day, to have the honor of meeting you or Mr Franklin at Mr Hoffmann's; I have therefore taken the liberty, by this mornings post, of appointing next Thursday,[6] at ten oClock to meet Mr Hoffmann at his own lodgings; & the Duke of Chaulnes will have the opportunity of another day, if that does not prove convenient.

With the strongest sentiments of gratitude & respect, I have the honor to be, Dear Sir, Your devoted humble Servt.

SAMUEL VAUGHAN JUNR.

Addressed: A Son Excellence / Monsieur Franklin, / Ministre Plenipotentiare des Etats / Unis &c &c, / a Passy, / pres de Paris.

Endorsed: To enquire & obtain this Package Ben's Books

Notation: Samuel Vaughan junior Paris 6 March 1783

4. Samuel Vaughan obviously did not realize that the "letters for my friends" acknowledged by Benjamin Vaughan in the excerpt quoted earlier referred to Darby and Grigby; see Benjamin Vaughan to BF, Feb. 25. Jay also gave the two men letters of recommendation; they arrived in Philadelphia in July: Morris, *Jay: Peace*, pp. 568–70; *Morris Papers*, VII, 682n; VIII, 342, 540; Jay to Livingston, April 8, 1783 (Library of Congress).

5. Richard Jackson (V, 148n; XXVI, 108n), whose sister Anne had married into the Darby family: x, 161n. In early April Richard Oswald forwarded a now-missing letter from Jackson to BF: W. A. S. Hewins, ed., *The Whitefoord Papers* . . . (Oxford, 1898), p. 186.

6. François-Joseph-Ignace Hoffmann (1730–1793) was the inventor of the polytype process (*DBF*). WTF and Samuel Vaughan, Jr., attended a demonstration on Thursday, April 10, with Faujas de Saint-Fond and others. BF visited Hoffmann two weeks later and had an inscription of his own reproduced by the new process: WTF *et al.*, specimen of polytype printing, April 10, 1783 (University of Pa. Library); BF's specimen, April 24, below.

From Catherine Turner[7]

ALS: American Philosophical Society

Dear Sir   Leigh the 7 April 1783

I Long since designd my self the Pleasure of writing to you, but Certain Circumstances prevented it you will no dout be suprize to have a Line from one you dont know but I hope you will have the Goodness to Exscuse the Liberty I have taken when I tell you that I once had the hapygness to Caul you my dear Uncel Franklin and I hope you will still promit me to caul you by that Name, I was Married to your Nephew John Mecom, I was a Long time at your House at Philadelphia with Mrs Franklin, and my dear Mrs Beache, thay ware very kind to me and I spent maney weeks at Burlinton with Governor Franklin, and his Lady, hose favours I shall never forgit, after the Death of Mr Mecom. I then Married Mr Turner, an Offecer, in the 47 Regement of Foot before this Unhappy war he was Wounded at Lexenton and at Bunkers hill, which he never recoverd, and departed this Life in June Last, he was one of the Best of Husbands and has Left me, a poor Lonly Widow. I was very happy but the Case is much Alterd, with me know, as I have not a relation, in this Country tho I have maney Friends ho has been very sivel to me, I should be very happy to return, to America and spend the remander of my Life there, for I have the rivited Affections of Nature to Struggel with, and would rather Live, in my Native Land Amongst my relations, but I Cant receve the Widows Penshon thare, and it is very Littel to Live on in this dear Country, if I Could Git a Friend, that had aney Intrest with the Secretary at War, to put me upon the Compassinate List, and endeavour, to Obtain the provision, made by that fund, for Officers Widow, I should do very well and be very happy. I saw in the papers, that you was Prepareing, to return to America, ware I am sure you, will make, thousand happy. God send you a safe Voige, and that you may spend the Eveing of your Life, in Peace and tranquility, and have every Blessing, this World Affords, and that of An-

---

7. The widow of John Mecom, who died in 1770 (I, lxii), and of Thomas Turner, a British officer with whom she apparently traveled to England: XXI, 348.

gels in the next, is the Prayers of your ever sencer and Affectionete Niec and most Obedent Humble Searvant

CATHERINE TURNER

PS I shall be much Obligd to you to Give my duty to my Mother Mecom and all our Friends and shall asteem it as a very Great favour to have a Line from you if I should be so happy you must Direct to me at Leigh nere Worrington Lancashire

Addressed: Hon: Benjn. Franklin. / Ministir Plenepotentiary from the / United States. / Paris.

From Benjamin Vaughan

Transcript: Massachusetts Historical Society

My dearest sir,   London, April 7, 1783.

I have received your several late favors by Mr Jonathan Williams & Mr. Penn, with many thanks.—[8] I cut out such parts of your newspapers as I judged proper to have published here, & was about to send them to some printer, but young Mr H. Laurens coming at the moment, I put them into his hands, as his father was well enough acquainted with the printer's most inclined to undertake the affair; & had expressed a wish to have the papers sent him after I had finished with them.

President Laurens goes over very well inclined to our new administration, (as I am told); which gives me pleasure on several accounts, particularly as it will facilitate business. Besides, I am glad to see Americans enough attached to us, to view with favorable eyes, even the bad or suspicious men among us. But I shall nevertheless trust to their good sense, to distinguish who have been the true friends to England & to *them;* & I hope that they will be no losers by our frequent revolutions here, as it has lately seemed to be a rule, that every administration must at least *begin* with some creditable measures. Ireland will probably suffer little by the present change, and England will at first only miss ecomony & enlargement of system.— I do not judge however

8. Jonathan Williams, Sr., and John Penn.

that a ministry which is neither relished by the people, nor relished by the king, & the parts of which do not relish each other can be very permanent; & the probability therefore is, that in three months they will either *less* agree, or *more* agree.

I am pretty indifferent about men, while I see measures going on well.

I am fully apprized of all your *general* reasonings about the Royalists; but if you will do me the favor to refer to my *letter* to you, in the last summer, respecting those gentlemen,[9] you will find that I made very little question about the *active* refugees; chiefly dwelling upon the hardships shewn to the absentees, neutral persons, & persons terrified into submission, or even that chose a wrong side on fair principles.— Having however heard much on the subject of retribution in this negotiation by the Amer Commissioners, I beg to be indulged in a word of apology for my own opinions, in addition to my former letter.

You are too well acquainted with the usual course of wars & of treaties concluding those wars; to believe that *justice* is the general rule by which either the one or the other are made or conducted. You know, on the contrary, that power & situation generally decide this business. If *England* therefore should now have acted with *complete justice,* it is more than she is to expect to receive from *other* powers; & *so far* it is a losing principle. I would *myself* however for one still act upon it; & I hope when it comes to *America's turn,* SHE will act upon it; & I believe, all things considered, that England has done pretty well in that line herself. But upon the footing of power & of the ordinary prejudices of states, I am well convinced that England has done very well by *you;* & that she has *not* made for herself *too* good a peace; but on the contrary, has given up some things to *future* policy; and has "omitted to avail herself of means, which might have improved her apparent, but temporary interests".— And the terms procured from her on all sides, certainly lessened the means which her ministers then had of serving the CONNECTION between the *two* countries (about which I am persuaded that we are *both* peculiarly interested;) as well as of serving our poor unfortunate race of human kind at large.

9. XXXVII, 719–25.

I believe there is a circumstance in your letters which goes still more beyond my propositions than the foregoing: for I do not wish to see the royalists "rewarded;" and I do not *ask* that America should "do them good".[1] I ask only, that certain persons among them should have "justice" (to use your own principle) "exhibited in their favor."— I think that I am not mistaken either in my facts or my principles, & I have no objection to avowing my opinions on this particular subject, for I cannot but think that the case will always sufficiently support me.

The inference which I would draw from the whole is, that America has *still* something to do on her side; & that in the interim, the American peace deserves to be kindly spoken of by America; the more especially, as factious people have been reprobated it in England.

I am, my dearest sir, Your ever devoted, affectionate & grateful   (signed) BENJN. VAUGHAN.

To Dr. Franklin at Passy.

(Copy.)

Crèvecœur to William Temple Franklin

ALS: American Philosophical Society

Sir,   Paris Monday 12: 0:clock [April 7, 1783?][2]
Agreable To your Grand Father's Promises, I beg you'd Send me by the bearer some Copies of the Interesting Map you Gave me the other Day which has been given to & has Singularly pleased the Mis. de Castries.[3]

1. See BF to Vaughan, *c.* March 21, above.
2. The first Monday after April 2, when BF was prompted to reply to Crèvecœur about his proposal for a packet boat service. BF's reply, [after April 2], enclosed an annotated copy of his Gulf Stream chart, the subject of this letter.
3. Castries had Crèvecœur translate BF's notes into French, and on April 10 sent them to Charles-Pierre Claret de Fleurieu, director of ports and arsenals, and head of the *dépôt des cartes* (*DBF*, under Claret). The cover letter said how useful it would be for navigation to have the Gulf Stream en-

I Remain very Respectfully, sir, Your Very Humble Servant
St. John

Addressed: A Monsieur / Monsieur Franklin Junior / Passy

From François Bowens   LS: American Philosophical Society

Ostend 8th April 1783./.

I have in Course received the honour of your Excellencies favour of the 24th. Ulto.[4] in Consequence of which I transmitted the necessary directions to London, on the 2d Currt. to prevent your Newspapers from being sent me in future[5] which I have no doubt will be paid proper attention to.

I am very sensible to the acknowledgements, Your Excellency, makes me on this Subject, which I must confess are highly agreeable to me, tho' I feel they are unmerited, as the little trouble I had, was amply recompensed by the pleasure I found, in the Idea that I was of use to your Excellency— I shall be happy to find opportunities of being more so than hitherto, & of meeting frequent opportunities by which I may convince you of the perfect respect with which I have the honour to be Your Excellencies Most obedt. & devoted servant   Pr. f. Bowens
Schoet[6]

His Excellency Dr. Franklin.

---

graved on a new (and presumably more accurate) chart. "The notes that are joined to the map are exactly what Mr Franklin gives me to understand," he wrote. "I beg you to examine everything, and if you have nothing better in your *dépôt*, mark this current and the observations and have the whole thing engraved." To our knowledge, a new chart was never produced: Ellen R. Cohn, "Benjamin Franklin, Georges-Louis Le Rouge and the Franklin / Folger Chart of the Gulf Stream," *Imago Mundi*, LII (2000), 136.

4. Not found.

5. Since 1780, Bowens had been receiving on BF's behalf various items sent from England. Most recently BF had asked him to procure and forward London newspapers: XXXII, 24–5, 422, 437, 500; XXXVI, 637. He must have contacted Samuel Potts, whose letter of May 9 addresses the same issue.

6. *Schout,* the Dutch term for bailiff.

Addressed: Son Excellence Le Docteur Franklin / en son hotel /
Passy / prés / Paris

From Ingenhousz   ALS: American Philosophical Society

                                        Vienna in Austria
My dear and Respectable Friend   April 8th. 1783.

As I have not heard from you this long while, I wish to know
whether you have recieved my letters, one accompanying a new
cast of my profil framed, an other by which I begg leave to dedicate to you my book, now under the press, at Paris, as I hope.[7] I
have not yet recieved the least intelligence from mr Wharton,
nor any from mr. Coffyn; so that I remain in some degree of anxiety about the money I entrusted with such unbounded confidence in the hands of mr. Wharton— I recieved, a few days
ago, a lettre from mr. Williams of Boston,[8] dated Boston Dec.
28. 1782, by which I am informed that from the produce of 500
Pound St., which mr. Williams of Nantes layd out for me in the
American trade, 7000 dollars have been put in the public loan
office at Boston on my name, the 15th of march 1779. I begg the
favour of acquainting me, whether I may flatter my self with the
safety of that money as to its Value. Doen't you think it advisable to leave it were it is, till every thing is in a settled situation?
I begg to forward the inclosed to mr. Williams, after having perused it.

I am dayly asked, whether you will soon come here—some
while ago the mr. *Veinbrenner* told me he had wrote a lettre to
you by order of the first minister of state Prince Kaunitz, of
which lettre I send the inclosed copy.[9] He had at that time wrote
to the same purpose to Count Mercy, to whom the Emperor has
now given official orders to invite you at his hous, and to treat

---

7. For the profile, whose accompanying letter has not been found, see
XXXVIII, 483. The dedication request is in Ingenhousz' letter of Jan. 28,
above.

8. JW's brother John; see our annotation of Ingenhousz' Feb. 26 letter.

9. This was Weinbrenner's own copy of his letter of Feb. 19, which is currently filed at the APS with the ALS.

you on the footing of a minister of a souverain power. Mr. Veinbrenner inform'd me also, that the imper. Ambassadour has orders to insinuate to you, that the Emperour is ready to aknowledge the united states as a souverain and independent power as
soon as you or any one authorised makes any Steps towards that
purpose.[1] Mr. Veinbrenner having not recieved any answer from
you, was advised by Pr. Kaunitz and an other state secretary to
speak me about it, and to request from me to press for the favour
of an answer, which I told him I should doe as soon as I should
write to you. This Morning that gentleman came to begg of me
to write you about it, delivring me the inclosed Copy. I told him
that I did not think any satisfactory answer could be given upon
the demand, as you could not probably judge of the solidity of
merchants in America; but, as he thinks you may perhaps be able
to give some directions on that head, that I will mention of it to
you.[2] I delight highly in seing by all this, that your joung Republic begins to be Courted by old souverains, who declined, not
a long while ago, her adresses— As they begged of me as a civility to endeavour to obtain an answer from you I could not
refuse it; and you may easily judge, that what ever satisfactory
or agreble intelligence I could communicate to the Emperour
from you, would not only be very honourable to me but would
also contribute to give me some degree of importance,[3] which I

1. See the annotation of Weinbrenner's Feb. 19 letter.

2. In his answer of May 16, BF said just what Ingenhousz predicted: that
he had been away from America too long to be able to evaluate the solidity
of mercantile houses. He recommended that Austria "send over a discreet,
intelligent Person" who could observe, evaluate, and advise. (Library of
Congress.) The Emperor had already appointed such a person, Baron
Frédérick-Eugène-François de Beelen-Bertholff (1729–1805), an official in
the council of finances of the Austrian Netherlands who had requested the
post. Beelen-Bertholff learned of his appointment on April 15, but did not receive his instructions until June. *Repertorium der diplomatischen Vertreter*, III,
284; Hanns Schlitter, ed., *Die Berichte des ersten Agenten Österreichs in den
Vereinigten Staaten von Amerika Baron de Beelen-Bertholff* (Vienna, 1891),
pp. 235–7; H. van Houtte, "Contribution à l'histoire commerciale des Etats
de l'empereur Joseph II (1780–1790)," *Vierteljahrschrift für Social und
Wirtschaftsgeschichte*, VIII (1910), 379–80; *Morris Papers*, VIII, 505–6.

3. Ingenhousz frequently communicated to the court political information
he received from BF. He described one of those communications in his letter

apprehend is reather in a declining Way, Since I submitted with reluctance to an arrangement by which I lost near a hundred P. a year against the conditions upon which I engaged to stay here.[4]

I think they will soon propose a commercial treaty with America, as it is their wish to get a share of that source of richess, enjoyed formerly by England alone. The articles of exportation from this Country are chiefly copper, steel, mercury and glass as fine as English. Hungarian wines begin also to be an object. From the low countries the chief exporting objects are lace and linnens.

Mr. Wharton promish'd me to send me some boston soap such as you gave me a piece of,[5] which it may very well be he has forwarded without it has come to my hands, as I See from the lettre of mr. Williams, that he has forwarded a lettre of myn to Boston which he took under his care.

I am very respectfully Your most obedient humble Servant and affectionate Frie   J. INGEN HOUSZ

I hear nothing of the printing of my book, nor even nothing of mr. LeBegue. Is he dead seck or absent? This vexes me not a little.

to his Exc. Benj. Franklin at Passy.

Endorsed: April 8. 83.

---

of Aug. 20, 1782; it was an extract of one of BF's recent letters, and a set of "reflections" based on views BF evidently expressed in a now-missing confidential letter: XXXVIII, 27. What appears to be Ingenhousz' draft of these reflections has recently been identified in the Yale University Library, where it had been misfiled under the erroneous date Ingenhousz gave it. Entitled "Remarque sur la lettre de monsieur Franklin du [*blank*] Nov. 1783," the two-page manuscript elaborates on the themes of England's arrogance and bellicosity, and the dangers to the "tranquilité" of Europe should any country— either England or one of the European nations—try to maintain political connections with North America, including Canada. An allusion to the ongoing War of American Independence obviously places this draft before November, 1782, and the subject matter and phraseology match the August description.

4. See XXXVIII, 365.

5. BF must have given him some of the family's crown soap.

From Le Roy   ALS: American Philosophical Society

Mardy au Soir [April 8 or 15, 1783][6]
Vous voulez bien mon Illustre Docteur donner à diner à une Jolie femme, qui meurt denvie de voir un grand homme de l'Amérique. Je crains que vous ne me trouviez bien indiscret en vous demandant la permission de vous mener jeudy par dessus le marché Un jeune Officier qui a le méme désir et non moins vivement, et qui est le fils d'un de nos bons amis M. Gueneau de Semur en Bourgogne[7] il est fort de la connoissance de M. Alexandre et vous avez surement entendu parler de lui par Ses différens ouvrages, Ayant Secondé M. De Buffon dans ses travaux et l'ayant Si bien imité mème que tout Paris y a été trompé. J'espere que les titres du Père feront un Passeport pour le fils, qui est d'ailleurs un jeune homme plein de raison, et bien fait pour vous admirer. J'espere dis-je que ces titres feront mon excuse.

J'ai vu aujourdhui une très Jolie femme qui m'a beaucoup demandé de vos nouvelles et qui m'a prié de la rappeller à votre Souvenir, Mde. Martin de Sette.[8] Elle espere bien que vous n'oublierez pas Son mari et d'autant plus qu'il paroît que Messieurs les Américains commencent à nommer leurs Consuls dans nos ports. Elle m'a assurré comme Une chose positive et que Son beau Pere lui a mandée que vous aviez nommè votre Consul pour Marseilles et que ce Consul est un Francois, M. Catelan.[9]

Voulez vous bien Mon Illustre Docteur que Je vous remercie en mon particulier et comme membre du Club de la belle Medaille dont vous lui avez fait présent.[1] J'ai été témoin ce Soir

6. The Tuesdays between April 6, the earliest date BF could have received the news of Dr. Hunter's death, and April 20, which was Easter.

7. The naturalist Philibert Guéneau de Montbéliard (Montbeillard). He and his wife collaborated on Buffon's *Histoire naturelle des oiseaux*. Their son, a young officer in the dragoons, was their only surviving child at the time of Philibert's death in 1785: XX, 219n; *DBF;* Larousse; *Jour. de Paris*, Dec. 16, 1785.

8. The wife of C. Barthélemy Martin fils aîné of Sète, presumably introduced to BF by Mme Le Roy on March 23; see Le Roy to BF, March 23, above.

9. M. Martin fils reported the same news in his letter to BF, April 11, below.

1. The medal was *Libertas Americana;* we have not identified the club.

des transports avec lesquels elle y a eté recue et il n'y a eu qu'une Voix pour me charger de vous exprimer, quand J'aurais l'honneur de vous voir, à quel point Le Club a été Sensible à une faveur Si flatteuse de votre part et qui marque l'opinion que vous avez de cette assemblèe Où votre nom a été celébré plusieurs fois d'une manière digne de vous. C'est tout dire.

J'ai recu Mon Illustre Docteur le billet de Monsieur votre petit-Fils par lequel il m'apprend la mort de M. Hunter et Vos voeux pour qu'il Soit remplacé dans L'Académie par M. Priestley.[2] Je me flatte que vous ne doutez pas de mes dispositions pour que ce remplacement se fasse comme vous le desirez et à cause de vous et à cause de lui Mais cette élection ne peut guère se faire qu'après Les Vacances de Paques Selon les formes que vous suivons ordinairement pour les élections.[3] Adieu Mon Illustre Docteur recevez les assurrances renouvellées des Sentimens d'attachement que je vous ai voués pour la Vie.   Le Roy

Mille et mille Complimens si vous voulez bien à Monsieur votre petit Fils.

From La Rochefoucauld   AL: American Philosophical Society

Mercredi au Soir. [April 9, 1783?][4]

Le Duc de la Rochefoucauld a l'honneur de faire Ses complimens à Monsieur franklyn; il a remis à l'Imprimeur le *Traité d'Alliance avec la france,* et *celui avec la hollande* pour lequel il S'est procuré la Gazette de Leyde; il prie Monsieur franklyn de vouloir bien lui

2. Samuel Vaughan, Jr., had communicated the news of Dr. Hunter's death with his brother Benjamin's wish that Priestley be put forward as his replacement in the Académie des sciences; see Samuel Vaughan, Jr., to BF, [April] 6.

3. See the letter from La Rochefoucauld, immediately below.

4. This letter had to have been written on a Wednesday between when the news arrived in Paris of William Hunter's death in London on March 30 (reported by Samuel Vaughan, Jr.: see note 2, above) and Easter Sunday, which in 1783 fell on April 20. Wednesday, April 16, is also a possibility, but the phraseology here seems to precede La Rochefoucauld's request of April 12, below.

envoyer le plutôt qu'il pourra le *Traité avec la suede,* et *la Pré-face,* s'il juge à propos d'en faire une.[5]

L'Academie vient d'élire M. Wargentin à la place vacante par la mort de M. Margraff;[6] l'élection à celle de M. hunter[7] ne Se fera qu'après Pâques: le Duc de la Rochefoucauld croit que M. Priest-ley y aura beau jeu et quand à lui, il Se fera un grand plaisir de Seconder les vues de Monsieur franklyn pour cet homme juste-ment celebre.[8]

Addressed: A son Excellence / Monsieur franklyn Ministre des / Etats-Unis d'Amerique / *A Passy.*

From William Mackinnen, Jr.[9]

ALS: American Philosophical Society

Sir   ruë La Jussienne Wednesday April 9th 1783

The enclosed letter I received in London from Mr Vaughn, with the flattering hope, of by this means being introduced to a Character for which I have so high a Veneration; I called at Passy last Saturday but had the mortification of not finding You at home, my stay in Paris has been so short and my knowledge of the multiplicity of Business you are engaged in, has been the cause of my not venturing a second intrusion; hoping at some

5. On April 5, above, Vergennes informed BF that Pierres had been granted permission to begin printing *Constitutions des treize Etats-Unis de l'Amérique.* In this and subsequent letters La Rochefoucauld asks BF for a preface, which he never wrote.

6. Meetings of the Académie des sciences were held on Wednesdays and Saturdays: *Almanach royal* for 1783, p. 529. Pehr Vilhelm Wargentin, an as-tronomer, replaced the chemist Andreas Sigismund Marggraf, who died on Aug. 7, 1782. Wargentin was installed on April 23, 1783: Institut de France, *Index biographique des membres et correspondants de l'Académie des sciences de 1666 à 1939* (Paris, 1939), pp. 307–8, 466.

7. William Hunter had been named an *associé étranger* on Feb. 3, 1782: *ibid.,* pp. 227–8.

8. Joseph Priestley was elected on Feb. 26, 1784, to replace Wargentin, who died on Dec. 13, 1783: *ibid.,* pp. 375, 466.

9. Introduced in a March 15 letter from Benjamin Vaughan; see the anno-tation there.

future period to have the happiness of an introduction to you I have the honor to be Sir your most obed hum ser

WILLIAM MACKINNEN JUR

Mr Vaughn in London a few Day before I left desired me to take charge of two large Books, containing charts of the Northern coasts of America, for Mr Adams in Paris; but my not knowing Mr Adam's Direction I took the Liberty of addressing them to You, and I now take the Liberty of desiring the favor, if you have received them, that you will acquaint Mr Adams with this circumstance.[1]

Addressed: A Monsieur / Monsieur Franklyn / á Passy / prés de Paris

Notation: Wm. Mackinnen Junr. Paris 9th. April 1783

To John Adams

L:[2] Massachusetts Historical Society

Passy, 10 Ap. 1783—

Since Mr. Adams's Departure Dr Franklin recd a Letter from Mr. Lawrens; the inclosed is a Copy of the Post-script, & which appears to be that mentioned to Mr. Adams in his Letter from Mr. Lawrens—[3]

Addressed: A son Excellence / Monsieur Adams / &ca &ca / Hotel du Roi / au Carouselle

Notations: Dr. Franklin. inclosing an Extract of a Letter from Mr. Laurens. / April 10. 1783.

1. Possibly Joseph Frederick Wallet Des Barres's *The Atlantic Neptune* (London, [1775–81]), which Benjamin Vaughan told JA on Feb. 25 that he would send by way of Charles Storer: *Adams Papers,* XIV, 296. Storer was in Paris by April 8; on that date BF issued a passport for him and a servant to go to Holland (The American Museum of Historical Documents, 1993).
   2. In WTF's hand.
   3. BF enclosed a copy (in L'Air de Lamotte's hand) of the postscript of Laurens' April 4 letter, above. That postscript was mentioned in Laurens' letter to JA of March 26[–April 4]: *Adams Papers,* XIV, 366.

From Mattheus Lestevenon van Berkenrode

AL: Library of Congress

ce Jeudi 10 Avril. [1783]

L'Ambassadeur de Hollande Sensible a L'attention obligeante de Monsieur Franklin, Le prie d'agreer tous Ses remercimens, et L'assurance de Son Sincere attachement.[4]

Addressed: A Monsieur / Monsieur Franklin. / Ministre plenipotentiaire / des Etats Unis, a La / Cour de France.

From Bartoli

ALS: American Philosophical Society

Monsieur   Paris ce 11 Avril 1783.

C'est avec la plus vive reconnoissance que je reçois le beau present dont il vous a plu de m'honorer.[5]

Le sujet, l'invention, l'execution de la Médaille, tout merite des eloges.

La manière même très-obligeante avec laquelle Vous avez bien voulu, Monsieur, me la faire parvenir, devançant le temps de la distribution, ajoute infiniment à ma gratitude. Pénètré de Vos bontés, et de la profonde estime que je Vous dois, j'ai essayé de faire en vers une *Description* de ce Monument à jamais glorieux.[6]

J'ai l'honneur de Vous la communiquer, en vous assurant en même temps du respect inviolable avec lequel je suis, Monsieur, Votre très-humble et très-obeissant Serviteur   BARTOLI

Notation: Bartoli 11. avril 1783.

---

4. On April 8 at Versailles, BF presented silver *Libertas Americana* medals to ministers of the French court and to foreign ambassadors.

5. The *Libertas Americana* medal.

6. Bartoli enclosed a 16-line poem entitled "Description de la Médaille sur l'Indépendance de l'Amérique, à l'occasion de la Paix." The final couplet concerns BF, whose voice soared to the heavens. For an English translation see Lester C. Olson, *Benjamin Franklin's Vision of American Community: a Study in Rhetorical Iconology* (Columbia, S.C., 2004), p. 169.

From Francis Coffyn

ALS: American Philosophical Society

Hond. Sir.   Dunkerque 11th. April 1783.

Since the letter I had the honnor to write your Excellency on the 9th. ultma. a great number of American prisonners arrived here from England, for whom I procured their passage, onboard of sundry vessells bound to different ports in America. Those mentioned in the enclosed receipts,[7] which were in great distress & destitute of every thing, I have assisted with a little money for their Subsistance during their Stay here, & to buy the necessairies for their passage.

£.[8]		
£.[8] 24.—.—.	Paid George Robinson	
" 32.—.—.	Do. John Garret.	
" 112.—.—.	Do. Saml. Solomons, Matw. Lower & Laurens Berry	The places of their abode &
" 32.10.—.	Do. Jonathan Foster.	the ships they
" 37.10.—.	Do. Olever Arnold.[9]	was taken in
" 42.—.—.	Do. John Green	are mentioned
" 25.—.—.	Do. Willm. Taylor.	at the back of
" 40.10.—.	Do. John Swan.	their respective
" 40.10.—.	Do. Joseph Bellony.	receipts.
" 33. 6.—.	Do. Francis Ware.	
" 31.10.—.	Do. Joseph Davis	
" 36.—.—.	Do. Richd. Lambert.	
" 34. 2.—.	Do. to the Penitent nuns for board at their Hospital, & funeral Expences of John Helatt, who died of the Small Pox.	

£. 520.18.—.   Together, which I have charged to your Excellency's Account.

This Sum added to £. 277.10.—. & £. 96.—.—. mentioned in my letters of 19th. Febry & 9th. march, make together £. 894. 8.—. which I have taken the liberty to draw on Your Excellency pble. 10 days after date, to the order of Messrs. Vandenyver fr.

7. Missing.
8. *I.e.*, *l.t.*
9. An Oliver Arnold and George Robinson were released from Forton Prison in 1781 to serve in the Royal Navy: Kaminkow, *Mariners*, pp. 6, 163.

& Cie, & request your Excellency will be pleased to honnor my drafts.[1]

Since the happy conclusion of the Peace, five vessells have been dispatch'd from this place to the ports of North America,[2] and Three more are now put up for Philadelphia, I hope my recommendations to the owners of these vessells in favour of the House of Messrs. Bache & Shee of said place, (which your Excellency recommended to me in 1779;)[3] will make these Gentlemen reep the first frutes of the peace, & that the assortment of the Cargos will convince the Subjects of the united States of the advantages the port of Dunkerque offers to the American Trade: Your Excellency may rely on my constant exertion to promote the interest of said House, & I hope my endeavours will not be fruitless.

One Capn. Coreil who has some time resided at Philadelphia & other parts of America during the war, has bought a brig here burthen 150 Tons, & is desirous of dispatching this vessell for said place under the name of General Washington, & under the colours of the united States of America, he intends to Sail in about three weeks for said destination, but as he can not proceed without a passport from your Excellency, he desired me to request your Excellency to grant him one; if his demand can be comply'd with, I humbly beg your Excellency will be pleased to send me Such a passport, the Crew of this ship will be composed of Americain Seamen, except the mate who was born in France. I hope Your Excellency will be pleased to favour me with an answer in order that the vessell may not be detained.[4]

I have the honnor to remain very respectfully Your Excellency's most obedient & most Humble Servant   F. Coffyn

S. E. M. B. Franklin a Passi.

1. Coffyn's previous letters are missing. His draft was paid on May 1: Account XXVII (XXXII, 4).

2. For two of these, the *Franklin* and the *Hazard*, see J. Torris & Wante to BF, [before Feb. 16] and Feb. 16, above.

3. BF had forwarded one of Bache & Shee's circular letters to Coffyn: "Houses Bache & Shees Circular Letters have been sent to," described in XXIX, 273n.

4. The arrival of the brig, commanded by "Le Conte de Coriel," was announced in the July 23, 1783, issue of the *Pa. Gaz.*

From Guillaume Grivel[5]

ALS: American Philosophical Society

Monsieur   Paris le 11 avril 1783.

Une incommodité Subite Survenue à M Canolle[6] ne lui a point permit d'aller chercher lui même la lettre que vous avez bien voulu lui promettre pour Londres.[7] Comme il espere pourtant que Son mal n'aura pas de Suite, il m'engage à vous prier d'avoir la bonté de la lui faire passer ici par la petite poste ce Sera une nouvelle obligation qu'il vous aura, et dont il vous Sera infiniment reconnoissant.

Permettez moi de me Servir de cette occasion, pour me renouveller dans votre souvenir et de vous assurer de l'estime très respectueuse avec laquelle J'ai l'honneur d'être Monsieur Votre très humble et très obéissant Serviteur   GRIVEL

l'adresse de M Canolle est chez M Garez rue de Verneuil fb. st germain

M Franklin Ministre des Etats unis

---

5. This is the only extant letter from Grivel (1735–1810), an author who published on a wide range of topics and who, at BF's suggestion, was elected a member of the APS in 1786: *DBF;* Larousse; BF's "List of Persons to be Recommended for Members of P. Society" (undated, Library of Congress); APS membership records.

6. According to the *DBF*, Canolle discovered peat bogs and coal deposits in the Limosin and went to England to study methods of extraction. On his return he set up a factory to make peat charcoal briquettes and in February, 1784, sought exclusive rights to his manufacturing process: *DBF*, under his son Jean de Canolle. We presume that at the time of the present letter Canolle was preparing to embark on the trip mentioned above. He had already demonstrated the advantageous burning properties of his substance (whatever combination of materials it was) to BF, who evidently approved; see Hutton to BF, May 2. In 1787 a scientific committee found Canolle's manufacturing process worthy of encouragement, but not a signficiant enough advance to merit a *privilège exclusif:* Antoine-Laurent Lavoisier, *Œuvres* (6 vols., Paris, 1862–93), IV, 462–7.

7. According to Hutton's May 2 letter, BF recommended Canolle to the geologist John Whitehurst, whose expertise in coal was well known. That letter is missing.

From Joly de Fleury

11. avril. [1783]

M. Joly de fleury ancien ministre des finances[8] a recue avec bien de la sensibilite la medaille[9] que Monsieur francklin a bien voulu lui addresser, et le prie de recevoir son sincere remerciement de cette delicate attention.

m franklin ministre plenip des etats unis — a passy

From C. Barthélemy Martin fils aîné[1]

Calais 11e: Avril 1783.

Suivant les ordres qu'il a plu à Son Excellence de me donner j'ay L'honneur de l'informer que de tous les Vaisseaux Anglo-americains qui etoient dans les Ports de *Cette* et de Marseille le dernier est parti de ce port depuis une 2one. de jours. Il s'apelloit le Hawke Captne. Bull, venant de Philadelphie avec un Chargement de Tabac d'ont la Ferme Royale fit achapt à 70 *l.t.* Tournois le quintal de Cent livres pezant.[2] Deux mois avant il etoit arrivé de Philadelphie Le Navire Le General Wolf Captne: Samuel Dutter [Butler] avec une Cargaison de Tabac que les Fermiers de Piemond acheterent.[3] On fait actuellement Cinq expeditions Francaises pour la Baye de Chesapeak, Baltimore, et Philadelphie. Il en est deja parti trois.

8. He was replaced as finance minister on March 29 by Henri-François-de-Paule Lefèvre d'Ormesson (1751–1807), who served until the following November: J. F. Bosher, *French Finances, 1770–1795: from Business to Bureaucracy* (Cambridge, 1970), pp. 177–8; Larousse, under Ormesson; John Hardman, *French Politics, 1774–1789: from the Accession of Louis XVI to the Fall of the Bastille* (London and New York, 1995), pp. 66–73, 145–50.

9. The *Libertas Americana* medal.

1. Who had sent BF a memoir in March; see Le Roy to BF, March 23.

2. The *Hawke* had arrived in January and returned by way of Gibraltar: XXXVIII, 591.

3. When the farmers general at Marseille offered only 60 *l.t.* per quintal for the *Wolf*'s tobacco, the Marseille firm of Rolland frères sought a higher price in Piedmont and other parts of Italy: XXXVIII, 180.

Le Congrés a bien voulu nommer pour Consul de la Nation à Marseille monsieur Cathalan Fils, de la même ville.[4] Son Excellence me permettra t'elle de lui faire observer que le Congrès ne reffuse pas sa Confiance à des Français? Je la merite par les Sentimens d'admiration que Son Excellence m'a inspiré et par Ceux d'ont je suis animé pour le bien de la Nation.

Le 23. de ce mois il sera vendu dans ce Port un Superbe Navire Anglais avec sa Cargaison. Son Excellence jugera de son Etat par l'affiche detaillée que je prends la liberté de lui envoyer. Ce Navire Construit en Amerique et destinné pour en faire la navigation est très propre pour ces voyages; on pense qu'il sera Vendu aux environs de Quarante Cinq à Cinquante mille Livres Tournois. Suivant le raport du Capitaine il n'a que Cinq Ans, & il a Couté quatre Vingt mille Livres Tournois.

Un Navire de Cette portée que l'on destinneroit pour l'Amerique pour etre Chargé annuellement à *Cette,* en Esprit de Vin, Eau de Vie, Vins, huilles, Savons, Farines, & draperies donneroit un grand bennefice aux interessés; les retours seroient aussy avantageux, les Sucres, les Rix, et les Tabacs sont des Objets essentiels, et d'une Vente proffitable.

Sy l'avis que je m'empresse à donner à Son Excellence peut l'engager à me donner ses ordres pour en faire L'achapt pour Son Compte, ou pour Celui de Ses amis reunis; je les rempliray avec Zelle. J'ose l'assurer que, pour l'objet des Cargaisons, et ventes des retours, Ses interets ne Sauroient être en meilleures mains que dans celles de mon Pere, Martin L'ainé de *Cette* qu'une longue experiance, et une parfaite Connaissance du Commerce mettent à même de travailler à la satisfaction publique. Quél avantage ne resulterait il pas aussy pour moy Sy Son Excellence daignoit m'honnorer du Titre de Consul de l'Amerique? Je lui demande pardon Si j'ose faire mention de moy dans ce moment—

4. In 1788, when Jefferson was reviewing consulships in France, he reported that Étienne Cathalan père (XXVI, 454) was serving as consul in Marseilles, though his son "has solely done the duties." Jefferson recommended that Etienne Cathalan fils be given the post. His rank would have to be vice consul, since in 1784 Congress had restricted consulships to American citizens: *Jefferson Papers,* XIV, 59–60; XV, 323; XVII, 246, 252, 497; XVIII, 583–7.

J'ay l'Honneur d'etre avec un Tres proffond, Respect de Son Excellence Le Tres Humble & tres Obeissant Serviteur

BARTHELEMY MARTIN FILS
de *Cette*.

ches Monsr. Vaillant receveur du Bureau de la Ferme Royale à Calais

From the Marquis de Ségur AL: American Philosophical Society

ce 11 avril 1783.

M de Segur a Reçu La medaille[5] que Monsieur franklin Lui a fait L'honneur de Lui envoyer, il le prie de vouloir bien en recevoir ses Remerciments./.

M. franklin

From Antoine-Jean Amelot de Chaillou[6]

ALS: American Philosophical Society

A Vlles. ce 12 avril 1783

J'ai reçû, Monsieur, La Médaille que vous avés eû la bonté de m'envoier,[7] je suis trés sensible à cette marque d'attention de votre part, je vous prie d'en agréer mes sincéres remercimens et Les assurances, de la parfaite considération avec laquelle j'ai Lhonneur d'être, Monsieur, votre trés humble et trés obeissant serviteur   AMELOT

M. Franklin a Passy

---

5. The *Libertas Americana* medal.
6. Who continued until November to serve as secretary of state for household affairs; for his forced retirement see John Hardman, *French Politics, 1774–1789: from the Accession of Louis XVI to the Fall of the Bastille* (London and New York, 1995), pp. 76–7.
7. The *Libertas Americana* medal.

From Michel-René Hilliard d'Auberteuil

ALS: American Philosophical Society

Monsieur   Paris le 12e. avril 1783.

Il y a bien longtems que je n'ai rendu mes devoirs à votre excellence.[8] Ce n'est de ma part ni defaut de zêle, ni de reconnaissance de toutes vos bontés, mais j'ai été attaqué d'une maladie longue et cruelle.

Je desirerais avoir le dessein des medailles frapées par ordre du congrès et ceux des mausolées érigés par vos soins,[9] vous me rendriez service de me les procurer. J'aurai l'honneur d'envoyer à ce sujet à votre excellence un dessinateur, Si vous me le permettez, ou je vous Suplierai de m'en confier les modeles, si vous le trouvez convenable.

Le sr. Charles Spener Libraire du Roi de prusse m'a écrit pour me demander une copie de ces desseins dont il est tres pressé pour un almanach qu'il veut faire à la commemoration de la revolution glorieuse à laquelle vous avez eu tant de part.[1] Je sais que votre excellence ne neglige rien de ce qui peut être flatteur pour les heros de la liberté qui ne peuvent trouver la recompense de leurs travaux que dans la louange des peuples; l'entreprise du sr. Spener me parait très propre à multiplier les éloges qui leur

8. He last wrote in August, 1782: XXXVIII, 20–1.

9. For the medals Congress actually commissioned, and the memorial to Gen. Richard Montgomery, see XXIV, 160n; XXX, 416n. Hilliard must also have had in mind the *Libertas Americana* medal, which was reported in the press as having been struck by order of Congress; see the headnote to "Explanation of a Medal," [*c.* May 5].

1. Johann Karl Philipp Spener (1749–1827) was director of the Berlin publishing firm Haude & Spener: *ADB.* He was currently preparing a new publication entitled *Historisch-genealogischer Calender oder Jahrbuch der merkwürdigsten neuen Welt-Begebenheiten.* Its first issue consisted of three parts, separately paginated: an almanac, a genealogy of the principal courts of Europe, and a history of the American Revolution by Matthias Christian Sprengel which would later be published independently. Spener wrote directly to BF on May 26, explaining the project in detail and requesting BF's assistance in providing illustrations (APS). For background on the publication see Eugene E. Doll, "American History as Interpreted by German Historians from 1770 to 1815," APS *Trans.,* new ser., XXXVIII (1948–49), 461–4; Horst Dippel, *Germany and the American Revolution, 1770–1800* . . . , trans. Bernhard A. Uhlendorf (Chapel Hill, N.C., 1978), pp. 52–3.

sont dus; et il me semble que Mr. Laurens en a jugé de même en lui envoyant deja le pavillon des treize états et le portrait de Mr. Payne qu'il a fait dessiner exprès d'après un tableau qu'il possede à Londres.

Permettez moi de vous envoyer le prospectus de l'histoire de la revolution de la hollande et l'introduction à cette Histoire.[2] En attendant que les faits historiques de la guerre Americaine aient acquis plus de maturité, j'ai cru devoir ofrir au Public l'histoire d'une autre revolution de la même nature, quoi que bien diferente par ses causes et ses circonstances.

Je Suis avec le plus profond respect Monsieur de votre Excellence Le très humble & très obeissant serviteur

HILLIARD D'AUBERTEUIL

Rue des fossés Montmartre no. 35

Notation: Hilliard Dauberteuil 12. avril 1783.

From La Rochefoucauld   AL: American Philosophical Society

samedi 12 Avril [1783]

Le Duc de la Rochefoucauld a l'honneur de faire tous Ses remercimens à Monsieur franklyn de Sa belle Médaille,[3] en attendant qu'il ait le plaisir de les lui renouveller de vive voix; il le prie de lui envoyer le plutot qu'il pourra, *le Traité avec la suede,* et *la Préface,* S'il le juge à propos;[4] l'Imprimeur attend après.

---

2. Hilliard wasted no time. The 32-page introduction was only approved for publication on April 11; BF's copy, with a title page and a map of the Low Countries, is bound with other pamphlets BF owned (Hist. Soc. of Pa.). The prospectus Hilliard enclosed in the present letter has not been located, but it was published in the *Jour. des Sçavans* for May, 1783, pp. 946–8. He proposed a three-volume work of approximately 400 pages, entitled *Histoire de la Révolution des sept Provinces-Unies des Pays-Bas,* which would be issued as soon as there were 500 subscribers. The work was never published.

3. A *Libertas Americana* medal.

4. As La Rochefoucauld had also requested in his letter of [April 9?], above.

From the Marquis de Castries L: American Philosophical Society

Versailles 13 avril 1783./.

M le Mis de Castries a l'honneur de prévenir Monsieur franklin que la flûte la Pintade va être Expédiée pour l'Amérique septentrionale.⁵ Il le prie de vouloir bien lui envoyer ses Paquets s'il en a qui ayent cette destination.⁶

From the Duchesse de Deux-Ponts

ALS: American Philosophical Society

dimanche 13 avril [1783]

Mr delisle⁷ home tres honette tres Aimable et qui a Lhoneur de Vous conoitre mon respectable amis Mais qui Na pas encor eut Celui de diner chez Vous, sest Mis sous ma protection pour Venir Vous demander a diner aujourdhui, Comme il est tres Lies avec Nous et avec La pluspart de Vos amis jai penséz mon cher amis que Vous Ne desaprouveriez pas que je Vous L'amenne, Mais jai Crue Cependant devoir Vous en prevenir en attendent Le bonheur de Vous Voir de Vous embrasser de Vous remercier de La Medaille⁸ et de Vous renouveller Mon fidel et tendre homage

M F DOUAIRIERE DU DUC DE DEUXPONTS

Addressed: a Monsieur / Monsieur franclin / Ministre pleinipotentiaire / des etats unis a La Cour / de france / *a passis*

---

5. The *Pintade* would carry back to France the last of Rochambeau's army, sailing from Baltimore on Oct. 5. Some 1,000 officers and soldiers sailed from the Chesapeake in May and June: Amblard-Marie-Raymond-Amédée, vicomte de Noailles, *Marins et soldats français en Amérique pendant la Guerre de l'Indépendance des Etats-Unis (1778–1783)* (2nd ed., Paris, 1903), pp. 339–41.

6. On April 16 Castries wrote again to acknowledge receipt of a packet from BF, which he promised to forward (APS).

7. There are no other clues to his identity. One possibility is the philosopher Jean-Baptiste-Claude Isoard, *dit* Delisle de Sales (1741?–1816), who knew both Voltaire and Helvétius. *DBF.*

8. The *Libertas Americana* medal.

From De Grasse[9]   LS: American Philosophical Society

Monsieur   a Paris le 13. avril 1783.
Je Suis tres flatté que Mes Services Pour la Liberté americaine,
m'ayent merité Les Temoignages flatteurs que Votre Republique
a Bien voulu m'en donner Par l'Envoy De la médaille[1] que Vous
avez eu la Bonte De M'addresser Comme son Ministre aupres de
sa majesté. Je m'estimeray toujours heureux D'avoir formè &
Executé Le projet De la Conquette D'Yorck-town qui a Decide
L'Indépendance D'un Peuple Si Digne De Se Gouverner Par Ses
propres Loix & qui En Temoigne une Reconnoissance Si Publique a Sa Majeste.
J'ay l'honneur D'Etre avec une consideration Respectueuse
Monsieur De Votre Excellence, Le Tres humble & tres obeissant
Serviteur   LE COMTE DE GRASSE

From Gabriel-Claude Palteau de Veimerange
                              LS: American Philosophical Society

                                    Ce 13 avril 1783./.
J'ay Reçu la Médaille que son Excéllence Monsieur franklin ma
fait L'honneur de menvoyer;[2] Je Suis infiniment Sensible à Son
attention et Je Supplie Son Excéllence d'en agréer mes Remerciments. J'ay L'honneur de lui renouveller en meme tems Les assurances de mon Respectueux attachement./.   VEIMERANGE

9. This is his last extant letter. At the end of April, the admiral was ordered to reside at Vannes while an inquiry was held at Lorient into responsibility for the 1782 defeat at the Battle of the Saintes. He was eventually acquitted, though his reputation suffered: Jean-Jacques Antier, *L'Amiral de
Grasse: Héros de l'Indépendance américaine* ([Paris], 1965), pp. 372–7.
1. The *Libertas Americana* medal.
2. He undoubtedly received one of the *Libertas Americana* medals in recognition of his having assembled supplies for the American army.

From Ernst Frederik von Walterstorff[3]

AL: American Philosophical Society

Sunday morning April 13th [1783]

Mr. de Walterstorff is very sorry he cannot have the honour of dining to-day with Dr. Franklin, owing to his being previously engaged; but will have the pleasure of waiting on Dr. Franklin sometime this forenoon, if possibly he can.[4]

From William Carmichael

ALS: Library of Congress

Dear Sir   Madrid 14th April 1783

I had the honor to address your Excellency some time ago by the Baron le Fort[5] and to advise you that I should find myself under the necessity of calling on you for the advances made by our Bankers here for the Public— After having delayed as long as possible these payments, as well to comply with the request you made Mr Jay to give you all the time in his power at the period you authorized him to draw on you for this purpose,[6] as on acct of the loss which would have arisen from the Depretiation of the paper money & the consequent effect it had on the course of exchange, I now find myself absolutely constrained to satisfy their demands & therefore Draw upon you this day for £s. 30000 in favor of Messrs. Cabarrus & Co. & for £s. 2254. 2 *s.* in favor of

---

3. Walterstorff (1755–1820), currently chamberlain of the king of Denmark, had met BF during a visit to Paris in 1782: BF to Livingston, April 15, below. His long career involved service in both Europe and the Danish West Indies. He was appointed a high court judge in St. Croix in 1780, and was named vice-governor of the island in 1785. He went on to serve as Danish minister in Stockholm (1797), London (1801), Paris (1810), and The Hague (1815): *Dansk Biografisk Leksikon* (16 vols., Copenhagen, 1979–84); *Repertorium der diplomatischen Vertreter*, III, 45, 46, 50, 55.

4. Walterstorff bore news from the Danish court that the king wanted to conclude a treaty of amity and commerce with the United States; see BF's April 15 letters to Livingston and Rosencrone.

5. Above, March 15.

6. XXXIV, 534.

Messrs. Drouilhet on the public Acct.[7] I transmit herewith the accompts of these Gentlemen to your Excy. lest Mr. Jay should have left Paris. I sent to that Gentleman Mr Cabarrus Acct in the month of Novr. Last and in the letter which I wrote him on that Occasion repeated a request mentioned in a former to have Copies of the receipts he took from Mr Cabarrus for the Sums placed in his hands— For these being cheifly in paper bearing a daily Interest and the payments having been often made some days after the receipt of the Money from Others, This Circumstance creates a difference in my Entries & Mr Cabarrus's Credits which cannot be ascertained so accurately as I desire without the receipts which that Banker gave to Mr Jay.[8]

I have compared the bills paid by these Gentlemen with their Accts and my Books & I find their Entries thereof as accurate & as correspondent with mine as the Time of their presentation for payment (frequently irregular) permitted.

I gave Mr Jay a State of the Accts of the Marquis de Yranda & Mr Gardoqui before he left this Country. I received from him my Salary in proportion I beleive as he received his from your Excy and I expected that when he settled his private Acct with you, he would have Informed you of the Amount of what he paid me, as he has my receipts for the same— I began to draw upon you in the Month of March 1782 when there was a considerable ballance due me.[9] The next Post you will receive my acct from that Period, for what precedes you will please to have recourse to Mr Jay.

In consequence of Advice which I have received from your

7. Jay had contracted these debts more than a year earlier. Etienne (Esteban) Drouilhet & Cie. was one of the banking firms that replaced François Cabarrus as bankers to the Spanish mission at the moment of Jay's default in March, 1782. Both firms operated in Madrid, but were French in origin: xxxvii, 7–8; Michel Zylberberg, *Une si douce domination: les milieux d'affaires français et l'Espagne vers 1780–1808* (Paris, 1993), pp. 130, 133–4, 139–43, 267–74; Wharton, *Diplomatic Correspondence*, v, 372.

On July 23 Ferdinand Grand paid 30,000 *l.t.* to Cabarrus & Co. and 2,454 *l.t.* 2 *s.* to Drouilhet's firm: Account XXVII (xxxii, 4).

8. Jay, however, claimed Carmichael had handled these transactions: Morris, *Jay: Peace*, pp. 682, 686.

9. See xxxvi, 466, 559, 604.

Grandson I take the Liberty of Drawing upon you for 7524 £s. 10 s. 8 Drs. in favor of Messrs. Drouilhets.[1]

Permit me to thank you for your kindness in accepting hitherto my bills. My situation otherwise would have been extremely embarrassing. The Marquis de la Fayette and others can Inform you that If I spend what Congress Allow me, It is more for their Service, than my own Pleasure.

I have waited hitherto for Mr Jay's answer to the Count de Arandas Communication of the present Disposition of this Court to regulate my Conduct thereby, But unless I hear soon from that Gentleman, I shall request the Minister to fix a day for my presentation to the King and Royal Family as Chargé des Affaires of the United States.[2] In every Other respect I am treated as such & have every reason to be personally satisfied with the Conduct of the Minister.

With the greatest respect and Affection I have the honor to be Your Excellencys Obliged & Humble Sert   Wm. Carmichael

His Excy Benjamin Franklin

From Jean-Baptiste-Jacques Elie de Beaumont

ALS: American Philosophical Society

Monsieur   Paris 14 avril 1783.

J'ai l'honneur de faire tous mes remercimens a votre excellence de la bonté qu'elle a eüe de m'envoyer la belle médaille frappée pour les Etats-unis.[3] C'est un monument du plus grand evenement qui soit dans les fastes du monde, et je ne vous dirai point en face quel est l'homme que cet evenement honore le plus. Vous avés plusieurs genres d'immortalité a la fois et Vous n'avés qu'a choisir.

La distance de nos demeures, et l'accablement de la perte cru-

1. On June 3 Grand paid 7,724 *l.t.* 10 s. 8 d. to settle Carmichael's bill: Account XXVII (XXXII, 4).

2. The Spanish Chief Minister was Floridablanca. Carmichael was not received by the court of Charles III until Aug. 23: Wharton, *Diplomatic Correspondence*, VI, 663–7.

3. The *Libertas Americana* medal.

elle que j'ai soufferte en perdant la femme la plus respectable[4] m'ont retenu depuis longtems chès moi avec ma douleur et mon fils[5] pour toute consolation, sans quoi je me serois fait un devoir de cultiver votre ancienne amitie. Je vous supplie de me faire dire quels sont les jours ou l'on vous trouve certainement a passy sans vous deranger j'aurois a vous entretenir de quelque chose d'interessant, mais j'ai besoin aussi de La certitude de vous trouver.

Je suis avec tout le respect que vous inspirès par vous même de votre excellence Monsieur Le tres humble et tres obeissant serviteur   ELIE DE BEAUMONT

From ———— Stockar zur Sonnenburg

ALS: American Philosophical Society

V. Excellence.   Schafhouse en Suisse du 14. Avr. 1783.

Je ne Sais ou je prends la hardiesse d'oser incommoder de nouveau Votre Excellence, Si ce n'est Son Extreme bonté qui me la donne. Ayant eu celle de m'honorer d'une reponse sur une question que je pris la liberté de Lui faire au Sujet de l'abbé Raynal et de ses Écrits,[6] mais Sa gracieuse condescendance devroit me rendre plus circonspect a Son Egard pour ne pas en abuser d'une maniere trop indécente.

Tout bien consideré l'abbé Raynal me paroit un ecrivain un peu trop romanesque pour un Historien et qui par son Elegance peut bien embellir un recit et le rendre interessant, mais qui peut etre n'en constatera jamais la verité par une persuasion plus solide; j'ay donc abbandonné le projet de traduire sa brochure en allemand d'autant plus que je viens d'apprendre que d'autres s'en occuppent[7] et que d'ailleurs la langue francoise est par-

4. His wife, Anne-Louise Morin du Mesnil Elie de Beaumont, a writer, died on Jan. 12: *DBF.*

5. Armand-Jean-Baptiste-Anne-Robert Elie de Beaumont (b. 1770): *DBF*, under Elie de Beaumont (family).

6. BF's reply to Stockar's questions about the reliability of Raynal's *Révolution de l'Amérique:* XXXVIII, 447–9.

7. F. H. Wernitz, *Staatsveränderung von Amerika*... (Frankfurt and Leipzig, 1782).

tout si connue aujourdhui qu'une telle traduction en devient presqu'un travail inutile— ce qui ne seroit pas le cas de quelque piece angloise tant Soit peu interessante et particulierement de celle dont je suis redevable a Votre Excellence[8] et que je preférerois de traduire, si Elle n'y trouve point d'inconvenient par d'autres considerations.

Ne seroit ce pas encore abuser des bontez de votre Excellence que de Lui proposer un sujet ou une Personne de ma connoissance pour le service des Etats Americains, qui Souhoitteroit d'y être placè en qualité de Chirurgien Major dont V.E. peut bien s'assurer qu'il seroit d'autant plus digne et plus capable que je n'aurois pas l'imprudence de le Lui recommander pour un pareil Emploi, Si Sa reputation n'étoit pas bien établie de ce coté la. C'est d'ailleurs un homme de bonne maison et un membre actuel de notre conseil souverain que rien que des raisons domestiques obligent de s'Expatrier. Il S'Est perfectionè dans Son art par une longue pratique quoiqu'il ne soit agè que de quarante et quelques années, outre qu'il a passè plusieurs années aux Services de L.L.H.H. Puissances. Rien que le desir d'Etre utile a un homme de bien me fait prendre la liberté de m'addresser a Votre Excellence pour ce sujet et j'aurois une extreme joye de recevoir une reponse consolante de sa part et de savoir de S.E. si mon susdit Ami ne pourroit etre employé sous la protection de S.E. a Philadelphie ou en quelqu'autre endroit des Etats Americains ou Son gout le porte préferablement que pour d'autres Services quelles Soient.

Si mon age qui approche de Soixante me permettoit encore de Si grandes courses je lui tiendrois volontiers Compagnie, quoique je n'aye pas besoin de Secours étrangers. Mais notre prètendue liberté Helvetique Se perd insensiblement et ne se nourrit plus que de vaines paroles; aprez avoir vu le Sort de geneve il est aisé de tirer l'horoscope sur notre ètat futur, car nos Bourgeois commencent trop a faire les gentilshommes pour n'être plus Sensibles qu'a la liberté.

Je fais cependant les plus sinceres Excuses a V. Excellence de l'impatience que je Lui donne peut être par mon babil et je suis

8. Most likely Paine's *Letter Addressed to the Abbe Raynal;* see BF's letter to Stockar mentioned above.

avec le plus profond respect. De Votre Excellence. Le tres humble et tres obbeissant Serviteur, STOCKAR ZUR SONNENBOURG.

To Robert R. Livingston

LS,[9] press copy of LS, and transcript: National Archives; AL (draft) and copy: Library of Congress

Sir,   Passy April 15. 1783.

You complain sometimes of not hearing from us. It is now near three Months since any of us have heard from America. I think our last Letter came with General de Rochambeau.[1] There is now a Project under Consideration for establishing Monthly Packet Boats between France & New-York, which I hope will be carried into Execution: Our Correspondences may then be more regular & frequent.[2]

I send herewith another Copy of the Treaty concluded with Sweden. I hope how ever that you will have received the former and that the Ratification is forwarded.[3] The King, as the Ambassador informs me, is now employed in examining the Duties, payable in his Ports, with a View of lowering them in favour of America, and thereby encouraging and facilitating our mutual Commerce.[4]

M. De Walterstorff, Chambellan du Roi de Dannemark, formerly Chief Justice of the Danish West India Islands, was last

9. In WTF's hand except for the postscript, which is in BF's hand.

1. Rochambeau arrived in France on Feb. 10 (Rice and Brown, eds., *Rochambeau's Army*, 1, 84n), bearing Livingston's letter to BF of Jan. 2 (XXXVIII, 537–8). Livingston had reproached BF for his silence the previous September; see XXXVIII, 68–9.

2. For the establishment of a packet boat service see BF to Crèvecœur, [after April 2].

3. See BF to Livingston, March 7.

4. On April 10 Ambassador Creutz wrote Gustavus III that BF had gratefully received the information about the king's proposed ordinances. BF assured Creutz that the United States wished to make trade as free as possible and that they did not intend to impose import duties higher than reciprocity demanded: Amandus Johnson, *Swedish Contributions to American Freedom, 1776–1783* (2 vols., Philadelphia, 1953–57), 1, 581, 590–1n.

Year at Paris, where I had some Acquaintance with him, and he is now returned hither. The News-Papers have mentioned him as intended to be sent minister from his Court to Congress; but he tells me no such Appointment has yet been made. He assures me however that the King has a strong Desire to have a Treaty of Friendship and Commerce with the United States; and he has communicated to me a Letter, which he received from M. Rosencrone the Minister for Foreign Affairs, expressing that Disposition. I enclose a Copy of the Letter, and if the Congress shall approve of entring into such a Treaty with the King of Denmark, of which I have told M. de Walterstorff I made no doubt, they will send to me or to whom else they shall think proper the necessary Powers and Instructions for that purpose.[5] In the meantime to keep the Business in Train, I have sent to that Minister, for his Consideration, a Translation of the Plan (*mutatis mutandis*) which I received from Congress for a Treaty with Sweden, accompanied by a Letter, of which I likewise enclose a Copy.[6] I think it would be well to make it one of the Instructions to whoever is commissioned for the Treaty, that he previously procure Satisfaction for the Prizes mentioned in my Letter.

The Definitive Treatys have met with great Delays, partly by the Tardiness of the Dutch, but principally by the Distractions in the Court of England, where for six or seven Weeks there was properly no Ministry nor any Business effected.— They have at

---

5. Walterstorff had requested an interview with BF in a note of April 13, above. The letter he had received from Rosencrone, the Danish Foreign Minister, dated Feb. 22, asked him to call on BF as soon as he arrived in Paris and attempt to gain BF's "confidence and esteem." The king wished to conclude a treaty of friendship and commerce as quickly as possible. Hoping that BF shared the view that this would be mutually beneficial, Rosencrone suggested that the fastest course would be to take the American-Dutch commercial treaty as a model. He hoped BF would communicate his ideas about any changes or additions. Once agreement had been reached and Congress had given its approval, an American representative presently in Europe could come to Copenhagen for final negotiations. (Copies of this letter are at the APS and the National Archives.)

This was not the first Danish approach, as the Danish chargé d'affaires at the Spanish court already had contacted William Carmichael: J. M. P. Fogdall, *Danish-American Diplomacy, 1776–1920* (Iowa City, 1922), p. 21.

6. BF to Rosencrone, immediately below.

last settled a Ministry but of such a Composition as does not promise to be lasting. The Papers will inform you who they are. It is now said that Mr. Oswald, who signed the Preliminaries, is not to return here, but that Mr. David Hartley comes in his stead, to settle the definitive.[7] A Congress is also talked of, and that some Use is therein to be made of the Mediation formerly proposed of the Imperial Courts.[8] Mr. Hartley is an old Friend of mine and a strong Lover of Peace, so that I hope we shall not have much difficult Discussion with him: but I could have been content to have finished with Mr. Oswald whom we always found very reasonable. Mr. Lawrens having left Bath, mended in his Health, is daily expected at Paris, where Messrs. Jay & Adams still continue. Mr Jefferson is not yet arrived, nor the Romulus in which Ship I am told he was to have taken his Passage.[9] I have been the more impatient of this Delay, from the Expectation given me of full Letters by him. It is extraordinary that we should be so long without any Arrivals from America in any Part of Europe. We have as yet heard nothing of the Reception of the Preliminary Articles in America, tho' it is now near 5. Months since they were signed. Barney indeed did not get away from hence before the Middle of January, but Copies went by other Ships long before him: He waited sometime for the Money he carried, and afterwards was detained by violent contrary Winds. He had a Passport from England, and I hope arrived safe; tho'

7. Fox informed Laurens of the appointment on April 5; see Laurens to BF, April 4, above.

8. Although Russian and Austrian mediation had been accepted by Britain and France, Fox, fearing the introduction of the principles of the League of Armed Neutrality into the discussions, was strongly opposed to Austrian and Russian involvement in the final treaty. He wished to conclude it as soon as possible. Vergennes concurred, hoping to finish before full powers arrived for the representatives of the mediators: Giunta, *Emerging Nation*, I, 827; Andrew Stockley, *Britain and France at the Birth of America: the European Powers and the Peace Negotiations of 1782–1783* (Exeter, 2001), p. 190.

9. Jefferson returned to Virginia instead of sailing on the *Romulus*, a French frigate which eventually carried French troops from Baltimore: XXXVIII, 537n; Amblard-Marie-Raymond-Amédée, vicomte de Noailles, *Marins et soldats français en Amérique pendant la guerre de l'indépendance des Etats-Unis (1778–1783)* (Paris, 1903), p. 340n.

we have been in some Pain for him on account of a Storm soon after he sail'd.

The English Merchants have shewn great Eagerness to reassume their Commerce with America: but apprehending that our Laws prohibiting that Commerce would not be repealed till England had set the Example by repealing theirs, the Number of Vessels they had loaded with Goods have been detained in Port, while the Parliament have been debating on the Repealing Bill, which has been alter'd two or three times and is not yet agreed upon. It was at first propos'd to give us equal Privileges in Trade, with their own Subjects repealing thereby, with respect to us, so much of their Navigation Act as regards Foreign Nations. But that Plan seems to be laid aside; and what will finally be done in the Affair is yet uncertain.

There is not a Port in France, and few in Europe, from which I have not received several Applications of Persons desiring to be appointed Consuls for America.[1] They generally offer to execute the Office for the honour of it, without Salary. I suppose the Congress will wait to see what Course the Commerce will take, and in what Places it will fix itself, in order to find where Consuls will be necessary, before any Appointments are made; and perhaps it will then be thought best to send some of our own People. If they are not allow'd to Trade there must be a great Expence for Salaries. If they may trade and are Americans, the Fortunes they make will mostly settle at last in our own Country. The Agreement I was to make here respecting Consuls has not yet been concluded.[2] The Article of Trading is important. I think it would be well to reconsider it.

I have caused to be struck here the Medal which I formerly mentioned to you, the Design of which you seem'd to approve. I inclose one of them in Silver for the President of Congress, and one in Copper for yourself: The Impression on Copper is thought to appear best; and you will soon receive a Number for the Members.[3] I have presented one to the King and another to

1. See XXXVIII, 314–17, and Pitot Duhellés to BF, Jan. 28, above.

2. See XXXVI, 484; XXXVII, 535; and Vergennes' Feb. 27 letter, above. For the question of consuls being allowed to trade see XXXVIII, 63.

3. George Fox, about to leave for the United States, was entrusted with 50

the Queen both in Gold; & one in silver to each of the Ministers,[4] as a monumental Acknowledgement which may go down to future Ages, of the Obligations we are under to this Nation. It is mighty well received, and gives general Pleasure. If the Congress approve of it, as I hope they will, I may add something on the Die (for those to be struck hereafter) to shew that it was done by their Order, which I could not venture to do 'till I had Authority for it.

A multitude of People are continually applying to me Personally and by Letters, for Information respecting the means of transporting themselves, Families and Fortunes to America.[5] I give no Encouragement to any of the Kings Subjects, as I think it would not be right in me to do it, without their Sovereign's Approbation: and indeed few offer from France, but Persons of irregular Conduct and desperate Circumstances whom we had better be without: But I think there will be great Emigration from England, Ireland, and Germany.

There is a great Contest among the Ports which of them shall be of those to be declared *Free* for the American Trade. Many Applications are made to me to interest myself in the Behalf of all of them:[6] But having no Instructions on that head, and thinking it a Matter more properly belonging to the Consul, I have done nothing in it.

I have continued to send you the English Papers. You will often see Falshoods in them respecting what I say & do, and write, &ca.[7] You know those Papers too well, to make any Contradiction of such Stuff necessary from me.

Libertas Americana medals addressed to Livingston: Fox to WTF, May 15, 1783 (APS).

4. BF presented the *Libertas Americana* medals at court on April 8; see the headnote to "Explanation of a Medal," [c. May 5]. The king and queen received the only two gold medals struck; see de Cotte to BF, March 26. In the second part of this sentence BF originally drafted "as a Mark of our Gratitude &c."

5. For such applications see XXXVIII, 195–7, and the headnote to Nivernois' letter of March 16.

6. See the letter from the Chamber of Commerce of Aunis, Jan. 31.

7. False or abusive articles about BF appeared in the British press throughout the war; for samples see Solomon Lutnick, *The American Revolution and the British Press, 1775–1783* (Columbia, Mo., 1967), pp. 43–5, 135–6.

Mr. Barclay is often ill, and I am afraid the Settlement of our Accounts will be in his hands a long Operation. I shall be impatient at being detained here on that Score after the Arrival of my Successor. Would it not be well to join Mr. Ridley with Mr. Barclay for that Service? He resides in Paris and seems active in Business: I know not indeed whether he would undertake it; but wish he may.

The Finances here are embarrass'd, & a new Loan is proposed by way of Lottery, in which it is said by some Caculators, the King will pay at the Rate of 7 per. Cent. I mention this to furnish you with a fresh convincing Proof, against Cavillers of the Kings Generosity towards us, in lending us six Millions this Year at 5 per Cent. and of his Concern for our Credit, in saving by that Sum the honour of Mr Morris's Bills, while those drawn by his own Officers abroad, have their Payment suspended for a Year after they become due.[8]

You have been told that France might help us more liberally if she would. This last Transaction is a Demonstration of the contrary. Please to shew these last Paragraphs to Mr. Morris, to whom I cannot now write, the Notice of this Ship being short; but it is less necessary, as Mr. Grand writes him fully.

With great Esteem, I have the honour to be, Sir, Your most obedient & most humble Servant.   B FRANKLIN

[*In Franklin's hand:*] P.S. Mr Laurens is just arrived.

The honble. Robt. R. Livingston Esqr Secy. for Foreign-Affairs.

Notation: Letter 15 April 1783. Doct B. Franklin— June 18. 1783 Referred to Mr Madison Mr Higgenson Mr Hamilton[9]

8. See the contract between BF and Vergennes, Feb. 25, and Joly de Fleury to BF, March 15.

9. Congressional delegates James Madison, Stephen Higginson, and Alexander Hamilton reported to Congress on July 24 about the present letter and the enclosed Swedish-American treaty: *JCC*, XXIV, 477n; XXV, 613–14.

To Marcus Gerhard Rosencrone[1]

Two press copies of LS, LS,[2] and transcript: National Archives; AL (draft),
copy, and press copy of copy: Library of Congress

Sir,   Passy, 15. April 1783.

M. de Walterstorff has communicated to me a Letter from
your Excellency to him,[3] which affords me great Pleasure, as it
expresses in clear and strong Terms the good Disposition of
your Court to form Connections of Friendship and Commerce
with the United States of America. I am confident that the same
good Disposition will be found in the Congress; and having acquainted that respectable Body with the Purport of your Letter,
I expect a Commission will soon be sent appointing some Person in Europe to enter into a Treaty with his Majesty the King
of Denmark, for the purpose desired. In the meantime, to prepare & forward the Business as much as may be, I send for your
Excellency's Consideration such a Sketch as you mention,
formed on the Base of our Treaty with Holland,[4] on which I shall
be glad to receive your Excellency's Sentiments. And I hope that
this Transaction when compleated, may be the means of producing and securing a long & happy Friendship between our two
Nations.

To smooth the Way for obtaining this desirable End, as well
as to comply with my Duty, it becomes necessary for me, on this
Occasion, to mention to your Excellency the Affair of our three

1. After diplomatic service in Stockholm, Dresden, and Berlin, Rosencrone (1738–1811) became Danish foreign minister in November, 1780, replacing Andreas Peter von Bernstorff. He served until April, 1784, when
Bernstorff again became foreign minister: *Repertorium der diplomatischen
Vertreter*, III, 51, 53, 54; *Gaz. de Leyde*, Nov. 28, 1780 (sup.), and April 30,
1784; *Dansk Biografisk Leksikon* (16 vols., Copenhagen, 1979–84).

2. We print from the press copy of a now-missing LS in WTF's hand. The
other press copy was taken from the surviving LS, also in WTF's hand, which
is misdated April 13.

3. See BF to Livingston, April 15, above.

4. According to BF's letter to Livingston cited above, he enclosed Congress' draft of a commercial treaty with Sweden, which was based on their
draft of a treaty with Holland; see the headnote on the Swedish-American
treaty published under [March 5].

Prizes, which having during the War enter'd Bergen as a neutral & friendly Port, where they might repair the Damages they had suffer'd, and procure Provisions, were by an Order of your Predecessor in the Office you so honourably fill, violently seized and deliver'd to our Enemies.[5] I am inclined to think it was a hasty Act, procured by the Importunity's & Misrepresentations of the British Minister, and that your Court could not on Reflection approve of it. But the Injury was done, and I flatter myself, your Excellency will think with me that it ought to be repaired. The Means and Manner I beg leave to recommend to your Consideration; and am with great Respect, Sir, Your Excellency's most obedient and most humble Servant.   B FRANKLIN

His Exy. M. Rosencrone

From the Comte de Mercy-Argenteau

L: American Philosophical Society

à Paris le 15. Avril 1783.

Note.

Le Professeur Märter chargé par L'Empereur[6] de recueillir dans les quatre parties du monde des animaux et des plantes pour la Ménagerie et les Jardins de Botanique de Sa Majesté, se propose de se mettre incessamment en route et de commencer sa tournée par les Provinces de la Domination des Etats unis de l'Amérique.

Persuadé que le Succès de son entreprise dépendra principalement des facilités et Secours qu'il trouvera dans les lieux où il aura des recherches à faire, il sent l'importance dont il seroit pour lui si Monsieur Franklin vouloit bien lui accorder sa recommandation auprès du Congrès général et de quelques particuliers dont les lumieres et conseils pourroient lui être utiles.[7]

5. BF had protested the Danish action to Bernstorff in 1779: XXXI, 261–5.
6. Joseph II.
7. BF obliged; see his April 22 letter to John Dickinson. Professor Franz Joseph Märter (1753–1827) left France in August; see our annotation of the

L'Ambassadeur de Sa Majté: l'Empereur chargé de concourir en ce qui dépendra de lui au Succès de la Commission du Sr. Märter, croit lui rendre un Service essentiel en adressant sa priere à Monsieur Franklin, et l'appuïant de Ses bons offices. L'Ambassadeur se flatte que ce Ministre accueillera favorablement une demande qui a pour but d'étendre les connoissances dans l'histoire naturelle, et qu'il voudra bien se prêter à lui adresser les recommandations susdites pour qu'il puisse les faire parvenir au Professeur Märter et le mettre en état de les présenter lui-même après Son arrivée en Amérique.

Ledit Ambassadeur saisit d'ailleurs avec un vrai plaisir cette occasion de présenter à Monsieur Franklin les assurances de son parfait attachement./.

Notation: Marter.

From Samuel Vaughan, Jr.   AL: American Philosophical Society

15 April, 1783.

Mr S Vaughan Junr. has the honor to present his most respectful compliments to Dr Franklin, & to send him, the 1 Number of Mr Linguets memoire, on the Bastile:[8] The 2 & 3 Numbers he will

---

letter just cited. His scientific expedition continued through 1788, taking him to Charleston and Louisville, among other places: *Morris Papers,* VIII, 627–8n; Hanns Schlitter, ed., *Die Berichte des ersten Agenten Österreichs in den Vereinigten Staaten von Amerika Baron de Beelen-Bertholff* . . . (Vienna, 1891), pp. 236–7, 406–8, 856–7.

8. Political journalist Simon-Nicolas-Henri Linguet (XXVIII, 106) was imprisoned in September, 1780, for attacking a member of the nobility. Upon his release in May, 1782, he went to London, where he resumed publishing his widely read *Annales politiques, civiles, et littéraires du 18ème siècle.* Despite having sworn not to write about his incarceration (a condition of his release), Linguet announced in January, 1783, his forthcoming *Mémoires sur la Bastille, et sur la détention de l'auteur dans ce château royal* . . . . Filled with lurid details, it was serialized in *Annales politiques* . . . , X (1783), nos. 73–75. Later that year it was issued as a pamphlet and became a best seller in numerous authorized and pirated editions, helping to popularize an image of monarchical administration in France as arbitrary and despotic: Darline Gay Levy, *The Ideas and Careers of Simon-Nicolas-Henri Linguet: a Study in*

do himself the pleasure of forwarding to him, as soon as they come to hand. He hopes Dr Franklin will excuse his requesting him, to return them as soon as perused, they being in great request, & borrowed.

From Thomas Greenleaf[9]   LS: American Philosophical Society

Monsieur,   Paris ce 16 avril 1783.

J'ai l'honneur de vous adresser Copie d'un Mémoire que je suis déterminé à présenter à M. Le Garde des Sceaux, à Monseigneur le Duc de Penthievre, à M. le Comte de Vergennes et à M. le Marquis de Castries, en faveur de notre Compatriote le Sr. fanning détenu dans la Prison de Dunkerque.[1] Il a commandé le Corsaire l'Eclipse, pendant qu'il étoit en croisière il a fait la visite de plusieurs Vaisseaux neutres; personne ne s'est plaint. Quelques mois après un François Passager sur l'un de ces neutres est venu a Dunkerque, il s'est plaint des Gens de l'Equipage du Corsaire l'Eclipse et leur a imputé de lui avoir volé de l'or, des Bijoux et autres effets précieux. Le Capitaine Fanning a voulu aller aux informations auprès de son Capitaine en second qui avoit commandé la partie de l'équipage chargée de la visite; ce Capitaine en second n'étoit plus en France depuis un certain tems. Faute de pouvoir se procurer des renseignemens M. Fanning a été forcé de ne donner aucune suite aux plaintes de ce François. Neanmoins [à] Son retour d'une nouvelle course qu'il

---

Eighteenth-Century French Politics (Urbana, Ill., 1980), pp. 200–9; Robert Darnton, The Literary Underground of the Old Regime (Cambridge, Mass., and London, 1982), pp. 24, 144–5.

9. The son of Joseph Greenleaf of Boston, Thomas was trained as a printer by Isaiah Thomas and during the Revolution served on numerous privateers. After the war he settled in New York and became an important newspaper publisher: DAB; XXVIII, 362n; JW Letterbook, Yale University Library. We cannot explain why this letter was sent in French; it is in the same secretarial hand as its enclosure.

1. See Nathaniel Fanning's letter of Jan. 27, above. The four-page enclosure, written in French and addressed to Miromesnil, the garde des sceaux, recapitulates the details of Fanning's case, argues for his innocence, and pleads for his release. APS.

entreprit aussitôt, M. Fanning a été arrêté au mois de 9bre. dernier. Si le vol a été commis par la partie de l'Equipage qu'il a chargée de faire la visite, il est toujours à l'abri de reproche, car il n'a pas quitté son bord; le delit ne Sauroit dont [donc] le regarder. Il n'est pas plus obligé à la reparation civile; mais en le Supposant pour un moment; pourquoi est il en Prison? Je crois qu'il est juste, Monsieur, que vous reclamiez la justice du Ministre du Roi, en faveur de M. Fanning et permettez de vous prier de vouloir bien vous en occuper.

Je suis avec respect Monsieur, Votre très humble et très obéissant Serviteur[2]   THOS: GREENLEAF

hôtel d'Orléans, Rue de Richelieu

From La Rochefoucauld   AL: American Philosophical Society

Mercredi matin [on or after April 16, 1783][3]
Le Duc de la Rochefoucauld a l'honneur de faire Ses complimens à Monsieur franklyn, et de le prévenir que l'impression des Traités avec la france et la hollande étant finie, l'imprimeur attend celui avec la suede pour terminer l'Ouvrage; le Duc de la Rochefoucauld prie Monsieur franklyn de vouloir bien le lui envoyer, ou lui mander Ses intentions à ce Sujet, ainsi que pour la Préface, il aura l'honneur de l'aller voir ces jours-ci.

2. Fanning was convicted on June 21; see XXXVIII, 341n. He claimed in his fictionalized memoir (for which see XXXVIII, 342n) that he was a frequent guest at Passy from late July to Aug. 9, when BF gave him a passport for Lorient, and that BF treated him "with the kindness of a parent": John S. Barnes, ed., *Fanning's Narrative: Being the Memoirs of Nathaniel Fanning, an Officer of the Revolutionary Navy, 1778–1783* (New York, 1912), pp. 241–50.

3. If Pierres had already finished printing the treaties with France and Holland, as La Rochefoucauld says here, then this letter was written on one of the Wednesdays following the Wednesday La Rochefoucauld wrote BF that he had given those treaties to the printer; that undated letter is above, under [April 9?]. The possibilities are April 16, 23, and 30. By Monday, May 5, the printing was complete; see Pierres to BF, May 5.

From Jonathan Williams, Sr.

ALS: American Philosophical Society

Hond sr   London April 16. 1783

I Wrote you that I Could not obtain a new addition of the Common prayer Book.[4] I have Since found one. I take this oppertunity to send it by the Bearrer mr. [*blank*]. Your friends Wh. are many have expectations of Seing you here some time in the summer & I belive you will find them as harty & prehaps more so then ever.

London is so much like home that I Cant but like it in preference to any place I ever Saw. I had rather decline going to France as the Journey is allmost as troblesom as going to America however if I Could be so happy as to go with you I would tarry here or go to France to Acommodate myself for Such a Passage—my love to your good Son & believe me ever Your Dutyfull Nephew & most Hble Servant   JONA. WILLIAMS

Addressed: His Excellency Benjamin Franklin / Passy near / Paris

From Beaujeu

ALS: American Philosophical Society

Très Réspéctable Ministre.   Champlitte ce 18. avril, 1783.

J'ai Recû, par le courier d'hier, la mèdaille que vous m'avès fait l'honneur de m'envoier;[5] et j'ai celui de vous en Remércier de toute mon âme. On s'emprèsse icy, a contempler ce monument qui intérèsse toute L'Europe et Éternise la gloire de L'amèrique.

Au Rèste, je dois prèvènir Votre Excéllence, qu'il ne m'èst pas possible de Repondre aux choses honnetes et gratieuses, que je présume être Renfermeè dans votre lettre, parce que je ne Sçai pas l'anglais et que personne icy ne l'entend.

---

4. On April 3, above.
5. BF must have sent Beaujeu a *Libertas Americana* medal.

Agreès je vous supplie Monsieur, toute la sinceritè de mes Vœux pour la complette prosperitè de tout ce qui vous intèrèsse.

C'est dans ces Sentimens que je suis avec bien du Réspéct Monsieur, de Votre Excellence, Le très humble et tres obèissant serviteur   LE CTE. DE BEAUJEU.

From William Hodgson   ALS: American Philosophical Society

Dear sir   London 18 April 1783
I take the liberty of inclosing you the Act for the Repeal of the prohibitory acts relative to America the Bill rec'd the Royal assent Yesterday,[6] there is another act in some degree of forwardness for taking away the necessity of certain documents that American Ships were required to bring—[7] I hope it will be all that at present is necessary to remove the Obstruction to mutual Intercourse betwixt the two Countries—it is said with some degree of Confidence that Mr Hartley is shortly to pay you a Visit to settle a Commercial Treaty, I hope it will be effected to mutual satisfaction— I am indebted to you upon Ballance of the Prisoners Acct something considerable about I believe £140— I

6. For the April 17 act repealing the Prohibitory Act, see *Journals of the House of Commons* (51 vols., reprint, London, 1803), XXXIX, 387. Copies retained by the American commissioners are at the Mass. Hist. Soc. and Library of Congress. BF instructed WTF to send a copy to Robert R. Livingston on April 26, the day he accompanied the newly-arrived David Hartley to Versailles; WTF's brief cover letter, also informing Livingston of Hartley's arrival, is at the National Archives. For background on the repeal, proposed by Fox on April 9, see the annotation of Laurens to BF, April 4.

7. On April 11 the House of Commons amended the bill abolishing certificates for American ships at the suggestion of William Eden, an opponent of liberal trade regulations, who worried about opening the carrying trade of the British West Indies to the United States. The documents were described in the bill as "any Manifest, Certificate, or other Document being required for any Ships belonging to the United States of America." Eden's amendment vested the king in Council with the authority to regulate all matters of British-American trade relations until Dec. 20. It passed in the House of Commons on April 25 and in the House of Lords two weeks later; the king gave his assent on May 12: *Journals of the House of Commons*, XXXIX, 387, 394, 409, 414, 415; Giunta, *Emerging Nation*, II, 92.

have not Time to night to send you particulars, but it is at your Command whenever you please to call for it—[8] I hope you will forward the Act to America the first Vessell it may have a Tendency to remove Difficulties I am very sincerely Dr sr your most Obliged Friend & Hble Servt WILLIAM HODGSON

His Excellency B. Franklin Esqr

Addressed: To / His Excellency / Benj: Franklin Esqr / Passy / Grand

From Kéralio   ALS: American Philosophical Society

A L'École Rle. [Royale] mre. [militaire] 18e. avril. 1783. Jusqu'à présent, mon respectable ami, vous m'avés constamment honoré de vos bontés; vous y mettés le comble en m'envoyant l'ingénieuse médaille qui éternisera Vôtre gloire et celle de Vôtre patrie.[9] Je n'ai pu y contribuer que par mes Vœux, mais je verserois mon sang pour la défendre.

Recevés l'hommage du tendre respect avec lequel je ne cesserai d'être, Mon respectable ami, Votre très humble et très obéissant Serviteur LE CHR. [CHEVALIER] DE KERALIO

From Daniel Duchemin   LS: American Philosophical Society

Monseigneur   ce 19 Avril 1783

Comme vous avez toujours eu des bontés pour moi, que ces mêmes bontés m'ont fait exister pendant bien du temps je vous prie de me les continuer en me faisant donner l'hôtel d'Invalide.[1]

8. Hodgson did not submit his account (XXXVII, 31n) until Oct. 24; it showed a balance of £49 7 s. 6 p. owed to BF.

9. A *Libertas Americana* medal. Four days earlier Kéralio had written WTF to inquire on behalf of a merchant friend whether Port Louis and Lorient were to be made free ports for trade with America (APS).

1. BF had recommended Duchemin, his former maître d'hôtel, for admission to the Hôpital de la charité that winter: XXXVIII, 611. The Hôtel royal des invalides was a home for wounded veterans of the king's armies: Pierre-Thomas-Nicolas Hurtaut, *Dictionnaire historique de la ville de Paris et de ses environs* (4 vols., Paris, 1779), III, 362–3.

Je présente un mémoire à Mr. de Ségur,[2] qui d'après votre recommandation et l'apostille que vous voudrez bien y ajouter, l'hotel me sera accordé. La bonté avec laquelle vous récompensez tous les français qui ont porté les armes pour votre patrie m'est un garand certain que vous allégerez l'indigence qui m'accable./. D. DUCHEMIN

A Monseigneur franklin Ministre Plénipotenciaire des Etats Unis de L'amérique Septentrionale près S.M. très Chrétienne

From Charles James Fox

Reprinted from William Temple Franklin, ed., *Memoirs of the Life and Writings of Benjamin Franklin* . . . (3 vols., 4to, London, 1817–18), II, 431.

Sir,   St. James's, April 19, 1783.
Although it is unnecessary for me to introduce to your acquaintance a gentleman so well known to you as Mr. Hartley,[3] who will have the honour of delivering to you this letter, yet it may be proper for me to inform you that he has the full and entire confidence of his Majesty's ministers upon the subject of his mission.[4]

2. As minister of war Ségur oversaw the administration of the Invalides: *Almanach royal* for 1783, pp. 190–1.
3. For Hartley's appointment as Oswald's replacement see the annotation of his letter of March 31. Hartley had been one of Fox's supporters in the House of Commons, had ties to North, and was hostile to Shelburne: XXXVI, 360–2; Butterfield, *John Adams Diary*, III, 135; George H. Guttridge, *David Hartley, M.P.: an Advocate of Conciliation, 1774–1783* (Berkeley and London, 1926), pp. 298–300. His relative liberalism on trade issues soon proved to be incompatible with Fox's orthodox mercantilism, however, and Fox, distrusting him, virtually ceased communicating: Andrew Stockley, *Britain and France at the Birth of America: the European Powers and the Peace Negotiations of 1782–1783* (Exeter, 2001), pp. 178–81.
4. Following the king's injunction, Fox gave Hartley written instructions on April 10 for concluding as quickly as possible an agreement concerning trade, whether a "treaty or provisional convention." They proposed that American produce be admitted to Britain under prewar duties and that British produce and manufactures be admitted to the United States on the same conditions. American manufactures, however, would not be admitted into

Permit me, Sir, to take this opportunity of assuring you how happy I should esteem myself if it were to prove my lot to be the instrument of compleating a real and substantial reconciliation between two countries formed by nature to be in a state of friendship one with the other, and thereby to put the finishing hand to a building, in laying the first stone of which I may fairly boast that I had some share.

I have the honour to be, with every sentiment of regard and esteem, Sir, your most obedient humble servant,   C. J. Fox.

From Elkanah Watson, Jr.[5]   AL: American Philosophical Society

London. 19th. Apl. 1783

Mr. Watson presents his respectfull compliments to His Excellency Doctr. Franklin & makes free to Send him a few papers.[6]

Britain, nor would foreign manufactures carried on American ships. Similar restrictions were proposed for American trade with the British West Indies, American ships being permitted to carry only American produce. Fox hoped that the repeal of prohibitory acts on American trade (as he was proposing to the House of Commons) would lead to reciprocal action by the Americans and the conclusion of a treaty or convention of intercourse: Giunta, *Emerging Nation*, II, 86–7; Fortescue, *Correspondence of George Third*, VI, 349.

On April 18 the king issued his own written instructions, authorizing Hartley to treat with the American commissioners on reciprocal opening of ports and arrangements of trade, and also to conclude a definitive peace treaty: Giunta, *Emerging Nation*, II, 91–2. Congress had instructed the commissioners on commercial articles to be included in a peace treaty, but they had no authority to make a separate commercial treaty: XXXVIII, 537; *JCC*, XXIII, 838.

5. Watson's business in Nantes was ruined by the French government suspending payment on American bills of exchange (for which see JW's letter of March 5 and Joly de Fleury's letter of March 15). He left the city on March 30 and relocated to England: Winslow C. Watson, ed., *Men and Times of the Revolution; or, Memoirs of Elkanah Watson* . . . (2nd ed., New York and London, 1857), pp. 212–13.

6. The same day, Watson also wrote to WTF and explained his idea for animating the lifesize figure of BF he had fashioned out of the wax head sculpted by Patience Wright and the suit of BF's clothes that WTF had sent him; see XXXVIII, 501–2. "I intend with the assistance of some ingenious mechanic, to contrive some kind of Clock machinery in the body, so as to give it a movement, & at the Same time, with the right hand, grind out electricity upon an

From the Baronne de Bourdic[7]

ALS: American Philosophical Society

a paris le 20 [April 1783?][8] rue jacob hotel de modene
Le desir que javois Monsieur davoir une Correspondance avec
vous me fit prendre avec empressement Les lettres que vous me

---

electrical machine I am in possession off": Watson to WTF, April 19, 1783,
APS. The eventual mechanism was more modest, but the hoax was a success.
Watson set the dummy by an open window with its head leaning out, until
passersby had taken notice; the following morning, the doctor's arrival was
reported in the London papers. Three men from Boston, who intended to
visit BF when they continued on to Paris, begged to be presented and were
told to come the following evening with their letters of introduction. When
they arrived, Watson warned them that BF was "deeply engaged in examining maps and papers" and might not be very responsive. He brought them
halfway across the room and introduced them to "Franklin," whereupon a
hidden friend manipulated wires that raised and lowered the head, causing
the figure to nod. Watson then led one of the awestruck guests, a certain "Mr.
B——," to approach the figure and offer his letter of introduction from
Samuel Cooper. When "Franklin" ignored the gesture, Watson berated the
figure for being rude, and horrified the guests by striking it a blow. "They
were all petrified with astonishment," Watson later wrote, "but B. never for-
gave me the joke." Winslow C. Watson, ed., *Men and Times of the Revolution...*, pp. 142–3. "B" was likely Oliver Brewster, who traveled to England
in July, 1783, in the company of Benjamin Austin, Jr.; both young men carried introductions to BF from Cooper dated July 19, 1783, which they eventually presented in person (APS).

7. This is the first of five surviving letters, partially dated at best, from
Marie-Anne-Henriette Payan de L'Estang (1744–1802), a poet from Nîmes
who spent most of 1783 in Paris, although the exact dates of her stay are unknown. Shortly after her arrival she made it her business to meet BF, and subsequently visited him as frequently as possible, "even at the risk of becoming troublesome," as she admitted upon her departure (Bourdic to BF,
undated, APS). She began writing poetry at the age of 16, after the death of
her first husband, the marquis d'Antremont. In 1777 she married the baron
de Bourdic. By the time she arrived in Paris, her reputation was established:
Voltaire was one of her correspondents and admirers, her poems appeared
regularly in the *Almanach des muses*, and in 1782 she was made a member of
the Académie de Nîmes. She so captivated the writer Blin de Sainmore that,
shortly after the date of the present letter, he published a 26-line poem in
praise of her talents (*Jour. de Paris*, May 8, 1783). See the *DBF*, under Bour-
dic-Viot; Gilbert Chinard, "Benjamin Franklin et la muse provinciale," APS
Proc., XCVII (1953), 493–510; Lopez, *Mon Cher Papa*, pp. 194–5.

8. Dated on the basis of the German letter she returns to BF along with her

483

chargeates de traduire; sans reflechir aux difficultes qui se sont presentees; pour une allemande qui a quitte Sa patrie depuis l'age de quatre ans⁹ la traduction d'une lettre de quatre pages devenoit un ouvrage; aussi ai je reste bien longtemps; vous Seul èties Capable de me donner asses de patience pour en venir a bout; jai lhonneur de vous lenvoŷer et vous demande un millions de pardons non de mon inexactitude mais de mon peu d'intelligence qui me force a emploŷer trois semaines pour une affaire de trois heures; malgrè mon peu de talent je mets un prix a mon travail je demande de voir encore une fois avant de retourner dans ma province un homme aussi interessant par ses vertus qu'etonnant par son genie deux mots de votre main pour massurer que Ce projet ne vous deplait point et vous verres bientot Celle qui a lhonneur detre Monsieur votre tres humble et tres obeissante Servante   DE LESTANG BARONNE DE BOURDIC
jadis La mse [marquise] dentremont

Endorsed: La Baronne de Bourdic A Paris

From Pio   AL: American Philosophical Society

à Paris ce 20. Avril 1783.
M. de Pio a reçu avec le plus grand plaisir La Medaille,¹ dont Monsieur Franklin a bien voulu lui faire le genéreux present. Il a l'honneur de Lui en faire tous ses remercimens, et de lui temoigner toute sa reconnaissance./.

---

translation, which she says took her three weeks to complete. The German original, by August Friedemann Rühle von Lilienstern, March 14, 1783, is summarized in the headnote to Martineau's letter of Jan. 25.

9. The baronne was born in Dresden, though she was descended from noble families of the south of France: *Dictionnaire de la noblesse*, XV, 529–30.

1. The *Libertas Americana* medal that he requested on March 20, above.

484

Robert R. Livingston to the American Peace Commissioners

Copy:[2] Massachusetts Historical Society; ALS (draft): New-York Historical Society; transcript: National Archives

Gentlemen,   Philadelphia 21st. April 1783.

Upon the receipt of the provisional Articles & a subsequent account bro't by a Vessel dispatched by Count d'Estaing,[3] I wrote the Letter No. 1. to Sr. Guy Carleton, & No. 2. to Admiral Digby: to which I recieved the Answers No. 3. & 4.[4] You will find them cold & distant— Those they wrote to the Minister of France, in answer to similar Communications made by him, were still more so, and contain the same illiberal doubts, which are mentioned in mine, expressed in much stronger terms. When they recieved an authentic account of the Treaty, they sent a Copy of it, no part being omitted, to Congress thro' the General. When the Proclamation for the Cessation of Hostilities was recieved at New York, it was sent to me by an Officer with the Letters No. 5. & 6., to which I returned the Answers No. 7. & 8.[5]

After this, two great questions were agitated in Congress—
1st. Whether they should proceed to the immediate ratification

2. Made by John Thaxter, Jr. The transcript indicates that the now-missing original was sent by Col. Ogden (for whom see Boudinot to BF, April 28) and the duplicate by the packet *General Washington*.

3. D'Estaing, commanding the French fleet at Cadiz, had sent the *Triomphe* to La Luzerne with news of the general peace agreement of Jan. 20; see Livingston to BF, March 26.

4. On March 24 Livingston had informed the British army and navy commanders of the general peace; see our annotation of Livingston's March 26 letter. Carleton and Digby responded on March 26 and 27, respectively: Wharton, *Diplomatic Correspondence*, VI, 346, 348.

5. On April 6 both Carleton and Digby informed Livingston that they had learned of the signing of the general agreement and would take the appropriate steps (apparently enclosures 5 and 6). Livingston responded on April 11 and 12 (apparently enclosures 7 and 8): Wharton, *Diplomatic Correspondence*, VI, 362–3, 367–70. On April 11 Congress proclaimed a cessation of arms, with only John Mercer of Virginia dissenting. It confirmed the commissioners' declaration of Feb. 20, above, and attempted to resolve the ambiguities as to when captures by privateers ceased to be legal: *JCC*, XXIV, 238–40; William T. Hutchinson *et al.*, eds., *The Papers of James Madison*, First Series (17 vols., Chicago and Charlottesville, 1962–91), VI, 450–2.

of the provisional Articles—and 2dly. whether they should release the Prisoners. Some maintained, with respect to the first of these points, that they knew not in what light to consider the provisional Articles, whether as Preliminaries, or a definitive Treaty— That the Preamble said they were to *constitute* the Treaty while at the same time they were only to be inserted in it—[6] These Terms they considered as contradictory, and they wished to have explanations from you on this head, to know what the operation of a ratification would be; and they inferred from your Silence, that none was necessary. They observed that no time was set for the Evacuation of New York— That the Ratification would in some measure compel them to release their Prisoners, & thus strengthen their Hands, when it was possible that the definitive Treaty might not take effect between Great Britain and France; and that the Ratification and the Restoration of Prisoners, if it left us nothing more to do, was in some sort to desert our Allies. To this it was answered, that the provisional Articles were only to be recieved as Preliminary—that from the very Nature of them they could not be definitive—that the Ratification would not alter the Nature of them, but confirm them as they stood—that they were confessedly very advantageous to Us— That the neglecting any such acceptation of them, as was necessary on our part, would give the Enemy a pretence for violating the Stipulations they contained—that the principal points between France & Great Britain being settled, we had no reason to apprehend a failure of a definitive Treaty—that it was important to shew, that we were determined to adhere in every particular to the Engagements you had made. These Arguments prevailed, & the Resolution No. 9. passed, directing the Ratification which I inclose.[7] It is probable that the definitive Treaty will be signed before this can reach you, otherwise it would be extremely desirable that some Ambiguities in the provisional Articles should be cleared up, and other Objects, which have

6. The preamble of the Nov. 30 Preliminary Articles says they were "To be inserted in, and to constitute the Treaty of Peace": XXXVIII, 382.

7. The articles were ratified on April 15: Giunta, *Emerging Nation*, 1, 823–4; *JCC*, XXIV, 243–51. The enclosure, marked "No. 9" (the April 15 resolutions, published in *JCC*, XXIV, 241–3), is at the APS.

been touched upon at different times in my public Letters, attended to. The sixth Article is not so precisely expressed as to point out to what time, the word *future* refers—whether to the Signature of the provisional Articles—whether to the Act which gave it the force of a Treaty, or to the definitive Treaty, tho' I should suppose the second to be the intention from the opposition between the word *now*, and the time of the ratification in America.[8]

The 7th. Article leaves the time for the evacuation of New York upon so loose a footing, that I fear our troublesome Guests will long continue to be such unless a day is fixed for their departure in the definitive Treaty. You can easily concieve the impatience that the distressed Inhabitants of New York feel at every moment's delay, & the fears & jealousies that prevail among them, lest it should be meant to retain these Posts as Pledges for the performance of the Stipulations in favor of the Tories— By the debates in Parliament on the third of March it is evident that they had then no Orders to evacuate.[9]

You will observe that the Ratification does not extend to the seperate Article. The Treaty between Spain & Great Britain renders it unnecessary—[1] And Congress not caring to express any Sentiment upon that Subject I refer you to my Letters to Dr. Franklin & Mr. Jay upon the Subject of a free Trade with the West Indies, and the Logwood Trade, which are important Objects here,[2] and I hope will be attended to in your definitive Treaty. It were to be wished that the Ambiguity with respect to the time of the cessation of Hostilities upon this Coast was cleared up, and the construction we put upon it adopted, to wit,

8. The sixth article prohibited future confiscations of Loyalist property or prosecution of Loyalists: XXXVIII, 386.

9. On March 3 David Hartley accused the government of not planning to evacuate New York before the end of the year. Secretary of State Townshend refused to set a date, citing the difficulty of finding the shipping to carry out so massive an evacuation of people and supplies: *Courier de l'Europe*, XIII (1783), 150.

1. For Livingston's criticism of the separate article see his letter to the commissioners, March 25.

2. Livingston to BF, Sept. 5, 1782 (XXXVIII, 71–2); and to Jay, Sept. 12, 1782 (Wharton, *Diplomatic Correspondence*, V, 721). See also XXXVIII, 332.

that by as far as the Canaries was intended the Latitude of the Canaries, which construction can be supported by a variety of Arguments, and is extremely important to Us, as a Number of our Vessels have been taken since the third of March.

I have the honor to be, Gentlemen, with great Esteem & Respect, your most obed. humble Servt.   ROBT. R. LIVINGSTON

Honble. John Adams, Benja. Franklin John Jay & Henry Laurens Esqrs.

No. 2.

2plicate.

(Copy)

Notation by John Adams: Mr Livingstone to the Ministers for Peace. 21. April. 1783.

From the Marquis de Brancas[3]

AL: American Philosophical Society

a paris lundi 21 avril. [1783]
Mr. le Mis. de brancas prie Mr. franclin de lui faire dire a qu'elle heure il pouroit avoir l'honneur de le voir le matin et quel jour lui conviendroit il s'interesse beaucoup a un jeune homme qui est a philadelphie et dont il voudroit lui parler.

3. Louis-Paul de Brancas, marquis de Brancas (1718–after 1791), son of Louis, *maréchal de France,* was a distinguished military officer. He was a *grand d'Espagne* and lieutenant general of Provence, a lieutenant general in the French army and *chevalier de l'Ordre du Saint-Esprit.* In 1785 he was named duc de Céreste and he retired to Provence: *DBF; Dictionnaire de la noblesse,* III, 982–3; *Almanach royal* for 1783, pp. 152, 186, 195, 202.

From the Duchesse de Deux-Ponts

AL: American Philosophical Society

paris Lundis [April] 21 a 2 heures [1783]
Mr le prince de deuxponts[4] desire Mon respectable amis d'avoir
Lhoneur de faire Votre Connessance d'autant quil est charge de
Vous parlér de La part des etats de baviere dun arrangement de
Comerce, avec Les etats unis.[5] Je Lui ait proposér de satisfaire
Son desir en vous donnant a dinee avec Lui il sera Libre jeudis
ous samedis. Voyéz, Mon charmant amis, Si Vous pouriez Me
faire Lhoneur de diner chez Moi Lun ous Lautre de Ces deux
jours avec Mr Votre petit fils? Recevez mon vertueux et cher amis
Lhomage dun Coeur qui Vous respecte autant quil Vous aime. M
de Keralio avec qui je Vais boire a Votre sante Vous presentes son
tendre homage. Je rouvre ma Lettre mon cher bon amis pour
Vous rendre mille actions de graces de 4 bouteille de rack [ar-
rack] quon Vient de me remettre de Votre part je vous en remercie bien tendrement.

Addressed: a Monsieur / Monsieur franklin / Ministre pleinipotentiaire / des etats unis a La Cour / de france / a passis

From Alice Izard

AL: American Philosophical Society

Hotel de Vendome 21st. April 1783.
Mrs. Izard presents her Compliments to Dr. Franklin, & requests
the favour of a passport for herself, & family, & Miss Stead, with
their Servants, to go to Bourdeaux, & from thence to America.[6]

---

4. Charles-Auguste (or Karl August, 1746–1795) succeeded his uncle, the
duchesse's late husband, Christian, as duc de Deux-Ponts (Zweibrücken) in
1775: XXVII, 556n; *ADB*. For his visit see also Kéralio's second letter of April
26 and the duchesse's letter of April 27.
5. Bavaria currently was ruled by another of Charles-Auguste's uncles,
Elector Charles-Théodore (Karl Theodor): XXVII, 536n; *ADB*. Charles-Auguste was his heir presumptive. For Bavarian interest in trade with the United
States see also Utzschneider's April 10 letter, discussed in our headnote to
Martineau to BF, Jan. 25.
6. Mary Stead was a daughter of the late Benjamin Stead, a London mer-

If Dr. Franklin has any commands for Philadelphia, Mrs. Izard will execute them with the greatest pleasure.[7]

Notation: Mlle. Beck chez la Mse D'Agne au Luxembourg

To John Dickinson

LS:[8] Historical Society of Pennsylvania; AL (draft):[9] American Philosophical Society

Sir,   Passy, April 22. 1783

M. Märter, Professor of Natural History in the Service of the Emperor, being appointed to make a Collection of Plants and Animals from the four Quarters of the World, for his Imperial Majesty's Botanic Gardens and Menagerie, proposes to begin his Operations by a Journey thro' the Countries under the Government of the United States of America. He is strongly recommended to me by his Excellency the Ambassador from that Court;[1] and I take leave to recommend him not only to the Civilities you are pleased in bestowing on Strangers of Merit but to all the Assistances and Facilities your Station and the Influence attending it may enable you to afford him in the Execution of his Commission, being persuaded that your Zeal for the Increase of useful Science, as well as the Respect due to his August Employer, will induce you to render Mr. Märter such Services with

---

chant and friend of Ralph Izard; her sister Elizabeth was married to Ralph Izard, Jr.: *Laurens Papers,* X, 102n; XV, 544n; XVI, 205n. The entourage left Paris on April 24. They expected to sail from Bordeaux to Philadelphia about May 10, but had difficulty obtaining proper accommodations for the trip: Smith, *Letters,* XX, 288; *Laurens Papers,* XVI, 203.

7. BF sent a passport the same day, along with several letters. These were sent under cover of a letter from WTF, a retained copy of which is at the APS.

8. In L'Air de Lamotte's hand, except for the portion of the complimentary close after "Sir" and the esquire line, which are in BF's hand.

9. In the margin of this unaddressed draft BF wrote "15 Copies." If he indeed supplied Märter with this number, the only one to survive is the present one to Dickinson, president of the Pa. Supreme Executive Council.

1. The comte de Mercy-Argenteau; his recommendation is above, April 15.

Pleasure.[2] I have the honour to be, very respectfully, Sir, Your Excellency's most obedient & most humble Servant

B FRANKLIN

His Excellency the Governor of Pennsylvania.

From Jacob Duché, Jr.   ALS: American Philosophical Society

Sir   Asylum, Lambeth, April 22, 1783

I return your Excellency my most sincere and hearty Thanks for your Kindness & Condescension in answering my Letter,[3] and for the candid & affectionate Manner in which you have given me your Advice on a Subject in which I feel myself deeply interested. This Advice shall be the Rule of my Conduct; and I will wait with Patience, till I hear from my Friends at Philada, to many of whom I have written within these few Days, by different Conveyances.

I must beg Leave to set your Excellency right with Respect to the Sentiments of my Congregations relative to my Departure. I left Philada. with their full Knowledge & Approbation. I did it in the most Public Manner, having called my Vestry, and acquainted them with my Motives for taking a Voyage to England, not doubting at that Time, but that a Plan of Reconciliation would have taken Place, and I should have been able to return to them in a few Months. I take the Liberty of enclosing a Copy of their Address to me on that Occasion.

The Vestry consist of 20 Gentlemen, the far greater Part of whom remained in the City with the British Army, were present at this Meeting, & signed this Address,[4] as well as an affection-

2. Märter and his traveling companion, Beelen-Berthoff (for whom see our annotation of Ingenhousz' April 8 letter), sailed from Le Havre on Aug. 1 on the packet *General Washington* and reached Philadelphia in early September: *Morris Papers*, VIII, 505, 627n; Hulbert Footner, *Sailor of Fortune: the Life and Adventures of Commodore Barney, U.S.N.* (New York and London, 1940), p. 147.

3. Of Jan. 28, above. BF's response has not been located.

4. Only nine of the twenty vestrymen showed up for that meeting, held on Dec. 9, 1777; Duché's own father did not attend. Many of the attendees,

491

ate Letter in my Favour to the Bishop of London, both of which stand entered in their Book of Minutes. I cannot, therefore, be said, to have deserted my Flock: But have every Reason to conclude, that if my Return depended on the Approbation of the Congregations, they, with their present good & friendly Rector, would immediately express their Desire of receiving me.

The whole must depend upon the Generosity of the Legislature; And I have the Satisfaction to hear, that several of my most intimate & valuable Friends are at this Time high in Office, and have no Doubt, but they will sollicit Government in my Favour— I have written particularly to Mr Dickinson, and to Mr Rob. Morris; and have also taken the Liberty of addressing a few Lines to General Washington.[5]

I should be happy indeed to have my Application honoured with the Sanction of your Excellency's Name; as I am very sure, that your Recommendation of my Case to the Notice of the Legislature by a Letter to their President, or by any other Method you may judge most proper, would add such Weight to the Sollicitations of my Friends, as would secure immediate Success.

---

listed at the end of this note, were Loyalists. They readily consented to Duché's request, and wrote an affectionate letter wishing him a safe voyage and speedy return. Duché copied that letter for BF in its entirety, leaving off only the signatory: church warden James Reynolds, a Loyalist who helped supervise the night watch during the British occupation of Philadelphia (Wilbur H. Siebert, *The Loyalists of Pennsylvania* [Columbus, Ohio, 1920], p. 44). Minutes of this meeting and the text of the letter are in Benjamin Dorr, *A Historical Account of Christ Church, Philadelphia, from Its Foundation, A.D. 1695 to A.D. 1841; and of St. Peter's and St. James's, until the Separation of the Churches* (New York and Philadelphia, 1841), pp. 163, 185–7. For the names of the other eight attendees we thank Sue Wright of the archives of Christ Church. They were Edward Shippen and Charles Stedman (Siebert, *Loyalists*, pp. 59, 86), Joseph Swift (Sabine, *Loyalists*, p. 638), Jonathan Browne (Lothrop Withington, "Pennsylvania Gleanings in England," *PMHB*, XXIX [1905], 95), Peter Knight, John Morris, Samuel Powel, and Alexander Wilcocks. See also Thomas H. Montgomery, "List of Vestrymen of Christ Church, Philadelphia," *PMHB*, XIX (1895), 519–26.

5. Duché's letter to Washington, dated April 2, asked his pardon and requested that Washington write to the Pa. legislature in favor of his return. Washington's response, written on Aug. 10, assured Duché that he bore no "personal enmity" but that he would leave the decision to the state of Pennsylvania: Worthington C. Ford, *The Washington-Duché Letters* (Brooklyn, N.Y., 1890), pp. 35–8.

But I will not presume too far. I know your Engagements must be numerous, and of the greatest Importance, and that you have various Applications to attend to, of much greater Consequence than mine.

Mrs Duché is much obliged to you for your kind Remembrance of her, and Answer to her Enquiries after Mrs Bache & her Children. We shall both be extremely happy to see you in England.

My Son, who is now in his 20th Year is a Pupil of my good Friend West, and most enthusiastically devoted to the Art, in which he promises to make no inconsiderable Figure.[6] As he is my only Son & a good Scholar, I wished to have educated him for one of the learned Professions. But his Passion for Painting is irresistible. West feeds the Flame with the Fuel of Applause: And his great Example has excited in my Boy an Ambition to distinguish himself in his Native Country, as his Master has distinguished himself here. The late Revolution has opened a large Field for Design. His young Mind already teems with the great Subjects of Councils, Senates, Heroes, Battles—and he is impatient to acquire the Magic Powers of the Pencil to call forth & compleat the Embryo Forms.

My eldest Daughter is in her 16th Year— My youngest in her 9th.[7] We have not been able to give them any other Advantages of Education, than our own Private Tuition. Indeed the Plan of Female Education in this Country is too expensive for our present contracted Circumstances; and at the same Time, has too much of the Ornamental, & too little of the Essential, to meet my Ideas or Inclinations.

I beg your Excellency to bear with this little Prattle about my Family— And have only to request the Favour of you, to peruse at your Leisure the enclosed Extract from my Letter to Mr Hopkinson, which will give you some Information with Respect to the State of Mind I was in, when I wrote the Letter to General

6. Thomas Spence Duché (1763–1790) was a student of Benjamin West (XXXIII, 196n): Albert F. Gegenheimer, "Artist in Exile: the Story of Thomas Spence Duché," *PMHB*, LXXIX (1955), 3–26.
7. Esther (b. 1767) and Elizabeth Sophia (b. 1774): *ibid.*, 10–11.

W. the Circumstances which attended the sending of it, and the Consequences to myself & Family.[8]

I have the Honour to be, With the greatest Respect Your Excellency's Most obliged & faithful Servant   J. Duché

Notation: S. Duche apl. 22. 1783.

From ——— Greissot(?)   ALS: American Philosophical Society

Monsieur   a Villeneuve L'archevesque Le 22. avril 1783.

J'ay L'honneur de vous adresser cy joint Un memoire du Nommé Jaques Blanchet cy devant Canonier de La Legion de Luxembourg,[9] Il Espere que Vous Voudréz Bien Luy faire Rendre La justice quil demande En Le faisant employer pour Sa cottepart dans l'Etat des prises dont est question, c'est Un Brave Soldat qui Sert depuis 17 ans dont 3 ont eté Employées a La navigation.

Je Suis avec un profond Respect Monsieur Votre tres humble Et tres obeissant Serviteur   Greissot(?)
Maire

8. Duché's letter to his brother-in-law Francis Hopkinson, eight pages of which he copied (the extract is undated), explained that his letter to Washington had been written at a time when he was under "the strongest Apprehensions of inevitable Danger impending over all my dearest Friends without the British Lines." He declared himself ready to return to Pennsylvania, where he intended to offer his allegiance to the state in the hope that a release from the attainder could be secured.

9. Blanchet is listed among the marines of the second company of the Luxembourg Legion: James A. Lewis, *Neptune's Militia: the Frigate* South Carolina *during the American Revolution* (Kent, Ohio, and London, 1999), p. 138. The enclosure, in Greissot's hand, explains that Blanchet embarked at the Texel in 1780 on the *South Carolina* but never received his share of the prize money. He subsequently sailed on the *Alliance;* Capt. Barry advanced him 16 guineas, but the balance of his prize money remains unpaid.

From Jean Hadenbrock ALS: American Philosophical Society

Monseigneur!   Bordeaux ce 22 avril 1783
    Permettez Monseigneur La Liberté que je prends De Vous
écrire que Sur Les Deux Lettre De recomandation que vous
m'avez fait L'honneur De me Donner pour Philladelphia et
Boston, Lorsqu'à mon arrivé ici Depuis Le 16 Du Courant, j'eus
L'avantage De trouver une Navire prete a Parter pour Philladelphia que est Desendû au Bas De la Reviére Le 18 et Partira au
Premier vend Convenable D'apres que Le Capetaine Desendera
avec moi jeudÿ prochain pour Le Susdit endroit Le Navir est Le
grand D'Estaing Capeteine Orée: De 600 tonneau 24 Canon 80
homme D'équipage D'après L'heureux arrive[1] Le Sir Rich Bach
vous écrira et j'aurai L'honneur De vous Dire tel que Le paÿs me
plait, ainsi que mes affaire se sont arengé, une Paquotille partera
aussi D'ici pour Boston à L'adresse Sir Williams,[2] et L'on n'est
au fait De travailler chez nous à force pour me faire Des éxpedi-
tion.
    Entre tems Vous D'aignéz De reçevoir mes tres humble re-
mercement. Je ferai usage De Vos cher recomandation Le plus
Sincers Dont j'espere La premiére Nouvelle vous rendra Satisfait, vous priant De ne retirer Votre bien Veillance De Celui
que se flatte D'etre tres Sinecerement De Monseigneur Votre
obeïsant & Digne Seviteur   JEAN HADENBROCK

Addressed: A Son Excellence / Monsieur Franklin / ministre
Plenipotentaire Des Etats unis / De LAmerique & &. / à /
Passÿ / près De Paris

1. The arrival of the *Grand d'Estaing*, Capt. J. Orr, was reported in the
Pa. Gaʒ. on June 11, 1783. One of the ship's owners, L. Lanoix, had written
to BF before its departure: XXXVIII, 391.
2. Jonathan Williams, Sr.

From the Comte de Lameth[3]

ALS: American Philosophical Society

Sir,   Paris. April. the 22th. 1783.

I Received with an innexpressible gratitude the pretious pledge of esteem with which america, and your Excellency, have daigned to Reward Services of So little importance as mine;[4] But which Could have deserved So great a favour: if the truest attachment, if the most Constant wishes for the Good Succes of So noble a Cause, if the tenderest veneration for the virtuous authors of So Glorious a Revolution, Could, in Supplying what I did not Perform, Give me Some Rights to the favour which america honours me with, I would not think myself quite unworthy of it: in the raptures of my just Gratitude I will not tell your excellency, I hope that a new war will afford me more opportunities of deserving So pretious a Reward: Such wishes Should be too Contrary to those of your excellency: undoubtedly you long ardently for the duration of a glorious peace, which Secures the felicity of your Country, to which you have So much Contributed: however, if the circonstances ever Permitted me to offer again my Services to america, I would think myself very happy in Keeping all the engagements I Contract with her in this day.

I hope, your Excellency, will grant me the permission to Pay my duties to him, and to lay down at his feet a new hommage of the warmest Gratitude, and of that most profond veneration with which I have the honour to be, of your Excellency, the most humble, and most obedient Servant.

LE CHR. [CHEVALIER] CHARLES DE LAMETH

cul de Sac notre dame des champs.

---

3. A member of a distinguished military family; for his parents see XXVI, 430n. Charles (1757–1832) had been seriously wounded at Yorktown; he and two brothers would be promoted to *maréchal de camp* in 1791–92 and later would serve Napoleon: *DBF;* Six, *Dictionnaire biographique;* Bodinier, *Dictionnaire.*

4. BF must have given him a *Libertas Americana* medal.

From Dominique-Louis Ethis de Corny

ALS: American Philosophical Society

Dear Sir   Paris the 23th. aprile 1783

I am Requested to introduce to your Excellency Mr. D'Acosta gentleman of Nantes, Vho has some Business Relating to the north america.[5] He Desires to have the honor of Waiting on your Excellency. If you Will Be so Kind as give me the notice of Day Vherein I may Lead this gentleman to Passy, in the Next Weeck, I shall traduce your Answer to Mr. D'acosta.

I have the honor to be With great respect and faithfull attachment Dear sir your Excellency's the most humble and Dutiful servant   DE CORNY

From Isabella Strange

ALS: American Philosophical Society

Sir   London April 23 1783

Permite me to join my most respectful compliments with Mr Stranges[6] and to return You my sincere thanks for the many favours I owe You for Your kind care of my corrosponce— I presume once more on Your goodness and beg the inclos'd may be forwarded. It contains the Coppy of a will by which my Cousin Mrs Hunter[7] and Her Family gets some Money by the Death of Her Grand-Father the Revd Dr Russell. I am with respect and esteem Sir Your very humb Sert

ISABELLA STRANGE

---

5. Fourteen months earlier, BF had accepted a bill of exchange from North America presented by D'Acosta (XXXVI, 566). The merchant may have had another to present or perhaps wished to renew trading (see XXIX, 365).

6. Her husband, Robert, wrote on March 29 (above).

7. Marianna Spence Hunter (XXXVII, 690n).

From George Washington

Draft:[8] Library of Congress

Sir [April 23, 1783]

I have the honor to inclose to you, a Letter and Memorial I have just reced from Baron De L'Estrade—an Old Veteran who served with us at the Seige of York—from my acquaintance with this Officer, joined to the general good Character he had—I feel strongly inclined to serve him but there may be many Reasons to render such an interference as he Requests improper—all I can do therefore is to submit the matter to you, with a wish that, so far as Circumstances and the rules of propriety will admit, you may interest yourself in his favor—[9]

Dr. Franklin

8. In the hand of staff officer Benjamin Walker: Fitzpatrick, *Writings of Washington*, XXVI, 356n. The dateline has been cropped; Fitzpatrick prints it as "Head Quarters, April 23, 1783." It is possible that BF never received this letter; see below.

9. Claude-Aimable-Vincent de Roqueplan (Roqueplant), baron de l'Estrade (1729–1819), was promoted to brigadier for his courage at Yorktown: Six, *Dictionnaire biographique;* Bodinier, *Dictionnaire;* Ministère des Affaires Etrangères, *Les Combattants français de la guerre américaine, 1778–1783* (Paris, 1903), p. 273. In March he wrote to Washington requesting the general's and BF's help in obtaining a command in St. Domingue. He enclosed a memoir asking Congress to order BF to support his application (National Archives). Washington answered on April 23 that he would forward the memoir and write the present letter to BF. He did so the same day, addressing to Boudinot the memoir, his letter to BF, and a forwarding letter which was read in Congress: Fitzpatrick, *Writings of Washington*, XXVI, 354–5; *JCC*, XXIV, 312n. It is not known whether Boudinot forwarded the material to BF; neither Washington's letter nor its enclosures are among BF's extant papers.

Franklin's Specimen of Polytype Printing[1]

ADS: Yale University Library

[April 24, 1783]

A Wit's a Feather, & a Chief's a Rod;
An honest Man's the noblest Work of God.

Pope.[2]

Passy, April 24, 1783 —BF.—

From Francis Coffyn

ALS: American Philosophical Society

Hond. Sir.   Dunkerque 24. April 1783.

I had the honnor to address your Excellency by my last letter of 11th. inst,[3] 13 receipts for monies disbursed for Sundry american prisonners, & to advise of my drafts on your Excellency of £. 894. 8.—., & at the Same time to communicate Capn Coreil's request to obtain a passport for his brig General Washington to proceed to Philadelphia; being Since deprived of the favour of your Excellencys answer, and Capn Coreil making dayly applications to me to know the result of his request, his vessell being now ready for Sea, I humbly beg your Excellency will be pleased to favour me with a few lines to inform me wether that Gentleman may expect the wish'd for passport, in order to avoid a prej-

---

1. On April 10, WTF and others had visited François Hoffmann and participated in a demonstration of his polytype process, a method of reproducing handwriting or line drawings. (See the annotation of Samuel Vaughan, Jr., to BF, [April] 6, above.) BF visited Hoffmann on April 24 and wrote this specimen. The polytype method involved having an individual write or draw on a highly-polished copper plate with special ink. The ink, which contained "an earthy substance," had sufficient contour that Hoffmann could press the copper plate onto another metal surface that would received its impression, creating a reverse image. This second "engraved" plate would be inked and used to print multiple copies: *Jefferson Papers*, X, 318–24.

BF would have recognized Hoffmann's method as similar in concept to what he had devised many years earlier in America; see XXXIII, 117.

2. BF had inscribed the same verse in Steinsky's autograph book on Jan. 27, 1781: XXXIV, 316.

3. Above.

udicial detention of his vessell in this Harbour; Capn. Coreil has promised me to give their passage to Sundry american prisonners which arrived here lately from England, enclosed I remit five receipts[4] from those I have relieved since my last, viz

£.	30.	—.—.	to James Manin
"	36.	—.—.	to Danl. Lockardy, John Ellebecker, & John Stevens
"	30.	—.—.	to Patrick Dolon,
"	84.	—.—.	to Michael Carr,
"	31. 5.—.		to Francis Peuwck, M. Russell & James Kelley,
£. 211. 5.—.			Together, which I have charged to your Excellencys Account.

I am Sorry to inform your Excellency that a ship onboard of which I procured a passage for four of the men whose receipts I sent in my last letter, has been drove onshore & wrecked the 22d. inst, and they narrowly escaped their lives; as these poor men stand now more then ever in need of assistance, I hope your Excellency will not desaprove that I supply them with a little more money for their absolute necessaries.

I have the honnor to remain with due respect Your Excellencys most obedient & most Humble Servant   F. COFFYN

His Excellency Dr. B. Franklin. a Passi.

From Robert Morris

Copy: Library of Congress

Sir,   Office of Finance 24. April 1783

I beg Leave to trouble your Excellency with the Delivery of the enclosed Letter which is left open for your Perusal that in Case the Baron should trouble you farther on the Subject you may be fully possessed of my Sentiments to him.[5]

---

4. Missing.

5. He enclosed a letter of the same day to Baron d'Arendt (*Morris Papers*, VII, 750) denying his right to interest on a bill of exchange paid by BF (for which see XXXVIII, 213n).

I am respectfully, your Excellency's most obedient and humble Servant   R M.

His Excelly. Benjm. Franklin

From Jonathan Shipley   ALS: American Philosophical Society

Dear Sir   Bolton Street Ap: 24th 83

I feel ashamd & distressd when I think how long I have left your most obliging & valuable Letter unanswerd. Indeed great part of the time I have been under the deep affliction of parting with our eldest & most deserving Daughter to the distance of Bengal.[6] I do not mean to depretiate the rest; but She had more of that domestick kindness & attention which You know how to value, & which an old Man wants & delights in. And tho' Sr Wm Jones is a worthy & indeed a superior Man; yet so total a Seperation with only a bare distant possibility of meeting again is as deeply & as tenderly affecting, if I can judge truely of my own feelings as her Death itself would have been.

I have had a very agreable visit from your very respectable Nephew Mr. Williams.[7] With a great tincture of Piety He seems to have preservd the old English Sense & Spirit, & Honesty, which the first Settlers exported in so large a quantity to America & have left an utter Scarcity of them here. You think too highly of us when You suppose that We have gaind Wisdom by all our misfortunes. We have discoverd many frauds & abuses; but corrected very few; & very little of the small savings We have made has been restord to the Publick. The old Rockingham Party, now headed by the D [Duke] of Portland are a set of up-

6. His daughter Anna Maria and her new husband, Sir William Jones, sailed for India three days after their wedding. There they remained until chronic ill health forced Anna Maria to return to England in late 1793. Jones was to follow as soon as he completed his digest of Hindu and Muslim law, but he died soon after she left, at the age of forty-seven. Garland Cannon, *The Life and Mind of Oriental Jones: Sir William Jones, the Father of Modern Linguistics* (Cambridge, New York, and Port Chester, N.Y., 1990), pp. 192, 196–9, 355–6, 384n.

7. Jonathan Williams, Sr.

right respectable Men but they have an aversion to every thing that they call a change in the Constitution; & yet without some change there can be no improvement. You know too as well as I, that these honest Men whom I lookd upon as the hopes of their Country[8] are united with Ld North & his meritorious Band, on condition that the latter shall share only in the profits without interfering in the measures of Government. But I own I tremble for the Event of a Union with Men, who protest against all Improvement, who think that Corruption is the main Spring of Government & that We have already weakend it too much; & from whom it would be folly to expect either good Faith or Moderation. How different is all this from the liberal Spirit with which your thirteen States have formd their Constitutions! availing themselves of the Lights & Experience of all former Times and Countries with the courage to hazard any great Trial that inventive Philosophy may suggest. My Mind looks with impatience & wonder towards the new Scenes that so many wise Institutions seem to promise; for I think that the Virtues & Understandings of Men are not only cultivated, but almost created by the Government they live under.

But these thoughts & a thousand more I hope soon to have the pleasure of discussing in free conversation with my dear & venerable friend. May your Stay with us be long; & after all your Labours & Triumphs may You find many days to enjoy repose at Twyford amidst your adopted Daughters in a Family that in affection is your own.

Your ever obligd & affectionate   J St Asaph

8. Charles James Fox and his followers. A year earlier Shipley had cautiously praised the new Rockingham government in which Fox was foreign secretary: XXXVII, 349.

From Jonathan Williams, Jr.

ALS: American Philosophical Society

Dear & hond Sir   Friday Evng. [April 25, 1783][9]
I shall give you pleasure by informing you that the Washington Capt Barney arrived at Phila the 12 March.[1] This Comes by
a Ship arrived at L'Orient from Virginia which brings no other
news.—
I suppose you know Mr Hartly is in Town.
I am as ever most dutifully Yours.   J WILLIAMS J

Addressed: A Son Excellence / Monsieur Franklin / A Passy. /
Payez au Porteur 24*s*.[2]

To Mary Hewson   ALS: Yale University Library

My dear Friend,   Passy, April 26. 1783
I received in its time your kind Letter of Feb. 22.[3] I am sensible of the Prudence of your Advice, respecting my coming to
England, and shall follow it.— Accept my Thanks for that, and
for your kind Invitation to Cheam when I do come; but the little
left of Life at my Age, will perhaps hurry me home as soon as I
can be quit of my Employment here. I should indeed have great
Pleasure in seeing you, and in being some time with you & your
little Family: I cannot have all I wish.
Mr Williams is now here with his Family. I shall mention to
him his not answering your Letter. We talk'd yesterday of you,
and of his Friend Dolly, whom I have not forgotten as she sup-

9. The first Friday after April 24, the day Hartley arrived in Paris. JW had
arrived at St. Germain on April 20, and was pleased to find his wife "exceeding well": JW to WTF, April 20, 1783 (APS); JW to James Moore, April 20,
1783 (Yale University Library).
1. The *General Washington* had left in January: XXXVIII, 560n.
2. On the address sheet, Antoine Bret, editor of the *Gazette de France*,
wrote his name and address: "M. Bret directeur de la Gazette Rue St. Lau-
rant no. 52." Beneath it BF wrote, "Medaille." For Bret see the *DBF;* Claude
Bellanger *et al., Histoire générale de la presse française* (5 vols., Paris, 1969–
76), I, 198–9.
3. Not found.

poses. He express'd the highest Esteem and Regard for you both. My Love to her when you see her.—[4]

I send you some more of the little Books,[5] and am ever, my dear Friend, Yours most affectionately   B FRANKLIN

Mrs Hewson

Endorsed: Franklin April 26. 83 / 41

From Mary Ann Davies[6]   ALS: American Philosophical Society

Dear Sir.   Florence April the 26th. 1783.

Notwithstanding I am at present a Being almost insensible to any Joy or Pleasure this miserable Life can afford, yet as I do still *Exist,* so do in me the strongest feelings of Gratitude, Respect, and Esteem, by which I must always be most sincerely attach'd to my ever dear & worthy Friend and Benefactor Doctor Franklin: & in consequence of such Attachment, every Event that contributes to his satisfaction, must rejoice me. 'Tis true I am almost dead to the World, as is the World to me; & am of course little inform'd of what passes: yet, if I comprehend right I think I may on this occasion Dear Sir congratulate You. I understand nothing at all of Politicks, but 'tis sufficient for me that I hear Matters are settled entirely to Your Wish.

4. JW and his wife and daughter had been at Passy since at least April 23: JW to Ward Boylston, and to Williams, Moore, & Co., April 23, 1783 (Yale University Library). "Dolly" was Dorothea Blunt (IX, 327n), who was part of the Craven Street circle.

5. Presumably installments of *L'ami des enfants;* see BF's Jan. 27 letter to Hewson. The series continued in 1783: *Jour. de Paris,* issues of Dec. 23, 1782, and Feb. 2, March 14, and April 5, 1783.

6. This is the first of only two extant letters from the instrumentalist and singer, who, in 1762, was the first person to perform in public on BF's newly invented glass armonica. She went on to popularize the instrument in concerts throughout Europe, often appearing with her younger sister Cecilia, a soprano: x, 118–23. We earlier referred to her as "Marianne," following the *DNB* and other sources, acknowledging that she signed her letters to BF otherwise: x, 120n. The *ODNB,* whose entry is substantially updated, has corrected the spelling to the one we use here, clarifying that she referred to herself as "Marianne" when writing in French.

Surrounded as You must be at this Epocha with crowds of elegant Congratulations, I should fear that mine (so much later than others & wanting even in the common Etiquette of Politeness &ca. &ca.) might offend rather than otherwise, were I not persuaded that the Person I write to is possess'd of that greatness of Soul which don't despise at any time the simple Dictates of a sincere Heart, tho' unadorn'd with Forms & Ceremony. This Opinion makes me hope you will not refuse writing me a Line or two that I may have the satisfaction of knowing more particularly about your Health &ca. &ca. than what one can by public report at this distance.— To hear from Yourself that you are perfectly well & happy will be the greatest pleasure I can enjoy, except that of seeing You again; in which I certainly would indulge myself, even now instead of writing were it in my power: but for this long time past, Fortune crosses all my Designs. Indeed since I had the pleasure of seeing You last,[7] both my Sister & I have gone thro' a great deal of Grief & Trouble of various kinds. After having the Affliction to see our Dear Affectionate Mother suffer a long & severe Illness, we had the Misfortune to lose Her: which was a Grief almost too much for us to bear. Since that, I had a violent return of my nervous complaints which brought me so low that there were little hopes of my recovery. I was near a twelvemonth confin'd to my Room, & most part of the time to my Bed.—[8] You will easily imagine what anxiety of mind this occasion'd my poor Sister; whose greatest foible is— being too much attach'd to me.— By this Illness of mine my Sister suffer'd much likewise in her Interests; for as she would not on any account quit me, she was oblig'd to decline several advantageous Offers in her Theatrical Profession. Misfortunes

7. The Davies sisters and their mother visited BF in 1778: XXV, 543–4, 550; XXVII, 456. They were living in Florence by August, 1782, when regular notices of Cecilia's performances appeared in the *Gazzetta Toscana:* John Ingamells, comp., *A Dictionary of British and Irish Travellers in Italy, 1701–1800* (New Haven, Conn., and London, 1997), p. 281.

8. Mary Ann was also unwell when the family was in Paris; see the references cited above. Her prolonged illnesses contributed to a popular misconception that the armonica caused nervous disorders: X, 125; Heather Hadlock, "Sonorous Bodies: Women and the Glass Harmonica," *Jour. of the American Musicological Soc.*, LIII (2000), 516, 520, 522, 524–5.

generally follow one another. At least we find it so.— A Person in whose hands my Sister & I had unluckilly placed our Money, fail'd.— So that we have as one may say to begin the World again. And to compleat our bad Luck, Death snatch'd away a Sovereign at whose Court (had I not been too giddy & fond of travelling some few Years ago) we might have been happily settled and to Whom had Fate spared Her to us, we might have had recourse at any time; particularly in our present lonely Situation!— The Great & Good Empress Maria Teresa would I am certain have even felt pleasure in taking into her Service those Orphans whose Parents as well as themselves She had formerly graciously deign'd to Patronize in a most particular manner.—[9] But She is gone!— In short we meet with nothing but Losses & Vexation. So much so that for my part I am heartily disgusted of the World.— But why do I intrude on your time with a tiresome description of my disagreable Situation?— Excuse Dear Sir such Liberty which proceeds from the Hopes I entertain that You still allow me some share in Your Friendship. And indeed to none but who I look upon as a very sincere Friend would I mention some of these particulars concerning our little Affairs (I mean as to Losses in Money Matters) for our System is, not to complain.—Therefore I must beg my Dear Sir You will not speak of that to any one: as my mentioning it is the natural impulse of an oppress'd mind which seeks consolation in venting itself with that open sincerity & confidence peculiar to Friendship.— I flatter myself likewise that having thus confided to You alone (even unknown to my Sister) an account of the unfortunate Circumstances in which I find myself, You will assist me with your good Advice.

I am destin'd to begin the World again, & *that* at a time when I did suppose my Career of Life was at an end. However since it

9. The sisters' father, the flutist and composer Richard Davies, had died in 1773; we do not know what patronage he owed to Empress Maria Theresa, who died in 1780 (XXXIV, 186n). While living in Vienna the sisters had been favorites at her court. In 1769 the empress commissioned for them a cantata for soprano and armonica, to be performed at a royal wedding. They sent BF a copy of the text, which is in Cecilia's hand: X, 120–3; *ODNB*, under Cecilia and Mary Ann.

must be so, I have once more got in practise of the Armonica, & make no doubt that if I could travel with it to different capital Cities & Courts as I have done before, 'twould be well worth my while: but unfortunately for me, my Situation is now so different to what it was then, that I dread undertaking to travel with that Instrument under my charge. Well I remember the difficulties & expence attending it, & the perpetual fear of its being damaged at each Custom House &ca. &ca.— Yet at that time I was happy in my poor Dear Father's continual care & attention. The Protection likewise of our Dear Parents made Travelling then appear to me quite in another light.— How can I now think of roving in that manner from one Country to another with only a Sister so much younger than myself?— Yet something I must do.— And really when I consider that I have the Prerogative (thro' your goodness) of being the first public Performer on that Instrument; & that even yet, by all I can get information of, no one else has made much progress on it, tho' some attempt it; these reflections give me courage. Were I but in Paris under your Protection!— Sometimes I have a mind to propose to my Sister for us to set off imediately towards Paris. But the knowledge I have of what one must spend in that City for Lodging, Living, &ca. &ca. and the inevitable Expence attending such a long Journey, soon deters me from proposing to undertake it merely upon Chance.

A Project however occurs to me, which if I have any good luck at all left, I should think might be brought to bear thro' your Interest.— The Queen of France is fond of Music— A small Annual Pension from her Majesty would attach to her Service the Original Performer upon an Instrument, the Invention of which being superiorly perfect, renders it worthy the Patronage of that Sovereign. And particularly so as the Inventor is universally ador'd by the French Nation. Now if You Dear Sir will but interest yourself for me with your usual Benevolence, what should prevent this being granted?— There might likewise probably arise some advantage for my Sister, in case there should be wanting a capital Singer for an Italian serious Opera, or the Queen's Concerts &ca. &ca.— I know Cecilia would willingly accept any reasonable Offer which would not require us to live separate. She is perfectly well in Health thank God, & her Voice still much stronger & finer than ever; 'tis amazing what power she has gain'd within these 2 or 3 last Years.— You could be of infinite Service to us both.— But I am really quite asham'd of being so importunate, & rely entirely on the benevolence of your disposition which I hope will pardon my opening my mind to You in this free manner, and applying as to a Parent for Advice & Assistance. I shall be unhappy 'till You favour me with a Letter which you will be so obliging to direct as on the other side. Thro' that Channel I shall be certain of receiving it safe, & without my Sister's knowledge. For I would not wish her to know of my troubling you about our Misfortunes, except I hear from You that there is a probability of succeeding in what I just now mention'd. At any rate I most earnestly request you will not fail writing to me soon as possible, as I shall wait here in Florence with the utmost impatience for your Advice.— Certainly Nobody living is so capable as You Dear Sir of striking out some Plan of Establishment to our advantage: & I know your goodness of Heart so well that I am sure You will think about it.— In short my whole Dependance is on You.— I ought to make a thousand apologies for the freedom with which I write, the length of this Letter &ca. &ca. but if You still have the Friendship for me, which I hope you have, *That* will excuse the faults of her who is with the highest Esteem & most sincere Attachment Dear Sir Your most oblig'd Friend & most humble Servant

MARY ANN DAVIES.

Madelle. Marianna Davies
ricapito dall' Illmo. Sigre.
Cancelliere Baretti
Firenze
Italia.

PS.— Since I am under the necessity of trying to gain a Livelyhood by the Armonica, I have another Favour to beg which I make no doubt You will be kind enough to grant. 'Tis that You will give me your Word that no other Person particularly in the musical Profession should have it in their power to boast of having instructions from Doctor Franklin either for making one of these Instruments, or for the method of playing on it. As that would just at present be the greatest detriment in the World to me. Pardon I beseech You this liberty.[1]

From Kéralio: Two Letters

(I) and (II) ALS: American Philosophical Society

I.

Samedi 26e. avril. 1783.

Vous vous rappellerés, mon Digne ami, que je vous ai parlé de Vin de Bourgogne que le supérieur de notre école militaire d'auxerre[2] vous proposoit. Quoique l'on préfére celui de Bordeaux dans votre patrie, Le Religieux qui vous remettra cette lettre vous donnera à ce sujet tous les renseignements possibles. Veuillés le recevoir avec votre bonté ordinaire et L'hommage du dévouement respectueux avec lequel je ne cesserai d'être Mon respectable ami Votre très humble et très obéissant Serviteur.

LE CHR. DE KERALIO

Addressed: A Monsieur / Monsieur Franklin. / à Passy.

II.

Paris, le 26e. avril. 1783. rue d'aguesseau, 9.h. du soir.

Du Thé vous a attendu pendant toute l'aprés-diner, mon respectable ami; mais vous l'étiés bien plus par la maitresse de la maison, ses enfants, le prince de Deux-ponts,[3] et votre serviteur.

1. BF did write a set of instructions for how to produce the best tone from the glasses; see XXXI, 311–14, where we observed that this request of Mary Ann's probably would not have been honored. On May 24 she advertised her armonica skills in the *Gazzetta Toscana:* "in view of her imminent departure from this city," she could give performances in private homes at a day's notice. Antonio Pace, *Benjamin Franklin and Italy* (Philadelphia, 1958), p. 280; Ingamells, *Dictionary of British and Irish Travellers in Italy,* p. 281. BF did not answer this letter, and Mary Ann wrote again on Oct. 17 begging for a response (APS).

2. Dom Rosman, who also was prior of the abbey of Saint-Germain, Auxerre: Ch. Moiset, "Le Collège royal militaire d'Auxerre," Société des sciences historiques et naturelles de l'Yonne *Bulletin,* XLVII (1893), 14–15.

3. For whom see the April 21 letter from the duchesse de Deux-Ponts.

Indépendamment de L'hommage que le prince vouloit vous rendre et qui vous est dû à tant de titres, il desiroit vous remettre la lettre ci-jointe,[4] et en causer avec vous.

Notre bonne amie[5] qui vous dit les choses les plus tendres vous demande Le jour que vous pourrés lui donner pour venir diner avec des américains dans la Semaine du 4e. mai au 10e inclus.

Rendez toujours justice, je vous en supplie, à L'attachement respectueux avec Lequel je ne cesserai d'être, mon Digne ami, Votre très humble et très obéissant Serviteur,

LE CHR. DE KERALIO

David Hartley to the American Peace Commissioners: Memorandum

D: Massachusetts Historical Society; copy: Public Record Office

David Hartley arrived in Paris on April 24. The following day he called on the individual American peace commissioners and found them eager to arrange for the opening of British and American ports to each other's trade and to conclude as quickly as possible a definitive treaty of peace.[6] On April 26 he went to Versailles, accompanied by Franklin, and informed Vergennes of his appointment as British minister plenipotentiary with authority to negotiate a final peace treaty. Vergennes reportedly turned to Franklin and said pointedly, "Il faut que nous finissions tous ensemble."

On the morning of April 27 Hartley met with the Americans to ex-

4. Possibly the letter from Joseph Utzschneider, April 10, written on behalf of a Bavarian merchant firm. It is summarized in our headnote to Martineau to BF, Jan. 25.

5. The duchesse de Deux-Ponts.

6. Hartley's instructions from Fox and his April 18 instructions from the king (which he showed the commissioners; see below) are discussed in annotation of Fox to BF, April 19. The information in this headnote, unless otherwise specified, comes from Hartley to Fox, April 27, 1783 (Giunta, *Emerging Nation*, II, 93–4).

change credentials and begin negotiations. They were furious to discover that Hartley's "credentials" consisted only of his April 18 instructions from the king. They refused to negotiate until he produced a commission under the great seal with full powers equal to their own, including the powers to conclude and ratify a peace treaty.[7] That day Hartley wrote to Fox requesting such powers. In the meantime he left with the commissioners two papers, copies of which he had given to Fox before leaving England. One was the proposed supplemental treaty he had sent Franklin on March 31 (above). The other is the present memorandum relating to it. The following day, evidently responding to Hartley's suggestion of an interim agreement, the commissioners informed him that they would give him a proposal that he could submit at the same time he requested his commission. They presented him with their proposed articles on April 29 (below).[8]

[before April 27, 1783]
General Memorandums relating to a proposed Supplemental treaty between Great Britain & the American States for the removal of the Troops and for opening the Ports without delay

The original Motive of proposing an intermediate & Supplemental treaty between the Provisional Articles and the definitive treaty proposed to be concluded between G. Bn. & the American States was to bring forward the intermediate connexion & correspondence between them, into a similar Situation to that of G. Bn. and France, during the period which may intervene between their preliminaries and their Definitive Treaty. The words in the preamble of the provisional Articles[9] relating to the proposed final treaty of peace, viz *but which Treaty is not to be concluded untill terms of Peace shall be agreed upon between G. Bn. & France* may admitt of Ambiguity viz. whether alluding to the definitive treaty, or to the settlement of preliminaries between G.

7. The king's April 18 instructions came under his own privy seal. Hartley was "to treat with the said [American] Ministers, for the Purpose of concluding a Definitive Treaty of Peace," and was to report regularly to Fox in order to receive further instructions: Giunta, *Emerging Nation*, II, 91–2; Butterfield, *John Adams Diary*, III, 112.

8. See JA and Jay to BF, April 28, and the commissioners' three proposed articles, April 29.

9. The preamble to the provisional peace agreement of Nov. 30, 1782 (XXXVIII, 382).

Bn. & France as it is [in][1] consequence of those Preliminaries, that all the parties have laid down their Arms by common consent. This latter is the interpretation which G. Bn. and the American States will put upon it, with the fullest grounds of justice, because the War is terminated by the provisional treaty in which *the independence of the united States is formally assured* and all parties have by *formal consent* agreed to lay down their Arms. And therefore the treaty of Alliance between France and the united States is accomplished and terminated.[2]

There is not the least reason to suppose that France would contend for any other interpretation. But in any case justice requires that all parties should be put upon similar and equal footings, For this reason the American States have a just right to Negotiate for the removal of the British Troops out of the heart of their country without delay and both G. Bn. and the American States are equally interested in an immediate revival of intercourse by Mutually opening their Ports to each other. When the Troops shall be removed and the intercourse revived, G. Bn. & America will be restored respectively to a similar repose of Situation, as that which subsists between France and G. Bn. since the signature of the Preliminary Articles between them. When this Supplemental treaty shall be settled for the removal of the Troops and for opening the Ports, which certainly may be settled in a few days; The two Parties will then proceed to the conclusion of the definitive treaty, All three Parties viz. G. Bn. France & the American States being then brought upon one equal footing & level together.

I have underlined the words extracted out of the 8th. Article of the treaty between France and the American States, upon which the Argument turns & by which I contend that the War is now terminated, according to the just sense & terms of that treaty.— The 8th. Article at full length runs thus— "Neither of the two parties shall conclude either truce or Peace with G. Bn. without the formal consent of the other first obtained, & they Mutually engage not to lay down their Arms untill the indepen-

---

1. Word supplied from the copy.
2. Hartley's assumption was unwarranted: XXXVII, 335n.

dence of the united States shall have been formally or tacitly assured by the treaty or treaties that shall terminate the war."[3]

As to the removal of the Troops from America it is to be observed that the Stipulation in the 7th. Provisional Article[4] on this point is not to take place till after the Ratification of the treaty in America, therefore a stipulation for their immediate removal with all convenient Dispatch is the most conciliatory Pledge of Good Dispositions towards America that can be given. The safe and speedy execution of such a Measure as the removal of a large Army consisting of various Nations and complicated with various civil as well as Military interests, which are too obvious to require enlargement, calls for the most consummate prudence & circumspection. Confidence therefore is necessary in such a case & the present Ministers of G. Bn. are entitled to that confidence for having come into the proposed Measure of removal without the least reluctance.

It has been proposed in support of the Stipulation expressed in words which if they came from suspicious Persons might admitt of some latitude (viz. the terms *convenient dispatch*) that a Public Declaration by a letter or some such Mode from the highest authority should be made that those words should not be construd beyond reasonable and necessary prudence, on the other hand it has been Proposed that the Troops should be removed to Long Island or Staten Island & that Congress should assist the Commander in Chief hiring Transports in America to facilitate & to expedite the removal of the Troops.[5] After so unequivocal a Measure on the British part as the restoration of New York to the Inhabitants and the retirement of the Troops to one of the

3. XXV, 589.
4. Of the Nov. 30 agreement (XXXVIII, 386).
5. At least one of the proposals was made by Henry Laurens, who suggested to Fox that some of the British troops be removed to Long Island or Staten Island: Laurens to BF, April 4 (above), and to Livingston, April 5 (*Laurens Papers*, XVI, 176). On April 10 Fox wrote to inform Hartley that the king had authorized Hartley "to give the strongest Assurances, that it is his Majesty's royal intention to give orders that the said removal [of the British Army from New York] shall be effected with as much dispatch as the nature of so great & difficult a business will admitt." Giunta, *Emerging Nation*, I, 817–18.

Islands, the Troops will be considered as in a State of Amity and hospitality. And it may be expected that all conveniences for their Voyage will be chearfully supplied to them. The restoration of the Port of New York to its Native Owners will of course be the token of throwing open all the Ports on both sides for the restoration of Mutual intercourse and Commerce. All further Prosecutions of the Loyalists which by the present State of the Provisional Articles are to continue in course till the definitive treaty should be immediately and for ever Abated. This condition should go hand in hand with the removal of the Troops. The Mutual release of all Prisoners as an Article of reciprocity cannot possibly meet with any difficulty or obstruction. In this State of Amicable Intelligence the foundation of future and perpetual conciliation may be laid. We may proceed to the second immediate & concurrent proposition viz. the opening the Ports on each side for intercourse and commerce. These two points viz. The removal of the Troops and the opening of the Ports are the two proposed objects of the Supplemental treaty.

The object of any temporary and provisional treaty of Commerce between G. Bn. & the American States would be simply to open the ports upon certain specified & known Conditions from which as I may say We may take our departure and which in the course & progress of things may be corrected and adjusted in such manner as the necessity or prudence of circumstances and the Dispositions of the respective parties may point out. But by no means should we enter previously into the detail of any System of commercial arrangements. If once we get into such a system of embarrassment we shall never get clearly into daylight again, or at best not for a great length of time, Regulations some of prudence some of jealousy, some of clashing interests, Many of extreme political intricacy &c &c. would employ the discussion of many Years, and if the Ports between Great Britain & America were to continue during that period obstructed or Shut, the course of the commerce itself would burst its way into some other & foreign channel, and it would probably so happen, in the end, that the two Nations of Great Britain & the united states of N. America, altho mutually possessed of the most substantial objects of commerce, the one towards the other, might nevertheless have the least proportion of direct intercourse between themselves, for all the great objects of National commerce Manufactures or Navigation.

Then let the ports be opened first and let any Regulations follow in order as the necessity or prudence of each particular case may require. It would not signify very much from what point you take your departure provided that point be Specified & Known. Because if any impracticability should occur or any material deviation from Principles of general justice or of reciprocity, arising from the great change of circumstances by the War, each particular case may be immediately provided for, as it arises, by some Specific regulation. In the mean while the ports may generally be open and the great objects of commerce such as Cloth Hardware lumber & provisions &c &c will be free and unimpeded in their important Movements, instead of the whole Trade being suppressed untill the last punctilio can be settled.

The case at present arising between Great Britain & the American States is totally novel and such as never has existed after the termination of any war between other Nations. As soon as preliminaries are signed by G. Britain with any independent states such as Spain France or Holland the course of mutual commerce emerges upon the same terms and conditions as were existing antecedent to the war. The Case between Great Bn. & the American States is very different because the American united states from being a dependent Nation before the War emerge an independent nation after the War. The basis therefore of any Provisional treaty between Great Britain & the American states should be simply to arrange such points as would emerge after the War impracticable and discordant to their newly established Independence, and to leave all others as much as possible untoucht. For instance that instrumental Regulations such as Papers bonds certificates & all other documents should be put between G. Bn. & the united States upon the same footing as between G. Bn. & any other independent Nation but that all duties rights privileges & all pecuniary considerations should emerge into action & effect as before the war. By these means the ports will be immediately & mutually opened upon specified & known conditions; And if the legislature of either Country thinks proper to introduce on its own part any new condition or regulation that will not shut the ports again generally but only operate according to the extent of the case on which side soever any novel condition should arise the other will likewise be at Liberty to make any corresponding regulation as between independent Nations. The great object is to open the ports between G Bn. & the American states immediately upon the Signature of preliminaries of peace as between France & Great Britain. By the proposition above stated GB. & France, & G.Bn. & the American states respectively on the subject of intercourse of commerce would emerge again after the war into situations relatively similar to their situations before the war.

[*In David Hartley's hand:*] Memorandums upon opening the ports April 1783

To Robert R. Livingston   LS[6] and transcript: National Archives

Dear Sir,   Passy, 27 Apl. 1783.

The Count Del Verme, an Italian Nobleman of great Distinction, does me the honour to be the Bearer of this. I have not the satisfaction to be personally acquainted with this Gentleman, but am much sollicited by some of my particular Friends, to whom his Merits & Character are known, to afford him this Introduction to you.——[7] He is, I understand, a great Traveller, and his view in going to America is merely to see the Country, & its

---

6. In WTF's hand.

7. Conte Francesco dal Verme of Milan (1758–1832) was a cousin of the Neapolitan ambassador to the British court. He was in the United States from June 30 to Dec. 21, bearing letters of introduction from JA and Laurens as well as BF. The Duke of Portland recommended him to the American commissioners, and David Hartley must have approached BF in person about a letter, as he did with JA: Smith, *Letters,* XX, 405; *Morris Papers,* VIII, 807n; Butterfield, *John Adams Diary,* III, 113–14; Francesco dal Verme, conte di Bobbio, *Seeing America and Its Great Men: the Journal and Letters of Count Francesco dal Verme, 1783–1784,* trans. Elizabeth Cometti (Charlottesville, 1969), pp. 5–62. Otherwise, we only know that BF was solicited in a highly circuitous way by several bankers (Caccia, Panchaud, and possibly Dangirard) who could hardly be considered "particular Friends": Ferry to Henry Grand, April 16, 1783; Henry Grand to WTF, [after April 16, 1783], both at the APS.

great Men:— I pray you will shew him every Civility, & afford him that Counsel which as a Stranger he may stand in need of.— With great Respect I am, Dear Sir, Your most obedient & most humble Sert.   B FRANKLIN

The honble R. R. Livingston Esqr

Notation: Letter 27 April 1783 Dr. B. Franklin Read July 8.[8]

From the Duchesse de Deux-Ponts

L:[9] American Philosophical Society

Dimanche 27e. avril. 10. h. du soir. [1783]
Made. La Douairiere de Deux-ponts embrasse son digne ami de tout son cœur; elle est bien fachée de ne pouvoir lui donner du Thé demain Lundi: mais elle va à la comédie italienne, et mardi à versailles pour le reste de la semaine: afin de se dédommager d'une privation aussi Longue, elle renouvelle sa priere à son ami de lui donner un jour dans la semaine prochaine pour venir diner avec m. Le prince de Deux-ponts, et des americains françois.[1]

Le secretaire intime présente ses tendres respects à m. Franklin et fait mille amitiés à m. son petit-fils./.

Addressed: A Monsieur / Monsieur Franklin. / à Passy.

8. The same day, July 8, President of Congress Boudinot wrote dal Verme a letter of introduction to Washington. Washington in turn introduced him to the merchant Nathaniel Tracy: Smith, *Letters,* xx, 405; W. W. Abbot *et al.,* eds., *The Papers of George Washington,* Confederation Series (6 vols., Charlottesville and London, 1992–97), I, 373–4n.

9. In the hand of Kéralio, the "secretaire intime" mentioned in the last sentence.

1. See her letter of April 21 and Kéralio's second letter of April 26.

From John Adams and John Jay[2]

AL:[3] Historical Society of Delaware

Monday April 28. 1783.

Mr Adams and Mr Jay present their Compliments to Dr Franklin and inform him, that they have just seen Mr Laurens and agreed with him upon a Meeting of the American Ministers Tomorrow at Eleven, at Mr Laurens's Lodgings. The Drs Company is desired, and Mr Franklin Junr is requested also to attend.[4]

Addressed: Son Excellence / Monsieur Franklin / Ministre Plenipotentiaire des / Etats Unis de L'Amerique / a Passy / Pres Paris

From Elias Boudinot

LS: American Philosophical Society; AL (draft): Library of Congress

Sir/   Philadelphia Aprill 28th. 1783.

The Bearer Coll: Ogdin of the New Jersey Line, a Gentleman who has been greatly distinguished for his Bravery & good Conduct, from the first commencement of the present War, having

---

2. This invitation to a meeting on April 29 gives no hint that JA, Jay, and Laurens had already agreed on the articles that they intended to present to Hartley, nor does it mention that they had already arranged for Hartley to join them. On the evening of April 27, after the Americans had met with Hartley (see the headnote to Hartley's memorandum to the commissioners, [before April 27]), JA called on Jay and invited him to come to his residence the next morning. At that time Jay reviewed the "Variety of Projects" JA had drafted concerning the topics under discussion: the removal of British troops from America, the opening of ports, "tranquilizing" the Loyalists, and articles concerning commerce. Jay and JA drew up propositions on the first three topics and called on Laurens, who approved them. They then called on Hartley, who was not at home. When Hartley later found them at Jay's residence, they invited him to a meeting the next day at 1:00 P.M. for the purpose of making him a proposition. JA and Jay then wrote the present invitation to BF and WTF: *Adams Papers*, XIV, 448–54; Butterfield, *John Adams Diary*, III, 113.

3. In JA's hand.

4. BF sent word that they would attend: Butterfield, *John Adams Diary*, III, 113. See the commissioners' proposed articles, below, April 29.

received the permission of Congress to make a Voyage to France, on his private concerns;[5] I must take the Liberty to recommend him to your Excellency's notice— He is of a good family in New Jersey, & having taken a very active part during the contest in this Country, deserves the favor & protection of every Friend to America.

He is one of those brave officers who persevered in the Journey thro' the Wilderness to Quebec in the Year 1775, and was wounded in the attack on that City—he also bore a share in the Laurels of York Town.

I have the Honor of inclosing a Letter from the Commander in Chief, which he has committed to my Care—[6] We are in daily and anxious Expectation of the Definitive Treaty, having been a long time without advices from our Ministers abroad, our last Letters being dated in February.

The terms of Peace give universal Satisfaction, her [here], except the article relative to English Debts, remaining silent, as to the time allowed our Citizens to make the payments—[7] The situation of our Country—The property of the Whigs being in the Public Funds, not a farthing of which can be had—The great Losses from the depreciated Money, and the stagnation of Trade for years past—make it absolutely necessary that three or four years should be allowed, for this purpose, in giving security for the Debts— If an immediate payment should be required, it will cast our Merchants so entirely into the power of the British Creditors as to be very injurious to the interests of France—

5. Matthias Ogden (1754–1791), the former colonel of the First New Jersey regiment, wished to establish trade connections with France: W. W. Abbot *et al.*, eds., *The Papers of George Washington*, Revolutionary War Series (18 vols. to date, Charlottesville and London, 1985–), I, 133n; *Morris Papers*, VII, 760n; Richard A. Harrison, *Princetonians, 1769–1775: a Biographical Dictionary* (Princeton, 1980), p. 330. He carried Livingston's letter to BF of May 9 (below) and his letter to the commissioners of April 21 (above), as well as copies of many earlier letters from him and Robert Morris. He also carried dispatches for Lafayette and Morris' letter of introduction of April 29, below: *Morris Papers*, VII, 761n; Idzerda, *Lafayette Papers*, V, 142.

6. Probably Washington to BF, April 23, above.

7. Article 4 of the preliminary treaty: XXXVIII, 385.

I have the honor to be with the greatest Respect & Esteem Your Excellency's Most Obedt. & very Hble Sert

ELIAS BOUDINOT

His Excellency Doctr. Franklin

private

Addressed: His Excellency Benjamin Franklin L L D / Minister-plenipotentiary from the United States / of America, at the Court of France / Paris. / ELIAS BOUDINOT

Notation: Boudinot 28 apl. 1783

From Claude-Gabriel de Choisy[8] and Pierre-François de Béville[9]

AL:[1] American Philosophical Society

ce 28 avril 1783.

Mrs. de choisy et de Béville Sont venu pour Saluer Son Excellence le Docteur Franklin et luy faire leur remerciments de la Medaille[2] qu'il a bien voulu leur envoyer./.

From the Marquis de Lafayette

L: American Philosophical Society

à Paris Ce 28. Avril [1783]

Le Mis. De la fayette fait Ses compliments à Monsieur franklin et le prie de lui faire lhonneur de Venir diner chez luy jeudy prochain[3] en Sa maison Rue de Bourbon.[4]

---

8. Choisy (b. 1723) was a *maréchal de camp* who had served with Rochambeau. Like Béville, he recently had returned to France aboard the frigate *Emeraude: DBF;* Bodinier, *Dictionnaire;* Six, *Dictionnaire biographique;* Rice and Brown, eds., *Rochambeau's Army,* I, 84n and *passim.*

9. For whom see Du Bouchet to BF, March 17.

1. In Choisy's hand.

2. Doubtless a *Libertas Americana* medal.

3. May 1. The other American peace commissioners went as well: Butterfield, *John Adams Diary,* III, 117.

4. Having reached the age of majority (25 years), Lafayette was able to purchase a house on the rue de Bourbon (now rue de Lille) in late 1782: Louis

From ———— Madlin[5]   ALS: American Philosophical Society

Monsieur   De paris ce 28. avril 1783
  Mil pardons De cette Liberte Mais La crainte de vous impor-
tuné De vive voix Mis oblige pour vous doner avis Dune petites
créance dont Monsieur vôtre fils Mes [m'est] redevable sen
doutes c'est pure oublie de sa part sil Ny à pas satisfait avant son
depart. Jôse éxpére Monsieur que voudré bien remarqué que Né-
tant point fournisseur ordinaire Je crois quils est apropos de vous
donner avis que cette petites dettes est pour réparation en fait de
sellerie et aûtre diférente petite fourniture par Moi fournie Montant a la somme de cent six livre dont Je fournirai le Memoir en
segond si Monsieur Lexige. Jose ésperé une réponce favorable et
suis en attendant avec toutes La soumission La plus réspéctueuse
qui vous est due Monsieur Votre très humble et très hobeisant et
soumis serviteur   MADLIN

Madlin sellier rue du bacq pres Les Jaccobin a paris

Addressed: a Monsieur / Monsieur francklin perre / en son
hôtelle a passis / a passi / Madlin

Notation: Madelin 28. Avril 1783.

————
Gottschalk, *Lafayette and the Close of the American Revolution* (Chicago,
1942), pp. 374–5; Howard C. Rice, Jr., *Thomas Jefferson's Paris* (Princeton,
1976), pp. 62–3.
  5. The saddler–carriage maker who had made repairs and supplied parts
for WTF's cabriolet the month before. He tried several more times to collect
payment from WTF: XXXVIII, 393n.

From Patience Wright

ALS: American Philosophical Society

Honred Sir   London [*torn:* April] 28th 1783

I had the pleasure to See your Son at my house govonour Franklin and acording to my Custom I had a long Chatt with him—as I am now in Fashon at Court or in other words am not in the Same Disgrace as while America was in *Rebelion*—Wherefore now I Can Speak out Such truths as may be useful to the honest Well meaning Rulers: who all own, they have not had truth laid before them—

The parliment is much devided with Regard to the Loyalists and their Clame being *Just* on the King—it is thought the people will Make him actt the honest Part by them; or Make an Enquirey: which nothing he *fears* So Much—for his *fears* of being Calld to an acount has been the Cause of all the Delays in Ministry and in acts of traed Repeals &c. great Care is taken to Keep up the Spirits of the people and all Parties are *Decevd* and *Deceving* Each other But Nothing is Determand by any PARTY but to Keep off Justice or the—*Retrospect:* Ld North has a promiss from all PARTIES to Keep him his *head*— The Bank the great Band of Society Keep all together untill you make us a visit Nothing will be Setteld.

The govonour looks well but old: and is very prudent: and he being Chose by New Jersey[6] will be Considerd by us that forward: the good Claim on the King; as much Strengtheng the Cause of the people against his tyranacall unjust treatment of all America: Friends and Enemies as their Case is now the Subject of Conversation.

I most heartly Joyne in Seting their Case in the Strongest light in favour of those well *Meaning* honest Men who Now Suffer for their Loyalty to the disgrace of Kings—

I hope those good opertunitys to unite all our force against tyrants Knaves &ca will be Now the bessiness of all great good men and help the people out of their present dificultys We Still look up to you and are with the Most Sincer Inthuzam your faithful Friend and very humbl Servant The People Joynd by Esteem
PATIENCE WRIGHT

6. See the annotation of Wright to BF, Feb. 22.

The Prince Wails Calld on us friday[7] Ld Dartmouth Ld Lusom with others Imploy My Son-in-Law to Paint thir Portrits[8]

Major Labilliere has his Christian Army almost Ready he Calls him Self a Christian Soldier

Addressed: His Exelency / Doctr Franklin / Passy / Paris

Notation: Wright 28 Apl. 1783

7. George Augustus Frederick, Prince of Wales (the future George IV), may have met the family through his art teacher, who was a mutual friend, or through the painter John Hoppner, who married Patience Wright's daughter Phoebe in 1781. Charles C. Sellers speculates that the prince's acquaintance with the Wrights may also have been an act of rebellion against his father: *Patience Wright: American Artist and Spy in George III's London* (Middletown, Conn., 1976), pp. 132, 151, 174.

8. Hoppner, who was made portrait painter to the Prince of Wales in 1789 and who painted SB's portrait in 1793, painted several children of the Earl of Dartmouth (XII, 362), including his eldest son, "Lord Lusom," *i.e.,* Lewisham (*ODNB*, under George Legge). We have found no record of his having painted the father. See William McKay and W. Roberts, *John Hoppner, R.A.* (rev. ed., London, New York, and Toronto, 1914), pp. 153–4.

The American Peace Commissioners: Three Proposed Articles[9]

Copies:[1] Massachusetts Historical Society (three), National Archives (two), William L. Clements Library, Archives du Ministère des affaires étrangères, Library of Congress; press copy of copy: American Philosophical Society; transcript and partial copy:[2] National Archives

[April 29, 1783]

No. 1.

Article[3]

It is agreed, that so soon, as his Britannic Majesty shall have withdrawn all his Armies, Garrisons and Fleets, from the United States of America,[4] and from every Port, Post, Place and Har-

---

9. For the drafting of these, and the April 29 meetings at which BF approved them and the Americans presented them to Hartley, see Adams and Jay to BF, April 28. Hartley immediately forwarded them to Fox as "articles drawn up between the American Ministers and myself," with comments that are cited in the annotation below: Hartley to Fox, April 29, 1783 (Giunta, *Emerging Nation*, II, 99–100). Four days later, when sending Fox duplicates of his correspondence, he referred to these as articles "for a supplemental or ulterior treaty . . . for the purpose of immediately opening the ports between Great Britain & the united states of America." As they were substantially the same as what Hartley himself had proposed to the Americans, he presumed that they would be approved by the British ministry: Hartley to Fox, May 3, 1783 (Giunta, *Emerging Nation*, II, 106).

1. We print a copy in L'Air de Lamotte's hand, corrected by WTF and with WTF's notation. (That same notation is part of every copy, sometimes serving as a title.) The press copy is from the copy at the AAE, which is also in L'Air de Lamotte's hand. The copy JA wrote into his diary (one of those listed at the Mass. Hist. Soc.) is in Butterfield, *John Adams Diary*, III, 115n.

2. Only article 1 of this copy survives, but on surrounding sheets are BF's notation, "Further Propositions to D. Hartley Esq," and WTF's notation, "We promised Mr. Hartley to forward these Papers to Congress."

3. This is an expanded, time-limited version of a suggestion the commissioners had made to Fitzherbert: above, [c. Feb. 20].

4. Hartley objected to this phrase, which made "an uncertain and conditional term to the commencement of future intercourse, and with a little aspect of Jealousy." He proposed instead that these issues be separated; he would sign an article for withdrawing the troops, and the next article would provide for the opening of American and British ports. In reporting this to Fox, he added that "This will be agreed to by the American Ministers, as soon as my Commission shall come with instructions to sign such an Article." He

524

bour within the Same, as stipulated by the 7. Article of the Provisional Treaty of 30. Nov. 1782,[5] Then, and from thenceforth, for and during the Term of [*blank*] Years,[6] all Rivers, Harbours, Lakes, Ports and Places, belonging to the United States, or any of them, shall be open and free, to the Merchants and other Subjects of the Crown of Great Britain, and their trading Vessels; who shall be received, treated, and protected, like the Merchants and trading Vessels of the State in which they may be, & be liable to no other Charges or Duties.

And reciprocally all Rivers, Harbours, Lakes, Ports and Places under the Dominion of his Britannic Majesty, shall, thenceforth be open and free to the Merchants and trading Vessels of the said United States, and of each & every of them, who shall be received, treated and protected, like the Merchants & trading Vessels of Great Britain, and be liable to no other Charges or Duties: Saving always to the Chartered Trading Companies of Great Britain, such exclusive Use and Trade of their respective Ports & Establishments, as neither the other Subjects of Great Britain, or any the most favoured Nation participate in.

No. 2.

Article

It is agreed that such Persons as may be in Confinement in the United States of America, for or by Reason of the Part which they may have taken in the late War shall be set at Liberty im-

---

asked Fox to send him the orders for troop withdrawal: Hartley to Fox, April 29, 1783, cited above.

5. XXXVIII, 386.

6. The American commissioners first suggested July 1, 1785, as a terminal date, but knowing that a bill was under consideration in the House of Commons that would give the king power to regulate commerce for a limited time period, they left this blank until the bill passed. Hartley received word from Fox on April 30 that the bill did pass, but it neglected to specify the time period: Giunta, *Emerging Nation*, II, 99–101, 101–2. (The king was given power to regulate commerce until Dec. 20, 1783; see our annotation of Hodgson to BF, April 18.)

mediately on the Evacuation of the said States by the Troops and Fleets of his Britannic Majesty.

And it is likewise agreed, that all such Persons who may be in Confinement in any Parts under the Dominion of his Britannic Majesty, for and by Reason of the Part which they may have taken in the late War, shall at the same time be also immediately set at Liberty.

No. 3.

Article

The Prisoners made respectively by the Arms of his Britannic Majesty & those of the United States of America, both by Land & Sea, shall be immediately set at Liberty without Ransom, on paying the Debts they may have contracted during their Captivity: And each contracting Party shall respectively reimburse the Sums which shall have been advanced for the Subsistence & Maintenance of their Prisoners, by the Sovereign of the Country where they shall have been detained, according to the Receipts & attested Accounts, & other authentic Titles, which shall be produced on each Side.

Notation by William Temple Franklin: 3 Articles proposed by the American Ministers & deliver'd to Mr. D. Hartley the 29. Apl 1783.

From Bowens
ʟs: Historical Society of Pennsylvania

Ostend 29 April 1783

Having received certain information from a friend of some Consequence at Bruxelles, that the Government of the Low Countries has taken the Resolution of sending a person of Rank to America in quality of a plenipotentiary to negotiate a treaty of Commerce between the united States & this Country— I most respectfully take the liberty of enclosing you a petition, & of begging your assistance in procuring the place of which it treats, & which I have the greatest ambition to be preferred to.—[7]

7. Bowens' petition, addressed to BF, is dated April 30 and expands on the themes in this letter. He renews his application to be appointed American

Your Excellency, is no Stranger, that during the War, & on every other occasion, I have done my utmost to be of Service to the Subjects of America, both by advancing them money, & giving them what advice they stood in need of, as my old friend Mr. Fras. Coffyn of Dunkirk can certify.

Your Excellency, may take any information you desire as to myself or my family, which I am convinced will turn out to my advantage— I have the honour of being personally acquainted with Mr. W. Lee of Bruxelles & am known to Mr. Laurens, to whom had the pleasure of paying my respects, as he past thro' this place.

I cannot Express, the Gratitude & obligation I shall have to your Excellency, in Case I should be so fortunate as to succeed in my petition, & merit your protection, in which I have the utmost Confidence—

I have the Honour to be with Sentiments of the utmost Respect & Esteem Your Excellencies Most obedt. & Devoted Servant F BOWENS

From Gerard Brantsen[8]   ALS: American Philosophical Society

Monsieur.   Paris ce 29. d'Avril 1783.

J'ai l'honneur de vous envoÿer ci jointe une lettre, qui m'ést venue a votre adresse dans mon paquet de Vienne.[1]

J'ai pareillement celui de vous faire bien de remercimens pour le cadeau de la medaille, que vous avez eue la bonté de m'envoÿer[2] et que LL. H.H. P.P.[3] viennent de me permettre d'ac-

---

consul in Ostend, recalls his service to Americans since the beginning of the war, claims to be proficient in most modern languages, and asserts that his family is one of the most distinguished in the country. Hist. Soc. of Pa.

8. Brantsen, Dutch minister plenipotentiary to the French court, was promoted on May 8 to the rank of ambassador extraordinary plenipotentiary: *Repertorium der diplomatischen Vertreter*, III, 263.

1. Possibly Ingenhousz' letter of April 8, above. He had forwarded an earlier letter from Ingenhousz: XXXVIII, 227.

2. A *Libertas Americana* medal.

3. Leurs Hautes Puissances, *i.e.*, the States General of the Netherlands (XXXIII, 447).

cepter. Je suis bien sensible, Monsieur, de cette attention de votre part et je conserverai avec un agreable souvenir le monument d'une epôque, qui en constatant l'independance de l'Amerique, fait honneur a votre nation, a votre nom et a votre sagacité.

Je vous prie d'agreër les assurences des sentimens distingués, avec lesquels j'ai l'honneur d'etre Monsieur Votre très humble et très Obeïssant serviteur   Brantsen

From Ingenhousz   ALS: American Philosophical Society

Dear friend   Vienna in Austria April 29 1783.
The bearer of this, Mr. james Robertson,[4] being arrived at Paris from a tour thro Italie, after having spent some time in Vienna, where he followed my experiments and became one of my friends, has begged the favour of me to send him an introductory lettre to you. As he is a very worthy and learned Gentleman, I can not refuse his request, and take the liberty to introduce him by this to your countenance and acquaintance. As he is thoroughly acquainted with a good deal of my perquisitions, he may inform you at a leasure hour with som of my transactions.

I have made a great deal of experiments with one of the strongest batteries, having three and tharty feet square surface coated, and have succeeded perfectly in imitating the phenomenon, which happened on the vane of a Steeple at Cremona.[5] I

4. James Robertson (c. 1753–1827), later Robertson-Barclay, who received a Radcliffe traveling fellowship upon earning his M.A. from Oxford in 1780. He was still in Paris in early June, 1783, when Charles Blagden dined with him (Blagden Papers, Yale University Library). Robertson received his medical degree from University College in October, 1783, and in 1785 was elected a physician at St. George's Hospital. He was made a fellow of the Royal College of Physicians in 1787 and a member of the Royal Society in 1790, and was appointed physician extraordinary to the Princess of Wales in 1799: *Alumni Oxonienses: the Members of the University of Oxford, 1715–1886* . . . (4 vols., London, 1887–88), III, 1210.

5. Ingenhousz was responding to BF's remarks on the lightning strike on the church in Cremona, which analyzed the strike and suggested further experiments: XXXVII, 504–12.

cut a vane of thin foil of this form and zize[6] I cut it in several pieces stikking one piece on the one side of a card and the following alternately at the opposit side of it, leaving between each Some space not covered, that is to say placing the pieces thus, that there was some space left between the edge of one piece and the edge of the Corresponding piece at the opposit side, so that the explosion was obliged to pass, not in a direct, but somewhat in a diagonal way thro the card to leap from one piece of metal to the other. The burr of all the holes was on both side of the Card but in general stronger at that side, where the flash went out to get at the metal piece on that Side. A great part of every piece of metal was partly exploded, partly melted, were it was melted only, Several small holes were observable, whose edges had been manifestly melted; and in those I could not distinguish which way the melted metal was chiefly driven outwards; but in some pieces of metal one hole, in some two were observed, whose edges were bended indifferently towards the one and the other Side the middel part of it being exploded. Some of those holes had a part of their edges turn'd the one way and an other part (in the same hole) the other way. Where I found two holes in one piece of metal, I found also two holes in the card opposit the holes struck in the metal. In some of these experiments I had Covered both Surfaces of the card with a piece of paper by means of sealing wax. But both those papers wher all torn to rags and the melted metal flew thro the room at the distance of several paces— I tryed also to imitate the phenomenon in this way: I flatted a copper wire by hamering it, and than Cut it in a tapering way: the explosion of the battery dissipated a great deal of it into smoak, the edges were ragged and had been in a melted Condition. But in none of them, I could as yet discover any real hole. Tho I think it not impossible to imitate the effect of the lightening at Cremona by directing an electrical blast thro a vane of this nature: and I will make more experiments to this purpose— In the last paper you was So good as to send me about the lightning of Cremona, you have proposed to give me, if I desire it, your opinion about the effect you mention there of an ex-

6. Here Ingenhousz drew a triangle similar to the one BF used to illustrate his own remarks: XXXVII, 505.

plosion of a battery by a discharging rod, by which explosion twelfe jarrs out of twenty where perforated notwithstanding the electric fire found an Open passage. Now I begg earnestly the favour of being instructed on this head. Give me leave allso to remind you of the theory of the new fire place in which the smoak is burn'd.

I have made some more capital discoveries in the laws of Nature, and have now a Stock of above 2000 experiments of which I will give an extract to the public. I would allready have done it, but mr. *le Begue de Presle* keeps My M.S. in hands and does not get it printed, of which delay I can not so Much as guess the reason.

I think it will be better to delay giving you an account of Some philos. papers which I took either from Conversing with you or from your own letters, till you are here, where I hope you will stay some weaks, as probably Some commercial or political arrangements with your new republic will be the Subjet of meetings you will have either with the Emperour or his ministers. But during your stay here I hope to have a good and even the best share of private Conversation with you. You can't grudge at some inconvience which must naturaly attend your exalted situation in life, by being Courted or plaged by Such, as out of respect, admiration or curiosity are extremely desirous of the advantage of being presented to you. Even a look of you now is become a desirable object. This inconvenience attending human grandour, which excites pride and vanity in men of the first rank, can not excite such passion in a man of your turn of mind and of your age. But this your Uncommon situation, at which many in every age have adspired but which was obtained by few, must excite in you some indulgence for an old friend, on Whom some rais of that splendor, which surrounds you, seem to be cast, proceeding from the friendship, with which you honour him. I am more and more Courted by people of every rang to present them to you. But what may be flattering to me, must be reather burtensom to you; and for that reason I will use on this head as much discretion as possible— A few days ago the greatest favourite of the Emperour Count *Lacy* marechal of our armies requested a favour of me, Viz. to ask you whether you Should think it would answer the purpose, if the famous Statuary mr. *Ceraqui* of Rome, who has work'd in London and has now finish'd an excellent bust of the Emperour of Marechal *Lacy, Laudun* &c. should goe over to America in expectation of being employed in erecting or making marmor[7] and Such like monuments, which the present Generation will probably erect to the perpetual memory of those eminent men who have had a great share in promoting the greatest revolution, which exist in human history, as also of the revolution it Self.[8] Marechal Lacy added, that, in case there was a prospect of finding employment there, and money should be Scarce, gouvernment could grant him land. Now, as it is very probable, that this Scheem derives from a superior hand, I could not refuse proposing you the question, and begging of you an answer as Soon as it will be convenient to you— I see in the papers that a medal has been struck at Paris by your direction.[9] None of them have yet arrived here.

Would you be so good as to engage Mr. Le Roy of the Royal academie to take Care of the printing of my books, in case Mr. Le Begue should be seck or dead, which I fear must be the case. Your intercession will Certainly have great wight with that gentleman, who is a learned and obliging man by nature. He will be at no expenses, as I can Send him the letters by the way of public ministers.

I am with due respect Your most obedient servant and affectionate friend   J INGEN HOUSZ

I have heard as yet nothing of mr. Sam. wharton. I write this post to mr. Coffyn of Dunkerque to inquire whether he has got some farther intelligence of mr. Wharton. Pray, if you see Dr. Bankroft, be so good as to give him this note and to engage him to

---

7. German for marble.
8. Sculptor Giuseppe Ceracchi (Cirachi), who had spent much of the 1770s in England, was at this time living in Vienna. He finally went to America in 1791 and produced a series of marble busts of prominent Americans, including BF: Jane Turner, ed., *The Dictionary of Art* (34 vols., New York, 1996). Franz Moritz, Count von Lacy, and Ernst Gideon, Baron von Loudon, were the two most celebrated generals of the Austrian army: Walther Killy, ed., *Deutsche Biographische Enzyklopädie* (12 vols., Munich, 1995–2000).
9. The *Libertas Americana* medal.

write me about what he knows of mr. Wharton and his transactions for our joint Concern.

I am sorry to see, that the King of England has chosen among his ministers those, who ruin'd and dismembred his empire, how [who] were the cause of so much blodshed, and how must, for that reason, be eternaly curs'd by America, whose friendship and protection they now implore with their hands still stained with its blod. I aknowledge your having been in the right by saying that that nation is Corrupted and degraded and therefore deserves to be ruin'd. They seem now to exercise still their hauhtiness against my Countrymen. Can France, Spain and America Suffre this, consistend with their honour?

to his Excellency B. Franklin Ministre Plenip. of the United States of America. at Passy

Endorsements: April 29, 83 / Mr Robertson Hotel d'Orleans. rue des petits Augustins / Answer'd May 17. 83

From Jane Mecom   ALS: American Philosophical Society

Dear Brother   Boston April 29 1783
    I have at Length recved a Leter from you in your own Hand writing, after a Total Silance of three years, in which Time Part of an old Song would Some times Intrude it Self in to my mind,
    Does He love & yet forsake me
    for
    can he forgit me
    will he Niglegt me.[1] This was but momentary at other times I concluded it was un Reasonable to Expect it & that you might with grate Propriety After my Teazing you so often, send me the

---

1. Mecom conflated two passages from an often-anthologized song known as "Guardian Angels," in which a young woman pines for her distant lover. The quoted lines are from the end of the second stanza and beginning of the third: "Can he forget me, Will he neglect me, Shall I never see him more! / Does he love, and yet forsake me, To admire a Nymph more fair?" *The Lark, Containing a Collection of Above Four Hundred and Seventy Celebrated English and Scotch Songs* (London, 1740), pp. 132–3.

Ansure that Nehemiah did to Tobias, & Sanbalet, who Endevared to obstruct His Rebulding The Temple of Jerusalem, I am doing a grate work; why Should the work Ceace whilest I Leave it & come *Down* to you.[2]

And a Grate work Indeed you have Done God be Praised. I hope now you, your Self, will think you have done enouf for the Publick, and will now Put in Execution what you have Sometimes wished to be premited to do; Sit down & Spend the Evening with your Friends. I am Looking Round me at Cambridge for a Comodious Seatt for you, not with any grat Hopes of your coming there I confes (but wishes) knoing you are Accomedated so much to your mind at Philadelphia, and have your children there. I Should However Expect a Share of your corispondence when you have Leasure; & Beleve me my Dear Brother, your writing to me gives me so much Pleasure that the grate, the very grate, Presents you have sent me[3] is but a Secondary Joy, I have been very Sick this winter at my Daughters,[4] keept my chamber Six weeks but had a Suficency for my Suply of Every thing that could be a comfort to me of my own before I recved any Intimation of the Grat Bounty from your Hand which your Leter has conveyed to me, for I have not been Lavish of what I before Posesed, knoing Sicknes & misfourtens might happen & Certainly old Age but I Shall now be So Rich that I may Indulg in a Small degree a Propencity to help Some Poor cretures who have not the Blesings I Injoy.

My Good Fortune came to me all to gether to comfort me in my weak State, for as I had been So unlucky as not to recve the Leter you Sent me throw yor Son Baches hands tho he In formes me he forwarded it Emediatly His Leter with a Drauft for twenty five Guneys came to my Hand Just before yours which I have recved[5] & cannot find Expreshon Suitable to acknolidg my Grat-

---

2. This answer to Tobiah and Sanballat is Nehemiah 6:3.

3. The bill of exchange and other promised funds, mentioned below.

4. Jane Mecom Collas' home in Cambridge, Mass.: XXXVIII, 506–7.

5. RB had written Mecom on Dec. 4; the letter (now missing) enclosed various bills of exchange, including a draft on John Hancock, and mentioned a letter he had forwarded to her from BF. On April 11 she wrote RB explaining that, although she had never received the forwarded letter, she had, in fact,

itude, How am I by my Dear Brother Enabled to live at Ease in my old Age (after a Life of care Labour & Anxiety) without which I must have been miserable.

The other Bills are not Paid yet & Corll Johonett is Absent & there is Some Demur about it but I Sopose it may turn out Right by & by His cousen Promises to call on me Prehap He will before I close this Leter, I have waited a fortnight and cannot git the bill Accepted nor a Sight of the Gentileman tho He has Promised many times He will come & talk with me, I am Informed Since I Came to Town that Mr. Williams had recved the other.—[6]

I yester day recved a Leter from Mrs Bache She Informs me She Expects you Home this Sumer that She & her chilldren are all well her Husband Gone to New York.

I was quite in a weak State when I came to Boston but find my Self gro Stronger Every Day Porpose to go to the State of Rhoad Island in about a Fortnight to Spend the Summer[7] I think if you come to America & come this way you will not Fail to call on me & our Good Friend Greene She Desiered me long ago to tell you how Happy She was in the Acquaintance of Some Gentleman you Recomended to them, how Exactly He ansured yor Discription, but I then forgot it & cant now Remember the Name. I heard from there Lately they are all well have an Increce of Grandchilldren which makes them very Happy.[8]

---

just received another from BF by post, undoubtedly the letter she acknowledges here: Van Doren, *Franklin-Mecom*, p. 218.

6. One bill, drawn on Col. Gabriel Johonnot for 1,026 *l.t.* 3 *s.* 6 *d.*, was reimbursement for money BF had spent on the colonel's son, Samuel Cooper Johonnot, and was to be paid directly to Mecom: XXXVIII, 482. Jonathan Williams, Sr., received payment for two other bills of exchange (both repaying BF for outstanding debts). One was Gabriel Johonnot's bill for £146, drawn on Andrew Johonnot (possibly the cousin mentioned here); the other was Winslow Warren's bill for £25, drawn on James Warren: XXXVII, 12; XXXVIII, 233; JW to Jonathan Williams, Sr., April 18, 1782 (Yale University Library).

7. At the home of Elihu Greene, widower of Mecom's granddaughter Jane Flagg Greene: XXXVII, 495; Jane Mecom to SB, May 18, 1783, in Van Doren, *Franklin-Mecom*, p. 223.

8. BF had recommended the comte de Ségur to Catharine Greene in April, 1782: XXXVII, 107. The following December she wrote BF two letters ex-

I percive Mr Williams is Highly Pleased with His Entertainment in France writs about going to England & not Returning in Less than a year[9] However that may be I Shall Chirish Some Hopes that you will come with Him tho on Second tho I think it will be two valeuable a Treasure among our famelyes to venture in won Botome but Shall depend on that Provedence which has hitherto Been your Preserver Protecter & Defender and am as Ever your affectionat and obliged Sister JANE MECOM

My Love to W T F whose Hand writing in your Leter & His name in the Signing the Trety as a Secratery gives me Pleasure

From Robert Morris   ALS: American Philosophical Society

Dear Sir   Philada. April 29th. 1783
When an Officer who has distinguished himself by a Series of Brave Actions in the defence of american Liberty wishes to be introduced to you, whose time & Labours have been exhausted in the same cause, it would be unjust to him to you and to myself not to afford him the opportunity of payg you his respects.

This introduction is in favour of Colo. Maths. Ogden of the New Jersey Brigade whose testimonial from the Commander in Chief justifies what I have said,[1] and I am confident you will not only countenance & advise, but also befriend him in any matters wherein you can with propriety become usefull to a deserving Young Gentleman.

With perfect respect & sincere regard, I am Dr sir Your Affectionate hble Servt   ROBT MORRIS

---

pressing pleasure at meeting Ségur and describing her growing family, which included a third grandson: XXXVIII, 417–18, 505.

9. Jonathan Williams, Sr., was in London by April 3: JW to BF, Feb. 23, above; Williams to BF, April 3, above. His plans for a long stay abroad changed; see his May 14 letter.

1. On April 19 Washington sent Ogden a certificate testifying to his military services. He also advised him that since his business in France was of a mercantile nature, he should not travel in uniform: Fitzpatrick, *Writings of Washington*, XXVI, 340. See also Boudinot to BF, April 28.

Addressed: His Excy / Benjn. Franklin Esqr. / Minister Plenipoy at the / Court of Versailles / by Colo Ogden

Notation: Robt. Morris apl. 29. 1783.

From Thomas Roberts[2]   ALS: American Philosophical Society

Sir   Dunkerke 29th Apl 1783
    Having Commanded Severel Privteers under the American and French Flagg during the late Ware and having been taken Prisoner in the Escamature by the Fly Sloop of Ware & Hunter Cutter on the 26th Septr last & Carried into yarmouth where I was Confined in Prison upwards of four Months and from there was removed to Newgate London where I remained till 31st Marh when I obtained my Liberty & returned to Dunkerke where I am out of all manner of employ & having expended Large Sums of Money in defending my Seelf on my Triel & on various unavoidable occaisions Shall ever esteem the Houner of your Protection in a Commisson to Saile under American Coullers for the future Suport of my Seelfe & Fameley I am Sir your Most Obedt &—very faithful Servt
                        THOS ROBERTS
                    at Mr Coffins American Agent Dunkerk

Addressed: His Excellency Lord Franklin / Plenipotentiary Ministere of the United / States of America at / Paris

2. In 1782 Roberts commanded the French privateers *Escamoteur* and *Trial:* Henri Malo, *Les Derniers Corsaires: Dunkerque (1715–1815)* (Paris, 1925), p. 281; Henri Malo, "American Privateers at Dunkerque," trans. Stewart L. Mims, United States Naval Institute *Proc.,* XXXVII (1911), 971.

From Richard Bache: Two Letters

(I) and (II) ALS: American Philosophical Society

I.

Dr. & Hond: Sir   Philadelphia 30th. April 1783.

The inclosed Letters were intended to be sent some time ago by Mr. Jefferson, who went as far as Maryland as a Commissioner for Peace, but he being recalled;[3] I now commit them to the care of Mr. Restife, a Gentleman that came over with the Minister of France,[4] he appears to be a good kind of Man, & has been very intimate in our Family— We are all well & happy in the blessings of Peace— I am ever Dear Sir Your affectionate Son   RICH: BACHE

Addressed: The Honble. / Dr. Benjamin Franklin / Minister Plenipoy. from the United / States of No. America / at Passy / Favored by Mr. Restive

II.

Dear & Hond: Sir   Philadelphia April 30h 1783.

This I hope will be handed you by Colonel Ogden of the Jersey Line, a Gentleman that has been in the Service of the United States since the commencement of the Contest with Great Britain, & has distinguished himself in the Service as a Soldier of high reputation, and unblemished Honor— As such I beg leave to recommend him to your Notice & Civilities not doubting you will find him highly deserving of them— I am ever Dear Sir Your affectionate Son   RICH. BACHE

Dr. Franklin

Addressed: The Honble. / Dr: Benjamin Franklin / Minister Plenipoy. from the / United States / at / Passy. / favored by Col: Ogden

3. See XXXVIII, 537n.
4. For Restif de La Serve, the second secretary at the French legation, see XXXVIII, 535n.

From Baron Otto von Blome

AL: American Philosophical Society

à Paris ce 30 avril 1783

M. de Blome a L'honneur d'assurer Monsieur Francklin de son sincere attachement et de Lui faire savoir qu'Il aura soin de faire parvenir à M. le Baron de Rosencrone La Lettre qu'Il Lui a adressé pour ce Ministre.[5]

Il fait en meme tems bien des remerciments à Monsieur Francklin de la Medaille qu'Il a eu la bonté de Lui envoyer,[6] et qu'Il accepte avec autant de plaisir que de reconnoissance.

From Vergennes

LS: Library of Congress; draft: Archives du Ministère des affaires étrangères

à Versles. le 30. Avril 1783.

Jai eu l'honneur, Monsieur, de vous adresser le 22. du mois dernier une lettre de Mr. le Mis. de Ségur accompagnée d'un Etat estimatif des effets d'artillerie apartenant au Roi qui Sont restés à Baltimore. Je vous ai prié en même tems de vouloir bien, le plustot qu'il vous Seroit possible, me dire votre Sentiment sur la proposition que faisoit le Ministre de la guerre de céder aux Etats Unis les effets dont il s'agit. J'attends Monsieur, vôtre réponse avec d'autant plus d'impatience que Mr. le Mis. de Ségur me presse beaucoup moi même de lui en donner une qui le mette en état de se décider sur les mesures qu'il peut y avoir à prendre relativemt. aux effets dont il est question.

J'ai l'honneur d'être très Sincéremt. Monsieur, votre très humble et très obéissant Serviteur   DE VERGENNES

Mr. francklin./.

5. Above, April 15.
6. A *Libertas Americana* medal.

From Messey[7]   LS: American Philosophical Society

Monsieur   [April, 1783?][8]
J'ai recu il y a quelques jours la Lettre dont vous m'avez honoré et la precieuse Medaile dirigée et frappée par vos Soins et
l'ordre des états unies de vôtre patrie de la Merique qui Catera-
trisa [caractérisera] dans tous les Sçicles [siècles] avenir la valeur
avec la quelle cette brave nation a acquise l'independance.

Je tient monsieur cette faveur et marque de distinction des
bontés avec les quels vous avez bien voulu m'accorder vôtre estime pendant le Sejour que jai fais a Passy, que jai employés avec
grand plaisir a vous rendre mes devoirs et faire la connoissance
de l'homme Le plus Celebre de nos jours.

Je regrette encore de n'avoir pas étés en même d'avoir cher-
ché a meriter cette grace au prix de partie de mon Sang pour le
Service de cette respectable patrie mais outre que j'avois quitté
le Service le Roi mon maitre en l'honorant de sa protection et
d'une partie de Ses Troupes na pas cru necessaire d'y faire passer
de la Cavalerie a y Servir comme volontaire.

A ce deffaut monsieur je vais consacrer a ma posterité cette
precieuse Medaile pour quelle ce Souvienne qu'un homme capable par ces grands talans d'avoir procuré l'independance a sa patrie m'ait trouvé digne de Ses bontés et j'oses vous demander la
grace de me les continuer.

Quand a celle que vous me faites de me dire les choses les plus
honnêtes et les plus flateuses dans la Langues françoise que vous
dites ne pas Savoir assez pour vous Exprimer comme vous le de-
sireriez monsieur, je me garderez bien quoique né avec l'usage
de cette Langue d'oser repondre á tous ce que faite l'honneur de
me dire crainte de ny pas mettre autant d'énergie de feu et de po-
litesses.

Je me renfermerés-donc monsieur a vous assurer du profond
respect et de toute la consideration avec le quel je suis pour la vie
monsieur Vôtre trés heumble et trés Obeissant Serviteur

MESSEY

7. Le Roy's father-in-law here acknowledges a now-missing letter from
BF. It may have been drafted by Le Roy, who on Feb. 10 had given BF a proposed version of an earlier letter to Messey.
8. The month BF distributed the first *Libertas Americana* medals.

Pardonné monsieur Si je me Sert d'une main etranger mais depuis le Carnaval[9] je suis attaqué d'un espece de Catare qui mait tombé Sur une Epaule quil a falu dechiqueté et enlevé partie des chaires jai été ord'Etat de faire une passe da.

Permetté que monsieur votre fils recoive ici monsieur les assurances de ma parfaites reconnoissance de l'honneur de Son Souvenir insy que mest très heumbles Compliments j'espere vivre encore assez quoi quen quatre vingt trois ans pour l'entendre renomé au nombre d'un des grands hommes de Sa patrie en vous imettant monsieur.

From Jean-André Mongez[1]   ALS: American Philosophical Society

Monsieur   paris mardi matin [April, 1783?][2]

Je me proposois depuis longtemps d'avoir L'honneur de vous remettre le troisieme volume de notre dictionaire d'agriculture dont vous avés bien voulu accepter les deux premiers; mais des affaires me retenant a paris, je vous prie de vouloir bien en accepter L'hommage, qu'il m'eut été bien flatteur de vous rendre moimeme.

J'apprends, Monsieur, que L'on vient de frapper des medailles pour la paix, et en signe d'union entre les etats de L'amerique et la france; vous connoissés notre cabinet de medailles et il a paru vous interesser quand vous L'avés visité.[3] Le moyen le plus sur

9. In 1783 Mardi Gras fell on March 4.
1. Mongez le jeune (1751–1788), *chanoine régulier* of Sainte-Geneviève and a student of natural history, had been the editor of the *Jour. de physique* since 1779. He collaborated with the abbé Rozier on *Cours complet d'agriculture . . . ou Dictionnaire universel d'agriculture* . . . (12 vols., Paris, 1781–1805), the third volume of which he sent under cover of this letter. Larousse; Quérard, *France littéraire*.
2. The month when vol. 3 of *Dictionnaire universel d'agriculture* was published: *Jour. de Paris* for April 10 and 26, 1783.
3. BF's visit to the famous library of Sainte-Geneviève, with its cabinet of antiquities, medals, and natural history specimens, is the subject of an undated note from Le Roy, who was certain that the visit was that very day, but he did not know at what time; see XXIV, 213, where the note is briefly described. Mongez's brother Antoine was the keeper of this important collec-

de L'enrichir seroit d'avoir La collection de ces medailles; elles commenceroient la classe des etats d'amerique n'y auroit-il point d'indiscretion de vous les demander?

J'ai L'honneur d'etre avec les sentimens de la plus haute consideration Monsieur Votre tres humble et tres obeissant serviteur

MONGEZ LE JEUNE;

chan. Reg. de ste Genevieve,
auteur du journal de physique

Notation: Mongez

To the Loge des Commandeurs du Temple[4]

ALS: Bibliothèque de Carcassonne

Passy, the 1st. of the 3d. Mo. 5783. [*i.e.*, May 1, 1783][5]

Dear Brethren,

I received your fraternal Letter dated the 21st. past, and am extremely sensible of your kind Congratulations, and of the Honour you propose to do me by an Act of Affiliation into your most respectable Lodge. I accept the Offer with great Satisfaction. And wishing you every kind of Felicity, particularly that your Power of doing Good may always be equal to your Inclination, I remain, Your very affectionate Brother   B FRANKLIN

To the Commanders of the Temple at Carcassonne.

Addressed by L'Air de Lamotte: A Monsieur / Monsieur David de LaSajeole, Avocat / en Parlement[6] / à Carcassonne.

---

tion: Larousse; *Almanach royal* for 1779, pp. 575–6, and for 1783, p. 500. The collection is described in Pierre-Thomas-Nicolas Hurtaut, *Dictionnaire historique de la ville de Paris et de ses environs* (4 vols., Paris, 1779), I, 55–7, 605.

4. The Carcassonne lodge that had invited BF to join in 1780: XXXIII, 304–6. He is here answering a recent invitation which has not been found.

5. For the masonic dating system see XXVIII, 475n.

6. BF's secretary misread the name of David de Lafajole, who received the lodge's mail: XXXVII, 647. His official function was listed as *maître des cérémonies: tableau des officiers,* described in XXXVII, 647n.

From the Vicomte de La Houssaye

ALS: American Philosophical Society

Monseigneur   Rennes 1er. May 1783

Comme tresorier principal de la Guerre En la province de Bretagne, jay Ete chargé de vous faire passer a Boston plusieurs millions,[7] je me Suis acquitté de Cette Commission avec autant d'exactitude que de zele, Comme Bon Citoyen Et amy des americains; j'ose vous suplier de vouloir Bien me faire Le Cadot d'une medaille qui me Servira de Reconnoissance Et de gage pretieux de votre Estime, j'en decoreray mon Cabinet et Garderay Soigneusement Et pretieusement la Lettre qui accompagnera Cette Liberalité.[8]

Je Suis avec un Respect infini de Votre Excellence Le tres humble & tres obeissant Serviteur

LE VICOMTE DE LA HOUSSAŸE

To Benjamin Franklin Bache

ALS: Yale University Library

My dear Child,   Passy, May 2. 1783.—

I have receiv'd several Letters from you, and in the last a Specimen of your Drawing, which I was pleas'd with, as well as with your Letters.[9] I am not going yet to England, as you supposed. When I do go there, I shall certainly take you with me. I send you the Medal you desire; but I cannot afford to give Gold Watches to Children. When you are more of a Man, perhaps, if you have behaved well, I may give you one or something that is better. You should remember that I am at a great Expence for your Education, to pay for your Board & Cloathing and Instruction in Learning that may be useful to you when you are grown up, and you should not tease me for expensive things that can be of little or no Service to you. Your Father and Mother and Brothers & Sisters were all well when I last heard from them: and I am ever Your affectionate Grandfather   B FRANKLIN

7. Doubtless the specie sent in 1781: XXXV, 28n, 421n.
8. There is no record of whether BF sent him a *Libertas Americana* medal.
9. BFB's letters of Jan. 30, Feb. 25, and March 30 are above.

Your young Friends the Morris's go to Geneva by this Opportunity,[1] and I recommend them to all your Civilities, and to those of Mr Cooper,[2] to whom I send my Love

Endorsed: Grandpappa Passy May 2 1783 B. F. B. Geneva May 24th 1783.

From James Hutton   ALS: American Philosophical Society

My good old friend   Pimlico 2 May 1783.
I thank you for your last kind Lr. which came I believe by mr Fitzherberts Conveyance with a charming book Memoires—sur Turgot.[3] Yes I rejoice at Peace. I have heard you was at the brilliant feast of the Paris Musæe on account of the Peace with my friend Court de Gebelin et Co. where your Bust by Houdon was[4]—does that Bust please? Mrs Hewson and I & Dolly B.[5] surely, if we were artists in Sculpture, could have thrown into it, what no Stranger ever could. Court de Gebelin was confined 4 months to his bed & cured at last by Dr Mesmers' invisible agent, supposed to be magnetical.[6] We have had here Shew-Men who

1. Robert Morris' sons Robert, Jr., and Thomas left Paris for Geneva with their guardian, Matthew Ridley, and their preceptor, Hugou de Bassville, on May 19: Matthew Ridley's Journal, entry of May 19, 1783 (Mass. Hist. Soc.).
2. Samuel Cooper Johonnot.
3. BF's letter is missing. The book he sent was doubtless Pierre-Samuel Du Pont de Nemours, *Mémoires sur la vie et les ouvrages de M. Turgot, ministre d'état* (2 vols., Philadelphia [*i.e.*, Paris], 1782). Du Pont de Nemours was an old friend of Hutton's: XXV, 413n.
4. See Court de Gébelin to the APS, March 15, above.
5. Dorothea (Dolly) Blunt, a friend of both Mary Hewson and Hutton: XXIX, 158–9; Hewson to BF, April 26, above.
6. Court de Gébelin had suffered acutely from kidney stones and a variety of other ailments since the winter of 1782. In March, 1783, a friend introduced him to Mesmer, who, in addition to applying animal magnetism, prescribed several conventional remedies such as exercise and cream of tartar. Claiming to have been cured within a week, Court de Gébelin published an enthusiastic endorsement of Mesmer, which he read to the Musée on July 31, 1783, and sent to his subscribers in lieu of the tenth volume of his *Le Monde primitif* (XXIII, 581n): Anne-Marie Mercier-Faivre, *Un Supplément à l' "Encyclopédie": le "Monde primitif" d'Antoine Court de Gébelin . . .* (Paris,

by means of a Magnet about them, used some how, by tapping a person on the Shoulder could make his watch stand, & by another Tap I suppose in another Direction return its movement as it was. I have heard that Dr Ingenhouse was Mesmers acquaintance[7] & that they had *both* laughd at father Hehls of Vienna's Ideas of Magnetism that way employd as Dr Mesmer now employs them, but it seems Dr Mesmer has thought more of the matter & gone farther.[8] The fact seems he has cured Court de Gebelin. Now you are Philosopher enough, if a Fact really is, not to dispute the Fact, though the quo modo has all appearance of Quackery. I wish to have your own thoughts about this matter after enquiry into certain alledged Facts. There is a possibility that there may be certain natural operations which produce certain effects, no miracle is pretended in this case, no peculiar Sanctity, no Grimace do I hear of, but I hear of Gebelin's real cure & am happy it is so.

Our worthy people at Labradore continue unweariedly employd in that vile Climate & succeed in general Civilisation.[9] & some take Christianity to heart & lose the fear of Death & Dye with Death before their Eyes without turning the Eye from that Object, else the most horrible to them.

Mrs Hewson has taken a house in Cheam, having left Kens-

1999), pp. 67–8; Frank A. Pattie, *Mesmer and Animal Magnetism: a Chapter in the History of Medicine* (Hamilton, N.Y., 1994), p. 186.

7. Ingenhousz had known Mesmer before the latter left Vienna and came to Paris in 1778, but he and others in the Viennese scientific community denounced Mesmer's theory of animal magnetism: XXVII, 506; Pattie, *Mesmer and Animal Magnetism*, pp. 41, 43–4, 61.

8. Maximilian Hell (Höll) (1720–1792), a Jesuit before the pope suppressed the order in 1773, was professor of astronomy at the University of Vienna. During the 1770s, he experimented with the manufacture of artificial magnets and was interested in exploring their medical applications. Mesmer, who initially adopted Father Hell's suggestions, later discontinued the use of magnets and developed his own peculiar theory of "animal magnetism": Pattie, *Mesmer and Animal Magnetism*, pp. 1–2, 7, 33–41; *Dictionary of Scientific Biography*, under Hell.

9. Since Hutton's last extant letter on the Labrador mission, written in the spring of 1780 (XXXII, 280–1), the Moravians founded a third mission at Arvertok, south of Nain: William H. Whiteley, "The Moravian Missionaries and the Labrador Eskimos in the Eighteenth Century," *Church History*, XXXV (1966), 86.

ington. She is happy in being near her sons, who are really lovely Children, to which place she has kindly invited me. & I wish I was able to get thither, for that good woman, your Disciple is really a most amiable person.

That tall Pensylvanian, whose only wish, in going to Cairo, was to get into Abyssinia, after several years waiting, *in vain,* is at last returnd to Germany, well & happy & respected. His name is John Antes, Son of Henry Antes,[1] late of Falkner Sewhamp Pensylvania. Our poor Indians to whom you had formerly after the Lancaster murthers, you yourself had been so kind a Protector,[2] have met with various fates, the last of which was truly dreadful.

While the *Crown Servants* had orderd them to move as *their* Indians wanted to strike your friends, were by a sad mistake, many of them murtherd by your friends against whom they would never combine were afterwards removed by the Crown Servants a vast way up the Country beyond Detroit to places supposed to be 800 miles from Bethlehem. Where they are now I know not, having heard lately no accounts of them.[3] Our White Brn. & Srs. have sufferd common Sufferings during the War, have been sometimes distressd & at others Relievd by the intervention of Congress, & the General Assembly of North Carolina has been kept in our Settlement in Salem there,[4] and I

1. John Antes wrote to BF from Cairo in July, 1779; see XXX, 89–92, where he is identified. His father, Henry (d. 1755), was prominent in the Moravian sect and helped found Bethlehem, Pa.: *DAB.*

2. BF had criticized the 1763 massacre of Indians in Lancaster County in "A Narrative of the Late Massacres . . . ": XI, 42–69.

3. BF was outraged at the news of this 1782 massacre of innocent Moravian Indians; see XXXVII, 586–8, 666, 734. The survivors sought sanctuary near Detroit, where the missionary leaders founded another settlement: Leonard Sadosky, "Rethinking the Gnadenhutten Massacre: the Contest for Power in the Public World of the Revolutionary Pennsylvania Frontier," in *The Sixty Years' War for the Great Lakes, 1754–1814,* ed. David C. Skaggs and Larry L. Nelson (East Lansing, Mich., 2001), pp. 196–200; Paul E. Mueller, "David Zeisberger's Official Diary, Fairfield, 1791–1795," Moravian Hist. Soc. *Trans.,* XIX (1963), 18–20.

4. When the N.C. Assembly met in Salem in late 1781 and early 1782, relations improved between the Moravians and the state officials. In April, 1782, the Assembly transferred the deed of the Wachovia tract, purchased by

thank God considering all things we are not ruined there. In Bethlehem I do not hear of any other difficulties much greater than occurrences war made common.

I have seen lately a Mr Canolles, a Limousin, who has invented a method of making a sort of combustible of marshy & clayish soil said to be cheap & burn well without the bad smell of Turf & Coals. & I heard you had tried the Materials & approved the Result. He shewd me a Lr. from you to a Mr Whitehurst without any farther Direction where to find him. Can you tell me any where Mr Canolles may hear of him?[5] Mr Court de Gebelin was so kind as to address this Mr Canolles to me. I liked the man & his Invention as far as I concievd it.

If you have Leisure to say any thing to me or send me any Lr. for Mrs Hewson in the French Ministers Packet, or send to Mrs Hewson, if you direct to her at Cheame near Epsom Surrey it will find her without expence except from London. The Count de Mustier[6] knows me as I did him several years ago here.

I shall be happy when ever I see you once again either at Paris or London, having very great obligations to you which I acknowledge with Pleasure as your affectionate friend & Obedient humble Servant   JAS. HUTTON

Addressed: To / Doctor Franklin / Passy / near Paris.

---

the Moravians in the early 1750s, to a local resident, thus securing the Moravian claim to nearly 100,000 acres of land. Originally, the deed had been in James Hutton's name, but as he was a resident of England, the land was subject to the Confiscation Act of 1777: Adelaide L. Fries, ed., "Records of the Moravians in North Carolina," N.C. Hist. Commission *Pub.*, IV (1930), 1784–6; Jerry L. Surratt, *Gottlieb Schober of Salem . . .* (Macon, Ga., 1983), pp. 15, 40n, 106.

5. For Canolle see Grivel to BF, April 11. BF's letter to Whitehurst has not been found.

6. Eléonore-François-Elie, comte de Moustier (1751–1817), served as interim minister to the British court between Feb. 7 and May 14, 1783. From 1787 to 1789 he served as minister plenipotentiary to the United States: Larousse; Lewis, *Walpole Correspondence*, XXV, 363n.

From David Hartley
ALS: Library of Congress

My Dear friend   Paris May 3 1783
   The Duke of Manchester[7] is come. I have seen Mr Adams &
Mr Jay[8] this Morning. They both intend to pay their respects to
his Grace I believe this evening or tomorrow morning—[9] I have
not seen Mr Jay but I presume he will do the same. I take the liberty to inform you of this.
Yours ever affecly   D H.

Addressed: To Dr Franklin / &c &c &c / Passy

Endorsed: Mr Hartley May 3. 1783

To Vergennes[1]
LS:[2] Archives du Ministère des affaires étrangères

Sir,   Passy, May 4. 1783
   I have considered the Proposal of M. le Mis. de Segur, to cede
to the Congress the military Stores left by M. de Rochambeau at
Baltimore; and I am of Opinion that it is probable a Part of them
may be acceptable, if not the whole; and that possibly some of
the different States may be enclined to purchase what the Congress should not want. But as I am ignorant of what may or may
not be wanted by the Congress, and have no Orders to purchase
or procure more Stores than have already been provided here, I
can enter into no Agreement respecting them. If a Power be sent

7. The new British ambassador to the French court; see his letter of May 7.
8. A slip of the pen; Hartley meant Laurens. JA was at Hartley's residence
on May 3 when Laurens came in. Their discussions about the English maintaining garrisons in North America and "carrying places" or portages for the
fur trade, and the need for clarifying the northeastern boundary of the
United States, are described in Butterfield, *John Adams Diary*, III, 118–19.
9. Ignoring French etiquette (which would have required that the "last
comer make the first Visit"), JA attempted to visit the duke that evening but
he was not at home. The duke returned the visit either the following day or
the day after that: Butterfield, *John Adams Diary*, III, 118–19.
1. In answer to Vergennes' second letter of March 22 and his reminder of
April 30, above.
2. In L'Air de Lamotte's hand. BF wrote the portion of the complimentary
close after "Excellency's" before signing.

to the Ambassador or Consul to treat with the Congress or the separate States concerning them, it may be the most probable means of disposing of them to Advantage. I am with Respect, Sir, Your Excellency's most obedient & most humble Servant

B FRANKLIN

M. le Comte de Vergennes.

From Sarsfield   ALS: American Philosophical Society

Dear sir.   rue pot de fer 4 may 1783

J'esperois avoir lhonneur de vous voir ce matin. J'en ai eté empeché par quelques affaires qui m'ont arretè Et Je me trouve forcé de vous ecrire parce que ce que J'ay a vous demander Demande un peu de Diligence.

Cest que Vous ayez la bonté de m'envoyer une lettre ou plusieurs de Recommandation en faveur de Jacques-Jean-patient Mazurié fils d'un maire de Landerneau En Bretagne qui va a Philadelphie dans L'intention d'y Etablir une maison de Commerce.³ Je ne le connois pas personellement mais Je prends le plus grand interet a Sa famille Et a Ses associes qui me Sont attachés depuis long tems.

Je fis l'autre jour une indiscretion En vous demandt. devant Mr De Brecquigny Si vous aviez Envoyé une medaille a Son academie.⁴ Je vous prie de vouloir bien en recevoir mes Excuses. Pour tacher de reparer mes torts, J'auray lhonneur de vous prevenir que quelqu'uns des officiers gaux. [généraux] de notre marine qui ont Eté a la baie de Chesapeak Lors de la prise du Ld Cornwallis Se proposent de vous En faire demander.⁵ Je me fais

3. He was undoubtedly related to the merchant Joseph Mazurié (XXVI, 210; XXXIII, 38).

4. The scholar Louis-Georges-Outard Feudrix de Bréquigny (1714–1794) was a member of both the Académie française and the Académie des inscriptions et belle-lettres: *DBF*. Four members of the latter academy thanked BF for a *Libertas Americana* medal the following month: Bon-Joseph Dacier *et al.* to BF, June 6, 1783 (APS).

5. De Grasse had two flag officers serving with him at the Battle of the Chesapeake, both with the rank of chef d'escadre: Louis-Antoine de Bou-

un plaisir de vous en avertir parce que, Si vous voulez leur en
donner, vous aurez le merite de les prevenir sinon Je tacherai de
Les detourner de leur demarche par quelque raison que vous me
suggererez. Je ne puis Encore vous indiquer que M Le Cher.
[chevalier] De Monteil mais les autres le suivroient. Il Est vray
que Je pourrois lui recommander de n'en point parler dans ce
moment cy.

Vous Connoissez my dear sir, les sentimens avec lesquels Jay
Lhonneur detre Votre tres humble Et tres obeissant serviteur

SARSFIELD

Franklin and Morellet: "Explanation of a Medal Struck by the Americans in 1782"

D: printed by Philippe-Denis Pierres, 1783[6]

Even before the *Libertas Americana* medal was struck, at the end of
March,[7] news of its design had spread throughout Europe and En-
gland by means of the following article published in the *Ga₹ette de
Leyde* on March 11 (in French) and widely reprinted:

If ever an event deserved to be recounted on a durable monument, it is undoubtedly the American War and the recognition of its Independence which
was the result. As a consequence, Mr. Franklin is having a medal struck here
relating to these great events. It represents Hercules in his cradle strangling
two serpents. A leopard, surprised by his strength, wants to pounce on him.
It is repelled by France, who, in the figure of Minerva, holds out her shield,
where there are three fleurs-de-lis. At the base are the years 1777 and 1781,
dates of the capitulations of the armies of Burgoyne and Cornwallis, repre-

---

gainville (XXXII, 73n) and François-Aymar, baron de Monteil: W. M. James,
The British Navy in Adversity: a Study of the War of American Independence
(London, New York, and Toronto, 1926), pp. 446–7. For the officers see
Christian de La Jonquière, *Les Marins français sous Louis XVI: Guerre d'in-
dépendance américaine* (Issy-les-Moulineaux, France, 1996) and Asa B. Gar-
diner, *The Order of the Cincinnati in France . . .* (n.p., 1905), p. 126.

6. Four-page brochure, with the second leaf blank; see Luther S. Livingston, *Franklin and his Press at Passy* (New York, 1914), pp. 178–80.

7. See de Cotte to BF, March 26.

sented by the two serpents. On the reverse is Liberty, represented by a beautiful woman, and in the exergue: Libertas Americana.[8]

Franklin presented the medals at court on April 8. The widely reprinted article reporting on that event, which first appeared in the *Gazette de Leyde* on April 18, changed several elements of the story. One of the key changes concerned who was responsible for having had the medal struck. Instead of crediting Franklin, as the initial article had correctly done, the second article credited the several "Commissioners of Congress":

Last Tuesday Mr. Franklin, Minister of the United States of America, had the honor of presenting to the King the medal which the Commissioners of Congress had struck here [*la médaille que les Commissaires du Congrès ont fait frapper ici*] commemorating their country's Independence. This medal, which will transmit to the remotest centuries the epoch of the most remarkable Revolution in the history of humankind, is the very one that we have already announced.

In translating that key passage, quoted above in the original and rendered literally, the British press added a phrase that strengthened the implication that Congress was behind the effort: the medal was "struck here *by order of* the Commissioners of the Congress."[9]

What accounts for the fact that in mid-April, the medal was perceived as having been struck by order of Congress, which it most certainly was not? The origin of this misunderstanding, we believe, was

8. The article carried a dateline of Paris, March 3. Within a week the story was reprinted in the *Courrier d'Avignon,* the *Jour. historique et politique de Genève,* the *Mercure de France* (in somewhat shortened form), the *Courier de l'Europe,* and, on March 15, in English translation in three London papers: Lester C. Olson, *Benjamin Franklin's Vision of American Community: a Study in Rhetorical Iconology* (Columbia, S. C., 2004), pp. 159–60. In Bachaumont, *Mémoires secrets,* March 19, a different first sentence was substituted: "Mr. Franklin, now that the independence already won de facto by the United States is legally confirmed by the peace treaty, is having a medal struck relative to this grand event." The *Gent. Mag.* for March, 1783 (p. 269), also changed the opening to something more neutral: "In commemoration of the American war, and the independence of America that succeeded it, Dr. Franklin has caused a medal to be struck."

9. The italics are ours. The earliest known English version appeared in the April 22–24 issue of the *London Chronicle.* An identical version appeared in the *Pa. Jour.* on June 18; this is the earliest identified instance of its reprinting in America: Olson, *Benjamin Franklin's Vision of American Community,* pp. 160–1. The article circulated throughout the American states until at least Sept. 13, when it appeared in the *South-Carolina Weekly Gazette.*

Franklin himself, by means of the French text presented here, which Morellet had first drafted at the end of March. That draft has not been located; what appears below is the text as printed by Pierres in May, when Franklin commissioned this dual-language brochure as he was preparing to send medals from a second striking to all the members of Congress.[1] As we explained in annotation to Morellet's letter enclosing the draft,[2] we believe that Franklin must have distributed handwritten copies of the French text when he presented the gold and silver medals at court on April 8. Why distribute such an interpretive description at all? Medals were generally self-explanatory. The answer, we believe, can be found by comparing Franklin's "Explanation of a Medal Struck by the Americans in 1782"—certain elements of which seem puzzling, on the surface—to the descriptions of the medal circulating in the press and quoted at the beginning of this headnote. We suspect that Franklin was countering that press coverage, and trying to ensure that both the iconography of the medal and his act of presenting it would be interpreted and reported in the way he intended.

The most curious element of the "Explanation" is the title itself. The *Libertas Americana* medal was struck neither "by the Americans" nor, obviously, "in 1782." It was entirely Franklin's idea: he selected the engraver, he approved the designs, and he financed the enterprise out of his slim discretionary funds. Livingston's enthusiasm about his initial concept had encouraged him but, as Franklin well knew, had not constituted an official endorsement. In fact, Franklin only sought the authorization of Congress on April 15, after the first group of medals had already been distributed.[3] Congress' refusal to endorse the medal came in the form of silence. Among themselves, members criticized the altered design of the allegory, which not only diminished America's role but also was historically inaccurate: Hercules had strangled his first snake at Saratoga long before France had even entered the war.[4]

1. See BF to Livingston, April 15, above.
2. From Morellet, [March 31].
3. For Livingston's initial reaction and BF's response to it see XXXVII, 432, 732. BF requested congressional authorization in his April 15 letter to Livingston, above.
4. The infant Hercules was "diminutive," Livingston complained, dwarfed by the towering figure of France who, instead of the nursemaid Franklin had originally imagined, was a warrior dominating the action by fending off a lunging British leopard — itself an element that had not figured in Franklin's original conception. Moreover, groused Livingston, the medal depicted a serious historical error: at the time of America's victory at Saratoga, France

Franklin's deliberately ambiguous phrase "by the Americans" achieved two related aims. First, it removed his own name from association with the production of the medal. Second, it suggested a message that he knew to be untrue, but that he believed to be vital to America's interests: that the medal was an official expression of gratitude to France on the part of the United States. The fact that Congress had not granted its approval was of secondary importance. Franklin created the impression that it had.

The title's claim that the medal was struck in 1782, on the other hand, seems to us to relate not to the Hercules allegory, celebrating the victories at Saratoga and Yorktown, but to the medal's obverse, portraying American Liberty. The newspaper article published in March had implied, incorrectly, that *Libertas Americana* was celebrating the preliminary peace signed on January 20, 1783, when Great Britain officially recognized American independence. Franklin never intended to commemorate England's grudging change of heart; in fact, he had designed the medal long before peace was assured. The obverse of the medal specifically celebrates America's declaring *itself* independent on July 4, 1776. By locating the medal in the year preceding the general peace agreement (which was the year he designed it), Franklin may have wanted to forestall all future confusion about this important distinction.

The fact that the text of the "Explanation" identified Liberty as the obverse of the medal, rather than the reverse, contradicted the description in the March newspaper article. This has to have been deliberate. It was also effective. By the end of April, when an article appeared in the *Correspondance littéraire*, the face portraying the head of Liberty was reported as the primary one. The image was described as "a portrait of a very beautiful head . . . with a frank and vigorous expression, her hair blowing in the wind, and the liberty cap atop a spear resting against her right shoulder."[5] This image of Liberty, for which we have found no precedent, seems to have been as much a creation of Franklin's as the Hercules allegory.[6] Its clear-eyed beauty, strength,

---

had not yet even entered the war, and was only offering "our infant Hercules . . . now & then a spoonful of pap." Livingston to Elias Boudinot, Sept. 29, 1783, quoted in Olson, *Benjamin Franklin's Vision of American Community,* p. 177.

5. Tourneux, *Correspondance littéraire,* XIII, 293–4. The Hercules allegory was dismissed as being of a "mediocre execution."

6. BF must have begun thinking about both sides of the medal during the summer of 1782, when he discussed the project with William Jones. BF's letter to Jones of March 17, above, credits him with furnishing "the mottos." His use of the plural indicates that Jones suggested the phrase "Libertas

and streaming tresses all suggest Franklin's metaphor of the virgin nation, and probably invoked for the French the same symbolic "naturalness" that they associated with Franklin and America. This was not simply "Libertas," but "Libertas Americana." With this image, we believe, Franklin was creating an entirely new and inspirational emblem for the United States.

This image of liberty was influential far beyond his lifetime on both sides of the Atlantic. In France, one of the first medals minted by the revolutionaries during Year One of the Republic (1792) adopted this same image, including a phrygian cap atop a spear, but substituted the legend "Liberté Francoise."[7] That same year, when the United States Mint was established, Congress decided that the new coins should display "a device emblematic of liberty." The earliest of these coins copied the portrait with free-flowing hair from the *Libertas Americana* medal.[8] For a legend, Franklin's Latin motto was translated and reduced to a single word, *Liberty,* which is still retained on United States coinage.

[*c.* May 5, 1783][9]

EXPLICATION *de la Médaille frappée par les Americains en* 1782.	EXPLANATION *of a Medal struck by the Americans in* 1782.
LA tête représente la Liberté Américaine, avec les cheveux	The Head representing American Liberty has its tresses

---

Americana" as well as the quote from Horace. As for the actual modeling of the head, Yvonne Korshak has suggested that Dupré was inspired by certain Hellenistic coins: "The Liberty Cap as a Revolutionary Symbol in America and France," *Smithsonian Studies in American Art,* 1 (1987), 61–2.

7. The 1792 Lyon Convention medal can be seen in V. G. [Victor Gadoury], *Monnaies française, Colonies, 1670–1942; Métropole, 1774–1942* (Versailles, 1937–42), p. 526.

8. As engraved by different artists over time, and for various denominations of coinage, these images vary in quality. Some include the liberty cap and pole; others do not. Among the best of the engravers was Joseph Wright, who had painted BF in Paris (XXXVII, frontispiece, xxvii, 626n). See *Walter Breen's Complete Encyclopedia of U.S. and Colonial Coins* (New York, London, Toronto, 1988), pp. 152–7, 161–5, 177–89. Yvonne Korshak, "The Liberty Cap as a Revolutionary Symbol in America and France" (cited above), is an insightful overview; see pp. 62–6 for the transition from American symbol to French.

9. See Pierres to BF, May 5.

flottans en arriere, pour montrer qu'elle est en action; & son emblême ordinaire, le Bonnet au bout d'une pique. Au-dessous on voit la date du 4 Juillet 1776, jour où les Etats-Unis se sont déclarés indépendans.

Au revers, les Etats-Unis sont représentés par un Hercule enfant, se levant du bouclier qui, dans Théocrite, lui sert de berceau, & étouffant dans ses mains deux serpens, emblême des deux armées angloises faites prisonnieres à Saratoga & à York-Town. Un léopard, représentant l'Angleterre, se jette en même tems sur l'enfant. Une Minerve armée d'un bouclier aux armes de France vient à son secours, & caractérise la protection généreuse que le Roi a donnée à l'Amérique.

La légende est un vers d'Horace dont le sens est: "Ce n'est pas sans le secours des Dieux que l'enfant montre ce courage".

Les deux dates du 17 Octobre 1777 & du 19 du même mois 1781 indiquent les deux capitulations de Bourgoyne & de Cornwallis.

Cette Médaille est destinée

floating in the air, to shew that she is in activity. The Cap carried on a Spear is her Ensign.

The Date underneath is that of the Declaration of Independence.

On the other Side, the United States of America are represented by an Infant Hercules, cradled in a Buckler to shew that they are nursed in War. A Leopard, representing England, comes with two serpents to destroy the Infant. France represented by a Minerva, comes armed to his succour, and under her protection he strangles the two serpents, while she guards him from the Leopard, by her shield marked with Fleurs-de-Lis.

The Legend is a line of Horace, importing that the Infant was not without divine assistance.

The Dates below are those of the two Capitulations of Saratoga & York-Town, whereby two entire English Armies that had enter'd and ravaged the United States with fire & sword, were extinguished.

This Medal is intended as a

à être un monument durable des événemens qui y sont désignés, ainsi que de la reconnoissance des États-Unis envers leur grand & généreux Bienfaiteur.

lasting Monument of those memorable events, and of the important aids afforded to America by her great & generous Benefactor.

To Vergennes ᴸˢ:[1] Archives du Ministère des affaires étrangères

Sir,   Passy, May 5. 1783
I have the honour to communicate to your Excellency herewith three Articles proposed between Mr. Hartley and the American Commissioners, respecting Commerce.[2] He has sent them to his Court for their Approbation. I doubt their Obtaining it; But we shall see. I am with Respect, Sir, Your Excellency's Most obedient & most humble Servant   B Franklin

M. le Comte de Vergennes.

From Vergennes

Copies:[3] Library of Congress, Massachusetts Historical Society, Archives du Ministère des affaires étrangères

Versailles le 5 May 1783
Je reçois, Monsieur, les deux Lettres d'hier et d'aujourd'hui que vous m'avez fait l'honneur de m'ecrire et la Copie des trois Articles debattus entre M.M les Commissaires des Etats Unis et M Hartley. Vous voudrez bien agréer que je prenne un temps competent pour les Examiner avant de vous proposer les Observations qui peuvent avoir trait a nos liens reciproques. Recevez en attendant, Monsieur mes sinceres Remercimens de cette communication confederal.

1. In the hand of L'Air de Lamotte. ʙꜰ finished the complimentary close before signing.
2. Above, April 29.
3. The first two listed are from the peace commissioners' letterbooks.

J'espere avoir l'honneur de vous voir demain a Versailles;[4] Je desire quil vous soit possible de vous rendre à l'assemblée des Ministres Etrangers. On observe que MM les Ministres et Commissaires des Etats Unis viennent bien rarement ici, et l'on en tire des Consequences que Je suis assuré que leurs Commettans desavoueroient s'ils en avoient Connoissance.

J'ai lhonneur d'etre avec un sincere Attachement, Monsieur, Votre tres humble et trés obeissant Serviteur   DE VERGENNES

A Monsieur Franklin

To Vergennes

> ALS: Archives du Ministère des affaires étrangères; copies: Library of Congress, Massachusetts Historical Society

Sir   Passy, May 5. 1783.

It was my Intention to pay my Devoirs at Versailles to-morrow. I thank your Excellency nevertheless for your kind Admonition. I omitted two of the last three Days from a mistaken Apprehension that being Holidays there would be no Court. Mr Laurens & Mr Jay are both Invalids;[5] and since my last severe Fit of the Gout, my Legs have continu'd so weak, that I am hardly able to keep Pace with the Ministers, who walk fast, especially in going up and down Stairs. I beg you to be assured that whatever Deficiency there may be of Strength, there is none of Respect, in Sir, Your Excellency's most obedient & most humble Servant

B FRANKLIN

His Excelly. the Count de Vergennes.

Notation: M. de R.[6]

4. A Tuesday, the usual day for ambassadors to attend the king at Versailles.

5. Jay had recently written to Livingston that he needed to restore his health, and asked permission to go to Spa and Bath as soon as the definitive treaty was settled. On July 19 he reported that the pain in his breast had abated and he no longer had a fever: Wharton, *Diplomatic Correspondence,* VI, 389; Morris, *Jay: Peace,* p. 563. Laurens was suffering from gout; on May 2 he wrote that his feet could scarcely carry him: *Laurens Papers,* XVI, 191.

6. Gérard de Rayneval was expected to draft a response.

My Friend Benjn. Franklin   Philad 5 mo. 5th. 1783

A good oppertunity offering, by a french Gentleman who
offers to take a letter to thee my kind Friend, I make use of it
affectionately to salute thee, wishing that the best of comforts,
indeed the only comfort worthy the notice of a rational mind;
the recollection of having done the best in our power for the true
welfare of mankind, in the promotion of Virtue & mutual love
amongst men, may be abundantly thy portion.

Inclose I send thee a petition from Francis Geay,[7] whose case
I believe thou art not unacquainted with, as the first account of
his becoming heir to his estate, was transmitted, thro' thee, by
letters to James Lovel then agent for foreign affairs;[8] I have
wrote many letters & sent several powers of attorney to his Relation Mr. Garos, Conseillier du Roy, at Fontenay le vicomte in
Poitou: but still a difficulty remains, his relations & heirs, who
are many not being willing to admit his heirship on account of
his having deserted from the french service, where he served
during thirteen years. He is between 60 & 70 years old, extreemly poor, & has been three times in the hospital, being dis-
sordered in his senses, as its thought from the effect of a cut he
received on the head at the battle of Dettinguen. M Barclay the
agent for the Congress, in France has been applied to by Mr Livingston,[9] now agent for foreign affairs. It was M Deponseau, M
Livingston's secretary drew the inclosed petition.[1] I dont doubt

7. François Geay, the French émigré whose inherited property in France
was being denied him on account of his having deserted the French army.
On Jan. 20 the French attorney Garos begged BF to use his influence at court
to obtain for Geay a pardon: XXXVIII, 608–10. Garos repeated that request
on May 1 (APS).

8. Garos had begun his campaign in 1781, sending a letter to the president
of Congress; this was forwarded to James Lovell. We have found no trace of
BF's involvement in that communication.

9. Robert Livingston wrote to Barclay on April 19, 1782: XXXVIII, 609n.
Some months later he sent to Barclay's care a letter from Benezet to Schweighauser concerning Geay. Barclay forwarded it, and promised to support
Geay's claim in any way he could: Livingston to Barclay, July 1, 1782; Barclay to Livingston, Oct. 19, 1782 (both at the National Archives).

1. The petition, addressed to BF and dated April 30, is in the hand of
Pierre-Etienne Du Ponceau (XXXVI, 581–2n). It summarizes the information

thy kind interposition in the poor fellow's favour. I intent to make a petition of the like import to the Chevalier de la Lucern the french Minister. We should have promoted his going over to France, but his wife cannot as yet be brought to consent. I also send thee a small Collection on the Plainness & Innocent Simplicity of the Christn. Religion[2] of which I request thy most serious perusal, when I am persuaded thou wilt agree with me, that the contents is worthy the most serious consideration, being such as is most likely to calm those aggitations of mind, which the viscituds which attend human life often occasion; the Indians mentioned at page 5. were our old friends, the moravian Indians formerly settled at Weehelusing, they were taken to Sandusky at the Wt. end of lake Ery, from whence the Wiandot King permitted them to return to their Home for corn, which they had left in great abundance; Our back inhabitants hearing of their return fell upon them, as thou remembers they did at Lancaster formerly, & murdered Ninety Six Men women & children who, after some time of prayer & siging hyms, quietly yielded to the knife & hatchet.[3] A plain instance that we are not at home, but only as pilgrims & strangers in this world canditats for a better as the greatest innocency & good will to men which was the case of these indiens, cannot protect us. Indeed the grievous effects of War, both with respect to the depravity of manners as well as the dreadful destruction it occasions, as particularly described in that of the last German War, as mentioned page 10[4] cannot but strike every considerate mind with horror, & is an amazing instance of the folly & dreadful corruption of the human heart as my country man de Voltaire denominates it War page 20th. *"Those legal murders which our abominable nature has made so necessary,"*[5] how will this compare in that awful period when all ap-

---

that Garos had already provided to BF, specifying that Geay has been in America for about 38 years. It asks BF, a fellow citizen of Pennsylvania, to obtain letters of pardon from the king's ministers. APS.

2. Anthony Benezet, *The Plainness and Innocent Simplicity of the Christian Religion* . . . (Philadelphia, 1782).

3. For this massacre see Hutton to BF, May 2.

4. The Battle of Kunersdorf during the Seven Years' War.

5. Voltaire, *Questions sur l'Encyclopédie* . . . (9 vols., [Geneva], 1770–72), v, 72, where Voltaire is discussing Tertullian.

pearances must give way to reality with the meek the loving disposition, so clearly enjoined us in the Gospel; which it appears the weldisposed amongst the ancient Heathens (so called) had a prospect of, as Numa Pumpilius[6] page 23 furnishes us a striking instance of, arising doubtless from his belief, in & trust of the goodness of that power which rulled the World the great dispenser of all events, whose special providence as Plutarch,[7] (tho' also called a heathen) well remarks was displayed in favour of Numa, so as to serve for a proof of what God in his mercy & love can do, in causing virtue to triumph over vice. But the passions & lusts of Men, from whence, as the Apostle remarks, Wars proceed,[8] have so far got the mastery as to overlay & silence that pure principle of truth, which God has dispensed to all Men & strongly drives people in the practice of what will rather satisfy their passions &c than what would be conducive to the real happiness of their fellow-men. This is the root of that unreasonable & irreligious assertion so common in the mouth of Politicians, that there is no other way to preserve the liberty & happiness of mankind by any other means but that horrid destruction & corruption which War occasions; which is charging the power justice & love of the compassionate & benevolent father of mankind, who under the Gospel Dispensation is denominated under the appelation of Love. *God is love,* says the Apostle, *& those who dwell in God they dwell in love.*[9] Happy if the Rulers & others would endeavour to imitate Numa & did by precept & example, inculcate in the people the true spirit of piety that fear of God & confidence in his goodness; that moderation & industry which was so eminently blessed in him. I have in prospect to make a translation of some part of this collection, if possible to rouse, in some of my country men, a consideration wherein true nobility consists, in opposition to that false prejudice so common amongst them, of slighting Labour & improvement in arts &c to pursue an empty notion of heroism,

6. Numa Pompilius, the second legendary king of Rome.

7. In *Lives,* Plutarch emphasizes Numa's piety and his favor among the gods.

8. Benezet is probably paraphrasing James 4:1–10.

9. I John 4:16.

which leads them to the neglect that true happiness & improvemt in virtue to be met with, only in social life, to seek after an imaginary & mad notion of gaining honour, or as we have of late so often heared it, publickly expressed immortal fame in warlike atchivements: *as vain a fanthom as ever danced before a mad man's eye.*

After teaching the youth in this city, near forty years, I have solicited & obtained the office of teacher of the Black Children & others of that people, an employment which tho' not attended with so great pecuniary advantages as others might be, yet affords me much satisfaction. I know no station of life I should prefere before it. Indeed my kind friend the object of Slavery is still an object worthy the deepest consideration, of a philosophic mind. Its sorrowfully astonishing that after the declarations so strongly & clearly made of the value & right of liberty on this continent, no state but that of Pennsylvania, & that imperfectly, have yet taken a step towards a total abolition of Slavery. I am at the point of publishing a small representation on the necessity of the Americans taking this important subject under the most serious consideration to put in the hands of the leading members of every state, introductory to some deep remarks of the Abbe Raynall on that important subject;[1] of these I will send thee a number. Might it not be profitably intimated to the leading people with you, the honour as well as the divine blessing which might be expected to attend them as a nation, if they would shew the example to the other European Nations, in putting an end to the infamous traffick of Slaves; a traffick so infamous & cruel in all its parts, that as the abbe Raynal well remarks it is a dishonour to reason even to endeavour to refute a practice so repugnant to all its dictates. The argument that the culture of their southern settlements cannot be carried on if that traffick ceases is as wicked as it is futile. Surely the number of Black people in their Islands & American Settlements with their offspring which would soon be large if due encouragement was given them would be sufficient to carry on their business. I should be glad if thou wouldst return & spend the remainder of thy time in re-

---

1. Benezet's 12-page *Short Observations on Slavery, Introductory to Some Extracts from the Writing of Abbe Raynal, on that Important Subject.*

tirement & quiet amongst thy old friends, when we might confer upon those weighty matters which can scarce be done by writing, matters quite different from those which the votaries of this world pursue either in pleasure or that foolish fanthom called fame arising either from knowledge or war: such as are indeed worthy the consideration of immortal spirits created for purity & happiness. With the best love I am capable of I remain in great haste thy affectionate friend ANTHONY BENEZET

Notation: Anthoy. Benezett. 1783

From Samuel Cooper: Extract[2]

Extract:[3] Archives du Ministère des affaires étrangères; press copy of extract: American Philosophical Society

[May 5, 1783]

Extract of a Letter from Dr. Cooper to B. Franklin Esqr, Dated Boston May 5th. 1782.—[4]

—"There is a Party among us disposed to avail themselves of every Incident, and of all personal Resentments to weaken and divide our public Counsils, and injure the Alliance. Regard to the general Good, as well as private, and the most constant Friendship oblige me to state Things as they are. It is then confidently whispered among us that Letters have been received from Paris, both in this State and at Philadelphia, which mention, that the

2. Cooper's letter has not survived. The most complete record of it is this extract, made by L'Air de Lamotte and obviously sent to Vergennes (given its location), though no cover letter is extant. BF seems to have received the letter around Sept. 10, 1783; on that day he sent identical letters to JA, Jay, and Laurens, quoting the passage about what was in the "Letters . . . received from Paris." Observing that those letters contained an "accusation, which falls little short of Treason to my Country," BF demanded that each of his fellow peace commissioners write him a certificate that would "destroy the Effect of that Accusation."

3. Also at the AAE is a French translation, with a notation explaining that it concerned the "intrigues de M. Adams pour accrediter dans l'amerique Seple. ses imputations et ses calomnies contre la france."

4. A slip of the pen. The French translation corrected the year to 1783.

Court of France was at Bottom against our obtaining the Fishery and Territory in that great Extent, in which both are secured to us by the Treaty. That our Minister at that Court favoured, or did not oppose this Design against us; and that it was entirely owing to the Firmness, Sagacity & Disinterestedness of M. Adams, with whom Mr. Jay united, that we have obtained those important Advantages.[5] I have not seen any of these Letters, and am considered I suppose as too much attach'd to the Alliance with France,[6] and that American Minister who so happily negociated it, to be trusted with such a Communication: they are said, however to come from some of our Plenipotentiaries at Paris, and particularly from Mr. Adams, a Gentleman against whom I never was prejudiced, having had a long Friendship and Respect for him.[7] It is certain some of his particular Friends here have believed and propagated these Reports, as they say, upon the best Authority. It has also been said from the same Quarter that the Court of France secretly traversed M. A.s Views in Holland, for obtaining of the United Provinces an acknowledgment of our Independence; and that the same Part has been acted in Spain and Russia.[8] All these Things are incredible to me, And tho' they make some Impression at present, Truth is great and will prevail. Care I hope will be taken both at Congress and in Europe, as far

5. One of these letters was undoubtedly the one JA wrote to Mass. congressional delegate Jonathan Jackson on Nov. 17, 1782, which contained all these accusations, and more. Vergennes was an enemy, France wanted to deprive America of the fishery and the western lands, BF was "plyant and Submissive," and Jay had been exemplary: *Adams Papers*, XIV, 61–4. On March 28, 1783, JA claimed in a letter to his wife that without his own efforts "our Cod and Haddock" would have been lost: *Adams Correspondence*, V, 111. His suspicions of the French government were largely unfounded: Orville T. Murphy, "The Comte de Vergennes, the Newfoundland Fisheries, and the Peace Negotiation of 1782: a Reappraisal," *Canadian Hist. Rev.*, XLVI (1965), 32–46.

6. Cooper secretly received a subsidy from La Luzerne to support the alliance: William C. Stinchcombe, *The American Revolution and the French Alliance* (Syracuse, 1969), pp. 119–23.

7. He had baptized JA's children: Butterfield, *John Adams Diary*, I, 339n; II, 7n.

8. These accusations appear in JA's letter to Jackson, cited above.

as public Prudence will permit, to state, as soon as may be, these Matters in a Just Light, and to prevent the public Mischiefs as well as private Injuries that may arise from Misrepresentations in Matters of such Moment. For myself, I stand and speak and act upon my old Ground, our Independence supported and deffended by the Friendship of France; and they who take the fairest and most effectual Measures to cultivate this Friendship, are most my Friends as being friendly to my Country. If through Ingratitude, Folly, Personal Piques, or Treachery, we loose so generous, so powerful, so faitful, and in our present Situation so natural a Friend as the King of France, we fall, and deservedly, into Contempt and Ruin. But I am persuaded there is good Sense and Virtue enough in the Government and People of America to prevent so shameful a Fall.

Mr. Adams wrote to Congress on Decr. 3.—resigning his Employments in Europe;[9] but has intimated in a subsequent Letter his Readiness to continue them, should he be appointed Minister to the Court of London:[1] Congress has not fill'd that Department that we have heard."—

From George Fox

AL: American Philosophical Society

Monday Eveng. [May 5, 1783][2]
Mr. Fox's most respectful compliments wait upon Dr. Franklin—takes the Liberty of informing him that he leaves Paris for Nantes on Thursday, and will do himself the honor of waiting upon him on the morning of that day to take his leave, & to request to be favored with his Commands for America, for which place he intends to embark in the Hannibal Capt Cunningham.[3]

9. JA to Livingston, Dec. 4, 1782 (Wharton, *Diplomatic Correspondence*, VI, 106).
1. On Feb. 5 JA advised Boudinot that the United States should send a minister to England, but he recommended Jay for the post: *Adams Papers*, XIV, 238–45.
2. Fox arrived in Nantes on May 13: George Fox to WTF, May 15, 1783 (APS). If he left Paris, as he says below, on the previous Thursday (May 8), then the present letter was written on May 5.
3. BF entrusted to Fox the *Libertas Americana* medals intended for Con-

Addressed: A Monsieur / Monsieur Franklin / Ministre Plenipotentiaire des / Etats Unis de l'Amerique / en son Hotel / a Passy

From Philippe-Denis Pierres

ALS: American Philosophical Society

Monsieur,   Paris 5 May 1783
    J'ai l'honneur de vous adresser les 300 Exemplaires de L'Explication de la médaille,[4] ainsi que le reste des feuilles qui Complettent les Constitutions.[5]
    Je me propose, Monsieur, d'avoir l'honneur de vous voir Mercredi, au Cas que vous soyez libre.
    Je suis avec autant d'attachement que de respect, Monsieur, Votre très humble & très obeissant serviteur   PIERRES

Je prie Monsieur Votre fils d'agréer mes très humbles Civilités.

Matthew Ridley to the American Peace Commissioners

ALS: American Philosophical Society

Honble Sirs   Paris Sunday Evening [before May 6, 1783?][6]
    On my return from Versailles I found a Letter from my Friend Mr. Joshua Johnson at Nantes covering the Inclosed Extract of

---

gress; see the annotation of BF to Livingston, April 15, above. Because the *Hannibal* was delayed, Fox took passage on the *Nancy,* Capt. Robert Shewell, which left Lorient in mid-June and sailed to Philadelphia by way of Lisbon: Fox to WTF, June 5 and 30, and Oct. 1, 1783 (APS); *Pa. Gaz.,* Feb. 5, 1783.

4. A dual-language imprint of BF's "Explanation of a Medal Struck by the Americans in 1782." See the headnote to the text, above, [c. May 5].

5. *Constitutions des treize Etats-Unis de l'Amérique.*

6. This letter has defeated our efforts either to date it precisely or to explain its contents. Because JA endorsed it, evidently before passing it on to BF, it must have been written when Ridley and JA were both in Paris and while Joshua Johnson was in Nantes. That puts the date somewhere between Oct. 26, 1782, when JA arrived from the Netherlands, and c. May 6, 1783, when Johnson left Nantes to come to Paris himself, on his way to London. (The

a Letter from Mr S Chase & sent him by his Brother the Governor of Maryland—[7] Mr. J. Johnson desires me to communicate the Intelligence it contains to you & also to the Ministers of the French Court—it being probably the only authentic hitherto received— The latter part of Mr. Johnson's request I must beg of you too, if you think it necessary.

I shall be much obliged to you to return me the Extract as I have not taken time to Copy it. I am respectfully Gentn Your most Obedient & most humble Servant   MATTW. RIDLEY

Mr. Johnson desires me to ask Dr. Franklin if he has rec'd any Letters from Mr Carroll covering others for him

Addressed: The Honble Commissioners / of the United States of / America

Endorsed by John Adams: Mr Ridley. [*Added by William Temple Franklin:*] Note from

From George Whatley   ALS: American Philosophical Society

London 6 May 1783

'Tis but lately My good old Friend that a Marylander lent, & on his Departure gave me, a Collection of Pieces, Political, Miscellaneous &ca.[8] said to be all Yours. I had never seen, or heard of

---

last letter Johnson wrote Ridley from Nantes is dated May 6; Ridley's endorsement suggests that he was in Paris by May 9: Mass. Hist. Soc.) The letters Ridley mentions from Johnson and Chase, and the one to Johnson from his brother "the Governor of Maryland" (former governor, in fact), are missing, as is the enclosed extract of Chase's letter, which was doubtless returned to Ridley. If that extract contained military intelligence, then this letter was probably written in the winter.

7. Thomas Johnson (XXVI, 227–8), the governor of Maryland from 1777 to 1779, had written to BF on Ridley's behalf in 1781: XXXV, 354. He was related to Md. assemblyman Samuel Chase (XXII, 148–9) through marriage; see the entries for both men in Edward C. Papenfuse *et al.*, *A Biographical Dictionary of the Maryland Legislature, 1635–1789* (2 vols., Baltimore and London, 1979–85).

8. *Political, Miscellaneous, and Philosophical Pieces* . . . (London, 1779); see XXXI, 210–13.

it. With great Pleasure I perus'd it; & it was enhanced by my finding the Notes, understood to be all Yours, as printed in the Second Edition of my Principles of Trade.[9] My Vanity is much flatter'd, as the Notes, from you, must sanctify my Work; & peradventure be an Inducement for it to be sought for.

I have the comfortable Vanity to find my Dedication, to the Second Edition, with only one Word *States* for *Kingdoms* will do for your most noble NOW great Country

"To all those who have the welfare & Prosperity of these States at Heart, the following Essay, containing, we hope, useful & uncontrovertible Principles on the Subject treated of, is very heartily, & afectionately inscribed."

So let them have it, if You please, as from a Citizen of the World.

The Text by the Notes is made yours as well as mine. Your Rulers have now full Elbow Room. Let all their Ports, be free Ports, to the utmost Extent, & leave to Wiseacres to make Rules & Regulations.

My Namesake Maddison[1] must see you. He will be able to satisfy you of common Occurences; so it will not take up, your, or my time; any farther than that some months since my poor Dear Woman, worn out with the Rheumatism to a Skeleton, left me. Pulvis & umbra sumus.[2] I feel old Age coming; but can yet do without Spectacles.

I have been now going 5 Years Treasurer of my favorite Charity, the Foundling.[3] It is of very little use, being so crampt as it is. I wish it otherwise. Some of my Brethren Governors are so extreamly narrow-Minded, because our Finances are very low, that lately they have restricted one half the Number of Children to be taken in annually, from *120* to *60*. I tell them if they spend

9. For BF's contributions to Whatley's *Principles of Trade*, a pamphlet published anonymously in 1774, see XXI, 169–77.

1. George Maddison (XIII, 545n), secretary of the newly arrived British ambassador to France, the Duke of Manchester.

2. We are shadow and dust. Horace, *Odes*, IV, 7.

3. Whatley had been associated with the charity for more than 25 years, and is listed as having served as treasurer from 1779 until his death in 1791: Ruth K. McClure, *Coram's Children: the London Foundling Hospital in the Eighteenth Century* (New Haven, Conn., and London, 1981), pp. 169–70.

every farthing we have, I think I can get you to take all the Children. I am laugh'd at for this Idea; but I go farther & Say you will buy them.

God bless you, & may you live as long as you like, in all Health & Happiness! is the Sincere Wish of Dear Sir Your Excellent Excellencys most afectionately devoted.

GEORGE WHATLEY.

Addressed: His Excellency / Benjn. Franklin / Esqr &ca &ca &ca. / Paris

From Gérard de Rayneval

AL: Library of Congress

à Versailles ce mercredy 7. may *1783*.
Mr. de Rayneval à l'honneur de prévenir Monsieur franklin, qu'il Se presentera chez-lui demain avant diner pour l'entretenir sur différents objets;[4] il renouvelle en attendant à Monsieur franklin les assûrances de son inviolable attachement.

Endorsed: Note M. de Raynevall May 7. 83

4. Vergennes may have dispatched Gérard de Rayneval to discuss the three draft articles BF had sent, especially if BF had not been able to go to Versailles on May 6 or if Vergennes was unprepared at that time to discuss them; see the exchange between BF and Vergennes, May 5. Rayneval surely would have reminded BF that by Article 2 of the Treaty of Amity and Commerce (xxv, 598), any concessions to British merchants would also have to be made to French merchants.

BF may also have broached with Rayneval the question of the excessive duties charged at Nantes for American tobacco, which JW and other American merchants had refused to pay beginning in the spring of 1782. The municipality of Nantes was suing JW for what he owed, even as the officials admitted that the rate was inappropriate and that other ports charged no duty at all: xxxvii, 486–7; xxxviii, 238–9. BF intervened with the French ministry in May, 1783, and probably before May 11, when Vergennes wrote to minister of finance Lefèvre d'Ormesson asking his view of the tariffs. BF requested that Nantes cease charging duty on American tobacco. This much is known from docketing on a May 14, 1783, letter from JW to Rayneval (AAE), written when JW learned that a ruling in the case was imminent, and if he lost, he would have to remit the full amount within twenty-four hours. Vergennes arranged for the judgment to be suspended: Vergennes to Antoine-Jean

From La Rochefoucauld

AL: American Philosophical Society

Mercredi 7. Avril [*i.e.*, May, 1783]⁵

Le Duc de la Rochefoucauld a l'honneur de faire Ses complimens à Monsieur franklyn, et de lui envoier un projet de lettre à M. le Garde des sceaux; il ne l'a pas terminée parce qu'il ignore le protocole des fins de lettre pour les Ministres Etrangers avec ce Ministre qui en a un particulier avec les Nationaux; il aura l'honneur d'aller chercher Monsieur franklyn aussitôt qu'il le pourra.

From the Duke of Manchester⁶

L: Library of Congress

Mercredi le 7 de Mai 1783

Le Duc de Manchester, Ambassadeur Extraordinaire et Plénipotentiaire de Sa Majesté Le Roi de la Grande Brétagne a l'honneur de faire part à Monsieur Francklin, qu'il a eu Mardi le 6 de ce Mois Ses premieres Audiences de Leurs Majestés Trés Chrétiennes,⁷ et de la Famille Royale.

Amelot de Chaillou, May 14, 1783; Amelot to Vergennes, May 15, 1783; Lefèvre d'Ormesson to Vergennes, May 19, 1783; all at the AAE.

5. The date as written is unmistakable but impossible: April 7 was a Monday. The draft letter to Miromesnil that La Rochefoucauld enclosed with the present letter is missing, but we suspect that it was written after all the sheets of *Constitutions des treize Etats-Unis de l'Amérique* were printed. Pierres completed them by May 5, when he sent a set to BF (see his letter of that date). It makes sense, therefore, that BF would have written to Miromesnil after reviewing them, to inquire about permission to publish the work. That permission was granted on May 11: Miromesnil to BF, June 16, 1783, AAE. The book was not published until July, however, because of delays that will be explained in vol. 40.

6. George Montagu, fourth Duke of Manchester, a former member of the opposition to Lord North, was named ambassador to France on April 9 and was soon issued instructions to conclude final peace treaties with the European powers: *DNB*, under Montagu; Harlow, *Second British Empire*, p. 462. He replaced Fitzherbert, who was sent to St. Petersburg: *Repertorium der diplomatischen Vertreter*, III, 162, 171–2. In mid-May Fox ordered him to prevent Hartley from "going so very fast" in his negotiations with the Americans: Andrew Stockley, *Britain and France at the Birth of America: the European Powers and the Peace Negotiations of 1782–1783* (Exeter, 2001), pp. 179, 190–9.

7. Louis XVI and Marie Antoinette.

To David Hartley

Copies: Public Record Office,[8] William L. Clements Library, Library of Congress, Massachusetts Historical Society

Although the American peace commissioners refused to conduct formal negotiations with David Hartley until he received a commission granting him full powers, they took advantage of his presence to exchange ideas. On April 29 (above) they discussed three proposed articles for a possible commercial treaty. The following day Adams conveyed to Hartley his own personal views about what the future relationship between their two nations ought to be, expressed his dissatisfaction with Franklin, and articulated his distrust of the French court, which he accused of wishing to perpetuate the animosity between Britain and the United States.[9] On May 3 Adams and Laurens talked with Hartley about Britain's maintaining garrisons or sharing portages on the American frontier.[1] And on May 7, as indicated in the present letter, Franklin discussed with Hartley the humanitarian initiatives he had drafted the previous summer and hoped would be incorporated into the Law of Nations and written into the definitive Anglo-American peace treaty. These guaranteed protection during wartime to all people laboring for the common good. By extension, and for the purpose of removing incentives to war, he argued for the prohibition of privateering and for the sugar colonies to be declared neutral countries under the general protection of all European nations.

Dear Friend   Passy May 8th 1783

I send you inclosed the Copies you desired of the Papers I read to you yesterday. I should be happy if I could see before I die, the proposed Improvement of the Law of Nations established.[2] The Miseries of Mankind would be diminished by it;— and the Happiness of Millions secured & promoted.— If the

8. In the hand of Hartley's secretary George Hammond.
9. Butterfield, *John Adams Diary,* III, 115–17.
1. See the annotation of Hartley to BF, May 3, above.
2. BF enclosed an extract of his July 10, 1782, letter to Benjamin Vaughan, beginning, "By the Original Law of Nations," and ending with the paragraph beginning, "This once established . . . " (XXXVII, 610), as well as his two related papers, "Thoughts on Privateering" and "Thoughts concerning the Sugar Colonies" (XXXVII, 617–20). See also BF's proposed article for the definitive treaty and BF to Oswald, Jan. 14, 1783: XXXVIII, 444–5, 584–5.

Practice of Privateering could be profitable to any civilized Nation, it might be so to us Americans, since we are so situated upon the Globe as that the rich Commerce of Europe with the West Indies, consisting of Manufactures, Sugars &c is obliged to pass before our Doors; which enables us to make short and cheap Cruizes, while our Commerce is in such bulky low-prized Articles as that ten of our Ships taken by you is not equal in Value to one of yours; and you must come far from home at a great expence to look for them. I hope therefore that this Proposition,[3] if made by us, will appear in its true Light, as having Humanity only for its Motive—I do not wish to see a New Barbary rising in America, and our long extended Coast occupied by Piratical States. I fear lest our Privateering Success in the two last Wars should already have given our People too strong a relish for that most mischievous Kind of Gaming mixed with Blood. And that if a Stop is not now put to the Practice, Mankind may be more plagued with American Corsairs than they have been and are with the Turkish. Try, my Friend, what you can do, in procuring for your Nation the Glory of being, though the greatest Naval Power, the first who voluntarily relinquished the advantage that Power seems to give them, of plundering others, and thereby impeding the mutual Communication among Men of the Gifts of God, and rendering miserable Multitudes of Merchants and their Families, Artizans & Cultivators of the Earth, the most useful, peaceable & innocent Part of the human Species.

With great Esteem and Affection, I am ever my Dear Friend Yours most sincerely   B FRANKLIN

D Hartley Esqr

Notations in different hands: Letter from Dr Franklin to Mr Hartley with enclosures 8th May 1783 / In Mr. Hartley's No. 12[4]

3. The abolition of privateering.
4. Hartley to Fox, No. 12, July 1, 1783 (Giunta, *Emerging Nation*, 1, 866–70).

From Sarah Bache ALS: American Philosophical Society

My dear Sir   Philad May 8. 1783

I cannot let Coll Cambray[5] go without a line to you tho I sit up to write in bed— I have had a fit of the Bilious Cholic that lasted twenty four hours, it went off yesterday but has left me very weak and with a bad head ake, I hope a good nights sleep will quite restore me, and then I shall be able to write you a long letter by Mr Oster[6] who goes in a day or two— Mr Bache went to Mr Kidds the day before yesteday just before I was taken and would have been home to night but for the rain, I never missed him more as he is realy the best nurse in the World. Little Deby is in the height of the Measles. She has it heavily, but I am in great hopes will do well, the rest have all had it and are well and hearty—we are sorry to part with Coll Cambray who is universaly liked here, both as a Soldier and a Gentleman, he flatters us that he shall return and live in America, I was sorry I could not see him this evening, having not learn'd as much of the French fashion as to see a Gentleman when I was in bed, I feel myself better than when first I took my pen in hand. I was thinking at first to make Will to write for me excuse this paper it was all that I had this evening—[7]

I am as ever Your Dutiful Daughter   S Bache

Addressed: Dr. Franklin / Coll Cambray

5. Cambray, who had been recommended by SB on Jan. 24 (above), sailed on the frigate *Gloire* on May 11, arriving in Brest on June 11: Lasseray, *Les Français,* I, 140.

6. Martin Oster (XXVII, 334n), the vice-consul of Philadelphia, was returning to France for health reasons: Abraham P. Nasatir and Gary E. Monell, comps., *French Consuls in the United States: a Calendar of Their Correspondence in the Archives Nationales* (Washington, D.C., 1967), pp. 566–7.

7. SB wrote on a sheet that her son Will had started to use for a letter of his own. He had gotten as far as "My Mama was much Desopointed that She." Beneath this SB explained, "Will had began a letter to Miss Beckwith."

From Anthony Benezet

ALS: American Philosophical Society

My friend Benjn Franklin   Philadelpa the 8th 5th mo 1783

I wrote a few days past, by a french Gentleman, but now my dear friend thy daughter having procured me an oppertunity, which appears more sure,[8] I make use of it to inform, that in my last was inclosed an earnest petition to thee from Francis Geay de la Gaconniere, the person to whom an Estate is fallen at Fontenay le Vicomte in Poitou, which I think thou art not unacquainted with, as the first letter came thro' thy channel to Jams Lovel, then employed in foreign affairs. I have wrote abt. twenty letters for him, & sent four powers of attorney, & am at last informed by His sister, that by his desertion, about forty years past, from the french service were he was a dragoon in the regiment of he has forfeited his right; to request thy assistance in procuring him letters of Rehibilation is the purport of his petition. He is extreemly poor, between 60 & 70 yr old & has been 3 times in our hospital, being at times disordered in his senses, owing as its thought to a cut he received on his head at the battle of Detinguin. I yesterday put in a petition to the same purport to the Chevalier de la Lucern Sally assuring me the bearer will deliver the packet without charge which I was afraid might occur if in danger of being put in the post office, I venture to send thee a number of Short Accounts of the Quakers Principles, their setlemt in America &c in French[9] which is not done so much from a desire of persuading people of the rectitude of their sentiments, as to strengthen in the people a disposition which appears to encrease of shaking the popish Nations from that dreadful yoke of implicite subjection to the tyranny of their church governmt, priest, monks &c and to give them an idea of that civil & religious freedom which So long did, & its hoped still will subsist in these parts. The difference of a simple innocent upright worship, in spirit & truth, which the Gospel proposes in opposition to that dead round of stupid practices in use, particularly in

8. SB sent her letter of the same date by the chevalier de Cambray-Digny. Benezet's letter of "a few days past" is above, May 5.

9. Undoubtedly his own *Observations sur l'origine, les principes, et l'etablisement en Amerique, de la societé connue sous la denomination de Quakers ou Trembleurs . . .* (Philadelphia, 1780).

the church of Rome I fear much for the maintenance of priest-craft than sincerely seeking God. I also send thee a couple of copies of a small Collection I lately published which I trust will not be disagreable to thee, upon the Innocency & Plainness of the Christian Religion,[1] in opposition to the crafts used in the church & the cruelty & horrid devastation & destruction by War, the armies &c illustrated in a small summary of the last German War at page 10th. also the effect of a contrary disposition in the instance of Numa Pompilius, who accepted of the crown of Rome, solely with a view of promoting the happiness of the people, whose virtue & love of his Maker & Fellow-Men was so blessed, that during forty three Years that he reigned his kingdom was preserved in peace; this Plutarch (tho called an heathen) has such a sense of the divine care over men, that he observes that, in Numa's happy reign, by a particular providence, (mark the expression) Heaven was pleased to preserve this happy reign, which is a plain proof of what God in his mercy & love can do, in rendering virtue triumphant over vice. Virtue, love, moderation & industry prevailed & even the nations around were so far from taking advantage of Numa's pacific temper to make war against him, that Plutarch remarks, a wonderful change prevailed amongst themselves & even in their differences they chose the Romans for their umpires; A clear instance this is, of what God in his love & mercy can & would doubtless do for mankind, if their heart & eye was to him; particularly when we consider they were under the monstrous prejudices which more or less attended on paganism, & that we are favoured with the precepts of the Gospel, and the example of a meek saviour who himself overcame by suffering. How vain are all expectations that mankind can establish themselves in safety & peace by force of arms & the number of their troops. Is the Emperor more secure with three hundred thousand men, whilst his competitors, the king of Prussia, or other potentates vie in raising an equal or greater number, if each of them had but a few hundred, they would be as strong; the encreasing the number does but increase the misery of the people, & destruction of

1. He also sent some of these pamphlets with his May 5 letter; see the annotation there.

Mankind; by those *Legal Murders, which our abominable nature has made so necessary* as Voltaire expresses it, as mentioned at page 20th; whereas if the disposition which was in Numa, was prevelant amongst Christians, there is the greatest reason to believe that the benevolent Power, who has dominion over the heart of man, which himself has made & whom the Apostle denominates under the appelation of *Love* God *is love & they that dwell in God they dwell in Love* would bless & preserve his creature man in a state of love to his Maker & one to another I believe it is not so much a disbelief in the power of God, to maintain order amongst men without that horrid corruption & destruction which war occasions, but it very much arises from an indulgence of the corrupt propensity of the heart, those lusts which the Apostle James says are the remote causes of war, that lust of power that pride, that desire of amassing wealth, must at any rate be satisfied, & while that continues to be the case & God consequently does not see cause to force men to act agreable to reason & humanity, the true Christian must mourn, like the Dove when out of the Ark & suffer as a pilgrim & stranger in this world, till their sighs & tears prevail. Happy would it be if some of the powers of Europe were favoured with the same prospect, which prevailed in Numa, doubtless the same blessing would attend, & as we are favoured wt the light of the Gospel exceed. How joyful would it be if thou could'st be the happy instrument in the promotion of this blessed work. I am the more free to express my self thus, as I am sensible there is something working in the minds of many thoughtful persons both french & germans, verging to this end; but I am afraid I shall if I have not already tire thee. Well Sally tells me she expects to see thee here this summer, which affords me satisfaction, & gives me hope that if thou wilt endeavour to promote such a blessed disposition, whilst thou hast the ear of the king of France, & other great ones, we shall have with pleasure to talk over of it, as of the Aurora of better times for mankind together by the fire side, before we put the Chairs in order and the long sleep will take place; when all great prospect peculiar to this world, but that of humility & love will sink into nothing & less than nothing.

I also send thee a letter wrote by Eliz Webb, mother to Jams.

Webb, thy old companion in the assembly,[2] which I am persuaded will be agreable to thee, & would I believe be so to many
pious people amongst the french, if in their language, there is
something agreably tendering & tending heaven ward in it.[3]
The continuance of the Slave Trade, is another avowed
abomination, could thou not give an item to the king of France
(& such of his ministers who are blessed with feeling hearts)
who I believe is a well disposed prince, what an honour it would
be to him & his country if he would take the lead in putting an
end to that unreasonable, inhuman & dreadful traffick; the plea
of necessity in its support is to Christians or even Philosophers
horrible beyond expression, besides it is not true; surely two
hundred & fifty thousands Negroes in the Island of Hispaniola,
& others in the same proportion is sufficient, with their encrease
if well used, to carry on their business: if a copy of this paragraph or something to the same purport was put in the hands of
the leading people, might it not be of service, for indeed we cannot expect peace will be of any long continuance whilst such
wickedness of so deep a dye, is so publickly maintained. In a former letter[4] I mentioned the case of the protestants in France, as
an object worthy thy notice, to endeavour out of charity to them,
as well as love to ourselves to endeavour the revocation of the

2. BF and Webb served together in the Pa. General Assembly from 1755
to 1762: VI, 256–61; Craig W. Horle *et al.*, eds., *Lawmaking and Legislators
in Pennsylvania: a Biographical Dictionary* (3 vols. to date, Philadelphia,
1991–), II, 373, 1049.

3. Benezet was responsible for the publication of *A Letter from Elizabeth
Webb to Anthony William Boehm, with His Answer* (Philadelphia, 1781), an
account of Webb's conversion experience and work as a Quaker minister. In
1783 Benezet was having it translated into German: George S. Brookes,
Friend Anthony Benezet (Philadelphia and London, 1937), pp. 346n, 349, 355,
375, 393–5, 402. Elizabeth Webb (1663–1727), from Gloucestershire, England, emigrated with her husband Richard to Philadelphia, becoming an
itinerant preacher and touring most of the American colonies. During a religious visit to Britain from 1710 to 1712, she met Anthony W. Boehm, chaplain to Prince George of Denmark, Queen Anne's husband: Rebecca Lar-
son, *Daughters of Light: Quaker Women Preaching and Prophesying in the
Colonies and Abroad, 1700–1775* (New York, 1999), pp. 296–8, 300.

4. Missing.

edicts still in force particularly those of May 14. 1725 confirmed by that of Jany. 17. 1750[5] by which it is enacted That all preachers who shall call assemblies, preach in them &c shall be put to death & the congregation sent the men to the gallies & the women to perpetual imprisonment; and by the same the Intendant of every province is impowred to give judgment in the last resort in the case of Protestants in consequence in 1752 Francis Benezet[6] was hanged at Montpellier for having held religious Meetings. Whilst these ordonances are in force we shall have reason to fear for our children & others who may travel in France. I have given memorials to the same effect to the Chevalier de la Lucern & to the Comte or Chevalier Chaleloux[7] who promised to make use of them in parte. With love I remain thy affectionate   ANTHONY BENEZET

Excuse innacuracie &c for I have not time to [*torn*]

5. Benezet probably means the royal declaration of May 14, 1724, imposing severe penalties against those who did not conform to the tenets of the Catholic Church. Louis XV signed two ordinances in February, 1745, imposing additional penalties on nonconformists: Guillaume de Félice, *History of the Protestants of France* . . . , trans. Henry Lobdell (New York, 1851), pp. 453–6, 478–9, 487; François André Isambert, *et al.*, eds., *Receuil général des anciennes lois françaises* . . . (29 vols., Paris, 1821–33), XXI, 261–70.

6. For François Bénézet, one of Benezet's distant relatives, see Brookes, *Friend Anthony Benezet*, pp. 4–5.

7. La Luzerne and Chastellux. Benezet also had communicated his sentiments on the persecution of Protestants in France to La Luzerne's secretary François Barbé de Marbois: Brookes, *Friend Anthony Benezet*, pp. 134, 456–7; Eugene P. Chase, ed., *Our Revolutionary Forefathers: the Letters of François, Marquis de Barbé-Marbois* . . . (New York, 1929), pp. 139–40.

From the Loge du Patriotisme, with a Note
from Nogaret[8]

ALS:[9] American Philosophical Society

à L'O∴[1] de la Cour le 8me. du 3me. mois de L'an
de la V∴L∴ 5783. [Versailles, May 8, 1783]
T∴ V∴ et T∴ ch∴ f∴[2]

La L∴ du Patriotisme regulierement assemblée pour arrêter
ce qui Sera convenable à l'inauguration de Son nouveau Temple,
laquelle doit Se faire Le *mercredi 14e.* jour de ce mois et S'occu-
pant des moyens d'illustrer une fête aussi intéressante a un-
animement député le T∴ ch∴ f∴ Nogaret vers vous pour vous
engager à lui faire la faveur d'assister ce jour à Ses travaux. Nous
esperons, T∴ R∴ f∴,[3] que vous voudrez bien répondre aux
Voeux unanimes de plus de Cent ff∴ qui envisagent comme une
jouissance aussi pretieuse que mémorable l'avantage de posseder
dans Leur Sein un f∴ qui mérite et fixe l'admiration et L'amour
des deux mondes. Nous avons la faveur d'etre avec les Sentimens
de la fraternité la plus distinguée en vous Saluant par tous l∴ N∴
et avec T∴ l∴ h∴ qui v∴ S∴ d∴[4]
T∴ V∴ et T∴ illustre f∴ Vos tres devoués, tres affectionnés
Serviteurs et ff∴

VAUCHELLE Vble
DE LAVILLE 2d. Surv.
TERRASSE orateur
MESNAGER:/:
LOUIS
D'LAVINÉ adjt a Secr.

8. The Loge du Patriotisme was constituted at Versailles in 1780. It held
public concerts to benefit its philanthropic mission, the relief of widows, orphans, and the infirm. Among its members, many of whom held bureaucratic
positions at court, were several musicians and composers. Nogaret, who had
joined the lodge the year before and would become the next venerable, wrote
the libretti for many of the lodge's operas: Le Bihan, *Francs-maçons parisiens*,
pp. 25, 376; Roger Cotte, *La Musique maçonnique et ses musiciens* (2nd ed.,
rev. and enl., Paris, 1987), pp. 22, 44–5, 49–50, 60–2, 80.
9. In Nogaret's hand.
1. L'Orient. The two abbreviations later in the dateline stand for Vraie Lumière. The masonic year began on March 1.
2. Très Vénérable et Très cher frère.
3. Très Respectable frère.
4. Les Nombres et avec Tous les honneurs qui vous Sont dûs, a variation
on the standard masonic closing (XXXVI, 113n).

S. Simon
Cuillié Secretaire
felix-Nogaret[5]

J'aurai la faveur de vous presenter Lundi mes respects, et de macquitter plus particulierement de ma Commission. Je vous re-mercierai en même tems du Cadeau que vous m'avez fait.[6]

F. FELIX NOGARET

From Robert R. Livingston

ls: University of Pennsylvania Library; al (draft): New-York Historical Society; transcript: National Archives

Sir, Philadelphia 9th. May 1783
We have yet had no information from you subsequent to the signature of the Preliminary Articles by France, Spain and Britain, tho' we have seen a declaration for the cessation of Hos-

5. The following members are listed in Le Bihan, *Francs-maçons parisiens:* François-André Vauchelle, venerable of the lodge, was *commis principal de la guerre;* Pierre Terrasse de Mareilles was *secrétaire de la feuille des bénéfices* and *garçon de la Chambre de la Reine;* Marie-Nicolas-Guillaume-Jacques Le Baillif Le Menager was a military officer; Louis Louis was a *commis* in the department of war; and Jean-Baptiste Cuillié was a *commis des finances.* Simon Simon, a harpsichordist and composer, was *maître de clavecin des enfants de France* as well as the instructor of the queen and the comtesse d'Artois: Stanley Sadie, ed., *The New Grove Dictionary of Music and Musicians* (2nd ed., 29 vols., London, 2001).

6. Probably a *Libertas Americana* medal. Once he received BF's acceptance, Nogaret invited WTF to accompany BF and stay for the banquet. Dress code was "costume noir," the hour was 11 A.M. (if WTF came later, he would miss the inauguration ceremony), and there was no admission fee: Nogaret to WTF, undated, APS. A four-page program of the inauguration entitled "Les Trois grades," in Nogaret's hand, is among BF's papers at the APS. The musical ceremony included a march, ariettas, recitatives, and a symphony for the reconstruction of the Temple. During the festivities that followed Nogaret recited a poem composed for the occasion ("A M. Franklin") in which he honored BF, a fellow brother, as the protector of humanity and the hero of liberty. It was printed in the *Almanach littéraire* for 1784, p. 264, where a note states: "Ces vers ont eté prononcés devant M. Franklin à Versailles, à une Fête patriotique qu'il embellit de sa presence."

tilities signed by you, Mr. Adams, and Mr Jay—[7] We grow every day more anxious for the definitive Treaty, since we have as yet discovered no inclination in the Enemy to evacuate their Posts— and in sending off the Slaves they have directly infringed the provisional Treaty,[8] tho' we on our part have paid the strictest regard to it— This will be more fully explained by the enclosed Copy of a Letter from General Washington containing a relation of what passed between him and General Carleton at a late interview—[9] let me again intreat that no doubt may be left in the Treaty relative to the time and manner of evacuating their Posts here— Without more precision and accuracy in this, than we find in the provisional Articles, we shall soon be involved in new disputes with Great Britain—

Our Finances are still greatly embarrassed—you may in part see our distress, and the means Congress are using to releive themselves from them, by the enclosed Pamplet, which I wish you and your Colleagues to read but not to publish—[1]

7. Above, Feb. 20.

8. The seventh article of the provisional treaty (XXXVIII, 386). In 1782–83 the British evacuated nearly 3,000 black people from Savannah and nearly 8,000 from Charleston, the vast majority of whom were enslaved to Loyalists. Moreover, at least 4,000 free blacks departed on evacuation ships from New York: Cassandra Pybus, "Jefferson's Faulty Math: the Question of Slave Defections in the American Revolution," *W&MQ*, 3rd ser., LXII (2005), 262–4; Sylvia R. Frey, *Water from the Rock: Black Resistance in a Revolutionary Age* (Princeton, 1991), pp. 174–9, 192–3.

9. This was undoubtedly Washington's May 8 letter to President of Congress Boudinot, enclosing a copy of his May 6 letter to Carleton and the minutes of their meeting earlier that day in which the subject of slaves was discussed: Fitzpatrick, *Writings of Washington*, XXVI, 402–6, 408–9, 410–12. Copies of all three documents are with BF's papers at the APS.

1. The pamphlet, *Address and Recommendations to the States, by the United States in Congress assembled* (Philadelphia, 1783), consisted of a circular letter Congress adopted on April 26 concerning the national debt (*JCC*, XXIV, 277–83) and supporting documents. Among the latter were excerpts from BF's letter to Robert Morris of Dec. 23, 1782, announcing the new French loan, and a copy of the July 16, 1782, financial contract between BF and Vergennes. Appended to the contract was Congress' ratification, signed by Elias Boudinot on Jan. 22, 1783. When answering the present letter on July 22, 1783, BF informed Livingston that the pamphlet was his first indication that the contract had been ratified, as the document itself had not arrived: Wharton, *Diplomatic Correspondence*, VI, 585.

The enclosed Resolution imposes a new task upon you,[2] I hope you will find no great difficulty in procuring the small augmentation to the Loan, which it requires—be assured that it is extremely necessary to sett us down in Peace—

None of the States tho' frequently called upon have sent me the Estimates of their losses by the Ravages of the British, except Connecticut and Rhode Island, and their Accounts are extremely imperfect, such as they are I enclose them;[3] For my own part I have no great expectation, that any compensation for these losses will be procured, however if possible it should be attempted— Commissioners might be appointed to assertain them here—great part of the Prisoners are on their way to New York, and the whole will be sent in a few days—[4] they will amount to about six thousand Men— Our Ports begin to be crouded with Vessels,[5] there is reason to fear that a superabundance of foreign Articles will in the end produce as much disstress as the want of them has heretofore occasioned—

I have the honor to be—sir, with great Respect and Esteem your most obedt humble servant, R R LIVINGSTON

Honble Benj: Franklin

No, 27.

From Samuel Potts[6] ALS: American Philosophical Society

My Dr Sir Genl Post Office May 9th. 1783

I should have acknowledged sooner the receipt of your letter of the 24 March but I have been in the Country for some time

2. A May 5 resolution directing that an application be made to Louis XVI for an additional 3,000,000 *l.t.*: *JCC*, XXIV, 328.

3. The enclosures are missing. The peace commissioners had requested the estimates the previous December: XXXVIII, 452.

4. A number of British officers had come to Philadelphia to conduct them: Smith, *Letters*, XX, 229.

5. During May there was a dramatic rise of ship entries into the port of Philadelphia: Richard Buel, Jr., *In Irons: Britain's Naval Supremacy and the American Revolutionary Economy* (New Haven and London, 1998), p. 246.

6. Comptroller general of the Inland Office of the British post office. He and his wife had entertained BF and WTF in Paris in 1780: XXXIII, 287.

past and therefore did not receive it till a few days since, I understand the News Papers have been regularly sent to you and in this, and all other occasions I shall be happy to obey your commands.[7] I trust you will not deem these only words of course, they flow from a very sincere and affectionate regard towards you and the intercourse we have had for many years will I flatter myself have proved the warmth of my friendship.

I have a matter in hand that I wish to take your opinion upon—in the year 1775 Mr. Antill[8] came to England and whilst he was here he borrowed of the two Mr. Foremans[9] of the Office of Ordnance myself and my Brother[1] the sum of Three Thousand Pounds which was to purchace a place in Philadelphia, which Mr. Morgan then held, from that time we have never heard anything towards paying the principle much less the Interest, and I therefore wish to know if you can be of service to us in any application to Congress. I have a mortgage of his which runs in this form. "Doth bargained sell and confirm to S. P. &c a certain Tract or parcel of Land containing Eight Thousand Acres in the county of Gloucester also one other Tract in the County of Albany also another Tract in the County of Charlotte in the province of New York and all other Tracts &c to hold &c"[2]— and further recites, "that being willing to give every other security for the payment of the money with Interest as aforesaid doth

7. BF's letter of March 24 is missing. On the same day, however, he wrote to Bowens about changing the way he would henceforth receive his London newspapers; see Bowens to BF, April 8. On June 10, 1785, Potts sent BF an account of two years' worth of forwarding the *Morning Chronicle* and *Lloyd's Evening Post*, beginning on March 30, 1783. APS.

8. The New Jersey Loyalist John Antill (XXI, 103–4n), who was now living in New York and considering a move to Nova Scotia: E. Alfred Jones, "Letter of David Colden, Loyalist, 1783," *American Hist. Rev.*, XXV (1919), 80–1.

9. The brothers Richard (bap. 1733–1794) and Anthony (1725–1802) Forman, both of whom were employed in the ordnance department of the army: *The Royal Kalendar . . . for the Year 1775* (London, 1775), p. 162; *ODNB*, under Forman family.

1. Possibly Henry Potts, one of the clerks of the roads for the British post office: *Royal Kalendar . . . for the Year 1775*, p. 119.

2. Gloucester County and a portion of Charlotte County eventually became part of Vermont.

bargain, transfer &c all his personal effects Bonds, Notes, Book Debts and any sums of money due to him towards discharging the sums due to Messrs. Foreman, Potts &c and gives them full power to sue for the same"—having thus given you the heads of the Mortgage I wish to have your opinion whether Congress will allow us to take possession of the Tracts, if you think the lands thus situated are worth our attention and whether you think [*torn:* it would(?)] answer any good purpose to put the Bonds(?) in force and if you can Aid and Assist us in this matter.

I beg your pardon for giving you this trouble but its of consequence to us and I hope you will excuse it.

Mrs. Potts and my Brother joins with me in best Compts. and beleive me to be Dr sir Your Most Faithful and Most Obed Servt.

SAM POTTS

Addressed: A son Excellence / Monsieur Franklyn / Passey / a / Paris

From William Wilkinson[3]   ALS: American Philosophical Society

Sir   Paris May the 9th. 1783.

Mr Philip Nicklin an English Gentleman, going to Philadelphia to establish a House in the Linnen Trade in Connection with that of Dickinson Lloyd. & Nicklin in London and being an entire Stranger there is desirous of having a few Letters to some Persons of Note in that City; as several of My Friends in England interest themselves much in his Wellfare being a deserving Young Man; I should be perticularly obliged to You, Sir, if You would be so kind as to procure him an Introduction to some of Your Friends there.[4] Being fully perswaded he will answer to

3. The English ironmaster: XXXIV, 175–6n.
4. We have no record of whether BF provided Nicklin (1760–1806) with a recommendation, but once in Philadelphia he reported that Nicklin had married and was "much esteemed": BF to Priestley, July 29, 1786 (Library of Congress). A native of Devonshire, England, Nicklin prospered as a merchant and was later appointed one of the directors of the Bank of Pennsylvania and the Insurance Company of North America: W. A. Newman Dorland, "The Second Troop Philadelphia City Cavalry," *PMHB*, XLIX (1925), 190–1; *Pa. Gaȥ.*, June 19, 1793.

the Utmost of Your Wishes the Obligation You will lay him under by this Favour; I have the honour to be very respectfully Sir Your most humble & obedient Servant[5] WILLIAM WILKINSON

a l'hotel du Parc Royal. Rue Colombier Faubourg St. Germains A Paris—

Addressed: A Son Excellence / Dr. Francklin / Ministre plenipotentiare des / Etats Unis de L'amerique septentrionale / A Passy

Notation: William Wilkinson Paris May 9. 1783

The Loge des Neuf Sœurs and Franklin: Announcement of a *Fête Académique*

Printed announcement: National Heritage Museum, Massachusetts[6]

Though the peace was publically celebrated all over Paris in the spring of 1783, this was the only celebration in which Franklin had a hand— or at least, to which he lent his name. Initially, the Nine Sisters planned to hold this *fête académique* on May 5 at its quarters on the rue Coquéron.[7] They sent printed invitations to the membership, dated April 8 and issued in the name of the lodge "de concert avec le T∴ C∴ F∴ *FRANKLIN, ex-Vénérable.*"[8] The festivities were to begin at five

5. Also on May 9 Wilkinson sent a note to BF accepting a dinner invitation for the following Sunday on behalf of himself and "Miss Wilkinson." APS. This might have been his sister Margaret (the only sister who was as yet unmarried, as far as we know), or perhaps his niece May (Mary): Norbert C. Soldon, *John Wilkinson (1728–1808), English Ironmaster and Inventor* (Lewiston, N.Y., Queenston, Canada, and Lampeter, Wales, 1998), pp. 23, 32–3, 212; H. W. Dickinson, *John Wilkinson, Ironmaster* (Ulverston, England, 1914), pp. 17–18.

6. Also at the National Heritage Museum is an example of the April 8 invitation described in the headnote. Both are addressed to the marquis de Pastoret (XXXVIII, 487n). Examples of both invitations are also in the Fonds maçonnique of the Bibliothèque nationale; see Amiable, *Une Loge maçonnique*, pp. 80–1 of the 2nd pagination.

7. BF was informed of the date by the marquis de La Salle d'Offémont on March 23; that letter, which has mostly to do with other matters, is described above in the headnote to Gebhard's letter of Jan. 22.

8. Très Cher Frère. BF served as *vénérable* from May, 1779, to May, 1781: XXIX, 528–30; XXXV, 88.

o'clock sharp; the price of admission for members and guests, and the controls on order and propriety, were the same as in the revised invitation published below. Reservations were being accepted through April 30.

Perhaps it was the volume of acceptances that made the lodge postpone the date and change the venue. Perhaps it was the clamor of nonmembers who wanted to attend. Whatever the case, even before they knew on which day in May the event would occur (they left the date blank), the lodge printed this revised invitation in the form of a general announcement. This time, as they emphasized in italics, one did not need to be a mason in order to attend. The venue would be the Redoute chinoise, and all the amusements in that garden would be available to the guests.[9]

The celebration took place on Monday, May 12. The marquis de La Salle, the current *vénérable*, began by reading a poem, and Elie de Beaumont delivered a speech on the peace. The marquis then presented Franklin with the medal illustrated on the facing page, engraved by lodge member Jean-François Bernier. There followed lectures and readings by various poets, artists, and members of the Academy of Sciences including Lalande, who presented a memoir on the new planet, Uranus, discovered in 1781 by William Herschel. The assembly then descended into the grotto and gardens to dine at café tables. Towards midnight they returned to the main hall where the Orchestre de l'Opéra performed an oratorio on the peace composed for the occasion, with lyrics by La Salle and music by Campan. The affair ended with a ball, and everyone who attended was given one of the medals that Franklin had earlier received. The *Journal de Paris*, which reported on the event, concluded that good order and "decency" had reigned, and that everything read and sung had pleased the elite crowd.[1]

9. Opened in 1781, the Redoute chinoise was similar to its counterparts in London, the Vauxhall and Ranelagh gardens. It offered a range of amusements and games, including swings, a dance hall, a restaurant, and a café set in an underground grotto: Louis-Sébastien Mercier, *Tableau de Paris*, ed. Jean-Claude Bonnet (2 vols., Paris, 1994), I, 536–7, 1433, 1658–9, 1864–5.
1. *Jour. de Paris*, May 18, 1783.

Franklin Medal

[before May 10, 1783]²

FETE ACADEMIQUE,

DONNEE, PAR EXTRAORDINAIRE,

A L'OCCASION DE LA PAIX,

PAR LA L.˙. DES NEUF-SŒURS,

CONJOINTEMENT AVEC L'EX.˙. V.˙. F.˙. FRANKLIN,

Le   Mai, à la Redoute Chinoise, Foire Saint-Laurent.

IL y aura Lectures, Concert, Hymnes relatifs à la circonstance, exécutés par les plus célebres Virtuoses; ensuite Bal. On entrera à quatre heures, & la séance commencera à six heures précises.

La Salle sera décorée de Tableaux, dont les sujets seront allégoriques à la gloire de la France, à l'indépendance de l'Amérique, & aux sentimens de la R.˙. L.˙.

Tous les Jeux contenus dans le local qu'on a choisi pour cette Fête seront à la disposition des Souscripteurs: il ne sera pas nécessaire d'être *Maçon* pour y être admis.

La Souscription sera de 24 livres. L'on aura la liberté d'y conduire une Dame, mais on paiera 6 livres de plus pour une seconde, & ainsi de suite pour chaque Dame qu'on présentera.

On pourra se faire inscrire jusqu'au 10 Mai, inclusivement, chez M. le Marquis *DE LA SALLE*, rue Saint-Roch, près celle Poissonnière, depuis neuf heures du matin jusqu'à midi, & chez M. *GAUCHER*, des Académies de Londres, Rouen, &c. rue Saint-Jacques, porte cochere vis-à-vis Saint Yves, depuis neuf heures du matin, jusqu'à cinq heures du soir.

Pour le maintien de l'ordre & de la décence, l'on sera obligé de déclarer, en souscrivant, ses qualités & demeure, ainsi que les noms & qualités des Dames qui seront admises; chaque Billet d'entrée portera le nom de la Personne qui le présentera.

Aucun Domestique ne sera introduit. La L.˙. se chargera de faire servir les Buffets.

2. The date by which acceptances were due.

From the Comte de Milly *et al.*[3]

AL:[4] American Philosophical Society

[before May 10, 1783]

Mrs. Le Cte. de Milly, Mis. De La Salle, & Cte. de Préaux[5] Vble. Ex vble. & Membres de La Loge des IX soeurs Sont venus pour rendre leurs devoirs a Monsieur Franklin & le prevenir que la fête a L'occasion de La paix qui Se donne le 12. mai a la redoute chinoise fbg. & foire st. laurent Commencera a 6. heures du soir, & qu'il est instemment prié d'y être rendû a 7. heures au plus tard. Suivant Son aveu & Sa promesse il est annoncé & le public Seroit desolé d'être privé de la presence du grand homme qui après avoir instruit l'univers a rompû les fers de sa patrie & donne des loix utiles & Sages au peuple nouveau qui lui doit Sa consistance & Sa liberté.

Addressed: A Monsieur / Monsieur Franklin Ministre des XIII. etats / unis de L'amerique / a Passy

To Robert R. Livingston[6]   LS:[7] New-York Historical Society

Dear Sir,   Passy, 10 May 1783.

Permit me to introduce to you the Bearer Mr. Hogendorff, of an illustrious Family, and Lieutenant in the Dutch Guards.[8] He

---

3. Three representatives of the Lodge of the Nine Sisters who called at Passy to impress on BF the importance of attending the *fête académique* whose invitations bore his name, and also, it seems, to make sure he arrived on time. The presentation of his medal came early in the ceremonies; see the preceding document.

4. In the hand of the marquis de La Salle.

5. Pierre-Antoine de Préaux was a former officer in the dragoons and a member of the Nine Sisters from 1778 to 1784: Le Bihan, *Francs-maçons parisiens;* Amiable, *Une Loge maçonnique,* p. 264 of the 1st pagination.

6. BF wrote an almost identical letter to George Washington on the same date (Library of Congress).

7. In WTF's hand.

8. Gijsbert Karel van Hogendorp (1762–1834) visited the United States from November, 1783, to June, 1784, befriending Jefferson and meeting Washington, Morris, and others. He later became a prominent conservative

is strongly recommended to me by Persons of Distinction, as a Gentleman of excellent Character: His principal Design in going to America is to make himself acquainted with the Country, & its Inhabitants: I beg you will favour him with your best Advice, & Counsels which as a Stranger he may stand in need of, and which you have a Pleasure in affording to Persons of Merit.—

With great Regard, I have the honour to be, Dear Sir, Your most obedt & most humble Sert. B FRANKLIN

R. R. Livingston Esqr.—

Endorsed: from Docr. Franklin

Ferdinand Grand to the American Peace Commissioners

Copies:[9] Massachusetts Historical Society, Library of Congress; partial copy: Library of Congress

Gentlemen, Paris, May 10 1783.

It is some Months ago since I had the honor to write you,[1] & am well persuaded, altho I received no Answer thereto, that it will have engaged your attention. I earnestly wish it may have been productive of an Improvement to the Finances of Congress which I then foresaw would be short of our Wants & which is unfortunately too much the case at present.

Last Month I remitted to the Honorable Rt. Morris the State of his Account, the Ballance of which were £413,892. 13. 9 due to me.[2] This added to the subsequent Payments I had to make

---

statesman in the Netherlands, playing a major role in the restoration of the House of Orange in 1813: Smith, *Letters,* XXI, 494n; *Morris Papers,* VIII, 813n; *Jefferson Papers,* VII, 80–3 and *passim;* Schulte Nordholt, *Dutch Republic,* pp. 253, 258–61, 278–9; *NNBW,* II, 587–93; Simon Schama, *Patriots and Liberators: Revolution in the Netherlands, 1780–1813* (New York, 1977), pp. 640–3 and *passim.*

9. All three copies are from the commissioners' letterbooks. Grand customarily wrote in French.

1. See his letters of Feb. 12 and 13, above.

2. The balance is in *livres tournois,* which is what Grand intended here and

would have thrown me in a State of Perplexity had it not been for the Assistance given me by the Garde du Tresor Royal.[3]

You will see, Gentlemen, by the State I have the honour to inclose for your Consideration that the Sums I am to pay exceed of one Million those that are to be paid me. And making even abstraction of all that is not M. Morris Bill there still remains a defect of £500,000 independent of the Allowance to be made for his usual Wants from Jany. 24 (date of his last Bills) up to the 12th of March.

I am happy to have it in my Power to say that I have exerted to this instant all that my Zeal & my Faculties could suggest me, did the last keep Pace with the former, I should never have applied but to them. However the State of Affairs is such now, that a Resolution must be taken relative thereto, & even without delay. The Bearers of M. Morris Bills growing so urgent upon me that rather than to have occasioned an Eclat before I could be informed with your Resolution, I prefferred accepting a further Sum of £54000 this Day.

I crave your Excellencies will honour me with a quick answer, meantime, I remain, most respectfully, Gentlemen, Your Most obedient & most humble Servt.   (signed) GRAND.

State of Congress's Finances at Paris
on the 10th of May 1783.—

Ballance due to me on the last Account	£413892.	13. 9
Sums paid by his Excelly Bn. Franklin's orders	172001.	5. 1
The Hble. Rt. Morris drafts to be paid	1,872,871.	1. 10

---

elsewhere by the £ symbol. He sent the account on April 15: *Morris Papers,* VIII, 315. A month later, before Morris received it, Morris directed his bankers in Amsterdam and Thomas Barclay to pay Grand whatever money they had: *Morris Papers,* VIII, 49–50.

3. Vergennes must have finally agreed to advance funds from the loan of 1783, as Grand had suggested in his letter to BF of Feb. 12. On April 12, after Harvelay, the *garde du Trésor Royal,* had told Grand that he would agree to the measure contingent on Vergennes' authorization, Grand wrote to Rayneval asking permission. The docketing on Grand's letter indicates that Vergennes' initial answer was negative, but by June 15 all the funds for the 1783 loan had been transferred to Grand: Ferdinand Grand to Rayneval, April 12, 1783 (AAE); Account XXVII (XXXII, 4).

His fresh drafts from Jany. 24 at 60 days sight,
of which I already accepted £54000.   804371 8.

                                                     £3263136. 8   8

Interest on the Dutch Loan   400000
Sabatier & Desprez Claim for
Furnitures to the La Fayette[4] 134,000

                                                          534000.

                                                     £3,797,136. 8. 8.

To the American Ministers for negotiating a Peace.

From Jean-Baptiste Artaud[5] ALS: American Philosophical Society

Monsieur.   Avignon 10 mai 1783.
  Ravir la foudre aux cieux, et le Sceptre aux tyrans,[6]
est une double gloire que l'univers n'a jamais vue Se reunir sur
une mesme téte, si ce n'est sur la votre.
  Daignés de grace laisser tomber un regard de bonté sur un
ecrivain qui a fixé avec autant de zele que dassiduité, pendant
tout le cours de la derniere guerre, linteret et les yeux de Ses
lecteurs, sur vos travaux et sur vos succés.
  J'ai celebré la conquette de la liberté faite par votre patrie,
mais le congrés ne me doit rien. J'ai fait venerer l'auteur de cette
noble entreprise, Sans aquerir aucun droit à votre bienveillance,

---

4. The merchant ship *Marquis de Lafayette* was captured in 1781 (XXXV,
192n). The clothiers Sabatier fils & Déprés contracted to provide various
items for the American Army: XXIV, 122–3; XXXV, 108n.
  5. Artaud (1732–1796) edited the *Courrier d'Avignon* from 1776 to 1784.
The paper supported the American cause from the outset, but tended to
blame Britain's "tyrannical," "despotic," and "arbitrary" actions on the ministry, rather than George III. Its sharp denunciations of the war and the ministry increased from late 1780 to the signing of the peace: *DBF;* Jack R.
Censer, "English Politics in the *Courrier d'Avignon,*" in *Press and Politics in
Pre-Revolutionary France,* ed. Jack R. Censer and Jeremy Popkin (Berkeley,
Los Angeles, and London, 1987), pp. 173, 184–99. This is Artaud's only extant letter to BF.
  6. A paraphrase of Turgot's famous epigram about BF (XXVII, xl).

enfin en faisant constament cherir la justice et la sagesse de la france ma patrie, je n'ai que rempli le devoir d'un sujet fidelle.

Cependant, Monsieur, j'ose vous suplier de m'acorder une medaille de l'independance si vous avés daigné lire mes ecrits, vous y avés trouvé une excuse a la liberté de ma demande.

Puissaije obtenir de vous ce monument de votre gloire, qui sera pour moi un monument de votre bonté. Je le leguerai à mes enfans; et ils diront aprés moi; "notre pere fut un françois fidelle à sa patrie et à ses alliés. Voila la recompense quil reçut du createur de la liberté americaine. Ce bienfait fut son unique consolation, avant quil mourut pauvre."

Je Suis avec un profond respect Monsieur. Votre trés humble et trés obeissant Serviteur   Artaud

auteur du courier d'avignon.

From Antoinette-Thérèse Melin Dutartre

ALS: American Philosophical Society

ce Samedy 10 de L'arbalêtre [May 10, 1783?][7]
Mon papa voila mon abbé qui part pour Londres ou il doit demeurer quelques Semaines avant de Retourner en irlande.[8] Voulez vous le charger de quelques commissions? Il S'en acquitera bien et avec grand plaisir: il ira vous voir de ma part. Avant Son départ Si vous pouvez Luy donner quelques lettres de recommendation, cela me fera plaisir, il meritte tout le bien que vous en pourrez dire et moi toutte l'amitié que vous avez pour moy: est ce que je ne vous vairez pas à mon arbalêtre? Venez mon papa, m'assurer que vous noublierez jamais celle qui a pour vous les plus tendres Sentiments   Melin Dutartre

mille choses à mon aimable cousine[9] dites lui que ma Santé est bonne mais que le gout d'ecrire ne m'est pas encore revenue il

7. The first month following Mme Dutartre's illness (alluded to below and mentioned in XXXVIII, 549), in which the 10th of the month fell on a Saturday. The next such month was January, 1784.

8. Mme Dutartre had introduced this Irish abbé to BF 18 months earlier: XXXVI, 47.

9. Mme Brillon.

faut une occation pressée comme celle ci pour forcer ma paresse
a déguerpir
   mon abbé ira prendre vos ordres un matin avant 10 jours
a l'arbalêtre par Ris à Ris route de fontenebleau

Addressed: A Monsieur / Monsieur franklin maison / de monsieur de chaumont rüe basse de passy près paris / à Passy

Notation: Dutartre

From Joachim-Marie de Pavola[1]

LS: American Philosophical Society

Monseigneur   Marseille le 10: may 1783
   Daignés nous pardonner la liberté que nous osons prendre, en
vous adressant avec la présente, les veux que nous n'avons cessé
de former pour la conservation des jours precieux de Votre Excellence; Puisque envieux depuis longtems de ce bonheur, nous
n'aurions pû encore y parvenir sans l'occasion favorable que
nous fournit Monsieur Jerome Manfrin, Fermier Général des
Tabacs a Venise;[2] Ce Seigneur Puissant par ses relations, Riche,
et grand Connoisseur en toutes sortes de Marchandises, et en-
tiérement porté pour seconder les Entreprises de Commerce; Par
une lettre qu'il nous a fait l'honneur de nous écrire, Il nous marque que Votre Excellence doit se rendre dans la ditte Ville pour
divers objets; En Consequence il nous temoigne qu'il seroit très
flatté, si durant le Séjour que vous aurés destiné d'y faire vous

---

1. Pavola served as consul of Ragusa at Marseille from at least 1759 to
1779: Louis Bergasse and Gaston Rambert, eds., *Histoire du commerce de
Marseille* (7 vols., Paris, 1949–66), IV, 534–5; *Almanach royal* for 1779, p. 507.
   2. Girolamo Manfrin (d. 1802), who received a tobacco monopoly in Dal-
matia in 1769, had made a large fortune by the mid-1780s, and became one
of the most important patrons and collectors in Venice: Vicenzo Fontana,
"Girolamo Manfrin e la manifattura tabacchi a Venezia di Bernardino Mac-
caruzzi," *Bollettino dei Musei Civici Veneziani*, XXII (1977), 51–63; Francis
Haskell, *Patrons and Painters: a Study in the Relations between Italian Art and
Society in the Age of the Baroque* (2nd ed., rev. and enl., New Haven and London, 1980), pp. 379–81.

vouliés bien accepter ses Services, et un Appartement chez lui. Il Emploira tout pour rendre a Votre Excellence et a Votre Rang les honneurs qui leurs sont dus, sans aucune autre Vuë que celle d'avoir l'heureuse Satisfaction de Votre Connoissance Personnelle, et de Vous seconder dans tout, sans le moindre interêt, Vû que l'honneur de Vous être utile luy est au dessus de toutes recompenses.

Voilà donc les motifs qui nous ont déterminés à Vous écrire, Persuadés que malgrés que nous n'ayons peut etre pas l'honneur d'etre Connus de Votre Excellence, vous voudrés bien accorder la préférence a l'offre que nous nous sommes chargés de Vous faire pour le susdit Seigneur, et agréer en même tems cette marque d'attention de nôtre Zele Pour Votre Chere Personne— Dans cette Esperence, Nous avons l'honneur d'être avec le plus profond respect—Monseigneur Vos très humbles et très Obeissants Serviteurs   DE PAVOLA

ancien Consul de Raguse

Endorsed: Marseilles

Notation: Pavola 10 May 1783.

From Stephen Thorogood   ALS: American Philosophical Society

Place of S. Mark. Venise May the [*blank*]

Most Honble. Sr.   [*c.* May 10][3] 1783.

I do not know with what foundation, that it is here generaly reported; that this Citty, will shortly be visited by You great Sr. Every one glow with pleasure at the thought of it, and Certainly I Should think it, one of the happyest period of my life, that moment in which I shall have the happiness, to know You personaly. In Jully eighty one, when I was on my travells from England,

---

3. Dated on the basis of Pavola's letter of that date, above, which mentions another Venetian's having heard rumors of BF's imminent arrival.

to this Place. I had resolved, to have that Satisfation, but peculiar reason prevented Me going so far, from my shortest Road.

Having allways made my favorite Study; Natural Phylosophy
few Moments Conversation with you Sr. would: Either sett me to
wright from that Oppinion, which I hold of the Eletrical fluid, or
We should have mark'd out some clearer reason to Account for
its very mestyrious action, in the change of the Leyden Bottle.

I Crave Earnestly to know, if We may entratain any hope of
Such report being true; if So; I Shall wait until I can personaly
communicate to You my thoughts, on this particular. If otherwise I must beg leave, to send them in Writing, which I hope You
will be able to well Compreand, althoue I am so deficient in the
English language. Fate having deprived Me of an English liberal
Education, being born of English Parents in this Citty, and lost
them in My Infancy.

It is true that at a time when Every moment of it, is Employd
by You for the wellfare of Your Contry; I should not intrude on
it, & unknown trouble You w. this present, but great as You are
in the Phylosophycal World, I am sure You must find a peculiar
satisfation in having comunicated to You, any new thought, or
Idea, by which it may be endevourd, to throw any new light on
the Study of Nature; being sensible, that to distract our Mind
from our greatest care is Even nessesary, and Serve only to recall Us to it w. Greater Spring & activity; I will hope that there
will be found a Moment in which You will Sr. be pleased to in-
spect them; and grant Me for the present the unmerrited honor
of Your obliging Answer. Remaining w. the profoundest Respect of Your Esselencys Most Obidient. Umble & Respectfull
Serv.   STEPHEN THOROGOOD

Addressed: His Exellency Ben. Frankilin Es. / Minister of the
United States of / Amarica to the Court of France / Paris.

From Edward Bridgen

ALS: American Philosophical Society

May 11 [1783][4]

As this will be delivered into your own hands by the bearer who is going to reside at Versailles I beg leave my Dr: Sir if she should have at any time occasion for your countenance I beg the favour that you will grant it her but I hope she will not want it. I wish Sir to know if there is any prospect of proceeding on the Copper Coin.[5]

May I also beg the favour of your Interest and Attention to Mr Parkers request he is a very honest Man but distressed on Acct: of laying out of his Property and his being a *steady* Friend I should hope would reccommend him to have his property restored May Health, Happiness and every good Attend you and *Yours* is the Sincere wish of Dr: Sir: Your faithful & Affect:

EDWARD BRIDGEN

Mr. Parkers papers are inclosed to Dr Bancroft

Notation: Bridgen—

4. The most plausible year, based on the three elements mentioned in this letter. In May, 1783, Bridgen was awaiting Congress' response to his proposal to supply America with copper coinage; British citizens were agitating to have their property in America restored; and Edward Bancroft (who is named in the postscript) was still in Paris. Bancroft left France in June, 1783, for a trip to America, and did not return until the following July: Bancroft to BF, June 20, 1783 (APS); *Conn. Jour.*, Oct. 8, 1783; *Morris Papers*, IX, 469.

5. For Bridgen's proposal, which the American commissioners sent to Livingston in December, 1782, see XXXVIII, 481–2.

From [Anne-Rose?] Cologan⁶

AL: American Philosophical Society

dimanche. 11 mai [1783]⁷

Mde de Cologan est bien fachée de ne pouvoir pas avoir l'honneur de Dejeuner aujourdhui avec Monsieur franklin, quelle aime de tout son Cœur. Elle le prie daccepter quelques bouteilles de vin de Canaries des terres de Mr de Cologan. Les unes sont du Vidonia et les autres du Malvoisia, elle espere que Monsieur franklin les trouvera de son gout, aussi bien que, Bai, Bai &C.⁸

Addressed: A Monsieur / Monsieur franklin / a Passy

6. Three partially dated letters in French survive from a "Mde de Cologan" who has ties to the Canary Islands wine trade. All are written in a familiar tone, and two of them seem to belong in 1783. We earlier identified her as the wife of Thomas Cologan, a member of a Canary Islands mercantile house (XXVII, 184, 553; XXXV, 153). Further research suggests that she was probably the wife of Thomas' brother John Cologan (1746–1799). John came to France as a young man to study for the priesthood, and married in Paris Anne-Rose Coghlan, the daughter of an English general who was in the French service. Cologan established himself in London as a merchant and a banker. Anne-Rose Coghlan Cologan is known to have been in Paris in 1783, and died in that city in January, 1784: *Jour. de Paris*, Feb. 2, 1784; *Gent. Mag.*, LIV (1784), 151; *Courier de l'Europe*, XV (1784), 113. If the "Mr. and Mrs. Cologan" who accepted BF's dinner invitation in 1781 was this couple (their letter, presumably written by the husband, is in English and in a different hand: XXXV, 153), it would mean that the wife had known BF for years before writing the present note. For these Cologans see Francisco Fernández de Béthencourt, *Nobiliario de Canarias* . . . (4 vols., La Laguna de Tenerife, 1952–67), I, 275; Augustín Guimerá Ravina, *Burguesia extranjera y comercio atlántico: la empresa comercial irlandesa en Canarias (1703–1771)* (Santa Cruz de Tenerife, 1985), pp. 85, 91, 93.

7. One of only two years during BF's stay when May 11 fell on a Sunday. The other was 1777, which seems unlikely.

8. Her two other letters are dated only "lundy 24" and "dimanche matin 24." The first is probably from early 1783 (the two possible months are February and March). It is a request for BF to write a letter of recommendation for John Shaw, a merchant who is about to leave London with a cargo that he plans to trade for wines at Tenerife, which he will then sell in Philadelphia and other American ports. John Cologan, though he is not mentioned in the letter, was undoubtedly involved in this scheme as he was trying to export wine to the United States in the spring of 1783: Agustín Millares Torres, *Historia general de las Islas Canarias* (6 vols., Las Palmas de Gran Canaria, 1975–

Lafayette to the American Peace Commissioners

Copies:[9] Massachusetts Historical Society, Library of Congress

Gentlemen, Paris, May 12th. 1783.

Having Yesterday conferred with Count de Vergennes upon some Public Concerns, He requested I would tell you what, instead of troubling you with the Demand of a meeting, I think better to mention in this Note.

The several Powers said he, are going to make up their Treaties, and when ready to sign, they will of Course meet to do it all together. The Mediation of the Emperor and that of Russia have been required, and under that Mediation the French Treaty will be signed, it now rests with America to know if She will conclude her Treaty under the Mediation, or chooses to let it alone. There is no Necessity for it, But in Case you prefer to have it, Count de Vergennes thinks it is time to join with England in making a combined Application to the Court of Vienna and that of Petersbourg.[1]

So far Gentlemen I have been requested to speak to you, I will add that from my last Conferences on the Subject, I hope we may get the Harbour of L'Orient, as we have wished, for the American Trade.

Be pleased to accept the Assurances of my great and affectionate Respect. (signed) La Fayette.

To the American Ministers for negociating a Peace.

---

81), IV, 150. The second letter is impossible to date: she bids BF farewell, as she had not the courage to say "ses adieux" in person, and thanks him for all his kindness on behalf of herself and her husband. Both letters are at the APS.

9. Both are in the commissioners' letterbooks.

1. On May 13 Hartley began writing a letter to Fox describing this offer. He concluded it on May 22, reporting that the American commissioners did not see any need for mediation and were surprised by the offer, as neither Russia nor Austria had acknowledged American independence: Giunta, *Emerging Nation*, 1, 858–9. Around this time both Fox and Vergennes were concerned that Russia might delay the signing of their final treaty, as the Russian envoy had proposed incorporating into it the principles of the League of Armed Neutrality: Andrew Stockley, *Britain and France at the Birth of America: the European Powers and the Peace Negotiations of 1782–1783* (Exeter, 2001), p. 190.

From the Baronne d'Ahax,[2] with Franklin's Draft of a Reply

AL: American Philosophical Society

paris le 12 may 1783

Monsieur apres avoir eu le bonheur de vous voir je desir de le renouveller et vous demande votre heurs la plus Comode ou je puis avoir la bonheur de vous revoir Seul car jai besoin dun Confidant et jesper de le trouver dans L'etre que je revere le plus au monde.

Jai l'honneur d'etre avec la plus grand veneration monsieur votre tres humble et tres obeisante servante

LA BARONNE D'AHAX

Je prie de vouloir avoir la bonte de mètre sur mon adresse L'envelope de Mr dupont directeur des subistance militairs au Bureau gènéral rúe charlot au marais a paris

Endorsed: Mr Franklin having much Business finds that previous Appointments of Days & Hours to see Persons on their private Affairs proves often inconvenient to him: And as it may be so to Madam la Baronne to come so far as Passy upon an Uncertainty, he submits it to her Consideration, whether if she has need of his Advice, it may not be best to state the Affair to him in a Letter, which he will immediately answer.

Notation: D'Ahas. 12 May 1783.—

2. The baronness had written once before, on March 8, to ask BF who Mr. "Jenjnis" (corrected from "Jenijns") actually was, and to beg for an appointment. BF should send his reply to the care of Mr. Cuny at the Hôtel d'Orléans. APS. On the day she wrote the present letter she also wrote to Henry Laurens and called on him in person. Laurens could not understand exactly what her grievances were, but the affair involved James Bourdieu and Edmund Jenings, who had duped her. Laurens judged her to be "some very high Personage," but excused himself as quickly as he could from further contact: *Laurens Papers,* XVI, 197.

From [Frederik Willem?] Boers[3]

AL: American Philosophical Society

a Paris ce 12 Mai 1783

M Boers a l'honneur de presenter ses respects a M le Ministre Franklin en lui assurant, qu'il est, on ne peut plus, sensible a la complaisance, que M Franklin a bien voulu avoir pour lui.

M Boers Sera toujours beaucoup flatté d'etre honoré des ordres de M Franklin et il les executera avec tout les sentimens de la reconnoissance, qu'il lui doit.

From Robert Morris

LS: American Philosophical Society; copy: Library of Congress

Sir   Office of Finance 12th May 1783

The Bills drawn by Congress in their Necessities press very heavily upon me, and one of the greatest among many Evils attending them is the Confusion in which they have involved the Affairs of my Department. I have never yet been able to learn how many of these Bills have been paid nor how many remain due neither am I without my fears that some of them have received double Payment.

To bring at length some little Degree of Order into this Chaos, after waiting till now for fuller Light and Information I write on the Subject to Mr. Adams and Mr. Jay and send Mr. Barclay to whom I also write a Copy of the enclosed Accounts directing him to Consult with your Excellency and with them to transmit me an Account of the Bills paid and of those remaining due and to take Measures for preventing double Payments.[4] The

---

3. This is the writer's only letter. We assume he is the representative of the Dutch East India Company who, in 1782, carried packets from Dumas and met BF: XXXVII, 160, 268, 316–17, 336–7.

4. Morris' letters to JA and Jay were nearly identical to this one. He sent copies of all of them to Barclay, along with the enclosed accounts, and instructed Barclay to confer with the commissioners and with Grand. All Morris' letters were written on May 12. For those letters and the enclosed accounts of bills of exchange drawn on the American commissioners and on BF see *Morris Papers*, VIII, 28–30, 32–5; *Adams Papers*, XIV, 476–7.

enclosed Accounts will inform you that of the Bills drawn for Interest and those for carrying on the current Service which have gone forward thro the Loan Offices amount the first to one Million six hundred and eighty four thousand two hundred and seventy eight Dollars equal to eight Million four hundred and twenty one thousand three hundred and ninety Livres and the second to two hundred and eighty six thousand seven hundred and thirty three and one third Dollars equal to one Million four hundred and thirty three thousand six hundred and sixty six Livres six Sous and eight deniers.

Let me intreat you Sir to forward these Views as much as possible for you will, I am sure, be Sensible how necessary it is for me to know the exact State of our pecuniary Affairs lest on the one Hand I should risque the public Credit by an Excess of Drafts or on the other leave their Monies unemployed while they experience severe distress from the Want. I am Sir with perfect Respect your Excellency's most obedient and humble Servant

ROBT MORRIS

His Excellency Benjamin Franklin Esqr. Minister Plenipotentiary of the United States.

Endorsed: Accounts of Drafts upon Commrs. & upon BF.

From Joshua and Catherine Johnson, and Matthew and Anne Ridley[5]

AL:[6] American Philosophical Society

Tuesday 13 May 1783.

Mr. & Mrs. Johnson presents their most respectfull compliments to Dr. Franklin & will do themselves the honor to wait on him.

5. Johnson's wife was Catherine Nuth (*c.* 1757–1811): Andrew Oliver, *Portraits of John Quincy Adams and His Wife* (Cambridge, Mass., 1970), p. 23. The Johnsons had recently arrived from Nantes and were on their way to London; see our annotation of Ridley to the Commissioners, [before May 6?]. Anne Richardson Ridley (XXXVI, 302n) had arrived in Paris from London on Dec. 13, 1782, and died there on Jan. 21, 1784: Matthew Ridley's Journal, entries of Dec. 13, 1782, and Jan. 21, [1784], Matthew Ridley Papers (Mass. Hist. Soc.).

6. Probably in Joshua Johnson's hand.

Mr. Johnson did not receive the honor of Dr. Franklin's Billet[7] til late last Evening or he would have returned an immediate answer.

Mr. & Mrs. Ridleys Compliments & will do themselves the honor to attend Dr. Franklin today.

From the Comte de Proli[8]   ALS: American Philosophical Society

Paris le 14 May 1783.

Le Cte. de Proli prend la respectueuse liberté de rappeller au souvenir de Monsieur Francklin qu'il a bien voulu lui promettre un passeport pour le navire Impl. [Impérial] la Capriçieuse, une lettre de recommandation pour le Capne. Simpson qui la commande et deux passeports en blanc pour les batiments qui la suivront.[9] Le Cte. de Proli ôse esperer que le depart precipité de la

---

7. Not found.

8. Pierre-Jean-Berchtold, comte de Proli (1750–1794), was the scion of a mercantile and banking family that had migrated from Milan to Antwerp. Accounts of his early career vary. At the time of this visit to Paris, he may have still been employed in the financial administration of the Austrian Netherlands, though his errand at Passy was on behalf of the ailing Compagnie de Trieste, founded in 1781 by his uncle, Charles-André-Melchior, also comte de Proli. By the end of 1783 Proli had established himself in Paris, where he engaged in international commerce and stock speculation, championed free trade, took part in the French Revolution, and in 1794 was denounced as a spy and died on the guillotine: Lüthy, *Banque protestante*, II, 654–5; Roland Mortier, "Un essai sur la liberté du commerce, ou le comte de Proli contre les 'économistes,'" in *Les Combats des Lumières: Recueil d'études sur le dix-huitième siècle* (Paris, 2000), pp. 354–67; *Biographie nationale . . . de Belgique* (44 vols., Brussels, 1866–1986), entries of Proli's uncle and father, Balthazar-Florent-Joseph.

9. Proli had requested these items in person, and left a record of them at Passy. His note, written in pencil on a blank leaf of an unrelated letter to BF (from Joseph Utzschneider, April 10, APS), provided details on the ship and captain (which BF incorporated into his certificate for the ship, published immediately below), requested the items listed in the present letter, and gave his address at the hôtel de Beauvais. He was representing the Compagnie de Trieste, which had requested papers for the *Capricieuse* from the Austrian court on May 1 but had received no response. On May 13 the company's Parisian bankers reported that Proli had been in Paris for a week and had

Capriçieuse, qui part dans le Courant de ce mois, lui fera pardonner Ses importunités. Sa reconnoissance Seroit infinie, Si Monsieur Francklin daignoit faire remettre au porteur les pièces desirées ou au moins les lui faire parvenir avant le depart du Courier de demain.[1]

Le Cte de Proli prie Monsieur Francklin d'agrèer les assurances de son respect P CTE DE PROLI

hôtel de Beauvais rûe des vieux Augustins

Notation: Cte. De Proli

----

finally seen BF, who not only promised the passports they were seeking, but also promised to write letters of recommendation for the company's ships. The Compagnie de Trieste had BF's certificate in hand by June 2, when they forwarded a French translation and an extract of their bankers' letter to the governor of Trieste (cited above). The governor forwarded their letter and its enclosures to Joseph II on June 7, adding his own plea for the required ships' papers, which were issued on June 12. The foregoing summary is drawn from French, Italian, and German documents relating to the *Capricieuse* which are filed together at the Hofkammerarchiv, Austria: Perrouteau, Delon & Cie. to the Compagnie Privée de Trieste et Fiume, May 13, 1783 (extract); French translation of BF certificate, May 14, 1783; Compagnie de Trieste to the comte de Brigido, June 2, 1783; comte de Brigido to Joseph II, June 2 (fragment) and June 7, 1783; reports of Austrian officials, June 12, 1783.

1. The only one of these papers that survives is BF's general recommendation, the "certificate" published immediately below. BF obviously issued this in lieu of a passport, which was unnecessary in peacetime. According to the dispatches of Baron de Beelen-Bertholff, the Austrian commercial agent in Philadelphia, Capt. Simpson carried letters of recommendation to RB (provided by BF) and Robert Morris. The *Capricieuse* reached Philadelphia in the fall of 1783, the first ship from Trieste to arrive. Simpson, who was part owner of the venture, consigned his cargo of clothing, foodstuffs, and copper to Bache & Shee. Most of it sold favorably: Hanns Schlitter, ed., *Die Berichte des ersten Agenten Österreichs in den Vereinigten Staaten von Amerika Baron de Beelen-Bertholff . . .* (Vienna, 1891), pp. 322–5.

Franklin: Certificate for the *Capricieuse*[2]

D (draft):[3] American Philosophical Society

[May 14, 1783]

To Persons[4] in Authority in any of the United States of America

The Imperial Ship the Capricieuse, *burthen about 350 Tons,* Commanded by Capt. Simpson being bound *from Trieste to Philadelphia, or some other Part of the United States,*[5] with Merchandize, *but* being uncertain what Port she may make; I hereby request that you would *on his Arrival,* favour the said Capt. Simpson with your Protection & Advice, for the Benefit of the Voyage & the Encouragement of Commerce with the friendly Nation to which he belongs.

Given at Passy this—&c

From John Adams

AL: American Philosophical Society

Wednesday May 14. 1783.

As there are Several Things which require the Deliberation of the American Ministers,[6] Mr Adams has the Honour to propose

2. Written in response to the preceding document.

3. In WTF's hand, with insertions by BF as indicated in italic type, and emendations as noted below. The wording is adapted from a certificate BF had written in 1777, which he characterized as a "General Recommendation of Ship & Cargo": XXIV, 478. On the first line of his draft of that certificate, BF crossed out the name of the ship and substituted "Imperial Ship the Capricieuse." Our predecessors were unable to explain this change (XXIV, 478n). It is now clear that BF gave this partially-emended draft to WTF in 1783 and asked him to draft a new certificate for the *Capricieuse*, which he then revised (the present document). A French translation of the now-missing fair copy, dated May 14 and indicating the full complimentary close and signature by BF, is in the Hofkammerarchiv, Austria.

4. WTF wrote "To all Persons," copying from the 1777 text. BF deleted "all."

5. WTF wrote simply, "to the said United States."

6. One of the items on the agenda probably was Lafayette's May 12 letter to the peace commissioners, above, which Laurens acknowledged on May 13. He told Lafayette that the commissioners would consider the matter as soon as JA scheduled a meeting: Idzerda, *Lafayette Papers*, V, 132n.

to Dr Franklin a Meeting at the Hotel du Roi Tomorrow at Eleven, if that time and Place are convenient to his Excellency. Mr A. will give notice to the other Gentlemen.

Addressed: Son Excellence / Monsieur Franklin / en son hotel / Paris

From the Abbé de La Roche   AL: American Philosophical Society

Auteuil ce 14.— [May 1783]

L'abbé de la Roche souhaite le bonjour à Monsieur franklin et le prévient que Made. et Mr. D'andlau partent demain à 7 heures du matin pour l'angleterre[7] et qu'ils Se chargeront volontiers des paquets et des commissions de Monsieur franklin pour ses amis ou connoissances d'angleterre. Made. d'andlau auroit été elle même les lui demander. Son depart inopiné la presse trop. Elle demeure faubourg st. honoré.

vera t'on ce soir Monsieur franklin à Auteuil?—

Addressed: A Monsieur / Monsieur franklin / A Passy

From Walterstorff   AL: American Philosophical Society

Paris the 14th. May 1783.

Mr de Walterstorff presents his respectfull compliments to Dr. Franklin and has the honour of returning to him the Constitution of the United States of America, begging leave at the same

---

7. Mme Helvétius' younger daughter, Geneviève-Adélaïde (1754–1817), and her husband, François-Antoine-Henri, comte d'Andlau (1740–1822), arrived in London on May 18, in the company of several other figures of the French court. Their visit, so soon after the preliminary peace treaty, did not go unnoticed, and the ladies in this company "ont émerveillé les Anglois au point de s'en attirer des éloges dans leurs papiers publics": Bachaumont, *Mémoires secrets,* XXIII, 52–3; *DBF,* under Mme Helvétius and Andlau; David Smith *et al.,* eds., *Correspondance générale d'Helvétius* (5 vols. Toronto, Buffalo, and Oxford, 1981–2004), III, 417–18n; IV, X, 100–1n.

time to appologize for not having sent this Collection back sooner, owing to his having lent some sheets of it to Baron de Blome. Mr. de W. gives his gratefull thanks to Dr. Franklin for having procured him the pleasure of being acquainted with those laws, which, if executed with the same spirit of philosophy and sound polity which framed them, will assure constant happiness to a Country, which, jusly proud of its well deserved liberty and Constitution, ought not to glorify less in its having given birth to a certain great Philosopher and truly amiable Statesman.

From Jonathan Williams, Sr.

ALS: American Philosophical Society

Hond. sr   London May the 14. 1783

Your favr. of apl. 23[8] Came to hand two day ago, note the Contents. I should have lik'd a passage with you; however the season is good & I have Concluded to Return hom to my own Country, Which I esteem to be the best that I ever Saw, I Shall sail in a few days for Boston, in the first ship that will be Cleard for that port, Wh. makes the Trade as Regular as it Can be before the Negotiations are finishd however I have On board this ship a quanty of Such goods as will be agreeable to aunt, & I think they are well Bot: On my arival she shall have the amo: of the money I Receiv'd of yours for Johnnot & Warrens Bills[9] at the first Cost, With the Charges that I pay & no other, I have Orderd Incurence— I think it best its about 2½ or 3 per Ct. I inclosd an Abrigment of the Common Prayer it is the Best state that Mr.

---

8. Not located. It was carried by Caleb Whitefoord, who left Paris on April 27 carrying letters from BF to friends in London. Before leaving he thanked WTF for the *Libertas Americana* medal, and requested more in silver and copper: Whitefoord to WTF, [April 26, 1783], May 9, 1783; Samuel Vaughan, Jr., to WTF, April 27, 1783 (all at the APS).

9. Following BF's orders: BF to Jane Mecom, Sept. 13, 1783, in Van Doren, *Franklin-Mecom*, pp. 224–5. For the bills of exchange see our annotation of Mecom to BF, April 29, above.

Wilkie[1] Could git it for me. Your friends here will be much diso-ponted, if you should not Visit them before you Return to Amer-ica in Particular the good Bishop of St Asaph Who expresses the highest Regard for you.[2] Wishing you the Blessings of every good & in your Own time a good passage to America & a happy Sight of your friends if Boston Should be your first Landing you will do me honour if you will make my house your hom, you will meat a harty wilcom from Your Dutyfull Nephew & most hble Servant my Love to Cousin William   JONA. WILLIAMS

To Doct Franklin

Addressed: His Excellency Benjamin Franklin / Passy near Paris

George III: Commission for David Hartley[3]

Copies:[4] Massachusetts Historical Society (four), Library of Congress, National Archives; transcript: National Archives

[May 14, 1783]

George R.

George the Third, by the Grace of God King of Great Britain, France and Ireland, Defender of the Faith, Duke of Brunswick

1. Doubtless the bookseller John Wilkie, who sold the edition; see XX, 343—5.

2. Jonathan Shipley told BF of his visit with Williams in his April 24 let-ter, above.

3. Fox sent these powers to Hartley on May 15 with a covering letter dis-cussing his objections to the three draft articles of April 29 (above). He ac-cused Hartley of either misunderstanding or ignoring his instructions, which stated that American ships would only be permitted to bring American pro-duce into British ports, and not any commodity that would be lawful for British vessels to bring. The first article was therefore inadmissable. He found the second and third articles unnecessary, given the sixth and seventh articles of the preliminary treaty. (In a private letter of the same day he called the third article both unnecessary and insidious.) He promised that no time would be lost in recalling the British troops still in America. As for the en-closed powers, he stressed that Hartley was not authorized to sign any treaty until the king approved it. Giunta, *Emerging Nation,* II, 118—20.

4. The one we print is in the hand of L'Air de Lamotte. All the copies were

and Lunenburgh, Arch Treasurer and Prince Elector of the Holy Roman Empire &c. To all to whom these Presents shall come GREETING.

Whereas for the perfecting and establishing the Peace, Friendship, and good Understanding so happily commenced by the provisional Articles signed at Paris the thirtieth Day of November last by the Commissioners of Us and our good Friends the United States of America viz, New-Hampshire, Massachusets-Bay, Rhode Island, Connecticut, New-York, New-Jersey, Pennsylvania, the three Lower Counties on Delaware, Maryland, Virginia, North Carolina, South Carolina and Georgia, in North America, and for opening, promoting and rendering perpetual the mutual Intercourse of Trade and Commerce between our Kingdoms and the Dominions of the said United States, We have thought proper to invest some fit Person with full Powers on our Part to meet and confer with the Ministers of the said United States now residing at Paris, duly authorized for the Accomplishing of such laudable & salutary Purposes. Now KNOW YE, that we reposing special Trust & Confidence in the Wisdom, Loyalty, Diligence & Circumspection of our Trusty & well beloved David Hartley Esquire, (on whom We have therefore confered the Rank of Our Minister Plenipotentiary) have nominated, constituted and appointed, and by these Presents do nominate, constitute and appoint our true, certain and undoubted Commissioner, Procurator & Plenipotentiary; Giving & granting to him all & all manner of Faculty, Power and Authority together with general as well as special Order (so as the general do not derogate from the special, nor on the contrary) for Us & in our Name, to meet, confer, treat & conclude, with the Minister or Ministers furnished with sufficient Powers on the Part of our said Good Friends the United States of America, of and concerning all such Matters and Things as may be requisite & necessary for accomplishing and completing the several Ends & Purposes herein before mentioned, and also for Us and in our

---

made from a now-missing one certified as a true copy and signed by Hartley on May 19, the day (as he wrote) that it was "delivered to the American Ministers." All copies listed here reproduce Hartley's certification.

Name to sign such Treaty or Treaties, Convention or Conventions, or other Instruments whatsoever as may be agreed upon in the Premises, and mutually to deliver and receive the same in Exchange, & to do & perform all such other Acts, Matters and Things as may be any Ways proper & conducive to the Purposes abovementioned, in as full and ample Form & manner, and with the like Validity and Effect, as We Ourself, if We were present, could do & perform the same: Engaging & promising, on our Royal Word that we will accept, ratify and Confirm in the most effectual Manner all such Acts, Matters and Things, as shall be so transacted & concluded by our aforesaid Commissioner Procurator and Plenipotentiary, and that we will never suffer any Person to violate the same, in the whole or in Part, or to act contrary hereto, In Testimony and Confirmation of all which, We have caused our Great Seal of Great Britain to be affixed to these Presents signed with our Royal Hand. Given at our Palace at St. James's, the Fourteenth Day of May in the Year of Our Lord, One Thousand seven hundred & Eighty three, and in the Twenty Third Year of Our Reign.

Notation by William Temple Franklin: Copy of Mr. Hartley's Full Power. exchanged with that of the American Ministers the 19 May 1783.

From Nathaniel Falconer[5]   ALS: American Philosophical Society

My Dear Sir   London May the 15 1783
   I Take the Liberty of informing you of my arrivall hear yesterday I left philadla the 12 of april in a vessell for ostend but Got put ashore at hasting I Expect to purches a ship hear and proceed to philadelphia if you have aney Commands hear that I Can Excute please to Let hear from you Mr Beach [Bache] was at Newyork when I Came away Mrs Beach was well Mr Williams[6] informs me you intend home which I am verey Glad to hear for

5. An old friend of BF's, who divided his life between the sea and public service: XII, 100n.
6. Jonathan Williams, Sr.

belive me whe Shall be much in want of your assistance on that
Side the watter and it is the wish of all your friends that you may
be there before october Next[7] I no youle Excuse the Liberty I
have Taken therfore will make no apologe for writing my Best
Compliments W T Franklin and Mr Hartly[8] who I understand is
now with you I am Dear Sir yr Hble Ser   NATH FALCONER

Addressed: Docter Franklin / at Paris

Notation: Falconer 15 May 178[*torn*]

From the Comte de Maillebois, with Franklin's Note for a Reply

ALS: American Philosophical Society

a Paris 15 may [1783]

Il y a bien longtemps, mon cher confrere,[9] que je me reproche de
n'avoir pas pu aller vous faire Moy mesme mes remerciments de
la medaille que vous aves eu la bonté de m'envoyer.[1] Vous scaves
que j'ay toujours eu dans le cœur la gloire du Congres, et les succes de mon respectable confrere et amy. J'aurais desiré d'y contribuer plus essentiellement.

M. de Banne, qui vous presentera ma lettre est un jeune
homme plein de zele et d'intelligence qui va voyager en amerique de L'aveu du gouvernement. Il me prie de vous engager a
luy donner des lettres de recommandation autant que vous le
pourres faire, je crois pouvoir vous reponde qu'il fera un usage
utile et sage des moyens qu'on luy donnera de s'instruire. C'est
ce qui m'engage a vous le recommander j'espere que je finiray
bientost mes proces et des que je seray libre, j'iray surement vous
renouveller moy mesme l'attachement bien sincere et inviolable,

---

7. As Falconer explained in a June 23 letter (APS), this is when Pennsyl-
vanians would vote for a new council of censors. One of its main functions
was to judge the operation of the Pennsylvania Constitution and, if necessary, to propose amendments: Robert L. Brunhouse, *The Counter-Revolution
in Pennsylvania, 1776–1790* (Harrisburg, Pa., 1942), pp. 15, 141–2.
8. To whom BF had introduced Falconer in 1775: XXII, 31–2, 196.
9. Both were members of the Académie des sciences: XXIII, 287n.
1. Doubtless one of the *Libertas Americana* medals.

avec lequel j'ay L'honneur d'etre, mon cher et respectable confrere, votre tres humble et tres obeissant serviteur

MAILLEBOIS

Endorsed: Give him a Letter to Dr Cooper[2]
Govr Greene
Mr. Livingston

2. The first two letters are extant, written on May 20; they will be discussed
in vol. 40.

Index

Compiled by Jonathan R. Dull.

(Semicolons separate subentries; colons separate divisions within subentries. A volume and page reference in parentheses following a main entry refers to an individual's first identification in this edition.)

Fitzwilliam, William Wentworth, Earl, 320
Fizeaux, Grand & Cie. (Amsterdam banking firm, XXIX, 455n): Morris draws on, 130; and F. Grand, 130; Herman Heyman's Sons cites as reference, 179; letter from, 130
Flesselles, Jacques de (*intendant* of Lyon), 79
Fleurieu, Charles-Pierre Claret de (director of ports and arsenals), 442–3n
Fleury, Pierre-Augustin-Bernardin de Rosset de Rocozel de (bishop), 16
Floirac, abbé ——— de, 10–11
Florida, 380, 383–4
Floridablanca, José Moñino y Redondo, conde de (Spanish chief minister, XXIII, 192n), 359n, 464n
Fly, H.M.S. (sloop of war), 536
Folger, Timothy, xxx, 427n
Forman, Anthony, 581–2
Forman, Richard, 581–2
Forquet, Charles (consulship seeker), 81
Forster frères (Bordeaux merchant firm), 308n, 367n, 423n
Forton Prison, 5n, 42n, 297n, 389, 452n
Fossé, Charles-Louis-François (army officer): BF discusses his stove design with, 372; sends essay, 372–3; letter from, 372–3
Foster, Jonathan (former prisoner), 452
Fothergill, John (physician, IV, 126–7n), 67, 294n, 295
Fottrell, John (Ostend shipowner): and Robeson, 194; asks advice on sending goods to America, passport for ship, 194–5; letter from, 194–5
Foundling Hospital (London), 566–7
Fournier, Simon-Pierre, le jeune (typefounder, xxx, 346), 37
Fox, Charles James: appointed secretary of state, 208, 320n, 428, 431n; is ally of North, 210, 214, 300, 316, 352n, 357n, 390, 502; and Portland, 320: Fitzwilliam, 320n: appointment of Hartley as peace negotiator, 413n, 432n, 469n, 481–2: Hartley's discussions with peace commissioners, 511, 513n, 524n, 525n, 568n, 570n, 596n, 605n: Manchester, 568n; Hartley arranges meeting between Lau-

rens and, 431–2n: is political supporter of, 481n; trade policy of, 431n, 479n, 481n; Laurens urges to conclude definitive treaty with U.S., 432–3; informs Laurens of Hartley's appointment as negotiator, 432n, 469n; opposes Austrian, Russian mediation, 469n; introduces Hartley, desires reconciliation, 481–2; praised by Shipley as member of Rockingham government, 502n; fears Russians will delay signing of final peace, 596n; admonishes Hartley for misunderstanding instructions about permissible American cargoes, 605n; promises no time will be lost in recalling British troops from America, 605n; letter from, 481–2
Fox, George (XXXII, 313n): dinner invitation to, 409; returns to America, 409n, 563; and WTF, 409n; carries *Libertas Americana* medals to Congress, 563–4n; letter from, 563–4; letter to, 409
France: BF ordered to seek, requests additional financial assistance from, lvi, 42–3, 141, 159, 176n, 580: argues that American union with, is foundation of U.S. importance in Europe, 302: describes *Libertas Americana* medal as acknowledgment of American obligations to, 470–1, 554–5: refrains from encouraging emigration to U.S. from, 471; government of, provides financial aid to Congress, lvi, 42–3, 141–2, 159–60, 164, 202–5, 301, 472, 579n, 588n: suspends payment of bills of exchange, lvi, 289–91, 301, 340–1, 374, 472, 482n: issues temporary embargo on shipping, 60n, 96n: chooses free ports, 106, 344n, 423–4, 471, 480n, 596: exchanges prisoners with British, 134: loans money to Beaumarchais for American supplies, 160–1n: requires French-owned ships to fly French flag, 175n: indemnifies Dalton for loss of ship, 199: gives subsidy to Maria Theresa during Seven Years' War, 204n: is criticized by JA, 301–2, 561–2, 569: is portrayed as arbitrary, despotic, 475n: advances Grand money from loan, 588; is not consulted

Franklin, Benjamin (*continued*)
bills, 97; approves Grand asking assistance of Dutch bankers, 170n; congratulates Barclay on his appointment to settle public accounts, 174; may assist A. Barry, 193; pays salaries of other ministers, 339, 396, 463: for S. Johonnot's education, 534n; answers questions about American trade, 363–4; appoints Morris as agent to receive, remit his salary, 396; salary of, 396n; cannot comment on solidity of American mercantile houses, 445n; forwards circulars from Bache & Shee, 453n; reimburses Coffyn for assisting prisoners, 453n; accepts d'Acosta's bill of exchange, 497n; bills of exchange, loan office certificates drawn on, presented to, cashed by, 500n; Grand accepts drafts of, 588
—character and reputation: is praised as legislator, 8–9: for his modesty, 71, 115: by Wheelock for his politeness, kindness, 176n: by Madison, 381; is reputed to have tender, good heart, 18; is blessed by gods, claims Saint-Auban, 22; is rumored to be preparing code of laws, 30; is called liberator of his country, 46, 71, 157: father of American states, 248–9: the American Lycurgus, 318; Ingenhousz wishes to dedicate book to, 89; James, Vaughan believe his autobiography will be example to others, 112–17; "chicanes ... upon the business of passports," claims Fitzherbert, 121n; Gastellier wishes to dedicate book to, 152–3, 166; Torris & Wante names ship after, 175; is compared to Sully, 207: Jupiter, 235n: Nestor, 241; is intolerant of Loyalists in "Apologue," 233n; jokes about his confusion about French genders, 236n; is held in high esteem by Gustavus III, 250; Hopkinson uncertain of public's gratitude for services of, 399–400; English newspapers publish false or abusive articles about, 471n; represents U.S. at fête académique, 583–6; Turgot poem about, quoted, 589
—earlier political and diplomatic career: conducts 1778 negotiations with Hutton,

24; works for repeal of Stamp Act, 116n; encourages German troops to desert, 144n; signs Franco-American Treaty of Amity and Commerce, 255; attempts to prevent American break with Britain, 295; at Cockpit hearing, 328n; as joint deputy postmaster general is involved with packet boat service, 425n; protests murders of Indians at Lancaster, 545
—family: coat of arms of, xxix; sends wine to RB, 61: books to BFB, 101, 206, 410, 438: bills of exchange, goods to J. Mecom, 532–3, 604; accused of unfair influence in appointment of WTF as secretary to peace commission, 65; may entrust BFB to Hewson's care, 67; plans to visit BFB in Geneva, 101; BFB wishes to accompany to London, 206; WF refuses to correspond with, during war, 211n: inquires about, 292n; hopes to visit Italy, Vienna with WTF, 218n; praises WTF for faithful service, tender filial attachment, 218n; and JW's financial difficulties, 289–91; asked to forward letter to RB, 304; recommends RB, J. Williams, Sr., to Schönfeld, 311–12n: Darby to RB, 361: Hadenbrock to RB, J. Williams, Sr., 495: Simpson to RB, 601n; RB considers joining for return voyage, 325; manumission of RB's slave Bob requested in will of, 345n; reads W. Bache letter to D. Montgomery, 345n; widow of John Mecom asks assistance of, 439; J. Williams, Sr., wishes to accompany on return voyage, 478; invited to visit Jane Mecom, 533, 535; SB expects to see in Philadelphia during coming summer, 534, 574; J. Williams, Sr., hopes for visit from, 605
—health: is conscious of his own mortality, lix; reportedly is a little lame, 25; sent various remedies for kidney stones, 25n, 91–2, 246; expects end of life not far distant, 69, 503; claims most of his life spent in health, vigor of mind, 69; Ingenhousz offers advice on relieving gout, kidney stones, 91–2; friends, colleagues inquire about, 99, 229, 334; age cited as reason for difficulty with French

Franklin, Benjamin (*continued*)
language, 157; past attacks of bladder or
kidney stones, 246n, 294; describes himself as quite recovered from late illness,
348; Vaughan sends castor oil to, 371;
BFB inquires about, 410; suffers from
gout, 556
—household: hires Finck as maître d'hôtel, 3; L'Air de Lamotte keeps records of
postage, errands for, 3–4; Finck lists
foodstuffs, supplies purchased for, 4;
Campo-de-Arbe recounts service in, asks
recommendation, 134–5; B. Vaughan
purchases, sends items for, 212; JW sends
rum, sugar, porter, but not cheese to,
375; assists Duchemin, 480n; sends ar-
rack to duchesse de Deux-Ponts, 489;
Burgundy (wine) offered to, 509; carriages owned by, 521
—memberships: in Neuf Sœurs masonic
lodge, xxx, lix, 14, 102, 157n, 583–6:
Göttingen Royal Society of Sciences,
145n: Club of Thirteen, 348; attends
Neuf Sœurs celebration of peace, xxx,
lix, 583–6; sent tickets to meeting of Société royale de médecine, 304; sponsors
Soulavie, Grivel for membership in
APS, 423n, 454n; presents "Maritime
Observations," Gulf Stream chart to
APS, 427n; recommends Priestley for
election to Académie royale des sciences, 437n, 448, 449; accepts affiliation
with Loge des Commandeurs du Temple, 541; was *vénérable* of Neuf Sœurs
lodge, 583
—minister to France: negotiates commercial treaty with Sweden, xxix, lv–lvii,
250–5, 300, 467; advises French on navigation into New England ports, xxx, lv;
asks for, receives French financial aid,
lvi, 42–3, 141–2, 159–60, 176n, 202–5,
301, 472, 579n; signs new contract for
repayment of loans, lvii, 43, 141–2,
159–60, 201–6, 301: initial contract
with Vergennes for repayment of American debt, 141, 159–60, 164, 202, 204;
and printing of *Constitutions des treize
Etats-Unis de l'Amérique*, lviii, 434–5,
448–9, 459, 477, 568; mollifies French

about signing of preliminary articles of
peace, lix; aids current, former American prisoners, 3–4; aid of, sought for
current or escaped prisoners, 41–2,
337–8; reportedly drafting letter to
king, 45; lobbied by various parties in
choice of free ports, 104–7; sends
American merchants circular concerning terms of armistice, 172n; Vergennes
copy of commissioners' proposals to
Hartley, 555, 567n; Vergennes extract of
Cooper letter about JA's accusations
against France, 561n; fears too frequent
requests for French financial aid, 176n;
is embarrassed by Dartmouth College's
appeal for foreign contributions, 177n;
Joseph II wishes overtures to, for commercial treaty, diplomatic relations with
Holy Roman Empire, 188n; reimburses
Hodgson for aiding prisoners, 209,
479–80; discharges British officers
from parole, 307; if necessary will pay
for ship for prisoner exchange, 308; presents Mazzei at court, 316n; relays
complaints of American merchants,
343–4; wishes to foster French-Ameri-
can trade, 344; dispatches, packets of,
364, 460; repeats request to resign, 381,
397; queried about proposed statue of
Louis XVI, 386; Austria supposedly
ready to recognize, negotiate commercial treaty with, 444–6; attempts to negotiate commercial treaty with Denmark, 462n, 467–8, 473; comments on
number of consulship applicants, 470;
protests Danish surrender of Bergen
prizes, 473–4; accompanies Hartley to
meeting with Vergennes, 479n, 510;
Ingenhousz anticipates will meet with
Joseph II or his ministers in Vienna to
discuss commercial treaty, 530; fails to
attend weekly audience for ambassadors, 556. See also *Libertas Americana;*
Passports
—music: invited by Houdetot to musical
performances, 22n, 133, 422: to *concert
des amateurs,* 119; B. Vaughan promises
to provide, should BF visit, 214; Vogler
presents theory of natural harmony to,